INVENTORY 98

 St. Louis Community College

Forest Park
Florissant Valley
Meramec

Instructional Resources
St. Louis, Missouri

GAYLORD

CHILDREN IN HISTORICAL AND COMPARATIVE PERSPECTIVE

Children in Historical and Comparative Perspective

AN INTERNATIONAL HANDBOOK AND RESEARCH GUIDE

Edited by Joseph M. Hawes
and N. Ray Hiner

GREENWOOD PRESS
New York • Westport, Connecticut • London

Library of Congress Cataloging-in-Publication Data

Children in historical and comparative perspective : an international
   handbook and research guide / edited by Joseph M. Hawes and N. Ray
   Hiner.
       p. cm.
   Includes bibliographical references and index.
   ISBN 0–313–25760–4 (lib. bdg. : alk. paper)
   1. Children—History—Cross-cultural studies.   I. Hawes, Joseph
M.   II. Hiner, N. Ray.
   HQ767.87.C48   1991
   305.2′3′09—dc20   90–38416

British Library Cataloguing in Publication Data is available.

Library of Congress Catalog Card Number: 90–38416
ISBN: 0–313–25760–4

First published in 1991

Greenwood Press, 88 Post Road West, Westport, CT   06881
An imprint of Greenwood Publishing Group, Inc.

Printed in the United States of America

The paper used in this book complies with the
Permanent Paper Standard issued by the National
Information Standards Organization (Z39.48–1984).

10 9 8 7 6 5 4 3 2 1

To
Philippe Ariès
and
Erik Erikson

CONTENTS

PREFACE

In his presidential address to the American Historical Association in 1988, Akira Iriye urged his colleagues to make greater efforts to internationalize history by searching "for historical themes and conceptions that are meaningful across national boundaries." Even when scholars from different countries get together to "exchange localized knowledge," he suggests that "they should keep in mind the question of what such information may mean to the rest of humanity." It was in this spirit that we undertook the creation of this volume on the history of children. We agree very much with Professor Iriye's belief that "whatever we do as historians will be of little value unless it has some meaning to readers in other parts of the world."[1]

Although our own research focuses on the history of American children, we have always understood that the field was international in its origins and scope, and that like other scholars in the area, we would benefit from a greater awareness of work being done on children in other countries. It seems clear to us that children and childhood are good examples of topics that cut across national boundaries and offer unique opportunities to enhance our understanding of the human condition.

As this volume clearly demonstrates, there is already an enormous volume of research on the history of children, even though it is not evenly distributed around the world. The field has advanced somewhat more rapidly in Western Europe and North America than in other areas where the historical profession is less well funded or where political conditions have inhibited such inquiry. We also would be the first to admit that not all of the significant research on the history of children is identified here. We regret very much the absence of a chapter on India, and several other areas deserve attention as well, including Spain and Spanish-speaking South America, Southeast Asia, sections of sub-Saharan Africa, Scandinavia, and Southern and Eastern Europe. We can only say that we view this volume as one step in the internationalization of the history of children. We are confident that it will not be the last.

Joseph M. Hawes and N. Ray Hiner

NOTE

1. Akira Iriye, "The Internationalization of History," *American Historical Review* 94 (February 1989): 2, 3, 9.

ACKNOWLEDGMENTS

This work is primarily that of the contributors whose chapters follow. Our task has been one of assembling and compiling and working with these scholars whose qualifications made them the logical choices for the various chapters. The project originated with a letter from Cynthia Harris, executive editor of Greenwood Press. We also acknowledge the assistance of Memphis State University and the University of Kansas.

CHILDREN IN HISTORICAL AND COMPARATIVE PERSPECTIVE

1

STANDING ON COMMON GROUND: REFLECTIONS ON THE HISTORY OF CHILDREN AND CHILDHOOD

N. Ray Hiner and Joseph M. Hawes

We haven't all had the good fortune to be ladies, we haven't all been generals, or poets, or statesmen, but when the toast works down to the babies, we all stand on common ground.[1]

—Mark Twain

Children now have a history—an incomplete and sometimes confusing history to be sure, but a fascinating and important history nonetheless. That much is clear from even a cursory reading of this volume. Few scholars, including historians of children, will fail to be surprised by how much has been learned about children in the past since the publication of Philippe Ariès' *L'Enfant et la vie familiale sous l'ancien régime* in 1960. One reason that the amount of published work on the history of children is unexpectedly large is that unlike some subfields in history, the history of children has not been dominated by one group or a single methodology, but has been the subject of inquiry by researchers in many fields, both inside and outside the discipline of history. The contributors to this volume have drawn on an astonishing variety of sources for their essays, including family history, women's history, demography, the history of education, psychohistory, labor history, art history, the history of medicine and health, folklore studies, legal history, the history of religion, intellectual history, literature, linguistics, anthropology, and sociology. Few of us, even those with the most Faustian appetites for scholarly reading, could be expected to be acquainted with the full scope of this burgeoning literature, certainly not for the entire world. Thus this volume has one clear purpose: to enable those interested in children to view their history in an international context and to learn from the questions, methods, and conclusions provided by scholars in the entire field.[2]

Of course the structural diversity of the history of children can be a source of serious weakness. The utter complexity and broad scope of the scholarship in the field, covering thousands of years, many cultures and nations, and based on different and sometimes contradictory assumptions and methodologies, almost defy comprehension. Anyone who approaches this literature with an obsessive need for obvious coherence and unimpeachable conclusions will be greatly disappointed. It would be extremely presumptuous for anyone to claim mastery of this enormous literature. We make no such claim.

Though the multidisciplinary character of the history of children precludes even a facile synthesis—at least at this point in the field's development—it does present some compensating advantages. The diversity of the history of children has, in the main, protected it from the narrowness of purpose, methodological bias, and intense focus that sometimes afflict new fields within history. Consequently the subject is less vulnerable to the caprice of changing academic fashions and politics within a particular field, which for any number of reasons might shift attention away from children. Even if social history, perhaps the major source of past and current historical interest in children, were to experience a noticeable decline in influence (a possible, if not probable, development), the effect on the history of children would be serious but not fatal because a significant amount of current historical research on children is not directly dependent on the assumptions, methodologies, or even the institutional position of social history.[3] Interest in the history of children has become so widely diffused and the volume of research has grown so large that it is highly unlikely children will ever again be overlooked as important historical subjects.

The extraordinary historiographical interest in children during the past three decades was encouraged by several factors, but among those cited most often are the youth movements of the 1960s and the efforts of historians to investigate the lives of those ''inarticulate'' groups, including children, who generally had been neglected or ignored by scholars.[4] Then, as research proceeded and knowledge about children grew, their importance as historical subjects became more evident and difficult to ignore. The sheer number of children who lived in the past, when the average age of human populations was considerably younger than it typically is in developed nations today, meant that the amount of time, energy, and resources that adults collectively and individually had to devote to the nurture and care of infants and young children was enormous.[5] Historians now understand that children in the past were central to the reproduction of class and the transmission of culture, important elements in the maintenance of political stability, and a significant source of labor for their families and communities.[6] In retrospect, it seems remarkable that until recently, children were virtually absent from our history, seldom seen or heard in our historical narratives.

This is not to say that the new history of children has been thoroughly integrated into the historical mainstream. Far from it. Indeed, this point is made by several of the contributors to this volume, even though most of them found a substantial body of research related to history of children in their respective countries. Patricia Rooke and R. L. Schnell describe Canadian child studies as "a truly marginal sub-specialty," and Mary Gibson agrees with the view expressed in 1980 by Marcello Flores that historians of Italy have "tended to portray children as appendages to the history of adults or institutions." David Ransel found so little historical literature focused directly on Russian children that he concludes, "Russia has no history of childhood." John Dardess strikes a more optimistic but still realistic note when he states that "the history of childhood in China has a shallow past, but surely a promising future." Similarly, Mary Jo Maynes and Thomas Taylor observe that although there has been little "room for children" in the works of German historians, children are now "poised to intrude noisily into German history." Perhaps only in France, England, and the United States, where interest in the history of children first developed and where the greatest volume of research on children exists, has there been much significant integration of children into general history. And even in these countries only a few scholars have begun to think through the implications of what we know about children for other, more traditional historical topics.[7] Clio's newest offspring is robust, but it is clearly still in its infancy.

Even in its immature state the history of children has raised some interesting issues for historians to ponder. Ariès, who did as much as anyone to legitimate the history of children as an academic enterprise and could justly be called its founder, left the field an important legacy. By making the point that childhood is, in large measure, a social construction that can vary in time and space, he established one of the bedrock assumptions on which the history of children could be build. As Linda Clark says in her essay on France, Ariès' work remains "central not only for historians of childhood but also for historians of the family, women, demography, education, social welfare and labor."

Still, it is one thing to say that childhood is part of the historical process, which now seems undeniable, and quite another to explain what this means for specific times and places. Hence some of Ariès' work has been subjected to intense criticism, especially his contention that there was probably "no place for childhood in the medieval world."[8] In his essay for this volume on "Childhood in Medieval Europe," David Nicholas gives credit to Ariès "for raising our consciousness of the importance of the history of childhood and providing a provocative synthesis," but he declares that "no medievalist still takes seriously his notion that people before the 'modern' period had no notion of childhood as a distinct period of human development." Valerie French speaks for historians of the ancient world when she says that Ariès committed "the literalist fallacy" when he concluded from paintings and other iconographic evidence that just because children were dressed as miniature adults, there was little, if any, recognition of "the difference between adults and children." As she explains, "one must consider here the artistic conventions of the culture. One would not argue that the ancient Egyptians really saw only one eye on a person's face simply because it was their convention to show only one eye in painting.'' Professor French further supports her critique of Ariès by citing evidence that shows striking similarities between ancient concepts of children and modern stage theories of child development. Sherrin Marshall also sees considerable continuity between the ''concerns and hopes'' of early modern European parents for their children and those of parents today. Finally, if Ariès' thesis about the absence of the concept of childhood does not hold for premodern Europe, there is even less evidence that applies to the non-Western world. In China, for example, John Dardess says that ''there never seems to have been much doubt, at least in a legal and ritual sense, about what a child was.'' Elizabeth Fernea notes that ''during the Islamic medieval period from 900 to 1200 A.D., several treatises were written on the method of raising a child.''

In view of the general rejection by ancient and medieval historians of Ariès' thesis concerning the emergence of childhood as a concept, it is more than a little ironic that he was actually somewhat nostalgic about the medieval period. He thought that the aggressive intrusiveness of modern schooling and social control deprived children of the freedom and spontaneity they allegedly enjoyed in medieval communities where they were not institutionalized as a special class. In contrast, Lloyd deMause, a scholar and publisher who exercised considerable influence on the early development of the history of children, finds little to admire in the treatment of children in premodern Europe, which he describes as an abusive nightmare. In fact, he argues that ''the further back in history one goes, the lower the level of child care, and the more likely children are to be killed, abandoned, beaten, terrorized, and sexually abused.''[9] Not surprisingly, the ancient and medieval historians, who rejected Ariès' relatively more benign view of the treatment of children during these periods, have roundly condemned deMause's psychogenic hypothesis as an unwarranted attack on the humanity of those they study. David Nicholas simply dismisses deMause's assessment of the Middle Ages as a ''hysterical lament.'' Valerie French does not question ''the grisly picture'' of murder and abuse that is presented by the evidence collected by deMause and others, but she does ''dispute deMause's contention that this evidence provides a full portrait of childhood in antiquity; deMause and his school ignore or distort evidence of positive attitudes and treatment of children.'' She believes that the historical record provides ''two contradictory portraits of childhood in classical antiquity'': one with a ''pattern of childrearing'' that was ''attentive, nurturing, valuing [of] the child'' versus another that was ''neglectful, destructive, demeaning [of] the child.'' Professor French doubts that, given ''the fragmentary nature of the evidence for reconstructing the lives of Greek and Roman children,'' it will ever be possible to determine which pattern predominated in the ancient Western world.

The record for child-rearing attitudes and behavior is no less equivocal for the premodern Far East. In both traditional China and Japan there is evidence of physical and sexual abuse of children, but this must be balanced against other evidence that shows a deep concern for children and their welfare, including a belief in the need for "placental instruction" in China or "womb education" in Japan and a preference for "gentle care" for infants in Japan or the "very powerful folk custom" in China "that set aside a certain liminal space in the earliest life of a child, and mandated its thorough, almost abject spoiling, such that every whim was satisfied, and its every tantrum yielded to." Similar illustrations can be drawn from the record of traditional, indigenous cultures in East Africa, Brazil, the Muslim Middle East, and North America.[10]

In sum, the available evidence seems to point to the presence of considerable continuity in parent-child relations throughout human history. Certainly that is the view of Linda Pollock, who maintains that "the barbaric system of child care described by many authors would be quite unique. The theory of prevalent systematic ill-treatment of children is highly unlikely." She supports this conclusion by questioning the representativeness of the evidence used to support the "Black Legend of childhood," by drawing on sociobiological theory to demonstrate how difficult, if not impossible, it is for truly widespread maladaptive behavior by parents to be maintained in any society for long periods. She also draws upon a systematic analysis of 496 British and American diaries and autobiographies written from the sixteenth through the nineteenth centuries. She concludes her book, *Forgotten Children: Parent-Child Relations from 1500 to 1900*, with the following statement: "Instead of trying to explain the supposed changes in parent-child relationship, historians could do well to ponder just why parental care is a variable so curiously resistant to change."[11]

The issue, however, is far from settled. Elizabeth Pleck, who reviewed the American sources included in Pollock's study before completing her own analysis of "110 reminiscences concerning children raised in the American colonies and the United States between 1650 and 1900," has questioned Pollock's reading of the evidence and her assumption that "the absence of information reflects the absence of punishment." Pleck notes that "cruel and abusive parents were not the kind of people who kept diaries."[12] Lloyd deMause has raised a similar objection to Pollock's methodology, commenting that "in order for abuse of children to be present for her [Pollock], it would have to have been written down by the perpetrator."[13]

Pollock admits in her preface that she "may be . . . placing too much emphasis on continuity in child-rearing practices," but she believes that these "changes should be investigated against the background of continuity. There may indeed be subtle changes in child care through the centuries—changes that so far lie hidden because of the prevailing interest to discover and argue for dramatic transformations."[14] This qualification seems prudent and useful, given the limited nature of the evidence used in the debate about child rearing.

Peter Petschauer has observed, with some justification, that most of those historians who have written about child rearing can be divided into two groups: "those who find tears and those who find smiles in the past." For him, "accuracy resides in both and neither side. One can indeed find empathy in the past and in the present. And one can find abandonment in the present and in the past."[15]

It may indeed be wise for historians of children to simply leave it at that, to accept for now this accurate, if somewhat unsatisfying, conclusion and proceed to explore other dimensions of children's lives in the past that lend themselves to more definitive conclusions.

What is most impressive about the debate over the quality of child rearing in the past is not only the difficulty in finding and interpreting valid evidence, but also the extent to which the debate has come to depend as much on what the participants think about human nature and what they value in human relations as on what empirical evidence they have collected and presented. Children are so fundamental to human life that to ask whether parents and other adults have grown in their capacity to nurture them is tantamount to asking whether there has been or can be human progress, however that may be defined. This is a profoundly important question, but it is not one that historians are equipped to answer in its current form. Historians of children can and should continue to investigate, describe, and assess changes and continuities in the historical experience of children, including child-parent relations, but they should resist the temptation to make global statements about whether these changes and continuities represent the advance or decline of human civilization, if for no other reason than the amount and quality of the evidence now available do not warrant making such judgments.

Fortunately the history of children is by no means synonymous with this interesting, but ultimately unresolvable debate about the quality of child rearing. Historians of children have undertaken a whole array of investigations of a wide range of other, equally interesting topics, which are summarized and discussed in the following chapters.[16] Although the results of this ongoing research are incomplete and often raise more questions than they answer, they do permit some tentative observations.

The most striking characteristic of the historical experience of children is its extraordinary variety. Each society and culture, each region and local community, each social class, ethnic group, and family, and each generation exerted its unique influence on children. The potential for variability seems almost infinite. Yet some patterns seem to have, to some degree, transcended the boundaries of time and culture. The vast majority of human infants have been and continue to be cared for primarily by females. Indeed, gender as a social construct has left its indelible mark on children throughout history, although its precise character has differed greatly from one time and place to another.[17] We know of no culture in which children did not play.[18] We know of no major culture in which some children were not abused (only the incidence of abuse is in question, not its existence).[19] In many, if not most, cultures children between the ages of six and eight have been assigned new roles and faced distinctly different expectations than younger children.[20] Similarly, few, if any, cultures have failed to take notice of the physiological changes associated with puberty and adolescence, although the degree and character of this recognition have been quite diverse.[21]

There are significant patterns of change as well as patterns of continuity in the history of children. These changes can be summarized most efficiently here by viewing them from a long-range, global perspective that compares conditions in premodern or traditional societies with those in contemporary, developed countries.[22] Children in developed countries today are more likely to be aborted before birth and less likely to be killed or die after birth, to become orphans, to experience the death of a sibling, or to suffer the effects of a fatal or debilitating illness or accident. They also are more likely to have surviving grandparents and divorced parents, and to live in a single-parent household than were children in the premodern world. ''Modern'' children have fewer siblings and are physically larger, healthier, better housed than were most children in traditional societies. After the age of five they are more likely to spend time in schools and engage in supervised play with children their own age than were children in the past, who were more likely to be in the presence of adults working and learning a craft, trade, or occupation. The parents of ''modern'' children are more likely to consult ''experts'' about child rearing than were their premodern counterparts. At home, children today are more likely to have access to their own ''private'' space than were children in premodern societies, where living space was at a premium. Also, the electronic media, especially television, have created a special world for children that was unimaginable in premodern times. Finally, children in developed countries are more likely to have a clearly defined legal status than were children in traditional societies, where kin and parental rights tended to be predominant.

To describe the patterns of change in the history of children in this highly abbreviated manner greatly oversimplifies and obscures the complex and uneven process by which these changes occurred. Certainly it is possible that children in some underdeveloped countries today have more in common with children of the premodern era than with children living in the world's most developed countries. Even so, it is important to remember that both ''the world we have lost'' and the world that, to some extent, has taken its place are worlds inhabited by children as well as adults, and that children are an important part of the transition from one to the other. The chapters that follow provide abundant evidence that this is so.

NOTES

1. We are indebted to Barbara Burn for drawing out attention to this Twain aphorism. See her introduction to *Metropolitan Children* (New York: The Metropolitan Museum of Art, 1984), a superb visual review of children in world art. Also see *Mark Twain Speaking*, ed. Paul Fatout (Iowa City: University of Iowa Press, 1976), p. 131.

2. We regret very much the person who agreed to prepare a chapter on India was unable to provide it.

3. Another case in point would be the changing relation between the history of childhood and psychohistory. In its early years the history of childhood was heavily influenced by psychohistory, but the apparent decline in psychohistory's prestige among

historians has not reduced historical interest in children. From this perspective, we have found it useful in this chapter to distinguish between the history of childhood as a social construction and the history of children, which includes the history of childhood, but also encompasses all aspects of children's lives. We hasten to add that this distinction is not recognized by everyone in the field or even by the contributors to this volume, most of whom treat the terms as interchangeable. One of the first scholars to make this conceptual distinction was Patricia T. Rooke, "The 'Child-Institutionalized' in Canada, Britain, and the United States: A Trans-Atlantic Perspective," *Journal of Educational Thought* 11 (August 1977):163.

4. See Peter N. Stearns, "Toward a Wider Vision: Trends in Social History," in *The Past Before Us: Contemporary Historical Writing in the United States*, ed. Michael Kammen (Ithaca, N.Y.: Cornell University Press, 1980), pp. 205–230; Lawrence Stone, "Family History in the 1980's: Past Achievements and Future Trends," *Journal of Interdisciplinary History* 12 (Summer 1981):51–87; N. Ray Hiner, "The Child in American Historiography: Accomplishments and Prospects," *The Psychohistory Review* 7 (Summer 1978):13–22. For an early overview of the field, see John Sommerville, *The Rise and Fall of Childhood* (Beverly Hills, Calif.: Sage Publications, 1982).

5. Most of the chapters in this volume review the demographic research on which this statement is based, but see especially the chapters by Valerie French, Elizabeth Kuznesof, David Nicholas, Sherrin Marshall, Mary Gibson, Mary Jo Maynes, and Thomas Taylor. The best review of this literature for the United States is Robert Wells, *Revolutions in America's Lives: A Demographic Perspective on the History of Americans, Their Families, and Their Society* (Westport, Conn.: Greenwood Press, 1982).

6. Again, these statements represent a summary of conclusions expressed throughout this volume.

7. For an excellent example of how valuable a children's perspective can be in understanding large historical events and processes, see Elliott West, *Growing Up with the Country: Childhood on the Far Western Frontier* (Albuquerque: University of New Mexico Press, 1989).

8. Philippe Ariès, *Centuries of Childhood: A Social History of Family Life*, trans. Robert Baldick (New York: Random House, 1962), p. 33. For recent reviews of the resp nse to Ariès' work, see S. Ryan Johansson, "Centuries of Childhood/Centuries of Paren .g: Philippe Ariès and the Modernization of Privileged Infancy," *Journal of Family History* 12 (1987):343–365; and Bruce Bellingham, "The History of Childhood Since the 'Invention of Childhood': Some Issues for the Eighties," ibid. 13 (1988):347–358.

9. Lloyd deMause, *The History of Childhood* (New York: Psychohistory Press, 1974), p. 1.

10. In addition to chapters in this volume by John Dardess, Kathleen Uno, Sara Harkness and Charles Super, Elizabeth Kuznesof, and Elizabeth Fernia, see Margaret Connell Szasz, "Native American Children," in *American Childhood: A Research Guide and Historical Handbook*, ed. Joseph M. Hawes and N. Ray Hiner (Westport, Conn.: Greenwood Press, 1985), pp. 311–342.

11. Linda A. Pollock, *Forgotten Children: Parent-Child Relations from 1500 to 1900* (Cambridge: Cambridge University Press, 1983), pp. viii–ix, 43, 69–70, 271.

12. Elizabeth Pleck, *Domestic Tyranny: The Making of Social Policy Against Family Violence from Colonial Times to the Present* (New York: Oxford University Press, 1987), pp. 44, 205, 237.

13. Lloyd deMause, "On Writing Childhood History," *Journal of Psychohistory* 16 (Fall 1988):161.

14. Pollock, *Forgotten Children*, p. viii.

15. Peter Petschauer, "The Childrearing Modes in Flux: An Historian's Reflections," *Journal of Psychohistory* 17 (Summer 1989):3.

16. We have suggested the following questions as guides to the range of topics and issues that historians of children can and should explore: (1) What have been the attitudes of adults toward children and childhood? (2) What were the conditions that shaped the development of children? (3) What has been the subjective experience of being a child in the past? (4) How have the children influenced adults and one another? (5) What have been the social, cultural, and psychological functions of children? See N. Ray Hiner and Joseph M. Hawes, eds., *Growing Up in America: Children in Historical Perspective* (Urbana: University of Illinois Press, 1985), pp. xx–xxii.

17. For discussions of gender and history, see Gerda Lerner, *The Creation of Patriarchy* (New York: Oxford University Press, 1986); Joan W. Scott, "Gender: A Useful Category of Historical Analysis," *American Historical Review* 91 (December 1986):1053–1075; and Linda Kerber, "Separate Spheres, Female Worlds, Woman's Place: The Rhetoric of Women's History," *Journal of American History* 75 (June 1988): 7–39.

18. Bernard Mergen, *Play and Playthings: A Reference Guide* (Westport, Conn.: Greenwood Press, 1981), pp. 176–221.

19. Robert B. Edgerton, however, suggests in the foreword to *Child Abuse and Neglect: Cross Cultural Perspectives*, ed. Jill E. Korbin (Berkeley: University of California Press, 1981), that child abuse may occur "very infrequently or not at all" in traditional societies. Still, Korbin concludes that "although idiosyncratic child abuse and neglect may be defined differently by [various cultural] groups and may occur with different frequencies, deviance in child care behavior is known cross-culturally as a possibility of human behavior." (p. 206) Also see John Demos' interesting discussion of this issue in his *Past, Present, and Personal: The Family and the Life Course in American History* (New York: Oxford University Press, 1986), pp. 68–91.

20. For examples, see the chapters in this volume by Valerie French, David Nicholas, Sherrin Marshall, John Dardess, and Elizabeth Fernea.

21. Ibid. There is a surprisingly large body of literature on adolescence in the West. Most of this literature is cited in the bibliographies for this volume.

22. This paragraph represents an effort to summarize some of the changes identified in this volume that affected children most directly, but it is certainly not a comprehensive list.

I

THE PREMODERN
WORLD

2

CHILDREN IN ANTIQUITY

Valerie French

Child rearing was the predominant occupation of women in classical antiquity; fathers also frequently played more than minor roles in caring for and educating their children. In addition, thousands of other adults contributed personally to rearing the young as midwives (who also served as pediatricians for babies), nurses (both wet and dry), tutors and companions (usually slaves, and most often of the same sex as the child), physicians, and teachers (not only for reading, writing, arithmetic, music, history, law, and rhetoric, but also for athletics and military training). Moreover, the laws of many ancient Mediterranean communities contained substantial provisions regulating the ways children were to be treated. In sum, there can be little doubt that child rearing was an important socio-political aspect of classical antiquity, an activity to which adults devoted large amounts of time and considerable attention.

Alongside this clear concern for and investment in the welfare of children stands an equally clear picture of thousands of children subjected to infanticide, sale, neglect, abandonment, and horrendous abuse (emotional, physical, and sexual). Nor can there be much doubt that ancient societies tended to devote more effort and resources to rearing male children.

Scholarly work to date has provided at least the sketches, and in some cases rich detail, for these two contradictory portraits of childhood in classical antiquity.[1] Given the fragmentary nature of our evidence for reconstructing the lives of Greek and Roman children, it is unlikely that a determination can be made as to which pattern of child rearing—attentive, nurturing, valuing the child versus neglectful, destructive, demeaning the child—predominated generally or within particular periods or specific cultures.

SOURCES AND METHODOLOGICAL ISSUES

Evidence for ancient childhood is surprisingly abundant, at least by the standards ancient historians use. The major difficulty in using the sources is that little nuggets of information about children, descriptions of and prescriptions for child rearing, and adult beliefs about and attitudes toward the young are widely scattered throughout written and material sources. Few writers treat childhood in any systematic manner; but important references to children are to be found in the work of poets, playwrights, novelists, philosophers, historians, biographers, essayists, and legal and medical writers. Material evidence such as children's toys, child-rearing equipment, artistic representations of children and their activities, inscriptions detailing legal provisions for children and funerary commemorations, and domestic architecture also is plentiful; but here, too, descriptions of this evidence must be located through excavation reports, volumes of epigraphic evidence, and museum catalogues.

For written sources, finding these nuggets requires careful combing of any potential source material; evaluating the many authors who speak of children means ascertaining, if possible, the individual's own experience with children and determining the cultural assumptions about children the writer is likely to have had. For material sources, the historian must be constantly aware of how modern assumptions about child rearing may affect interpretation of artifacts and the significance of their provenance. Finally, an aristocratic male bias heavily colors the literary evidence; and most artifacts, even those related to the lower classes, were designed and produced by men.

Historians have begun to develop a clear and agreed-on set of standards for drawing reliable inferences from this evidence. There is consensus that the variables of gender, class, and particularly culture must be factored into interpretation; that overly literal readings of the evidence are suspect[2]; and that using modern Western theories about children and child rearing can be fraught with uncertainty. But in matters of interpreting the affective qualities of the relations between adults and children, there is significant disagreement. Moreover, historians have barely begun to explore why communities adopted and maintained their child-rearing practices, why those practices changed, and the effects of changes in child-rearing practices on succeeding generations.

THE FAMILY, REPRODUCTION, AND THE STATE

The family was the primary unit of social and economic organization in ancient Greece and Rome; and to a significant extent, political life was an extension of the private family into the public realm.[3] Over time and across socioeconomic strata, most families used a reproductive strategy that kept them relatively small; two or perhaps three children would survive to adulthood. This strategy was apparently motivated by different concerns, depending on socioeconomic status. Without primogeniture, the wealthy tried to maintain the size of their estates;

they avoided dividing them among too many heirs and paying out too many dowries. Among the poor, limited resources and poor health worked to constrain family size.[4] Times of war, famine, and pestilence were particularly difficult for the poor.

Sometimes family planning, although privately, not publicly, determined, became a matter of public concern, particularly when there was fear that some portion of the state's population was not replenishing itself.[5] The Spartans of the archaic and classical eras (ca. 700–350 B.C.E.) were well known not only for promoting procreation among the full citizens, but also for a system of eugenics; an older or infirm Spartan husband could choose to have his wife impregnated by a younger, more robust Spartan; and babies with congenital defects were supposed to be exposed.[6]

The Romans were much concerned about two problems that came with limiting the size of families—failure of the aristocracy to reproduce itself and lack of manpower for the legions. Romulus was believed to have decreed that all boys and at least one girl were to be raised. The emperor Augustus tried through legislation, the *Lex Julia de maritandis ordinibus* of 18 B.C.E. and the *Lex Papia Poppaea* of 9 C.E., to coerce marriage and procreation among the upper classes and to reward parents of all classes for bearing three or more children; the laws met with much resistance and were largely ineffective.

The emperors of the early second century C.E., Nerva, Trajan, and Hadrian, established state-supported subsidies (the *alimenta*) to help those who had small farms rear their young; private benefactors set up similar programs to aid the children of the poor. These welfare efforts were prompted by both a desire to increase the birthrate among families likely to provide legionnaires and a genuine concern for the health and well-being of children reared in near poverty. Confined mainly to Italy, the subsidy programs favored males over females (e.g., boys got more money for food and remained eligible for aid longer) and undoubtedly alleviated the hunger of some children. But there is no evidence that these child welfare programs increased family size.[7]

ADULT KNOWLEDGE OF, BELIEFS ABOUT, AND ATTITUDES TOWARD CHILDREN

Knowledge of Children

Given the ubiquity of references to children throughout the ancient written sources, it is a fair inference that adult males observed and gained considerable knowledge of children and their lives. The dramatist Aeschylus clearly describes how difficult it is to discover what a crying baby wants; the comic playwright Aristophanes shows us a father who can understand his son's baby talk and take care of his toilet training; the philosopher and politician Cicero notes the competitiveness of young boys in their play; the poet Horace comments on how balky a two-year-old can be; the teacher of Marcus Aurelius, Fronto, writes that one of a baby's first words is likely to be "da"—"give me."[8]

The correspondence of men such as Cicero, Pliny the Younger, and Fronto shows real parental concern for and interest in the young, as does a third-century C.E. letter from a wife to her husband, who is apparently caring for their son while she attends to a household move: "Many salutations to the little Theon. Eight toys have been brought for him by the lady to whom you told me to give your salutations."[9]

Greek vase paintings, particularly on little jugs called *choes*, regularly depict young children (usually plump little boys) at play with wagons, pets, and toys. Other artistic evidence—terra-cotta statues, clay models, funerary stelae—also provide pictures of children and their activities.[10] These activities range from babies in cradles, to toddlers being carried on adults' shoulders, to boys playing with knucklebones, to a young girl getting a cooking lesson from (presumably) her mother.

The Roman visual evidence also attests to adult male observation of the young. The Roman sarcophagi of the late republic and imperial periods provide especially interesting pictures; these reliefs show groups of boys roughhousing and groups of girls in more sedate play; they show a range of toys such as hoops, spinning tops, wagons, and scooters.[11]

The best evidence for adult knowledge about the young comes from philosophers and medical writers. According to Greek tradition, the earliest lawgivers were concerned with the way the young should be reared and educated; Roman tradition about its founder, Romulus, also credits him with legislation on child rearing and education. Whether there is any truth in these traditions is impossible to ascertain. But political philosophers of the fourth century B.C.E., principally Plato and Aristotle, devoted considerable attention to children and how to make sure that their education and training equipped them for life as good citizens.[12] From these discussions we can see the establishment of a philosophical tradition that both describes the development of children and prescribes the proper treatment for each stage of their development.[13] Let us look first at this tradition's empirical descriptions of the development of children from infancy to early adulthood.

As described by Plato and Aristotle, five stages of childhood represent both physical and psychological growth; the psychological development encompasses both emotional and cognitive maturation. Babyhood lasts from birth to about two years of age, when the child is weaned and can talk. The baby's inability to express its needs and wants was particularly frustrating to both Greeks and Romans.[14] Aeschylus vividly describes this problem in a speech given by Cilissa, Orestes' nurse:

> A baby is like a beast, it does not think
> but you have to nurse it, do you not, the way it wants.
> For the child still in swaddling clothes cannot tell us

if he is hungry or thirsty, if he needs to make
water. Children's young insides are a law to
themselves.[15]

The next stage might be called an early preschool period; children from about
two to three or even five years of age are described as beginning to separate
themselves from their mothers or nurses and becoming more physically active.
They are easily frightened and highly impressionable. Such children begin to
devise games and play by themselves. The biographer and philosopher Plutarch,
an especially sympathetic observer of the young, described the activities of his
two-year-old daughter Timoxena: "She would invite the nurse to offer the breast
and feed with it not only other infants, but even inanimate objects and playthings
she took pleasure in, as though serving them at her own table."[16]

Real preschoolers, children from three to six or seven, are portrayed as very
active and forming their own social networks with friends and games. Play,
often in games that replicate adult activities, predominates in their day-to-day
lives. At the age of six or seven children begin school and enter a stage that
lasts until puberty. Competition (among boys) is an important element in their
activities, both in school and outside of it. The final stage of development is
adolescence, until the child reaches the late teens or early twenties.[17]

This scheme of development clearly shows the androcentric nature of our
sources. Given the early age of marriage for girls in most ancient societies (the
Spartans were a notable exception), it is doubtful that we can legitimately speak
of a female adolescence.[18] However, a fragmentary work called "The Distaff"
by the fourth-century B.C.E. poetess Erinna from Telos suggests a friendship
between two girls that lasted into early adolescence. Erinna describes their play
as younger children (dolls, cavorting in the sea, riding horses), implying that
the two friends had moved to a new stage of their lives. Erinna then says, "But
when . . . you forgot all that you heard as a child from your mother, dear Baucis
. . . forgetfulness . . . Aphrodite," suggesting a friendship that was ended by Baucis' marriage, probably at thirteen to fourteen years of age.[19]

The philosophical tradition articulated by Plato and Aristotle carried over into
the Greco-Roman and Roman world. Cicero, the great teacher of rhetoric Quintilian, Plutarch, St. Augustine, and the late pagan writer Macrobius, authors
whose works span some five centuries (early first B.C.E. to early fifth C.E.)—
all these writers' descriptions of the growth and development of children follow
the earlier model with but few modifications.[20]

Any argument that this philosophical tradition represents valid knowledge
about children—their stages of development and the characteristics of each
stage—depends, of course, on the validity of the standards used to test the ancient
knowledge. Several decades of research on child development and psychology
posit models to which the ancient tradition bears striking resemblances. The only
stage the ancient tradition seems to miss is what is now called toddlerhood,
although the early preschool phase shares some of toddlerhood's characteristics.

To the extent that we accept modern theory about child development, we conclude that the ancient tradition represents a valid body of knowledge about the young.

The medical writers provide additional evidence of adult knowledge of children. At least ten pediatric treatises are known to have been written and demonstrate that pediatrics was recognized as a distinctive branch of medicine; of them, only that by Aëtius of Amida and a substantial fragment by Soranus are extant. Other medical writers also discussed children.[21] Many childhood diseases were recognized, demonstrating that adults had a solid working knowledge of the medical afflictions suffered particularly by children and their greater vulnerability to disease and infection.[22]

Although the ancient medical writers represent the gamut of medicine, from the best medical thinking to common folk wisdom, they all concurred with this observation expressed by Celsus:

Indeed in general children ought not to be treated like adults. Therefore, as in any other sort of disease, we must set to work with more caution in these cases: not let blood readily, not readily clyster, not torment by wakefulness and by hunger or by excess of thirst, nor is wine as a treatment very suitable.[23]

The ancient works show a solid empirical knowledge of childhood diseases and their likely outcomes. Although modern pediatricians are not likely to prescribe ancient treatments for sick children,[24] they would recognize the validity of the ancient observation that children have their own diseases and often require a different kind of medical care.

Adult Beliefs about Children

Knowledge and belief are, of course, often inextricably intertwined. The distinction I want to draw here is that between verifiable observation (knowledge) and conclusions drawn from those observations (beliefs). The case of pediatrics—ancient and modern—illustrates the importance of this distinction. The empirical observations of ancient medical writers seem reliable, but many of their beliefs about efficacious treatment do not.

We can best evaluate ancient beliefs about the most effective methods of child rearing with this distinction between observations of children's characteristics at various stages of development and prescriptions for appropriate child care. For example, noting the baby's inability to speak and do much for itself, the philosophical tradition said that babies need much attention and affection and minimal discipline. Observing that children between ages two and six are easily frightened and upset, the tradition contended that during these years, children should be shielded from base or corrupting influences.[25]

The tradition's beliefs about the relation between observed characteristics and appropriate child care can be most conveniently summarized in the following chart:

OBSERVED CHARACTERISTICS	PRESCRIBED TREATMENT
1. Most children pass through stages of physical and mental growth—infancy or babyhood; preschool years; elementary school years; puberty and adolescence.	1. Tailor treatment to suit the specific stage of growth.
2. Although there are characteristics and needs that apply to children generally, there are inherent differences among children.	2. Look for these differences, and tailor treatment to meet the needs of the individual child.
3. Most children are plastic, impressionable, moldable.	3. Begin to mold children in early infancy into the kind of adults the society desires by providing proper role models and keeping children away from base influences.
4. Most young children are fragile, damageable.	4. Protect them from harsh treatment, and spare them from harsh punishment.
5. School-aged children and adolescents are reasonably strong and sometimes headstrong.	5. Use firm, even harsh, discipline to instill proper attitudes and behavior.[26]
6. Most children are playful and sometimes competitive.	6. Provide constructive play and, when appropriate, allow their competitive instincts to push them toward desired achievements.

These propositions form the foundation of the tradition's belief in the efficacy of nurture, of the importance of the environment in rearing the young. The tradition, however, also believes in the role of nature. Because they belong to the general category of children, the young naturally have certain characteristics. In addition, children differ from one another naturally. It is interesting that the ancient tradition's discussion of nature and nurture does not, as is so often the case in our own time, posit a nature *versus* nurture controversy; there appears to be no argument over the primacy of one or the other. Rather, nature and nurture are believed to operate together, each playing a significant role and suggesting appropriate guidelines for child-rearing practices.[27]

Because the tradition encompasses the work of men from a variety of philosophical schools—Academics, Peripatetics, Stoics, the Roman Sophists—we can be reasonably confident that these views permeated the upper classes and were adopted by men and women privileged enough to obtain more than an elementary education.[28] But we have no idea of the extent to which the general populace shared the beliefs about children and child rearing found in this philosophical tradition.

Adult Attitudes toward Children

Here we move into the realm of affect, with all the attendant difficulties of determining how a person feels about something. Ancient historians who investigate childhood and family life fall into two camps: those who eschew an attempt to determine the quality of feelings within families, and those who, like myself, acknowledge the problems but believe that they can recover some reasonably reliable pictures of this critical element of human experience.[29] We can find a common ground if we limit discussion to expressed attitudes toward children, and thereby push to one side the question of what a particular adult or group of adults felt about their own children or children generally.

I propose to separate adult attitudes into two broad categories: those that suggest a positive and those that express a negative view of the child. These categories imply the imposition of a system of values, a system shared by modern western societies.

Positive Views of the Child

The extensive treatment of child rearing by the ancient philosophers itself suggests a positive attitude: children are educable and their education is worth the investment of time and effort. Indeed, one finds over and over in ancient literature an affirmation of the importance of the child. The child is seen as both the individual family's and the larger community's link to the future. The family without children is incomplete[30]; the evidence indicates that thousands of babies were either formally adopted or cared for by foster parents. And both Greeks and Romans believed that only by proper education of children would the society be able to perpetuate itself.

In addition to the value children had as embodying the family's and community's future, they were described as a source of pleasure for their parents and caregivers. One of the most poignant expressions comes in Plutarch's letter of consolation to his wife when their little daughter Timoxena died.

The delight [our love for our children] gives is quite pure and free from all anger or reproach . . . just as she was herself the most delightful thing in the world to embrace, to see, to hear, so too must the thought of her live with us and be our companion, bringing with it joy in greater measure, nay in many times greater measure, than it brings sorrow.[31]

Corroboration for Plutarch's view that children provide pleasure comes from a variety of evidence. Scattered throughout the literature are references such as Plato's portrait of a country farmer's feast with his children, Catullus' description of the smoothness of a baby's earlobe, and Fronto's request to Marcus Aurelius that he kiss his little daughters' hands and feet.[32] Hundreds of funerary epitaphs for children from the Roman period describe the child as sweet or announce the parents' grief over their loss. Two examples suffice to illustrate this kind of evidence.

Stop, traveler, and read what is written here. A mother was not allowed to enjoy her only daughter. Some god, I don't know which, begrudged her to me. Since I, her mother, was not allowed to dress her while she was alive, I performed this task as was fitting after she died, when her time on earth was over. A mother has honored with this memorial the daughter whom she loved.[33]

And

To the gods of the dead, the tomb of Junia Procula, daughter of Marcus. She lived eight years, eleven months, five days. She left in sorrow her unhappy father and mother.[34]

If one can hazard an inference about the attitudes toward children expressed by artists and artisans, one sees in these renderings a real interest and delight in children at play.

In the Roman period we find another expression of the importance of children: they are examples of Nature and Nature's plan, and hence of the divine. Cicero, for example, says "My own school, more than others, go to the nursery, because they believe that Nature reveals her plan to them most clearly in childhood."[35] We see this theme developed in early Christian writers, such as St. Augustine, who contends that "for these things hast thou hid from the wise and prudent, and hast revealed them unto babes."[36]

Negative Views of the Child

One of the major expressions of a negative view of children is infanticide. There can be no doubt that infanticide was regularly and widely practiced throughout classical antiquity. The willful exposure of infants no doubt reflected an attempt both to regulate population and to eliminate at the beginning children too weak or malformed to survive.[37] Moreover, evidence attests to some people's dispassionate view of the act. For example, in a first-century B.C.E. annulment of a marriage contract in Alexandria, the settlement provides that the pregnant wife "is permitted to expose her baby and to join herself in marriage to another husband." A soldier wrote home to his wife: "If it is a boy, let it live; if it is a girl, expose it."[38]

There were but few attempts to curtail infanticide. Only the Greek cities of Thebes and Ephesus banned the act, and ancient writers seldom condemn it.[39] Roman law, largely in response to the influence of Christianity, made infanticide a capital offense only in 374 C.E. Even with all the evidence for the widespread practice of infanticide, it is nonetheless impossible to arrive at any firm conclusions about how often and under what circumstances families resorted to it.

Another expression of a view that devalues and tends to destroy children is the sale of young children into slavery.[40] Such a sale could consign a child to life as a household drudge or a farm laborer—or worse. Evidence exists that both male and female children were sold to brothels to be used by pedophiles of any sexual orientation; they also were sold to professional beggars, who maimed them to make them more pitiable, and thus more likely to elicit coins from passersby.

The many injunctions of ancient writers to avoid excessive and abusive punishment have been taken to imply that spankings, beatings, whippings, and the like were common methods of discipline in most households. The inference may well have considerable validity, but we cannot determine just how frequently parents and caregivers used violent, even brutal, measures.

More particularly, an inference about latent maternal hostility toward male children in classical Athens has been advanced by Philip Slater. The inference rests on his interpretation of the powerful female figures in classical Greek tragedy. The argument runs as follows. Greek men, and hence Greek tragic poets, were misogynic and homosexual because of their mothers' frustrations with their restricted lives; the mothers projected their sexual and social frustrations onto their young boys because as wives, they dared not voice such frustrations to their husbands; the young boys (who were, according to Slater, under their mothers' sole care until they went to school) sensed and internalized their mothers' hostility, causing them both to become narcissistic and to fear, and therefore come to hate, women. The powerful women of Attic drama are, then, a projection of narcissistic male fears of their hostile mothers.[41] Most feminist scholars of Greek drama and the lives of ancient women have rejected Slater's arguments by advancing alternative explanations of the role of women in tragedy or by demonstrating that Slater's contention that fathers were uninvolved in the lives of their young sons is invalid.[42]

Finally, an argument can be made that the ancient societies' emphasis on education was not for the sake of the child, but for the perpetuation of the state and community. There is some merit to this contention. Seldom do classical Greek writers extol education as serving the interests of the child who receives it; the work of Plato and Aristotle (particularly Plato's dialogues), however, takes as a given that whatever benefits the state also benefits the individual. Later writers, such as Quintilian and Plutarch, do speak about the pleasure children can take from their studies.

Unfortunately the fragmentary nature of the evidence does not permit any conclusions about the relative prevalence of positive versus negative adult attitudes toward their own children or children in general. We are probably safe in assuming that within each society, both positive and negative attitudes existed simultaneously; perhaps the same could be said for most people.

RECONSTRUCTING THE LIVES OF ANCIENT CHILDREN AND THE FUTURE OF THE STUDY OF ANCIENT CHILDHOOD

The next stage in the study of ancient children is the evaluation and synthesis of the disparate studies carried out to date. One object of such work is reconstructing the kinds of experiences children of different ages, different genders, and different socioeconomic status were likely to have had. This work might well try to take the children's perspective, at least in describing what kinds of activities went on around them and what they might be doing. This reconstruction, however, cannot do anything more than speculate on children's reactions to or feelings about their experiences. The voices of but a few ancient women have survived; ancient children are totally silent.

Some preliminary work towards attaining this goal has been done by scholars whose work I have been discussing. Additional discussions can be found in a genre of studies that treat the lives of women and daily life in various ancient communities.[43] We already know, for example, a good deal about child-rearing paraphernalia such as infant feeding bottles, cradles, cribs, and potty chairs; about nursing and nurses and lullabies; about children's clothing from swaddling bands to footgear and jewelry; about the incredible range of children's toys, pets, games, and songs; about tutors and companions; about birthday parties and other festivities that included children; about school curricula; about the kinds of stories children heard; about the numerous gods and goddesses who presided over childhood and to whom it is likely that children and their parents offered prayers; and about pediatric treatments.

Sorting out how this information is to be correlated with the age, gender, class, and particular culture of children is yet to be accomplished. Studies of the childhoods of famous people may help to determine how the general evidence about children and childhood is to be applied to the upper classes. Although evidence about any particular person's childhood is sparse, it can, on occasion, suggest explanations for that person's adult behavior and attitudes.[44] More work along these lines can and will certainly be done.

Yet to be achieved also is a careful historical treatment of ancient childhood, an investigation of how and why child-rearing practices either persisted or changed over time; when one considers that classical antiquity conventionally spans well over a millennium (from ca. 800 B.C.E. to 400 C.E.), the need for a historical approach becomes self-evident. Finally, once a historical study is in place, historians can turn their attention to tracing, where possible, the effects of changes in child-rearing practices on the larger society.

This last task promises a way to integrate the study of ancient childhood into the fabric of the study of classical antiquity generally. For example, I have for some time been working on an argument that significant changes in the way young Spartan children were reared and socialized provide at least a partial explanation for the decline of Spartan power in the fourth century B.C.E. and an important component of any explanation for the Spartans' inability to reform their state and return to the ways of an earlier period.

It is through such investigations that the history of ancient children—most certainly worthy of study in its own right and inherently interesting—will take its rightful place alongside the well-established narratives of politics, warfare, and diplomacy, and will illuminate the lives of another important group of silent people.

NOTES

As this work goes to press, two important new books have appeared and mark significant advances in scholarship: Mark Golden, *Children and Childhood in Classical Athens* (Baltimore: Johns Hopkins University Press, 1990), and Thomas Wiedemann, *Adults and Children in the Roman Empire* (New Haven: Yale University Press, 1989).

My indebtedness to colleagues working in the field of childhood and family history is apparent from my discussion. In particular, I thank Judith P. Hallett for her support, both intellectual and personal.

All quotations in this chapter, unless otherwise noted, are from Loeb Classical Library editions. The Loeb editions of classical authors are by far the most accessible and convenient to use.

1. For work that emphasizes the positive (from a late-twentieth-century, Western perspective), see Valerie French, "History of the Child's Influence: Ancient Mediterranean Civilizations," in *Child Effects on Adults*, ed. Richard Q. Bell and Lawrence V. Harper (Hillsdale, N.J.: Lawrence Erlbaum, 1977), pp. 3–29; "Birth Control, Childbirth, and Early Childhood," in *Civilization of the Ancient Mediterranean*, v. 3, ed. Michael Grant and Rachel Kitzinger (New York: Charles Scribner's, 1988), pp. 1355–1362. For the position that Greek and Roman children lived in a nightmare of neglect and abuse, see Lloyd deMause, "The Evolution of Childhood," *History of Childhood Quarterly: Journal of Psychohistory* 1 (1974):503–575; R. Etienne, "La Conscience medicale antique et la vie des enfants," *Annales de demographie historique* (1973):15–61.

2. Ancient historians have, in my view, correctly rejected the literalist fallacy that appears in the early work of Philippe Ariès. For example, rendering a young child as a miniature adult does not of necessity mean that adults did not recognize the difference between adults and children. One must consider here the artistic conventions of the culture. One would not argue that the ancient Egyptians really saw only one eye on a person's face simply because it was their convention to show only one eye in the painting.

3. For substantial discussion of ancient families, see Judith P. Hallett, *Fathers and Daughters in Roman Society: Women and the Elite Family* (Princeton, N.J.: Princeton University Press, 1984); W. K. Lacey, *The Family in Classical Greece* (Ithaca, N.Y.: Cornell University Press, 1968); Beryl Rawson, ed., *The Family in Ancient Rome* (Ithaca, N.Y.: Cornell University Press, 1986); Suzanne Dixon, *The Roman Mother* (Norman: University of Oklahoma Press, 1988).

4. For a description of second-century B.C.E. population decline among the poor in Greece, see Polybius, *Histories* 36.17.5–11.

5. On methods of contraception, see French, "Birth Control," p. 1356, and bibliography, p. 1362.

6. For the Spartan approach to family planning, see the first sections of Plutarch,

Lycurgus; and the initial sections of Xenophon, *Constitution of the Lacedaemonians*, trans, J. M. Moore, *Xenophon and Aristotle on Democracy and Oligarchy* (Berkeley: University of California Press, 1975), pp. 75–79.

7. On this ancient child welfare program, see R. P. Duncan-Jones, "The Purpose and Organization of the *Alimenta*," *Papers of the British School at Rome* 32 (1964): 123–146. For ancient welfare programs in general, see A.R.W. Hands, *Charities and Social Aid in Greece and Rome* (London: Thames & Hudson, 1968).

8. Aeschylus, *Libation Bearers* 753–757; Aristophanes, *Clouds* 1381–1385; Cicero, *de finibus* 5.15.42; Horace, *Satires* 2.3.258–259; Fronto, *Letters to Friends* 1.12.

9. In Mary R. Lefkowitz and Maureen B. Fant, *Women in Greece and Rome: A Source Book in Translation* (Baltimore: Johns Hopkins University Press, 1982), p. 237.

10. For visual evidence on Greek childhood, including the *choes*, see Anita Klein, *Child Life in Greek Art* (New York: Columbia University Press, 1932). For the Hellenistic period, during which children were a popular subject, see Margaret Bieber, *The Sculpture of the Hellenistic Age* (New York: Hacker Art Books, 1981), pp. 136–139 and figures nos. 534–558.

11. There is no work comparable to Klein's for Roman children. This description of the visual evidence comes from my own survey of museums, museum catalogues, and excavation reports.

12. The preoccupation with male children hardly needs comment. Both Plato and Aristotle do, on occasion, mention girls. For example, Plato says that girls should learn gymnastics also (*Laws* 694D).

13. For Plato, the most important discussion comes in *Laws* 789E–795E; for Aristotle, it is *Politics* 1336a-b and 1338b.

For a detailed discussion of these schemes of development, see French, "History of the Child's Influence," pp. 17–18.

14. One of the common Greek adjectives used to describe young children was "nepios," which means "not yet speaking." The Latin *infans* also means "incapable of speech."

15. Aeschylus, *Libation Bearers* 753–757, trans. Richmond Lattimore.

16. Plutarch, *Moralia* 608D.

17. Because the focus of my own research has been on young children, before they go to school, I have concentrated on them throughout this chapter. Moreover, there are a number of excellent studies of Greek and Roman education and the development of children from early school years through adolescence. See, for example, Frederick A. G. Beck, *Greek Education 450–350 B.C.* (London: Metheun, 1964); Stanley F. Bonner, *Education in Ancient Rome: From the Elder Cato to the Younger Pliny* (Berkeley: University of California Press, 1977); M. L. Clarke, *Higher Education in the Ancient World* (London: Routledge & Kegan Paul, 1971); Robert A. Kaster, "Notes on 'Primary' and 'Secondary' School in Late Antiquity," *Transactions of the American Philological Association* 113 (1983):323–346; H. I. Marrou, *A History of Education in Antiquity* (London: Sheed & Ward, 1956).

These studies share the androcentric bias of our sources. For a study of the education of girls, see Susan G. Cole, "Could Greek Women Read and Write?" in *Reflections of Women in Antiquity*, ed. Helene P. Foley (New York: Gordon and Breach Science Pub., 1981), pp. 219–245.

18. See, for example, the remarks and evidence presented by Jo-Ann Shelton, *As the Romans Did: A Sourcebook in Roman Social History* (New York: Oxford University Press,

1988), pp. 209–291. Spartan brides usually were at least eighteen years old. The later age of marriage for females was probably a result of Spartan concern with eugenics; they appear to have recognized a higher infant mortality rate for births to very young mothers.

19. For Erinna's poem, see Lefkowitz and Fant, *Women in Greece and Rome*, p. 7.

20. For the Greco-Roman and Roman schemes of development, see French, "History of the Child's Influence," pp. 24–27.

21. The pediatric works of Antigenes, Apollonius of Byblos, Aristanax, Damastes or Damnastes, Demetrius, Mnesitheus, Moschion, and Oribasius are either entirely gone or exist only in fragments. More well known authors treating children's health and illnesses are Aretaeus, Cassius, Celsus, Galen, Hippocrates and the Hippocratic school, Pliny the Elder, and Rufus.

22. For a discussion of childhood diseases recognized by ancient physicians, see George F. Still, *The History of Paediatrics* (London: Oxford University Press, 1931), pp. 6–12, 18–20, 28–31.

23. Celsus, *de medicina* 3.7.1C.

24. For some ancient remedies, see Still, *History of Paediatrics*, pp. 19–20.

25. For Plato, the most damaging influences came from Greek epic tradition, with its violence and overt sexuality; according to Plato, children needed protection from Homer! Aristotle shared Plato's concern about the effects of sex and violence on preschoolers; he believed that these base influences could produce childhood depression and abnormal and unhealthy behavior in adults; *Nichomachean Ethics* 1148b.

26. Quintilian, unlike most writers in this philosophical tradition, cautions against flogging and other abusive punishment, *Institutio Oratoria* 1.3.13–17. Aristotle and Plutarch recommend delaying harsh punishment until after puberty.

27. Perhaps the most comprehensive essay on ancient children is a work attributed to Plutarch, *de liberis educandis* (*On the Rearing of Children*), found in the corpus of Plutarch's philosophical writings, *Moralia*, 1A–14C.

28. In the Hellenistic and Roman imperial periods, a good many slaves and freedmen had been given advanced educations; moreover, upwardly mobile families who acquired some wealth through trade, industry, and commerce provided an advanced education for their sons so that they would have a better opportunity to rise to an even higher social status. The celebrated poet Horace is an example of a son of a poor freedman, who, through education (and talent!), rose to a high social position; Horace tells the story of his father's efforts in *Satires* 1.6.65–92.

29. For the minimalist approach to Roman family life, see Keith R. Bradley, "Child-care at Rome: The Role of Men," *Historical Reflections* 12 (1985):485–523; Beryl M. Rawson, "Family Life Among the Lower Classes at Rome in the First Two Centuries of the Empire," *Classical Philology* 61 (1966):71–83; R. P. Saller, "Familia, Domus, and the Roman Conception of the Family," *Phoenix* 38 (1984):336–355; R. P. Saller and B. D. Shaw, "Tombstones and Roman Family Relations in the Principate: Civilians, Soldiers, and Slaves," *Journal of Roman Studies* 74 (1984):124–156.

For a study that centers on affective ties within aristocratic Roman families, see Hallett, *Fathers and Daughters*; Hallett makes a persuasive argument that the strongest affective bond within upper-class families was that between fathers and their daughters. The work of Suzanne Dixon, *The Roman Mother*, contends that maternal bonds to their children tended to be rather weak because of a number of factors: the early age of female marriage and Roman law gave women the status of a child relative to their husbands; the high rate of death in childbirth left many children to grow up without their biological mothers; in cases of divorce, the father legally had the children. There are, nonetheless, a large number of examples of apparently strong ties between mothers and their children.

Historians of Greek family life tackle the nature of affective ties within families much more readily, perhaps because family emotional dynamics loom so large in Attic drama. See the discussion on Slater's thesis about the mother-son relationship in classical Athens.

30. See, for example, Homer, *Iliad* 2.701 and *Odyssey* 19.399–412; Aristotle, *Politics* 1.3; Plutarch, *Moralia* 258D; Dio Chrysostom, *Discourses* 15.8.9–10. A funerary inscription put up by a husband for his wife laments their childlessness: "We longed for children which an envious fate denied us," in Lefkowitz and Fant, *Women in Greece and Rome*, p. 210.

31. Plutarch, *Moralia* 608C and E. Plutarch also devoted an entire essay to the subject of natural parental affection for the young, extending his argument beyond humans to the animal kingdom; *de amore prolis*, *Moralia* 493–477E.

32. Plato, *Republic* 1.343A; Catullus, 25.1–2; Fronto, *ad M. Caesar* 5.42.

33. Shelton, *As the Romans Did*, p. 205.

34. Lefkowitz and Fant, *Women in Greece and Rome*, p. 257. A great many Roman epitaphs record the exact age of the child at death.

35. Cicero, *de finibus* 5.20.55.

36. St. Augustine, *Confessions* 7.12.

37. The literature on ancient infanticide is extensive. For a summary of recent work, see French, "Birth Control," p. 1362. It seems likely that more females were subjected to infanticide than males.

Some real difficulty in interpretating material evidence, particularly the hundreds of small pots in which the bones of infants have been found, comes from the fact that the final decision on whether to rear a baby was not made until about a week after its birth; a baby did not become an official member of the family—and probably not a person— until the ceremony in which the father accepted it was performed. When a baby died in the days between its birth and its official acceptance, it was not always a case of infanticide; it seems probable that many of these "potted" skeletons represent babies who died before official acceptance. Neonatal mortality rates must have been very high. For care of the neonate, see Valerie French, "Midwives and Maternity Care in the Roman World," *Helios* 13 (1986):79–80.

38. For the annulment, see Berlin papyrus 1104, in Lefkowitz and Fant, *Women in Greece and Rome*, p. 60. For the soldier's instructions, see Oxyrhynchus Papyri 744, in Shelton, *As the Romans Did*, p. 28.

39. Philo Judaeus is a clear exception; he argues that infanticide is murder; *On Special Laws* 3.108–109.

40. For the most comprehensive treatment of this evidence, see deMause, "Evolution of Childhood," pp. 503–575. Although no one would contest the grisly picture that this evidence paints, I do dispute deMause's contention that this evidence provides a full portrait of childhood in antiquity; deMause and his school ignore or distort evidence of positive attitudes and treatment of children.

41. Philip E. Slater, *The Glory of Hera: Greek Mythology and the Greek Family* (Boston: Beacon Press, 1968); and "The Greek Family in History and Myth," *Arethusa* 7 (1974):9–14.

42. For an alternative interpretation of tragedy, see Sarah B. Pomeroy, *Goddesses, Whores, Wives, and Slaves: Women in Classical Antiquity* (New York: Schocken, 1975),

pp. 93–119. For the rearing of small boys in Athens, see Valerie French, "Sons and Mothers," *Helios* 4 (1976): 54–56.

43. For example, see J.P.V.D. Balsdon, *Roman Women* (New York: Barnes & Noble, 1962), pp. 190–199; F. R. Cowell, *Everyday Life in Ancient Rome* (New York: G. P. Putnam, 1961), pp. 35–44, 72–77; Marjorie and C.H.B. Quennell, *Everyday Things in Ancient Greece* (New York: G. P. Putnam, 1954), pp. 130–141, 218–255; T.B.L. Webster, *Athenian Culture and Society* (Berkeley: University of California Press, 1973), pp. 58–67, 78–79.

44. See, for example, J. R. Hamilton, "Alexander's Early Life," *Greece and Rome* 12 (1965):117–124; Arthur D. Kahn's, *The Education of Julius Caesar: A Biography, A Reconstruction* (New York: Schocken, 1986), suggests how historians can attack the problem.

REFERENCES

Balsdon, J.P.V.D. *Roman Women*. New York: Barnes & Noble, 1962.
Beck, Frederick A. G. *Greek Education: 450–350 B.C.* London: Metheun, 1964.
Bonfante, Larissa. "Dedicated Mothers." *Visible Religion* 3 (1984): 1–17.
Bonner, Stanley F. *Education in Ancient Rome: From the Elder Cato to the Younger Pliny*. Berkeley: University of California Press, 1977.
Bradley, Keith R. "Childcare at Rome: The Role of Men." *Historical Reflections* 12 (1985):485–523.
———. "Child Labour in the Roman World." *Historical Reflections* 12 (1985): 311–330.
Clarke, M. L. *Higher Education in the Ancient World*. London: Routledge & Kegan Paul, 1971.
Cole, Susan G. "Could Greek Women Read and Write?" In *Reflections of Women in Antiquity*, edited by Helene P. Foley, pp. 219–245. New York: Gordon and Breach Science Pub., 1981.
Cowell, F. R. *Everyday Life in Ancient Rome*. New York: G. P. Putnam, 1961.
deMause, Lloyd. "The Evolution of Childhood." *History of Childhood Quarterly: Journal of Psychohistory* 1 (1974):503–575.
Dixon, Suzanne. *The Roman Mother*. Norman: University of Oklahoma Press, 1988.
Duncan-Jones, R. P. "The Purpose and Organization of the *Alimenta*." *Papers of the British School at Rome* 32 (1964):123–146.
Etienne, R. "La Conscience medicale antique et la vie des enfants." *Annales de demographie historique* (1973):15–61.
French, Valerie. "Sons and Mothers." *Helios* 4 (1976):54–56.
———. "History of the Child's Influence: Ancient Mediterranean Civilizations." In *Child Effects on Adults*, edited by Richard Q. Bell and Lawrence V. Harper, pp. 3–29. Hillsdale, N.J.: Lawrence Erlbaum, 1977.
———. "Midwives and Maternity Care in the Roman World." *Helios* 13 (1986):69–84.
———. "Birth Control, Childbirth, and Early Childhood." In *Civilization of the Ancient Mediterranean*, Vol. 3, edited by Michael Grant and Rachel Kitzinger, pp. 1355–1362. New York: Charles Scribner's, 1988.
Hallett, Judith P. *Fathers and Daughters in Roman Society: Women and the Elite Family*. Princeton, N.J.: Princeton University Press, 1984.

Hamilton, J. R. "Alexander's Early Life." *Greece & Rome* 12 (1965): 117–124.

Hands, A.R.W. *Charities and Social Aid in Greece and Rome*. London: Thames & Hudson, 1968.

Harris, W. V. "The Roman Father's Power of Life and Death." In *Studies in Roman Law in Memory of A. Arthur Schiller*, edited by R. S. Bagnall and W. V. Harris. Leiden: de Grueyers, 1986.

Joshel, S. "Nurturing the Master's Child: Slavery and the Roman Child Nurse." *Signs* 12 (1986): 3–22.

Kahn, Arthur D. *The Education of Julius Casear: A Biography, A Reconstruction*. New York: Schocken, 1986.

Kaster, Robert A. "Notes on 'Primary' and 'Secondary' School in Late Antiquity." *Transactions of the American Philological Association* 113 (1983):323–346.

Klein, Anita. *Child Life in Greek Art*. New York: Columbia University Press, 1932.

Lacey, W. K. *The Family in Classical Greece*. Ithaca, N.Y.: Cornell University Press, 1968.

Lefkowitz, Mary, and Maureen B. Fant. *Women in Greece and Rome: A Source Book in Translation*. Baltimore: Johns Hopkins University Press, 1982.

Manson, M. "The Emergence of the Small Child in Rome (Third Century B.C.–First Century A.D.)." *History of Education* 12 (1983):149–159.

Marrou, H. I. *A History of Education in Antiquity*. London: Sheed & Ward, 1956.

Pomeroy, Sarah B. *Goddesses, Whores, Wives, and Slaves: Women in Classical Antiquity*. Schocken: New York, 1975.

Quennell, Marjorie, and C.H.B. Quennell. *Everyday Things in Ancient Greece*. New York: G. P. Putnam, 1954.

Rawson, Beryl. "Family Life Among the Lower Classes at Rome in the First Two Centuries of the Empire." *Classical Philology* 61 (1966):71–83.

———., ed. *The Family in Ancient Rome*. Ithaca, N.Y.: Cornell University Press, 1986.

Saller, R. P. "*Familia, Domus*, and the Roman Conception of the Family." *Phoenix* 38 (1984):336–355.

Saller, R. P., and B. D. Shaw. "Tombstones and Roman Family Relations in the Principate: Civilians, Soldiers, and Slaves." *Journal of Roman Studies* 74 (1984):124–156.

Shelton, Jo-Ann. *As the Romans Did: A Sourcebook in Roman Social History*. New York: Oxford University Press, 1988.

Slater, Philip E. *The Glory of Hera: Greek Mythology and the Greek Family*. Boston: Beacon Press, 1968.

———. "The Greek Family in History and Myth." *Arethusa* 7 (1974):9–14.

Still, George F. *The History of Paediatrics*. London: Oxford University Press, 1931.

Webster, T.B.L. *Athenian Culture and Society*. Berkeley: University of California Press, 1973.

3

CHILDHOOD IN MEDIEVAL EUROPE

David Nicholas

Summarizing the history of childhood in any thousand-year period is a formidable undertaking. Sources are scarce, since virtually everything that we have about children is from the pens of adults. Most writers of childhood memoirs were trying to make a point about human nature or the particular treatment they received. Just as it is true today, many children were abused and many others were loved, even pampered. Theories of child rearing beg the question of actual treatment. In striking contrast to the current situation, few parents were aware of the latest notions of proper child rearing. Even within the same family, parents might have different attitudes toward the children and how they should be raised. Social "class" also is no infallible key. Most aristocratic parents took a less active role in raising their children than did the poor, and were at least as likely to mistreat them. Although most children worked for their parents or were put out to service, they also played; the city of York in 1376 prohibited owners from letting their horses run loose because of the many children playing in the streets.[1] All scholars credit Philippe Ariès for raising our consciousness of the importance of the history of childhood and providing a provocative synthesis; however, no medievalist still takes seriously his idea that people before the "modern" period had no notion of childhood as a distinct period of human development. His disciples have gone much farther, perhaps culminating in Lloyd de Mause's hysterical lament that childhood in the Middle Ages was "a nightmare of abuse and murder."[2]

CHILDHOOD IN THE EARLY MIDDLE AGES

We know little of childhood in early medieval Europe. The treatment of children in works of art suggests affection, sympathy, and adults' horror at the violence often visited on the young.[3] Children were clearly distinguished from adults in the Germanic law codes. Under the mid-seventh-century laws of the Visigoths, a free male baby in his first year had a blood price (wergeld) of 30 solidi, which had grown to 90 solidi by his tenth year. Between ages ten and fifteen the price increased 10 solidi per year, and between ages fifteen and twenty it grew by 30 solidi per year, until at age twenty, when he was considered mature, he was worth 300 solidi. The contrast between the child and the adult was more marked with women, whose blood prices rose only during the child-bearing years: girls under fifteen had half the wergeld of males, but between ages fifteen and forty the wergeld had risen to five-sixths. A similar contrast is found among the Salian and Ripuarian Franks.[4]

Princes, including the Merovingian kings, had schools in their palaces, but we have no evidence of how the children were treated. Charlemagne's famous legislation ordering local priests to offer training in letters shows that there also were private schools. But most of our knowledge of how children were treated in the early Middle Ages comes from the pens of monks. Pierre Riché has credited them with the "discovery of the child," and with modifying the harsh pedagogical doctrines of the ancients.[5] The practice of giving boys to monasteries as oblates was declining in the eleventh century and stopped in the twelfth; but before this the monasteries were educating numerous boys whose personal inclinations or whose intellectual and physical limitations might not have led them to the personal choice of this vocation.[6] Hildemar, who wrote a commentary in the ninth century on the Benedictine Rule, realized that boys were incapable of the physical asceticism demanded of adult monks, particularly regarding diet. Care was given to their hygiene, and the younger children were given extended periods of rest. Virtually all monasteries provided play time outside the cloister for the boys. The innocence of young children appealed to Hildemar, as it had to St. Benedict himself, Paul the Deacon, and Pope Leo the Great; as they reached adolescence they had more inclination to sin. Their training thus had to begin early, when they were malleable. Four masters were given responsibility for ten children, for education of the young was considered the responsibility of the entire community. At age fifteen the boys were no longer considered infants, and were given instead to a "senior" for further training, particularly in controlling anger and their incipient sexuality. Although the masters and seniors could use corporal punishment, this was not emphasized.[7] After 1215 the church discouraged monasteries from receiving boys younger than fourteen into their schools, and in fact by the twelfth century the abbeys were educating few boys not destined for the monastic life.[8] The fact that they had so little experience with children may explain the hostility toward them expressed by many monks after this time.

CHANGES OF THE HIGH MIDDLE AGES

Evidence becomes more abundant in the eleventh century, when there also are suggestions of a change in attitude toward children. Perhaps as a result of the increasing veneration of the holy family, the cult of infant Jesus, and the nursing Madonna, there are more literary references to kindness toward children, playing with babies, and descriptions of the child's first steps. Several sources note children's responsiveness to music. The biographer of St. Hugh of Lincoln claimed that he was particularly effective with children, for he and they were attracted by each other's innocence and good humor.[9] David Herlihy has noted that the new sense of "social investment" in children occurred in two phases: a first, concerned with education and training of children, and a second, discernible mainly from the late fourteenth century onward, in which private charity and institutions exhibited "concern for the child's survival and health under difficult hygienic conditions."[10]

Yet the new evidence poses its own set of problems. Children leave no records until they are literate, and we must be careful to note the age of the "children" meant in all sources. Virtually all moralists and most autobiographers were sympathetic toward innocent infants but hostile toward adolescents, who were disliked by the patriarchs for their independence and by the clergy for their sexuality. Furthermore, given the high birth rates, "only" children were unusual. Yet most literary references, biographies, autobiographies, and parental expressions of attitude about children are by or about youngest children of either sex, such as the abbot Guibert of Nogent, or eldest sons, such as Peter Abelard. Property transactions and criminal records provide some corrective for the later Middle Ages.

A central problem of our inquiry is definitional. The situation of the child in law was comparable to that of the woman: he or she was under the father's guardianship until reaching the age of majority or leaving home. The age of majority varied. It was twelve under most regional custumals, but the Golden Bull of 1356 set majority at age eighteen. Roman law, which was being used increasingly in the later Middle Ages, had children under seven completely incompetent legally. Thereafter, they were limited but not totally incompetent. This distinction is close to the provision of the *Schwabenspiegel* that children were not legally punishable for their actions until after age seven.[11]

The terminology of the sources also poses problems. The words usually translated "child" (*puer*, *liber*, *puella*, *enfant*, *kind*) can mean young children, but they also can refer to adolescents or even to young adults, particularly those "uprooted" or without a fixed position in society. In many sources infancy lasted until age seven, then was followed by puerility, which lasted until fourteen, and then youth, extending to age twenty-eight. Other sources, however, simply omit youth and extended puerility to twenty-eight.[12] Medical doctors distinguished three "ages": true infancy, lasting from birth to anywhere from seven months to two years, depending on when the child began to speak; from infancy to age seven; and puerility, to age fourteen.[13] Other sources speak of "adolescence" as a stage that could last into the thirties or forties, depending on when the person was emancipated by or from the father.

TWO FAMOUS CHILDHOODS

In attempting to determine the attitudes of "typical" parents toward their children, scholars have paid considerable attention to saints' lives, in which mothers usually are portrayed sympathetically, and fathers appear as ogres who are trying to keep their boys away from a religious vocation. The balance is only redressed to some extent in the Italian *ricordi* of the late Middle Ages, which show close relationships between fathers and sons.[14] In particular, two well-documented childhoods that probably were not typical have given rise to a psychoanalytical literature: St. Peter Damian and Abbot Guibert of Nogent.

St. Peter Damian was a youngest child whose mother was "worn out by child-bearing." His older brother reproached her for having added yet another potential heir to a too large household. The mother then fell into postpartum depression and neglected the baby. A priest's wife or concubine accused the mother of unnatural behavior, freed the baby from swaddling bands, and cured it of rash or scabies. As soon as the infant had recovered, the mother showed true solicitude and nursed it, and there were no further problems during the parents' lives. Characteristically, the parents seem to have raised their children themselves, with some help from outsiders. When they died the older siblings took care of the younger; the future saint was raised by an older brother and the latter's wife, who mistreated him and eventually turned him out to be a swineherd. At about age twelve he was placed in the care of a second brother, Damian, later archpriest of Ravenna, who had him educated. Peter Damian himself mentioned in another context an older sister who had been "like a mother" to him. Thus two siblings treated him well, and a third did not. Such cases show the folly of generalizing about either good or bad treatment.[15]

Abbott Guibert of Nogent left a revealing autobiography. He was clearly the baby of the family: he had at least two older brothers. Because they are mentioned only as being absent, he must have been the youngest by some years, indeed the only child left in the household by the time his coherent recollections begin. He was the child of a mother in her thirties whose frigidity had driven her knightly husband to seven years of impotence. He admits that he was his mother's favorite, noting "a mother's natural affection for her last-born" and "how greatly she provided me with the care of nurses in infancy and of masters and teachers in boyhood, with no lack even of fine clothes for my little body, so that I seemed to equal the sons of kings and counts in indulgence." Guibert makes it plain that he loathed his brother, who was a knight. Guibert was bitter at his mother's lack of tenderness but was attached to her. His sexual fixations, particularly his disgust of himself during his adolescence—"with the gradual growth of my young body, as the life of this world began to stir my itching heart with fleshy longings and lusts to suit my stature''—have evoked Freudian interpretations.[16] It is clear that Guibert's case was highly individual and that no generally applicable patterns can be derived from it.

There can be little doubt that most parents in the Middle Ages valued their children and cherished them, even if the parents' means of disciplining their children seem unenlightened to modern eyes. Our few sources detailing the grief of parents at the loss of children are highly emotional. The Massacre of the Innocents often was portrayed in medieval art, and the theme was taken up by the Corpus Christi cycles at the end of the period. Englishmen in the fifteenth century evidently placed such a high emotional value on children that the rumored fate of the princes in the Tower helped to cause the fall of Richard III.[17] That few parents or children wrote down their sentiments about each other proves nothing; not many do so now, when literacy is much more widespread. Most couples desired children. The marriage of Francesco Datini of Prato foundered because it was childless, evidently because of the wife's infertility (Datini sired bastards). The attitude of Datini's friend Ser Lapo Mazzei was probably typical. He had a large family and saw his children as a financial burden, but he loved them and was attentive to all of them.[18]

INFANCY

Most sources agree that parents swaddled their newborns, although not at all times. Gerald of Wales is the only exception, in saying that the Irish babies are ''abandoned to ruthless nature,'' and he clearly thought that their mothers were being negligent. Virtually all manuals on childhood recommended regular and frequent baths, usually two or three a day, perhaps a reflection of the sanitary problems of swaddling. Medieval medical literature gave less attention to swaddling than to feeding and bathing, and to the need of avoiding trauma and abrupt transitions. In contrast to the ancients, medieval physicians advocated having the mother nurse her own infants, although actual practice was different. There was a certain sexism in medical writing, for girls were to be nursed less long than boys; boys should be rubbed hard and girls softly. Some writings also demonstrate a practical concern with the child's first steps and how adults could guide them.[19]

Infants were kept in cradles, including the portable variety, and the number of injunctions by the English bishops that the children should be kept in cradles until at least age three, to avoid the dangers of overlaying or suffocation, show that most children and their nurses or their parents slept in the same room. The need of play and toys for children was recognized. Various sources mention playing ball, peek-a-boo, or hide-and-seek with a parent, almost always the mother. The biographer of Aelred of Rievaulx mentions him coming home as a small boy "from the games that small boys play with their fellows." By the thirteenth century, writers recognized the value of play in combating boredom. Some grave art shows children playing, particularly with dogs, birds, toy horses, dolls, puppets, wagons, and tops. Clay figurines were popular. Hobby horses are found, evidently to imitate knights. Although earlier scholars thought that such toys were limited to the upper classes, archaeological excavations show that they were used more generally. Children of both sexes played together, although it irritated moralists.[20]

Women who could afford to do so usually sent their infants to wet nurses, but laborers seldom did. Aristocratic and noble parents were seldom attached to their children in their children's early years, for the children were put out to a nurse from birth. Care was taken in the choice of a nurse, since the child was thought to take in the nurse's character with her milk. The father usually located the nurse through his network of clients. He, rather than the mother, decided when the child would be weaned. The child was wholly dependent on the nurse, for there is little evidence that the parents visited him or her much, and the nature of this care varied. Sometimes there were several nurses in succession. The duration of time under the nurse varied, for the child might return to its birth family at any time between roughly ages two and seven; the nurse thus raised many children after weaning. When the child returned to his biological family it was to a group of strangers. It is clear that emotional bonds between infants and children were much stronger among the lower orders, who could not afford nurses, than among the wealthy.[21]

THE MEDIEVAL HOUSEHOLD

The problems of the nature and composition of the household, and the number of children in it, are thus crucial to the question of how children within it were treated. Rural families tended to have more children than urban, and in both rural and urban sectors the rich had more children than the poor. The population of most cities was young. Almost 39 percent of the inhabitants of Florence in 1427 were age fourteen or under, although the proportion of children in rural Tuscany was lower. Most Italian households contained only the nuclear family, even among the upper orders; but the father usually was considerably older than the mother, and some households contained a large and varied population, including his bastards, less frequently children from a previous marriage, and, above all, servants, many of them from poor branches of the family who used domestic service as a means of accumulating money for a dowry. Although in England and the Low Countries the age gap between the parents usually was much less than in Italy, the use of time in service was widespread. Girls, particularly farm girls who came to the city, normally entered service in the concluding stage of childhood at about age twelve. English poll tax records suggest that many adolescents, particularly in the cities, did not live in their parents' homes. This can be explained by underreporting to avoid the tax as well as by their absence in domestic service.[22]

The sex ratio strongly favored boys at birth, but in the late teens the records become distorted; fathers inflated their daughters' ages (eighteen was considered optimal for marriage) and deflated those of their sons (liability to the head tax began at eighteen). Thus in the late teens the sex ratios briefly favored girls. In Italy girls married early, usually in the late teens, whereas marriage was delayed into the twenties in the North. In the intervening years, between the return from the wet nurse and the age when provision for the child's adulthood had to be made, "adults tended to ignore, neglect, and forget their offspring; infants in early life possessed a kind of transparency."[23]

Another frequent complication in the lives of medieval children was the stepparent. In an age of high death rates few people survived until adulthood with both parents still alive. In Tuscany it was unusual for widows to remarry; it was considered reprehensible, among other reasons, because if they did, or indeed if they returned to their natal families, their children stayed with the late husband's kinspeople, as belonging to them. In some exceptional cases the children stayed with the mother's kin, and the latter were paid for the children's maintenance. Hence many adult children of remarried mothers accused their mothers of cruelty for having abandoned them. This pattern was less common in the North, where many widows remarried. The determinant seems to have been the stepfather's attitude, rather than whether the paternal lineage wanted the children. The Flemish sources are unclear about whether a widower who did not want to support his children could leave them with the mother's family without paying for their support. An important part of the situation, however, is that most occupations—certainly among the master artisans, the largest group marrying and producing children—were conducted in the home. Thus, whereas in the modern age, fathers, most of whom work outside the home, have difficulty raising very young children, that was not true in the Middle Ages. Artisans' children, just as the offspring of peasants, were useful as laborers. The frequency of remarriage in Flanders also meant the custody of orphan children frequently was divided. The extended family evidently decided each case on the basis of what would be most advantageous for the child or the family or both. There was a tendency, but not an invariable rule, for boys to be situated with men, and girls with women; older brothers frequently took care of their siblings. There also was a tendency in cases of divided custody to leave younger children with the mother, with the legal guardian either supporting the older ones or farming them out into service or apprenticeship.[24]

SEXISM AND INFANTICIDE

The problem of attitudes toward children is linked to two problems to which no entirely satisfactory answer can be given: whether boys were valued more highly than girls, and whether unwanted children, and particularly girls, were frequent victims of infanticide. There is some evidence, although it is by no means conclusive, that sons were preferred over daughters. Girls were in the majority in the foundling hospitals. Balancing this is the fact that urban girls spent more time at home than their brothers did, for the boys were sent away for an education, albeit often only to a day school, usually at age seven. The girls stayed at home and developed strong emotional bonds with their parents, for it was unusual for girls to be educated outside the home by the fifteenth century.[25]

Few went as far as St. Bernadino of Siena, who thought that girls should be turned into household drudges. The number of admonitions from moralists that mothers should never leave their little girls alone for fear for their chastity suggests less that girls were sequestered than that there was a problem. Narrative sources and art works show girls dressed well and pampered. Yet the problem of providing dowries for girls, particularly in Mediterranean Europe, doubtless contributed to a certain disenchantment with female children. By 1200 the bride-price, which was given to the bride by the groom, had yielded in most areas to the dowry, given by the bride's family to the groom. The dowry amounts, which were thought necessary to attract a proper husband, became so enormous that kinsmen often had to assist the parents in providing the dowry. In the fifteenth century Florence established a dowry fund in which the girls' parents could invest. In Flanders the premarital settlement usually was smaller.[26]

Literary sources suggest that infanticide was widespread among the Romans— at least among the poor—although the Romans clearly cared deeply about the children whom they did allow to survive. The Christian church condemned infanticide, abortion, and contraception, but the number of references in the penitentials suggest that these practices were widespread. The common practice of having young children sleep in the parental bed led to smothering by "overlaying." This offense figures prominently in the penitentials, for the clergy suspected, probably correctly, that parents sought to remove unwanted children by faking such accidents. Overlaying was still the main cause of infant death in the ecclesiastical province of Canterbury in the fifteenth century. Infanticide was tried in church courts until very late, for it was considered a sin rather than the crime of homicide. Emily Coleman has used the extremely high ratio of boys to girls on the estates of Saint-Germain-des-Prés in the ninth century to suggest widespread killing of girl babies, and this is certainly supported by increased evidence of concern in the Carolingian penitentials about infanticide. Overlaying and exposure of infants became the objects of a serious campaign in the penitentials, intensified in the eleventh and twelfth centuries. Infanticide did not cease to be a problem after the twelfth century. Most documented cases were committed by unwed mothers anxious to avoid shame. Yet the prevailing sexual climate seems to have conditioned the extent of infanticide. In the Low Countries, where there was a high incidence of bastardy and little social stigma was attached to it, infanticide cases were extremely rare, although the secular arm took jurisdiction over them.[27]

BASTARDY AND ABANDONMENT

The problem of infanticide is linked to bastardy. In virtually all parts of Europe the father's illegitimate children were part of the household, often as servants but sometimes as fully recognized members of the family. In an age of widespread sexual license illegitimacy seems to have carried no particular social stigma among the upper orders of society and little among the upper bourgeoisie, but rather more among the poor. Still, bastards were not placed on the same footing as legitimate children. Illegitimacy barred children from direct inheritance in most parts of Europe (they could be remembered in testaments) and from holy orders.

Illegitimate children were especially likely to be abandoned. The first known orphanage dates from 787 in Milan. At Florence there were two hospitals that accepted foundlings along with the sick: San Gallo (founded at the end of the thirteenth century) and La Scala (founded in 1316). But the problem of foundlings grew so astronomically in the late Middle Ages that in 1421, Florence decided to establish a separate foundling hospital, the Innocenti, which only opened its doors in 1445. At Rome the hospital of Santo Spirito accepted all needy people when Pope Innocent III founded it in 1201, but it was reformed around 1450 as a foundling hospital. Bologna got its first orphanage in 1459, Pavia in 1449, Paris in 1363. By 1450 most large cities of Europe had orphanages. At Ghent an orphan was defined in law as a child who had lost either parent. The city had only two orphanages, both of them small, since the powerful lineages of the city apparently took care of their own foundlings. A suggestion that any surviving blood relations were expected to help raise orphans also is found at Montpellier, where the city government undertook to care for abandoned children whose relatives could not be identified by hiring professional wet nurses as municipal employees.[28]

OF PUERILITY AND ADOLESCENCE: THE CHILDREN OF THE NOBLES

The nobility constitutes a peculiar case, but there are striking parallels in their attitudes toward child rearing and those of the middle and lower orders. Most noblewomen did not nurse their children. The boys were sent at the age of six or seven to the courts of other lords for education in the chivalric arts, or, in some cases, to episcopal or monastic schools. They invariably were boarders, and thus lived away from the parents. Males, at least from the twelfth century, passed from the stage of "boy" or "adolescent," in which they were trained as warriors, into that of "youth": their training was finished, so they lived as knights errant on the tournament circuit for a year or two, supported by their parents, but remained unmarried. Then the youth would come back to the parental home to live, and conflicts with the father often resulted. With this group, as with the upper bourgeoisie, marriage was the onset of adulthood.

Girls of the nobility, too, were sent away from home: some went to nunneries, and some of those who were betrothed early—a practice limited to the nobility—were sent to the future husband's home for rearing. In the notions and, to a great extent, the practice of the time, noble girls passed directly from childhood to womanhood, with earlier marriage than even among the upper Italian bourgeoisie. Among the nobles, as among the upper bourgeoisie, but not the lower bourgeoisie and the peasantry, the mother did most of the child rearing as long as the child was at home. But the need to prepare children for adulthood and the right of lords over their wards limited the biological mother's role severely; although some noblewomen tried to buy the wardships of their own children, most seem to have accepted the desirability of having them leave home.[29]

There can be no doubt that many noble children were thrust into adult roles early, before the teenage years, but this seems to have been determined, predictably, by whether their parents lived long or chose to marry them off early. The chronicler Lambert of Ardres reports that the count of Guines' fourteen-year-old wife "still liked to play with dolls."[30] In areas dominated by Roman law it was not unusual for sons to be unemancipated and under their fathers' control into their late twenties or even beyond. Yet a case in the Limousin has a noble boy of about ten participating actively—not simply passively as a witness—in a land transaction; but after he became a knight, around age twenty, he tried to revoke the grant in question, so he may have acted under duress. The same area also shows considerable conflict between elderly fathers and even grandfathers and their adult sons, since men seem to have been rather long-lived there. The future Count of Flanders, Robert "the Frisian," witnessed a charter in 1039, when he may have been as young as seven.[31] The childhood of King Philip "the Fair" of France (1269/85–1314) was essentially devoid of affection. As a second son in a family tainted by allegations of sexual impropriety and in the shadow of an idealized grandfather (St. Louis IX), Philip became a moralistic, rigid adult determined to establish his own claim to greatness in the face of profound emotional insecurity.[32]

CHILDREN IN SCHOOL

Much of our evidence of childhood during the years of adolescence is of two types: school regulations and episodes, and the use of children in the work force. It is well known that in the late eleventh century, just as we begin to discern changing attitudes toward children, there was a sudden increase in the amount of primary education available. The emergence of specialized occupations meant that more care had to be taken with educating the young. Writing around 1115 of his youth, around 1070, Abbot Guibert of Nogent related that

there was a little before that time, and in a measure there was still in my youth, such a scarcity of teachers that hardly any could be found in the towns, and in the cities there were very few, and those who by good chance could be discovered had but slight knowledge and could not be compared with the wandering scholars of these days.

Probably all too typically, Guibert studied under a tutor who compensated for his own ignorance by beatings that seem to have been severe even by the standards of the time, and the abbot advocated a milder regimen as more effective. Interestingly, although Guibert saw his own vocation as holy, he realized that contrary inclinations were natural

While others of my age wandered everywhere at will and were unchecked in the indulgence of such inclinations as were natural at their age, I, hedged in with constant restraints and dressed in my clerical garb, would sit and look at the troops of players like a beast awaiting sacrifice.

Other authors, such as John of Salisbury, note the repetitive character of the arts and the brutality of even the most enlightened instructors. Under the circumstances, it is small wonder that students were boisterous.[33]

Contrary voices were heard. When an abbot complained to St. Anselm that his pupils kept getting more unruly, although his monks never stopped beating them, Anselm, perhaps drawing on his own childhood experiences, replied that the boys simply thought that the abbot and monks hated them and wished them ill. Although enlightened for the time, this has some background in the works of Alcuin and Theodulf of Orleans, who recommended affection as well as discipline, and urged, as Anselm did, that the teachers recognize the children as human beings.[34]

It was imperative that the sons of merchants and nobles gain at least the rudiments of literacy, and all major cities had private and church-sponsored schools. Schooling usually began at age seven, and the master replaced the father as disciplinarian. Giovanni Villani claimed that in Florence during the 1330s, between eight thousand and ten thousand children, or more than 50 percent of their number, attended grammar schools. Girls were not educated beyond grammar school unless they were destined for nunneries, but between one thousand and two thousand boys went on to six secondary schools, where they prepared for business careers. Several hundred others attended four "large schools," which gave access to the universities and the professions.[35] Late in our period the notions of the Italian humanists began to affect educational practice, particularly in mitigating harsh disciplinary regimens and urging parents to consider their children's inclinations in choosing their occupations.[36]

Most municipal schools were day schools, and contact was not lost with the natal family. But it is important to realize that just as apprenticeship and the period of knight errantry were a transitional stage of adulthood for urban and aristocratic boys, respectively, the arts course fulfilled this function for those entering the learned professions, which were increasingly in demand. Students who were away from home might get parental assistance, but they still had to arrange for most of their own accommodations and books and get their own food by their early teens.[37] Some moralists, fearful of temptations of the flesh, cautioned fathers against sending their sons away to school, and with reason. The authorities at Toulouse in the fifteenth and sixteenth centuries became concerned because the brothel was near a grammar school. Similar complaints were voiced at Dijon in 1426 and at Venice and Montpellier and in Germany in the sixteenth century.[38] It is clear that schoolboys used their independence to gain sexual experience.

CHILDREN IN THE WORK FORCE

Particularly in Germany, most town and guild regulations of the late Middle Ages required children and wives, as well as adult men, to swear not to violate economic regulations. Both sexes were expected to begin working or to train for eventual employment at an early age. At this social level, below the merchant aristocracy, boys' break with their natal families might have been less brutal than that of girls, some of whom were put into service as early as age eight; in these cases the employer provided the dowry. Boys usually were not apprenticed before the teen years, although there were violations, and years of service might precede formal apprenticeship. But in contrast to the situation in the North, most Italian apprentices lived with their natal families. Orphan children at Ghent were expected to pay for their support with the income of their property if it sufficed. If not—and in many cases even if it did—they were expected to take jobs as they got older. A common theme was for the young person to "earn his own bread," so that the income from his or her estate would simply be reinvested and accumulate as enforced savings. Nowhere was emancipation automatic when the age of majority was attained, but it was not delayed unreasonably, except in Mediterranean Europe. Although the earnings of Flemish adolescents were under the jurisdiction of their guardians, most of them were given allowances, not touching their principal property; in such cases many took their own lodgings. If they managed their property responsibly, emancipation would follow. Although statistics are impossible for Flanders, child labor was quite ordinary, although we do not get the impression of wholesale farming out of children into live-in service, as in Tuscany. The wage-earning children of the middle and lower orders escaped adults' tutelage in ways that were impossible for aristocratic children, who did not work, and thus did not perform the services that would make them valued as adults or gain them emancipation. For these people, as we have seen, "childhood ended when the father died."[39]

The generally low level of technology meant that most child labor was used in the family shop, and in many respects the master and his wife replaced the natural family. Indeed, they might be part of the extended family group, since children often were apprenticed to older siblings or uncles. The master was to provide material support, moral and intellectual education, and professional training. Personal concerns usually were formulaic in apprenticeship contracts. The master was to keep the apprentice from cold and hunger, and usually agreed to treat the apprentice as his own child. The overwhelming majority of apprentices were boys. Some guilds did admit women as masters, but this became restricted in most places to occupations of low status by the fifteenth century. Illness usually did not annul the contract if there was a reasonable chance that it would be cured; if it persisted, the child might be taken back to the parents until cured.

Apprenticeship obligation included lodging, laundry, lighting, and usually, but not invariably, food. Some contracts obliged the master to send the apprentice to school, but this was found only in the early years of the apprenticeship, except when the master was in an "intellectual" field, as chirurgie. The master's wife also had the right to punish the apprentice, but the courts recognized this as her husband's legal responsibility. The lawsuits that survive over bad treatment of apprentices, usually brought by their parents or other kin, show that in fact apprentices had little recourse against brutal masters. Some contracts bound the parents to contribute toward the child's support, but this diminished the longer the apprenticeship lasted, as the child paid his own way by his labor. The parents normally paid nothing in the last year or two of the training.[40]

PEASANT CHILDREN

Recent studies have deepened considerably our knowledge of child rearing among the lower orders. The peasants, whether through poverty or inclination, were more likely to keep their children at home and raise them personally than were burghers and nobles. Although some sent their daughters away into domestic service, most did not, and from the earliest years children were given tasks around the home. An English statute of 1388 shows that boys and girls worked as carters and behind plows, although evidence from the coroners' rolls suggests that they more often tended animals and fowl, at least until they were teenagers. Literary sources, such as *Piers Ploughman*, *Arme Heinrich*, and *Meier Helmbrecht*, all note the economic burdens that too many children placed on a family, but they also show that the children were affectionately regarded, and the burdensome aspect lacks the rancor that we find with churchmen. If attitudes toward children were becoming more affectionate in the late Middle Ages, the evidence for it is clearer among the peasants than among the townsmen or the nobility.[41]

The shepherds of Montaillou, in the Pyrenees, had large families at the end of the thirteenth century. Wet nurses were used only by the richest, or by poor girls who had to arrange care for their babies while they worked as servants; indeed, because peasant women often functioned as nurses for city women, nursing seems to have been largely confined to the nobility and the bourgeoisie. The parents seem to have had a considerable and at times almost hysterical affection for their children. By the early teens at the latest boys began helping their fathers at work. From age eighteen they were grouped with the men. Parents seem to have begun to look seriously for husbands when their daughters started menstruating; girls thus married even earlier here than in the Italian cities.[42]

Barbara Hanawalt has used the English coroners' rolls to reconstruct "typical" peasant childhoods. Boys seem to have been more adventurous than girls: although most victims of infanticide were girls, boys died nearly twice as often as girls in accidents. Infants often were left alone in a cradle by the fire, sometimes in the care of older siblings, while the parents worked outside. Fire from cradle accidents was the most common killer of newborns. From age two children had better motor skills; they wandered out and fell into wells or streams. Toddlers, like infants, were left alone rather often, and wandered off, but the number of accidental deaths drops sharply after age four, when they seem to have tagged along after the adults more often and were given small jobs. Still, most accidents that involved children through age six were play-related, rather than work-related. The problem in accidental deaths seems to have been that both parents had jobs to do and could not watch constantly over infants. The child's life changed dramatically between ages eight and twelve. The same age was a turning point in urban childhood, but there it more often meant school or apprenticeship. Most lived at home, and got work-related and sex-specific tasks. Girls worked around the home, baked and brewed, and did some gathering, while boys herded and fished. After age thirteen their work routines were close to those of adults.[43]

Literary evidence shows that peasant and urban teenagers alike had their own societies, clubs, festivals, and flirtations. Court fines suggest widespread teenage sex, and the records of the church courts suggest a casual attitude toward pre-marital intercourse, although pregnancy was relatively infrequent. The situation seems to have been somewhat less blatant than in the cities, where young men openly admitted "frolicking" in bathhouses and public brothels in what seems to have been part of a rite of passage, as was membership in youth gangs. Respectable young women were not allowed to experiment sexually before marriage.[44]

English peasant children, who have been more thoroughly studied than their continental counterparts, gradually assumed adult roles in the teenage years, with the distinction that boys joined a tithing group at age twelve and assisted others as pledges in civil actions, whereas girls did not. Both sexes, at least among the more prosperous peasants, were given some property and gradually assumed more independence of their parents during adolescence, corresponding to what we find in the cities. Marriage, which ended childhood, usually was arranged by the parents, but with the couple's consent.[45]

CONCLUSION

Our information before the eleventh century is extremely limited for all groups except monastic oblates. Thereafter, we find that most parents in medieval Europe tried conscientiously to prepare their young for assuming the burdens of adult-hood. The adulthood in question usually was one that the parents' circumstances and logical aspirations suggested was a likely eventual situation for the child: peasant children were not educated in elegant manners, and noble children were not trained to stand behind a plough. The fact that the upper orders gave their children to wet nurses and had a rather complex and mobile household structure meant that these parents' emotional bonds to their children were somewhat distant. Artisan and peasant parents, whether through economic necessity or personal inclination, more often kept their children at or near home, and participated more directly in their upbringing.

In a sense, the conclusion to this essay must be that no general conclusion is possible. We must maintain detachment and historical perspective, avoiding above all the trap of rigid typologies and ideological reconstructions. The physical circumstances of life were difficult in medieval Europe. Because most adults were the victims of considerable gratuitous violence and emotional and economic deprivation, at least when compared with standards in the contemporary Western world, it should occasion no surprise that children, as legal and physical dependents of those adults, would suffer even more. Standards of discipline in the home, and even more in the schools, were undeniably much severer than now, but this does not mean that most children were deliberately mistreated or exploited. Most normative literature before the fourteenth century was written by people who had little contact with children and was read by few parents. The individual personalities of particular parents and children counted for much more than principles of child rearing. The "modern" period brought no magic dawn of enlightenment to the European child.

NOTES

1. Ordinance cited by Lorraine C. Attreed, "From Pearl Maiden to Tower Princes: Towards a New History of Medieval Childhood," *Journal of Medieval History* 9 (1983):47.

2. Philippe Ariès, *L'Enfant et la vie familiale sous l'ancien régime* (Paris: Plon, 1960), translated as *Centuries of Childhood: A Social History of Family Life* (New York: Alfred Knopf, 1962); Lloyd de Mause, ed., *The History of Childhood* (New York: Harper & Row, 1975), p. 1. F. Xavier Baron, "Children and Violence in Chaucer's *Canterbury Tales*," *Journal of Psychohistory* 9 (1979–80):77–103, finds that adults showed helpless compassion, at times in a sort of stereotypical sentimentality, toward children victimized by violence. Peter Petschauer, "On Phillipe Arises and the History of Childhood," *Journal of Psychohistory* 13 (1985–86):358, notes that the proliferation of records of feelings about children in the modern period may show nothing about attitudes, but rather a rise in literacy.

3. Ilene H. Forseth, "Children in Early Medieval Art: Ninth Through Twelfth Centuries," *Journal of Psychohistory* 4 (1976):31–70.

4. Cited by David Herlihy, "Medieval Children," in *The Walter Prescott Webb Memorial Lectures. Essays on Medieval Civilization* (Austin: University of Texas Press, 1978), pp. 115–116.

5. Pierre Riché, *De l'éducation antique à l'éducation chevaleresque* (Paris: Flammarion, 1968), pp. 30–31.

6. John E. Boswell, "*Exposito* and *Oblatio*: The Abandonment of Children and the Ancient and Medieval Family," *American Historical Review* 89 (1984):21.

7. Mayke de Jong, "Growing Up in a Carolingian Monastery: Magister Hildemar and His Oblates," *Journal of Medieval History* 9 (1983): 99–128.

8. Nicholas Orme, *English Schools in the Middle Ages* (London, 1973), p. 225.

9. Mary Martin McLaughlin, "Survivors and Surrogates: Children and Parents from the Ninth to the Thirteenth Centuries," in de Mause, *Childhood*, pp. 117–18.

10. Herlihy, "Medieval Children," p. 124.

11. From Klaus Arnold, *Kind und Gesellschaft in Mittelalter und Renaissance, Beiträge und Texte zur Geschichte der Kindheit* (Paderborn: Ferdinand Schöningh, 1980), pp. 24–25.

12. This misunderstanding explains one ludicrous historical malapropism concerning medieval children: see Peter Raedts, "The Children's Crusade of 1212," *Journal of Medieval History* 3 (1977), especially 295–300, superseding older works.

13. Arnold, *Kind und Gesellschaft*, p. 19. See also Nicholas Orme, *From Childhood to Chivalry. The Education of the English Kings and Aristocracy, 1066–1530* (London: Methuen, 1984), p. 5.

14. James Bruce Ross, "The Middle Class Child in Urban Italy, Fourteenth to Early Sixteenth Century," in de Mause, *Childhood*, pp. 200–204.

15. McLaughlin, "Survivors," pp. 103–105.

16. John F. Benton, ed., *Self and Society in Medieval France. The Memoirs of Abbot Guibert of Nogent (1064?–c. 1125)* (New York: Harper & Row, 1970), pp. 12, 41, 68, 82, 95; following Benton in Freudian interpretation is Jonathan Kantor, "A Psychohistorical Source: The Memoirs of Abbot Guibert of Nogent," *Journal of Medieval History* 2 (1976):281–304; for a critique of the Freudian interpretation, see M. D. Coupe, "The Personality of Guibert de Nogent Reconsidered," *Journal of Medieval History* 9 (1983): 317–329.

17. Attreed, "From *Pearl* Maiden to Tower Princes," especially pp. 50–55. Children were highly valued and their upbringing carefully watched in Jewish communities; see Kenneth R. Stow, "The Jewish Family in the Rhineland in High Middle Ages: Form and Function," *American Historical Review* 92 (1987):1085–1110.

18. Iris Origo, *The Merchant of Prato. Francesco di Marco Datini* (London: Peregrine Books, 1963), pp. 161, 215–217.

19. McLaughlin, "Survivors," pp. 114, 136–137; Luke Demaitre, "The Idea of Childhood and Child Care in Medical Writings of the Middle Ages," *Journal of Psychohistory* 4 (1977): 461–490.

20. Cases cited in McLaughlin, "Survivors," pp. 153, 167; James Bruce Ross, p. 202; Arnold, *Kind und Gesellschaft*, pp. 39–40, 67–76.

21. Ross, "Middle Class Child," pp. 184–198; McLaughlin, "Survivors," pp. 116–117; Shulamith Shahar, *The Fourth Estate. A History of Women in the Middle Ages* (London: Methuen, 1983), pp. 183–187. Christiane Klapisch-Zuber, "Blood Parents and Milk Parents: Wet Nursing in Florence, 1300–1530," in her *Women, Family, and Ritual in Renaissance Italy* (Chicago: University of Chicago Press, 1985), pp. 132–164.

22. Maryanne Kowaleski, "The History of Urban Families in Medieval England," *Journal of Medieval History* 14 (1988):53–54.

23. David Herlihy and Christiane Klapisch-Zuber, *Tuscans and Their Families. A Study of the Florentine Catasto of 1427* (New Haven, Conn: Yale University Press, 1985), pp. 138–144, 145, 198. See also P.J.P. Goldberg, "Female Labour, Service and Marriage in the Late Medieval Urban North," *Northern History* 22 (1986):18–38.

24. David Nicholas, *The Domestic Life of a Medieval City. Women, Children, and the Family in Fourteenth Century Ghent* (Lincoln: University of Nebraska Press, 1985), pp. 124–125.

25. Shahar, *Fourth Estate*, p. 186; Christiane Klapisch-Zuber, "Childhood in Tuscany

at the Beginning of the Fifteenth Century,'' in *Women, Family, and Ritual*, pp. 104–106, finds that virtually all evidence suggests that girls in Tuscany were less valued than boys and were cared for less well, a fact that may explain why sex ratios there favored boys.

26. Jack Goody, *The Development of the Family and Marriage in Europe* (Cambridge: Cambridge University Press, 1983), p. 258; Diane Owen Hughes, "From Brideprice to Dowry in Mediterranean Europe," *Journal of Family History* 3 (1978): 262–296; Stanley Chojnacki, "Dowries and Kinsmen in Early Renaissance Venice," *Journal of Interdisciplinary History* 5 (1975): 571–600, reprinted in *Women in Medieval Society*, ed. Susan M. Stuard, pp. 173–198 (Philadelphia: University of Pennsylvania Press, 1976); Nicholas, *Domestic Life*, pp. 112–113.

27. McLaughlin, "Survivors," pp. 120–121; Emily Coleman, "L'infanticide dans le Haut Moyen Age," *Annales E.S.C.* 29 (1974):315–335, translated as "Infanticide in the Early Middle Ages," in Stuard, *Women in Medieval Society*, pp. 47–70; Richard C. Trexler, "Infanticide in Florence: New Sources and First Results," *History of Childhood Quarterly* 1 (1973):259–284, however, finds that the number of boys and girls killed was roughly equal. See also Frances Gies and Joseph Gies, *Marriage and the Family in the Middle Ages* (New York: Harper & Row, 1987), pp. 27, 40–41, 60–62; Pablo Fernandez, "Het verschijnsel kindermoord in de Nederlanden (XIVe–XVe eeuw)," in *Sociale structuren en topografie van armoede en rijkdom in de 14e en 15e eeuw. Methodologische aspecten en resultaten van recent onderzoek*, ed. W. Prevenier, R. van Uytven, and E. van Cauwenberghe (Ghent: RKFO, 1986), particularly pp. 111–112, 127–128; Richard Helmholtz, "Infanticide in the Province of Canterbury During the Fifteenth Century," *History of Childhood Quarterly* 2 (1975):379–390.

28. Herlihy, "Medieval Children," p. 124; McLaughlin, "Survivors," pp. 122–124; Nicholas, *Domestic Life*, p. 115; Leah L. Otis, "Municipal Wet Nurses in Fifteenth-Century Montpellier," in *Women and Work in Preindustrial Europe*, ed. Barbara A. Hanawalt (Bloomington: Indiana University Press, 1986), p. 83; Herlihy and Klapisch-Zuber, *Tuscans*, p. 145. On orphanages in the German cities in the fourteenth century, see Arnold, *Kind und Gesellschaft*, p. 40.

29. Shahar, *Fourth Estate*, pp. 138–145; Georges Duby, "Dans la France du Nord-Ouest. Au XIIe siècle: les 'jeunes' dans la société aristocratique," *Annales. E.S.C.* 19 (1964):835–846, translated as "In Northwestern France. The 'Youth' in Twelfth-Century Aristocratic Society," in *Lordship and Community in Medieval Europe*, ed. F. L. Cheyette (New York: Holt, Rinehart, & Winston, 1968), pp. 198–209; Sue Sheridan Walker, "Widow and Ward: The Feudal Law of Child Custody in Medieval England," in Stuard, *Women*, pp. 159–172; Walker, "Proof of Age of Feudal Heirs in Medieval England," *Mediaeval Studies* 35 (1973), particularly pp. 312–316.

30. Case cited by Gies and Gies, *Marriage and the Family*, p. 197.

31. Jane K. Beitscher, " 'As the Twig Is Bent' . . . :Children and Their Parents in an Aristocratic Society," *Journal of Medieval History* 2 (1976): 184–188; Charles Verlinden, *Robert Ier le Frison, comte de Flandre. Etude d' histoire politique* (Antwerp: De Sikkel, 1935), pp. 11, 14.

32. Elizabeth A. R. Brown, "The Prince Is Father of the King: The Character and Childhood of Philip the Fair of France," *Mediaeval Studies* 49 (1987): 282–334.

33. Benton, *Self and Society*, pp. 11, 45–46; John of Salisbury, *The Metalogicon*, trans. Daniel J. McGarry (Gloucester, Mass.: Peter Smith, 1971), pp. 67–69; Herlihy, "Medieval Children" p. 120.

34. McLaughlin, "Survivors," pp. 131, 173 n. 191.

35. Herlihy, "Medieval Children," p. 122. Orme, *From Childhood to Chivalry*, p. 16, notes that some aristocratic fathers involved themselves directly in their children's education, or at least recognized an inclination toward a particular vocation; but this was more usual farther down the social scale, where parents and children were in more constant contact.

36. Christian Bec, *Les marchands ecrivains. Affairs et humanisme à Florence 1375–1434* (Paris: Mouton, 1967), pp. 286–299.

37. C. H. Haskins, "The Life of Medieval Students as Illustrated by Their Letters," and "Manuals for Students," both reprinted in his *Studies in Mediaeval Culture* (New York: Frederick Ungar, 1965), pp. 1–35, 72–91. On schooling in general, see Orme, *English Schools*.

38. Leah L. Otis, *Prostitution in Medieval Society. The History of an Urban Institution in Languedoc* (Chicago: University of Chicago Press, 1985), pp. 79, 199 n. 17; Jacques Rossiaud, "Prostitution, Youth, and Society in the Towns of Southeastern France in the Fifteenth Century," in *Deviants and the Abandoned in French Society. Selections from the Annales . . . 4.* (Baltimore: Johns Hopkins University Press, 1978), pp. 1–50.

39. Klapisch-Zuber, "Childhood," pp. 97, 107–108; Nicholas, *Domestic Life*, pp. 134–140.

40. Philippe Didier, "L'apprentissage médiéval en France: formation professionnelle, entretien ou emploi de la main-d'oeuvre juvenile?" *Zeitschrift der Savigny-Stiftung für Rechtsgeschichte, Germanistiche Abteilung* 101 (1984):200–255; on the occupations of women, see Martha C. Howell, *Women, Production, and Patriarchy in Late Medieval Cities* (Chicago: University of Chicago Press, 1986), pp. 174–183.

41. The theme of shared tasks reinforcing bonds of family affection is emphasized especially by McLaughlin, "Survivors," pp. 138–139, on the basis of literary evidence. For an example of attitudes among peasants toward their children—in this case toward a daughter who was the youngest child—see "Der arme Heinrich," in *Peasant Life in Old German Epics. Meier Helmbrecht and Der arme Heinrich*, trans. Clair Hayden Bell (New York: W. W. Norton, 1968), especially pp. 101–105. See also Shahar, *Fourth Estate*, pp. 230–232.

42. Emmanuel Le Roy Ladurie, *Montaillou. The Promised Land of Error* (New York: Random House, 1979), pp. 210–218.

43. Barbara A. Hanawalt, "Childrearing Among the Lower Classes of Late Medieval England," *Journal of Interdisciplinary History* 8 (1977): 1–22; Barbara A. Hanawalt, *The Ties That Bound: Peasant Families in Medieval England* (Oxford: Oxford University Press, 1986), pp. 156–204.

44. Rossiaud, "Prostitution," p. 23.

45. Judith M. Bennett, *Women in the Medieval English Countryside: Gender and Household in Brigstock Before the Plague* (Oxford: Oxford University Press, 1987), pp. 66–67; Hanawalt, *Ties That Bound*, pp. 188–197.

REFERENCES

Alberti, Leon Battista. *I Libri della Famiglia*. Translated in *The Family in Renaissance Florence* by Renée Neu Watkins. Columbia: University of South Carolina Press, 1969.

Ariès, Philippe. *Centuries of Childhood: A Social History of Family Life.* New York: Alfred Knopf, 1962.

Arnold, Klaus. *Kind und Gesellschaft in Mittelalter und Renaissance.* Paderborn: Ferdinand Schöningh, 1980.

Attreed, Lorraine C. "From *Pearl* Maiden to Tower Princes: Towards a New History of Medieval Childhood." *Journal of Medieval History* 9 (1983):43–59.

Baron, F. Xavier. "Children and Violence in Chaucer's *Canterbury Tales.*" *Journal of Psychohistory* 7 (1979–80):77–103.

Bec, Christian. *Les marchands écrivains. Affairs et humanisme à Florence 1375–1434.* Paris: Mouton, 1967.

Beitscher, Jane K. " 'As the Twig Is Bent' . . . :Children and Their Parents in an Aristocratic Society." *Journal of Medieval History* 2 (1976):181–191.

Bennett, Judith M. *Women in the Medieval English Countryside: Gender and Household in Brigstock Before the Plague.* Oxford: Oxford University Press, 1987.

Benton, John F. (ed.). *Self and Society in Medieval France. The Memoirs of Abbot Guibert of Nogent (1064?–c. 1125).* New York: Harper & Row, 1970.

Billar, P.P.A. "Birth Control in the Medieval West." *Past and Present* 94 (1982):3–26.

Boswell, John E. "*Expositio* and *Oblatio*: The Abandonment of Children and the Ancient and Medieval Family," *American Historical Review* 89 (1984):10–33.

Brissaud, Y. B. "L'infanticide à la fin du moyen âge," *Revue historique de droit français et étranger* 50 (1972):229–256.

Brown, Elizabeth A. R. "The Prince Is Father of the King: The Character and Childhood of Philip the Fair of France." *Mediaeval Studies* 49 (1987):282–334.

Chojnacki, Stanley, "Dowries and Kinsmen in Early Renaissance Venice." *Journal of Interdisciplinary History* 5 (1975):571–600.

Coleman, Emily R. "Medieval Marriage Characteristics: A Neglected Factor in the History of Medieval Serfdom." *Journal of Interdisciplinary History* 2 (1971):205–219.

Coupe, M. D. "The Personality of Guibert de Nogent Reconsidered." *Journal of Medieval History* 9 (1983):317–329.

de Jong, Mayke. "Growing Up in a Carolingian Monastery: Magister Hildemar and His Oblates." *Journal of Medieval History* 9 (1983):99–128.

Demaitre, Luke. "The Idea of Childhood and Child Care in Medical Writings of the Middle Ages." *Journal of Psychohistory* 4 (1977): 461–490.

de Mause, Lloyd, ed. *The History of Childhood.* New York: Harper & Row, 1975.

Didier, Philippe. "L'apprentissage médiéval en France: formation professionnelle, entretien ou emploi de la main-d'oeuvre juvenile?" *Zeitschrift der Savigny-Stiftung für Rechtsgeschichte, Germanistische Abteilung* 101 (1984):200–255.

Duby, Georges. "Dans la France du Nord-Ouest. Au XIIe siécle: les 'jeunes' dans la société aristocratique," *Annales, E.S.C.* 19 (1964):835–846, translated as "In Northwestern France. The 'Youth' in Twelfth-Century Aristocratic Society." In *Lordship and Community in Medieval Europe*, edited by F. L. Cheyette, (New York: Holt, Rinehart, & Winston, 1968) pp. 198–209.

Duby, Georges, and Jacques Le Goff, eds. *Famille et parenté dans l'occident médiéval.* Paris, 1978.

Fehr, H. *Die Rechtsstellung der Frau und der Kinder in den Weistümern.* Jena, 1912.

Fernandez, Pablo. "Het verschijnsel kindermoord in de Nederlanden (XIV-XV eeeuw)."

In *Sociale structuren en topografie van armoede en rijkdom in de 14e en 15e eeeuw. Methodologische aspecten en resultaten van recent onderzoek*, edited by W. Prevenier, R. van Uytven, and E. van Cauwenberghe, pp. 111–133. Ghent: RKFO, 1986.

Flandrin, J. "Repression and Change in the Sexual Life of Young People in Medieval and Early Modern Times." In *Family and Sexuality in French History*, edited by Robert Wheaton and Tamara K. Hareven. Philadelphia: University of Pennsylvania Press, 1980, pp. 27–48.

Forseth, Ilene H. "Children in Early Medieval Art: Ninth Through Twelfth Centuries." *Journal of Psychohistory* 4 (1976):31–70.

Geis, Frances, and Joseph. *Marriage and the Family in the Middle Ages*. New York: Harper & Row, 1987.

Goldberg, P.J.P. "Female Labour, Service and Marriage in the Late Medieval Urban North." *Northern History* 22 (1986): 19–38.

Goodich, Michael. "Childhood and Adolescence Among the Thirteenth-Century Saints." *History of Childhood Quarterly* 1 (1973):285–309.

Goody, Jack. *The Development of the Family and Marriage in Europe*. Cambridge: Cambridge University Press, 1983.

Gransden, Antoine. "Childhood and Youth in Medieval England." *Nottingham Medieval Studies* 16 (1972):3–19.

Grey, Ursula. *Das Bild des Kindes im Spiegel der altdeutschen Dichtung und Literatur mit textkritischer Ausgabe von Metlingers 'Regiment der jungen Kinder.'* Europäische Hochschulschriften, Reihe I, Deutsche Literatur und Germanistik 91. Bern: Herbert Lang; Frankfurt: Peter Lang, 1974.

Hanawalt, Barbara A. "Childrearing Among the Lower Classes of Late Medieval England." *Journal of Interdisciplinary History* 8 (1977):1–22.

———. *The Ties That Bound: Peasant Families in Medieval England*. Oxford: Oxford University Press, 1986.

———. ed. *Women and Work in Preindustrial Europe*. Bloomington: Indiana University Press, 1986.

Haskins, Charles H. *Studies in Mediaeval Culture*. New York: Ungar, 1965.

Helmholtz, Richard M. *Marriage Litigation in Medieval England*. Cambridge, 1974.

———. "Infanticide in the Province of Canterbury During the Fifteenth Century." *History of Childhood Quarterly* 2 (1975):382–389.

Herlihy, David. "Medieval Children." In *The Walter Prescott Webb Memorial Lectures: Essays on Medieval Civilization*. Austin: University of Texas Press, 1976, pp. 109–141.

Herlihy, David, and Christiane Klapisch-Zuber. *Les Toscans et leurs familles. Une étude du Catasto florentin de 1427*. Paris: Editions de L'Ecole des Hautes Etudes en Sciences Sociales, 1978. Abridged translation as *Tuscans and Their Families. A Study of the Florentine Catasto of 1427*. New Haven, Conn.: Yale University Press, 1985.

Hughes, Diane Owen. "Domestic Ideals and Social Behavior. Evidence from Medieval Genoa." In *The Family in History*, edited by Charles E. Rosenberg. Philadelphia: University of Pennsylvania Press, 1975, pp. 115–143.

———. "From Brideprice to Dowry in Mediterranean Europe." *Journal of Family History* 3 (1978):262–296.

John of Salisbury. *The Metalogicon*. Translated by Daniel J. McGarry. Gloucester, Mass.: Peter Smith, 1971.

Kantor, Jonathan. "A Psychohistorical Source: The *Memoirs* of Abbott Guibert of Nogent." *Journal of Medieval History* 2 (1976):281–303.

Kellum, B. "Infanticide in England in the Later Middle Ages." *History of Childhood Quarterly* 1 (1974):367–388.

King, P. D. *Law and Society in the Visigothic Kingdom*. Cambridge: Cambridge University Press, 1972.

Klapisch-Zuber, Christiane. *Women, Family, and Ritual in Renaissance Italy*. Chicago: University of Chicago Press, 1985.

Kowaleski, Maryanne. "The History of Urban Families in Medieval England." *Journal of Medieval History* 14 (1988):47–63.

Krull, Jerome. "The Concept of Childhood in the Middle Ages." *Journal of the History of Behavioural Sciences* 13 (1977):384–393.

Laslett, Peter. *The World We Have Lost, Further Explored*, 3rd ed. New York: Charles Scribner's Sons, 1984.

Le Roy Ladurie, Emmanuel. *Montaillou. The Promised Land of Error*. New York: Random House, 1979.

McLaughlin, Mary Martin. "Survivors and Surrogates: Children and Parents from the Ninth to the Thirteenth Centuries." In de Mause, *Childhood*, pp. 101–181.

Nicholas, David. *The Domestic Life of a Medieval City. Women, Children, and the Family in Fourteenth-Century Ghent*. Lincoln: University of Nebraska Press, 1985.

Origo, Iris. *The Merchant of Prato. Francesco di Marco Datini*. London: Peregrine Books, 1963.

Orme, Nicholas. *English Schools in the Middle Ages*. London, 1973.

———. *From Childhood to Chivalry. The Education of the English Kings and Aristocracy, 1066–1530*. London: Methuen, 1984.

Otis, Leah L. *Prostitution in Medieval Society. The History of an Urban Institution in Languedoc*. Chicago: University of Chicago Press, 1985.

———. "Municipal Wet Nurses in Fifteenth-Century Montpellier." In Hanawalt, *Women and Work*, pp. 83–93.

Peasant Life in Old German Epics. Meier Helmbrecht and Der arme Heinrich. Translated by Clair Hayden Bell. New York: W. W. Norton, 1968.

Peiper, A. *Geschichte der Kinderheilkunde*. Leipzig, 1956.

Petschauer, Peter. "On Phillipe Arises and the History of Childhood." *Journal of Psychohistory* 13 (1985–86):357–359.

Raedts, Peter. "The Children's Crusade of 1212." *Journal of Medieval History* 3 (1977): 279–323.

Riché, Pierre. *De l'éducation antique à l'éducation chevaleresque*. Paris: Flammarion, 1968.

Ross, James Bruce. "The Middle Class Child in Urban Italy, Fourteenth to Early Sixteenth Century." In de Mause, *Childhood*, pp. 183–228.

Rossiaud, Jacques. "Prostitution, Youth, and Society in the Towns of Southeastern France in the Fifteenth Century." In *Deviants and the Abandoned in French Society. Selections from the Annales . . . 4*, pp. 1–50. Baltimore: Johns Hopkins University Press, 1978.

Shahar, Shulamith. *The Fourth Estate. A History of Women in the Middle Ages*. London: Methuen, 1983.

Stow, Kenneth R. "The Jewish Family in the Rhineland in the High Middle Ages: Form and Function." *American Historical Review* 92 (1987):1085–1110.

Stuard, Susan M., ed. *Women in Medieval Society*. Philadelphia: University of Pennsylvania Press, 1976.

Trexler, Richard C. "Infanticide in Florence: New Sources and First Results." *History of Childhood Quarterly* 1 (1973):98–116.

———. "The Foundlings of Florence, 1395–1455." *History of Childhood Quarterly* 1 (1973):259–284.

Walker, Sue S. "Proof of Age of Feudal Heirs in Medieval England." *Mediaeval Studies* 35 (1973):306–323.

——— "The Marriage of Feudal Wards in Medieval England." *Studies in Medieval Culture* 4 (1974):209–233.

4

CHILDHOOD IN EARLY MODERN EUROPE

Sherrin Marshall

Childhood in early modern Europe is a controversial subject. Debate has raged among historians, sociologists, and anthropologists for more than two decades over how well or badly children fared in European society from the mid-fifteenth through the end of the eighteenth century. This chapter provides an overview of the major controversies related to childhood in early modern Europe, discusses the diverse types of source materials used to reach very different conclusions, and presents examples of evidence that can be used to reconstruct the reality of children's lives in early modern Europe.

Research on the history of childhood during this period burgeoned with the important seminal work of Philippe Ariès, *Centuries of Childhood*, in 1962.[1] In that book Ariès reached what has become a famous series of interconnected conclusions: that children, especially young children, were unimportant members of the family because they died so easily during these centuries; that they were in fact regarded as "miniature adults" in many important ways such as dress; and that they were subject to strict disciplinary practices that often bordered on cruelty. Ariès' conclusions were elaborated on in the later studies of Lloyd de Mause, Lawrence Stone, and Edward Shorter, who all outlined an increasingly bleak picture for children.[2]

Other models for the history of childhood have appeared. These have relied more on primary sources, often in manuscript form, frequently located in archives, to offer alternative views. The early modern period in European history, like that of the Middle Ages, is not rich in extant source material, particularly for the earlier phases. Much evidence has been lost. Historians, therefore, ground their reconstructions of the past in what is often fragmentary evidence, the only evidence they have. For example, one study used the diary of a seventeenth-century Puritan clergyman, Ralph Josselin, that was kept from 1641 to 1683, while a second investigated the records of Richard Napier, who treated men and women for mental illness in England between 1597 and 1634.[3] Each of these sources is unique. Some historians have questioned the extent to which generalizations that are purportedly valid for an entire society can be based on a single source. Others have suggested that these records reveal so much of the society that perhaps generalizations based on them *are* possible. Still other scholars simply reiterate that as long as historians are forced to reconstruct the past confronted with a dearth of materials, questions of interpretation will arise.

A second method of reconstructing the history of childhood, used to counter excessive reliance on one source, is that of utilizing different, but comparable sources. Such studies have focused on groups of biographies and autobiographies—some of which were actually written by children themselves—or court cases, for example. Although criticism has been leveled at this approach as well—not everyone wrote an autobiography, so how typical could be the children who did?—other scholars reiterate that when historians are obliged to rely on scanty and scattered sources for their reconstruction of the past, differences of interpretation will continue to arise.

What other types of evidence are used by historians examining the history of childhood in early modern Europe? When historians investigate *printed* and *archival* (or manuscript) sources, they turn to chronicles maintained by parents—usually fathers—that often are found in Bibles, birth registers, and genealogies. They rely on memoirs, journals, diaries, and autobiographies, some few of which were kept by children, as well as letters, to and sometimes from children. Children may figure in the testamentary dispositions of their parents or in court cases. The latter might tell us whether child-beating and infanticide were grounds for litigation during the early modern period.

A second group of sources that yield useful information on children can be termed *iconographic*. These sources include portraits of children and children portrayed within a family grouping. Early modern European genre paintings depict life, in the words of sixteenth-century Dutch artist Pieter Breughel, "as I saw it." Before artists such as Breughel the masters of the Italian Renaissance had pioneered in realistic portrayals of people's lives. Sometimes visual as well as verbal images of childhood appear on gravestones.

Statistical sources reveal more abstract evidence about the reality of childhood. What was infant and child mortality in early modern Europe? What effect, if any, did mortality have on child-spacing patterns within the family? How can we measure, demographically, the transition from childhood to adulthood? What was the age at first marriage for children? In all the above are there gender differences for boys and girls? Did differences exist from one European country to another?

Finally, sources that reflect attitudes *toward* children should be taken into consideration. Because many of these are prescriptive, in the form of sermons, for example, or advice-books on child rearing, they must be used with caution. Our emphasis is on reality, verifiable insofar as it is humanly possible. Prescriptive sources, however, reveal a society's norms and values, and can thus be a useful aid in reaching an understanding of the ways in which a society nearly five hundred years removed from us thought children *should* be raised, or believed that children *should* behave.

All the above suggests that the reconstruction of childhood in early modern Europe must be multifaceted, especially if our goal is to depict the actuality of children's lives. These sources are used collectively here to examine the following stages of life: birth, infancy (approximately one to four years), childhood (five to eleven years), adolescence (twelve years and beyond), and the transition to adulthood, the years of which were variable. Even these stages of life reflect twentieth-century views on age boundaries. For the early modern period some historians suggest the following division: infancy (which encompassed newborns, infants, and toddlers, one to seven years), childhood (seven to fourteen years), and adolescence (fifteen to twenty-five years), as three of the "seven ages of man."[4]

The birth experience during this epoch was fraught with danger to mother and child alike, particularly when even the smallest complication occurred. Babies were delivered by midwives, whose skills ran the gamut from highly accomplished to minimal.[5] Premature births, especially, were difficult: in Holland, Oda van Zuylen's seventh son and tenth child—nonetheless, a person important enough to have been noted by the sixteenth-century chronicler—"was born eleven weeks too early, and thus died."[6] By the end of the early modern period such births were still problematic. In 1800 Madame de la Tour du Pin, an aristocrat exiled by the French Revolution, wrote that she "gave birth to a small and very frail baby girl, who had completed only a seven and a half months term. She was so thin and delicate that I hardly dared to hope that she would live."[7] Overall, projections vary with regard to maternal and infant mortality. One recent demographic estimate compares the English maternal mortality rate in 1979, 0.12 per one thousand births, with that of the sixteenth and seventeenth centuries, about twenty-five per thousand births.[8] Additional evidence on maternal mortality, in this instance from sixteenth- and seventeenth-century Holland, reveals that the majority of married women outlived their husbands, even when one calculates first marriages of wives.[9] Thus, although childbirth was a potentially dangerous experience, it was perhaps not so demographically catastrophic as has sometimes been posited.

In addition to those who perished in childbirth, many children died in infancy. Although it has been suggested that high mortality rates have been exaggerated, statistics for Holland and Germany indicate that about one-third of all children died in birth or infancy, before reaching their fifth birthday.[10] The uncertainty of life for young and old alike clearly contributed to the joy in new birth and hopefulness of continuing life. Successful childbirth was a joyous event, remarked on in many family registers, journals, and even genealogies. Not all babies survived, as we have seen. Contrary to earlier conclusions, evidence suggests that the deaths of babies affected parents deeply. The Nuremberger Johannes Beringer's *Hauschronik* recorded the birth of his first son, Theophilus, in 1525, and the child's death the next year: "Through God's will, taken from this world."[11] Many memoirs and journals recorded specific details of death for young children as well as those for children who were maturer. Birth defects were noted: Clara van Lauwick, a sixteenth-century Dutch gentlewomen, bore only one child in her first marriage, noted the chronicler, "and the child came badly misshapen into the world; so much so that there would have befallen great distress if it had lived."[12] Death came from diseases, such as chicken pox. Joost van Heemskerck died in 1647, "age three years less seven days," as his bereaved father wrote in the family chronicle. "He'd had a high fever for days, and was completely covered with the chicken pox, and although most of these had in fact dried up, still his fever didn't diminish. Finally, his body was worn out, and the fever claimed his life."[13] Plague and other epidemic diseases swept across Europe periodically. Smallpox, too, was dreaded, and it was not until the end of the eighteenth century that large numbers of infants began to be inoculated against it.

Accidental death was attributable to many causes. Infant suffocation, or overlaying, occurred when a baby died because the parent or caregiver lay too close or on top of it in bed. On occasion such deaths had sinister connotations— such as deaths of illegitimate babies born to unwed mothers—but other episodes appear to be accidental. Living and sleeping arrangements in early modern Europe favored overlaying. Beds were few, and it also has been speculated that having the baby sleep with the mother or caregiver was a reaction to high infant mortality rates.[14] Other mishaps were similar to those documented for the Middle Ages. Hermann von Weinsberg of Cologne was nearly drowned in 1522 at age four when he fell into a barrel of water; Willem van Boshuysen drowned near Leiden at the age of five, "through misfortune and terrible luck," wrote his father.[15]

Parents, seem, on the whole, to have been more strongly affected by the deaths of children as their offspring matured. This should not encourage us to infer that mothers and fathers were unaffected by the deaths of infants and very young children. In *Forgotten Children*, a "study of Parent-child relations from 1500–1900," Linda Pollock documents a wide range of individual responses on the part of English parents whose diaries recorded the deaths of children.[16] William Brownlow, writing at the end of the sixteenth century, lost numerous children shortly after birth; but this did not make him "indifferent." Upon the deaths of two sons who had survived only a few years, Brownlow wrote, "O Lord thou has dealt bitterlie with mee and broken me with breach upon breach, when wilt thou comfort mee." Nehemiah Wallington (1598–1658) wrote on the death of his four-year-old daughter: "The grief for this child was so great that I forgot myself so much that I did offend my God in it; for I broke all my purposes, promises, and covenants with my God, for I was much distracted in my mind, and could not be comforted, although my friends speak so comfortably unto me."[17]

Similarly, the reformer Martin Luther wrote of the death of his daughter Elizabeth at the age of eight months: "I so lamented her death that I was exquisitely sick, my heart rendered soft and weak; never had I thought that a father's heart could be so broken for his children's sake."[18] As saddened as Luther was by this event, he was devastated by the death of another daughter, Magdalena, who died in 1542 at age thirteen. In fact, he asked his friend Justus Jonas to pray to God, giving thanks for Magdalena's deliverance from "the flesh, the world, the Turk, and the Devil," for Luther said he and his wife were "unable to do this without crying and grieving in our hearts . . . (for) the force of our natural love is so great. . . . The features, the words, and the movement of our living and dying daughter, who was so very obedient and respectful, remain engraved in our hearts; even the death of Christ . . . is unable to take all this away as it should."[19] When Madame de la Tour du Pin's daughter, Cecile—whose successful premature birth had caused her mother to marvel at her survival in the first place—perished, her mother's diary noted: "I had her with me for seventeen years, only to see her die at the very moment when she was able to enjoy to the full all the gifts of beauty, character, intelligence and charm with which she was blessed. God took her away from me—may His blessed will be done."[20]

It cannot be said that most parents did not mourn the deaths of young children. The difference in all these cases is only one of degree. The expression of sorrow, in early modern Europe or today, is a particularly personal concern. Several diarists failed to display depth of feeling over the deaths of their *adult* children, whereas others exhibited such grief intensely. In early modern Europe personal expression of grief also was framed by religious dimensions. Protestant and Catholic alike regarded excessive grief as a failing, albeit one that was understandable and all too human. Belief in an afterlife and God's will moderated inward feelings, or made grief-stricken parents feel that they *should* moderate such feelings. Contemporary historians may have mistaken this outward evidence of self-control for apathy or even nonchalance. Pollock notes, for example, that another sixteenth-century diarist, Nicholas Assheton, failed to comment on the death of his child shortly after birth. She observes, however, that he attended the infant's funeral and laid the child in his grave.[21] Although Pollock speculates that he may have suffered from an inability to articulate his feelings, and was perhaps unable to express his grief, it also is probable that the issue of religious seemliness was paramount for many parents. Although Nehemiah Wallington revealed an inconsolable grief on the death of his toddler daughter, his wife chided him by saying, "I do as freely give it again unto God, as I did receive it of him."[22] Our religious frame of reference differs so greatly from that of parents in early modern Europe that we can see why differing viewpoints may have been derived from the same evidence, and why historians must guard against drawing ahistorical conclusions.

Autobiographies and diaries not only provide valuable information on parental reactions to the birth and death of newborns and young children, but also reveal much detail about these other aspects of infancy. Once again, they demonstrate that parents concerned themselves with the smallest details of their progeny's progress. Examination of child-rearing practices in early modern Europe also has led to varying conclusions. A number of scholars stress what they regard as the sorry plight of children who were farmed out to wet nurses, swaddled so as to inhibit their growth, routinely beaten, abused, and harshly disciplined.[23] Maternal breast-feeding was endorsed by medical and religious opinion, but wet nursing was a fact of life among the upper classes and lowest, in particular. Evidence demonstrates that infant mortality was highest among such infants. Once again some historians have urged caution in the interpretation of wet-nursing practices, for differences clearly existed. By the seventeenth century maternal breast-feeding had become fashionable among the aristocracy in many countries, and at least some mothers were eager to nurse their own infants. Some have linked this new emphasis with the rise of puritanism, or the religious shifts during the Reformation and Counter-Reformation. Other distinctions to be drawn are those of choice of wet nurse, and economic circumstances of the parents. Some parents had the commitment and economic wherewithal to locate and retain a satisfactory wet nurse. On the birth of Madame de la Tour du Pin's son in 1790 she observed in her diary that "when he was born, he seemed to be only skin and bone, but a good foster-mother (i.e., wet-nurse) took charge of him and he soon gained weight."[24] Even if a woman chose to nurse herself, she might encounter difficulties. In Scotland the young Countess of Eglinton found a wet nurse for her daughter in 1618 after (or so she believed) her own milk supply had failed; her mother-in-law wrote, "I am very glad that you have gotten a young milk woman for her, seeing her mammy proved not sufficient. You have done very wisely in doing the same."[25] Finding the right wet nurse could be a time-consuming process; in the meantime the infant undoubtedly suffered. One eighteenth-century diarist, born in 1744, wrote of his own life:

Four different wet-nurses were alternately turn'd out of doors on my account, and to the care of whom I had been entrusted, my poor mother being too weak a condition to suckle me herself. The first of these bitches was turn'd off for having nearly suffocated me in bed; she having sleep'd upon me till I was smother'd, and with skill and difficulty restored to life. The second had let me fall from her arms on the stones till my head was almost fractured, & I lay several hours in convulsions. The third carried me under a moulder'd old brick wall, which fell in a heap of rubbish just the moment we had passed by it, while the fourth proved to be a thief, and deprived me even of my very baby clothes.[26]

In another instance an eighteenth-century mother weaned her child early because, as she put it, "the nurse's conduct has been so very reprehensible that I must part with her."[27] It is unclear how usual such concerned behavior was in the early modern period. Most parents who employed wet nurses failed to exercise the same care, or at the very least failed to note that care was taken. Clearly, many infants died in the care of wet nurses. As might be expected, the most at-risk were illegitimate infants, especially those from destitute backgrounds, for whom the mortality rates were astronomical. In *The Poor of Eighteenth Century France*, Olwen Hufton documents hundreds of deaths of illegitimate children.[28] These included foundlings, who often were abandoned at birth, as well as other unwanted illegitimate children, typically farmed out to wet nurses who might be "nursing" a dozen infants at once. In eighteenth-century England poor laws gave responsibility for foundling infants to the parish. A number of contemporary studies documented widespread abuses in the system, such as a parliamentary report of 1716:

A great many poor infants and exposed bastard children are inhumanely suffered to die by the barbarity of nurses, who are a sort of people void of commiseration or religion, hir'd by the churchwardens to take off a burthen from the parish at the cheapest and easiest rates they can, and these know the manner of doing it effectually.[29]

Farming out babies to wet nurses had been viewed as a socially acceptable form of infanticide. How were cases of infanticide treated legally in early modern Europe? Unwed mothers figure in a number of criminal prosecutions of those apprehended for infanticide. A study of twenty-four cases of alleged infanticide in eighteenth-century Amsterdam reveals that no less than twenty-two cases involved servant girls, who often were penniless and always defenseless.[30] Society and social attitudes did not overlook such cases: infanticide was a serious criminal act.[31] Notwithstanding, punishment was often severer in theory than in actuality. The circumstances that brought women to such acts were recognized, as well as the reality of unfeeling treatment of unwanted illegitimate infants. Infanticide was not rampant or commonplace in early modern Europe, but rather provoked by extenuating circumstances.

Autobiographies, diaries, journals, and letters provide information on aspects of infancy other than breast-feeding, such as weaning, swaddling, eating and sleeping habits, walking, and talking. Weaning usually occurred in the second year of life, and was a gradual process that included the introduction of pap and mashed vegetables into the diet. Swaddling, another child-rearing practice that has been attacked, took place from birth through the first year of life. When a baby was swaddled he or she was placed on a large square of material, usually woolen, that was folded over the feet. It was held in place by long strips of cloth, which were tightly wound around the legs. A second piece of cloth, called the waistcoat, was placed around the chest and arms, with additional strips of cloth wound around the upper half. An additional band held the head steady and kept it from wobbling. After a few months the upper portion was left off, but the swaddling clothes themselves were only gradually removed, usually during the second year. Did swaddling render impossible the search for autonomy that psychologists consider so important for babies, or does swaddling express a fundamental level of concern, and, especially for infants, recreate much of the womb's security? Both opinions have their adherents.

The most important events that marked the child's transition from infant to

child involved training and education. Of the case studies that Pollock utilizes
for the early modern period, 33 percent of her sixteenth-century examples contain
information on education, compared with 46 percent for the seventeenth and
eighteenth centuries. She itemizes 24 sources for the sixteenth century, 80 for
the seventeenth, and 245 for the eighteenth—in itself an excellent statistical piece
of evidence demonstrating that sources for the later period are vastly more
comprehensive.[32] Religious instruction was closely linked with education in
general throughout the period, although the emphasis differed in time and geographical locale. Many, perhaps most, children received their early education
at home. The spread of the Renaissance, and particularly the impact of humanistic
principles, affected education throughout Europe. Before the Reformation many
schools had already altered their curricula, moving away from the medieval
texts. Notwithstanding, at the end of the fifteenth century, boys of six or seven
began their studies in Latin as well as German in Nuremberg. The Reformation
brought with it an incorporation of moral and political ends into the students'
studies in that city. In Protestantized Germany boys and girls were both sent to
primary schools.[33] This represented no break with the past in many locales, for
girls and boys alike in Renaissance Italy seem to have attended primary school.[34]
The difference was the end to which education was to be put: with the advent
of the Reformation many reformers argued that girls as well as boys should be
literate, the better to read the Bible and instruct their children.

Throughout early modern Europe, there was no standard age for starting
school, and class differences were marked. Children of the artisanal classes had
some education, but the line between education and apprenticeship was often
blurred. Further up the social ladder, educated parents frequently were devoted
to the education of their offspring. On occasion they assumed responsibility for
it themselves, with varied consequences. The clergyman Ralph Josselin also was
a schoolmaster, and oversaw the early education of his children in the 1640s
and 1650s. Schooling for the Josselin children began early: his daughter Mary
was said in her father's diary to have had a "towardlyness to learn" and "an
aptness to her booke" in 1646, aged four years. At five years ten months
Josselin's son Thomas was described as a "good speller, apt to learne, and
attaine the hardest words in his bible or accidence in which he reads." This
same source also yields information on learning to write: most often writing was
learned after reading, so that girls, who had less formal education than boys,
might well learn to read, but be unable to write. Josselin's diary alludes to receipt
of a first letter from one of his daughters, when she was fourteen and had already
been away at school for four years. Repeatedly, Josselin spells out the prime
importance of education for his children. The goal was to raise them up in God's
sight as godly beings.[35]

The context in which child rearing, training, and education occurred has been
of interest to historians. Discipline, as a measure of control forced on children,
also has been the subject of historical investigation into childhood and has
similarly been linked with religious instruction. Was obedience enforced with

brutality? Was the immediate goal of religious instruction and education first and foremost to "break the child's will"? Conflicting evidence and interpretations abound. One sixteenth-century English diarist, John Dee, wrote of his eight-year-old daughter's ear being boxed by her mother, and stated that she "bled at the nose very much, which did stay for an houre and more." A contemporary of Dee's who lived from 1498 to 1563 wrote of the pillorying of a woman "for beytyng of her chyld with rodes," as well as noting that a master who beat his young apprentice so severely that the skin was taken off the youth's back was himself whipped in the pillory until "blude ran downe."[36]

Excess in corporal punishment was in fact a criminal offense, subject to fines. The punishment of such behavior was noteworthy to the diarist, who clearly regarded such action with approbation. Similarly, most parents did not record their satisfaction at physically punishing their children. On the contrary, most often they noted their chagrin and disappointment in themselves. In the early modern period there was a close, yet flexible tension between religious attitudes, societal expectations, and actual practices. As Stephen Ozment puts it:

Moderate corporal punishment was a regular and encouraged part of discipline both at home and at school in Reformation Europe, especially during the formative years between six and twelve. Both children and adults, however, viewed harsh and arbitrary discipline as exceptional and condemned it, while outright brutality brought firings and fines and even deep personal remorse.[37]

Ozment's conclusions are valid for particular circumstances, speaking of discipline within the family and at school. Although society relegated apprentices to a role analogous to that of children in many ways, children of higher social status—within the artisanal and middle classes—were not often physically abused. Apprenticeship served as an important rite of passage well into the early modern period. The age of entry into apprenticeship was laid down as not younger than ten or older than eighteen years; Houlbrooke estimates that the age of entry into service and apprenticeship in England rose over time. Possibly, he speculates, the rise in age of apprentices resulted from a limiting of numbers of those entering crafts as time passed.[38] The master was responsible for teaching rules and skills of his craft, as well as bringing up the apprentice to be an honorable member of the guild. One eighteenth-century trade charter reminded the master that "the apprentice has been given into your care by the guild to look after him, body and soul, as the rules provide. You will have to render account for this apprentice, and you must look after him as you would look after your own child!"[39] Many parents offered continuing support and devotion during the period of apprenticeship, which lasted for ten years or more. Most poor children, especially orphans, who were apprenticed lacked familial resources of concern and support. Additionally, economic and social changes diminished the value of apprenticeship by the early modern period. The sixteenth-century reformers had altered religious practices considerably with regard to charitable institutions.

Some problems related to apprenticeship arrangements were revealed, for the reformers thought that these should be ameliorated. Lucas Hackfurt was appointed welfare administrator in Strasbourg in 1523; in a memorandum of 1532 to the Town Council he wrote:

The citizens complain that young boys and girls go up and down the streets begging so that no one can eat in peace. One boy pulled the bell off of some one's house. . . . But who has offered to take these young people during this harsh period of inflation when even those who have had servants for a long time dismiss them and give them leave? . . . Where can the parents go with them? . . . Nor is there any craftsman who would teach such a lad for no pay. That is why it is so difficult for the welfare board to hire out young boys for trade. . . . This is why they must become miserable beggars, because they receive no help in their youth.[40]

It was not only in sixteenth-century Germany, racked as it (and the rest of Europe) was by inflation, that appeals for change in the treatment of apprentices were heard. By the eighteenth century abusive treatment of poor apprentices was a prevalent social ill, although yet again conflicting evidence abounds. Just as the English parish was responsible for sending orphans to wet nurses as infants—an action that condemned many to certain death—it also apprenticed them when they grew old enough to work. The apprenticeship of parish children was regulated by the Act of 1601; workhouses were prevalent after 1722. A great deal of parliamentary testimony spoke to the failure of this system for these unwanted children and young people, and the need for urgent reform. Beyond the very real abuses some historians also have documented continuing opportunities as apprentices for girls and boys alike. K.D.M. Snell observes that further down the social scale, between 23 and 35 percent of parish apprentices in the eighteenth century were girls, whereas for those apprenticed by their families the number fell to under 10 percent. Further, his evidence reveals that female apprenticeship was nearly as costly as for boys, and demonstrates that apprenticeship offered comparable employment opportunities for members of both sexes even as late as the eighteenth century.[41]

Apprenticing teenagers was, additionally, a means of controlling their behavior in some instances. Evidence demonstrates that adolescents, and particularly adolescent males, could be unruly in early modern Europe. Discipline clearly failed to achieve the desired end on numerous occasions. In addition, the expression of such behavior was socially acceptable under certain circumstances. Activities of adolescents in what were known as youth-abbeys have been studied. Natalie Zemon Davis traces the existence of these groups—which participated in village rituals, such as charivaris, and games, such as *soules*, a kind of football—throughout Europe back at least as far as the twelfth century.[42] The presence of youth gangs has been documented in Renaissance Italy.[43] Youths later appear in the religious upheavals of the sixteenth century and as participants in riots, often arising from economic grievances. They represented diverse social classes, for the sons of "good upstanding citizens" as well as destitute orphans were observed in riots in seventeenth- and eighteenth-century Holland.[44] In the religious violence that ensued from the Reformation and Counter-Reformation, youths were visible in crowds, as instigators in episodes of iconoclasm, and even in the socially sanctioned murder of religious opponents. Boys as young as ten to twelve were involved.[45] More than a few youths exploited the ways in which society was in upheaval and undergoing rapid change at the time.

All of this should help to place in perspective the emphasis on "discipline" of children and youths in the early modern period. Did broad differences in approach to parent-child relations exist throughout Europe? Robert Muchembled links a solidification of parental, and particularly paternal, authority with the rise of the absolutist state in France. He surveys legal changes during this time as well as pedagogical techniques, and concludes that "all life in society, in a word, diffused royal authority, divine authority, and paternal authority." Jean-Louis Flandrin concludes that "the authority of parents and their powers of coercion of their children increased from the sixteenth century onwards," documenting his case through religious writings and sermons.[46] In England, too, the father's role has been viewed as authoritarian and patriarchal, but Ralph Josselin's seventeenth-century diary reveals far more complicated emotions. Josselin not only documents his relations with his wife and young children, but also includes a great many details of his misery, frustration, and despair over his second son, John, who drank, swore, and fell into debt. Although Josselin repeatedly threatened to disinherit his son, on his father's death the bulk of the family estate in fact passed to John, who seems finally to have attained a shaky, but permanent truce with his father.[47]

By the eighteenth century, attitudes toward discipline in child rearing seem to have altered. A number of historians who paint a gloomy picture of childhood in the past regard this century as the most crucial time of transition, and even describe some parents as permissive. The religious dimension in character formation lessened, although "training the child" remained an important goal. Many parents strove for a balance between severity and indulgence. As in the earlier period, enormous variation can be seen in individual examples. One English father wrote in the mid-eighteenth century:

I have thought a great deal on "Train up a child in the way he should go." I have considered the New Testament precepts on the same subject; and I have endeavored to practise them. . . . I recollected my being a child myself; how I behaved to my father and how he behaved to me. . . . I laboured to preserve the love, esteem and affection of my children. . . . I made a practice of talking with my children, to instruct them to impress their minds. . . . I then understood how unreasonable and cruel it was in parents to scold and beat their children for acting in such and such a manner; when they had taken no pains to instruct them that such actions were wrong.[48]

Or, as his contemporary, an English mother, wrote:

Little benefit can arise from mere compulsion, either in doing or forbearing, further than as it may gain time for the understanding and judgement to ripen. . . . To keep children in the proper state of obedience, without having them stand in too much awe, is sometimes difficult. I have always wished that they should be afraid of doing wrong, but not afraid of me. . . . I am, from judgement, no great disciplinarian; if I err, I had rather it should be on the lenient side. Fear and force will, no doubt, govern children while little, but having a strong hold on their affections will have the most influence over them in their progress through life.[49]

Here as well the realities of family life urge caution on us as we consider how parents hoped and wanted to rear their children. As in the earlier period, the battle of the wills was not so much with young children, but with adolescents. Lady Mary Wortley Montagu was a pioneer in the inoculation of children against smallpox; her son, then six, was inoculated in 1714. He turned into an unruly youth, and ran away from school at thirteen, considering himself already qualified for Oxford. "After a good deal of search," Lady Mary wrote her sister, "we found and reduced him, much against his will, to the humble condition of a schoolboy." This escapade was only the beginning. The boy ran away to sea as a cabin boy a year later; a distraught Lady Mary advertised in newspapers for information on his whereabouts. He was only discovered when he boasted to the crew of his noble birth and displayed his inoculation scars as proof.[50] Was it parental permissiveness that brought about this state of affairs? Or was it the absence of a strong father in the boy's life, coupled with a mother unsure of how to proceed? Such a conclusion might be reached in the twentieth as well as the eighteenth century.

Although the religious dimension shifted in the eighteenth century, practices themselves do not seem to have altered significantly. Considerable continuity was in evidence, with advice books and prescriptive literature advocating behavioral practices that may have been difficult for parents to implement in actuality. Writing on England from 1450 to 1700, Ralph Houlbrooke concludes that "the blending of humanist ideas with the corrective precepts emphasized in the literature of Christian duty encouraged parents to avoid the extremes of severity and indulgence and to pursue the classical ideal of moderation in all things."[51]

Education and training in the early modern period structured the transition from childhood and adolescence to adulthood. In some ways adolescents were children, in others, adults. What characteristics marked the individual as an adult? One important criterion was the attainment, or ability to attain, economic independence or stability. By the end of the early modern period educational experiences were drastically altered among the elite. Fewer and fewer children were sent out to be educated or serve in another household. By the end of the seventeenth and beginning of the eighteenth centuries more youths entered university. There seems to be little evidence that children were sent away to school because they were of little value or concern, any more than the medieval evidence supports the claim that they were sent into other households for the same reason. At the very least, definitive generalizations are impossible. Parents put forward a number of rational, pragmatic arguments for these practices. Boys would receive a better education at school, which would lead to their advancement. As we have seen, sons in particular needed discipline that often was difficult to provide at home, especially for adolescents. As learning became the prerequisite for professional success and career advancement, parents felt compelled to provide every available advantage for their sons. Although the educational training was in and of itself of prime importance—it became necessary, for example, for legal and diplomatic careers—contacts made and friendships fostered were probably equally important. Early modern European society relied on networks, grounded not only in kin relations, but also in ties of clientage. This rationale for sending one's offspring away to school was real, and functioned on many levels for parents.

Although physically absent, children often were in their parents' thoughts. Johan van Ewsum, who lived in the northern province of Groningen in the Netherlands in the mid-sixteenth century, wanted his sons to enjoy the same educational advantages he had himself been fortunate to acquire. This meant that he was obliged to send the children away, for efforts to find a tutor for them closer to home failed repeatedly. Johan's letters to his sons' tutors demonstrate his concern with every aspect of their lives, from the books they would study to their need for clean linens and a room with a good working fireplace.[52] Parents were anxious about the environment in which their children lived, and their watchfulness was revealed in many respects. On reaching adolescence, children were expected to emulate certain standards and ideals of mature conduct. Parental laments over children who failed to measure up to expectations were frequent, and parental pressure was at least as often totally ineffectual. By the time children had grown to young adulthood, parents had done what they could to assist them in the attainment of economic independence and stability.

Choice of marital partner was another momentous event in the progression from child to adult. The making of a suitable marriage was important in early modern Europe—socially, economically, and religiously. The Reformation and Counter-Reformation in the sixteenth and seventeenth centuries diminished the practice of clandestine marriage and greatly reduced the number of arranged marriages. It has been assumed that parents had near total control of their children's marriage partners, but recent research has not borne out this conclusion. Parental pressure to choose an appropriate partner was real, but so were the choices that young people made for themselves. It was theoretically possible for marriage to occur very early; in many countries the minimum legal ages for binding marriage were twelve for women and fourteen for men, and couples could be betrothed at the age of seven.[53] In most areas of Europe, however, to marry at such a tender age was not considered "fitting," and was remarkable. The ideal of "parity," reflected in the use of the word "match" to describe a satisfactory union, also was reflected in the theme of balance or reciprocity in some accounts of interpersonal relations. Marriage, after the religious upheaval and transition that occurred during the early modern period, was no longer a sacrament in the Protestantized regions of Europe, but regulated by the secular authorities.[54]

Early modern European parents had some of the same concerns and hopes for their children as parents do today. They wanted their children to "turn out well," to grow to be a credit to them and a source of pride. Their hopes and fears for their children often are couched in terms that we have no difficulty grasping. Similarly, children in early modern Europe are recognizable to us as children— teething, taking their first steps and learning to talk, playing children's games, going off to school, and growing up. The crucial differences between our society and that of early modern Europe appear in factors that structured that world very differently from our own. Demographic realities brought death more readily in childbirth, through diseases such as plague, or more "ordinary" diseases such as chicken pox, measles, and smallpox. Those unlucky enough to have been orphaned had few familial resources, if any, to fall back on; Cinderella was no fairy tale, but sad reality.[55] The "idea of the family" itself was very different in early modern Europe, and included stepparents, stepchildren, servants, and apprentices.[56] Accidental death and economic hardship, especially for the poor, occurred in some ways that are beyond our ken. Many of these realities in fact are difficult for us to fully comprehend; the same can be said of religious values and practices, and the formality of relations between parents and children. None of this should preclude our awareness of the real warmth of feelings between parents and children. As one of Ralph Josselin's recorded sermons put it in 1669:

What have we received from our parents? We received from them our life under god, & our bringing up, & education, with a great deal of care & labor, & with all love & tenderness, Now to returne that love & tenderness to your parents with all willingness, this is to requite them; & this is well pleasing to god.[57]

Almost every feature of the history of childhood in early modern Europe is subject to controversy. There have been a number of interpretations—many of which are diametrically opposed—of each childhood development and child-rearing practice examined in this chapter. It seems clear that controversy will continue over childhood in early modern Europe. Not all children were loved or well treated, then as now. Then as now, contemporaries had difficulty with behavior that failed to conform to prevailing pieties about the family and parental concerns. To understand accurately this "world we have lost," different in so many ways from our own and yet similar in so many others, requires tact, sensitivity, and caution on the part of historians and those who seek to understand that world of the past.[58] Early modern Europeans found strength, succor, and solace in the ideal of reciprocity. That ideal of balance, of give and take, of mutuality, tempered other important ideals of authority and hierarchy, and encouraged sentiments of love and devotion that would not appear unfamiliar to us today.

NOTES

1. Philippe Ariès, *L'Enfant et le vie familiale sous l'ancien régime* (Paris: Plon, 1960), translated as *Centuries of Childhood: A Social History of Family Life* (New York: Alfred Knopf, 1962).

2. Edward Shorter, *The Making of the Modern Family* (New York: Basic Books, 1977); Lawrence Stone, *The Family, Sex and Marriage in England 1500–1800* (New York: Harper & Row, 1977); Lloyd de Mause, ed., *The History of Childhood* (New York: Harper & Row, 1974).

3. Alan MacFarlane, *The Family Life of Ralph Josselin* (New York: W. W. Norton, 1970); Michael MacDonald, *Mystical Bedlam: Madness, Anxiety, and Healing in Seventeenth-Century England* (Cambridge: Cambridge University Press, 1981).

4. Ariès, *Centuries of Childhood*, pp. 21, 66; MacFarlane, *Family Life*, p. 91.

5. For useful information on this subject, particularly as it pertains to childbirth and its attendant difficulties, see Merry E. Wiesner, *Working Women in Renaissance Germany* (New Brunswick, N.J.: Rutgers University Press, 1986); Steven Ozment, *When Fathers Ruled: Family Life in Reformation Europe* (Cambridge, Mass.: Harvard University Press, 1983); Keith Thomas, *Religion and the Decline of Magic* (New York: Charles Scribner's Sons, 1971).

6. Sherrin Marshall, *The Dutch Gentry 1500–1650: Family, Faith, and Fortune* (Westport, Conn.: Greenwood Press, 1987), p. 49.

7. *Memoires of* (Henrietta-Lucy,) *Madame de La Tour du Pin*, trans. Felice Harcourt (New York: McCall Publishing Co., 1971), p. 338.

8. Ralph A. Houlbrooke, *The English Family 1450–1700* (London: Longman, 1984), p. 129.

9. Marshall, *Dutch Gentry*, pp. 54–56.

10. Linda A. Pollock, *Forgotten Children: Parent-Child Relations from 1500 to 1900* (Cambridge: Cambridge University Press, 1983), p. 51; Marshall, *Dutch Gentry*, pp. 15–16; H.F.K. van Nierop, *Van ridders tot regenten* (Amsterdam: De Bataafsche Leeuw, Hollandse Historische Reeks 1, 1984), p. 77.

11. In Klaus Arnold, *Kind und Gesellschaft in Mittelalter und Renaissance* (Paderborn: F. Schöningh, 1980), pp. 182–183.

12. Marshall, *Dutch Gentry*, p. 49.

13. R.E.O. Ekkart, "Familiekroniek van Heemskerck en van Swanenberg," *Jaarboek Centraal Bureau voor Genealogie* 32 (1978):65.

14. Pollock, *Forgotten Children*, p. 137.

15. Ozment, *When Fathers Ruled*; W.J.J.C. Bijleveld, "Oude genealogische gegevens omtrent het geslacht van Boschuysen in Rijnland," *Nederlandsche Leeuw* 43 (1925):14. The overall situation with regard to accidental death did not differ greatly from that documented by David Nicholas for the Middle Ages in the preceding chapter. For the Netherlands, additional substantiation on children's accidental deaths can be found in P.C.M. Hoppenbrouwers, "Maagschap en vriendschap," *Holland-Regionaal-historisch tijdschrift* 17 (1985):102. I owe this citation to H.F.K. van Nierop.

16. Pollock, *Forgotten Children*, pp. 134–139.

17. Ibid., pp. 134–135.

18. Quoted in Ozment, *When Fathers Ruled*, p. 168.

19. Ibid.

20. *Memoires*, p. 338

21. Pollock, *Forgotten Children*, p. 134.

22. Ibid., p. 135

23. This approach is taken by de Mause, as well as Stone and Shorter. See, for example, de Mause's introductory essay, *History of Childhood*, pp. 35–39; Stone, *Family, Sex and Marriage*, in which selections on pp. 68–70, 161–174, and 479–480 are all indicative of the more detailed and extensive interpretations in his work; Shorter, *Making of Modern Family*, pp. 175–186, 196–199. For France, see also Elisabeth Badinter, *L'Amour en Plus* (Paris: Flammarion, 1981), which condemned wet nursing and its effect on children; R. Mercier, *L'Enfant dans la Societe du 18e Siècle* (Paris, 1961); George Sussman, "The Wet-Nursing Business in Nineteenth Century France," *French Historical Studies* 9 (1975), deals with a later period, but emphasizes that if anything, his conclusions are more valid for the early modern period; Houlbrooke, *English Family*, pp. 132–133.

24. *Memoires*, p. 140.

25. Rosalind K. Marshall, *Virgins and Viragos* (Chicago: Academy Chicago, 1983), p. 117.

26. Quoted in Pollock, *Forgotten Children*, p. 218.

27. Ibid.

28. Olwen Hufton, *The Poor of Eighteenth-Century France 1750–1789* (Oxford: Clarendon Press, 1974), pp. 320–349, as well as the citations in n. 23 above.

29. Quoted in M. Dorothy George, *London Life in the Eighteenth Century* (New York: Harper & Row, 1964), p. 217.

30. Donald Haks, *Huwelijk en gezin in Holland in de 17de en 18de eeuw* (Utrecht: Hes, 1985), pp. 82–86; S.Faber, "Kindermoord, in het bijzonder in de achttiende eeuw te Amsterdam," *Bijdragen en mededelingen betreffende de geschiedenis te Amsterdam* 93 (1978):224–240.

31. See, for example, the case cited in Robert Muchembled, *Popular Culture and Elite Culture in France 1400–1750*, trans. L. Cochrane (Baton Rouge: Louisiana State University Press, 1985), p. 194, of the father and his two daughters who committed infanticide together in 1530: all three were executed. Claude Delasselle, "Les enfants abandonnés à Paris au XVIIIe siècle," *Annales E.S.C.* (Jan.–Feb. 1975):185–210.

32. R. K. Marshall, *Virgins and Viragos*, pp. 117–120; Pollock, *Forgotten Children*, pp. 215–216; Stone, *Family, Sex and Marriage*, pp. 426–432.

33. Gerald Strauss, *Nuremberg in the Sixteenth Century* (Bloomington: Indiana University Press, 1976), pp. 234–235.

34. Georges Duby, ed., *A History of Private Life: Revelations of the Medieval World* (Cambridge, Mass.: Harvard University Press, 1988), pp. 240–241.

35. MacFarlane, *Family Life of Ralph Josselin*, p. 91.

36. Pollock, *Forgotten Children*, p. 144.

37. Ozment, *When Fathers Ruled*, p. 149.

38. Houlbrooke, *English Family*, pp. 166–178, as well as the remainder of ch. 7.

39. Quoted in Michael Mitterauer and Reinhard Sieder, *The European Family* (Chicago: University of Chicago Press, 1983), p. 105.

40. Miriam Usher Chrisman, "The Urban Poor in the Sixteenth Century: The Case

of Strasbourg,'' in Chrisman and Otto Gründler, eds. *Social Groups and Religious Ideas in the Sixteenth Century* (Kalamazoo, Mich.: The Medieval Institute, 1978), p. 63.

41. K.D.M. Snell, *Annals of the Labouring Poor. Social Change and Agrarian England, 1660–1900* (Cambridge: Cambridge University Press, 1985), p. 294, and esp. ch. 6.

42. "The Reasons of Misrule," in Davis, *Society and Culture in Early Modern France* (Stanford, Calif.: Stanford University Press, 1975), pp. 97–123.

43. Duby, *History of Private Life*, p. 243. The issue of control is paramount to this discussion. Terence R. Murphy's interesting article, "Woful Childe of Parents Rage: Suicide of Children and Adolescents in Early Modern England, 1507–1710," *Sixteenth Century Journal* 17 (1986):259–270, documents several hundred suicides reported to King's Bench between 1485 and 1714, and postulates that in a society where parents and masters literally had the upper hand, suicide was one desperate means by which children and adolescents could control their own destiny.

44. Rudolf Dekker, *Holland in beroering* (Baarn: Amboboeken, 1982), p. 39.

45. Natalie Davis, *Society and Culture*, pp. 163, 183; Robert Mandrou, *Introduction to Modern France, 1500–1640*, trans. R. E. Hallmark (New York: Harper & Row, 1977), pp. 133–134.

46. Muchembled, *Popular Culture*, p. 228; Jean-Louis Flandrin, *Families in Former Times*, trans. Richard Southern, (Cambridge: Cambridge University Press, 1979), pp. 130–140.

47. MacFarlane, *Family Life of Ralph Josselin*, pp. 120–125.

48. Quoted in Pollock, *Forgotten Children*, p. 157.

49. Ibid.

50. Robert Halsband, *Life of Lady Mary Wortley Montagu* (New York: Oxford University Press, 1960), pp. 124–125.

51. Houlbrooke, *English Family*, pp. 143–144.

52. S. Marshall, *Dutch Gentry*, p. 17.

53. Martin Ingram, *Church Courts, Sex and Marriage in England, 1570–1640* (Cambridge: Cambridge University Press, 1987), pp. 128–131; 173–174.

54. Haks, *Huwelijk en gezin*, pp. 9–11; John Bossy, "The Counter-Reformation and the People of Catholic Europe," *Past and Present* 47 (1970):54–57; Ingram, *Church Courts*, pp. 140–145.

55. Peter Laslett, *Family life and Illicit Love in Earlier Generations* (Cambridge: Cambridge University Press, 1977), pp. 160–173.

56. Snell, *Annals of the Labouring Poor*, pp. 320–322.

57. MacFarlane, *Family Life of Ralph Josselin*, p. 223.

58. The phrase is that of Peter Laslett, *The World We Have Lost* (New York: Charles Scribner's Sons, 1965).

REFERENCES

Ariès, Philippe. *Centuries of Childhood: A Social History of Family Life*. New York: Alfred Knopf, 1962.

Arnold, Klaus. *Kind und Gesellschaft im Mittelalter und Renaissance*. Paderborn: Ferdinand Schöningh, 1980.

Burke, Peter. *Popular Culture in Early Modern Europe*. New York: Harper & Row, 1978.

Carlton, Charles. *The Court of Orphans*. Leicester: Leicester University Press, 1974.

Davis, Natalie. *Society and Culture in Early Modern France*. Stanford, Calif.: Stanford University Press, 1975.

Dekker, Rudolf. *Holland in beroering*. Baarn: Amboboeken, 1982.

de Mause, Lloyd, ed. *The History of Childhood*. New York: Harper & Row, 1974.

Duby, Georges, ed. *A History of Private Life: Revelations of the Medieval World*, vol. 2. Cambridge, Mass.: Harvard University Press, 1988.

Flandrin, Jean-Louis. *Families in Former Times*, translated by Richard Souther. Cambridge: Cambridge University Press, 1979.

Forster, Robert, and Orest Ranum, eds. *Family and Society*. Selections from the Annales. Baltimore: Johns Hopkins University Press, 1976.

Goody, Jack. *The Development of the Family and Marriage in Europe*. Cambridge: Cambridge University Press, 1983.

Goody, Jack, Joan Thirsk, and E. P. Thompson, eds. *Family and Inheritance*. Cambridge: Cambridge University Press, 1976.

Houlbrooke, Ralph A. *The English Family 1450–1700*. London: Longman, 1984.

Laslett, Peter. *Family life and Illicit Love in Earlier Generations*. Cambridge: Cambridge University Press, 1977.

MacDonald, Michael. *Mystical Bedlam: Madness, Anxiety, and Healing in Seventeenth-Century England*. Cambridge: Cambridge University Press, 1981.

Macfarlane, Alan. *The Family Life of Ralph Josselin*. New York: W. W. Norton, 1977.

Mandrou, Robert. *Introduction to Modern France, 1500–1640*, translated by R. E. Hallmark. New York: Harper & Row, 1977.

Marshall, Rosalind K. *Virgins and Viragos*. Chicago: Academy Chicago, 1983.

Marshall, Sherrin. *The Dutch Gentry 1500–1650: Family, Faith, and Fortune*. Westport, Conn.: Greenwood Press, 1987.

Mitterauer, Michael, and Reinhard Sieder. *The European Family*. Chicago: University of Chicago Press, 1983.

Muchembled, Robert. *Popular Culture and Elite Culture in France 1400–1750*. Baton Rouge: Louisiana State University Press, 1985.

Peeters, H.F.M. *Kind en jeugdige in het begin van de moderne tijd ca 1500-ca 1750*. Meppel: Boom, 1966.

Pinchbeck, Ivy, and Margaret Hewitt. *Children in English Society*. 2 vols. London, 1969.

Pollock, Linda A. *Forgotten Children: Parent-Child Relations from 1500 to 1900*. Cambridge: Cambridge University Press, 1983.

Outhwaite, R. B., ed. *Marriage and Society*. New York: St. Martin's Press, 1981.

Ozment, Steven. *When Fathers Ruled: Family Life in Reformation Europe*. Cambridge, Mass.: Harvard University Press, 1983.

Rotberg, Robert, and Theodore K. Rabb, eds. *Marriage and Fertility: Studies in Interdisciplinary History*. Princeton, N.J.: Princeton University Press, 1980.

Schucking, Levin L. *The Puritan Family*. London, 1969.

Shorter, Edward. *The Making of the Modern Family*. New York: Basic Books, 1977.

Snell, K.D.M. *Annals of the Labouring Poor: Social Change and Agrarian England*. Cambridge: Cambridge University Press, 1983.

Thomas, Keith. *Religion and the Decline of Magic*. New York: Charles Scribner's Sons, 1971.

Wrightson, Keith. *English Society 1580–1680*. London: Hutchinson, 1982.

5

CHILDHOOD IN PREMODERN CHINA

John Dardess

The history of childhood in China is a subject wholly untouched until recently. The potential body of source materials for such a study—or indeed series of studies—is large to the point of unmanageability, and scattered over a variety of written genres, both native and foreign.

I shall open up the topic by introducing some of the principal kinds of written works that deal with childhood in whole or in part. I have in mind the reader who may not be familiar with Chinese history and society, but who may have a vague sense that a Chinese childhood will have been lived in obedience to some unfamiliar order of rules and expectations. Western-language sources are considered first, followed by a review of the topic from within the resources that Chinese civilization has itself produced over the past millennium or so.

Among the most accessible of sources are those that detail childhood as lived inner experience. There exist a number of reminiscences written or dictated by Chinese for the Western reading public. One of the earliest of these is Yan Phou Lee's *When I Was a Boy in China* (Boston, 1887). Many of these autobiographies are memorable, even searing. Katherine Wei and Terry Quinn, *Second Daughter. Growing Up in China, 1930–1949* (New York, 1984), contains, among other things, an exceptionally frank and vivid account of a girlhood visit to a traditional-style, upper-class extended household in rural south central China in the early 1940s. Chiang Yee, *A Chinese Childhood* (1940, reprinted New York, 1953), gives a bittersweet collection of vignettes of upper-class life on the mid-Yangtze early in this century. Martin C. Yang, *A Chinese Village. Taitou, Shantung Province* (New York, 1945), relates at absorbing length his childhood experiences as a member of a north China peasant family. One also may mention Ida

Pruitt's *A China Childhood* (San Francisco, 1978), an extraordinary story of her life as a child growing up quasi-Chinese in the same province of Shantung, also around the turn of the century. These citations are meant as examples only, as they by no means exhaust the genre.

There also is childhood as collective social manifestation as observed by outsiders, in the early days Christian missionaries, whose intended readership appears primarily to have been the churchgoing youth of their own home countries. Most books of this sort are profusely illustrated. Examples include Mary Isabella Bryson's *Child Life in Chinese Homes* (London, 1885), later republished in altered format as *Childhood in China* (London, 1900). Mrs. Bryson, an English missionary, was for many years posted in Wuchang on the mid-Yangtze, about 150 miles west of Chiang Yee's home city of Kiukiang, and her carefully executed account gives special attention to differences between the rich and the poor in the way they handled their children, as well as to the separate treatment accorded boys and girls, especially in the wealthier families. Also useful are the several works of Isaac Taylor Headland (1859–1942), an American Methodist missionary and teacher with some close connections in the Manchu court in Peking in the early 1900s. He is sunnier and more ebullient about his subject than Bryson, who tends to stress the unpleasant. His *The Chinese Boy and Girl* (New York, 1901) is, in a way, an attempt to describe a distinct Chinese children's culture, with its own special games and amusements. Headland's *The Young China Hunters* (West Medford, Mass., 1912) is a peculiar work, or so it appears now, in that it consists in an imaginary visit to Peking by a delegation of American children, who speak either among themselves or to the American teachers who accompany them and explain authoritatively every strange sight they encounter. Nowhere do the American children directly engage their Chinese counterparts, nor is any Chinese child given a participatory role. At the end Headland offers his own verse translations of two primers used in the households of the Peking elite, the *Ti-tzu kuei* ("Rules for Sons and Younger Brothers") and the *Nü-erh ching* ("Classic for Girls"). The point of all this, one gathers, was to interest American children in supporting foreign missions, or perhaps in the possibility of future careers as China missionaries.

Seventy or so years later it was in a very different spirit and with a very different readership in mind that the attention of outsiders was once again directed to the question of childhood in China. For one thing, the recent emergence of "childhood" as a singular and compelling focus of inquiry in its own right, as between the covers of this and many other Western books, has in no small degree been the outcome of a sense of crisis occasioned by an erosion of religious values, an apparent weakening of family competence and solidarity, and the rise of learned professional specialties such as child psychology, early childhood education, social work, and the like, all of which aim, often in conjunction with state authority, to ease the disastrous results of family incapacity or mismanagement in the rearing of its children. It is social scientists or professional practitioners who have been the most recent commentators on childhood in China.

Unlike the missionaries earlier, the latest writers have not brought to China an unproblematical sense of the superiority of Western culture, or even unbounded faith in the ability of their own techniques to improve much the general quality of childhood in their home societies. A prime example is William Kessen's *Childhood in China* (New Haven, Conn., 1975), a thoughtfully edited collection of reports by the American Delegation on Early Childhood Development in the People's Republic of China, which made its visit in 1973, late in the Mao era. The visitors saw in childhood in that immeasurably older society visually striking, intellectually puzzling counter-examples to all the disorder and anomie that seemed to infect the lives of children in America. Neither the visitors nor their hosts could explain how the children of the families, nurseries, kindergartens, and primary schools they saw all managed to become so "emotionally expressive, socially gracious, and adept," so controlled and well ordered even in the apparent absence of any conscious, deliberate guidance or programming. Evidently the place and purpose of childhood in the larger picture of human and social development were perfectly, if tacitly, understood and accepted, such that "the ideology of expectations often becomes the fact of child behavior."[1]

Kessen suggests that the extraordinary "concentration, orderliness, and competence" of the children must stem in some way from "the older stabilities of Chinese culture," rather than from Marxism-Leninism, or the Maoist doctrines of the moment. Indeed, that may be true. Yet it is by no means clear *how* it may be true because when one considers the "older stabilities," one is immediately confronted with the problem that the institutional matrix of childhood in the later dynastic era was so very different from the vast array of state-run nurseries, kindergartens, and primary schools of the 1970s. The upbringing and early education of children were family matters into which the Confucian state seldom, if ever, intruded directly.

Even though the big question, how one arrives here from there, currently is unanswerable, the whole matter of child raising in China's past is well worth a look in its own right, in part because so much in it is at variance with Western tradition and practice. Unlike the case in the early West, there never seems to have been much doubt, at least in a legal and ritual sense, about what a child was. A person's age normally was carefully reckoned in *sui*: an infant was one *sui* at birth, and turned two on the first day of the next lunar new year. Criminal liability began at seven *sui*, and became, by degrees, heavier until finally legal adulthood and full culpability was reached at sixteen *sui*.[2] China's self-contained "Confucian civilization" indeed placed certain definite expectations on children. Even though China's historical experience was never such as to raise childhood out of its familial and educational nexus to anything like the same degree of singularity we find about us in America nowadays, it is nevertheless possible to discern signs of broad historical change in the matter, especially during the sixteenth and seventeenth centuries, when efforts were made to ease some of the harsher standards of earlier times.

Before I introduce some of the relevant literature, let me sketch in some general context. Given the immense size of China, its huge population, and the sheer length of its recorded history, any topical inquiry such as "childhood" must sooner or later founder on the jagged edges of regional, temporal, and social variation. A sense of the realities demands that one proceed circumspectly. Let "later imperial China" take in the Sung (960–1279), Yüan or Mongol (1279–1368), Ming (1368–1644), and Ch'ing or Manchu (1644–1911) dynasties. The early boundary (tenth and eleventh centuries) is marked by a doubling of the population to the hundred million range; a surge of economic development and enrichment; the spread of cheap printed texts; and the revival and reworking of the Confucian doctrinal heritage, a broad movement known as neo-Confucianism.

As for social context, it is convenient (and also culturally relevant) to focus one's attention on the upper class. The label "upper class" poses grave problems of definition, but by it I mean the social element known in Chinese as *shih* or *shih-ta-fu*, variously rendered in English as literati, scholar-gentry, or scholar-officials—anyone, in short, with something approaching a classical Confucian education and often, but not necessarily, at an upper or middle level of income usually, but not always, derived from landholding. *Shih-ta-fu* were expected to assume leadership roles of some sort: as imperial officials, as teachers, as local elders, or as managing heads of lineages or extended families. Any of these roles might be assumed by the same man at different stages in his life, and one or more of them might involve him in questions of child management.

The orthodox, extended, upper-class Chinese household (or family) was, in theory and often enough in fact, an autonomous socioeconomic unit. Depending on one's direction of vision, it was either the original model or a microcosm of the imperial political system. "It is within the family," as Benjamin Schwartz has put it, "that we find the root of *public* virtue."[3] A positive view of the equivalency of state and family as ordered systems was early on advanced by Lü Pen-chung (1048–1145) in a tract called "Instructions for Children" (*T'ung-meng hsun*):

Serving the ruler is like serving one's parents. Serving one's official superiors is like serving one's older brothers. Associating with official colleagues is like associating with all the members of one's family. You treat the clerical underlings just like you treat [domestic] slaves and servants. You cherish the common people the same as you cherish your wife and children. You manage state affairs just like you manage family affairs. If you can do things like this, then you can say you have taken your mind to its limits. If you fall short in the slightest, then you have not yet done all you can.[4]

Lü, as most writers of instructions for families or children, was a purveyor of Confucian doctrine. Sometimes it is appropriate to think of the Confucianists as constituting a kind of national superprofession: a knowledge elite trained in an abstract and generalized body of principles, in their case ethical, applicable to all aspects of collective existence, and demanding to be put to disinterested use to remedy any and all collective ills. Confucian writers wrote with an authority that consciously transcended the ad hoc and the merely customary, and as such it may not be going too far to understand them as distant cousins to the professional social theorists and practitioners of our own time and place. The Confucian writers certainly shared some of the same anxiety over their efficacy as any of the members of Kessen's delegation. The Confucians themselves did not regard Confucian civilization as in any way an achieved condition. It was, rather, a distant goal that demanded a difficult, unrelenting uphill struggle against the forces of social disorder and chaos, a battle in which the successes were few and the failures many. Childhood was certainly one crucial battlefront in this struggle, and the Confucian texts—advice books, medical books, family instructions, primers, and the like—that deal at all with children should be read in this light. What one will discover in the literature is the fashioning by Confucian writers of a number of strategies and techniques aimed at fostering in children as quickly and efficiently as possible the adult Confucian virtues of self-restraint, altruism, and sober and discriminating moral judgment.

In theory, such instruction might start while the child was yet in the womb. Ancient ritual detailed a regimen called "placental instruction" (*t'ai-chiao*), in which the pregnant mother sought to shape the character of the coming child by restricting her activities, avoiding bitter or spicy foods, and listening to refined music and elevated moral discourse. I am not at all sure how widespread this procedure was in later imperial times; I found it prescribed but once, in a book of family instructions by Hsu Hsiang-ch'ing (1479–1557).[5] One may note, however (and this is part of a configuration of new developments in child handling), in the sixteenth and seventeenth centuries the rise of nearly a dozen Confucian medical writers who were, among other things, eager to intrude into the previously neglected territory of infancy and earliest childhood. Although it was clear to them (as it also was clear to Mrs. Bryson) that the health of the children of the lower classes often was more robust because they were free to run and play outdoors, the medical writers nevertheless strongly prescribed the strict confinement of upper-class children for the sake of their moral development. They also looked to emotional and behavioral lapses in the nursing mother as the principal sources of the diseases of infancy and early childhood.[6] In an important study Charlotte Furth has shown in detail the close subordination of gynecology and pediatrics in late imperial times, not so much to the pursuit of health for its own sake as to the overriding need to sustain and strengthen the patriarchal Confucian family system.[7]

One way to gauge the place of children in that system is to consider the fairly small number of family instructions or household management guides that were originally intended for the use of specific families, but were published and widely circulated, and thus served as inspirational models nationwide. Of these guides the one that gives the most attention to children, young boys almost exclusively, is the *Family Instructions* of Huo T'ao (1487–1540), an imperial official and Confucian moralist from the countryside near Canton.[8] I have reproduced elsewhere the ground plan of this walled, carefully guarded extended-family compound, together with an explanatory key.[9] Huo T'ao's elaborate layout is intended to provide architectural reinforcement for the Confucian sociomoral order, and as such it resembles nothing so much as a well-designed prison camp.

Inside the Huo compound sexes and age cohorts are strictly segregated. Sixteen two-room apartments have been reserved for nuclear families of childbearing age, and one notes how the wives' rooms open into "females' streets," which are at every point walled off from the streets used by the males. Each sex has been assigned separate dining areas, separate latrines, separate assembly halls, and separate routes to access to the quarters of the husbands' parents. Huo T'ao has assumed that by age fifty parents have become grandparents, and accordingly he moves them to special quarters toward the front of the compound. The moral imperative of filial piety (*hsiao*) comes into its fullest play here, between these older and younger married adults, and not within the nuclear families as such. The babies and young children are clearly expected to live with their parents, although at some point boys are expected to "follow" their fathers, and girls, their mothers. No age is specified for this, but the Chiang family rules, for example, compel the sex segregation of siblings at age ten.[10]

Huo T'ao has no interest in infants. For him, Confucian sociomoral instruction begins with toddlers. As soon as the child can "walk and talk," Huo T'ao demands that its parents begin teaching it the rudiments of filial piety by taking it along on their required morning and evening visits to the husband's parents' quarters, so that it may learn by observing and itself practice asking after its grandparents' warmth and comfort, just as its parents do.

From earliest childhood, moreover, the little one should be taught to identify his elders, and to yield to them his seat, his place at table, and his position in a group. "Whenever he sees his elders in the morning," wrote Huo, "he must bow solemnly. He must respond [to orders] with assent. He must be taught to be factual, deliberative, reverential, and conscientious. If he practises these things from childhood, they will come naturally to him." The tot also learns how to identify teachers, or dignified figures who resemble teachers, and is shown on such occasions how to "come forth, bow, and stand for a while at left or right." Further, little boys should be taken by their elders twice monthly to the ancestral temple, so that they can watch the elders as they perform the obeisances, and gradually learn to participate themselves.[11]

Huo T'ao had no tolerance for play. Instead, children must practice treating one another as adults. Here is what he mandates:

Revering friends: As for families with children, as soon as a child is able to walk and talk, it must be taught not to play with other children. When [children] see each other in the morning, they must be taught to bow solemnly to each other. When they enter primary school, they must be taught to order themselves by age-rank. When they see each other do good, they must increase their respect for each other. They must not gang together to make jokes, laugh, or cavort. They must learn good from each other, and warn each other against evil. They must not slander each other, or compete with each other.

The ancients benefited from their friends, whereas nowadays people are harmed by them. If these things are taught from childhood, then [the boys] will nourish and preserve an upright nature. This is the basis for suppressing human desires and extending Heaven's principles. This is why I write "revering friends," not "closeness with friends."[12]

Thus the little Huo boys were to be deliberately and persistently molded into the orthodox Confucian morality and behavior from their earliest conscious moments. It is apparent here that by itself, the nuclear family nest is quite inadequate to this task, and that the "public" character of Confucian familial values requires a larger and wider social context for their realization. Similarly, all punishments were to be inflicted by the extended family as a whole or its representatives, never by the child's own parents. "Whenever sons and nephews are guilty of transgressions," wrote Huo, "their crimes may be punished only in the ancestral temple. Private families may not beat or curse them, as to do so would damage the atmosphere of harmony."

Huo T'ao was by no means alone in his determination to implant Confucian styles of deportment into children so early, and to do it within the context not of the nuclear, but of the large and extended family. At the same time, however, there persisted a powerful folk custom (noted as early as the twelfth century by that acute observer of attitudinal tendencies within families, Yuan Ts'ai, and still much in evidence at the present day[13]) that set aside a certain liminal space in the earliest life of a child, and mandated its thorough, almost abject spoiling, such that its every whim was satisfied, and its every tantrum yielded to. "[A]lmost every Chinese child," noted Isaac Taylor Headland, "is a little tyrant."[14] Yan Phou Lee (b. 1861, and, like Huo T'ao, from the Canton region) stated that "babyhood is the most enjoyable stage in the life of an Oriental. It is the only period when his wishes are regarded and when demonstrations of affection are shown him. The family regulations are such that so soon as a child begins to understand, he is not only taught to obey, but also loses his freedom of action."[15]

The aim of rule book writers like Huo T'ao was, if not to eliminate spoiling altogether, to put an end to it as early as possible. Thus P'ang Shang-p'eng (ca. 1524–ca. 1581, also from the Canton region) laid it down that boys from the age of five will no longer be permitted to act as they please, and will memorize and daily chant the P'ang family's own trimetrical jinglet (called "Song for the Instruction of Boys"), with its strident ethical propaganda.[16] Hsu Hsiang-ch'ing (1479–1557, from the Chekiang coast east of Hangchow) advised that:

as soon as a child can walk and talk and eat, he will begin to show traces of good conscience (*liang-chih*). This is the right time to ensure that he does not become willful and unrestrained. Confucius said that the road to sagehood begins with the nourishing of uprightness in childhood. This means that the child must constantly be taught not to engage in silly behavior, that he must eat after his elders, that he should always yield the nicer and accept the poorer, and that, as for clothes, he should always be taught to take the plain and spurn the fancy.[17]

Establishing disciplined procedures for handling infants lay in the province of the medical writers, or of the writers of Confucian advice books for brides. Thus Ch'en Ch'ueh (1604–1677, a native of the same place as Hsu Hsiang-ch'ing) counseled brides not to coddle infants or overdress them, and to feed them on strict schedule, not on demand.[18] Writers of family management guides never ventured that far, and babyhood seems on the whole to have preserved its freedoms pretty much intact.

Elementary education for boys constituted, in late imperial times, a Confucian subspecialty in its own right, with its own large literature of scholarly methodology, syllabi, primers, and so on. There were traditionally recognized two stages in formal education: elementary (hsiao-hsueh, literally small studies, lesser learning) and advanced (ta-hsueh). The orthodox neo-Confucian belief, as stated by its principal exponent, Chu Hsi (1130–1200), was that in the golden age of antiquity there had existed a national system of elementary schools that every male child in the realm from the ages (sui) of eight to fifteen was required to attend. These schools gave instruction "in the chores of cleaning and sweeping, in the formalities of polite conversation and good manners, and in the refinements [of the Six Arts] of ritual, music, archery, charioteering, calligraphy, and mathematics."[19]

As with most of the rest of the antique inheritance, this elementary education had been neglected for millennia, and the neo-Confucian revivers of the heritage found themselves only with bits and fragments of the original curriculum and its texts to work with. Thus part of the literature on elementary education is purely scholarly, in the sense that it simply tried to research and recapture the ancient system, for example Chu Hsi's Hsiao hsueh, actually done by Liu Ch'ing-chih (1130–1195) under Chu Hsi's direction, and a small cottage industry of later scholars laboring to improve on Chu Hsi.

This work was important. It had the effect of establishing in principle the idea that elementary education was an essential component of a fully civilized society. It provided guidelines for practical efforts at reform. And it sanctified the idea that although elementary study should be open to all boys, there must follow at about the age of fifteen a rigorous winnowing, so that only boys of privileged status "together with the gifted from among the populace" might undertake advanced instruction.[20]

Hand in hand with the scholarly effort to repossess the antique program of primary instruction there also was set in motion a long series of concrete attempts to set up elementary schools in the here and now. These reforms did not, as a rule, try to reimpose the antique system literally. The idea was, rather, to adapt its more practicable elements to the much changed social conditions of later imperial times. Practical guides to elementary schooling, which are legion, drop most of the "Six Arts," for example. And as elementary education was not state-controlled or regulated in late imperial times, it pretty much has to be established on a case-by-case basis whether and when a young child was tutored by his elder kinsmen or a hired tutor (classes usually were held in the family's ancestral hall), or attended classes in a privately endowed community school (*she-hsueh* or *i-hsueh*), as Huo T'ao arranged for his kin. In addition, as Alexander Woodside has pointed out, the elementary curriculum was never wholly standardized.[21] Thus there existed flexibility, and a choice of methodologies that earlier tended to reflect the mainly "adult" proclivities of the neo-Confucian scholars, but later, from around the sixteenth century, came to embody a growing concern for children's special needs.

Thus the approach of Chu Hsi, or at least of the *T'ung-meng hsu-chih* ("What Children Must Know") ascribed to him, was alternately prohibitory and hortatory in tone. It aimed at implanting adult standards in children as early as possible, without making much in the way of particular concessions to child mentalities. There is a good deal of later literature in this same vein. For example, Chen Te-hsiu's (1178–1235) often-reprinted *Chiao-tzu-chai kuei* ("Regulations for the Studio Where I Teach My Sons"), among other things, gives detailed instructions on sitting, walking, standing, speaking, bowing, reciting, and writing. The little ones are exhorted always "to walk slowly with the arms held within the sleeves, with no waving of the arms or jumping," and to recite "with the undivided mind upon the words, enunciating the phrases slowly, so that each word is distinct and clear; don't look about you or play with things with your hands."[22]

Some family rules (not all of them) contain variations or extensions of these themes of deportment: the fourteenth-century Cheng rules enjoin a comely gravity on all male children (no leaping, arguing, joking, slouching, or using vulgar language); and Huo T'ao's rules list no less than *fifteen* stipulations governing the child's control of his facial expressions, his bodily postures, and his speech.[23]

That this pressure toward instilling solemnity and self-control early on in children may have had some effect is evidenced in Lee Yan Phou's reminiscence, in which he discusses the early disciplines imposed on him and others of his class, with the result that, as he writes, "the Chinese boy at sixteen is as grave and staid as an American grandfather."[24] And Mrs. Bryson noted in the 1880s that "all violent exercise is discouraged, and a boy is taught that the more dignified and grave his deportment, the greater approbation he will receive from his elders."[25]

Yet these were the fruits of a pedagogy that often enough came into being at the price of deep-seated resentments among the children who experienced it. Lee asserted that the too-early repression of children "does foster a sullenness and a spirit of rebellion that fear alone keeps under. But the Chinese deem this method absolutely necessary for the preservation of authority."[26]

Lee was not, apparently, aware that the method had been called into question long before his own time. In fact, a more "liberal" approach to early childhood education goes back at least to the early sixteenth century and Wang Yang-ming, the philosopher and statesman whose thesis was that education was not something imposed as strictures from without so much as it was the result of ethical self-discovery and self-realization unfolding from within, the gradual or sudden awakening of the "good conscience" (*liang-chih*) of each individual. Wang was one early exponent of the view that early childhood learning posed special problems, principally that the purely physical energies of children had to be provided some outlet, which he insisted should take the form of singing, dancing, and ritual. Children who were repressed, he observed, develop smouldering hatreds that they inevitably vent in sly and underhanded ways.[27]

The idea that elementary education should be better adapted to children's natures also found expression in the discovery that children liked rhymed jingles and learned them easily. Confucian writers of repute, including especially Lü Te-sheng (d. 1568) and his son, Lü K'un (1536–1618), worked a number of elevated moral injunctions and bits of practical wisdom into popular jingle form. These often were reprinted.[28] The "Trimetrical Classic" (*San-tzu ching*) was composed by someone now unknown perhaps as early as the thirteenth century, but it appears to have achieved true popularity as a primer only from around the seventeenth century onward. This little text, which Lü K'un liked and used, delivers fundamental neo-Confucian doctrine to primary pupils in the form of short and easy rhymes.[29]

Children also loved stories and pictures, and some observant pedagogues, seizing on this fact, put together some morally uplifting illustrated texts for them. An example of this (which seems to have had a regional rather than a national vogue) is the *Jih-chi ku-shih* ("Stories for Daily Memorization") of 1542, by Hsiung Ta-mu, himself a primary teacher by profession. The stories are biographies, arranged in sixty-one categories, and presented as true history, with names and dates and specific settings. Its sober moral lessons may or may not have impressed young minds, but most of the accounts are actually quite interesting, and perhaps Hsiung had some success holding the attention of his pupils with this primer.[30]

Somewhat surprisingly, in all the general guides to elementary education I found, the storytelling approach is conspicuous for its absence. At least for some writers, the reason seems to have been that storytelling bordered too closely on common culture, the vulgar world of opera and professional narration, and was, accordingly, more an enticement to dissipation than an effective vehicle of instruction. Lu Shih-i (1611–1672, from the Yangtze Delta region of Kiangsu province) stated as much:

Chu Hsi, in his remark on the hexagram *meng* ("childhood"), wrote: "Take away external temptations, so as to preserve intact true purity." These are eight marvelous words. As a child, one is most susceptible to outside temptations, things like playing gambling games, watching operas, or listening to story-tellers. These very easily lead people into permanent dissipation. The good teacher of children won't allow this, nor will he even let them get close to such outside enticements.[31]

There was no place for stories in Lu's own program of education, which he divided into three phases, each lasting ten years. The primary phase was for children from five to fifteen *sui*, that is, as early as four by Western reckoning.

Lu argued that one must begin as early as that nowadays because children are much more sophisticated ("attracted to knowledge and transformed by material things") than they were in ancient times, when primary instruction began at eight or nine.[32] Still, Lu assailed Chu Hsi for having made the idea of "seriousness" (ching) central to his revival of elementary education. "Seriousness" was all well and good for older students; it was not something to impose on the little ones. Lu Shih-i was no follower of Wang Yang-ming, but he, too, thought, as Wang had, that the youngest pupils had to be handled leniently and lured into learning through appropriate methods, which in the case of formal subjects (the *Four Books* and *Five Classics* of Confucianism, plus astronomy, geography, history, and computation) meant the memorization and recitation of rhymed songs. The psychological theory of education that underlay this methodology, as stated by Lu Shih-i and echoed by others, was that children up to the age of about fifteen have an innate capacity for memorization (*chi-hsing*) that educators should certainly exploit. After the age of about fifteen that capacity fades and is supplanted by a new capacity for understanding (*wu-hsing*). At that point pedagogical technique must shift to new ground. "When [the pupils] grow older," wrote Lu, "their calculating intelligence grows, at which time enticements will just make them uncontrollable. Then you must be strict with them. Otherwise, they become unruly. Each method works for a specific age."[33]

At the end of elementary education it was the responsibility of the upper-class extended families themselves to conduct evaluations of each boy's aptitude, and place him in some appropriate career (*yeh*). It seems to have been the expectation that only a few boys in any family would show true diligence or talent for book-learning or meditative study. The rest will not. Slight, but interesting differences among families arise in connection with the question of what to do about the young washouts.

Huo T'ao's solution was, as far as I know, unusual in its enthusiasm for physical labor. Primary school was mandatory for all boys at age seven, but at age ten they also were made to do farmwork, either fulltime in spring and summer or halftime through the year. "Most of the sons and nephews," he wrote,

dislike farmwork and are unaware that if they do it in youth, they will learn its hardships, and will not develop a mind for luxuries. If one practices farming when young, one's habits will become solid and honest, and one will have no mind for depravities. By undergoing physical toil, one develops a mind for goodness, and will not do the kinds of things that entail censure. So the sons and nephews must work at farming.[34]

So far, so good. But at age fifteen farmwork changed from a meritorious exercise to a kind of penalty for the academically inept. Boys who, on reaching the age of fifteen, began study for the imperial civil service examinations were excused from all farm labor. But if at age twenty-five they had no success at that, then they were forced to become farmers for life, a pursuit that counted for little in the Huo family's merit rating system, and rendered them ineligible for posthumous commemoration in the family's ancestral temple.

Almost all the family rules contained provisions that were designed in one way or another to facilitate the early discovery of academic talent, and to foster it by various kinds of preferential treatment. For Huo T'ao it was either advanced study or farming, decided at age fifteen. The fourteenth-century Cheng rules established a cutoff point at age twenty-one, whereat the "dull" ones left school and were placed in one or another management position in family government. No one was expected to farm.[35] Hsu Hsiang-ch'ing offered failing youth several choices: farming, crafts, commerce, painting and calligraphy, medicine, or fortune-telling and geomancy—all respectable, if second-rate, income-producing careers.[36] A few rule books single out, at the opposite end of the spectrum, unusually gifted youth as a cause, not for pride, but for trepidation, owing to the likelihood that such boys would easily escape all discipline, turn frivolous and arrogant, and in the end bring themselves and their families to ruin.[37]

Model households of the upper class usually had in their rules provisions for the ancient "capping" ceremony, a formal coming-of-age ritual for boys. Details for conducting the rite were available in a text such as Chu Hsi's Chia li ("Family Rituals"). Capping was by no means automatic. Huo T'ao's rules clearly restricted it to boys of twenty who passed tests on the Four Books and the Huo Family Instructions, and whose record of behavior was considered acceptable. The Cheng rules put capping between the ages of sixteen and twenty-one, whenever the boy had "memorized the Four Books and one of the [Five] Classics in orthodox text, and can explain the general meaning." He could be uncapped later if he became remiss in his studies.[38]

And what of girls? Chinese girlhood has a history very different from that of boys, although to be sure there are points of parallel development. There seems no doubt that a separate, subordinate female culture, with its own folkways and uncanonical rituals, was a standard component of upper-class family life through the whole late imperial period. Family instructions, written by and for men, typically have little to say about or to women, beyond laying down sex segregation as a primal principle of family organization. The Confucian classic called the Book of Rites sanctioned this arrangement, prohibiting all contact, direct or indirect, between any male and female except the very young, the very old, and husband and wife. All sharing of objects and giving of gifts, even passing objects from hand to hand, was forbidden. This is why, for example, the ground plan of the Huo family compound featured a set of rotating food buckets installed in such a way that the women and girls in the kitchen and the male servants in the men's dining rooms could pass things back and forth without so much as even eye contact being made. The Cheng rules (in an early version at least) also featured just such a device.

The rigid sequestration of women was certainly conducive to and perhaps even guaranteed the formation of a separate female culture. There were repellent and even shocking aspects to that culture, as it was within female circles, and not in any Confucian rule books, that such things as female infanticide, foot-binding, mother-in-law tyranny, and the cruel treatment of family servants (often children) were common practice. By their reticence in these matters the Confucian rule books chose in effect to leave that female culture to itself, intact and unchallenged.[39]

Some of the writers of family instructions positively denied to women access to the higher civilization of the men, including in particular such things as painting, calligraphy, or belles lettres. For example, Hsu Hsiang-ch'ing ordered that girls from the age of seven were to be confined henceforth to the women's quarters. Next, at the age of eight, they were to be taught to read the "female teachings," a generic term that probably has in mind such texts as the *Lieh-nü chuan* ("Biographies of Women," by Liu Hsiang, B.C. 77–6) and the *Nü chieh* ("Commandments for Women," by Pan Chao, herself a woman, d. 116 A.D.). This was so that the girls will know "the right way of being a woman." However, added Hsu, "do not let [the girls] become adept at writing, or study lyrical composition."[40] Madame Wen, nee Lu (seventeenth century), in a little book of homespun advice recorded by her son, is quoted as having said: "Women should just learn to recognize a few characters, like those for fuel, rice, fish, meat, and the like; to learn more is of no benefit, and may even be harmful." Chiang I (1631–1687, from the Yangtze Delta region of Kiangsu), in his book of family instructions, ruled that girls "are to be allowed only to recognize written characters, and are to be taught filial behavior and ritual restraint. They needn't read a lot of books." Yao Shun-mu (1548–1627, from northern Chekiang province), however, insisted that the daughters be taught cooking, weaving, embroidery, plainness, and reticence, and said nothing of literacy.[41]

The fourteenth-century Cheng rules also made no provision for female literacy, but did subject the women to regularly scheduled Confucian preaching. Presumably daughters sat by their mothers during the twice-monthly lectures, when male students read and explained to them the *Lieh-nü chuan*, and at the daily morning assemblies, when a young, uncapped male repeated aloud the Cheng family's "instructions for women" (*nü-hsun*). A hair-pinning ritual, wholly a female ceremony, was mandated for daughters as they came of age.[42] The rules have no more to say about the upbringing of daughters.

These strictures, designed to maintain a clear boundary between the women's world and that of the men, did not necessarily forbid women direct access to the Confucian texts studied by the men, but there was in this connection a definite expectation that women would not progress far in their studies. Lü K'un quotes with approval Ssu-ma Kuang (1019–1086) on this point:

When the girl is six, she should start practicing easy women's work. At 7, she should recite the *Classic of Filial Piety* and the *Analects*. At 9, she should learn the meaning [of those texts] plus the *Commandments for Women* and texts of that sort. She should have some general idea of the larger meaning. Nowadays some people teach their daughters songs and poetry and vulgar music, and that is not appropriate.[43]

Nuances aside, the prescriptive literature of Confucian household management is consistently resolute in its determination not only to segregate the female membership, but also to exclude it from the higher culture and intellectual life of the nation (learned or cultured women were, typically, not of the upper class, but courtesans whose status was servile). Participation by upper-class women in China's higher civilization would have required close, sustained, and collegial or personal relations with men, and that would have imperiled the very foundations of social order. Normative social order (*li*, "ritual," "propriety") was based in a series of discriminatory distinctions—youth and age, scholar and peasant, master and servant, Chinese and barbarian, male and female, and so on—whose necessary points of contact required strict limitations and controls.

And "human inclinations" (*jen-yü*) always challenged these distinctions. In 1360 K'ung Ch'i finished a book he called the "Straight Remarks" (*Chih chi*). This was not the usual guide to family management, but rather a collection of raw materials (e.g., anecdotes and observations) whose purpose was in part to show why strict segregation within the upper-class family was absolutely necessary. K'ung Ch'i's own family, by his own testimony in utter disarray, owing to the negligence of his father and the rise of one of his concubines, often was used by him as a source of negative examples. From him one can see how much the Confucian sociomoral order depended on a vigilant policing of people and of the environment they lived in. Thus he strongly urged that anything conducing to sexual arousal be removed from the family compound, including domestic animals of mixed gender, whose shameless and unsightly copulations were especially unwholesome for young children and young servants to look at.[44] He would forbid young daughters from crossing status lines and playing with the children of wet nurses: "This is sure to cause family disorder," he warned. "It is up to some knowledgeable male in the family to put a stop to this right away, and see to it that the wives do not injure [the principle] of great righteousness with their permissiveness."[45] If young daughters play with the servants' children, they will become contaminated by "the light-minded attitudes of the marketplace, and by the time those daughters have grown up, they will have become habituated to intimacy and casualness in their relationships, and surely then some unwelcome things may take place."[46]

K'ung Ch'i feared the lower, servant class as a source of moral pollution; he held exactly the same view of Turks and other foreigners common in China in his day—as people who were otherwise acceptable, but who did not practice sex segregation, and who, therefore, should never be met socially because of the fatal attraction their lax customs had for women and other weak-willed elements in the Chinese upper classes.

Among the members of the upper-class household itself there were dangers too. K'ung relates a story about a wealthy family in which lived a son with his daughter, and his sister with her son. Brother and sister teased the two little cousins about their someday becoming husband and wife. Now, marriage between paternal cousins was absolutely immoral and illegal; but what was meant only as a joke ended in the two children becoming strongly attracted to each other, and the story ends in tragedy.[47] No wonder that the common rule was that daughters, on marriage, must leave the paternal home for good.

Unmarried, nubile daughters also raised problems. K'ung Ch'i related an official case that he had heard from his father, which had to do with an unmarried girl of pinning age (around fifteen) who became pregnant, even though careful investigation determined that she had never had a lover. What had happened was that the girl had overheard the noises of desire her parents had made while engaged in intercourse. Her emotions were moved. Shortly after, the mother urinated in a basin, and the daughter followed and urinated in the same basin. The "lingering air" penetrated her and so caused a fetus to form. To us this explanation looks like an elaborate cover-up for incest; to K'ung Ch'i it showed that "the ancients had a reason for establishing the rule that inner and outer must not share baths and latrines."[48] More important, it showed that whatever the circumstances, unmarried daughters must leave their parents' quarters and live strictly by themselves:

As for unmarried daughters, their housing must be especially secluded and quiet. They must not visit the rooms of their parents, or those of their brothers' wives, for fear they'll witness common or intimate goings-on, which would be most inappropriate. This is an example of what the ancients meant by "stopping trouble before it starts."[49]

In view of the likely shortage of such secluded housing in extended-family compounds, the most convenient remedy for the problem was to marry off the daughters about as soon as they came of age physically. Although child brides may have been disapproved (although only Hsu Hsiang-ch'ing's rules explicitly forbid them), daughters were commonly married off in their mid to late teens. Hanley and Wolf estimate, in Western-style years, "a premodern mean age at marriage of approximately 17.0."[50]

Upper-class marriages in late imperial China were matters of negotiation between senior heads of families. In view of the sequestration of daughters, there was no way even the boy's elders could get to know the prospective bride ahead of time. The girl was rather a blank quantity until she actually arrived as a bride at her husband's gate. Therefore, the family management guidebooks could do no more than offer rules of thumb in arranging the marriages of sons. It was urged by most guides that rich or powerful families be avoided, despite the generous dowries and other advantages they might offer. Hu Yuan (993–1059, a neo-Confucian father quoted approvingly by Lü K'un) advised that one marry one's daughters into families better than one's own, and select brides from families not as good, in the expectation that this class asymmetry would help to ensure that the new bride would render diligent and careful service to her parents-in-law.[51] Chiang I's rules stated that one should select girls whose parents are known to be virtuous, and that the bride should be a girl of virtue, not of "talent and allure."[52]

It is known that upper-class families were expected to evaluate the aptitudes of their sons and nephews and direct them into one or another appropriate career. It would be surprising if, given their sequestration, the senior womenfolk did not do the same for their daughters and nieces. The matter requires further research, but it is likely that the daughters will have varied greatly: some stolid and ugly, some shy and yielding, some frivolous and pretty, some formidable young dragon-ladies. Of these, some may well have been especially prepared for conventional upper-class marriage, and others for roles as concubines, courtesans, nuns, or tradeswomen. The prescriptive literature is silent, but the social demography of upper-class families—the extreme lopsidedness of their reported son-daughter ratios, with many more unaccounted-for daughters than female infanticide alone can explain—seems to point in that direction.[53]

It is symptomatic of a larger process of social change under way in China that from about the late sixteenth century, something of a "women's problem" came more and more to the attention of Confucian writers. Recent research has begun to point this up. Joanna F. Handlin has demonstrated Lü K'un's pioneering role in trying to convey Confucian ethics more effectively to girls and women by composing songs and tracts addressed specifically to them in an interesting and affective literary style.[54] Mary Backus Rankin has further pointed out how, down to the early nineteenth century, and well before the onslaught of Western ideas, Confucian writers came increasingly to challenge the old orthodoxies and oppressions—"such evils as bound feet, seclusion, curtailed education, and a rigid one-sided morality, epitomized in the cults of chastity and virginity."[55]

The publication of Lü K'un's illustrated *Kuei fan* ("Models for the Women's Quarters") in the late sixteenth century was one of the earliest significant Confucian inroads into the autonomy of women's culture. This, as well as the later efforts of others in the same direction, was not a guidebook for use within any particular family, but a tract directed at the sequestered society of women in general, with nothing less than the aim of effecting its moral and spiritual reformation along Confucian lines.

Lü's observation was that the moral education of upper-class women had fallen much too far below the ancient standards. Women had become vain, arrogant, self-indulgent, flippant, and even violent, to the point that family order was everywhere in jeopardy. To reimpose that order, Confucian intervention into the upbringing of daughters by their mothers was essential. What Lü thought lacking was reading materials that girls might enjoy as well as learn from. The traditional texts of female instruction (most of them, incidentally, composed by women[56]) he found to be "too long, too difficult, too miscellaneous, or too flavorless to win the reader's respect." His new *Kuei fan* presented lively, well-executed stories of model females (arranged by social role: daughters, mothers, sisters, sisters-in-law, stepmothers, wet nurses, maids, and so on) with the idea that these should have a suasive impact, and so elevate women's attitudes and behavior. Lü's father contributed to the overall project of women's uplift by composing easy rhymes for girls to learn and recite.[57]

In a recent and pathbreaking study Mark Elvin has reproduced woodcut illustrations from a Ming edition of the *Kuei fan*, and has further shown that the educational efforts of people like Lü K'un had some definite social effect. More and more, the imperial state officially canonized women for leading virtuous private lives, often at great and sometimes at extreme personal sacrifice. Female Confucian virtues were most meritorious when expressed in defiance of the inappropriate demands of men. An explosion of official honors occurred in the eighteenth and nineteenth centuries, as women of the lower classes came to gain recognition as well.[58] It is historically significant that the moral uplift of girlhood and womanhood by way of an improved and appealing pedagogy paralleled in time the development of comparable techniques directed at the youngest male pupils, as noted earlier.

In case the daughters and brides missed this new education, or were unmoved by it, then one notes a deepening concern by Confucian writers, especially in the seventeenth century, for placing controls on female misbehavior, in particular the savage cruelties often inflicted by upper-class wives and daughters on young serving maids.

That the wives and daughters, themselves a suppressed and culturally deprived class in the context of the extended family, were especially prone to abuse female servants, who ranked at the bottom of the family social hierarchy, was noted as early as the twelfth century by Yuan Ts'ai.[59] In the seventeenth century (late Ming) Wang Yen-ch'ou described at length, with convincing psychological realism, the "living hell" that some brutal women continued to inflict on young family maids.[60] The sanctions Wang and others recommended for this problem ran from the bride's early breaking in to the family rules ("teach the bride when she first comes" was the often-repeated adage), to expulsion from the family, to legal action before the local magistrate. Advice books for brides, such as the *Hsin-fu p'u* by Lu Ch'i (b. 1614), devoted much space to normalizing women's management of family maids.[61]

Surely a childhood spent as a servant, male or female, was not enviable. There seems to have been no place allotted in it for education, for play, or even for leisure.[62] Confucian moral doctrine, that in the sixteenth and seventeenth centuries came to be presented in a more and more positive way to the regular womenfolk, seems never to have descended any further down the family social hierarchy. Confucian doctrine should, in theory, have been fairly easy to simplify for servants; Confucian ethics always emphasizes the acceptance of status, high or low, and the devoted performance of duties that status requires. Yet not even a morally inspiring jingle seems ever to have been written for serving children. Was it perhaps enough to persuade the women to go easier with their punishments? Or was the moral emancipation of servants on some future Confucian agenda, never fulfilled?

In sum, the upper-class extended household of late imperial China was something more than simply an enterprise dedicated to the maintenance and perpetuation of a patrilineal kinship group. Its internal structure and mode of operation were strongly shaped by a need to uphold and make manifest Confucian so-ciomoral values as expressed through the principles of *li*, which set senior apart from junior, male from female, and people of ability and stature from people without it.

Children and youth were, because of the imperative of *li*, divided among themselves within a single extended family. It did not matter so much that one was a child. What mattered was that one was a son or daughter, older or younger than the next child, and a regular family member or a child of the servant class. Each child had its proper *place*.

Children were discouraged from banding together simply as children. Free play was frowned on, as was the mixing of children across sex and status lines. The rules of social hierarchy and discrimination were among the earliest lessons children were taught. Yet there did exist something of a children's culture: nursery rhymes and tales, games, puppet shows, kites, toys, and so on.

The Confucian distinctions were, by all indications, maintained within the family only by dint of constant effort, constant vigilance, and what K'ung Ch'i liked to call "steel guts" (*kang ch'ang*) on the part of those in positions of family authority. Human desires and passions often ran in one direction, whereas the body of Confucian principle cut in quite another.

The upper-class family probably maintained an outward display of rank and order without great difficulty. In part this was possible because social rank and order were embodied in the architecture and layout of the extended-family com-pound. But the actual state of affairs must always have fallen short of the ideal in some way or another. Human passion and desire thwarted the ideal system not by way of any frontal challenge to its basic principles and outer form, but by subterfuge and concealed subversion. That, too, was a lesson learned and practiced from childhood. Perhaps the eerie absence of American-style confron-tation and overt disruption in the primary schools of Mao's China, the childish orderliness that so impressed Kesson's group, was in some way a continuation of that tradition.

NOTES

I thank N. Ray Hiner, organizer of the seminar "Children and Youth: Problems, Myths, and Perspectives," held under the auspices of the Hall Center for the Humanities at the University of Kansas in spring 1987, for the opportunity to present some of these ideas and to hear others.

1. William Kessen, ed., *Childhood in China* (New Haven, Conn.: Yale University Press, 1975), p. 220.

2. Ann Waltner, "The Moral Status of the Child in Late Imperial China: Childhood in Ritual and Law," *Social Research* 53 (Winter 1986):667–687.

3. Benjamin Schwartz, *The World of Thought in Ancient China* (Cambridge, Mass.: Harvard University Press, 1985), p. 70.

4. Quoted in Chang Po-hsing (1652–1725), *Hsiao-hsueh chi-chu* (Collected Annotations on the Elementary Education), Cheng-i t'ang ed., 5.18a.

5. Hsu Hsiang-ch'ing (1479–1557), *Hsu Yun-t'un i-mou* (The Bequeathed Plans of Hsu Hsiang-ch'ing), Yen-i chih-lin ed., 1b.

6. Angela Kiche Leung, "Autour de la naissance: la mère et l'enfant en Chine aux xive et xviie siècles," *Cahiers internationaux de sociologie* 76 (1984):51–69.

7. Charlotte Furth, "Concepts of Pregnancy, Childbirth, and Infancy in Ch'ing Dynasty China," *Journal of Asian Studies* 46 (February 1987):7–35.

8. Huo T'ao (1487–1540), *Huo Wei-yai chia-hsun* (Huo T'ao's Family Instructions), Han-fen-lou mi-chi ed. Author's own translation.

9. John Dardess, "The Management of Children and Youth in Upper-Class Households in Later Imperial China." Unpublished seminar paper, 1987, pp. 7–8.

10. Chiang I (1631–1687), *Chiang-shih chia-hsun* (Chiang Family Instructions), Chieh-yueh shan-fang hui-ch'ao ed., 6a.

11. Huo T'ao, 23a–24a, 26b.

12. Ibid., 24ab.

13. Patricia Buckley Ebrey, tr., *Family and Property in Sung China. Yuan Ts'ai's Precepts for Social Life* (Princeton, N.J.: Princeton University Press, 1984); Martha Nemes Fried and Morton Fried, *Transitions. Four Rituals in Eight Cultures* (Harmondsworth: Penguin Books, 1980), p. 82.

14. Isaac Taylor Headland, *The Chinese Boy and Girl* (New York: Fleming H. Revell Co., 1901),. p. 36.

15. Yan Phou Lee, *When I Was a Boy in China* (Boston: Lothrop Publishing Co., 1887), p. 17.

16. P'ang Shang-p'eng (ca. 1524–ca. 1581), *P'ang-shih chia-hsun* (P'ang Family Instructions), Ling-nan i-shu ed., 5a, 12b–13a.

17. Hsu Hsiang-ch'ing, 1b–2a.

18. Ch'en Ch'ueh (1604–1677), *Hsin-fu p'u pu* (Supplement to Lu Ch'i's *Guide for Brides*, Hsiang-yen ts'ung-shu ed., 3rd ser., 3.18a.

19. Daniel K. Gardner, *Chu Hsi and the Ta-hsueh. Neo-Confucian Reflection on the Confucian Canon* (Cambridge, Mass.: Harvard University Press, 1986), pp. 79–80.

20. Ibid., pp. 80–81, quoting Chu Hsi.

21. Alexander Woodside, "Some Mid-Qing Theorists of Popular Schools: Their Innovations, Inhibitions, and Attitudes Toward the Poor," *Modern China* 9 (January 1983):3–36.

22. Quoted in Ch'en Hung-mou (1696–1771), *Wu-chung i-kuei* (Bequeathed Guidelines of Five Kinds), Ssu-pu pei-yao ed., sec. 1, A.13b, 14a.

23. John W. Dardess, "The Cheng Communal Family: Social Organization and Neo-Confucianism in Yuan and Early Ming China," *Harvard Journal of Asiatic Studies* 34 (1974):27; Huo T'ao, 21a–22b.

24. Lee, *When I Was a Boy*, p. 34.

25. Mary Isabella Bryson, *Child Life in Chinese Homes* (London: The Religious Tract Society, 1885), pp. 59–60.

26. Lee, *When I Was a Boy*, p. 19.

27. Wing-tsit Chan, tr., *Instructions for Practical Living and Other Neo-Confucian Writings by Wang Yang-ming* (New York: Columbia University Press, 1963), pp. 182–184.

28. Joanna F. Handlin, *Action in Late Ming Thought. The Reorientation of Lü K'un and Other Scholar-Officials* (Berkeley: University of California Press, 1983).

29. James T. C. Liu, "The Classical Chinese Primer: Its Three-Character Style and Authorship," *Journal of the American Oriental Society* 105 (April–June 1985):191–196.

30. Original edition reproduced in the series *Chung-kuo ku-tai pan-hua ts'ung-k'an* (Old Chinese Illustrated Books) (Shanghai, 1959).

31. Quoted in Ch'en Hung-mou, sec. 1, B.21b–22a.

32. Ibid., B.19ab.

33. Ibid., B.19b–20a.

34. Huo T'ao, 28a.

35. Cheng Chi (fourteenth century), *Ching-i pien* (Compilation for Manifesting Righteousness, i.e., the Cheng Family Rules), Chin-hua ts'ung-shu ed., 2.6b–7a.

36. Hsu Hsiang-ch'ing, 3a.

37. Lu Yu (1125–1210), *Fang-weng chia-hsun* (Lu Yu's Family Instructions), Chih-pu-tsu chai ts'ung-shu ed., 10a; Hsu Hsiang-ch'ing, 2b.

38. Huo T'ao, 13b; Cheng Chi, 1.13a.

39. For perspectives on this matter, see the contributions of David Johnson and Evelyn Rawski, in *Popular Culture in Late Imperial China*, ed. David Johnson et al. (Berkeley: University of California Press, 1985).

40. Hsu Hsiang-ch'ing, 3b.

41. Wen I-chieh (seventeenth century), *Wen-shih mu-hsun* (Wen Family Maternal Instructions), Hsueh-hai lei-pien ed., 2a; Chiang I (see n. 10), 6a; Yao Shun-mu (1548–1627), *Yao-shih yao-yen* (Medicinal Words for the Yao Family), Chih-chin-chai ts'ung-shu ed., 2b.

42. Cheng Chi, 1.3ab, 2.1a, 2.13a.

43. Quoted in Ch'en Hung-mou, sec. 4, B.7a.

44. K'ung Ch'i (fl. 1360), *Chih-cheng chih-chi* (Straight Remarks), Yueh-ya t'ang ts'ung-shu ed., 3.21ab.

45. Ibid., 1.8b.

46. Ibid., 3.23b–24a.

47. Ibid., 1.7b–8b. On early adolescent dalliances, cf. Ann Waltner, "On Not Becoming a Heroine: Lin Dai-yu and Cui Ying-ying," *Signs* 15:1 (Autumn, 1989):61–78.

48. K'ung Ch'i, 1.7a.

49. Ibid., 1.33b–34a.

50. Susan B. Hanley and Arthur P. Wolf, eds., *Family and Population in East Asian History* (Stanford, Calif.: Stanford University Press, 1985), p. 4. Child marriage is well covered in Arthur P. Wolf and Chieh-shan Huang, *Marriage and Adoption in China, 1845–1945* (Stanford, Calif.: Stanford University Press, 1980).

51. Ch'en Hung-mou, sec. 4, B.7a.

52. Chiang I, 3b, 5b.

53. John Dardess, "Ming Historical Demography: Notes from T'ai-ho County, Kiangsi," *Ming Studies* 17 (1983):60–77.

54. Joanna F. Handlin, "Lü K'un's New Audience: The Influence of Women's Literacy on Sixteenth-Century Thought," in *Women in Chinese Society*, ed. Margery Wolf and Roxane Witke (Stanford, Calif.: Stanford University Press, 1975), pp. 13–38.

55. Mary Backus Rankin, "The Emergence of Women at the End of the Ch'ing: The Case of Ch'iu Chin," in ibid., pp. 39–66 (the quotation is from p. 40).

56. See Marina H. Sung, "The Chinese Lieh-nü Tradition," in *Women in China*.

Current Directions in Historical Scholarship, Richard W. Guisso and Stanley Johannesen (Youngstown, N.Y.: Philo Press, 1981), pp. 63–74; M. Theresa Kelleher, "The *Nü ssu-shu*, or *Four Books for Women*," paper presented to the Neo-Confucian Seminar, Columbia University, April 3, 1987.

57. Ch'en Hung-mou, sec. 4, B.1a ff.

58. Mark Elvin, "Female Virtue and the State in China," *Past and Present* 104 (1984):111–152.

59. Ebrey, *Family and Property*, p. 290.

60. Ch'en Hung-mou, sec. 4, C.1b–3a.

61. Lu Ch'i, *Hsin-fu p'u* (Guide for Brides), Hsiang-yen ts'ung-shu ed., 3rd ser.

62. Some illuminating examples are translated and discussed in Lien-sheng Yang, "Schedules of Work and Rest in Imperial China," *Harvard Journal of Asiatic Studies* 18 (December 1955):301–325.

A NOTE ON FURTHER READING IN WESTERN LANGUAGES

As a topic for scholarly inquiry, the history of childhood in China has a shallow past, but surely a promising future. The larger social structures that encompass childhood have recently been the subject of some major gains: note especially Patricia Buckley Ebrey and James L. Watson, eds., *Kinship Organization in Late Imperial China 1000–1940* (Berkeley: University of California Press, 1986), and Charlotte Furth, "The Patriarch's Legacy: Household Instructions and the Transmission of Orthodox Values," to appear in *Orthodoxy in Late Imperial China*, ed. K. C. Liu (forthcoming). Also in process is a major undertaking, Patricia Ebrey's annotated translation of Chu Hsi's *Chu-tzu chia li*, under the title *The Family Rituals of Master Chu*.

On childhood in Mao's China, one also may consult Iris Bubenik-Bauer, *Kollektive Kleinkinderziehung. Aspekte der Erziehung in der Volksrepublik China* (Veröffentlichen aus dem Ubersee-Museum Bremen, Reihe D Band 3, Bremen, 1977), and Ruth Sidel, *Women and Child Care in China* (New York: Hill & Wang, 1972). For Taiwan there is a large anthropological literature; one important example, which deals with the upbringing of girls, is Margery Wolf, *Women and the Family in Rural Taiwan* (Stanford, Calif.: Stanford University Press, 1972). Richard W. Wilson has written two books on the political socialization of children in Taiwan; note in particular his later one, *The Moral State. A Study of the Political Socialization of Chinese and American Children* (New York: Free Press, 1974).

Missionary accounts, diligently researched, would surely turn out to contain a great deal more about childhood in China than I have cited in this chapter. One place to start is Jane Hunter, *The Gospel of Gentility. American Women Missionaries in Turn-of-the-century China* (New Haven, Conn.: Yale University Press, 1984).

Literature and the visual arts also are rich sources. The famous eighteenth-century novel *Dream of the Red Chamber* has been translated in whole or in part several times, most recently by David Hawkes as *The Story of the Stone* (5 vols., Bloomington: Indiana University Press, 1979). The novel deals centrally with the interactions of early adolescents in a declining upper-class household. Those who enjoyed the film *The Last Emperor* might be inspired to consider the more prosaic boyhood of an imperial ancestor, the Ch'ien-lung emperor (1711–1799); see Harold Kahn, "The Education of a Prince: The Emperor Learns His Roles," in *Approaches to Modern Chinese History*, ed. Albert Feuerwerker et al. (Berkeley: University of California Press, 1967), pp. 15–44.

Children also were represented with some frequency in traditional Chinese painting; the whole question of *how* they were depicted, by whom, when, and for what purpose awaits study and analysis. As one example only, the thirteenth-century artist Li Sung seems to look at children quite outside the bounds of Confucian orthodoxy in his "The Knick-Knack Peddler," in which a bunch of little rich children accompanied by a wet nurse eagerly surround a well-stocked itinerant toy merchant. See Ellen Laing, "Li Sung and Some Aspects of Southern Sung Figure Painting," *Artibus Asiae* 37 (1975):5–38, and figures no. 3–11, 14, 15.

REFERENCES

Bryson, Mary Isabella. *Child Life in Chinese Homes*. London: The Religious Tract Society, 1885.

Chan, Wing-tsit, tr. *Instructions for Practical Living and Other Neo-Confucian Writings by Wang Yang-ming*. New York: Columbia University Press, 1963.

Chang Po-hsing (1652–1725). *Hsiao-hsueh chi-chu* (Collected Annotations on the Elementary Education). Cheng'i t'ang ed.

Ch'en Ch'ueh (1604–1677). *Hsin-fu p'u pu* (Supplement to Lu Ch'i's *Guide for Brides*). Hsiang-yen ts'ung-shu ed.

Ch'en Hung-mou (1696–1771). *Wu-chung i-kuei* (Bequeathed Guidelines of Five Kinds). Ssu-pu pei-yao ed.

Cheng Chi (fourteenth century). *Ching-i pien* (Compilation for Manifesting Righteousness, i.e., the Cheng Family Rules). Chin'hua ts'ung-shu ed.

Chiang I (1631–1687). *Chiang-shih chia-hsun* (Chiang Family Instructions). Chieh-yueh shan-fang hui-ch'ao ed.

Chiang Yee. *A Chinese Childhood*. New York: John Day, 1953.

Dardess, John. "The Cheng Communal Family: Social Organization and Neo-Confucianism in Yuan and Early Ming China." *Harvard Journal of Asiatic Studies* 34 (1974):7–52.

———. "Ming Historical Demography: Notes from T'ai-ho County, Kiangsi." *Ming Studies* no. 17 (1983):60–77.

———. "The Management of Children and Youth in Upper-class Households in Later Imperial China." Unpublished seminar paper, 1987.

Ebrey, Patricia Buckley, tr. *Family and Property in Sung China. Yuan Ts'ai's Precepts for Social Life*. Princeton, N.J.: Princeton University Press, 1984.

Elvin, Mark. "Female Virtue and the State in China." *Past and Present* 104 (1984):111–152.

Fried, Martha Nemes, and Morton Fried. *Transitions. Four Rituals in Eight Cultures*. Harmondsworth: Penguin Books, 1980.

Furth, Charlotte. "Concepts of Pregnancy, Childbirth, and Infancy in Ch'ing Dynasty China." *Journal of Asian Studies* 46 (1987):7–35.

Gardner, Daniel K. *Chu Hsi and the Ta-hsueh. Neo-Confucian Reflection on the Confucian Canon*. Cambridge, Mass.: Harvard University Press, 1986.

Guisso, Richard W., and Stanley Johannesen, eds. *Women in China. Current Directions in Historical Scholarship*. Youngstown, N.Y.: Philo Press, 1981.

Handlin, Joanna F. *Action in Late Ming Thought. The Reorientation of Lü K'un and Other Scholar-Officials*. Berkeley: University of California Press, 1983.

Hanley, Susan B., and Arthur P. Wolf, eds. *Family and Population in East Asian History*. Stanford, Calif.: Stanford University Press, 1985.

Headland, Isaac Taylor. *The Chinese Boy and Girl*. New York: Fleming H. Revell Co., 1901.

————. *The Young China Hunters*. West Medford, Mass.: The Central Committee on the United Study of Missions, 1912.

Hsiung Ta-mu (fl. 1542). *Jih-chi ku-shih* (Stories for Daily Memorization). Reprinted in *Chung-kuo ku-tai pan-hua ts'ung-k'an* (Old Chinese Illustrated Books). Shanghai, 1959.

Hsu Hsiang-ch'ing (1479–1557). *Hsu Yun-t'un i-mou* (The Bequeathed Plans of Hsu Hsiang-ch'ing). Yen-i chih-lin ed.

Huo T'ao (1487–1540). *Huo Wei-yai Chia-hsun* (The Family Instructions of Huo T'ao). Han-fen-lou mi-chi ed.

Johnson, David., et al., eds. *Popular Culture in Late Imperial China*. Berkeley: University of California Press, 1985.

Kelleher, M. Theresa. "The *Nü ssu-shu*, or, *Four Books for Women*." Paper presented to the Neo-Confucian Seminar, Columbia University, April 3, 1987.

Kessen, William, ed. *Childhood in China*. New Haven, Conn.: Yale University Press, 1975.

K'ung Ch'i (fl. 1360). *Chih-cheng chih-chi* (Straight Remarks). Yueh-ya t'ang ts'ung-shu ed.

Lee, Yan Phou. *When I Was a Boy in China*. Boston: Lothrop Publishing Co., 1887.

Leung, Angela Kiche. "Autour de la naissance: la mère et l'enfant en Chine aux xivᵉ et xviiᵉ siècles." *Cahiers internationaux de sociologie* 76 (1984):51–69.

Liu, James T. C. "The Classical Chinese Primer: Its Three-Character Style and Authorship." *Journal of the American Oriental Society* 105 (April-June 1985):191–196.

Lu Ch'i (b. 1614). *Hsin-fu p'u* (Guide for Brides). Hsiang-yen ts'ung-shu ed.

Lu Yu (1125–1210). *Fang-weng chia-hsun* (The Family Instructions of Lu Yu). Chih-pu-tsu chai ts'ung-shu ed.

P'ang Shang-p'eng (ca. 1524–ca. 1581). *P'ang-shih chia-hsun* (P'ang Family Instructions). Ling-nan i-shu ed.

Pruitt, Ida. *A China Childhood*. San Francisco: Chinese Materials Center, 1978.

Schwartz, Benjamin. *The World of Thought in Ancient China*. Cambridge, Mass.: Harvard University Press, 1985.

Waltner, Ann. "The Moral Status of the Child in Late Imperial China: Childhood in Ritual and Law." *Social Research* 53 (Winter 1986):667–687.

————. "On Not Becoming a Heroine: Lin Dai-yu and Cui Ying-ying." *Signs* 15:1 (Autumn 1989):61–78.

Wei, Katherine, and Terry Quinn. *Second Daughter. Growing Up in China, 1930–1949*. New York: Holt, Rinehart, & Winston, 1984.

Wen I-chieh (seventeenth century). *Wen-shih mu-hsun* (Wen Family Maternal Instructions). Hsueh-hai lei-pien ed.

Wolf, Arthur, and Chieh-shan Huang. *Marriage and Adoption in China, 1845–1945*. Stanford, Calif.: Stanford University Press, 1980.

Wolf, Margery, and Roxane Witke, eds. *Women in Chinese Society*. Stanford, Calif.: Stanford University Press, 1975.

Woodside, Alexander. "Some Mid-Qing Theorists of Popular Schools: Their Innovations,

Inhibitions, and Attitudes Toward the Poor." *Modern China* 9 (January 1983):3–36.

Yang, Lien-sheng. "Schedules of Work and Rest in Imperial China." *Harvard Journal of Asiatic Studies* 18 (December 1955):301–325.

Yang, Martin C. *A Chinese Village. Taitou, Shantung Province*. New York: Columbia University Press, 1945.

Yao Shun-mu (1548–1627). *Yao-shih yao-yen* (Medicinal Words for the Yao Family). Chih-chin chai ts'ung-shu ed.

II

THE MODERN WORLD

6

AUSTRALIA AND NEW ZEALAND

Mary McDougall Gordon

Since the late 1970s Australian historians have published any number of studies in fields with significant implications for the history of childhood: the family, women, education, demography, social policy, urbanization, and religion. This scholarly interest reflects recent developments in social history, including new perceptions of issues and the mining of sources long neglected by "traditional" historians. Only a minority of these studies focus on childhood. Moreover, seldom are they informed either by the different interpretations of childhood history formulated in Europe and the United States over the past twenty-five years or by conceptual approaches forged to analyze the Australian experience. This dearth of synthetic scholarship and the absence of historical debate so characteristic of other fields in Australian social history impede any critical analysis of the current state of the literature in childhood history.

Only two scholarly essays that discuss the differing overseas interpretations of childhood history have been published. Jan Kociumbas' "Childhood History as Ideology" appeared in 1984, and Judith Keene's "Excavating the Sand Pit in Search of the History of Childhood" in 1986.[1] Keene's essay, a critical assessment of interpretations and methodologies in studies of European childhood, is a useful introduction for those who are unfamiliar with the historiography. She concludes that neither the sociohistorical approach (exemplified by Philippe Ariès and Lawrence Stone) nor the psychohistorical approach (among whose leading exponents are Erik Erikson and Lloyd de Mause) is "a guarantee of analytical success." Keene does not offer her own guidelines or discuss existing scholarship on Australian childhood, although in a footnote she refers to the Kociumbas essay as one that "includes Australian work."[2]

Jan Kociumbas' study is the more significant of the two. The author's specialty is childhood history. She wrote her Ph.D. thesis on "Children and Society in New South Wales and Victoria, 1860–1914," and has published two articles derived from the thesis.[3] More important, in this essay Kociumbas advances her own interpretation and suggests ways in which her model might be applied to the history of Australian childhood.

The bulk of "Childhood History as Ideology" is devoted to a closely reasoned critique of the work of such well-known European and American interpreters of family and childhood history as Ariès, Erikson, de Mause, Stone, David Hunt, Peter Laslett, Christopher Lasch, and Edward Shorter.[4] Like Judith Keene's, this critique covers familiar ground and finds serious weaknesses in the different interpretations. Along with many other critics, Kociumbas sees "fundamental" problems in Philippe Ariès' pathbreaking book, *Centuries of Childhood*, published first in French in 1960 with an English translation in 1962. Nevertheless his central thesis, that "childhood is a social construction varying over time in accordance not with biological or psychic needs but with the changing views of various groups of adults," provides the basis for her own approach.[5] She proposes that Ariès' thesis be modified and clarified in two ways. First, she writes, it must be recognized more explicitly that children's needs render them different from and dependent on adults. Because that is a timeless and universal phenomenon, it therefore is not open to historical inquiry. Rather, historians must examine the way those needs have been defined and met, since *that* is changeable over time. Second, scholars must express more explicitly that all societies socialize their children, although the degree and nature of socialization may vary. They must examine, too, concepts and changing methods of socialization, and ask questions about the groups and individuals who create the changing images of childhood, probing for their motives—especially as they relate to power and wealth—and testing the effectiveness of the transmission of ideology. Examination of such agencies of socialization as families, schools, and institutions catering to the poor also is an "important part of the story."[6]

Kociumbas only briefly describes "Australian work" on childhood and the related fields of family and women's history, and she finds conceptual and methodological weaknesses in the few studies she cites. These studies, essentially descriptive and lacking explanation of structural and attitudinal change, she asserts, adopt either sociological or psychohistorical approaches that look to the past to illuminate problems of the present or project back into the past present-day assumptions about the importance of the family. Thus, Kociumbas writes, in *Children and Families in Australia*, written in 1979 by the psychologists Ailsa Burns and Jacqueline Goodnow, the "overall theme" is the necessity of establishing the "child-centred" family in the face of harsh colonial conditions. In a 1981 essay on the colonial family the historians Patricia Grimshaw and Graham Willett argue that the extended family, allegedly common to all classes in the preindustrial period, was superior to the modern nuclear family. Miriam Dixson, in *The Real Matilda*, uses a psychohistorical approach in a pioneering (1976)

overview of women's experiences, and she claims that the early convict environment, lacking the stable family that modern theory deems essential for healthy
personality growth, caused severe emotional damage to children that carried over
the generations to the present. In another early work (1971), *The Great Australian
Stupor*, the psychologist Ronald Conway bemoans the decline of the family
because of the diminished role of the modern father.[7]

In the final pages of "Childhood History as Ideology" Kociumbas proposes
a model for the study of Australian childhood. She suggests that one starting
point for scholars' research might entail the study of private philanthropy's early
challenges to the church's traditional role in the moral training of the young and
the care of children of the poor. For the later nineteenth century, her own period
of special interest, she gives more detailed suggestions. Research here might
focus on the expansion of child-saving groups as the state took over the role of
the church and as members of an emergent managerial-professional class, inspired by the ideas of overseas social scientists, became new experts who advised
the state on strategies directed toward children. Kociumbas stresses that connections must be made between these developments and the broader patterns of
social and economic change. By the 1880s, for example, economic expansion
had encouraged the growth of a middle class whose families could provide stable,
protected lives for their children and "translate ideology into action." The growth
of the middle class drew attention to the presence of children of the poor, seen
by theorists and observers as a separate species whose lack of a "standard"
childhood rendered them potential threats to life and property. Consequently the
experts advised the state to expand its facilities so as to rescue and reform these
children. Composed of doctors, lawyers, and later, academics, and supported
by creative writers and journalists, the new professional class increased in influence in the early twentieth century as the state sought to meet the challenges
of economic change and the potential threat of class conflict. The passage of
Children's Protection Acts, the kindergarten movement, child study and infant
welfare organizations, children's courts, and "new education" were manifes-
tations of new attitudes and policies toward children. Kociumbas warns, however, that historians must guard against attributing only self-serving motives to
the theorists and child-savers. Although certainly engaged in forms of social
control, the experts saw themselves as creators and transmitters of "a body of
humane and scientific law" that promised to remedy the problems of the age
and, by saving the child, preserve the existing structure of society.[8]

Although Kociumbas does not say so, her focus on the role of the experts in
the remaking of childhood actually places her work more in the tradition of the
French scholars Michel Foucault and Jacques Donzelot and their American counterparts Barbara and John Ehrenreich and Christopher Lasch than in the tradition
of Philippe Ariès. Foucault, Donzelot, the Ehrenreichs, and Lasch all direct their
attention to the increasing involvement in family matters by the state and by
different agencies such as the therapeutic professions. The price paid for the
bourgeois creation of the family as a private nuclear haven, they argue, was the

eventual intrusion of official and professional guardians who policed the family in ways hitherto unknown.[9]

Without providing any citations, Kociumbas observes that few Australian studies explore the crucial issue of child socialization. Historians who have examined the decline of the church with respect to the state, for example, ignore the way this created a vacuum filled by the new experts. State education has "a large historiography," yet the role of the teacher in eroding and counteracting parental values and authority has been neglected. The function of children's books, school texts, and Sunday school hymns in the transmission of values, and the "vested interest" of the medical profession in child training and institutional care similarly remain unexplored. Further, historians who describe the expanding role of the state in providing asylums, reformatories, and foster care "rarely depart from the vision of the professionals and child savers themselves," viewing change as evolutionary progress toward enlightenment.[10]

"Childhood History as Ideology" is a landmark essay in that it presents the first theoretical guide for future research in a vitally important area of childhood history. It provides the salutary reminder that, like other groups, children are part of a larger society and culture that places demands on them and attempts to order their behavior and experience. It also serves as a corrective to those who accept a more benign notion of progress. As the American historian John Demos has suggested, attitudes toward childhood can become "a kind of yardstick for measuring historical trends of the most profound consequence."[11] But in its approach to the history of changing attitudes toward children, the essay leaves a number of questions unresolved. For example, were the new experts really such a coherent, monolithic group in the late nineteenth and early twentieth centuries? What was the experts' relationship with officials who represent "the State"? Did the experts' power and influence vary in the different states? Were they equally concerned with all stages of childhood, from infancy to youth? Were their strategies directed only toward children of the poor, as Kociumbas implies? A troubling omission, too, is the part played by "the Church." Its traditional role in child socialization may have been usurped by the state, but the influence of the different denominations surely remained significant. After the establishment of "secular" state educational systems in the late nineteenth century, the Catholic church expanded its own school system to inculcate a subculture antithetical in many ways to Protestantism and the scientific rationalism endorsed by the experts. There is a good deal of evidence, too, that members of the Protestant clergy and reformers with a religious background played important roles in child-saving movements.

Furthermore, Kociumbas does not address the criticism leveled against Ariès that a focus on socialization assumes that ideology is synonymous with behavior and experience. With respect to Australia, for example, we need to know how and why middle-class parents "translated ideology into action." It should not be assumed, either, that the middle class is a homogeneous group with identical interests and goals. Further, families of any class are not passive objects in the historical process. They may accept, resist, or modify imposed values and institutions. For the period under review some examples of behavior inconsistent with presumptive class interests immediately come to mind: the continuing decline of the birthrate among the urban middle class despite the warnings of "race suicide" by eugenicists and government officials; evidence of maternal lack of response to new child-rearing advice and the continuing strength, especially in rural areas, of the traditional family; some parents' rejection of sex education for their children; and the resistance of urban working-class and rural parents to compulsory schooling.[12]

What is even more important, a single-minded focus on socialization leaves other areas unexplored and produces a truncated history of childhood. To Kociumbas, ideology *is* childhood history. She asserts that such history "cannot be child-centered" because childhood is a social construction varying over time with the changing attitudes of groups of adults.[13] But concentration on ideology, although an essential foundation for any comprehensive history of childhood, ignores other significant issues. For example, children and childhood in turn have influenced adults and society. The rates of infant and child mortality, the proportions of children in a population, the emergence of a youth culture with its own icons and values, and the effects of childhood experiences on adult character and aspirations are important aspects of this countervailing influence. Additionally, for a broader understanding of childhood we need to identify major "turning points" in its history, and to be sure if structural constraints are less important than ideological ones. We need to explore the significance of class, gender, and regionalism; the "life course" transitions; the interaction between the child, the family, and the community; and the ways in which the lives of minority children may differ from those of the dominant race or ethnic group. Only then can we decide which issues are irrelevant.

Although lacunae in the historiography of Australian childhood are wide indeed, more useful studies exist than Kociumbas indicates; some of these have appeared since the publication of her landmark essay. Fragmented and reflecting the current limitations of the field, these studies nevertheless constitute the foundation stones for a future scholarly edifice. Before proceeding to review the literature, five generalizations can be offered. First, most studies deal with the period from European settlement in 1788 to World War I, a time that spans the colonial era and the early decades of nationhood after the federation of the colonies in 1901, and neglect the era after World War II when Australia entered a maturer phase of urban industrialism and experienced considerable and economic change.[14] Second, a major turning point in childhood history clearly emerges in the late nineteenth and early twentieth centuries, a formative period in Australian history. Third, most studies emphasize the socialization of children, probably the easiest of tasks for historians of childhood. Fourth, most focus on urban areas in the more populous regions of New South Wales and Victoria; generalizations about the "Australian" experience frequently rest on evidence from these two eastern states. Finally, historians have neglected the experiences of "ethnic" and Aboriginal children; those studied invariably are children of British stock.[15]

For the early colonial period two interesting studies that direct attention toward childhood have appeared in recent years, and should be read in conjunction with each other: Portia Robinson's *The Hatch and Brood of Time: A Study of the First Generation of Native-Born White Australians, 1788 to 1828* and Michael J. Belcher's doctoral thesis, "The Child in New South Wales Society: 1820 to 1837."[16] Both scholars have conducted intensive research in primary sources and both rely heavily on the first true census, that of 1828. Neither examines childhood in Van Diemen's Land (later Tasmania), separated from New South Wales only in 1825.

Robinson's research is impressive in family reconstitution, and her findings accentuate the complexity and fluidity of early colonial society, with its mixture of convicts, ex-convicts, soldiers, military and civil officials, and free settlers. Her conclusions emphasize the extraordinary stability of family life in a penal colony where males heavily outnumbered females, the comparatively low infant and child mortality rates, the parental concern for children, the differing experiences of children from all classes, the role differentiation for boys and girls, the honest and industrious qualities of youth, and the ways in which native-born children, unlike their parents, were shaped by colonial conditions. It is a remarkably rosy view, aggressively advanced and presented as a "new" interpretation.[17]

In agreement with Robinson on many points, Michael Belcher nevertheless is more ambivalent about colonial-born children and their families. He includes thoughtful analyses of parental responses to the reigning middle-class ideology of marriage and child rearing, demographic influences, children and the law, relationships within families, and children's responses to their experiences. Children in fact emerge as actual presences far more than in Robinson's work. Belcher concludes that although it is difficult to gain an accurate picture, there was a "high-degree" of family instability. He locates the cause more in the harsh conditions of pioneering life than in the brutal convict environment. Less convinced than Robinson of the high-mindedness of colonial youth, he claims that they were "a mixed bunch."[18]

Belcher hesitates to confirm that affection for children was widespread. He cautions that parental affection is difficult to determine, and that even though most children appear to have remained at home until boys achieved early economic independence and girls married young, prolonged contact within households is a necessary, but not sufficient condition for loving contact.

Moreover, Belcher tempers his optimistic view of children's lives by carrying his research into the late 1830s, when he sees a decline of opportunity as native-born boys matured. With little access to land, and facing a more competitive adult world and depressed economic conditions in the 1840s, poorly educated youths of the middling classes "sank slowly" to become a landless urban work force.[19]

Nonetheless his research reveals that only a "tiny minority" of parents was actively unwilling or unable to care for its children. Mining family letters and journals to good effect he finds evidence of closeness and affection within literate and well-to-do families, and from other sources "glimpses" of loving concern within the ranks of the inarticulate. Struggling parents, for example, demanded welfare and assistance in ways "undreamed of" by the Home Government but met by colonial officials. Further, those parents frequently treated the residential institutions as child-care centers from which they retrieved their children when fortunes improved. All in all, Belcher concludes, the first generation of colonial-born children bore "all the hallmarks of a closely scrutinized and privileged minority."[20]

The positive conclusions by these two historians (although more restrained in Belcher's case) question the interpretations of those who maintain that the barbarity of a penal colony colored subsequent history or inflicted long-term psychic damage on children. Moreover, by placing children at the center of inquiry, the two provocative studies provide an essential foundation for the study of childhood in the early nineteenth century.

Pioneering studies of the Australian family from the perspective of family history have proved unsatisfactory, as Kociumbas points out in "Childhood History as Ideology."[21] Quite simply, the necessary research is lacking to support Australian scholars' early generalizations. Some recent studies reveal more sophisticated methodologies and more intensive research. A number have been collected in *Families in Colonial Australia*, edited by three social historians and published in 1985.

All essays in this volume, the editors tell us, are informed by one or more categories suggested by the influential English historian of the family, Michael Anderson: family demography; changing meanings or "sentiments" in family relationships; and household economics or interpretations of "family structure and personal behaviour in the context of material bonds within the family and of economic change outside it."[22] The essays range from demographic studies of families in the future states of Queensland, Victoria, and Western Australia to examinations of family life in rural and gold-mining communities in Victoria, in a mining and dairying district in New South Wales, and in the city of Sydney. The essays on family demography face real problems because of the lack of detailed manuscript census returns, but a number of the contributors effectively use such rich and neglected sources as rate books, probate and court records, and land maps. In a final summation one of the editors, Ellen McEwen, is properly tentative about advancing generalizations based on the findings of these "pioneers" in the "new field" of family history. She does see some common threads: the significance of class divisions, the prevalence of nuclear families, and the ubiquity of child labor among rural and working-class families. But McEwen emphasizes that the evidence suggests considerable variety in colonial family life (as indicated by the word "families" in the title of the book) and in family adaptation to social and economic change.[23]

Some of these essays are far too brief, contain inadequate documentation, read as little more than works in progress, or fail to reveal a conceptual framework despite the editors' assurances. But fortunately a number are based on intensively researched doctoral theses or are shortened versions of thoughtful published or forthcoming works. This augurs well for continuing interest and productivity in family history. Community and regional studies such as these are essential foundations for more comprehensive treatment of family life in Australia. For students of childhood history the most useful essays are "Marriage and Children in Western Australia, 1842–1849" by Margaret Anderson (Grellier), who has published a more detailed demographic analysis of Western Australian families and is engaged in research on families in Western and South Australia; "Family and Community in Nineteenth Century Castlemaine" by Patricia Grimshaw and Charles Fahey, a version of a larger study of the V⁚ 'orian community; Ian Davey's "Growing Up in a Working-Class Community," part of a larger study of children in a suburb of Adelaide, South Australia; and an examination of families and children in a district of New South Wales by Winifred Mitchell and Geoffrey Sherington, which has been expanded into a book, *Growing Up in the Illawarra*.[24]

The largest body of work concerned directly with colonial childhood deals specifically with the socialization of children. Michael Belcher's thesis is a broad treatment of childhood in the early years of the penal colony of New South Wales, and it examines such socialization agencies as families, schools, and institutions catering to children of the poor. But other scholars have studied more closely the institutions caring for children "at risk." The best of this work, one that surveys the colonial era in New South Wales as a whole, is John Ramsland's recent book, *Children of the Back Lanes*, based on a doctoral thesis.[25]

Ramsland traces the development of the British model of "Bentham-inspired barracks" and its abandonment in the late nineteenth century in favor of the boarding-out system of foster care. He clearly demonstrates that the aim of the early child-savers was to remove children from "corrupt influences" by incarcerating the young wards in closed environments and training them to become part of "a respectable, religious, obedient labouring class."[26] Haphazard at first, the institutional system became highly centralized after the economic depression of the 1840s, the gold rushes of the 1850s, and the growth of a middle class determinedly seeking a more orderly society. Ramsland provides careful descriptions of the regimen within the government and privately sponsored orphanages, asylums, industrial schools, and reformatories, and effectively describes the realities of life for children within the "total" institutions. He skillfully traces the increasing involvement of the state, culminating in legislation in 1866 giving officials wide police and regulatory powers and in the establishment in 1873 of a Royal Commission on Public Charities. Ramsland sees the recommendations of the Commission, many in operation today, as representing a turning point in child welfare. Well versed in innovations abroad, the Commission of notable citizens attacked the institutional model as inhumane and "at utter variance with the family system." Athough some institutions, chiefly reformatory, survived into the twentieth century, by 1880 the "surrogate family" system of boarding-out replaced the old model and ushered in the modern age of child welfare.[27]

Ramsland has written elsewhere on institutional care in Tasmania and on the development of boarding-out in the Australian colonies.[28] It is regrettable, therefore, that he did not expand his book into a badly needed comparative study of child welfare throughout the colonies. Moreover, this book is not without flaws. Ramsland does not address the question of poverty itself or probe deeply into the motivations of the different groups of child-savers who chose to treat the symptoms rather than the causes of poverty. Nor does he discern the roots of attitudes and policies that would lead to the ever-increasing involvement of the state and the professionalization of child welfare in the early twentieth century. The insights of such urban historians as A.J.C. Mayne and Anne O'Brien and of scholars in women's history who have explored the "feminization" of poverty might have contributed to a more penetrating analysis of colonial child welfare.[29]

Studies that examine colonial attitudes and policies toward children of the poor in other regions include Joan C. Brown's 'Poverty Is Not a Crime' on social services in Tasmania, Brian Dickey's book on social welfare in South Australia, Margaret Barbalet's Far from a Low Gutter Girl on the "forgotten world" of state wards in South Australia, and an examination of the foundations of child welfare legislation in Victoria in Neglected and Criminal, by Donella Jaggs. Barbalet's book is remarkable for its evocation of the life of a child in a state institution. The charity network of reformers from the "old bourgeoisie," more interested in the "deserving" than the "undeserving" poor, is explored most thoroughly in Victoria, where voluntary agencies played a larger role than government in child welfare. Sheila Bignell, Graeme Davison, Anthea Hyslop, Richard Kennedy, Shurlee Swain, and Deborah Tyler are among those who have written on these charitable activities. Swain's work, based on a 1976 thesis on the Victorian charity network, is especially valuable. Her article "Destitute and Dependent: Case Studies in Poverty in Melbourne, 1890–1900" graphically depicts the effects of charity on parents and children from the ranks of the "deserving" poor.[30]

Although there is a large literature on social welfare in Australia, few works focus on child welfare in the twentieth century. One book that attempts to include a coherent description of attitudes and policies toward children throughout Australia is No Charity There!, by Brain Dickey.[31] But the book is essentially an introductory survey of welfare from the convict era to the present, and Dickey's discussion of developments in child welfare after 1916 is frustrated by a lack of scholarly studies on the period. As in many other areas, much work needs to be done on child welfare for the later decades of this century.

As we know, a broader study of changing attitudes toward children that carries over into the twentieth century has been written by Jan Kociumbas. The two articles derived from her thesis on children and society in New South Wales and

Victoria from 1860 to 1914 are titled "The Management of Children: Medical Advice on Child Care in New South Wales and Victoria, 1860–1900" and " 'What Alyce Learnt at Nine': Sexuality and Sex Roles in Children's Literature to 1914."[32] The first article briefly examines the emergence of physicians in the late nineteenth century as new experts in child rearing by scientific "laws of health," and the transformation of their role to one analogous to that of the clergy. The logic underlying medical prescription for the mental, moral, and physical health of the young, Kociumbas asserts, was that social improvement and national survival did not require any redistribution of wealth and power. It began rather with individual child training at home by a full-time mother in touch with expert opinion.[33] The second and much longer article explores changes in children's literature, a genre "always intimately related to what certain groups of adults believe the young ought to know." Here Kociumbas focuses on another group of experts, the educational theorists and creative writers who emerged in the late nineteenth and early twentieth centuries. Concerned with the alleged problems of premature sexuality in children, these experts advocated "the scrutiny of the full-time mother and the prolonged dependence and segregation of the child." The writers and theorists were supported by influential physicians, teachers anxious to prolong children's education, administrators of state and charitable institutions, and some Protestant clergy. These experts' influence was sustained by an expansion of the market for children's literature beyond the families of the middle class through inclusion of their work in new school textbooks.[34]

Kociumbas provides useful information, thoughtfully presented within the context of her thesis on socialization, concerning prescriptive literature on the training deemed proper for the young. But the dynamics of professionalism and the connections between ideology and the broader patterns of social and economic change remain unclear. Moreover, despite her admonitions against ascribing only self-serving motives to the new experts, the dominant theme of her work is the unequivocal middle-class imposition of new methods of social control. All the issues above are explored more satisfactorily in *The Disenchantment of the Home: Modernizing the Australian Family, 1880–1940*, by Kerreen Reiger. Published in 1985, the book is a revision of a thesis on the "rationalization" of domestic life in Victoria. The author gathered some additional evidence from other regions (chiefly New South Wales), but her generalizations rest primarily on documentation from Victoria. Nevertheless it is an important book that, unlike much sociological work, provides impressive evidence from primary sources. Reiger's approach is similar to that of Kociumbas, although apparently she is unfamiliar with the latter's work.[35]

Reiger, like Kociumbas, examines the role of an emergent class of "professionals, technocrats and experts" in the socialization of families, and her "core argument" deals with the connections between change in familial and personal relations and the wider patterns of economic, social, and cultural change. She sees these connections as part of a general extension of "technical rationality" in modern Western societies, referred to by Max Weber as the "disenchantment" of the world. With respect to Australia (actually Victoria), Reiger firmly places the role of the new professional class, to include psychologists after World War I, within the wider context of transition from a basically preindustrial colonial economy to a modern one, with the interwar years representing the "first waves" of the advancing industrial and consumerist culture characteristic of Australian society after World War II.[36] Reiger acknowledges her debt to Jacques Donzelot, Christopher Lasch, and the Ehrenreichs, and argues along with these overseas scholars that the experts extended scientific principles beyond the public world to the private world of the family. Unlike the oveseas scholars, however, Reiger asserts that women as well as men played an active role in rendering the domestic sphere more compatible with the world of commerce and industry. She proceeds to examine the strategies of doctors, teachers, "kindergartners," and domestic science and child guidance specialists in the professionalization of contraception, childbirth, and child rearing, and in the efforts to remove "the veil of prudery and silence" from sexuality.[37]

Reiger focuses on the reorganization of the family and the pivotal role of the mother, but also analyzes the development of new notions of childhood and the ways in which changing attitudes and policies toward the family changed the lives of many children. Reiger finds "extraordinary" contrast between nine-teenth- and twentieth-century sources. She notes that the lives of children were changed by the modern emphasis on the complexity of the mother's child-rearing tasks, the importance of socializing all children, and the influence of psycho-logical theory after World War I. Moreover, she sees an "enormous" shift from the nineteenth-century view that children were responsible moral agents to the modern conception of children as "victims" or "patients."[38]

Although Reiger's work meshes with that of Kociumbas, she confronts some of the issues the latter fails to address. Reiger finds ambivalence in the reform message and in varieties of class and gender responses. She sees, for example, a good deal of tension and conflict among the different groups of the middle classes. The new experts, she also points out, were determined to transform all families, unlike the reformers (chiefly women) from the old bourgeoisie who were part of the charity network inherited from the nineteenth century and primarily concerned with imposing their values on the "deserving" poor. Fur-ther, the new experts' model of the "rationalized" family threatened cherished values, and profoundly undermined the nineteenth-century bourgeois conception of the home as a moral and emotional haven from the cold and calculating world of commerce and industry. Moreover, in the process of modernization, women were hardly "passive puppets" or "unwitting dupes of a male ruling-class programme." Many actively participated in the reorganization of home and family, sometimes taking the initiative, as in the founding of crèches, infant welfare centers, domestic science education, and kindergartens. Others resisted or adapted the "decrees" of the experts.[39] All in all, Reiger sees the process of change as slow, uneven, and complex.

Other studies supplement Kociumbas' and Reiger's work on the socialization of children during the early twentieth century. A number of scholars, for example, link the child welfare movement with the population debate and the eugenics movement, and see the interrelationship as part of a wider campaign for national efficiency. A recent article by Stephen Garton, "Sir Charles Mackellar: Psychiatry, Eugenics, and Child Welfare in New South Wales, 1900 to 1914," is particularly illuminating.[40] Brian Gandevia's *Tears Often Shed*, a brief but useful text on child health and welfare movements in Australia, directs attention to the emergence of the specialty of pediatrics and the formation of such organizations as the Boy Scouts, which trained youths in patriotism, manliness, and middle-class virtues through healthy outdoor activities rather than prescriptive literature. The baby health movement also has been examined by M. Lewis, and by Philippa Mein Smith, who focuses on the teachings of Dr. Truby King, advocate of a regimen requiring the ministrations of a full-time mother. A fine article by Peter Spearritt explores the evolution of the kindergarten movement.[41] As yet there are no studies on the growth of professionalism and the quest for national efficiency comparable in scope to those by G. R. Searle in Great Britain and Andrew Abbot and Thomas Haskell in the United States.[42] In conceptual grasp, skillful interplay between theory and evidence, and persuasive argumentation, Kerreen Reiger's work on the "remaking" of childhood in *The Disenchantment of the Home* is the most sophisticated analysis to date of changing attitudes and policies toward children as the new nation entered the modern age.

An institution important in the lives of all children, at least in the modern era, is the school. Much has been written on education in Australia, but most studies focus on the development in the late nineteenth century of highly centralized state systems, their administration, and their curricula. "Traditional" historians see the evolution of state education as the enlightened outcome of liberalism and democracy. Some revisionists recently have attacked this "Whiggish" interpretation, and argue instead that compulsory schooling was another form of social control imposed on the lower classes to promote a more harmonious society.[43]

It is clear that a major turning point in public education, varying in time and intensity in the different colonies, occurred during the 1870s and 1880s. Under the slogan of free, compulsory, secular education, colonial governments ceased granting aid to church schools and established centralized control of schools under departments of education. With the federation of the colonies in 1901 and the end of a long economic depression, vigorous educational theorists and administrators, advocates of the "new education" then reshaping British schooling, agreed that the state schools had failed to train pupils satisfactorily in the skills and moral values deemed essential for the new nation. Reforms in education, part of the larger reform movement discussed earlier, included the introduction of medical inspection of children, kindergartens, physical culture, and changes in the elementary curriculum so as to reduce rote learning and cultivate self-expression. School fees were abolished for primary schooling, and requirements for compulsory minimum attendance tightened. Teacher training became more formalized, and for a minority of children secondary schools offered technical, vocational, and academic training to meet the respective needs of commerce, industry, and the professions. The transmission of social values remained a paramount aim of "progressive" education. As Peter Board, the director of education in New South Wales contended, schools were "the nurseries of morality."[44]

Few studies in educational history focus on the schools as socialization agencies, the development of schooling in response to changing ideas on childhood, the responses of parents to the advent of compulsory schooling, or the school experiences of the children themselves. The most detailed study of the transmission of ideology through the schools remains an article, "Social Values in the New South Wales Primary School, 1880–1914," published in 1970 by S. G. Firth. Firth examines school texts and sees continuity as well as change in the values taught between the late colonial and early Commonwealth eras. The "new education," he argues, simply made the school a more efficient transmitter of values. Ignoring the literature directed specifically toward young girls (the essay's date of publication may explain this lapse), Firth maintains that the ideal pupil of 1914 remained much the same as in the nineteenth century: a self-reliant, patriotic British gentleman. Nevertheless Firth demonstrates that major changes occurred in school texts used in the state schools. An "implicit Christianity" (for secular did not mean godless) replaced the "explicit theology" of earlier texts. Further, after the foundation of the Commonwealth, textbooks fostered Australian as well as British loyalties, and the wattle, the kangaroo, and the Australian flag joined the Union Jack and the crown and orb as national symbols.[45]

Firth compares and contrasts these social values with those transmitted in Catholic schools, expanded into an autonomous system after the introduction of "secular" state schooling. The Catholic schools, like the state schools, he writes, preached the virtues of thrift and hard work but, unlike the state schools, emphasized survival rather than a "success ethic." Moreover, for Catholics, the motherland was Ireland, and their religion was indispensable to morality. Strongly anti-British in the nineteenth century, textbooks by 1910 taught an Irish-Australian patriotism. Their adventure stories and tales of heroic exploits did not glorify the British Empire. Rather, they pointed up religious lessons, and the heroes were saints and martyrs instead of British statesmen, soldiers, and explorers. If the major aim of state schooling by World War I was the production of good citizens, Firth observes, the aim of Catholic schooling was to produce good Catholics.[46]

Firth's examination of Catholic textbooks is supplemented by a broader treatment of socialization in Edmund Campion's book, *Australian Catholics*.[47] Campion (a priest) agrees with Firth that Australian Catholicism was Irish Catholicism and that the hierarchy in the late nineteenth century aimed to produce "a united Catholic mind." Campion pays a great deal of attention to Catholic education, especially in its heyday from 1900 to World War II, since he sees the schools, permeated by religion, as the key to an understanding of the religious life of Australian Catholics. In striking descriptions of school life, he evokes the sights, sounds, smells, and solidarity of the Catholic faith, absorbed as an "atmosphere" by schoolchildren well before they recognized the religion as dogma.[48]

The socialization of girls, neglected by Firth, has received some attention in recent years, undoubtedly because of the influence of women's history. Edmund Campion, Beverly Kingston, Noeline Kyle, and Jan Kociumbas, for example, have explored the ways in which young girls were trained for their future roles as wives and mothers.[49] School textbooks stressed the glories of motherhood, the virtues of self-sacrifice, humility, and altruism, and the punishments awaiting those who transgressed the bounds of "femininity," as did the books written for a burgeoning children's market by such popular authors as Ethel Turner and Mary Grant Bruce. Gender-specific education, exemplified by the "cult" of domestic science, firmly entrenched in the school curriculum after World War I, has been examined by Jill Matthews and Kerreen Reiger.[50] Other historians, such as Alison Mackinnon in her study of the Advanced School for Girls in Adelaide, *One Foot on the Ladder*, and Ailsa Zainu'ddin in a history of the private Methodist Ladies' College in Melbourne, deal with secondary schooling for girls that aimed at academic excellence and preparation for higher education in the universities.[51] Zainu'ddin's book, *They Dreamt of a School*, is especially interesting. Established in 1882, the Methodist Ladies' College provided an education similar to that given to boys in the neighboring Wesley College. Unlike most of the private schools that educated so many girls of the upper classes, it was headed by a succession of male headmasters and, because of its low fees, attracted a cross section of pupils seldom seen in its more exclusive counterparts. But the school in other ways was typical of its kind. Although it provided opportunities for learning, liberating experiences, and participation in student self-government and female rituals and ceremonies, the school also preached the traditional values of home and family and the importance of the role of the full-time mother. The mixed message given to the young women exemplified the conflicts they would face in the future if they attempted to combine professional careers with marriage and motherhood.

There are, too, a number of histories of private boys' schools. Founded mainly by major Protestant denominations in the late nineteenth century, these schools educated upper-class youths and prepared many students who entered the universities before World War II. Such histories are chiefly celebratory studies of individual schools written by "old boys," Geoffrey Sherington's *Shore*, a critical history of the Sydney Church of England Grammar School, is a notable exception.[52] But there is no broad study of these schools (or of the girls' schools) comparable in scope to James McLachlan's book on American boarding schools, institutions catering to sons of the *haute bourgeoisie* and probably closer in ambience to the Australian private schools than to the famed public schools of England.[53] In an approach that could foster more critical inquiry into the influential Australian boys' schools, McLachlan points out that the American institutions were forerunners in the modern institutionalization or dependency of adolescent youths. Moreover, he focuses on their importance as cultural institutions training future leaders in society who would set the tone of public and social life. He demonstrates the ways in which the schools fostered esprit de corps, an image of the school as a family, the building of character through organized sports, participation in student self-government, and the inculcation of muscular Christianity, patriotism, middle-class virtues, and gentlemanly behavior.

Some provocative and interesting work on South Australian public education has been produced in recent years by a group of Adelaide historians, among them Pavla Cook, Ian Davey, Denis Grundy, Malcolm Vick, and Kerry Wimshurst. Influenced by the American historian of education Michael Katz (at one time a faculty member at the University of Toronto), these revisionist scholars have examined the responses of working-class parents in Adelaide to state laws on education passed between 1875 and 1915, and their work is closely linked to the neglected issue of child labor.[54]

In 1875 South Australia passed an education act establishing its system of free, secular, and compulsory schooling. The law required that children between the ages of seven and thirteen attend school for thirty-five out of forty days each quarter. Between 1899 and 1905, however, "an alliance of child savers and Liberal and Labor politicians" passed a series of acts limiting urban children's opportunities for casual work and tightening minimum attendance requirements to four out of five days a week. The reformers claimed that the earlier attendance law allowed children too much free time to roam aimlessly through the streets, where they acquired "vicious" habits in the "gaslit" environment. Clearly, reformers were disturbed by the perceived dangers of city life and the potential threat to the social order posed by bands of roving, idle children.[55] Studies produced by South Australian historians demonstrate that despite reformers' claims, most children in commercial Adelaide were far from idle, and they provide revealing glimpses into the exhausting lives of children from working-class families. Many of these children engaged in "meaningful and important casual labour," and contributed to the survival of their families, the most desperate of which were headed by single parents. Some sold race cards, matches, newspapers, flowers, or fruit, and fetched and carried in small contracting businesses. Others helped with such semirural activities as grape-cutting, fruit-picking, and carting stock to market. Because of the customary sexual division of labor, young girls helped their mothers or released them for work outside the home. Some at the age of twelve entered domestic service or apprenticeships in occupations like dressmaking.[56]

Parents of these children, writes the historian Kerry Wimshurst, were "quite prepared to utilize state schooling as much as economic circumstances and work patterns of family and community would allow." The "great majority" of children complied with the minimum attendance laws, although it is clear that after the more stringent requirement of 1905, children worked longer hours before and after school. But many parents actively and energetically opposed continuing attempts to introduce full-time compulsory schooling. More stringent regulations, they argued, would place "extra burdens" on struggling parents and represent an unwanted intrusion by the state.[57]

The Adelaide group, intent on revising the traditional interpretation that sees educational reform as part of the advance of liberalism and democracy, initially emphasized the burdens placed on struggling parents and the attempts by parents to circumvent unwelcome laws, and their evidence is persuasive. Yet more recent work by this group indicates that middle-class authorities frequently supported the parents. Local school boards proved to be flexible when children failed to meet minimum attendance requirements, especially when there was sickness at home or when children were "usefully and profitably employed."[58] In a recent article the demographer Ann Larson finds similar conflict and interaction between authorities and working-class parents in colonial Melbourne after Victoria in 1872 passed an education act that established free, secular, and compulsory education and another in 1890 that tightened minimum attendance requirements. Larson concludes that before 1900, although parents valued a basic education for their children, they did not value attendance or a lock-step process of schooling. They forced the authorities to conform to the "external realities" of families' economic needs and "the subjective beliefs about when a child ceased to be a child."[59] Further research may disclose similar responses in other states, although South Australia's educational system in some ways veered from those established elsewhere. Nevertheless, as Kerry Wimshurst observes, the period between 1890 and 1914 did see "the evolution of a concept of schooling and a vision of childhood which severely restricted the alternatives open to children both in and out of school hours." In 1915 this process culminated in the passage of an education act, under a Labour government that restructured South Australia's school system. The act established the leaving age at fourteen, made full-time attendance compulsory, limited children's casual work outside school hours, and introduced technical and domestic science courses that, the historian Ian Davey asserts, gave "institutional expression to class and gender divisions in society." The aim of the Education Act of 1915, Davey continues, was "to reproduce the social order in a more 'scientific' and 'efficient' manner; its effect was to establish the institutional machinery for the invention of working-class adolescence."[60]

This revisionist work thus places educational reform firmly within the wider framework of the middle-class progressivism described earlier. Further, it revises the more benign notion that the extension of schooling was part of the advance of democracy. The revisionists, however, fail to explain satisfactorily why reforms were accepted so enthusiastically by the Labour party, and they do not explore the attitudes of other members of the working class or classes who may have seen education reforms as creating better opportunities for their children. Moreover, Wimshurst concludes that after 1915, "children were abstracted from an environment permeated by family and street culture and placed full-time in the closed community and artificial nursery of the school."[61] This conclusion assumes that family and street cultures were "natural" nurseries, and therefore provided richer and more diverse experiences for children participating in "the adult world of work." We do not know what the children themselves, whose lives were fashioned by adults, thought about these cultures. There is a fairly large literature, however, of autobiographies and memoirs of childhood in the country and outback and scholarly studies on the urban poor that suggest other versions of childhood experiences in the family and "the adult world of work." In these accounts childhood was frequently blighted by hardship, exhaustion, and little hope for the future. Moreover, after passage of the Education Act of 1915, most children left state schools at fourteen. They would not attend secondary schools until the massive expansion of state secondary schooling after World War II. This suggests that adolescence and prolonged dependence lasted only a few short years for large numbers of Australian children.[62]

Although education in Australia has "a large historiography," it is clear that neither the "Whig" nor the "social control" interpretations satisfactorily explain the development of and responses to educational reform. Moreover, as in other areas of childhood history, recent studies are regional, and focus on urban schooling in the period between 1890 and World War I. This is yet another indication that although some thoughtful and challenging work is appearing that surely will lead to further research and historical debate, the study of childhood in Australia is only in its infancy.

If the field of childhood history in Australia is in its infancy, in New Zealand it is yet in the gestation stage. Much of the work concerned with children can be found only in unpublished theses, a scattering of articles in scholarly journals and anthologies, and histories of education primarily concerned with the development and administration of school systems. Some historians demonstrate familiarity with interpretations and methodologies developed overseas by historians of the family, and place changes in the family and the consequent effects on children within the larger context of a changing society. Few appear familiar with advances in the history of childhood or design conceptual frameworks to analyze the New Zealand experience. The problem is compounded by a scarcity of sophisticated studies in related fields of social history.

Given these forbidding limitations, some generalizations nonetheless can be offered on current scholarship in childhood history. First, the largest body of work, much of it unpublished, is in the areas of education and child welfare. Second, there is a marked turning point in attitudes and policies toward children in the late nineteenth and early twentieth centuries, a critical transition period in New Zealand history. Third, most of the scholarship focuses on this transitional period, roughly from 1890 to 1920. Finally, existing studies concentrate on "European" children, the majority of British stock.[63]

Although traders and missionaries had arrived decades before, formal European settlement began with the British annexation of New Zealand as a crown colony in 1840. Composed of the North and South Islands, the new colony was basically rural, characterized by mixed farming in the north and large pastoral holdings in the south. Nevertheless, by 1881, 42 percent of the population lived in urban areas with more than one thousand inhabitants. In 1870 the central government, to revive a flagging economy, initiated a deliberate policy of modernization. It built roads, railways, bridges, harbors, and public works, instituted a vigorous immigration policy, laid a cable to Australia, and inaugurated steamship service to San Francisco. In one decade the European population doubled to 490,000 (about one-half the population of the Australian colony of Victoria), the civil service and middle class expanded, the number of small landholdings increased, manufacturing and service industries employed a larger work force, and the population of the native people, the Maoris, reached its nadir in 1880, chiefly through epidemics of European diseases, dislocation, and declining fertility and high infant mortality.[64] Thus by the end of the first fifty years of colonization the outline of modern New Zealand society had appeared. European hegemony was assured, the country's prosperity depended on a rural economy and British markets, a large population lived in urban areas, the people accepted an active government, and most white families were British in origin.

Little is known about these pioneering families. In the 1970s two collections of essays on the New Zealand family appeared, each edited by a sociologist, but most of the essays concentrate on the modern era and contemporary "problems."[65] The most ambitious attempt at a historical overview is an essay in one of the collections titled "Towards a History of the European Family in New Zealand," by Erik Olssen and Andrée Lévesque, who observe that "virtually nothing" has been written on the family. The authors are familiar with the interpretations of a few English and American family historians and apply some of those concepts to their own study. The essay ranges in time from 1840 to 1970, and Olssen and Lévesque acknowledge that their history is "brief and tentative." They devote only a few pages to the period of early colonization, from 1840 to 1879, and rely chiefly on a small collection of printed memoirs, scholarly articles, and unpublished theses.[66] In another essay in the same collection, "Children and Young Persons in New Zealand Society," Dugald J. McDonald, a sociologist, adopts a "social values" approach and "encapsulates" the dominant attitudes toward children in four separate periods from 1840 to 1970. McDonald, who also devotes only a few pages to the early period, concludes that the colonial child was a "chattel," undertaking adult tasks at an early age and having no identity beyond that conferred by masters or parents.[67] These brief accounts can be supplemented by other studies that include material on colonial families and children, notably those by Rollo Arnold, Stevan Eldred-Grigg, Jeanine Graham, P. J. Whelan, and historians of education, among them A. E. Campbell, J. C. Dakin, Ian and Alan Cumming, and David McKenzie.[68]

From all these accounts some generalizations emerge about the pioneering families and their children. Until the late 1860s males greatly exceeded females, and many men, especially in rural and gold-mining settlements, remained single. In 1874, 95 percent of women over thirty were married, and although families were relatively small in number, they included broods of children. In 1881 children made up 42 percent of the population, a percentage augmented by the family migration of the 1870s and the relatively low rate of child mortality. In the towns and small cities families lived under a good deal of communal supervision, and few settlements lacked a church or a jail. Contemporary observers' accounts make frequent references to class distinctions and, writes Jeanine Graham in a chapter on "Settler Society" in the *Oxford History of New Zealand*, "from the outset distinctions of birth, education, income and occupation were acknowledged." But as Claire Toynbee points out in a thoughtful assessment of the scholarship on class and social structure in colonial New Zealand, historians have "failed to construct a coherent picture of nineteenth century social structure and process."[69]

There is no question that the large landholders who produced the colony's major export, wool, were at the top of the social heap, and in Stevan Eldred-Grigg's book, *A Southern Gentry: New Zealanders Who Inherited the Earth*, the clearest picture of these families emerges. In such circles intermarriage was common, and fortunes frequently were consolidated by judicious matches fostered in an exclusive social life that emulated the pursuits of the English country gentry. Of 360 landowners in the South Island, for example, 112 had attended British universities, and prolonged education for the gentry's offspring was taken for granted. Some were taught by tutors and governesses, others attended private schools, and boys' schools modeled on the public schools of England, like Christ's College in the small city of Christchurch, were founded in the early years of settlement. Some older boys and girls sailed "home" to such prestigious schools as Rugby and Cheltenham, and youths received a "final polish" at Oxford or Cambridge. For those who stayed behind, education culminated at university colleges founded in the late 1860s and early 1870s in the leading provinces of Otago and Canterbury.[70] Private schooling would remain the preferred form for children of the gentry and an emergent commercial and professional elite. McDonald's description of the child as a chattel does not apply to upper-class children. For them childhood was extended, dominated by schooling and the leisurely pursuits of a privileged class. Nor does the description of the child as a chattel, Rollo Arnold argues, fit many children on family farms, who early in life developed a strong sense of self-reliance, independence, and self-worth.[71]

Some glimpses of the less privileged children who lived on the farms in the small towns and in the four main cities of Auckland and Wellington in the North Island and Christchurch and Dunedin in the South Island emerge in histories of education. During the crown colony era from 1840 to 1852 education was fitful, a combination of schooling at home by mothers if they were competent (one-quarter of the early migrants were illiterate), dame schools, Sunday schools, denominational schools partly supported by the government, and common schools established in a few regions. In 1852 control of education was placed in the hands of provincial governments when the British Parliament granted New

Zealand representative government. A constitution divided the country into six initial provinces with elected governments and superintendents for each province, and created a central government, the General Assembly, with an elected House of Representatives and a Legislative Council or Upper House nominated by the governor.[72]

Under the constitution provincial governments were instructed to establish district schools supervised by local boards and committees and divided into six grades or standards, a plan similar to Great Britain's Irish National system and the early school systems in colonial Australia. Richer and more populous provinces in the South Island immediately established or enlarged their school systems, and in 1864, for example, an estimated 70 percent of the children in the exceptional province of Nelson were enrolled in school. In the North Island, where many homesteads were devastated by the Anglo-Maori wars, little was done about schooling. In Auckland, the major province, the government established a school system only in 1869. Nevertheless it is clear that public rhetoric favored a basic education for children, and most provincial governments were prepared to establish schools.

Although histories of education are descriptive rather than analytical, certain trends can be recognized. First, the role of the churches in schooling steadily declined, apparently because of "sectarian bickering," and the schools became increasingly secular. By the early 1870s daily Bible reading sufficed for religious instruction during school hours, although the Irish National and Royal Readers were heavily moralistic and Protestant in tone. Second, because all schools charged fees, a basic education was denied to children of the poor. Third, and this surely is linked to the declining role of the churches, state responsibility for education was widely accepted. Finally, many families in urban and rural areas, as David McKenzie observes, "refused to take school attendance seriously." An estimated 58 percent of all children between the ages of five and fifteen were enrolled in the schools by the early 1870s, and of those only 38 percent attended regularly. Clearly the school was not an important institution in the lives of many children.[73]

In 1876 the General Assembly abolished the provincial governments (although provincial loyalties remained strong), replacing them with a "confused multitude" of local boards and councils that to this day manage local affairs.[74] One year later the government passed an education bill establishing a national system of free, compulsory, and secular schooling for children from ages seven to thirteen years, legislation similar in many respects to measures passed in the same decade in Great Britain and in the Australian colonies. Thus the New Zealand government fell into step with British policies, signifying that the state was prepared to play a more coercive role in education and in the extension of childhood. At the same time the government moved to curtail the factory employment of children aged ten to fourteen to half-day shifts or alternate full days.[75]

The period of early colonization also witnessed the increasing role of the government in child welfare. Although most families achieved some degree of "plain comfort" in their lives (by the 1870s the standard of living was higher than in Australia and the United States), there were always those unable or unwilling to support their children. During the crown colony era benevolent societies and the churches, with aid of the government, took care of the poor chiefly through outdoor relief. By the 1860s there was considerable social dislocation caused by gold rushes in the provinces of Otago and Westland in the South Island, the Anglo-Maori wars in the North Island, and depressed conditions in leading urban centers.[76]

P. J. Whelan devotes the major portion of a 1956 thesis on child welfare in the nineteenth century, the only detailed study of child welfare in the early years of colonization, to the provincial period, and painstakingly describes developments after 1852 in each province. Outdoor relief continued to suffice in smaller settlements, but in more populous and hard-hit regions the churches and private charity, with government support, housed children in orphanages and industrial schools. At the height of the gold rush in Otago in 1867 the provincial government, apparently responding to "public demand," authorized the building of an industrial school for "neglected" and "criminal" children. Canterbury province followed suit, and a Naval Training School to fit boys from ten to fifteen for the mercantile marine, was established in Auckland.[77] Other institutions, seven in all, were privately sponsored or partly supported by the government. Some provinces, like Wellington in the North Island, "exported" children to Catholic orphanages in Nelson or the industrial school in Otago. All these institutions came under the control of the department of justice when the General Assembly abolished the provincial governments, and in 1880 this control was transferred to the department of education.

Whelan provides some information on the lives of children in these institutions. All endured hard labor, rigid discipline, and indifferent schooling. Except for the inmates of the Naval Training School, boys left at the age of twelve for apprenticeships or agricultural labor, and girls for domestic service. Newspapers in the late 1870s began reporting on abuses at the institutions, and some indication of the children's responses to conditions can be gained by the "wave" of absconding in that decade.[78]

What does not emerge from Whelan's thesis is any understanding of the composition of community and provincial groups that favored "Bentham-inspired barracks," or of the process by which the state began to assume the "traditional" responsibilities of families, churches, and communities. Nor do we learn what constituted "neglect" or "criminal" behavior, or what the responses of parents were to policies that removed children from their care and, in some cases, transported them far away.

Whelan does provide evidence that local and provincial leaders' primary concerns by the 1860s were the potential threat to social order and community moral standards posed by children of "disreputable" parents from "hereditary pauper" origins, the desire to separate these contaminated children from the more respectable elements in society, and the determination to train them in industrious work habits for a future place in society as rural and domestic "servants."[79]

It is in the years between 1890 and 1920 that children assumed a new importance in New Zealand society, and it is this period that is the focus of most studies on children. The historian Erik Olssen, in a thoughtful chapter titled "Towards a New Society" in the *Oxford History of New Zealand*, offers the most acute analysis of changing attitudes and policies toward the family and children, and places change within the larger context of the transformation of society. During this period the process of modernization begun in 1870 accelerated, and by the 1920s New Zealand exhibited many of the features of modern industrialized societies. The country prospered, although wealth was distributed unevenly, and the population increased as did the manufacturing and service industries, although lack of iron precluded large-scale industrialization. Urbanization proceeded at a rapid pace, with more than 40 percent of the population by 1921 living in areas with more than eight thousand inhabitants. Generous government land and credit policies opened up large areas for closer land settlement, refrigeration stimulated the dairying industry, and the Liberal party, in power between 1891 and 1911, began a series of "state experiments" that, writes the historian Keith Sinclair, gave the country its reputation of being "the most radical state in the world."[80]

Olssen sees society in these years as characterized by urbanization, bureaucracy, specialization, and organization. Nowhere, he writes, was "the extent of modernization more evident than in the changing structure and role of the family." In broad strokes he describes the major change as a "spectacular" decline in fertility and family size in the urban middle class (spreading to the working classes after World War I and to rural families by the late 1930s), increasing assumption of welfare responsibilities by state and voluntary agencies, introduction by the medical profession of scientific procedures on child rearing that required the attention of a full-time mother, the expansion of schooling, and legislation for the protection of children. All these changes were evidence that children had become "social assets."[81]

The theme of "social capital" is taken up by Dugald McDonald in his "encapsulation" of changes in attitudes toward children from the turn of the century to World War II. McDonald sees an ideological shift of "revolutionary" proportions after 1900, when "the gradually increasing intervention in the private world of the family was predicated upon the notion that the adult contribution of citizens, the society's *social capital*, was related to the degree of care given in childhood." Child rearing, McDonald concludes, was deemed too important to be left to the discretion of the family. In a brief account he cites some of the examples also given by Olssen, and concludes that the Liberal party era spelled "the end of the inalienable right of the family to decide the quality of life of its children."[82]

Other studies explore in more detail aspects of changing attitudes toward children, although few scholars place their work in a larger framework. Jeanine Graham traces the development in the 1890s of Liberal party legislation on the factory employment of children. In 1901 these laws were consolidated into a measure that prohibited the employment of children in factories and small workshops before the age of fourteen or on completion of standard five in the primary schools, thus linking the law to compulsory schooling. The government also passed a Children's Protection Act in 1890 that controlled the presence of children in licensed premises and prevented boys under fourteen and girls under sixteen from working as "mendicants." Graham points out that the Liberals were "socially and politically circumspect." They did not interfere with unpaid labor on family farms, domestic service in middle-class households, or paid labor before and after school hours. The laws, as David McKenzie makes clear, had little impact on parental attitudes. Although the numbers of children employed in factories were never large, nearly as many children (1,632) worked in 1901 as in 1890. Only more stringent school attendance laws eventually would restrict the growth of this kind of employment.[83]

Graham briefly discusses the importance of women's groups in agitating for these and other laws, ranging from bills legitimizing children born out of wedlock if the parents eventually married, allowing adoption by a wide range of prospective parents if the natural parent or parents consented, and protecting infants from "baby farming" to granting police the right to interfere in cases of neglect and abuse, and raising the age of consent for girls to sixteen years.[84]

The emergence of middle-class women's organizations, stimulated by the granting of women's suffrage in 1893, and the "cults of domesticity and true womanhood" have been examined by others, among them Phillida Bunkle, Phyllis Levitt, and Erik Olssen and Andrée Lévesque. Bunkle explores the origins of the Women's Christian Temperance Union (WCTU), founded in 1885 and the first national women's organization. She argues, along with Raewyn Dalziel, who has written an article on women's role and the vote in the nineteenth century, that women did not seek equality, but "elevation of a separate sphere and expression of peculiarly female values." Women in the WCTU, Bunkle observes, were "tireless" in the interests of child care, education, and the young.[85] In a doctoral thesis on "public concern" for young children in the city of Dunedin from 1879 to 1889, Levitt discusses the activities of a variety of women's organizations, including the establishment of a Young Women's Christian Association, a day nursery for "wearied mothers," the first free kindergarten, and agitation against baby farming. Olssen and Lévesque briefly describe the emergence of the ideology of domesticity and true womanhood that gave women a new importance in the home and as moral guardians and altruistic social servants.[86]

All these studies demonstrate that although women were indignant about the treatment of children of the poor and filled with compassion for "little ones," they were obsessed with the "purity" of the child and the evils of moral contagion. Levitt writes that women's primary aim in founding a free kindergarten in Dunedin was to guard "gutter children," burdened with "evil tendencies," from the thriftlessness, disease, pauperism, and crime of their surroundings.[87]

These indications of middle-class anxieties that focused on the children of the poor who would grow up to become New Zealand citizens are elaborated in a research essay, "Saving the Children of New Zealand: A Study of Social Attitudes Towards Larrikinism in the Later Nineteenth Century," written in 1975 by P. A. Gregory.[88] She examines the "rule makers" who set out to bring a range of youthful activities under government control, and subject "larrikins" (an Australasian term for troublesome youths) and their irresponsible parents to much needed discipline. A network of women's organizations, headed by the WCTU and the Society for the Protection of Women and Children (later changed to Home and Children), joined with other citizens in agitation that in the 1890s bordered on hysteria. The campaign centered on behavior not classified as criminal: "cheeky" boys smoking cigarettes, "blocking thoroughfares," using "filthy language," and engaging in "mischief." Although more extreme measures, like a Curfew Act, failed to pass because of opposition from the public (including women) to unwarranted interference with personal liberty, Gregory sees the moral crusade as important in influencing such later developments as the formation of School Cadets and the introduction of compulsory physical and moral instruction in the schools, the passage of a law against juvenile smoking, the Juvenile Offenders Act that introduced separate courts for children, and the establishment of Boys' Institutes and the Boy Scouts. Gregory concludes that the proposals of moral crusaders were all directed toward conservative ends. She argues that their diagnoses of wrongdoing tell less about delinquency than about aspects of the new society that caused alarm: urbanization, social change, the decline of religion, and the weakened role of the family.[89]

In a doctoral thesis on "Indigence and Charitable Aid in New Zealand, 1885–1920" and in articles derived from the thesis, Margaret Tennant sees middle-class anxieties and the repressive tendencies behind much of what represented reform as not peculiar to women, but part of deeply rooted attitudes toward the poor. She asserts that the reputation of New Zealand as a "social laboratory" obscures the "poor law" aspects of welfare, with its notions of dependency and deservedness, and the fear of pauperism and degeneracy in the New World.[90] This mixture of compassion and repression in attitudes and policies toward the poor emerges in Jan Beagle's thesis, "Children of the State: A Study of the New Zealand Industrial School System, 1880–1925." Beagle expands on Whelan's study of industrial schools in the nineteenth century, beginning with the passage of the Industrial Schools Act of 1882, which drew heavily on British procedures, introduced the new element of foster care, and aimed at firmer central control of state-sponsored and privately sponsored institutions. Continuing revelations about conditions in these schools and a scandal about the excessive punishments and mistreatment of children at a Catholic school in Nelson run by the Marist Brothers resulted in a Royal Commission in 1900. Women's organizations such as the National Council of Women declared that "life in its cruellest shape" was typical of a state ward's experience. Recollections of former inmates portrayed their life as "torture" and "sterilizing hell," and Phyllis Levitt finds that destitute mothers in Dunedin dreaded the incarceration of their children.[91]

Despite the government's advocacy of foster care in 1882 after the inspector general of schools, William J. Habens (a Congregational minister), visited Australia to study its boarding-out scheme, only 30 percent of state wards were in foster care by 1900, and the church institutions harboring children frowned on the practice. Moreover, the state continued to build institutions, including the first reform school for girls. Beagle sees major changes occurring only with the emergence of "a new class of professional public servants," the most important of whom was John Beck, appointed officer in charge of industrial schools in 1916 after years of administrative experience and close study of child welfare abroad, especially in the United States. By the end of Beck's term in 1924 the education department had closed four of the institutions, appointed the first juvenile probation officer, and established probation homes. Fifty percent of state wards were in foster care by 1925, and Beck forced private institutions to board out about 20 percent of their charges. In 1925 a "new era" began with the passage of a Child Welfare Act, which created children's courts with preventative rather than punitive purposes and established a child welfare branch staffed with professional officers.[92]

All these government experts thought in terms of reforming government policies and custodial arrangements rather than of helping families to retain their children or of keeping children within their communities. Beagle sees increasing government intervention as a "more natural" phenomenon than in Great Britain because of the heritage of state action.[93] Margaret Tennant, the most critical of historians of welfare, implies that administrators like John Beck were more enlightened than local communities. She writes that present-day nostalgia for "community care" presupposes that the community "care." Tennant and the historian Olssen are in agreement that a "deep reluctance" to admit the existence of social problems, including those of destitute and wayward children, stemmed from the ingrained belief that most of the problems of the Old World did not exist in "God's own Country," but if present were rooted in flaws of character or a pauper heritage.[94]

The historian Graham, in her article on child employment, warns that a focus on children of the poor distorts the picture of childhood. Evidence from oral histories and genealogies provides an "important counterweight" to the negative impression left by a focus on exploitation. Thousands of New Zealand children, she points out, were untouched by the laws or by hardships in a country with one of the highest standards of living in the world. These children grew up "secure in the knowledge" that they were loved and cared for, and that New Zealand was "a good place to be born and raised."[95] Rollo Arnold, in his essay on the country child in late Victorian New Zealand, also issues a caveat. Arnold argues that the modern concept of childhood, with its essential criteria of dependence, protection, segregation, and delayed responsibility, does not apply to rural children in this critical era.[96] Much work needs to be done on rural children.

There are no studies of the new class of experts who emerged at the turn of the century comparable to those by Australian scholars. But Olssen, who briefly describes the significance of professionals in "Towards a New Society," examines the influence of the medical profession in the "remaking" of the family and childhood in an article on Dr. Frederick Truby King and the Plunket Society.[97] Truby King of Dunedin founded in 1909 the Society of Promoting the Health of Women and Children, popularly known as the Plunket Society. King, Olssen observes, linked "the care of babies to the health of the family, nation and Empire," and his prescriptions became "orthodoxy." The society, which the government subsidized, addressed major anxieties of urban and rural leaders—national growth and greatness, concern about urban disorder, and signs of degeneracy in the "white race." Central to King's philosophy were the notions of discipline, self-control, and the importance of mothers, who would become the "executives" of a new society by raising their children scientifically, with the clock as the key to a regulated life. The ideology gave mothers a sense of purpose and "cosmic importance," and the society became a beloved institution in New Zealand life. It gained the loyalties of women of all classes, and by 1945, 85 percent of non-Maori children were Plunket babies. At the heart of the ideology, Olseen writes, was "the older cult of motherhood" subtly altered so that the mother became subject to control by outside experts who represented "a new form of authority."[98]

In an article on "Natural Directions: The New Zealand Movement for Sexual Differentiation in Education During the Twentieth Century," Margaret Tennant discusses the importance of King and other members of the medical profession in influencing the introduction of cooking and dressmaking courses in the primary schools and "home science" as a compulsory subject for girls in secondary schools. In 1909 an endowed chair in home science was established at the University of Otago, in King's bailiwick. Girls were discouraged from taking the "hard" sciences, and by 1918 home science came close to botany as the main science in girls' schools. The education in "womanly qualities," Tennant observes, "meant not only an education for home-life and maternity, but, more subtly, an education in mathematical, scientific, and technical ineptitude, and a lasting constraint on girls' choices for future lifestyles."[99]

Standard histories of education recount the changes that occurred in public schooling after the 1890s, when an effective primary system was finally "in place" after the end of the long depression. Under George Hogben, the Liberal party's choice for inspector general of schools, the power of the education department increased and the prolongation of childhood was accomplished. The department established teacher-training schools, a common syllabus for each standard, a *School Journal* to supplement selected readers, and a national examination system that controlled children's entry into future occupations. It tightened attendance requirements in 1894 and 1901, raised the school-leaving age to fourteen in 1901, and in 1910 required children to attend school each day. In 1901 the department allowed "free places" in secondary schools, all of which charged fees. These schools were rigorously academic, but in 1905 the first technical day school opened to train boys in vocational work and girls in commercial courses. Although considered of inferior status, by 1921 the technical high schools enrolled 18 percent of postprimary pupils. The limited enrollment in academic high schools, by 1920 13 percent of children in the age-group, opened entry into an expanded university system. With the important Education Act of 1914, the department took over from local boards the control of school inspectors as well as the power to appoint and dismiss teachers, crucial steps in centralizing administration. By 1920 the national school system closely resembled the highly centralized state systems in Australia.

"Traditional" education historians, as in Australia, portray these developments as steps in the gradual realization of educational opportunity. A recent book by Roy Shuker, *The One Best System?*, challenges this "Whig" interpretation and places schooling in the context of modernization and the "hegemony" of the middle class. He sees the period before World War I as critical in laying the foundations of a system that offered only the appearance of opportunity and actually perpetuated the power relations and social arrangements of New Zealand society. Shuker advances some telling criticisms of school reform but relies almost entirely on secondary sources and the ideas of revisionist historians abroad, especially in the United States.[100]

The most comprehensive study of socialization of children is Colin Mc-George's doctoral thesis, "Schools and Socialization in New Zealand, 1890–1914," written in 1985. He provides detailed chapters, replete with impressive evidence, on such topics as teachers as exemplars, school texts, the *School Journal*, the efforts to "tame the playground" and the children and to foster love of empire and a growing pride in New Zealand, instruction in middle-class morality, and the socialization of girls for their future roles as wives and mothers.[101]

Although McGeorge acknowledges that the impact of socialization on the children is difficult to determine, he sees varying results, citing, for example, the evidence of children's sexual precocity and vulgarity in inspectors' reports, and the amusingly ineffective attempts by teachers and administrators to rid children of their "colonial twang."[102] McGeorge echoes a number of Shuker's criticisms about school reform but asserts that explanations of reform as a reflection of the growth of democracy or as a movement toward more efficient social control simplify the picture. He argues that the schools were "contested grounds" not always at the service of middle-class respectability, and that policies were not always implemented effectively or, if they were, failed to achieve the desired results. Some of the examples he gives are the failure of religious groups to overturn the secular clause in the 1877 Education Act, the permissiveness toward attendance laws, especially in rural areas, of teachers and parents, and the inability of George Hogben to introduce more "practical" courses in academic high schools because of parents' resistance. McGeorge quotes the historian McKenzie's contention, in an article on "Ideology and the History of Education," that a "hubble and bubble" of interest groups rather than a single, clearly defined group acted to affect the schools. He goes on to argue that the continuing debate over education was not conducted along class lines. Even the most radical wing of organized labor, the "Red Federation," failed to develop a critique of the schools.[103]

McGeorge concludes that from a broad perspective, education reform must be seen as a general extension of childhood and as a "major factor in establishing a national identity." Moreover, he observes, it is easy to see the discipline and didacticism of the schools as middle-class control and forget that it was "adult control of children and supported by widely shared attitudes toward the young."[104]

Much work remains to be done on the history of childhood in Australia and New Zealand, and its historians must depend on future advances in related fields in social history. What emerges most clearly from existing studies on childhood is that there are definite turning points in attitudes and policies toward children in both countries at the end of the nineteenth century, a process similar in many ways to developments in other Western societies. Yet what sets Australia and New Zealand apart from Great Britain and the United States, for example, is that these changes occurred at a time of increasing urbanization, not as a result of industrialization. Although Australia and New Zealand differ in many ways— most notably in size, population, settlement policies, and the diversification of the economy and population in recent decades—the similarities and the common British heritage are striking. Scholarly interchange between the two countries can yield only fruitful results in the field of childhood history. Furthermore, there is a wealth of sources on children and childhood that awaits the scholars of Australia and New Zealand.

NOTES

I thank the American Philosophical Society and Santa Clara University for grants that aided my research in Australia and New Zealand, and Barbara Molony, Jo B. Margadant, and Steven Gelber of the history department at Santa Clara for helpful comments. In Australia I thank the librarians of the Public Library of New South Wales, especially those at the Mitchell Library, and the staffs of the Rare Book Room and Interlibrary Loan at the Fisher Library, University of Sydney. For valuable advice and help, I also am indebted to Jan Kociumbas of the department of history and especially to Kenneth Cable, former head of the department and an old friend from undergraduate days at the university. In New Zealand thanks are due to the wonderful librarians of the National Library, which includes the Alexander Turnbull Library, to Bill Gaynor and Brent South-gate of the department of education in Wellington, to Rollo Arnold, and especially to Jeanine Graham of the department of history, University of Waikato, Hamilton, for many kindnesses and useful advice. None of the scholars mentioned above is responsible for my conclusions.

1. Judith Keene, "Excavating the Sand Pit in Search of the History of Childhood," *Australian Historical Society Bulletin* 47 (1986):9–20; Jan Kociumbas, "Childhood History as Ideology," *Labour History* 47 (1984):1–19.

2. Keene, "Excavating the Sand Pit," p. 17, n. 2. See, for example, Philippe Ariès, *Centuries of Childhood: A Social History of Family Life* (New York: Alfred Knopf, 1962); Lawrence Stone, *The Family, Sex and Marriage in England, 1500–1800* (New York: Harper & Row, 1977); Erik H. Erikson, *Childhood and Society* (New York: W. W. Norton, 1950); Lloyd de Mause, ed., *The History of Childhood* (New York: Harper & Row, 1975). These are only samples of Keene's citations. In this essay I use "childhood" as a broad term embracing the stages from infancy to adolescence because the field has not yet developed to the point where historians examine specific stages of childhood in any detail.

3. Jan Kociumbas, "Children and Society in New South Wales and Victoria, 1860–1914" (Ph.D. thesis, University of Sydney, 1983); "The Management of Children: Medical Advice on Child Care in New South Wales and Victoria, 1860–1900," *Australia 1888* 9 (1982):14–19; " 'What Alyce Learnt at Nine': Sexuality and Sex Roles in Literature to 1914," *History of Education Review* 15 (1986):18–36.

4. See, for example, David Hunt, *Parents and Children in History: The Psychology of Family Life in Early Modern France* (New York: Basic Books, 1970); Peter Laslett and Richard Wall, eds., *Household and Family Life in Past Time* (Cambridge: Cambridge University Press, 1972); Christopher Lasch, *Haven in a Heartless World: The Family Besieged* (New York: Basic Books, 1977); Edward Shorter, *The Making of the Modern Family* (New York: Basic Books, 1975). Kociumbas is well read in the history of childhood, especially in European sources; the books listed above are only samples of her citations.

5. Kociumbas, "Childhood History," p. 7.

6. Ibid., pp. 11, 14.

7. A. Burns and J. Goodnow, *Children and Families in Australia: Contemporary Issues and Problems* (Sydney: Allen & Unwin, 1979); Patricia Grimshaw and Graham Willett, "Women's History and Family History," in *Australian Women: Feminist Perspectives*, ed. Norma Grieve and Patricia Grimshaw (Melbourne: Oxford University Press, 1981), ch. 12; Miriam Dixson, *The Real Matilda: Women and Identity in Australia, 1788–1975* (Ringwood, Vic.: Penguin Books, 1975); Ronald Conway, *The Great Australian Stupor: An Interpretation of the Australian Way of Life* (Melbourne: Sun Books, 1971). Kociumbas also briefly comments on *Damned Whores and God's Police: The Colonization of Women in Australia* (Ringwood, Vic.: Penguin Books, 1975), by Anne Summers, and Patricia Grimshaw's "Women and the Family in Australian History," in *Women, Class and History: Feminist Perspectives on Australia, 1788–1978*, ed. E. Windschuttle (Melbourne: Fontana, 1980). See Kociumbas, "Childhood History," pp. 7, 8, 10.

8. Kociumbas, "Childhood History," pp. 14, 16.

9. See Barbara Ehrenreich and John Ehrenreich, "The Professional-Managerial Class," *Radical America* 11 (1977):7–31; Michel Foucault, *The History of Sexuality*, vol. 1 (New York: Vintage, 1981); Jacques Donzelot, *The Policing of Families* (New York: Pantheon Books, 1979); Lasch, *Haven in a Heartless World*. Kociumbas, who

cites the Ehrenreichs and Lasch, acknowledges that Lasch identifies the role played by doctors, teachers, psychologists, and officers of the juvenile courts in the United States from 1900 to 1930 but argues that he offers no explanation for their motivations, and that her use of the concept of professionalism differs from his because Lasch denies that professionals constituted a class. See "Childhood History," pp. 8–9, 16 n. 51.

10. Kociumbas, "Childhood History," p. 17.

11. John Demos, "Developmental Perspectives on the History of Childhood," in *Growing Up in America: Historical Experiences*, ed. Harvey J. Graff (Detroit: Wayne State University Press, 1987), p. 84.

12. See, for example, N. Hicks, *This Sin and Scandal: Australia's Population Debate, 1891–1911* (Canberra: Australian National University Press, 1978); Kerreen Reiger, *The Disenchantment of the Home: Modernizing the Australian Family, 1880–1940* (Melbourne: Oxford University Press, 1985), especially pp. 62–63, 71–72, 171, 175, 182, 212–217; Kerry Wimshurst, "Child Labour and School Attendance in South Australia, 1890–1915," *Historical Studies* 19 (April 1981):388–411.

13. Kociumbas, "Childhood History," p. 14.

14. The colonies of Queensland, New South Wales, Victoria, Tasmania, South Australia, and Western Australia federated in 1901 into the Commonwealth of Australia. Tasmania (Van Diemen's Land), Victoria (Port Phillip), and Queensland (Moreton Bay) became autonomous colonies in 1825, 1850, and 1859, respectively. Western Australia and South Australia were settled in 1829; neither of these two colonies was founded as a penal settlement, although Western Australia accepted convicts between 1850 and 1868. General histories of Australia include C.M.H. Clark, *A History of Australia*, 6 vols. (Melbourne: Melbourne University Press, 1962–1987); F. K. Crowley, ed., *A New History of Australia* (Melbourne: William Heinemann, 1974). For early Commonwealth history see Stuart MacIntyre, *The Oxford History of Australia: 1901–1942, the Succeeding Age*, vol. 4 (Melbourne: Oxford University Press, 1986); this volume is the only one in the series published to date, and Gavin Souter, *Lions and Kangaroo: The Initiation of Australia, 1901–1919* (Sydney: Collins, 1976). Scholars have not carried the study of children beyond World War I except in a general way. Most studies that do so are sociological, examine contemporary problems, and lack historical perspective and research. One exception, which examines attitudes toward childhood after 1890 and carries the study into the interwar years, is Reiger's *Disenchantment of the Home*. Because of the lack of coherent studies, this review concentrates only on the years from British settlement to World War I.

15. Studies on ethnic or Aboriginal children are so few, and in the case of Aborigines so controversial, that no summary is attempted here. Ethnicity is particularly relevant for post–World War II Australia when considerable non-British European migration occurred, and the abolition of the "White Australia" policy in 1972 opened the doors for non-European migrants. Some studies on ethnicity are R. G. Brown, ed., *Children Australia* (Sydney: Allen & Unwin, 1980); Morag Loh, *With Courage in Their Cases* (Melbourne: F.I.L.E.F. Publications, 1980); Wendy Lowenstein and Morag Loh, *The Immigrants* (Melbourne: Hyland House, 1977). In the past few decades an impressive amount of revisionist work on Aboriginals has appeared. But Aboriginal history currently is a sensitive, controversial, and rapidly changing field. Research on women, family, and kinship has been conducted chiefly by white female anthropologists; a good collection on women is *Fighters and Singers: The Lives of Some Australian Aborigines* (Sydney: Allen & Unwin, 1985), edited by Isabel White, Diane Barwick, and Betty Meehan. Of

more direct interest is *Aboriginal Child Rearing in North Central Arnhem Land* (Canberra: Australian Institute of Aboriginal Studies, 1981), by Annette Hamilton. For reminiscences collected by anthropologists that include descriptions of childhood see Janet Mathews, ed., *The Two Worlds of Jimmie Barker: The Life of an Australian Aborigine, 1900–1972 (Canberra: Australian Institute of Aboriginal Studies, 1977);* J. B. Roberts, ed., *The Mapoon Story by the Mapoon People* (Melbourne: International Development Action, 1975). See also Margaret Tucker, *If Everyone Cared* (Sydney: Ure Smith, 1977), and the moving description of his childhood in James Miller's *Koori: A Will to Win* (Sydney: Sydney University Press, 1985). A fine thesis by Heather Goodall, "A History of Aboriginal Communities in New South Wales, 1909–1939" (Ph.D. thesis, University of Sydney, 1984), devotes a good deal of attention to the children. Goodall is especially good on the enforced separation of children from their families by governmental action.

16. Portia Robinson, *The Hatch and Brood of Time: A Study of the First Generation of Native-Born White Australians, 1788 to 1828*, vol. 1 (Melbourne: Oxford University Press, 1985); Michael J. Belcher, "The Child in New South Wales Society, 1820 to 1837" (Ph.D. thesis, University of New England, 1982).

17. Robinson's interpretation has been anticipated to some extent by Michael Sturma, *Vice in a Vicious Society: Crime and Convicts in Mid-Nineteenth Century New South Wales* (St. Lucia: University of Queensland Press, 1983); see also K. Macnab and R. Ward, "The Nature and Nurture of the First Generation of Native-born Australians," *Historical Studies* 10 (1962):298–308. Debate about the stability of society in the early years of the penal colony by no means is resolved. For a summary of Robinson's conclusions see *The Hatch and Brood of Time*, Introduction.

18. Belcher, "Child in New South Wales Society," pp. 167–172, 197, 203.

19. Belcher, "Child in New South Wales Society," pp. 13–14, 148, 300, 313. Approximately 38 percent of the population in 1833 were convicts. Transportation ended in 1840 and in eastern Australia as a whole by 1853.

20. See also Reiger, *Disenchantment of the Home*, p. 12, in which Reiger observes that "much of the new family history" has been "descriptive and uninformed by any clear theoretical framework."

21. Ibid., ch. 2, especially pp. 14–21; see also pp. 174–198, 304–305, quotation on p. 198. There are valuable deposits of family papers in the Mitchell Library (ML), Sydney, the National Library of Australia (NLA) in Canberra, and in the different state libraries and university archives. Particularly useful for the early colonial periods are the papers of the Bedford, Close, Duguid, Hassall (excellent), Marsden, McDougall, Stephen, and Suttor families (all in ML), and the Bate family (NLA). Useful published journals include C. E. Blomfield, ed., *Memoirs of the Blomfield Family* (Armidale, N.S.W.: n.p., n.d.); H. Morton, ed., *Annabella Boswell's Journal* (Sydney: Angus & Robertson, 1965); Peter Cowan, ed., *A Faithful Picture: The Letters of Eliza and Thomas Brown at York in the Swan River Colony, 1841–1852* (Fremantle, W.A.: Arts Centre Press, 1977). For New South Wales both Belcher and Robinson provide excellent bibliographies.

22. Patricia Grimshaw, Chris McConville, and Ellen McEwen, eds., *Families in Colonial Australia* (Sydney: Allen & Unwin, 1985), quotation from Introduction, p. xiii; see also Michael Anderson, *Approaches to the History of the Western Family* (London: MacMillan, 1980).

23. For McEwen's essay see Grimshaw, et al., *Families in Colonial Australia*, ch. 6.

24. Ibid., chs. 6, 9, 10, 14 for the essays by Anderson, Grimshaw and Fahey, Mitchell

and Sherington, and Davey, respectively. For other published works by, first, Anderson under the name of Margaret Grellier, see "The Family: Some Aspects of Its Demographic Ideology in Mid-Nineteenth Century Western Australia," in *A New History of Western Australia*, ed. C. T. Stannage (Nedlands: University of Western Australia Press, 1981), pp. 473–510; second, Grimshaw and Fahey's study in *Australia 1888* 9 (1982):88–125; third, versions of the Davey study in "Transitions: School and Work in the Family Economy," *Australia 1888* 10 (1982), and in P. Cook, I. Davey, and M. Vick, "Capitalism and Working-Class Schooling in Late Nineteenth Century South Australia," *Journal of the Australian and New Zealand History of Education Society* 8 (1979):36–48. For Mitchell's and Sherington's book see *Growing Up in the Illawarra: A Social History, 1834–1984* (Wollongong, N.S.W.: University of Wollongong Press, 1984). This book, unfortunately, is disappointing, and bears all the earmarks of a hastily produced work. Paperbound with many illustrations, the book provides more "background" than analysis of childhood and lacks a conceptual framework. Strictly chronological, it relies chiefly on "personal memories" for the twentieth century. Other works that focus on or include material on colonial families and children are Lindsay Benfell, "Juvenile Crime in Western Australia in 1888," *Australia 1888* 12 (1983):23–30; Cowan, ed., *Faithful Picture*; C. T. Stannage, *The People of Perth: A Social History of Western Australia's Capital City* (Perth: Perth City Council, 1979), pp. 73–101; E. McEwen, "Family, Kin and Neighbours: The Newcastle Coalmining District, 1860–1900," *Australia 1888* 4 (1980):68–86; J. Cole, "The Social Dynamics of Lifecourse Timing in Historical Perspective: Transitions in an Australian Rural Community, Boonah [Queensland], 1850–1978" (Ph.D. thesis, University of Queensland, 1981).

25. John Ramsland, *Children of the Back Lanes: Destitute and Neglected Children in Colonial New South Wales* (Kensington: University of New South Wales Press, 1986). Other studies of colonial child welfare in New South Wales include Brian Dickey, "The Establishment of Industrial Schools and Reformatories in New South Wales, 1850–1875," *Journal of the Royal Australian Historical Society* (henceforth *JRAHS*) 25 (1939):89–128, 169–213; N. Williamson, " 'Hymns, Songs and Blackguard Verses': Life in the Industrial and Reformatory School for Girls in New South Wales, 1869 to 1887," *JRAHS* 67 (1982):312–324, and " 'Laundry Maids or Ladies?: Life in the Industrial and Reformatory School for Girls in New South Wales, 1887–1910," *JRAHS* 68 (1983):375–387; S. Willis, " 'Made to Be Moral' at Parramatta Girls' School, 1898–1923," in *Twentieth Century Sydney: Studies in Urban and Social History*, ed. J. Roe (Sydney: Hale & Iremonger, 1980), pp. 178–192; Elizabeth Windschuttle, "Women and the Origins of Colonial Philanthropy," in *Australian Welfare History: Critical Essays*, ed. Richard Kennedy (Melbourne: MacMillan, 1982), pp. 10–31.

26. Ramsland, *Children of the Back Lanes*, quotations on pp. 3, 11, 58.

27. Ibid., quotation on p. 162.

28. John Ramsland, " 'A Place of Refuge from Dangerous Influences': Hobart Town Industrial School for Girls, 1862–1945," *JRAHS* 71 (1985):207–217; "The Development of Boarding-Out Systems in Australia: A Series of Welfare Experiments in Child Care, 1860–1910," *JRAHS* 60 (1974):186–198. The boarding-out system was instituted in Great Britain and on the continent in the middle of the nineteenth century; South Australia was the first colony to institute the system in 1872. Until the "professionalization" of foster care in the early twentieth century, "lady" visitors made inspections. It is clear that rural areas were favored for foster homes; the fear of the dangers of city life for children as well as the desire to rid the cities of seemingly idle children are mixed with compassion

in the writings of philanthropic women. For more on boarding-out see Catherine Helen Spence, *An Autobiography* (Adelaide: W. K. Thomas, 1910), and *State Children in Australia: A History of Boarding-Out and Its Developments* (Adelaide: Vardon & Sons, 1907); for a more critical assessment, see Brian Dickey, *No Charity There! A Short History of Social Welfare in Australia* (Melbourne: Thomas Nelson, 1980), ch. 4.

29. See, for example, A.J.C. Mayne's fine article, " 'The Question of the Poor' in the Nineteenth Century City," *Historical Studies* 20 (1983):557–573; Anne O'Brien, "The Poor in New South Wales, 1880–1918" (Ph.D. thesis, University of Sydney, 1983); J. Allen, "Octavius Beale Reconsidered: Infanticide, Baby-Farming and Abortion in New South Wales, 1880–1939," in *In Pursuit of Justice: Australian Women and the Law, 1788–1979*, ed. J. Mackinolty and H. Radi (Sydney: Hale & Iremonger, 1979). Most studies on poverty in Australia discuss only urban poverty.

30. Joan C. Brown, *'Poverty Is Not a Crime': The Development of Social Services in Tasmania, 1803–1900* (Hobart: Tasmanian Historical Research Association, 1973); Brian Dickey, with Elaine Martin and Rod Oxenbury, *Rations, Residences, Resources: A History of Social Welfare in South Australia Since 1836* (Adelaide: Wakefield Press, 1986); M. Barbalet, *Far from a Low Gutter Girl: The Forgotten World of State Wards, South Australia, 1887–1940* (Melbourne: Oxford University Press, 1983); Donella Jaggs, *Neglected and Criminal: Foundations of Child Welfare Legislation in Victoria* (Bundoora, Vic.: Phillip Institute of Technology, 1986). For the charity network in Victoria see Sheila Bignell, "Orphans and Destitute Children in Victoria Up to 1864," *Victorian Historical Magazine* 44 (1972):5–18; Graeme Davison, "The City-Bred Child and Urban Reform in Melbourne, 1900–1940," in *Social Process and the City*, ed. Peter Williams (Sydney: Allen & Unwin, 1983):143–174; Anthea Hyslop, "Christian Temperance and Social Reform: The Women's Christian Temperance Union of Victoria, 1887–1912," in *Women, Faith and Fêtes: Essays in the History of Women and the Church in Australia*, ed. Sabine Willis (Melbourne: Dove Press, 1977):43–62; Richard Kennedy, *Charity Warfare: The Charity Organization Society in Colonial Melbourne* (Melbourne: Hyland House, 1985); Shurlee Swain, "The Victorian Charity Networks in the 1890s" (Ph.D. thesis, University of Melbourne, 1977) and "Destitute and Dependent: Case Studies in Poverty in Melbourne, 1890–1900," *Historical Studies* 19 (1980):98–107; Deborah Tyler, "The Case of Irene Tuckerman: Understanding Sexual Violence and the Protection of Women and Girls, Victoria, 1890–1925," *History of Education Review* 15 (1986):52–67. For Sydney see J. Godden, "Philanthropy and the Women's Sphere: Sydney, 1870-circa 1900" (Ph.D. thesis, Macquarie University, 1983). For the Protestant churches in the late nineteenth century, whose clergy frequently were more socially concerned than the congregations, see J. D. Bollen, *Protestantism and Social Reform in New South Wales, 1890–1910* (Melbourne: University of Melbourne Press, 1972); R. Broome, *Treasure in Earthen Vessels: Protestant Christianity in New South Wales Society, 1900–1914* (St. Lucia: University of Queensland Press, 1980). See also H. R. Jackson, *Churches and People in Australia and New Zealand, 1860–1930* (Wellington: Allen & Unwin, 1987).

31. Brian Dickey's *No Charity There!* is a general survey that includes sections on child welfare except for the later decades of the twentieth century; predictably the largest section deals with the period from 1890 to World War I. Books on general social welfare that treat child welfare briefly include Francis G. Castles, *The Working Class and Welfare: Reflections on the Political Development of the Welfare State in Australia and New Zealand, 1890–1980* (Sydney: Allen & Unwin, 1985); Jill Roe, ed., *Social Policy in Australia: Some Perspectives* (Stanmore, N.S.W.: Cassell, 1976). See also Sydney Labour

History Group, eds., *What Rough Beast? The State and Social Order in Australian History* (Sydney: Allen & Unwin, 1982).

32. See n. 3 above.

33. Kociumbas, "Management of Children," especially pp. 17, 18. This article is weakened by its focus on the late nineteenth century, when the role of physicians as new experts on child rearing was less significant than in the early twentieth century.

34. Kociumbas, " 'What Alyce Learnt at Nine,' " pp. 18, 19. The quotation in the title comes from *What Alyce Learnt at Nine*, one of a number of circumspect tracts in the "Mother's Perplexity Series" telling young girls the facts of life, all by Ina L. Austen. Kociumbas' essay includes discussion of Sunday school hymns, school texts, and popular novels and for the popular literature is superior in analysis to a well-known older work by H. M. Saxby, *A History of Australian Children's Literature, 1841–1941* (Sydney: Wentworth Books, 1969).

35. Reiger, *Disenchantment of the Home*. The book is a revision of Reiger's Ph.D. thesis "The Disenchantment of the Home: The Rationalization of Domestic Life in Victoria, 1880–1940" (La Trobe University, 1982). See also Reiger's "Women's Labour Redefined: Child Bearing and Rearing Advice in Australia, 1880–1930," in *Worth Her Salt: Women at Work in Australia*, ed. M. Bevege, M. James, and C. Shute (Sydney: Hale & Iremonger, 1982). Reiger does not cite Kociumbas' 1983 thesis in her bibliography or the article Kociumbas published in 1982; Kociumbas includes only Reiger's article "Women's Labour Redefined" (1982) in the bibliography of her thesis. The failure of these two scholars to read each other's thesis is extraordinary, given the paucity of material on Australian childhood and the similarities between the two scholars' approaches.

36. Reiger, *Disenchantment of the Home*, Introduction, especially pp. 2, 3.

37. Ibid., pp. 16–20, 167, and especially p. 211, where Reiger notes the "antifeminism" of Donzelot and Lasch (unshared by the Ehrenreichs) and writes that in none of these accounts, including the Ehrenreichs', "do women play an active role." Reiger's examination of the active role played by women in the modernization of the family questions the polemical thrust of much of women's history in Australia, where themes of women's oppression and victimization still dominate the literature. Another book that explores the role of experts (this time the psychiatric profession) in defining "femininity" unequivocally sees women as victims of a conscious conspiracy; see *Good and Mad Women: The Historical Construction of Femininity in Twentieth-Century Australia* (Sydney: Allen & Unwin, 1984), by Jill Julius Matthews.

38. Reiger, *Disenchantment of the Home*, chs. 7, 10; quotations on pp. 20, 34, 215. In chs. 2 and 7 Reiger provides interesting descriptions of middle- and upper-class family life, contrasting nineteenth-century methods of child rearing with those advocated by the new experts. She provides a good bibliography of sources on childhood and child rearing, as does Jan Kociumbas in the bibliography to her thesis, "Children and Society in New South Wales and Victoria." Among useful sources on family life, child rearing, and the ideology of the home, chiefly among middle- and upper-class families, see David Adams, ed., *The Letters of Rachel Henning* (Ringwood, Vic.: Penguin Books, 1969); Dymphna Cusack and Norman Freehill, *Dymphna Cusack* (Melbourne: Thomas Nelson, 1975); Mary Edgeworth David, *Passages of Time: An Australian Woman, 1890–1974* (St. Lucia: University of Queensland Press, 1975); Graeme Davison, *The Rise and Fall of Marvellous Melbourne* (Melbourne: Melbourne University Press, 1979); Miles Franklin, *Childhood at Brindabella: My First Ten Years* (Sydney: Angus & Robertson, 1963); Donald Horne, *The Education of Donald* (Sydney: Angus & Robertson, 1967); B. Kingston, *My Wife,*

My Daughter and Poor Mary Ann (Melbourne: Nelson, 1975); Brian Lewis, *Sunday at Kooyong Road* (Melbourne: Hutchison, 1976); Hal Porter, *The Watcher on the Cast Iron Balcony: An Australian Autobiography* (London: Faber & Faber, 1963); and Bernard Smith, *The Boy Adeodatus* (Ringwood, Vic.: Allen Lane, 1984). Mary Edgeworth David's autobiography is especially interesting because she was raised in a "progressive" household. Useful ms. collections include the A. Deakin Papers (NLA); the V. Scantlebury Brown Papers, Melbourne University; and Memoirs of Eliza Chomley, State Library of Victoria. Two collections of oral histories, Jacqueline Kent's *In the Half-Light: Life as a Child, 1900–1970* (Sydney: Angus & Robertson, 1988) and Wendy Lowenstein's *Weevils in the Flour: An Oral Record of the 1930s Depression in Australia* (Melbourne: Hyland House, 1978) contain vivid recollections of childhood. These books are marred by a failure to explain their methodologies or to offer interpretations of the material.

39. Reiger, *Disenchantment of the Home*, Part II ("Socialization") and Part III ("Sexuality"); quotations on pp. 168, 169. Reiger's failure to examine rural families narrows her scope. It is likely that traditional ways in the family remained tenacious outside the cities.

40. Stephen Garton, "Sir Charles Mackellar: Psychiatry, Eugenics and Child Welfare in New South Wales, 1900–1914," *Historical Studies* 22 (1986):21–34. See also C. Bacchi, "The Nature-Nurture Debate in Australia, 1900–1914," *Historical Studies* 19 (1980):199–212; M. Roe, *Nine Australian Progressives: Vitalism in Bourgeois Social Thought, 1890–1960* (St. Lucia: University of Queensland Press, 1984); Mary Caute, "Craniometry and Eugenics in Australia: R.J.A. Berry and the Quest for Social Efficiency," *Historical Studies* 22 (1986):35–53.

41. Brian Gandevia, *Tears Often Shed: Child Health and Welfare in Australia from 1788* (Sydney: Pergamon Press, 1978); M. Lewis, " 'Populate or Perish': Aspects of Infant and Maternal Health in Sydney, 1870–1939" (Ph.D. thesis, Australian National University, 1976); Philippa Mein Smith, "Truby King in Australia: A Revisionist View of Reduced Infant Mortality," *New Zealand Journal of History* 22 (1988):23–43; Peter Spearritt, "The Kindergarten Movement: Tradition and Change" in *Social Change in Australia: Readings in Sociology*, ed. Donald E. Edgar (Melbourne: Cheshire Publishing, 1974), pp. 583–596.

42. G. R. Searle, *The Quest for National Efficiency* (London: Oxford University Press, 1971); Andrew Abbott, *The System of Professions: An Essay on the Division of Expert Labor* (Chicago: University of Chicago Press, 1988); Thomas L. Haskell, *The Authority of Experts: Studies in History and Theory* (Bloomington: University of Indiana Press, 1984).

43. The best standard history of education is *A History of Australian Education* (Melbourne: Oxford University Press, 1980), by Alan Barcan; see also his *A Short History of Education in New South Wales* (Sydney: Martingale Press, 1965). For colonial education see A. G. Austin, *Australian Education, 1788–1900; Church, State and Public Education in Colonial Australia* (Melbourne: Pitman, 1961); John Cleverly, *The First Generation School and Society in Early New South Wales* (Sydney: Sydney University Press, 1971); J. S. Gregory, "Church and State Education in Victoria to 1872," in *Melbourne Studies in Education*, ed. E. L. French (Melbourne: Melbourne University Press, 1960), pp. 3–88. For books that question the "Whig" interpretation and see the Victorian Education Act of 1872 as a means of establishing social control over working-class families, see B. Bessant, *Schooling in the Colony and State of Victoria* (Melbourne: La Trobe University Press, 1972); Denis Grundy, *"Secular, Compulsory and Free": The Education Act of*

1872 (Melbourne: Melbourne University Press, 1972). For a recent critique of the neo-Marxist approach see G. Dow, "Family History and Educational History: Towards an Integration," *Historical Studies* 21 (1985):421–431, especially pp. 429–431. For a history of Catholic education see R. Fogarty, *Catholic Education in Australia, 1806–1950*, 2 vols. (Melbourne: Melbourne University Press, 1959); see also Patrick O'Farrell, *The Catholic Church and Community in Australia* (Melbourne: Thomas Nelson, 1977). A point worth noting is that, unlike in Western societies, school systems in Australia were established after urbanization rather than industrialization.

44. For the quotation on Peter Board see S. G. Firth, "Social Values in the New South Wales Primary School, 1880–1914: An Analysis of School Texts," in *Melbourne Studies in Education*, ed. R.J.W. Selleck (Melbourne: Melbourne University Press, 1971), p. 125. For school reform in this era see MacIntyre, *Oxford History of Australia*, vol. 4, pp. 108–109.

45. Firth, "Social Values in the New South Wales Primary School," especially pp. 128–134. For evidence that children had their own subculture characterized by vulgarity, mocking of parental values, sexual precociousness, and frank bigotry, see Wendy Lowenstein, *Shocking, Shocking, Shocking: The Improper Play Rhymes of Australian Children* (Prahran, Vic.: Fish & Chip Press, 1974).

46. Firth, "Social Values in the New South Wales Primary School," especially pp. 158–159.

47. Edmund Campion, *Australian Catholics: The Contribution of Catholics to the Development of Australian Society* (Ringwood, Vic.: Penguin Books, 1987). Campion's analysis of Catholic education is the strongest section in a book that, on the whole, downplays sectarian and doctrinal strife.

48. Ibid., quotations on pp. 67, 156.

49. Campion, *Australian Catholics*, pp. 106–109; Beverly Kingston, "The Lady and the Australian Girl: Some Thoughts on Nationalism and Class," in *Australian Women: New Feminist Perspectives*, ed. Norma Grieve and Ailsa Burns (Melbourne: Oxford University Press, 1986), ch. 2; Noeline Kyle, *Her Natural Destiny: The Education of Women in New South Wales* (Kensington: University of New South Wales Press, 1986); Jan Kociumbas, " 'What Alyce Learnt at Nine'," pp. 22–30.

50. For Turner and Bruce see Ethel Turner, *Seven Little Australians* (London: Ward, Locke, 1894), the most famous of her many novels, and Mary Grant Bruce, *A Little Bush Maid* (London: Ward, Locke, 1910), one of the "Billabong" series.

51. Alison Mackinnon, *One Foot on the Ladder: Origins and Outcomes of Girls' Secondary Schooling in South Australia* (St. Lucia: University of Queensland Press, 1984); Ailsa C. Thomson Zainu'ddin, *They Dreamt of a School: A Centenary History of Methodist Ladies' College, Kew, 1882–1982* (Melbourne: Hyland House, 1982). See also Marjorie Theobald, " 'Mere Accomplishments'? Melbourne's Early Ladies' Colleges Reconsidered," *History of Education Review* 13 (1984):15–29; Alison Mackinnon, "Educating the Mothers of a Nation: The Advanced School for Girls, Adelaide," in *Worth Her Salt*, ed. Bevege, James, and Shute, pp. 62–71. In *Her Natural Destiny* Kyle reaches the same conclusions as Zainu'ddin in her analysis of private schooling for girls in New South Wales between 1788 and 1920.

52. See C.E.W. Bean, *Here, My Son: An Account of the Independent and Other Corporate Boys' Schools of Australia* (Sydney: Angus & Robertson, 1950); Geoffrey Sherington, *Shore: A History of Sydney Church of England Grammar School* (Sydney: Sydney Church of England Grammar School/Allen & Unwin, 1975).

53. James McLachlan, *American Boarding Schools: A Historical Study* (New York: Charles Scribner's Sons, 1970).

54. Michael Katz is quoted regularly in studies by the Adelaide group; one of the group, Ian Davey, has collaborated with Katz in comparative educational studies. In his research in Canada, Katz has modified the approach advanced in his first book, *The Irony of Early School Reform: Educational Innovation in Mid-Nineteenth Century Massachusetts* (Cambridge, Mass.: Harvard University Press, 1968), in which he set out to demolish the "myths" of popular education in America and saw the emergence of school reform purely as the imposition of middle-class social control over a reluctant community.

55. First quotation from Ian Davey, "Growing Up in a Working Class Community," in *Families in Colonial Australia*, ed. by Patricia Grimshaw, Chris McConville, and Ellen McEwen (Sydney: Allen & Unwin, 1985), p. 171; second quotation from Wimshurst, "Child Labour and School Attendance," p. 390.

56. For some studies by the Adelaide group see Davey, "Growing Up in a Working Class Community"; Wimshurst, "Child Labour and School Attendance"; Cook, Davey, and Vick, "Capitalism and Working-Class Schooling"; D. Grundy, "Free Schooling and the State in South Australia, 1875–1898," in *Melbourne Studies in Education*, ed. I. Palmer (Melbourne: Melbourne University Press, 1983); quotation from Wimshurst, "Child Labour and School Attendance," p. 389.

57. For quotations from Wimshurst see "Child Labour and School Attendance," pp. 389, 403.

58. See Ann Larson, "Who Wants to Go to School? The Effects of Free and Compulsory Education in Mid-Nineteenth Century Victoria," *History of Education Quarterly* 15 (1986):1–2.

59. Ibid., pp. 1–15, quotations p. 15.

60. Quotation from Wimshurst, "Child Labour and School Attendance," p. 411; quotations from Davey, "Growing Up in a Working Class Community," p. 172.

61. Wimshurst, "Child Labour and School Attendance," p. 411.

62. See, for example, John Shaw Neilson, *Autobiography* (Melbourne: National Library of Australia, 1978); Henry Lawson, "Early Days," in *Stories and Poems of Henry Lawson*, ed. Marjorie Pizer (Melbourne: Australian Book Society, 1957); Jacqueline Kent, *In the Half-Light*, ch. 2; D. J. McDonald, "Child and Female Labour in Sydney, 1876–1898," *Australian National University Historical Journal* nos. 10, 11 (1973–1974):40–49. Accounts of schooling after World War II, including the massive expansion of state schooling and the emergence of a multicultural society, are found only in general histories of education such as Barcan, *History of Education in Australia*, and in scattered articles in anthologies such as *Melbourne Studies in Education*. These accounts are primarily concerned with administrative and curricular change.

63. As with Australian Aboriginal history, Maori history has become increasingly sensitive and controversial, with Maoris regarding their history, written almost exclusively by whites, as yet another *pakeha* (white) perspective on the Maori experience. There is a large historiography on Maoris but fewer studies, chiefly by anthropologists, psychologists, and education historians, on Maori children. Because of the sensitivity of the issue, this review discusses only studies of European children. The chapters on Maoris in W. H. Oliver with B. H. Williams, eds., *The Oxford History of New Zealand* (Wellington: A. H. & A. W. Reed, 1976), provide extensive bibliographies. On Maori schooling see J. M. Barrington and T. H. Beaglehole, *Maori Schools in a Changing Society: An Historical Review* (Wellington: New Zealand Council for Educational Research, 1974).

Two autobiographies by Maoris that give poignant accounts of their childhoods are *Tangi*, by Witi Ihimaera (Auckland: William Heinemann, 1973), and *Amiria: The Life Story of a Maori Woman* (Wellington: A. H. & A. W. Reed, 1976), by Amiria Manutahi Stirling and Anne Salmond. There is little information on children of small clusters of German, Scandinavian, Yugoslav, Asian, and Pacific Island migrants; many of these children's experiences were similar to those of rural children. For some recollections of childhood see A. Batistich, *The Olive and the Vine* (Wellington: Department of Education, 1962); C. G. Petersen, *Forest Homes* (Wellington: A. H. & A. W. Reed, 1956); A Trlin, *Now Respected, Once Despised: Yugoslavs in New Zealand* (Palmerston North, N.Z.: Dunmore Press, 1979).

64. Useful histories are Oliver, ed., *Oxford History of New Zealand*; Keith Sinclair, *A History of New Zealand* (Auckland: Penguin Books, rev. ed., 1988). See also D. Ian Pool, *The Maori Population of New Zealand, 1769–1971* (Auckland: Auckland University Press/Oxford University Press, 1977).

65. Stewart Houston, ed., *Marriage and the Family in New Zealand* (Wellington: Sweet & Maxwell, 1970); Peggy G. Koopman-Boyden, ed., *Families in New Zealand Society* (Wellington: Methuen Press, 1978).

66. Erik Olssen and Andrée Lévesque, "Towards a History of the European Family in New Zealand," in Koopmann-Boyden, ed., *Families in New Zealand Society*, pp. 1–25; quotations on pp. 1, 20. Olssen and Lévesque cite the work of family historians Christopher Lasch, Tamara Hareven, and Edward Shorter (U.S.) and Peter Laslett (U.K.).

67. Dugald J. McDonald, "Children and Young Persons in New Zealand Society," in Koopman-Boyden, ed., *Families in New Zealand Society*, pp. 44–56; quotations on p. 45.

68. Rollo Arnold, "The Country Child in Late Victorian New Zealand," in *Australasian Victorian Studies Association: Conference Papers*, ed. Helen Debenham and Warren Slinn (Christchurch: University of Canterbury Press, 1983); Stevan Eldred-Grigg, *A Southern Gentry: New Zealanders Who Inherited the Earth* (Wellington: A. H. & A. W. Reed, 1980); Jeanine Graham, "Settler Society," in Oliver, ed., *Oxford History of New Zealand*, ch. 4, and "Child Employment in Colonial New Zealand," *New Zealand Journal of History* 21 (1987):62–78; P. J. Whelan, "The Care of Destitute, Neglected and Criminal Children in New Zealand, 1840–1900" (M.A. thesis, Victoria University, 1956); A. E. Campbell, *Educating New Zealand* (Wellington: Department of Internal Affairs, 1941); Ian Cumming and Alan Cumming, *A History of State Education in New Zealand, 1840–1975* (Wellington: Pitman, 1978); J. E. Dakin, *Education in New Zealand* (Newton Abbott, Engl.: David & Charles, 1973); J. David S. McKenzie, *Education and Social Structure: Essays in the History of New Zealand Education* (Dunedin: New Zealand College of Education, 1982).

69. Quotations in Graham, "Settler Society," p. 134, and Claire Toynbee, "Class and Social Structure in Nineteenth Century New Zealand," *New Zealand Journal of History* 13 (1979):66. Graham provides an excellent bibliography of nineteenth-century sources from the Auckland Museum, the Auckland Public Library, and the Taranaki Museum. The Alexander Turnbull Library in the National Library of New Zealand in Wellington is a treasure trove of manuscript collections, as is the Hocken Library, University of Otago, Dunedin. The N.Z. Genealogical Society also has records of many families, as do other university and city archives.

70. Eldred-Grigg, *Southern Gentry*, pp. 9, 20, 68, 78, 83–85, 122, 157–158. See also Lady Mary Anne Barker, *Station Life in New Zealand* (London: MacMillan, 1870)

and *Station Amusements in New Zealand* (London: William Hunt, 1873); G. H. Schole-field, ed., *The Richmond-Atkinson Papers*, 2 vols. (Wellington: Government Printer, 1960). Sir James Elliott's *Firth of Wellington* (Auckland: Whitcombe & Tombe, 1937) is the biography of a celebrated headmaster of a boys' preparatory school.

71. Arnold, "Country Child."

72. The six initial provinces were Auckland, New Plymouth (later Taranaki), and Wellington in the North Island and Nelson, Canterbury, and Otago in the South Island. Later the creation of other provinces, Hawke's Bay in the north and Westland and Marlborough in the south, brought the total to nine; Southland broke away but later rejoined Otago province.

73. McKenzie, *Education and Social Structure*, pp. 1–2. The province of Nelson in 1858 abolished fees and levied an annual householders' tax. Much work needs to be done on religion; most publications are histories of individual denominations, many published by the churches. The most recent book, *Churches and People in Australia and New Zealand*, by Hugh Jackson, despite its title and useful material on church attendance and Catholic and Protestant relations, is heavily weighted toward Australia and does not discuss the churches' roles in education or welfare, and is actually a history of institutions.

74. Sinclair, *History of New Zealand*, p. 103.

75. For the series of legislative acts passed in the 1870s, see Graham, "Child Employment," pp. 62–63.

76. Sinclair, *History of New Zealand*, p. 103.

77. Whelan, "Care of Destitute, Neglected and Criminal Children," pp. 24–29.

78. Ibid., pp. 68, 103–108, 141–142.

79. Ibid., pp. 26–29. Whelan's thesis is quoted regularly, but it is a descriptive rather than an analytical study, and welfare in this period needs reexamination.

80. Erik Olssen, "Towards a New Society," in Oliver, ed., *Oxford History of New Zealand*, ch. 10; see also Tom Brooking, "Economic Transformation," in Oliver, ed., *Oxford History of New Zealand*, ch. 9. Quotations from Sinclair, *History of New Zealand*, p. 187.

81. Olssen, "Towards a New Society," pp. 258, 260.

82. McDonald, "Children and Young Persons," p. 47.

83. Graham, "Child Employment," p. 69. Graham notes that the laws reflected a lack of uniformity about when a child became an adult, but that twelve was the most commonly adopted age of demarcation. By 1900 fourteen years was more accepted. A Royal Commission of 1900 on relations between employers and employed, commonly known as the Sweating Commission, contains information on employment and conditions of work for children; see *Appendices to the Journals of the House of Representatives*, 1890, H–5. For parental attitudes see also McKenzie, *Education and Social Structure*, pp. 26–27.

84. Graham, "Child Employment," pp. 74–75.

85. Phillida Bunkle, "The Origins of the Women's Movement in New Zealand: The Women's Christian Temperance Union, 1885–1895," in *Women in New Zealand Society*, ed. Phillida Bunkle and Beryl Hughes (Auckland: Allen & Unwin, 1980), pp. 52–76, quotations on pp. 52, 73; Raewyn Dalziel, "The Colonial Helpmeet: Women's Role and the Vote in Nineteenth Century New Zealand," *New Zealand Journal of History* 11 (1977):112–123. For a contrasting view of women's attitudes toward equality see Patricia Grimshaw, *Women's Suffrage in New Zealand* (Auckland: Auckland University Press/ Oxford University Press, 1972). See also Erik Olssen, "Women, Work and Family:

1880–1926," in Bunkle and Hughes, eds., *Women in New Zealand Society*, pp. 159–183. Much work is needed on New Zealand women and their organizations. For a second collection of essays on women see Barbara Brookes, Charlotte Macdonald, and Margaret Tennant, eds., *Women in History: Essays on European Women in New Zealand* (Wellington: Allen & Unwin, 1986). See also Jan Beagle, "Children of the State: A Study of the New Zealand Industrial Schools, 1880–1925" (M.A. thesis, University of Auckland, 1974), pp. 157–159, for women's criticisms of the industrial schools. Papers of the WCTU are in the Alexander Turnbull Library, National Library of New Zealand, Wellington.

86. Phyllis Levitt, "Public Concern for Young Children: A Socio-Historical Study of Reform, Dunedin 1879–1889" (Ph.D. thesis, University of Otago, 1979), pp. 49, 78, 132; Olssen and Lévesque, "Towards a History of the European Family," pp. 6–11.

87. Bunkle, "Origins of the Women's Movement," pp. 61–63, 73; Levitt, Public Concern," p. 78.

88. Penelope Ann Gregory, "Saving the Children of New Zealand: A Study of Social Attitude Towards Larrikinism in the late Nineteenth Century" (research essay, Massey University, 1975). This essay, an undergraduate honors paper, is remarkably sophisticated in its analysis and well researched.

89. Ibid., quotations on pp. 2, 7, 66. See also Stevan Eldred-Grigg, *Pleasures of the Flesh: Sex and Drugs in Colonial New Zealand, 1840–1915* (Wellington: A. H. & A. W. Reed, 1984).

90. Margaret Tennant, "Indigence and Charitable Aid in New Zealand, 1885–1920" (Ph.D. thesis, Massey University, 1981); "Duncan McGregor and Charitable Aid Administration, 1886–1896," *New Zealand Journal of History* 13 (1979):33–40; "Mrs. Grace Neill in the Departments of Asylums, Hospitals and Charitable Institutions," *New Zealand Journal of History* 12 (1978):3–16. See also a suggestive article by W. H. Oliver, "Social Welfare: Social Justice or Social Efficiency?" *New Zealand Journal of History* 13 (1979):25–33, in which Oliver asserts that the interest in children was motivated as much by ideas of discipline, control, and order as by humanitarian concern.

91. Beagle, "Children of the State," pp. 92, 119. See also Levitt, "Public Concern," p. 51. For a harsh indictment of the life of a state ward see John A. Lee, *Children of the Poor* (London: Werner, Laurie, 1934).

92. Beagle, "Children of the State," p. 246. See also Olssen, "Towards a New Society," pp. 260–262. There is no scholarly study of foster care. A "Centennial Report" of the New Zealand Foster Care Federation, 1983, in the National Library in Wellington, provides some historical background and recollections of former foster children, many of whom had unhappy memories.

93. Beagle, "Children of the State," p. 246.

94. Tennant, "Indigence and Charitable Aid," ch. 1 and p. 400.

95. Graham, "Child Employment," p. 77.

96. Arnold, "Country Child," pp. 3, 13. See also Jeanine Graham, "Country Children," paper presented before the Conference of the New Zealand Society of Genealogists, March 1988.

97. Olssen, "Towards a New Society," pp. 257–259; "Truby King and the Plunket Society: An Analysis of a Prescriptive Ideology," *New Zealand Journal of History* 15 (1981):3–23.

98. Olssen, "Truby King and the Plunket Society," pp. 4, 7, 20–21. On the Plunket Society see also Philippa Mein Smith, *Maternity in Dispute: New Zealand, 1920–1939* (Wellington: Department of Internal Affairs, 1986); Jock Phillips, *A Man's Country? The Image of the Pakeha Male, a History* (Auckland: Penguin Books, 1987), pp. 223–224. For the spread of Plunket Society ideas to the country see H.C.D. Somerset, *Littledene: A New Zealand Rural Community* (Auckland: Whitcombe & Tombe, 1938), pp. 70–71, and for memories of the pervasiveness of the ideology see Hector Bolitho, *My Restless Years* (London: Max Parrish, 1962).

99. Margaret Tennant, "Natural Directions: The New Zealand Movement for Sexual Differentiations in Education During the Early Twentieth Century," *New Zealand Journal of Educational Studies* 12 (1977):150–152, quotation on p. 152. Although Truby King gained fame (and a knighthood) for his work with infants, he spoke out on a wide range of matters concerning women. Tennant writes (pp. 148, 150) that King's and other male doctors' views did not go unchallenged by female physicians and women's groups. These women fought for advanced education and the right to enter professional life, but they also agreed that woman's primary role was that of wife and mother. For one woman's resentment about her schooldays see T. Rhoda Barr, *Within Sound of the Bell* (Christchurch: Whitcombe & Tombs, 1953), especially pp. 7, 42.

100. Roy Shuker, *The One Best System? A Revisionist History of State Schooling in New Zealand* (Palmerston North, N.Z.: Dunmore Press, 1987). For contemporaries who clearly saw that the future paths of children separated after standard six in the primary schools, when most left school and others secured entry into higher standards, see Jean Boswell, *Dim Horizons* (Christchurch: Whitcome & Tombs, 1955), p. 105, and H. P. Kitson, *A Nelson Boyhood* (Wellington: Department of Education, 1969), pp. 16–17.

101. Colin McGeorge, "Schools and Socialization in New Zealand, 1890–1914" (Ph.D. thesis, University of Canterbury, 1985), especially chs. 4, 7, 9, 11, 16, 19, 20, 22. For the "taming of the playground" see also Brian Sutton-Smith, *A History of Children's Play in New Zealand* (Wellington: New Zealand Council for Education Resedarch, 1981), and *A History of Children's Play: The New Zealand Playground, 1840–1950* (Philadelphia: University of Pennsylvania Press, 1981). For the *School Journal* see also E. P. Malone, "The New Zealand School Journal and the Imperial Ideology," *New Zealand Journal of History* 7 (1973):12–27. The department of education's library in Wellington has back issues of the *School Journal*. McGeorge's thesis, although very long and somewhat discursive, is essential reading for the schools in the Edwardian period, and it contains an excellent bibliography. The Dorothy Neal White Room at the National Library of New Zealand has a large collection of school textbooks dating back to the nineteenth century as well as children's books and annuals. For children's literature see Betty Gilderdale, *A Sea Change: 145 Years of New Zealand Junior Fiction* (Auckland: Longman Paul, 1982).

102. McGeorge, "Schools and Socialization," pp. 165, 527–534. See also F. Bennett, *A Canterbury Tale: The Autobiography of Dr. Francis Bennett* (Wellington: Oxford University Press, 1980), p. 42; Elizabeth Gordon and Tony Deverson, *New Zealand English* (Auckland: William Heinemann, 1985).

103. McGeorge, "Schools and Socialization," chs. 3, 14 and pp. 740–744. See also J. David S. McKenzie, "Ideology and the History of Education," *New Zealand Journal of Education History* 19 (1984):2–9.

104. McGeorge, "Schools and Socialization," p. 750.

REFERENCES

Adams, David, ed. *The Letters of Rachel Henning*. Ringwood, Vic.: Penguin Books, 1969.

Alford, Katrina. *Production or Reproduction? An Economic History of Women in Australia, 1788–1850*. Melbourne: Oxford University Press, 1984.

Allen, J. "Octavius Beale Reconsidered: Infanticide, Baby-Farming and Abortion in New South Wales, 1880–1929." In *Pursuit of Justice: Australian Women and the Law, 1788–1979*, edited by J. Mackinolty and H. Radi. Sydney: Hale & Iremonger, 1979.

Anderson, Margaret [Grellier]. "Marriage and Children in Western Australia, 1842–1849." In *Families in Colonial Australia*, edited by Patricia Grimshaw, Chris McConville, and Ellen McEwen. Sydney: Allen & Unwin, 1985.

Appendices to the Journals of the House of Representatives, New Zealand. H–5, 1890.

Arnold, Rollo. "The Country Child in Late Victorian New Zealand." In *Australasian Victorian Studies Association: Conference Papers*, edited by Helen Debenham and Warren Slinn. Christchurch: University of Canterbury Press, 1983.

Austin, A. G. *Australian Education, 1788–1900: Church, State and Public Education in Colonial Australia*. Melbourne: Pitman, 1961.

Bacchi, C. "The Nature-Nurture Debate in Australia, 1900–1914." *Historical Studies* 19 (1980):199–212.

Barbalet, M. *Far from a Low Gutter Girl: The Forgotten World of State Wards, South Australia, 1887–1940*. Melbourne: Oxford University Press, 1983.

Barcan, Alan. *A History of Australian Education*. Melbourne: Oxford University Press, 1980.

———. *A Short History of Education in New South Wales*. Sydney: Martingale Press, 1965.

Barker, Lady Mary Anne. *Station Life in New Zealand*. London: MacMillan, 1870.

———. *Station Amusements in New Zealand*. London: William Hunt, 1873.

Barr, T. Rhoda. *Within Sound of the Bell*. Christchurch: Whitcombe & Tombs, 1953.

Barrington, J. M., and T. H. Beaglehole. *Maori Schools in a Changing Society: An Historical Review*. Wellington: New Zealand Council for Educational Research, 1974.

A. Bastistich. *The Olive and the Vine*. Wellington: Department of Education, 1962.

Beagle, Jan. "Children of the State: A Study of the New Zealand Industrial School System, 1880–1925." M.A. thesis, University of Auckland, 1974.

Bean, C.E.W. *Here, My Son: An Account of the Independent and Other Corporate Boys' Schools of Australia*. Sydney: Angus & Robertson, 1950.

Bedford Family. Papers. Mitchell Library, Sydney.

Belcher, Michael. "The Child in New South Wales Society, 1820 to 1837." Ph.D. thesis, University of New England, 1982.

Benfell, Lindsay. "Juvenile Crime in Western Australia in 1888." *Australia 1888* 12 (1983):23–30.

Bennett, F. *A Canterbury Tale: The Autobiography of Dr. Francis Bennett*. Wellington: Oxford University Press, 1980.

Bessant, B. *Schooling in the Colony and State of Victoria*. Melbourne: La Trobe University Press, 1972.

Bignell, Sheila. "Orphans and Destitute Children in Victoria Up to 1864." *Victorian Historical Magazine* 44 (1972):5–18.

Blomfield, C. E., ed. *Memoirs of the Blomfield Family*. Armidale, N.S.W.: n.p., n.d.

Bollen, J. D. *Protestatnism and Social Reform in New South Wales, 1890–1910*. Melbourne: University of Melbourne Press, 1972.

Bolitho, Hector. *My Restless Years*. London: Max Parrish, 1962.

Boswell, Jean. *Dim Horizons*. Christchurch: Whitcombe & Tombs, 1955.

Brooking, Tom. "Economic Transformation." In *Oxford History of New Zealand*, edited by W. H. Oliver with B. R. Williams. Wellington: Oxford University Press, 1981.

Broome, R. *Treasure in Earthen Vessels: Protestant Christianity in New South Wales Society, 1900–1914*. St. Lucia: University of Queensland Press, 1980.

Brown, Joan C. *'Poverty Is Not a Crime': The Development of Social Services in Tasmania, 1803–1900*. Hobart: Tasmanian Historical Research Association, 1973.

Brown, R. G., ed. *Children Australia*. Sydney: Allen & Unwin, 1974.

Brown, V. Scantlebury. Papers. Melbourne University Archives.

Bruce, Mary Grant. *A Little Bush Maid*. London: Ward, Locke, 1910.

Bunkle, Phillida. "The Origins of the Women's Movement in New Zealand: The Women's Christian Temperance Union, 1885–1895." In *Women in New Zealand Society*, edited by Phillida Bunkle and Beryl Hughes. Auckland: Allen & Unwin, 1980.

Burns, A., and J. Goodnow, *Children and Families in Australia: Contemporary Issues and Problems*. Sydney: Allen & Unwin, 1979.

Campbell, A. E. *Educating New Zealand*. Wellington: Department of Internal Affairs, 1941.

Campion, Edmund. *Australian Catholics: The Contribution of Catholics to the Development of Australian Society*. Ringwood, Vic.: Penguin Books, 1987.

Castles, Francis G. *The Working Class and Welfare: Reflections on the Political Development of the Welfare State in Australia and New Zealand, 1890–1980*. Sydney: Allen & Unwin, 1985.

Caute, Mary. "Craniometry and Eugenics in Australia. R.J.A. Berry and the Quest for Social Efficiency." *Historical Studies* 22 (1986):35–53.

Chomley, Eliza. Papers. State Library of Victoria.

Clark, C.M.H. *A History of Australia*. 6 vols. Melbourne: Melbourne University Press, 1962–1987.

Cleverly, John. *The First Generation School and Society in Early New South Wales*. Sydney: Sydney University Press, 1971.

Close Family. Papers. Mitchell Library, Sydney.

Cole, J. "The Social Dynamics of Lifecourse Timing in Historical Perspective: Transitions in an Australian Rural Community, Boonah, 1850–1978." Ph.D. thesis, University of Queensland, 1981.

Cook, P., I. Davey, and M. Vick. "Capitalism and Working Class Schooling in Late Nineteenth Century South Australia." *Journal of the Australian and New Zealand History of Education Society* 8 (1979):36–48.

Conway, Ronald. *The Great Australian Stupor: An Interpretation of the Australian Way of Life*. Melbourne: Sun Books, 1971.

Cowan, Peter, ed. *A Faithful Picture: The Letters of Eliza and Thomas Brown at York in the Swan River Colony, 1841–1852*. Fremantle, W.A.: Arts Centre Press, 1977.

Crowley, F. K., ed. *A New History of Australia*. Melbourne: William Heinemann, 1974.

Cumming, Ian, and Alan Cumming. *A History of State Education in New Zealand, 1840–1975*. Wellington: Pitman, 1978.

Cusack, Dymphna, and Norman Freehill. *Dymphna Cusack*. Melbourne: Thomas Nelson, 1975.

Dakin, J. E. *Education in New Zealand*. Newton Abbott, Engl.: David & Charles, 1973.

Dalziel, Raewyn. "The Colonial Helpmeet: Women's Role and the Vote in Nineteenth Century New Zealand." *New Zealand Journal of History* 11 (1977):112–123.

Davey, Ian. "Transitions: School and Work in the Family Economy." *Australia 1888* 10 (1982).

———. "Growing Up in a Working Class Community." In *Families in Colonial Australia*, edited by Patricia Grimshaw, Chris McConville, and Ellen McEwen. Sydney: Allen & Unwin, 1985.

Davison, Graeme. "The City-Bred Child and Urban Reform in Melbourne, 1900–1940." In *Social Process and the City*, edited by Peter Williams. Sydney: Allen & Unwin, 1983.

———. *The Rise and Fall of Marvellous Melbourne*. Melbourne: Melbourne University Press, 1979.

Deakin, Alfred. Papers. Australian National Library, Canberra.

Dickey, Brian. "The Establishment of Industrial Schools and Reformatories in New South Wales, 1850–1875." *Journal of the Royal Australian Historical Society* 25 (1939):89–128, 169–213.

———. *No Charity There!: A Short History of Social Welfare in Australia*. Melbourne: Thomas Nelson, 1980.

——— with Elaine Martin and Rod Oxenbury. *Rations, Residences, Resources: A History of Social Welfare in South Australia Since 1836*. Adelaide: Wakefield Press, 1986.

Dixson, Miriam. *The Real Matilda: Women and Identity in Australia, 1788–1975*. Ringwood, Vic.: Penguin Books, 1975.

Dow, G. "Family History and Educational History: Towards an Integration." *Historical Studies* 21 (1985):421–431.

Duguid Family. Papers. Mitchell Library, Sydney.

Edgeworth David, Mary. *Passages of Time: An Australian Woman, 1890–1974*. St. Lucia: University of Queensland Press, 1975.

Eldred-Grigg, Stevan. *A Southern Gentry: New Zealanders Who Inherited the Earth*. Wellington: A. H. & A. W. Reed, 1980.

———. *Pleasures of the Flesh: Sex and Drugs in Colonial New Zealand, 1840–1915*. Wellington: A. H. & A. W. Reed, 1984.

Elliott, Sir James. *Firth of Wellington*. Auckland: Whitcome & Tombs, 1937.

Firth, S. G. "Social Values in the New South Wales Primary School, 1880–1914: An Analysis of School Texts." In *Melbourne Studies in Education*, edited by R.J.W. Selleck. Melbourne: Melbourne University Press, 1971.

Fogarty, R. *Catholic Education in Australia, 1806–1950*. 2 vols. Melbourne: Melbourne University Press, 1959.

Foster Care Federation Centennial Report, 1983 (n.p.).

Franklin, Miles. *Childhood at Brindabella: My First Ten Years*. Sydney: Angus & Robertson, 1963.

Gandevia, Brian. *Tears Often Shed: Child Health and Welfare in Australia from 1788*. Sydney: Pergamon Press, 1978.

Garton, Stephen. "Sir Charles Mackellar: Psychiatry, Eugenics and Child Welfare in New South Wales, 1900–1914." *Historical Studies* 22 (1986):21–34.

Gilderdale, Betty. *A Sea Change: 145 Years of New Zealand Junior Fiction.* Auckland: Longman Paul, 1982.

Godden, J. "Philanthropy and the Women's Sphere: Sydney 1870-circa 1900." Ph.D. thesis, Macquarie University, 1983.

Goodall, Heather. "A History of Aboriginal Communities in New South Wales, 1909–1939." Ph.D. thesis, University of Sydney, 1984.

Gordon, Elizabeth, and Tony Deverson. *New Zealand English.* Auckland: William Heinemann, 1985.

Graham, Jeanine. "Settler Society." In *Oxford History of New Zealand*, edited by W. H. Oliver with B. R. Williams. Wellington: Oxford University Press, 1981.

———. "Child Employment in Colonial New Zealand." *New Zealand Journal of History* 21 (1987):62–78.

Gregory, J. S. "Church and State Education in Victoria to 1872." In *Melbourne Studies in Education*, edited by E. L. French. Melbourne: University of Melbourne Press, 1960.

Grellier, Margaret. "The Family: Some Aspects of its Demographic Ideology in Mid-Nineteenth Century Australia." In *A New History of Western Australia*, edited by C. T. Stannage. Nedlands: University of Western Australia Press, 1981.

Grimshaw, Patricia. "Women and the Family in Australian History." In *Women, Class and History: Feminist Perspectives in Australia, 1788–1978*, edited by E. Windschuttle. Melbourne: Fontana, 1980.

———. *Women's Suffrage in New Zealand.* Auckland: Auckland University Press/Oxford University Press, 1972.

——— and Charles Fahey. "Family and Community in Nineteenth Century Castlemaine." In *Families in Colonial Australia*, edited by Patricia Grimshaw, Chris McConville, and Ellen McEwen. Sydney: Allen & Unwin, 1985.

———, Chris McConville, and Ellen McEwen, eds. *Families in Colonial Australia.* Sydney: Allen & Unwin, 1985.

——— and Graham Willett. "Women's History and Family History." In *Australian Women: Feminist Perspectives*, edited by Norma Grieve and Patricia Grimshaw. Melbourne: Oxford University Press, 1981.

Grundy, Denis. *"Secular, Compulsory and Free": The Education Act of 1872.* Melbourne: Melbourne University Press, 1972.

———. "Free Schooling and the State in South Australia, 1875–1898." In *Melbourne Studies in Education*, edited by I. Palmer. Melbourne: Melbourne University Press, 1983.

Hamilton, Annette. *Aboriginal Child Rearing in North Central Arnhem Land.* Canberra: Australian Institute of Aboriginal Studies, 1981.

Hassall Family. Papers. Mitchell Library, Sydney.

Hicks, N. *This Sin and Scandal: Australia's Population Debate, 1891–1911.* Canberra: Australian National University Press, 1978.

Horne, Donald. *The Education of Donald.* Sydney: Angus & Robertson, 1967.

Houston, Stewart, ed. *Marriage and the Family in New Zealand.* Wellington: Sweet & Maxwell, 1970.

Hyslop, Anthea. "Christian Temperance and Social Reform: The Women's Christian Temperance Union of Victoria, 1887–1912." In *Women, Faith and Fêtes: Essays in the History of Women and the Church in Australia*, edited by Sabine Willis. Melbourne: Dove Press, 1977.

Ihimaera, Witi. *Tangi*. Auckland: William Heinemann, 1973.

Jackson, H. R. *Churches and People in Australia and New Zealand, 1860–1930*. Wellington: Allen & Unwin/Port Nicholson Press, 1987.

Jaggs, Donella. *Neglected and Criminal: Foundations of Child Welfare Legislation in Victoria*. Bundoora, Vic.: Phillip Institute of Technology, 1986.

Keene, Judith. "Excavating the Sand Pit in Search of the History of Childhood." *Australian Historical Society Bulletin* 47 (1986):9–20.

Kent, Jacqueline. *In the Half-Light: Life as a Child, 1900–1970*. Sydney: Angus & Robertson, 1988.

Kingston, B. *My Wife, My Daughter and Poor Mary Ann*. Melbourne: Thomas Nelson, 1975.

———. "The Lady and the Australian Girl: Some Thoughts on Nationalism and Class." In *Australian Women: New Feminist Perspectives*, edited by Norma Grieve and Ailsa Burns. Melbourne: Oxford University Press, 1986.

Kitson, H. P. *A Nelson Boyhood*. Wellington: Department of Education, 1969.

Kociumbas, Jan. "Children and Society in New South Wales and Victoria, 1860–1914." Ph.D. thesis, University of Sydney, 1983.

———. "The Management of Children: Medical Advice on Child Care in New South Wales and Victoria, 1860–1900." *Australia 1888* 9 (1982):14–19.

———. " 'What Alyce Learnt at Nine': Sexuality and Sex Roles in Literature to 1914." *History of Education Review* 15 (1986):18–36.

Koopman-Boyden, Peggy, ed. *Families in New Zealand Society*. Wellington: Methuen Press, 1978.

Kyle, Noeline. *Her Natural Destiny: The Education of Women in New South Wales*. Kensington: University of New South Wales Press, 1986.

Larson, Ann. "Who Wants to Go to School? The Effects of Free and Compulsory Education in Mid-Nineteenth Century Victoria." *History of Education Quarterly* 15 (1986):1–15.

Lawson, Henry. "Early Days." In *Stories and Poems of Henry Lawson*, edited by Marjorie Pizer. Melbourne: Australian Book Society, 1957.

Lee, John A. *Children of the Poor*. London: Werner Laurie, 1935.

Levitt, Phyllis. "Public Concern for Young Children: A Socio-Historical Study of Reform, Dunedin 1879–1889." Ph.D. thesis, University of Otago, 1979.

Lewis, Brian. *Sunday at Kooyong Road*. Richmond, Vic.: Hutchison, 1976.

Lewis, M. " 'Populate or Perish': Aspects of Infant and Maternal Health in Sydney, 1870–1939." Ph.D. thesis, Australian National University, 1976.

Loh, Morag. *With Courage in Their Cases*. Melbourne: F.I.L.E.F. Publications, 1980.

Lowenstein, Wendy. *Weevils in the Flour: An Oral Record of the 1930s Depression in Australia*. Melbourne: Hyland House, 1978.

———. *Shocking, Shocking, Shocking: The Improper Play Rhymes of Australian Children*. Prahran, Vic.: Fish & Chip Press, 1974.

——— and Morag Loh. *The Immigrants*. Melbourne: Hyland House, 1977.

McDonald, D. J. "Child and Female Labor in Sydney, 1876–1898." *Australian National University Historical Journal* 10, 11 (1973–1974):40–49.

McDonald, Dugald J. "Children and Young Persons in New Zealand Society." In *Fam-*

ilies in New Zealand Society, edited by Peggy Koopman-Boyden. Wellington: Methuen Press, 1978.

McDougall Family. Papers. Mitchell Library, Sydney.

McEwen, Ellen. "Family, Kin and Neighbours: The Newcastle Coalmining District, 1860–1900." *Australia 1888* 4 (1980):68–86.

———. "Family History in Australia: Some Observations on a New Field." In *Families in Colonial Australia,* edited by Patricia Grimshaw, Chris McConville, and Ellen McEwen. Sydney: Allen & Unwin, 1985.

McGeorge, Colin. "Schools and Socialization in New Zealand, 1890–1914." Ph.D. thesis, University of Canterbury, 1985.

McKenzie, J. David S. *Education and Social Structure: Essays in the History of New Zealand Education.* Dunedin: New Zealand College of Education, 1982.

———. "Ideology and the History of Education," *New Zealand Journal of Education History* 19 (1984):2–9.

MacIntyre, Stuart. *Oxford History of Australia, 1901–1942, the Succeeding Age.* Vol. 4. Melbourne: Oxford University Press, 1986.

Mackinnon, Alison. *One Foot on the Ladder: Origins and Outcomes of Girls' Secondary Schooling in South Australia.* St. Lucia: Queensland University Press, 1984.

———. "Educating the Mothers of a Nation: The Advanced School for Girls, Adelaide." In *Worth Her Salt: Women at Work in Australia*, edited by M. Bevege, M. James, and C. Shute. Sydney: Hale & Iremonger, 1982.

Macnab, K., and R. Ward. "The Nature and Nurture of the First Generation of Native-born Australians." *Historical Studies* 10 (1962):298–308.

Malone, E. P. "The New Zealand School Journal and the Imperial Ideology." *New Zealand Journal of History* 7 (1973):12–27.

Marsden Family. Papers. Mitchell Library, Sydney.

Mathews, Janet, ed. *The Two Worlds of Jimmie Barker: The Life of an Australian Aborigine, 1900–1972.* Canberra: Australian Institute of Aboriginal Studies, 1977.

Matthews, Jill Julius. *Good and Mad Women: The Historical Construction of Femininity in Twentieth-Century Australia.* Sydney: Allen & Unwin, 1984.

Mayne, A. J. C. " 'The Question of the Poor' in the Nineteenth Century City." *Historical Studies* 20 (1983):557–573.

Mein Smith, Philippa. "Truby King in Australia: A Revisionist View of Reduced Infant Mortality." *New Zealand Journal of History* 22 (1988):24–43.

———. *Maternity in Dispute: New Zealand 1920–1939.* Wellington: Department of Internal Affairs, Historical Publishers Branch, 1986.

Miller, James. *Koori: A Will to Win.* Sydney: Sydney University Press, 1985.

Mitchell, Winifred, and Geoffrey Sherington. *Growing Up in the Illawarra: A Social History, 1834–1984.* Wollongong, N.S.W.: University of Wollongong Press, 1984.

———. "Families and Children in Nineteenth Century Illawarra." In *Families in Colonial Australia*, edited by Patricia Grimshaw, Chris McConville, and Ellen McEwen. Sydney: Allen & Unwin, 1985.

Morton, H., ed. *Annabella Boswell's Journal.* Sydney: Angus & Robertson, 1965.

Neilson, John Shaw. *Autobiography.* Melbourne: National Library of Australia, 1978.

O'Brien, Anne. "The Poor in New South Wales, 1880–1918." Ph.D. thesis, University of Sydney, 1983.

O'Farrell, Patrick. *The Catholic Church and Community in Australia: A History*. Melbourne: Thomas Nelson, 1977.

Oliver, W. H., with B. R. Williams, eds. *The Oxford History of New Zealand*. Wellington: Oxford University Press, 1981.

―――. "Social Welfare: Social Justice or Social Efficiency?" *New Zealand Journal of History* 13 (1979):25–33.

Olssen, Erik. "Towards a New Society." In *Oxford History of New Zealand*, edited by W. H. Oliver with B. R. Williams. Wellington: Oxford University Press, 1981.

―――. "Truby King and the Plunket Society: An Analysis of a Prescriptive Ideology." *New Zealand Journal of History* 15 (1981):3–23.

―――. "Women, Work and Family." In *Women in New Zealand Society*, edited by Phillida Bunkle and Beryl Hughes. Auckland: Allen & Unwin, 1980.

――― and Andrée Lévesque. "Towards a History of the European Family in New Zealand." In *Families in New Zealand Society*, edited by Peggy G. Koopman-Boyden. Wellington: Methuen Press, 1978.

Petersen, C. G. *Forest Homes*. Wellington: A. H. & A. W. Reed, 1956.

Phillips, Jock. *A Man's Country? The Image of the Pakeha Male, a History*. Auckland: Penguin Books, 1987.

Pool, D. Ian. *The Maori Population of New Zealand, 1769–1971*. Auckland: Auckland University Press/Oxford University Press, 1977.

Porter, Hal. *The Watcher on the Cast Iron Balcony: An Australian Autobiography*. London: Faber & Faber, 1963.

Ramsland, John. *Children of the Back Lanes: Destitute and Neglected Children in Colonial New South Wales*. Kensington: University of New South Wales Press, 1986.

―――. " 'A Place of Refuge from Dangerous Influences': Hobart Town Industrial School for Girls, 1862–1875." *Journal of the Royal Australian Historical Society* 71 (1985):207–217.

―――. "The Development of Boarding-Out Systems in Australia: A Series of Welfare Experiments in Child Care, 1860–1910." *Journal of the Royal Australian Historical Society* 60 (1974):186–198.

Reiger, Kerreen. *The Disenchantment of the Home: Modernizing the Australian Family, 1880–1940*. Melbourne: Oxford University Press, 1985.

―――. "Women's Labour Redefined: Child Bearing and Rearing Advice in Australia, 1880–1930." In *Worth Her Salt: Women at Work in Australia*, edited by M. Bevege, M. James, and C. Shute. Sydney: Hale & Iremonger, 1982.

Roberts, J. B., ed. *The Mapoon Story by the Mapoon People*. Melbourne: International Development Action, 1975.

Robinson, Portia. *The Hatch and Brood of Time: A Study of the First Generation of Native-Born White Australians, 1788 to 1828*. Vol. 1. Melbourne: Oxford University Press, 1985.

Roe, Jill, ed. *Social Policy in Australia: Some Perspectives*. Stanmore, N.S.W.: Cassell, 1976.

Roe, M. *Nine Australian Progressives: Vitalism in Bourgeois Social Thought, 1890–1960*. St. Lucia: Queensland University Press, 1984.

Saxby, H. M. *A History of Australian Children's Literature, 1841–1941*. Sydney: Wentworth Books, 1969.

Scholefield, G. H., ed. *The Richmond-Atkinson Papers*, 2 vols. Wellington: Government Printer, 1960.

Sherington, Geoffrey. *Shore: A History of Sydney Church of England Grammar School*. Sydney: Sydney Church of England Grammar School/Allen & Unwin, 1975.

Shuker, Roy. *The One Best System? A Revisionist History of State Schooling in New Zealand*. Palmerston North, N.Z.: Dunmore Press, 1987.

Sinclair, Keith. *A History of New Zealand*. Auckland: Penguin Books, rev. ed., 1988.

Smith, Bernard. *The Boy Andeodatus*. Ringwood, Vic.: Allen Lane, 1984.

Somerset, H.C.D. *Littledene: A New Zealand Rural Community*. Auckland: Whitcombe & Tombs, 1958.

Souter, Gavin. *Lions and Kangaroos: The Initiation of Australia, 1901–1919*. Sydney: Collins, 1976.

Spearritt, Peter. ''The Kindergarten Movement: Tradition and Change.'' In *Social Change in Australia: Readings in Sociology*, edited by Donald E. Edgar. Melbourne: Cheshire Publishing, 1974.

Spence, Catherine Helen. *An Autobiography*. Adelaide: W. K. Thomas, 1910.

———. *State Children in Australia: A History of Boarding-Out and Its Developments*. Adelaide: Vardon & Sons, 1907.

Stannage, C. T. *The People of Perth: A Social History of Western Australia's Capital City*. Perth: Perth City Council, 1979.

Stephen Family. Papers. Mitchell Library, Sydney.

Stirling, Amiria Manutahi, and Anne Salmond. *Amiria: The Life Story of a Maori Woman*. Wellington: A. H. & A. W. Reed, 1976.

Sturma, Michael. *Vice in a Vicious Society: Crime and Convicts in Mid-Nineteenth Century New South Wales*. St. Lucia: University of Queensland Press, 1983.

Summers, Anne. *Damned Whores and God's Police: The Colonization of Women in Australia*. Ringwood, Vic.: Penguin Books, 1975.

Sutton-Smith, Brian. *A History of Children's Play: The New Zealand Playground, 1840–1950*. Philadelphia: University of Pennsylvania Press, 1981.

———. *A History of Children's Play in New Zealand*. Wellington: New Zealand Council for Education Research, 1981.

Swain, Shurlee. ''The Victorian Charity Networks in the 1890s.'' Ph.D. thesis, University of Melbourne, 1977.

———. ''Destitute and Dependent: Case Studies in Poverty in Melbourne, 1890–1900.'' *Historical Studies* 19 (1980):98–107.

Suttor Family. Papers. Mitchell Library, Sydney.

Sydney Labour History Group, eds. *What Rough Beast? The State and Social Order in Australian History*. Sydney: Allen & Unwin, 1982.

Tennant, Margaret. ''Indigence and Charitable Aid in New Zealand, 1885–1920.'' Ph.D. thesis, Massey University, 1981.

———. ''Duncan MacGregor and Charitable Aid Administration, 1886–1896.'' *New Zealand Journal of History* 13 (1979):33–40.

———. ''Brazen Faced Beggars of the Female Sex.'' In *Women in History*, edited by Barbara Brookes, Charlotte Macdonald, and Margaret Tennant. Wellington: Allen & Unwin, 1986.

———. ''Natural Directions: The New Zealand Movement for Sexual Differentiations in Education During the Early Twentieth Century.'' *New Zealand Journal of Educational Studies* 12 (1977):142–153.

Theobald, Marjorie. '' 'Mere Accomplishments?' Melbourne Early Ladies' Colleges Reconsidered.'' *History of Education Review* 13 (1984):15–29.

Toynbee, Claire. "Class and Social Structure in Nineteenth Century New Zealand." *New Zealand Journal of History* 13 (1979):65–80.

Trlin, A. *Now Respected, Once Despised: Yugoslavs in New Zealand.* Palmerston North, N.Z.: Dunmore Press, 1979.

Tucker, Margaret. *If Everyone Cared.* Sydney: Ure Smith, 1977.

Turner, Ethel. *Seven Little Australians.* London: Ward, Locke, 1894.

Tyler, Deborah. "The Case of Irene Tuckerman: Understanding Sexual Violence and the Protection of Women and Girls, Victoria, 1890–1925." *History of Education Review* 15 (1986):52–67.

Whelan, P. J. "The Care of Destitute, Neglected and Criminal Children in New Zealand, 1840–1900." M.A. thesis, Victoria University, 1956.

White, Isabel, Diane Barwick, and Betty Meehan, eds. *Fighters and Singers: The Lives of Some Australian Aborigines.* Sydney: Allen & Unwin, 1985.

Williamson, N. " 'Hymns, Songs and Blackguard Verses': Life in the Industrial and Reforming School for Girls in New South Wales, 1869 to 1887." *Journal of the Royal Australian Historical Society* 67 (1982):312–324.

———. "Laundry Maids or Ladies? Life in the Industrial and Reforming School for Girls in New South Wales, 1887–1910." *Journal of the Royal Australian Historical Society* 68 (1983):378–387.

Willis, S. " 'Made to Be Moral' at Parramatta Girls' School, 1898–1923." In *Twentieth Century Sydney: Studies in Urban and Social History*, edited by J. Roe. Sydney: Hale & Iremonger, 1980.

Windschuttle, Elizabeth. "Women and the Origins of Colonial Philanthropy." In *Australian Welfare History: Critical Essays*, edited by Richard Kennedy. Melbourne: MacMillan, 1982.

Zainu'ddin, Ailsa C. Thompson. *They Dreamt of a School: A Centenary History of Methodist Ladies' College, Kew, 1882–1982.* Melbourne: Hyland House, 1982.

7

BRAZIL

Elizabeth Anne Kuznesof

The family as an institution has dominated Brazilian society since the first years of Portuguese colonization. The prevalence of the private sphere as compared with the public or official organization of life is a common theme of Brazilian historiography. Even the clergy has relatively less influence and from the seventeenth through the nineteenth centuries was largely absorbed within the family chapels in the shadow of the Big House. Further, the description of the family (often called a *clan* or *clã*, although not in the strictly anthropological sense) invariably includes reference to *numerous* kindred. Despite these characteristics, contemporary historical references to children and to childhood before the twentieth century are few and usually occur as part of a more general description of society.

The position of the state—whether Royal, Imperial, or Republican—has been that the care and nuturing of children is a private function. When the state has intervened—as in prohibiting women from willfully aborting or abandoning children in the eighteenth century (although fathers *were* allowed to abandon children)—the concern was primarily one of the paternal right over the lives of offspring, rather than a concern for the children themselves. Similarly the function of the *juíz dos orphãos* was to protect the property of each of the two extended families represented. Throughout the colonial period the issue of support for orphanages for abandoned children was constantly debated, with local governments as much as possible placing the responsibility for these inconvenient children with brotherhoods of the Santa Casa de Misericórdia, although Royal legislation stated that it was a community responsibility.

Certain issues have been especially emphasized in the literature as having had an important impact on the history of childhood. The first is how the child was viewed within his or her society of origin. Was childhood seen as a separate stage of life, or simply as a preparation for adulthood? Were children "angels," or "devils"? Was a child born with specific capacities or tendencies? What was the role of education in the socialization of children?[1]

Other historians have focused on the changing relations of parents to children over time. In this approach it usually is argued that affective relations between parents and children were distant in the preindustrial past because of the emotional risks involved in very high levels of infant and child mortality.[2]

A third approach looks at the world of experience of the child in a historical context, including the ways in which the child acted as a creative historical force in his or her own right. For this third group of historians important areas of influence might include religious beliefs, war, and the position of women in society.[3] This study is an attempt to describe the world of Brazilian childhood by a combination of the approaches described above, but most emphasis is placed on the experience of childhood within its historical context, as much as possible from the child's perspective.

CHILDHOOD IN THE THREE FORMATIVE CULTURES: INDIGENOUS, AFRICAN, AND PORTUGUESE

Much of the material culture, attitudes about everyday practices, and beliefs about the supernatural evinced in Brazilian families in the colonial period can be traced to either the indigenous or the African culture. Although the Portuguese were politically supreme in Brazil and dominated institutional life of all kinds, women of the indigenous and African cultures were extremely important in the care and nurture of children of all backgrounds. A description of the ideological and social context of childhood in each of these formative cultures provides a deeper sense of the complex spiritual and socioeconomic reality of Brazilian childhood as it emerged in the colonial period.

Most Brazilian children were of indigenous background in the early sixteenth century, and even those with Portuguese fathers usually had indigenous mothers. Indigenous customs of childbirth and care, and ideas about the appropriate roles of women and children, therefore, strongly influenced social practice. Africans began to arrive in Brazil about 1550, but because of the effects of sex ratio (predominantly male) and the isolated circumstances of their plantation lives, Africans had less cultural and demographic impact on Brazilian society than did the Indians until the mid-eighteenth century. At that time the free colored population in Brazil began to be of numerical significance, and miscegenation and migration became much more common.[4] African culture was highly heterogeneous, involving many languages, traditions, and religions. Therefore, the influence also was both complex and diverse.

In the indigenous societies of colonial Brazil, magic, totemism, and rituals to protect children and other tribal members from "bichos" (beasts of the jungle) were central to their cultures. Children were seen as having sprung from the seed of their fathers, with the mothers acting as so many sacks to carry the children as they developed in embryos. For that reason, kinship was recognized only on the paternal side. Mothers usually worked in the fields until parturition, giving birth in the fields alone (or perhaps with the father acting as midwife) and washing the child in the river. The father—when he knew that birth was imminent—lay down in his hammock and was waited on by relatives and friends (and his wife when she had given birth) for about eight days. The reason for this special treatment was the difficult and dangerous work of the father in the first days of the life of the child, which was to give birth to the child's spirit.[5]

After birth the child was brought to the father to cut the umbilical cord with his teeth or with sharp stones.[6] The father also chose the first of several names that were given a child, a name that should ensure that the child would grow strong and inspire fear in its enemies. Often the name selected also was a name that had been successful in the father's past.[7] Many times children were given names of animals, fish, or trees; these names were seen as magical, reportedly only spoken in low, religious tones. Other nonpoetic "nicknames" were used in everyday discourse, names such as Guarquinguará (bird's behind), Miguiguacú (big buttocks), and Cururupeba (little toad). These names were supposed to render the people bearing them repugnant to demons.[8] Many indigenous tribes thought that they were descended from other forest creatures, and young children were viewed as little different from these creatures. For that reason they were especially in danger of being seduced or kidnapped.[9]

From the time of birth the child was placed in a *tipoia*, or small hammock that was fastened to the back of its mother and in which it spent most of its first two years. If the newborn were male, the father attached a bow with flowers and a bundle of herbs or grasses to the hammock-cradle. Also, cotton was commonly placed on the child's head, and the child's palms were rubbed with bird feathers and sticks of wood so that the child would grow and prosper. Neighbors who assisted the father at the time of the child's birth were considered to be in a special relation to the child, rather like godparents, according to the Portuguese Jesuit Fernão Cardím.[10] Cardím emphasized how much the Indians loved their children, even saying that "they [felt] it [was] more important to do well for their children, than for themselves."

Indigenous women nursed their children between eighteen months and, by some reports, seven years. Women labored constantly, planting in the fields, preparing flour and other foods, spinning cotton, making clay pots, preparing body dyes for menfolk and children and applying them, washing clothes and hammocks. Young children accompanied their mothers during all these activities. In their early lives Indian children were not subject to corporal punishment.[11] They were, however, taught to fear demons and beasts, and were taught games and songs that emphasized the dangers of these creatures to young children. The tribes also possessed devil masks that represented demonic jungle creatures (possibly the spirits of people who had died) and that were used in ritual dances. The Indians had a series of customs that were intended to guard them all, but especially the children, from the evil spirits. They included body painting; the perforation of the lips, nasal septum, and ears; the insertion of plugs, spindles, and/or stalks into orifices of the body; and the stringing of animal teeth about the neck.[12]

At puberty both boys and girls had their hair cut short. The boys were then segregated in special houses called *baito* in which they were instructed in various rituals of manhood and the appropriate relations between men and women. Women were not allowed near these houses on pain of death. Boys were put to trials of survival and torture during their initiation to manhood, and they were instructed in hunting, war, house construction, and the traditions of the tribe. Although children were not spanked or punished for misbehavior, sometimes boys were beaten as part of their education to make them brave and strong.[13]

According to Hans Staden, the Tupiniquins promised their daughters in marriage while they were still children. At puberty the young girl's hair was cut, and her skin was scratched or cut and treated in such a way that black patterns remained on her skin when she was healed. When her hair had grown long again and her wounds had healed, she was given to her fiance with little ceremony.[14]

The great number and variety of African societies and cultures that fed into the Brazilian population through the slave trade make an evaluation of the impact of African culture on Brazilian childhood seem an impossible task. It has been convincingly argued, however, by a number of African anthropologists and historians, that there existed a common central African culture with certain constellations of basic symbols, beliefs, values, and rituals that had overriding importance in all the tribal societies.[15] Among the common aspects of African culture were the beliefs in charms and rituals to protect the community from disease and death.[16] Central Africans focused their religious lives on the cult of spirits of recently deceased ancestors—the shades. Monica Shuler argues that the shades were "the source of social values and order, and through the ritual of Kumina, or 'the African dance,' the Central Africans communed with them and thus ensured their beneficence to the group. Today Kumina involves dancing, drumming and singing, culminating in possession by the shades."[17] An eighteenth-century native of the Niger, Ibo Olaudah Equiano, also described a society of villages united by religious beliefs with an emphasis on ancestor cults and a myth of patrilineal descent from a common founder or founders.[18] Africans in colonial Brazil evinced a preoccupation with burial rites because of their belief "in the indispensability, for happiness in the world beyond, of the care of the descendants of the dead person in giving him an adequate funeral and in observing rigorously the prescribed rituals which will assure for him a worthy position with his ancestors."[19] According to an account by an ex-slave captured on the Nigerian coast about 1810, the religion of that people included a "king of heaven who was immaterial and had neither temples nor statues" and a great number of secondary gods, called *orisa*. These latter were represented by wooden images in sacred compounds, and each had special powers and followers. There also was a belief in evil spirits, or genie. Offerings to the orisa included chickens, a sheep, or an ox.[20] Craemer (et al.) points out that although for Christianity the belief system predominates, for Africans ritual and charm were primordial.[21] Among African Christians, the sacraments, the music, and the ritual prayers also were emphasized.

Among Central Africans, the exchange of women between tribal societies through marriage was an important part of the culture. Because women were the primary socializers of children, culture and beliefs were spread through marriage. This flexibility of Central African culture and its propensity to accept new rituals, symbols, beliefs, and myths also facilitated the communication and acceptance between different African traditions within Brazil.[22]

Childbirth in Central Africa ordinarily was accompanied by the women of the family or the neighborhood, who delivered the child and knotted the umbilical cord. For six days the mother lay on her mat with her child and washed neither herself nor the child. On the seventh day the room was cleaned from top to bottom. Even the cinders of the hearth were taken and thrown into the river. An *alase*, or priest, then rubbed palm oil on the head of the child, and bathed him in the container in which the cinders were thrown away. The priest dissolved a few grains of salt in his own mouth and, blowing a few drops of saline saliva on the forehead of the child, called aloud the name the child's father had told him in advance.[23] Selection of the baby's name was important, and was determined through communion with the spirits, often in possession or a dream.[24] The wrong name could lead to "spirit sickness" and bad luck.

In Central Africa nursing lasted for at least one year and usually three years, according to a document dated 1810. Often the infant was tied to the mother's back with a knotted cloth while she worked in the fields. The child had no separate cradle, but slept by its mother covered with cloths. Male infants were circumcised in Central African culture in a religious ceremony at the age of six or seven. Children of both sexes also were scarified at that time, being incised with knife marks that represented their particular tribes.[25]

Children of both sexes under fifteen years of age wore no clothes.[26] Among the Niger Ibo, residence was patrilocal, and families lived in either nuclear or extended family groups. Authority was based on age grading among both sexes. Men, women, and children worked on the farms. Corporal punishment for children was rare.[27]

Marriages in Central Africa often were the result of an agreement between the two families when the children to be married were seven or eight years old. Among Nigerians, the groom's family paid a bride-price to the bride's father for his bride, and polygamy was allowed. The Niger Ibo also expected that the bride would bring with her all the property and gear needed by a married woman. Adultery by the wife was sometimes punished by slavery or death, as the husband decided, but husbands were not required to be physically faithful to wives.[28]

Portugal in the sixteenth century was an ethnically and religiously diverse cultural environment, dominated by Catholicism but including substantial Jewish and Muslim populations.[29] Religion influenced every aspect of life from birth to death. All unexplained events were attributed to supernatural forces. Devotion to particular saints was strong, and varied by locale. Numerous secular priests ministered to the population while the landscape was liberally studded with monasteries and nunneries. Nevertheless, much of religious life was not mediated by the clergy, but practiced by lay people at shrines to local saints in the countryside and at the private altars arranged for prayer in every "palace, mansion and humble residence" with images of the saints and votive lights.[30]

As peasants and townspeople struggled with environmental threats to their collective well-being, they turned to the saints for assistance in epidemics, droughts, plagues of locusts, and other disasters. With the introduction of images in the twelfth century, votive devotion was no longer tied to churches, and the countryside was soon dotted with shrines to Mary and other saints. Community disaster frequently was met by conjuring of saints to avoid storms or locusts, by petitionary processions and novenas, by vows to fast or build a chapel or give to charity. Often the people of the town in question would conclude that the occurrence of the disaster—whatever it was—was the result of neglect of a particular saint, who had to be petitioned to overcome the disaster and prevent future problems.[31] Thus the beliefs involved included recognition of a series of powerful semidieties with substantial powers to cure illness and effect environmental disaster. Devils and evil spirits also formed part of this belief system even within Catholicism. Many practices linked to the ancient gods persisted in common usage, especially among the lower classes. Many of them were forms of nature worship disguised as devotion to Catholic saints or Catholic feasts. Such superstitious beliefs common to the time included belief in witches, vampires, fairies, the Evil eye, omens, fortune tellers, incantations, demons, spells, love potions, and the like.[32] Thus, for example, when Father Anchieta was told about devils who populated the forests in Brazil and plagued the indigenous peoples in the sixteenth century, he did not view this as evidence of paganism, but as fact.[33] In certain ways Catholicism, with its emphasis on the pope and the crucifixion, seems very different from either the indigenous or the African religion. Looked at from a local and individual perspective in historical context, however, there were substantial similarities.

Burial rites and mourning customs also included many superstitions and beliefs of "pagan" origin, including the belief in tormented souls, in ghosts, in the revenge of the dead, and in spiritualism.[34] These beliefs bore substantial similarity with the African preoccupation with the influence of the dead in the lives of the living.

The Portuguese child was baptized eight days after birth, regardless of class. Baptism ordinarily was performed by a priest. In most cases a child had three godparents (*compadres*) at the ceremony (two men and a woman if the child were male and two women and a man if the child were female). The child's forehead was sprinkled with salted water during the ceremony. Other religious rituals of childhood included confirmation (which might have occurred as early as age five) and the first haircut, which was accompanied by a blessing, special prayers, and sometimes new godparents.[35]

The Catholic view of the family and of childhood in sixteenth-century Brazil was strongly influenced by the thought of St. Augustine and, especially, St. Thomas Aquinas.[36] For Augustine the primary purpose of marriage was procreation, which had the value of tempering "the concupiscence of the flesh" by causing lustful couples to instead "think of themselves as mother and father."[37] Children, according to Augustine, were both conceived and born with original sin. What this meant, as interpreted by Blustein, is not that children were born unjust and immoral (this was impossible, since children were seen as having no concept of right and wrong or of reason until age seven), but that children were "willful and passionate and [needed] the firm tutelage of a stern master."[38] Aquinas accepted Augustine's views on the sinfulness of children because of the doctrine of original sin. Aquinas, however, emphasized in addition that parents and children had rights and duties toward each other. For example, parents were obliged to provide their children with physical, mental, moral, and religious education, as well as the material necessities of life. Children also had duties toward their parents: duties of obedience lasting until maturity, and duties of piety, which were permanent.[39] Blustein, interpreting Aquinas, says on this issue:

Parents have eminence, and ought to be revered (not just respected by their children, because of the kind of benefits that children receive from them). Next to God, parents are the "closest sources of our existence and development" (question 101, article 1), surpassing even country, for it is only because parents give their children existence, food, the support needed for life, and education, that they are able to share in the benefits of homeland. Since the benefits parents bestow touch the whole of our existence, our entire personality and not just one relatively minor aspect of it, the degree of our indebtedness to them is particularly great, and it is incumbent on us to revere them in a special way, to acknowledge and pay back our debt to them by the virtue of piety. Whenever we are dependent on another for a whole side of our life, piety comes into play, and filial piety shows itself, first, through honor or appreciation, which involves a certain attitude of mind toward one's parents as well as the outward manifestation of this attitude when occasion requires; and second, through actual service, which entails assisting parents when in need, visiting them when sick, caring for them in their old age.[40]

The Portuguese family system is most vividly portrayed by the principle of *patria potestad*, enunciated in fifteenth- and sixteenth-century law codes, which compelled obedience of children to parents and of wives to husbands for the general good of the family. The rights of lineage became gradually subordinated (beginning in about the thirteenth century) to the autonomy of the nuclear household and to the authority of the head of household (in the nineteenth century), particularly if that person were male.[41] Within the elite family these relations were dramatized in the forms of address; the son called his father and mother *Senhor pai* and *Senhora mae* (father, my lord and mother, my lady), and addressed them as *Vossa Mercé* (your worship). The children asked for the parents' blessing at morning, at night, and always when they met. The form followed through the nineteenth century was one in which the child, with bowed head and folded hands, said, "Louvado" or "Louvado seja" (in a shortened form of blessed be our Lord Jesus Christ.) To this the father responded, "Para sempre seja louvado" (Blessed be forever), or more simply, "God bless you." Older children also had great authority over younger ones, and often were named godparents of their younger siblings. Parental authority was practically unlimited, and children were subject to their father as long as he lived. History even records extreme cases in which fathers ordered the deaths of their sons or daughters for disobedience or supposed immorality. Cases of this kind, with no attempt at prosecution of the father, are found as late as the nineteenth century.[42]

The three cultures that informed the development of Brazilian childhood—the indigenous, the Portuguese, and the African—were all characterized by extreme levels of religiosity and belief in diverse supernatural beings, both benign and malicious. Although men were dominant in all three cultures with respect to family authority, political organization, and lineage, the economic and social roles of women, particularly in indigenous and African tribal societies, were critical. The Portuguese believed that children were born in original sin, were willful and passionate, and needed a "stern master." This emphasis on discipline contrasted with the customs of both indigenous peoples and African tribes, who reportedly did not use corporal punishment on children before the Portuguese expansion to the New World. Authority was strongly associated with age and sex in both Portuguese and African cultures, with older brothers having considerable control over the activities of younger siblings.

In the context of Portuguese colonization the Jesuits made substantial efforts to assimilate the indigenous people and the African slaves into the Portuguese culture, the Catholic religion, and the Christian way of life. For the Indians the method most often used was that of separating Indian children into schools and educating them in their own language apart from their parents, which often resulted in dissension between the generations. The second group of Jesuits brought Portuguese orphans raised in their Lisbon school with them, and placed them together with the Indian children so that they would learn each other's language and the Portuguese children would teach the Indians the catechism and Christian precepts.[43] The Jesuits also encouraged the Indians to settle in sedentary villages, to wear European clothes, and to learn European occupations. The missionaries utilized music, religious theater, ceremonies, and processions to transmit Christian ideas and Catholic rituals to the indigenous peoples.[44] The worst difficulty, according to Father Anchieta, came from the disinterest of the Portuguese population in the Christianization of the Indians and the bad example that the Portuguese set for them. Indians who lived with the Portuguese on their plantations received less Christian teaching than those who lived in Indian villages, according to Anchieta.[45]

If the indoctrination of the indigenous people was slow and incomplete, the evangelization of the African slaves was even less successful. The bulk of the slaves lived on plantations, socially and culturally separate from their Portuguese masters. In the words of René Ribeiro, "with the mass of slaves continually changing in numbers due to continual losses through epidemic, flight, or sicknesses and bad treatment, it was a difficult and ungrateful task to Christianize the slaves."[46]

According to colonial law, new slaves arriving in Brazil had to be baptized within a certain period of time, and most of the slaves were baptized on arrival in slave ships. If this was not possible, the Jesuits catechized the slaves on the plantations until they were ready for baptism. In this work they encountered considerable resistance from the plantation owners, who were loathe to lose a day's work during the introduction of the slaves in Christian principles.[47] Masters also attempted to segregate the slaves from religious services by arguing that the churches were small, that the slaves were naked, and that "because of their bad odor they did not allow their masters and the Portuguese to remain either within or without the churches."[48] This superficial exposure to Christianity left ample time and opportunity for the practice of African religious rites, especially as they had among themselves "African sorcerers, brought to Brazil as slaves, who secretly continued to practice witchcraft."[49] By the 1840s only a minority of owners continued to baptize slaves. Nevertheless, Africans in Brazil were anxious to be baptized. Mary Karasch suggests that the large volume of water used in African baptisms by black priests implies that the ceremony may have had a purification significance.[50] Shuler reports that Africans in Jamaica particularly valued baptism by immersion in the river because "the river is the home of African spirits." The ritual also is believed to provide the protection of a powerful spirit.[51] According to Karasch, baptism "had the character of an initiation ceremony in the sense of integration into a black community, for Rugendas observed that baptized slaves treated the unbaptized Africans as 'savages' until they had undergone the ritual."[52]

MORTALITY, CHILD ABANDONMENT, AND ADOPTION

High levels of fertility and of infant mortality were characteristic of both the free and the slave populations in Brazil from the sixteenth century until the end of the nineteenth century. Data on this subject are difficult to locate, and tend to be anecdotal. For example, Dutch traveler Johan Nieuhoff, in the 1640s, lamented the high infant mortality in Pernambuco, and Gilberto Freyre cites Fernandes Gama as saying that "the Portuguese women at first reared very few children" since "two thirds of them died shortly after birth."[53] Authors commonly state that half the children born in Brazil to the end of the nineteenth century died before their fifth birthday. Life expectancy for the total population in Brazil was estimated to be only two-thirds that of the U.S. population in the late nineteenth century, and Brazilian male slaves had roughly half the life expectancy of U.S. slaves in the same period.[54]

In the nineteenth century the causes of infant mortality were considered important enough to warrant several studies by the hygienists of the period.[55] Diverse opinions were cited in these articles, with substantial emphasis being placed by many on the prevalence of wet nursing by slaves, many of whom were reputed to be syphilitic and to have worms. Others emphasized lack of sufficient clothing, the custom of allowing children to go naked, the "dampness of dwellings," improper diet, lack of medical care, hunger, and the neglect of childhood diseases.

Undoubtedly mortality was an important and constant dimension of everyday life. Not only was mortality among infants very high, primarily from dysentery, malnutrition, and starvation, as well as from infectious diseases, but approximately one in five births reportedly resulted in the death of the mother.[56] Diseases related to childbirth, but especially puerperal fever, constituted 154.4 per 1,000 deaths listed in São Paulo from 1799 to 1809.[57] Therefore, it is not only true that children were born with little chance to survive, and often witnessed the deaths of siblings, cousins, and playmates, but a child also was very likely to lose his or her mother at an early age. Gilberto Freyre describes the marriages of fifteen-year-old female members of the Brazilian aristocracy to men fifteen or twenty years older than they, which resulted in one pregnancy after another and the early deaths of the young brides to childbirth. Often the husbands married their dead wives' sisters or cousins within a matter of weeks and repeated the same pattern, so that each elite husband finally had four or five wives and twenty or more children.[58]

It is difficult to say much about the constant presence of death, the disappearance of loved ones, in the lives of Brazilian children. Brazil's great writer João Guimarães Rosas (1968) has described the emotions of a young boy in the presence of the death of a turkey he had seen and admired: "All eternity, all certainty, was lost; in a breath, in the glimmer of a sigh, that which is most precious is taken from us. . . . In the infinitesimal null speck of a minute's time, a feather's weight of death entered the child's soul" ("The Thin Edge of Happiness"). As time went on "he felt more and more tired; unable to respond to what he was shown. . . . His fatigue turned from repressed emotion to secret fear: he was discovering the possibility that there might be other misfortunes lurking in the mechanical world, in hostile space, and beginning to see that only a hair's breadth lies between contentment and disenchantment." In another story, "Treetops," the little boy is sent to visit his uncle and aunt because his mother is sick. Guimarães Rosa describes his fear: "He knew that his mother was ill. That was why they were sending him away, surely for a long time, surely because they had to. That was why they had wanted him to bring his toys. . . . It was like this: something bigger than everything else in the world might happen, was going to happen."[59]

Novelist José Lins do Rêgo also wrote of death in his autobiographical trilogy on plantation life in northeastern Brazil—the deaths of his mother, his father, his cousin, his playmates, his pet ram, and others on the plantation. His mother died while the novelist was a young child. "My mother's death filled my whole life with a hopeless sense of melancholy. . . . This arbitrary force—destiny—was to make me a difficult boy tormented by ugly visions.''[60]

In these families the black wet nurse was universally employed to raise the young. Children of the elite reportedly had relatively little contact with their mothers, and learned everything in the laps of the black slaves. Perhaps it is not surprising that observers report a ''lack of maternal tenderness'' on the part of elite Brazilian mothers and that little grief was felt at the death of very young children.[61]

Mme. Emma Toussaint commented that

the burial of a child calls forth no mournful thought. Convinced that they are angels, who go to heaven, the Brazilians, after having exposed the child dressed in white and crowned with roses, place it in a little pink or red coffin. This casket is placed across the two door curtains of a *sega* (a kind of coupe, driven by two horses by a postilion) painted red, and at each side of the carriage four or six men on horseback, in red liveries, and large burning tapers in their hands, accompany the body to the cemetary. . . . It is not in the customs of the country that the parents should follow the body. On all the routes of the procession, the Brazilian ladies throw roses to the little angel: it is very touching.[62]

Dr. Teixeira reported that parents often told him that ''the death of children is a blessing.''[63] Children who died soon after birth were ''angels.'' The elite buried them in sky blue or carnation-hued caskets in ''pagan'' cemeteries. But the popular classes more often wrapped them in a cloth and buried them near the bushes by the gate. José Lins do Rêgo wrote:

I thought how children on the plantation were raised. They suffered with dysentery days on end and then one day they died. They were angels, but few people paid any attention to the poor little creatures. They were buried close to the house, unbaptized, pagan. I never knew why the preferred place for burial was by the bushes at the gate. It was God's will that they should escape life. They were buried there so the worms would not starve.[64]

Anthropologist Alceu Maynard Araujo points out that unbaptized babies could not be buried in the cemetery because it was sacred ground. Therefore, the unbaptized babies were/are buried at road crossings or somewhere near the house. People commonly believed that the baby needed to be near the house so that if the infant were heard to cry, holy water might be taken to baptize it. It was believed that the child would cry within seven years, and for the child to go to heaven, a Christian must hear the cry and baptize the child.[65]

We might ask why babies died without baptism, since any Christian could baptize a baby in an emergency—that is, if death were imminent. It is clear that parents in all three formative cultures ideally waited a minimum of eight days after birth for baptism or naming ceremonies. In the indigenous and African cultures there was a belief that the soul or spirit of the child was created by the father during that period. For the Portuguese the custom may have derived from the ancient religious customs, rather than from Catholicism. It also is notable that despite frequent clerical admonitions against delaying baptism, baptism in the church often was postponed months or even years. One possible explanation for this lies in a custom that has recently been documented for three generations of twentieth-century nonelite families in Porto Alegre—the custom of home baptism. According to anthropologist Claudia Fonseca, the home ritual provided a means of rewarding or acknowledging as ritual godparents people who were close to the affections of the family, but who would not perform the economic and social functions of godparenthood, as recognized by the church. In addition, home baptism protected the soul of the infant without incurring enormous expense. The expensive clothes and gifts and elaborate feast connected with a church baptism could be delayed to a more convenient time, and sometimes siblings were baptized together. For children born of consensual unions the occasion of church baptism might be deferred until after the parents were wed.[66]

The difficult social and material conditions of eighteenth- and nineteenth-century Brazil are nowhere so poignantly demonstrated as in the overwhelming proportions of child abandonment in this period. In part this phenomenon was related to the issue of mortality, in that children, particularly those of single mothers who died in childbirth, were vulnerable to abandonment. The majority of abandoned children were newborn or very young, and probably were abandoned because the mother thought that she could not care for the child. The development of foundling houses in Brazil from the seventeenth to the early nineteenth centuries was a response to this problem, but it also undoubtedly facilitated abandonment, since parents could be more assured that some effort would be made to care for the child.

The first historical references to abandoned children are from the early eighteenth century. In this period unwanted children were left at the doors of private homes, in churches, often at close relatives' houses, or at the homes of people known to be charitable, or even in garbage heaps. Many of these children were baptized and raised as "god-children."[67] In the late eighteenth century the growing number of abandoned children in São Paulo was "alarming."[68] Official complaints concerning this phenomenon were common from 1800 on, including the observation that the vast majority of abandoned newborn infants failed to survive. Laima Mesgravis utilized parish baptismal records to estimate the proportion of abandoned children among births, and arrived at a figure of 17 to 24 percent for the parish of the Sé in São Paulo from 1800 to 1824. Renato Venâncio similarly estimated that 21.1 percent of baptized infants in urban Rio de Janeiro were abandoned children in the last half of the eighteenth century. Other impressionistic contemporary estimates have placed the level of abandonments at an unbelievable two out of every three births in São Paulo in the early nineteenth century. *Expostos*, or abandoned children, were a common household element in the eighteenth-century census manuscripts, particularly in households headed by women.[69]

Although São Paulo baptismal records do not distinguish the abandoned children by color, the records of the Salvador, Bahia, foundling house suggest a predominance of white foundlings for the late eighteenth century, perhaps because "social circumstances" were more likely to force white mothers to "hide" the birth. In many cases placing a child in the turning wheel was seen as the alternative to starvation. In some cases the parents would leave a note with the child, saying that they would reclaim it with "better times." Another factor was the large number of women, living in consensual unions, deserted by their "husbands," who left for the mines or to return to Portugal, or to migrate to areas of newly developing commerical agriculture within Brazil.[70]

In Salvador, Bahia, the foundling house, supervised by the Brotherhood of the Santa Casa de Misericórdia, took reponsibility for foundling children for three years, during which time it paid wet nurses to care for them in their homes. There was no supervision, and on several occasions the Santa Casa removed a child from a wet nurse because of ill treatment. Mortality was disproportionately high among foundlings, which may in part have resulted from the abuse of wet nurses. The nurses also were irregularly paid, and sometimes they sold their charges or returned them to the turning wheel and then claimed pay for two nurselings. In some cases they may have even murdered the children.[71]

After three years the brotherhood placed the children in a home where they were raised. A boy might be apprenticed in a trade or taken on as help in a retail store, or enlisted in the army. Many girls worked as domestics in homes, an arrangement that sometimes was a problem. If it was deemed that a young woman's honor was in danger, she may have been withdrawn from the home and placed in another home or in the retirement house. As a final act of charity the brotherhood often would finance a dowry for a female foundling.[72]

Child abandonment unfortunately has continued to be a significant social problem in Brazil, with available assistance still meager. It is impossible to estimate the magnitude of this problem or to trace quantitative trends. The problem was considered alarming enough to be portrayed in a realistic novel by Jorge Amado in 1937, entitled *The Captains of Sand* (Capitães de Areia). In this novel a gang of more than 100 boys between the ages of eight and fourteen lived in an abandoned sugar mill near the beach and dedicated themselves to a life of theft and violence.

The novel begins with an editorial in the Sergipe newspaper demanding the help of the police and the juvenile court to end this terror. Each of these authorities responds to the newspaper that some other agency is responsible for handling the problem. As we learn in the novel, in some cases the children had deliberately been abandoned by their parents; in others they had simply been neglected to the point that they resolved to leave home. Or the resources in their families were so few that they thought they should leave so as not to continue to be a burden to their families. Amado relates how the children sought comfort in various ways, from religion or women or making love to one another, to stealing useless things. Even as they seemed to face the world almost as adults, defending and feeding themselves, making business deals with criminals, their needs for nurturance and for fantasy are revealed in their relations and in their incredible response to a merry-go-round that comes to town. The newspaper editor and the authorities blame the parents for not showing "Christian feelings" for the up-bringing of their children.

It should not, however, be assumed lightly that maternal feelings were lacking among Brazilian women. The same conclusion of "indifference" presented first by Ariés for medieval society and repeated—with some alterations in chronology by Edward Shorter and Lawrence Stone—is currently being challenged by Stephen Wilson and Linda Pollock. Wilson points out that the historiography on this point is inconsistent "for, while attitudes are assumed to derive from the demographic context in the traditional or pre-industrial milieu, the opposite assumption, that a change in attitudes brings about demographic change, is made for the modern milieu." Wilson argues that customs associated with deaths and naming of children as well as with wet nursing may be understandable within their own context, not as indifference and neglect, but as having positive cultural meaning within the specific situation. For example, the custom that parents should not follow the casket of a child to its burial place may be understood as a desire not to attract death to the other children in the family.[73]

Pollock (1983) utilizes sociobiology to demonstrate the systematic abuse of the kind suggested by some authors (particularly Lloyd de Mause, 1975) would not have been possible. She says: "For parental care to have been as drastically different in the past societies as has been suggested, would mean parents acting in direct opposition to their biological inheritance. . . . The barbaric system of child care described by many authors for previous centuries would be quite unique." Although in some ways the resort to sociobiology as a response to a historical interpretation on childhood may seem extreme, the use of the biological approach does provide some useful observations. For example, although living things would naturally be concerned with reproduction and the rearing of off-spring, Trivers (1974) points out that such concern does not prevent conflicts of interest between parents and particular offspring. Therefore, although evolutionary theory predicts that parent behavior in general would be to the advantage of children, it might not always be optimal for each child. Illustrating this idea, Pollock points out that in cases of infanticide, for example, anthropological data suggests that "surviving children are well cared for." In a similar vein Daniel Smith, discussing eighteenth-century Chesapeake families, suggested that infan-ticide and abandonment "may have been actions taken regretfully by parents to limit family size, at a time soon after birth before attachment bonds had strongly developed."[74]

One kind of Brazilian evidence that would seem to support a positive attitude toward children is the considerable emphasis in folklore, witchcraft, and sorcery on love and on fecundity. These traditions originated from Portugal and Africa, and include charms and spells for fertility as well as to protect the lives of the pregnant woman and the child. The mandrake root was said to attract fecundity and to undo evil spells against the home and reproduction. Altar stones, herbs, toads, crayfish, bats, snakes, doves, rabbits, and hoot owls also were believed to be useful for various kinds of sexual magic, including the attraction of a lover or husband, the consummation of a marriage, the impregnation of a woman, and the successful birth and survival of a child.[75] The numerous prenatal and even more numerous postnatal taboos also attest to the significance and care given to mothers and infants at the time of childbirth.[76]

Common among Brazilians today as in the colonial period is the use of the *promessa*, or promise, to a saint to fulfill wishes. Many images of the virgin Mary in particular are devoted to aspects of conception and childbirth. Some examples of these are Our Lady of Conception, of the Blessed Event, of Birth Pangs (das Dores), of the Expectation, of the Favors. If the favor is completed by the Virgin, the woman promises to do something in return, such as name the newborn child after her. Maria is surely the most common name for Brazilian girls and as a middle name also a common one for boys historically and today. Other promises might concern future participation in a parade carrying a cross or with the child dressed as an angel. Women who want to be or are pregnant also offer dolls made of wax or wood to images of the Virgin, known to be protective of fertility and maternity.[77]

An iconographic study of "Our Lady of Expectation or of 'O' " (1985) by Eduardo Etzel demonstrates the local importance of the cult of the virgin on the brink of childbirth at nine months of pregnancy for São Paulo, from the seventeenth to the end of the nineteenth century. Large images for chapels of the seventeenth century were replaced by small images for private oratories at the end of the eighteenth century and during the nineteenth century. The seventeenth-century images were copied in the nineteenth century because of the local persistence of the cult among country people, even though it no longer was followed in Europe. The relatively high level of mortality among infants and during childbirth explains the continuation of the popularity of the enormously pregnant 'O,' while women in areas of declining mortality had tended to move their devotions in the nineteenth century to the modest and more optimistic virgin of the "good birth," shown with the infant in her arms.[78]

Modern studies on Brazilian families firmly attest to a strong positive value for children.[79] For example, Ruth Cardoso states:

If marriage is desirable, it is because it leads to a family, and by that is meant procreation. . . . Children are an integral and necessary part of the family, because they bring greater pleasure, or because they will care for the parents in their old age, or even because they will impose a welcome and ennobling degree of suffering. . . . Children are seen to be a source of worry as much as of happiness, but they are inevitable. It is unthinkable to form a family without the desire to have children.[80]

In addition to the general desirability of children for both men and women, motherhood often is seen as the "essential attribute" of women. In her research among São Paulo agricultural workers Stolcke concluded:

The ideal number of children has diminished, but both men and women share the conviction that one should have children, and if one cannot have them oneself one should adopt them. One woman who had adopted a boy underlined the women's ideal of having children with the graphic proverb "bananeira que não da cacho merece ser cortada" (a banana plant that does not give bananas should be cut down).[81]

Fostering or adopting children is a widespread custom that has a long history in Brazil and also European roots. Two forms have existed historically: one of complete absorption of a child into a family different from his or her own, the other a form of "child exchange" or "lending" for purposes of socialization and apprenticeship and to provide service, usually in a household that is in a higher socioeconomic strata than that of the child's household of origin. The first form continues to be significant in Brazilian society today, whereas the second form was important for both sexes into the latter half of the nineteenth century and has gradually disappeared in the twentieth century. It is difficult to tell these two forms of fostering apart in the historical context, since they take on similar characteristics during adolescence. A major difference is that in the first case, the child is adopted because it has no parents or the parents are unable to care for it; adoptions of this kind are common among the poor as well as the better-off segments of society. Undoubtedly the incidence of adoption has been strongly correlated historically with poverty and the high level of mortality. The lucky orphan was adopted by neighbors or kin of the original parents, but the unlucky orphan joined the abandoned children placed daily in the turning wheel of the city orphanage.

Within the historical context the documentation of the incidence of the "*filho de criacâo*" (child of upbringing) is difficult, except through the use of censuses. Eighteenth-century censuses do commonly list orphans as household members, as well as other related or nonrelated extended household members, with orphans constituting about 5 percent of household members in urban São Paulo in 1765.[82] This could be a low estimate, since it includes only those among the extended household members who were specifically designated as orphans. For example, it is quite possible that orphans who were kin of the head of household might be designated as "cousin" or "kinsman" (parents) without designating them as orphans.

Twentieth-century community studies by anthropologists emphasize the frequency of adoption in Brazilian society. In some cases children are adopted by childless couples who treat them exactly as if they were their own. On the other hand when parents raise "orphans" in addition to their own offspring the "orphans" most often do the chores. For the most part children are adopted into families of an equal or higher socioeconomic strata, which tends to lead to a difference in treatment.[83]

Charles Wagley reported from 1940s data on adoption in the Amazon region:

The frequent adoptions in Itá and the free way people allow their children to be adopted cannot therefore be explained entirely in terms of poverty or of the usefulness of children to their foster parents. Adoption has the same human basis in the Amazon as it does elsewhere. But, in many parts of the world, a mother who would give up her child so easily as the one mentioned above would be considered lacking in maternal feelings, and in many societies even poverty-stricken mothers cling desperately to their children. In the Amazon, the "giving away" of a child is understandable behavior motivated by the acquisition of benefits for the child. And in Itá the attitudes of foster parents toward their children differ from those of foster parents in other Western societies. . . . In Itá people never predict that an adopted child may become a social deviant or be unsuccessful in life because of its parentage. More credence seems to be given to social environment than to biological heredity in Itá. Further, these attitudes toward adoption and toward allowing children to be adopted seems to reflect a fundamental attitude of parents toward children in Itá. People love children, but they can allow them to be taken by others when their own poverty makes adoption beneficial.[84]

In very different circumstances in the shantytown families of Rio de Janeiro in the 1970s the fostering of children also is found to be prevalent. Cardoso reports: "Adoption is so frequent among the lower classes that almost all our informants had at least one case in their family." Most social scientists interpret frequent adoptions among poor populations as instrumental devices for survival by the use of children as labor, but Cardoso finds this explanation insufficient. She argues that fostering is burdensome, and it is done primarily to create kinship ties and only secondarily to provide labor.[85] The expansion of kinship ties among the migratory poor increases their means of support and assistance within uncertain circumstances.

EARLY CHILDHOOD IN BRAZIL

According to traditional folklore, for seven days after birth the child must be kept in a darkened room to avoid the seven-day sickness, which often ended in death.[86] This disease (which country people believe also can attack on the fourteenth day or during the fourteenth year) has been identified in modern times as a tetanus infection, and the prohibitions are still followed in many places.

The mother was to follow a complex series of postnatal taboos, including six weeks of convalescence and restriction of her diet for eight days to a particular variety of chicken with broth, porridge of manioc flour, cooked plantain, and tea with herbs. Some foods had to be avoided during the entire convalescence, as did washing of the genitals or the hair.[87] Visitors were limited to women with babies, who would not look enviously at the newborn and give it the "evil eye" (*mal de ojo*).

Breast-feeding normally was begun on the second day and preceded on demand. For colonial families that could afford it the hiring or purchase of a black nanny to nurse the child was the preferred procedure.[88] Freyre states that the custom of using wet nurses came from Portugal. The nineteenth-century author of the *Medical Guide*, Imbert, counseled the use of black wet nurses because, he said, Brazilian mothers, who are still very young, could not endure the strain of a long period of nursing.[89] The remarks of nineteenth-century observers on the black wet nurses emphasize the resilience and patience of these women, as well as the abundance and richness of their milk. The general picture is that the first three years of a child's life were ones of constant attendance by a black nanny who provided the breast on demand, and who stayed up all night comforting crying babes, carrying them around from one place to another. It often is said about Brazilian children that for the first two years their feet never hit the ground. Traveler Lino d'Assumpção referred to the black nannies as "automatons" and "nursing machines" (machina de amamentar).[90]

The significance of baptism and of the relations of ritual kinship created through baptism as well as a number of other life rituals, such as christening, first cutting of nails, and marriage, also is much remarked on. Baptism ensured the salvation of an infant, and it was observed above that unbaptized babies could not be buried in sacred ground. Taking this further it was believed that a child was an animal (*bicho*) or a pagan (*pagão*) until baptized. As such he or she could not really be a civilized human being and could not either act "with respect" toward others or be "respected" by them. Parents must show respect toward their children by baptizing them before the children can learn to act with respect toward their parents.[91] Although the Catholic Church sees baptism as a form of cleansing of original sin, many Brazilians think that baptism confers a soul on a child more than it cleanses the one the child already has. Unbaptized children were believed to be special prey of mythical monsters often characterized as "wild" and "lost."

Mythical monsters and bogeymen plagued the lives of badly behaved young children. Some, such as the *Caca*, the *Papão* (or liver-eating man), and the lobisomem (*werewolf*), were of Portuguese origin.[92] Freyre argues that these monsters were multiplied and transformed in the mouths of the black nurses and Brazilian-born mothers.

New fears, brought over from Africa or assimilated from the Indians by the white colonists and by the Negroes, were now added to the Portuguese obsessions having to do with the bogeyman, the goblin, the werewolf . . . the man-with-the-seven-sets-of-teeth and surrounded by a greater number of ghostly forms, and more terrible ones, than any other children in the world. . . . All of these goblins were used to frighten disobedient children who cried, smeared themselves with jelly in the pantry or failed to take a bath in the morning.[93]

In the Brazilian view children were mischievous and irresponsible; that was their nature. It was their parents' responsibility to raise (criar) them so that they would act with respect, consideration, and shame (respeito, consideração, vergonha). These are qualities that it was hoped children acquired within their household and family and for which they must show gratitude to their parents. Respect refers to a public way of treating other people. Among Brazilian children the most obvious sign of this was in the kissing-of-the-hand ritual that was followed by Brazilian children for centuries, morning and night.[94] Along with that was the frequent request for a blessing from adults considered to be of more position, age, or respect.

Consideration is a private way of considering another person, thinking about their needs. Shame (vergonha) is the idea of taking responsibility for your acts, the awareness of the rights of other people in the world.[95] In the colonial period whippings were common for children over age five, and modern families continue to keep paddles (palmatorias) that are to be used to strike the hand of a disobedient child, but corporal punishment is not commonly used any more. Nevertheless, the question of upbringing is a serious one in the lower classes as well as in the upper classes. It is expected that children will behave badly unless they are properly raised. That is the responsibility of the parent, and it is a sacrifice for which the children must be eternally in debt.

The importance of kinship to the lives of young Brazilian children in the colonial past will hardly be judged surprising. In the Brazilian case, however, kinship has not only been important, but also a dominating principle for social and economic exchanges. Particularly in the colonial period the extended bilateral kinship system, including relatives with different kinship terms for ten generations of kin, was the major form of social organization. During the colonial period and the nineteenth century kinship obligations and exchanges were recognized across all these groups, including blood relatives and affines.[96] Although most families lived in nuclear households the clustering of families by kin group was notable.[97]

Kinship links were significantly reinforced and supplemented in the eighteenth century by *compadrio*, or ritual kinship. *Compadrio*, a chosen relationship, as compared with kinship, a given relationship, was even more closely linked to the practical aspects of everyday life. Lia Fukui affirms, for example, that in Laranjeiras, a rural *bairro* of the municipality of Itapecerica da Serra in São Paulo, there was a definite preference for choosing kin as *compadres*. More important than kin, however, was the criteria of proximity of residence of the prospective *compadre*. If there were no appropriate kin in the neighborhood, the tendency was to choose as *compadre* someone who lived close enough to help out in times of need.[98] A further criteria—especially important in urban areas—was the economic or political situation of the person selected.[99] The idea was to develop strong links of mutual assistance with those people who had the greatest capacity to help in critical life situations.

In quantitative terms each child had two *compradres* of baptism, one of christening and usually the two people selected to stand up with the bride and groom at their wedding were considered *compadres*, totaling five primary compadres. Parents were also ritual kin to the *compadres* of each child. It was thus possible for any given household to be linked to a majority of the households in the *bairro* in this way.[100]

Compadrio functioned as a means of developing bonds of trust and political, economic, and social exchange patterns within the *bairro*. Kinship links within the *bairro* were reinforced through *compadrio*, the term *compadre* frequently replacing the kin term as a form of address. In the same way *compadrio* integrated unrelated people in the *bairro* and newcomers into neighborhood patterns of mutual assistance.[101] In essence, *compadrio* acted as a kind of amalgam between kinship (a blood connection) and neighbor (a place connection), combining the level of trust and the sense of obligation and expectation of kinship with the practical convenience of locational proximity for the satisfaction of day-to-day needs for ready and easily available help. Young children were thus provided at an early age with special dyadic relations—in addition to their formal kinship relations—with people who were sworn to protect them and help them whenever possible. These relations, which considerably expanded the kinship networks of the entire family in addition to those of the child, also have frequently been cited as a reason for having or adopting children. Particularly for poor people, the expansion of the kinship network and the network of mutual assistance and obligations is their primary defense against poverty.[102]

Boys and girls are treated differently in Brazil from early childhood. For example, it is common for boys in the popular classes to run around nude until they are four or five years of age. But little girls' genitals are covered by diapers from within a few weeks of birth. As little girls become older they are dressed in colorful cotton underpants. By the time they reach the age of three their mothers keep them in shirts or dresses and attempt to instill some sense of modesty or shame (*vergonha*) in their young daughters.[103] From the beginning daughters are watched much more closely than sons, kept close to home and under family supervision.

Social activities and play have always been important aspects of Brazilian life, organized within neighborhoods, villages, plantations, and private homes. Much of this socializing is organized around the fourteen or more religious holidays of each year, most of them celebrated by the family and its kindred as a group. These festivities usually involve enormous quantities of food and drink as well as fireworks, dancing, and games. Birthdays also are celebrated in an extravagant manner, with entire families of kindred and friends invited in for fantastic feasts and party favors, often far beyond what the family can afford. In addition to the festivities in which all the family participates there are a variety of games played by children. Many of these are differentiated by gender. Little girls play circle games as well as games with dolls. The games of boys include kites—which they fabricate themselves from sticks and colored paper—and a number of games that involve pushing, running, shouting, and generally besting one another in physical play.[104]

Carlinhos, the protagonist of *Plantation Boy*, by José Lins do Rêgo, arrived on his grandfather's plantation at age four and spent most of his time for several years playing with the boys who worked on the plantation, called *moleques* (black ragamuffins). With these boys he picked oranges and guavas out of the orchard, rode bareback on horses, went swimming in the river, and chased and even murdered birds. Although the "moleques" had chores to do in the morning,

Carlinhos had none. He was supposed to study with his tutor, but he says he learned nothing until he went away to boarding school. His position as grandson of the *senhor* protected him from punishment.

On the plantations during the colonial period children of the Big House grew up playing with slave and free colored children from families that worked on the plantation. Often the sons of the plantation owner were given male slave "playmates" while they were still young. According to Koster,

as soon as a child begins to crawl a slave of about his own age, and of the same sex, is given to it as a playfellow or rather as a plaything. They grow up together, and the slave is made the stock upon which the younger owner gives vent to his passion. The slave is sent upon all errands, and receives blame for all unfortunate accidents; in fact the white child is thus encouraged to be overbearing, owing to the false fondness of its parents.[105]

The work role of the child in the subsistence household was of great importance. By the age of six or seven the child was expected to help with domestic tasks and was allowed access to the household tools.[106] Assimilation into the household work force was gradual, paralleling the development of the child's strength and skills. Because the necessary skills were rudimentary, the child had only to imitate his elders. Working beside his parents he learned how to plant beans, corn, and manioc, how to work the soil, how to care for the animals. Subtler knowledge concerning the appropriate times for the planting of different crops, how to choose the best soils, and how to manufacture domestic utensils also was acquired by age nine or ten.[107] The importance of child labor within the household of the poor subsistence farmer in eighteenth- and nineteenth-century São Paulo was potentially high. It was, in these terms, rational for a subsistence farmer to want numerous children in the household, particularly with high levels of mortality, and when there were already children present to alleviate the difficulties of caring for the next.

CONCLUSION

Children over age seven in the colonial period and the nineteenth century became increasingly differentiated from one another—the slaves and the lower classes from the elites, and the girls from the boys. Slave children and children in the popular classes gradually were integrated into the work force. Elite children began to receive serious training for their social role, and male elite children often were sent away to school. Young elite women were increasingly cloistered and supervised to ensure that their "honor" would not be jeopardized.

Religious beliefs of various origins had an important impact on both the concept of childhood and the way young children were socialized. The concepts that children were "born in sin" (Portuguese Catholic), were spiritually akin to wild animals or forest demons at birth (indigenous Brazilians), or were born without a soul (African culture) resulted in an early preoccupation with the physical and spiritual safety of young children and a belief in a "stern" upbringing. Both African and indigenous women routinely carried their infants on their backs as they labored in the fields and at home. Because most of the child care in Brazil during the first 300 years was handled by indigenous, African, or mixed-blood women, it is not surprising that most Brazilian children have spent (and continue to spend) the first year or two of their lives being carried around by their female kinfolk.

Baptism and the use of ritual kinship or co-parents (*compadrio*) were originally Catholic rituals adopted universally by all ethnic groups in Brazil. The birth and naming rituals of all three cultures included the concepts of acquiring a soul and forms of protection against evil beings. To these were added ideas of purification or contact with powerful protective spirits through baptism. In addition to its spiritual dimensions, baptism functioned as a ritualistic means of integrating a child into society through the celebration of the new family member and the assignment of godparents for that child. Similarly, Brazilians believe that the baptism ceremony "shows respect" for the child who can then learn "respect" for his or her parents and kinfolk. Respect, consideration, and shame are thought to be the major virtues or attitudes that good parents should instill in their children.

In this chapter I have attempted a general discussion of the history of early childhood in Brazil. Although infant mortality and child abandonment statistics in the past have been grim, these facts of preindustrial life seem insufficient to argue that Brazilian families in this period were "indifferent" to their children. To the contrary, it is clear from a variety of sources that children were and are considered essential in every family and that motherhood is viewed by many as the essential attribute of a woman. Birth and death were constant preoccupations in Brazil until well into the twentieth century. The common customs of child exchange and ritual kinship and the importance of neighborhood and kindred religious festivals must have meant that children were given a wide exposure to adults and children outside their immediate family as they grew up. Also the tendency for racial mixture among children as they played must have something to do with the general level of comfort that Brazilians ordinarily feel with racial mixture. Another aspect of that mixture, the tendency to manifest social differences between races and classes in the context of child's play, would seem also to have had antidemocratic results in terms of socialization.

NOTES

1. The classic statement of this approach is Philippe Ariès, *Centuries of Childhood: A Social History of Family Life* (New York: Alfred A. Knopf, 1962).

2. See Stephen Wilson, "The Myth of Motherhood a Myth: The Historical View of European Child-Rearing," *Social History* 9:2 (May 1984):181–198, and Linda A. Pollock, *Forgotten Children: Parent-Child Relations from 1500 to 1900* (Cambridge: Cambridge University Press, 1983), for a critical view of this literature.

3. Examples of this approach are John Demos, *A Little Commonwealth: Family Life*

in *Plymouth Colony* (New York: Oxford University Press, 1970), and Erik H. Erikson, *Childhood and Society* (2nd ed.; New York: W. W. Norton, 1963).

4. Roger Bastide and Florestan Fernandes, *Brancos e negros em São Paulo* (São Paulo, 1959), p. 12.

5. Gabriel Soares de Sousa, *Tratado descriptivo do Brasil em 1587* (3rd ed.; São Paulo: Companhia Editôra Nacional, 1938), pp. 370–371.

6. Fernão Cardim, *Tratados da Terra e Gente do Brasil* (2nd ed., São Paulo: Companhia Editôra Nacional, 1939), p. 149.

7. Hans Staden, *Duas Viagens a Brasil* (São Paulo: Publicações da Sociedade Hans Staden, 1942), p. 170.

8. Soares de Sousa, *Tratado descriptivo do Brazil*, pp. 370–371.

9. Gilberto Freyre, *The Masters and the Slaves (Casa-Grande & Sensala): A Study in the Development of Brazilian Civilization*, trans. Samuel Putnam (New York: Alfred A. Knopf, 1946), pp. 147, 151–153.

10. Cardím, *Tratados da Terra e Gente*, pp. 149–150.

11. Serafim Leite, *Novas cartas jesuiticas* (São Paulo: Companhia Editôra Nacional, 1940), p. 166.

12. Freyre, *Masters and the Slaves*, p. 143.

13. Ibid., pp. 149–150; Soares de Sousa, *Tratado descriptivo de Brazil*, pp. 370–371.

14. Staden, *Duas Viagens a Brazil*, pp. 171–172.

15. Willy de Craemer, Jan Vansina, and Reneé C. Fox, "Religious Movements in Central Africa: A Theoretical Study," *Comparative Studies in Society and History* 18:4 (October 1976):458–475, 463; Mary Karasch, "Central African Religious Tradition in Rio de Janeiro, *Journal of Latin American Lore* 5:2 (1979):233–253.

16. Craemer et al., "Religious Movements in Central Africa," p. 469.

17. Monica Shuler, *"Alas, Alas, Kongo"; A Social History of Indentured African Immigration into Jamaica, 1841–1865* (Baltimore: Johns Hopkins University Press, 1980), pp. 71–72.

18. G. I. Jones, "Olaudah Equiano of the Niger Ibo," in *Africa Remembered*, ed. Philip Curtin (Madison: University of Wisconsin Press, 1967), p. 63.

19. René Ribeiro, "Relations of the Negro with Christianity in Portuguese America," *Americas* 14:4 (April 1958):469.

20. M. d'Avezac, "Notice sur le pays et le peuple des Yebous, en Afrique," translated by Philip Curtin, in Curtin, ed., *Africa Remembered*, pp. 274–275.

21. Craemer et al., "Religious Movements in Central Africa," p. 471.

22. Karasch, "Central African Religious Tradition," p. 235.

23. d'Avezac, "Notice sur le pays," p. 255; see also Ayuba Suleiman, "Capture and Travels of Ayuba Suleiman," in Curtin, ed., *Africa Remembered*, p. 50.

24. Shuler, *"Alas, Alas, Kongo,"* p. 79.

25. d'Avezac, "Notice sur le pays," p. 256; Suleiman, "Capture and Travels," p. 50.

26. d'Avezac, "Notice sur le pays," p. 155.

27. Jones, "Olaudah Equiano," pp. 60–69.

28. d'Avezac, "Notice sur le pays," pp. 258–259; Jones, "Olaudah Equiano," pp. 67, 71.

29. A. H. de Oliveira Marques, *Daily Life in Portugal in the Late Middle Ages*, trans. S. S. Wyatt (Madison: University of Wisconsin Press, 1971), pp. 206–208; William

A. Christian, Jr., *Local Religion in Sixteenth-Century Spain* (Princeton, N.J.: Princeton University Press, 1981), pp. 14–20.

30. Thomas F. Glick, "The Ethnic Systems of Premodern Spain," *Comparative Studies in Sociology* 1 (1978):157–171.

31. Christian, *Local Religion in Sixteenth-Century Spain*, pp. 20–22.

32. Oliveira Marques, *Daily Life in Portugal*, p. 226.

33. Padre Jose de Anchieta, *Carta fazendo a descripcão das innumeras coisas naturães* (São Paulo: Typ da Casa Ecléctica, 1900), pp. 47–48.

34. Oliveira Marques, *Daily Life in Portugal*, p. 276.

35. Ibid., pp. 206–207.

36. On this point see João Cruz Costa, *A History of Ideas in Brazil*, trans. Suzette Macedo (Berkeley: University of California Press, 1964), p. 16, and the discussion of Richard Morse, "The Heritage of Latin America," in *The Founding of New Societies*, ed. Louis Hartz (New York: Harcourt Brace and World, 1964), pp. 153–157.

37. *The Good of Marriage*, trans. C. T. Wilcox (New York: Fathers of the Church, 1955), p. 13.

38. Jeffrey Blustein, *Parents and Children: The Ethics of the Family* (New York: Oxford University Press, 1982), p. 54.

39. *Summa Theologiae*, XLI, trans. T. C. O'Brien (New York: Blackfriars, 1972), q. 104, art. 2.

40. Blustein, *Parents and Children*, pp. 58–59.

41. See the discussion of this in Elizabeth Kuznesof and Robert Oppenheimer, "The Family and Society in Nineteenth-Century Latin America: An Historiographical Introduction," *Journal of Family History* 10 (Fall 1985):217–219.

42. Antonio Cândido, "The Brazilian Family," in *Brazil: Portrait of Half a Continent* ed. T. Lynn Smith (New York: Dryden Press, 1951), pp. 204–205; see also Freyre, *Masters and the Slaves*, pp. 404–419; Alcântara Machado, *Vida e Morte do Bandeirante* (Belo Horizonte: Ed Itataía, 1980), pp. 151–164.

43. Julio Cesar de Morães Carneiro, *O Catolicismo no Brasil* (Rio de Janeiro: Livraria Agir, 1950), pp. 93–95, 100–101; Serafim Leite, *Páginas de Historia do Brasil* (São Paulo: Companhia Editôra Nacional, 1937), p. 16; Joseph de Anchieta, *Cartas, Informações, Fragmentos Históricos e Seramões* (Rio de Janiero: Civilização Brasileira, 1933), pp. 67, 71, 79, 85, 88, 98, 145, 201, 322, 333.

44. Robert Ricard, "Comparison of Evangelization in Portuguese and Spanish America," *Americas* 14:4 (April 1958):453.

45. Anchieta, *Cartas*, pp. 333–334.

46. Ribeiro, "Relations of the Negro," p. 460.

47. Serafim Leite, *História da Companhia de Jesus no Brasil*, II (Rio de Janeiro, 1938–1948), p. 592, as cited in Ribeiro, "Relations of the Negro," p. 458. For details of slave evangelization and catechism see the documents published by the archbishop of Bahia in 1707, translated and published in Robert E. Conrad, *Children of God's Fire* (Princeton, N.J.: Princeton University Press, 1983), pp. 154–159.

48. Cristovão Gouveia, in Leite, *História de Companhia*, p. 355, as cited in Ribeiro, "Relations of the Negro," p. 461.

49. Henry Koster, *Viagens ão Nordeste do Brasil* (São Paulo: Companhia Editora Nacional, 1942), p. 326.

50. Mary Karasch, *Slave Life in Rio de Janeiro, 1808–1850* (Princeton, N.J.: Princeton University Press, 1987), pp. 255–257.

51. Shuler, "*Alas, Alas, Kongo,*" p. 36.

52. Karasch, *Slave Life*, p. 257; João M. Rugendas, *Viagem Pitoresca Através do Brasil*, trans. Sergio Milliet (São Paulo, 1967), pp. 134–135, as cited by Karasch, *Slave Life*, p. 257.

53. Freyre, *Masters and the Slaves*, p. 386.

54. Thomas W. Merrick and Douglas H. Graham, *Population and Economic Development in Brazil: 1800 to the Present* (Baltimore: Johns Hopkins University Press, 1979), pp. 56–57.

55. Jose Maria Teixeira, *Causes of the Mortality of Children in Rio*, 1887; Baron de Lavradío, "Some Considerations of the Causes of Mortality in the Children of Rio de Janeiro and the Diseases Most Frequent in the First Six or Seven Months of Life," a series of articles in the *Jornal de Acadêmia Imperial*, 1847.

56. Freyre, *Masters and the Slaves*, pp. 366, 378–379; Maria Luiza Marcílio, *La Ville de São Paulo* (Rouen: Rouen Nizet, 1968), p. 205.

57. Elizabeth Kuznesof, *Household Economy and Urban Development: São Paulo 1765–1836* (Boulder, Colo.: Westview Press, 1986), pp. 58–61.

58. Freyre, *Masters and the Slaves*, p. 379.

59. João Guimarães Rosa, *The Third Bank of the River and Other Stories* (New York: Alfred A. Knopf, 1968), pp. 7–8, 227–228.

60. José Lins de Rêgo, *Plantation Boy*, trans. Emmi Baum (New York: Alfred A. Knopf, 1966), p. 6.

61. Freyre, *Masters and the Slaves*, p. 378.

62. Mme. Toussaint-Samson, *A Parisian in Brazil* (Boston: James H. Earle Publisher, 1891), pp. 130–131.

63. As cited by Freyre, *Masters and the Slaves*, p. 388.

64. Lins do Rêgo, *Plantation Boy*, p. 350.

65. Alceu Maynard Araujo, *Cultura Popular Brasileira* (São Paulo: Edições Melhoramêntos, 1973), p. 150.

66. Claudia Fonseca and Jurema Brites, "O Batismo em Casa: Uma Prática Popular no Rio Grande do Sul," unpublished manuscript.

67. Laima Mesgravis, *A Santa Casa de Misericórdia de São Paulo, 1599?–1884: contribuição ão estudo da assistência social no Brasil* (São Paulo: Conselho Estadual de Cultura, 1976), pp. 178–179; Sérgio Buarque de Holanda, "Movimentos da População em São Paulo no Século XVIII," *Revista do Instituto de Estudos Brasileiros* 1 (1966):79.

68. Alfonso de E. Taunay, *Historia da Cidade de São Paulo no Século XVIII: 1735–65*, vol. 1, p. 2 (São Paulo: Coleção do Departamento de Cultura, 1949), pp. 107–136.

69. Mesgravis, *A Santa Casa de Misericórdia*, p. 172; Renato Pinto Venancio, "Infancia sem Destino: O Abandono de Criancas no Rio De Janeiro do Seculo XVIII" (Dissertacáo de Mestrado Dep. de Historia, USP, São Paulo, 1988), p. 30; Kuznesof, *Household Economy*, pp. 73, 156–157; Lucila Herrmann, "Evolução da estrutura social de Guaratinguetá num período de trezentos anos," *Revista de Administracao* 2 (March-June 1948):28, 34.

70. A.J.R. Russell-Wood, *Fidalgos and Philanthropists: The Santa Casa de Misericordia of Bahia, 1550–1755* (Berkeley: University of California Press, 1968), pp. 309, 313; Kuznesof, *Household Economy*, p. 73, n. 102.

71. Russell-Wood, *Fidalgos and Philanthropists*, p. 316.

72. Ibid., p. 317.

73. Wilson, "Myth of Motherhood," pp. 182, 189.

74. Pollock, *Forgotten Children*, pp. 43, 51; Robert Trivers, "Parent-off-spring conflict" *American Zoologist* 14 (1974), pp. 249–64; Daniel Smith, "Autonomy and Affection: Parents and Children in Eighteenth-Century Chesapeake Families" *The Psychohistorical Review* VI (1977):32–51.

75. Pedro McGregor, *Jesus of the Spirits* (New York: Stein Day, 1967), pp. 59–61.

76. Charles Wagley, *Amazon Town: A Study of Man in the Tropics* (New York: Macmillan, 1953), p. 246; Marvin Harris, *Town and Country in Brazil* (New York: Columbia University Press, 1956), p. 165.

77. Araujo, *Cultura Popular Brasileira*, pp. 143–145; McGregor, *Jesus of the Spirits*, pp. 61–63.

78. Eduardo Etzel, *Nossa Senhora da Expectaçâo ou Do Ó* (São Paulo: Bolsa de Valores de São Paulo, 1985), p. 52.

79. Wagley, *Amazon Town*, pp. 176–177; Ruth C. L. Cardoso, "Creating Kinship: The Fostering of Children in Favela Families in Brazil," in *Kinship Ideology and Practice in Latin America*, ed. Raymond T. Smith (Chapel Hill: University of North Carolina Press, 1984), pp. 198–199; Verena Stolcke, "The Exploitation of Family Morality: Labor Systems and Family Structure on São Paulo Coffee Plantations 1850–1979," also in Smith, ed. *Kinship Ideology*, p. 286; Nevin O. Winter, *Brazil and Her People of Today: An Account of the Customs, Characteristics, Amusements, History and Advancement of the Brazilians and the Development and Resources of Their Country* (Boston: Page Co., 1910), p. 204.

80. Cardoso, "Creating Kinship," pp. 198–199.

81. Stolcke, "Exploitation of Family Morality," p. 286.

82. Kuznesof, *Household Economy*, pp. 156–157.

83. Wagley, *Amazon Town*, pp. 180–183.

84. Ibid., pp. 183–184.

85. Cardoso, "Creating Kinship," pp. 200, 202. For an interpretation emphasizing the role of child labor in adoption proceedings see Claudia Fonseca, "A Circulação de Crianças em Grupos Populares de Porto Alegre no Inicio do Seculo: Um Exame de Processos Juridicos de Apreensão de Menores (1900–1926)," unpublished manuscript.

86. Harris, *Town and Country in Brazil*, p. 155.

87. Wagley, *Amazon Town*, pp. 246–247.

88. Freyre, *Masters and the Slaves*, p. 379; Tomaz Lino da Assumpação, *Narrativas do Brasil (1876–1880)* (Rio de Janeiro: Livraria Contemporânea de Faro e Lino, 1881), p. 49; Toussaint-Samson, *A Parisian in Brasil*, pp. 44–45.

89. As cited in Freyre, *Masters and the Slaves*, p. 336.

90. Assumpçaô, *Narratives do Brazil*, p. 49.

91. Eugene Keith Galbraith, "Facets of Social Experience: Household, Family and 'Compadrio' in a Northeast Brazilian Community" (Ph.d. diss., John Hopkins University, 1983), pp. 119–120. On the twentieth-century practice of home baptism in Rio Grande do Sul (in addition to church baptism) see Fonseca and Brites, "O Batismo em Casa."

92. Stuart B. Schwartz, "The Uncourted *Menina*: Brazil's Portuguese Heritage," *Luso-Brazilian Review* 2:1 (Summer 1965):78.

93. Freyre, *Masters and the Slaves*, pp. 292–293.

94. Assumpçaô, *Narrativas do Brazil*, p. 48.

95. Galbraith, "Facets of Social Experience," pp. 110–120.

96. Emilio Willems, "The Structure of the Brazilian Family," *Social Forces* 31:4

(1953):341–345; Lia Fukui, "Parentesco e família entre sitiantes tradicionais" (Ph.D. diss., University of São Paulo, Social Sciences, 1972), pp. 47–86.

97. Elizabeth Kuznesof, "Clans, the Militia and Territorial Government: The Articulation of Kinship with Polity in Eighteenth-Century São Paulo," in *Social Fabric and Spatial Structure in Colonial Latin America*, ed. David J. Robinson (Ann Arbor: University Microfilms, 1979), pp. 204–217.

98. Fukui, "Parentesco e familia," pp. 250–254; Robert W. Shirley, *The End of a Tradition: Culture Change and Development in the Municipio of Cunha* (New York: Columbia University Press, 1971), pp. 39–40.

99. Maria Isaura Pereira de Queiroz, *Barrios rurais paulistas* (São Paulo: 1973), pp. 39–40; Donald Ramos, "A Social History of Ouro Preto: Stresses of Dynamic Urbanization in Colonial Brazil, 1695–1726" (Ph.D. diss., University of Florida, 1972), pp. 242–254.

100. Donald Pierson, *Cruz das Almas* (Rio de Janeiro, 1966), pp. 280–282.

101. Pereira de Queiroz, *Barrios rurais paulistas*, p. 40.

102. Cardoso, "Creating Kinship," pp. 196–203.

103. Galbraith, "Facets of Social Experience," pp. 121–122.

104. Wagley, *Amazon Town*, pp. 187–214.

105. Henry Koster, *Travels in Brazil* (1st ed., 1817; London, 1916), as cited in Freyre, *Masters and the Slaves*, p. 350.

106. Fukui, "Parentesco e familia," p. 237; Sidney Mintz, *Worker in the Cane* (New Haven, Conn.: Yale University Press, 1964).

107. Antonio Candido, *Os parceiros do Rio Bonito* (Rio de Janeiro: Livraria Duas Cidades Ltda, 1964), pp. 117–118.

REFERENCES

Amado, Jorge. *Los Capitanes de la Arena*. Buenos Aires: Editorial Futuro, 1956.

Araujo, Alceu Maynard. *Cultura Popular Brasileira*. São Paulo: Edições Melhoramêntos, 1973.

Ariès, Philippe. *Centuries of Childhood: A Social History of Family Life*. New York: Alfred A. Knopf, 1962.

Ariños, Alfonso. *Lendas e Tradições Brasileiras*. 2nd ed. Rio de Janeiro: F. Briguiet & Co., 1937.

Arriaga, Eduardo E. *Mortality Decline and Its Demographic Effects in Latin America*. Westport, Conn.: Greenwood Press, 1976.

———. *New Life Tables for Latin American Populations in the Nineteenth and Twentieth Centuries*. Westport, Conn.: Greenwood Press, 1976.

Assumpção, Tomaz Lino da. *Narrativas do Brasil (1876–1880)*. Rio de Janeiro: Livraria Contemporânea de Faro e Lino, 1881.

Azevedo, Fernando de. *A Cultura Brasileira*. São Paulo: Ediçoes Melhoramêntos, 1964.

Belmartino, Susana M. "Estructura de la Familia y 'Edades Sociales' en la Aristocracia de Leon Y Castilla Segun las Fuentes Literarias e Historiograficas (Sigos X-XIII)." *Cuadernos de Historia de España* (Buenos Aires) 47–48 (1968):256–328.

Bennett, Frank. *Forty Years in Brazil*. London: Mills & Boon, 1914.

Callcott, Maria Dundas Graham, Lady. *Journal of a Voyage to Brazil, and Residence There, During Part of the Years 1821, 1822 and 1823*. New York: Praeger, 1969.

Candido, Antonio. *Os parceiros do Rio Bonito*. Rio de Janeiro: Livraria Duas Cidades Ltda., 1964.

Cardoso, Ruth C. L. "Creating Kinship: The Fostering of Children in Favela Families in Brazil." In *Kinship Ideology and Practice in Latin America*, edited by Raymond T. Smith. Chapel Hill: University of North Carolina Press, 1984, pp. 196–203.

Carvalho Franco, Maria Sylvia de. *Homens Livres na Ordem Escravocrata*. São Paulo: Publicaçao do Instituto de Estudos Brasileiros, 1969.

Coimbra, Creso. *Fenomenologia da Cultura Brasileira*. São Paulo: LISA-Livros Irradiantes S.A., 1972.

Cooper, Clayton Sedgwick. *The Brazilians and Their Country*. New York: Frederick A. Stokes Co., 1917.

De Mause, Lloyd. "The Revolution of Childhood." In *The History of Childhood*, ed. de Mause. London: Souvenir Press, 1976: pp. 1–74.

Demos, John. *A Little Commonwealth: Family Life in Plymouth Colony*. New York: Oxford University Press, 1970.

Denslow, David, Jr. "Sugar Production in Northeastern Brazil and Cuba, 1885–1908." Ph.D. diss., Yale University, 1974.

Edmundo, Luiz. *O Rio de Janeiro do Meu Tempo*. Rio de Janeiro: Imprensa Nacional, 1938.

Erikson, Erik H. *Childhood and Society*. 2nd ed. New York: W. W. Norton, 1963.

Finkelstein, Barbara. "Uncle Sam and the Children: History of Government Involvement in Childrearing." *Review Journal of Philosophy and Social Science* (India) 3 (1978):139–153.

———, ed. *Regulated Children/Liberated Children: Education in Psychohistorical Perspective*. New York: Psychohistory Press, 1979.

Fonseca, Claudia. "A Circulação de Criancas em Grupos Populares de Porto Alegre no Inicio do Seculo: Um Exame de Processos Juridicos de Apreensão de Menores (1900–1926)." Biblioteca Setorial de Ciencias Sociais e Humanidades, UFRGS, manuscript.

Fonseca, Claudia, and Jurema Brites. "O Batismo em Casa: Uma Prática Popular no Rio Grande do Sul." Biblioteca Sectorial de Ciencias Sociais e Humanidades, UFRGS, manuscript.

Fox, Vivian C., and Martin H. Quitt, eds. *Loving, Parenting and Dying: The Family Cycle in England and America, Past and Present*. New York: Psychohistory Press, 1980.

Freyre, Gilberto. *The Masters and the Slaves (Casa-Grande & Senzala): A Study in The Development of Brazilian Civilization*, translated by Samuel Putnam. New York: Alfred A. Knopf, 1946.

Fukui, Lia. "Parentesco e família entre sitiantes tradicionais." Ph.D. diss., University of São Paulo, Social Sciences, 1972.

———. *Sertão e Bairro Rural. Parentesco e Familia entre Sitiantes Tradicionais*. São Paulo: Editôra Atica, 1979.

Galbraith, Eugene Keith. "Facets of Social Experience: Household, Family and 'Compadrío' in a Northeast Brazilian Community." Ph.D. diss., Johns Hopkins University, 1983.

Greven, Philip. *The Protestant Temperament: Patterns of Child-Rearing, Religious Experience, and the Self in Early America*. New York: Knopf, 1977.

Harris, Marvin. *Town and Country in Brazil*. New York: Columbia University Press, 1956.

Hawes, Joseph M. *Children in Urban Society: Juvenile Delinquency in the Nineteenth Century*. New York: Oxford University Press, 1971.

Hendrick, Harry. "The History of Childhood and Youth." *Social History* 9:1 (January 1984):87–96.

Herrmann, Lucila. "Evolução da estrutura social de Guaratinguetá num período de trezentos anos." *Revista de Administraçao* 2 (March-June 1948): 3–333.

Hiner, N. Ray, and Joseph M. Hawes. *Growing Up in America: Children in Historical Perspective*. Urbana: University of Illinois Press, 1985.

Holanda, Sérgio Buarque de. "Movimentos da População em São Paulo no Século XVIII." *Revista do Instituto de Estudos Brasileiros* 1 (1966):55–111.

Koster, Henry. *Travels in Brazil, 1809 to 1815*. 2 vols. Philadelphia, 1817.

Kuznesof, Elizabeth. "Clans, the Militia and Territorial Government: The Articulation of Kinship with Polity in Eighteenth-Century São Paulo." In *Social Fabric and Spatial Structures in Colonial Latin America*, edited by David J. Robinson. Ann Arbor: University Microfilms, 1979, pp. 181–226.

———. "The Role of the Female-Headed Household in Brazilian Modernization." *Journal of Social History* 13:4 (June 1980):589–613.

———. "Property Law and Family Strategies: Inheritance and Corporations in Brazil: 1800–1960." Paper presented at the American Historical Association Convention in Chicago, December 30, 1984.

———. *Household Economy and Urban Development: São Paulo 1765–1836*. Boulder, Colo.: Westview Press, 1986.

Kuznesof, Elizabeth, and Robert Oppenheimer. "The Family and Society in Nineteenth-Century Latin America: An Historiographical Introduction." *Journal of Family History* 10 (Fall 1985):217–219.

Levi, Darrell. *A Família Prado*. São Paulo: Cultura 70, Editôra Brasiliense.

Levine, David. *Family Formation in an Age of Nascent Capitalism*. New York: Academic Press, 1977.

Lins do Rêgo, José. *Plantation Boy*, translated by Emmi Baum. New York: Alfred A. Knopf, 1966.

McCracken, Grant. "The Exchange of Children in Tudor England: An Anthropological Phenomenon in Historical Context." *Journal of Family History* 9 (Winter 1983):303–313.

McGregor, Pedro. *Jesus of the Spirits*. New York: Stein & Day, 1967.

Malvido, Elsa. "El Abandono de los Hijos: Uma Forma de Control de Tamaño de la Família y del Trabajo Indigena, Tula, 1683–1730." *Historia Mexicana* 29:4 (1980):521–561.

Marcílio, Maria-Luiza. *La ville de São Paulo: peuplement et population 1750–1850*. Rouen: Rouen Nizet, 1968.

Martinho, Lenira Menezes. "Organização do trabalho e relações sociais nas firmas commerciais do Rio de Janeiro: primeira metade século XIX." *Revista do Instituto de Estudos Brasileiros* 18 (1976):41–62.

Mattosos, Katia M. de Queirós. *Bahia: A Cidade do Salvador e Seu Mercado no Século XIX*. São Paulo: Editora Hucitec Ltda.; Salvador: Secretaria Municipal de Educação e Cultura, 1978.

Mechling, Jay. "Advice to Historians on Advice to Mothers." *Journal of Social History* 9 (1975):44–63.

Merrick, Thomas W., and Douglas H. Graham. *Population and Economic Development in Brazil: 1800 to the Present*. Baltimore: Johns Hopkins University Press, 1979.

Mesgravis, Laima. "A 'roda' da Santa Casa de São Paulo: a assistencia social ãos enjeitados no seculo xix." Paper presented at I Congreso de Historia, São Paulo, 1972.

———. *A Santa Casa de Misericórdia de São Paulo, 1599?–1884; contribuição ão estudo da assistência social no Brasil*. São Paulo: Conselho Estadual de Cultura, 1976.

Mesquita, Eni de. "O papel do agregado na região de Itu, 1798–1830." *Coleção Museu Paulista*, serie de historia, VI. São Paulo, 1977, pp. 1–105.

Minge-Kalman, Wanda. "The Evolution of Family Productive Changes During the Peasant to Worker Transition in Europe." Ph.D. diss., Columbia University, 1977.

Mintz, Sidney. *Worker in the Cane*. New Haven, Conn.: Yale University Press, 1964.

Moacyr, Primitivo. *A instrução e as províncias*. 3 vols. São Paulo: Companhia Editora Nacional, 1936–1940.

Moncorvo, Filho. *Historico da Protecção a Infancia no Brasil 1500–1922*. 2nd ed. Rio de Janeiro: Empresa Graphica Editôra, Departamento da Crianca no Brasil, 1926.

Morse, Richard M. *From Community to Metropolis: A Biography of São Paulo, Brazil*. Gainesville: University of Florida Press, 1958.

Mulhall, Michael G. *The Progress of the World*. London, 1880.

Pereira de Queiroz, Maria Isaura. *Bairros rurais paulistas*. São Paulo: Livraria Duas Cidades, 1973.

Pierson, Donald. *Negroes in Brazil: A Study of Race Contact at Bahia*. Chicago: University of Chicago Press, 1942.

———. *Cruz das Almas*. Rio de Janeiro: J. Olympio, 1966.

Pollock, Linda A. *Forgotten Children: Parent-Child Relations from 1500 to 1900*. Cambridge: Cambridge University Press, 1983.

Ramos, Donald. "A Social History of Ouro Preto: Stresses of Dynamic Urbanization in Colonial Brazil, 1695–1726." Ph.D. diss., University of Florida, 1972.

Rendôn, José Arouche de Toledo, "Reflexões sobre o estado em que se acha a agricultura na capitania de São Paulo (1788)." *Documentos interessantes* 44 (1930):195–215.

Rosa, João Guimarães. *The Third Bank of the River and Other Stories*. Translated by Barbara A. Shelby. New York: Alfred A. Knopf, 1968.

Rothstein, Frances. "Capitalist Industrialization and the Increasing Cost of Children." In *Women and Change in Latin America*, edited by June Nash and Helen I. Safa. South Hadley, Mass.: Bergin and Garvey, 1986, pp. 37–52.

Russell-Wood, A.J.R. *Fidalgos and Philanthropists: The Santa Casa da Misericórdia of Bahia, 1550–1755*. Berkeley: University of California Press, 1968.

Santos Filho, Lycurgo de Castro. *Historia da medicina no Brasil*. 2 vols. São Paulo: Editôra Brasiliense, 1947.

Schwartz, Stuart B. "The Uncourted *Menina*: Brazil's Portuguese Heritage." *Luso-Brazilian Review* 2:1 (Summer 1965):67–80.

Scrimshaw, Susan. "A Study of Changing Values, Fertility and Socio-Economic Status." In *Population and Social Organization*, edited by M. Nag. The Hague, 1975, pp. 135–151.

Shirley, Robert W. *The End of a Tradition: Culture Change and Development in the Município of Cunha.* New York: Oxford University Press, 1971.

Slater, Peter G. *Children in the New England Mind in Death and Life: From the Puritans to Bushnell.* Hamden, Conn.: Archon Books, 1977.

Smith, Daniel B. "Autonomy and Affection: Parents and Children in Eighteenth-Century Chesapeake Families," *The Psychohistorical Review* 6 (1974):249–264.

Stolcke, Verena. "The Exploitation of Family Morality: Labor Systems and Family Structure on São Paulo Coffee Plantations 1850–1979." In *Kinship Ideology and Practice in Latin America,* edited by Raymond T. Smith. Chapel Hill: University of North Carolina Press, 1984, pp. 264–296.

Suzannet, Conde de. *O brasil em 1845* tradução de Marcia de Moura Castro. Rio de Janeiro: Editôra de Casa do Estudante do Brasil, 1957.

Taunay, Alfonso de E. *História da Cidade de São Paulo no Século XVIII 1735–1765,* vol. 1, p. 2. São Paulo: Coleção do Departmento de Cultura, 1949.

Tilly, Louise, and Joan Scott. *Women, Work and the Family.* New York: Holt, Rinehart and Winston, 1978.

Toussaint-Samson, Mme. *A Parisian in Brazil,* translated by Emma Toussaint. Boston: James H. Earle Publisher, 1891.

Trivers, Robert. "Parent-Offspring Conflict." *American Zoologist* 14 (1974):249–264.

Venancio, Renato Pinto. "Infancia sem Destino: O Abandono de Criancas no Rio de Janeiro do Século XVIII." (Dissertação de Mestrado em Historia, FFLCH, USP) São Paulo, 1988.

Wagley, Charles. *Amazon Town: A Study of Man in the Tropics.* New York: Macmillan, 1953.

Willems, Emilio. "The Structure of the Brazilian Family." *Social Forces* 31:4 (1953):341–345.

Wilson, Stephen. "The Myth of Motherhood a Myth: The Historical View of European Child-Rearing." *Social History* 9:2 (May 1984):181–198.

Winter, Nevin O. *Brazil and Her People of Today: An Account of the Customs, Characteristics, Amusements, History and Advancement of the Brazilians and the Development and Resources of Their Country.* Boston: Page Co., 1910.

8

CANADA

Patricia T. Rooke and Rudy Schnell

Seventy years ago [children] would have been scattered like chaff the sport
of disease, death, crime and infamy.

Winnipeg Tribune
October 20, 1938

Although it would be wrong to describe the history of Canadian child studies
as a contested area of scholarship, it is nevertheless fraught with ambiguity,
conceptual confusion, and incompleteness. To what extent these problems are
inherent defects in the area of scholarly inadequacies remains to be seen. As a
new and exciting interest in the late 1960s and 1970s, child studies attracted a
mixed bag of workers in Canada. And soon, partly because of the field's proximity to other interests—for example women's and welfare history—the academics wandered off into adjacent fields; and the more marginal workers—
journalists and others—were merely exercising their professional talents on another bit of human interest.

Canadian historical scholarship has never exhibited a strong interest in theory
or methodological precision, and child studies history, a truly marginal subspecialty, is no exception. When the first studies were started, however, major
waves of historical revisionism were beginning to shift Canadian scholarships.
In particular, the history of education began its steady drift to a more critical
stance regarding conventional wisdom about the intentions and motives of educational promoters, the latent and manifest functions of schooling, the relation
of schooling and class interests, and the crude belief in the reciprocal relation

of schooling and civilization, to name a few. Much of this heady skepticism was occasioned by the appearance in 1966 of Michael B. Katz at the Ontario Institute for Studies in Education (OISE).[1]

During his years in Canada, Katz proved to be both an inspiration and a gray eminence. His *Irony of Early School Reform* (1968) set a high standard for the new revisionists, and his energetic research program in social history helped to generate interest in the newer methods associated with recent social history and to inspire a generation of graduate students at OISE, who later filled important posts in Canadian institutions. Because Katz mixed scholarship and radical reform so powerfully, he was a compulsive force in all areas of social history in Canada, even with those who rejected his vision of history and social change. Part of the Katzian presence was a push toward a social control—in a vulgar sense, interpretation of historical events, rhetoric, and motives. Some scholars of childhood moved perceptibly in harmony with the push, and others, when push came to shove, remained outside the game and thus outside the mainstream of the dominant view. Nevertheless, both as a graduate adviser and a researcher, Katz encouraged and carried out some of the first research on children in Canada.[2]

The point of this discussion is that history of education moved from a rather quaint study carried on by a few scholars in faculties of education to a topic of interest to educationists and scholars in the social science departments.[3] Moreover, because Katz was clearly a major scholar in social history, educationists, particularly those associated with him at OISE and later York University, enjoyed a substantial rise in peer esteem. The social history project, which went well beyond the old parameters of chalk and desks, helped to legitimize a much broader conception of education, and thereby opened the door to the inclusion of child studies, family, and welfare history as both research and teaching specialties in faculties of education.[4]

The 1980s witnessed the decline of a close relation between educationists and historians in part because historians moved on to new, ''hot'' areas once social reform lost its central position and education its supposed role as a major instrument of reform. One need only examine national history conferences to see the flight by historians from education. In turn, historians of education in faculties of education have responded to changing views of universities by shifting their work back to more school-based topics. Some of the practitioners of child studies history in education faculties, however, have stubbornly refused to fully give up their work.

At this point it is probably wise to suggest the limits of this essay review. With the event of mass, compulsory schooling, no history of children in family or institutionalizations is possible without a consideration of the history of formal education. Indeed, we are convinced that a history of children with their families is, in a large part, a history of their lives in schools. The institutional framework makes adolescent subculture possible, the organization and rhythm of school life interact pervasively with family and social life, and the school is so determinate in defining and presenting children and adolescents that it is truly the locus of those stages of human life—at least in Western industrial societies. Nevertheless, although the history of Canadian education is not remarkably rich, we have consciously decided to eschew any sustained examination of the literature and to limit our survey to those areas typically found in the history of child studies, such as child-saving, care and protection of neglected and dependent children, identification and treatment of delinquent children, child health and hygiene, child development, child labor, and the migration of unaccompanied children from Britain to Canada. A related interest, poorly conceptualized but of enduring concern, is the provision of human services for all children and the growing tendency to use the "normal child" as the standard for community action. Therefore, the review essay focuses on these topics.[5]

Another limitation or perhaps characteristic of recent Canadian studies is that scholars and amateurs alike have been responsive to the location and organization of archival sources. No need, in Canada, the admonition to avoid theory and to concentrate on case studies. This penchant for archival research is rooted in an older tradition of political history that dominated Canadian scholarship until the 1970s, the high profile of the new social history at places such as OISE, and a generous program of research support provided first by the Canada Council and then by the Social Sciences and Humanities Research Council (both federal funding agencies) to doctoral students and academic staff. Moreover, Canadian archives—the National Archives (NAC; formerly the Public Archives [PAC]) of Canada and the provincial archives—were and are good places to work. The relatively small size of even the NAC (PAC) meant that the staff could provide personal attention. Because of the extraordinary financial backing for Canadian doctoral students (most of whom, unlike those in the United States, are supported by their departments and universities, or through scholarships and federal research grants throughout programs that sometimes extend to three years and longer), the number of Canadian-produced studies of Canada and Canadians finally outstripped the production in Great Britain and the United States in the past decade.[6] Nevertheless, the actual volume of dissertations in the history of Canadian child studies remains small. Consequently we have cited those that treat appropriate topics and even on occasion work reported in progress.

The reliance on archival collections has grounded much of child studies history on a solid base of documentary evidence, encouraged local, regional, and institutional studies, and, finally, strange to say, fostered a Whig rendering of history. The reasons for this tendency are interesting and confusing to say the least. First is the fact that archivists process documents, and thereby give them an appearance of growth, development, and evolution. Indeed, the best collectors and producers of documents are government offices, large private agencies, and nice limited voluntary societies. With the government documents we see the diversification and sophistication of the office, surely something to inspire a belief in progress! The same is true of most large private agencies with their changes of names and function in response to new conditions. Even for the more fragile voluntary societies—even those who have gone onto their reward—their demise reassures us in the inevitable failure of passe forms of social organization and practice, the triumph of the fittest, and prompts us to believe in the past as the present writ small.

Second, the very topic, child studies, lends itself to a progressive interpretation. Who can doubt progress with the proliferation of child protection acts, child-saving institutions, public health initiatives, child-rearing literature, the appearance of child study and development, and, worse yet, universal schooling with its mushrooming apparatus of services and trained licensed personnel? Some commentators have seen this not as progress, but as social control. The problem is that progress and social control essentially are labels for the same events and stories, and that progress fits better than social control in the elimination of childhood diseases, the prevention of exploitive child labor, and provision of pleasant places for children. Additionally, it is difficult, if not impossible, to stand outside one's own conceptual givens, and not to judge past events, ideas, and actors in one's own terms. Thus they fall short of our state of grace and reveal themselves as wanting. Even those who choose alternative life-styles usually can do so only because the larger community provides the infrastructure that makes separatism possible.

The following is a discussion of the three major themes that have come to dominate Canadian childhood history: the child-saving movement with nineteenth-century antecedents and twentieth-century transformations; the juvenile immigration movement; and juvenile delinquency.

CHILD-SAVING

For this theme we depart momentarily from a decision not to discuss doctoral dissertations to make an exception of one of the earliest contributions to childhood history, that of Terrence Morrison, "The Child and Urban Social Reform in Late Nineteenth Century Ontario" (University of Toronto, 1971). Morrison's work suggestively signposted a territory that had been largely uncharted and pointed to directions yet to be explored. The study, reflecting the new American scholarship such as Anthony Platt's *The Child Savers* (1969), tackled changing views of childhood and attitudinal shifts during the period from 1870 to 1900, a time of rapid urbanization and demographic growth in Ontario. Besides the skillful use of a variety of previously untapped sources and approaches, Morrison borrowed such concepts as "maternal/social feminism" and the "cult of true womanhood" from American scholars such as William O'Neil and Barbara Welter to focus the argument and successfully transcend the descriptive frameworks preferred by more traditional historians.[7] These concepts were to be advantageously explored by historians engaged in the new women's history in Canada in the 1970s.[8] In light of Morrison's original study it remains puzzling that it was never revised for publication, although several articles were taken from it.[9]

Morrison's study is concerned with those reform groups (sanitary reformers, women's rights advocates, proponents of applied Christianity, child-savers, and new educationists) that were involved in larger social problems that affected the urban child—"physical debilitation, delinquency, truancy, impiety, ignorance, neglect, immorality and intemperance."[10] He argues that the family model, which included a romantic appreciation of children, a stress on child rearing as the essential function of the family, and "a chivalrous veneration of women," was the ideal "reformers hoped to translate into existence as the institutional foundation of society."[11] He relates this to the early women's rights movement, which argued for the moral benefits to be derived from extending the maternal sphere to the public domain through feminine social action.

To date there are three sustained scholarly studies whose theme is based in the changes from child-saving sentiment to child welfare policy under the auspices of federal, provincial, and municipal governments. The first and most cited of these is Neil Sutherland, *Children in English-Canadian Society: Framing the Twentieth Century Consensus* (1976), which analyzes an impressive range of printed sources. Sutherland's discussion, starting in the 1880s and concluding in the 1920s, is *national* in scope. Moreover, a broader range of topics than Morrison's reflects a sensitivity to changing societal attitudes manifested in various forms of child-saving—reformatories and family homes, the public health movement, and schooling. His work with the health movement (and later that of Norah Lewis, whom he trained) is a particular strength.[12] Another strength lies in his explication of the attitudes of middle-class reformers toward family life and their ideal of childhood, which manifested in wide-ranging reform efforts fueled by the idealism of applied Christianity expressed in the social gospel movement. The fear of social disintegration produced a medical metaphor that connected the health of family life to the overall health of society. He, too, emphasizes the reformers' belief in the "right family environment" and the ideal of "motherhood," which was projected into the children's aid society model and the treatment of delinquents. In brief, he argues a "cause and effect relationship between economic change and patterns of childrearing and family organization."[13] What distinguishes Sutherland's explanation from Morrison's is that the latter is critical of the assumptions behind the reform movement, the motivations of the reformers, the often ambiguous consequences of their actions, and the increasing intervention and infringement on individual rights; whereas Sutherland appears to accept these as legitimate and reads the printed sources as if their rhetoric is reality. That one cannot take such historical documents on face value is amply demonstrated by a careful scrutiny of J. J. Kelso's papers, which belie the claim that the first superintendent of dependent and neglected children in Ontario "displayed administrative abilities of a high order."[14] Morrison, too, however, although critical of the rhetoric, is inclined to assume that the rhetoric is actually being implemented as described. It is only in the interpretation of the evidence that Morrison and Sutherland dramatically differ.

As the subtitle of this book suggests, Sutherland sees a uniformity of Anglophone attitudes and treatment of children in place by the 1920s with only fine-tuning necessary to refine the mechanisms. This is an improbable view in light of Kelso's own words in 1921 that after three decades of organizing children's aid societies, "there was no system, no unity, no method" (even in *Toronto!*) and that "all kinds of organizations are at work but there is no harmony or co-ordination. They are all working at random."[15] Sutherland's and the following study of Kelso represent what might be loosely described as "consensus" history in that conflict is minimized unless it is satisfactorily resolved in events and policies deemed to be "progressive."

A thorough biography of the public life of Canada's best-known child-saver is Andrew Jones and Leonard Rutman's *In the Children's Aid: J. J. Kelso and Child Welfare in Ontario* (1981). A factual and sympathetic rather than an analytical account, it overlooks or is unaware of the complexities of the man, or of the perceptions of his work by many of his associates. Although the authors reflect the obsession of English-Canadian history with Ontario, in fact much of Kelso's work as Ontario's superintendent of neglected and dependent children (1893–1935) or as leading promoter of the provincial and children's aid society system provided the impetus for the transfer of models and philosophies to other provinces. Therefore, this is a crucial study to understanding such a transplantation, despite the authors' failure to spell out the connections. The predominance of sources are from Kelso's papers and the documents of his office as superintendent with a dependence on secondary sources—unpublished theses—for the historical background.[16] Judging by the authors' generous citations of Sutherland's work and the similarity of their conclusions about Kelso's work and the reform movement, as well as a similar tendency with other scholars, *Children in English-Canadian Society* has indeed framed a consensus on the nature of Canadian child-saving. There is no reason to suppose that it will not continue to do so, given the prevailing lack of interest in published studies on the subject.

Kelso was not an "original" in any sense, although he was a pioneer on the Canadian child-saving scene. Jones and Rutman missed an opportunity to place him on a much broader stage where so many of his ideas were derived from the social ferment of countries such as the United States and Great Britain. He was a somewhat imitative social reformer whose presence was ubiquitous rather than compelling. Nevertheless, he is to Canada what Charles Loring Brace is to the United States. Moreover, he is a representative of charity organization, that intermediary mode of social welfare organization that existed between the former mode of private philanthropy and the later one of state control. His style was highly personal with a sincere idealism reminiscent of the florid sentimentality of nineteenth-century popular "enthusiasm." Nor do the authors adequately grasp that by the first decade of the twentieth century, both Kelso's style and the mode of social welfare organization he represented were under attack from the next generation of child-savers—the professionalizers, those ambitious and social-scientifically oriented practitioners whose interests were in coordinating child rescue agencies under central voluntary and government-assisted structures headed by trained personnel. Consequently, long before his superannuation,

Kelso was considered both an embarrassment and an anachronism by this new reform group.

Although few child-savers have left behind the boxes of materials of a Kelso, or much less that of a later child welfare advocate, Charlotte Whitton, the work of Rutman and Jones points the way to *prosopography*, or collective biography, of similar figures such as Ernest Blois of Nova Scotia and Minnie Campbell of Manitoba (both of whom were active in campaigning for a Canadian children's bureau), Laura Holland in British Columbia child welfare, or F. J. Reynolds of Saskatchewan, also a superintendent of dependent children.

It is imperative at this juncture of writing child studies history that revisions are made to the glowing accounts of the various aspects of child-saving that perpetuate themselves like time-worn cliches. For example, Henry C. Klassen's article, "In Search of Neglected and Dependent Children" (1981), a discussion of the Calgary Children's Aid Society, repeats the standard Whig interpretation that children who were indiscriminately as well as discriminately taken from their families, punished for trivial offenses, and coerced into conformity, and whose domestic lives were invigilated by well-meaning home visits, were happy with this state of affairs. The contrast between this and Rebecca Coulter's revisionist interpretation of similar data and events on the provincial level is a welcome antidote to the prevailing Whiggism. In "Not to Punish But Reform" (1982) Rebecca Coulter ironically observes:

But if central Canadians selected one idea from here and one idea from there to construct a child welfare system that they *knew* was superior, as Sutherland suggests, then Albertans, at least, exhibited that same smug attitude towards Ontario's system. Ontario's system was good but Alberta's was better.[17]

It is in light of this situation that the third sustained study can be seen as an attempt to rectify the imbalance.

Coming after Morrison, Sutherland, and Jones and Rutman, it was to be expected that a third book would revise some of the previous scholarship. Patricia T. Rooke and R. L. Schnell, in *Discarding the Asylum: From Child Rescue to the Welfare State in English-Canada, 1800–1950* (1983), attempt such a revision and include a substantial coverage of a neglected period in Canadian childhood history, the "colonial" or pre-Confederation years.

Although their time period is more ambitious, Rooke and Schnell do not cover such topics as public health, education, or juvenile delinquency. When they deal with the role of Kelso or the efficiency of the children's aid societies, they depart radically from the views of the previous authors.[18] Indeed, their interpretation rejects any suggestion—except at the rhetorical level—that a national *consensus* in philosophy, policy, or practice was in place by the 1920s. Their argument is based on an analysis of of archival collections from Victoria to St. John's relating to institutions, child rescue agencies and child welfare advocates, and interest groups.

Discarding the Asylum places the post-Confederation period in the middle of a century and a half of child-saving in a discussion that examines the voluntaristic and sporadic child-saving precedents to "scientific" charity. It examines provinces other than Ontario, in which the bulk of research has concentrated, and goes beyond the 1920s, where most studies end. In many cases Rooke and Schnell find the "consensus" decidedly wanting, thus agreeing with similar views expressed by such child welfare advocates as Charlotte Whitton, who campaigned until the late 1940s to standardize child welfare structures, legislation, and practices. Moreover, the authors claim as fundamentally ahistorical and self-congratulatory the assertion that Canadian child welfare groups initially developing alongside their British counterparts "subsequently reach[ed] their level of proficiency and eventually pass[ed] them."[19] This book sees child-saving as part of the rescue motive, whose influence is considerable, well before the late nineteenth century and that contributed to the transformation of relief and charity into more systematic methods. By correlating the rescue motive to asylum-building generally, it demonstrates how ideas on institutionalization were projected into patterns of social reorganization, thus expanding the temporal, spatial, and moral boundaries of the asylum (as a place of rescue and refuge) to an ideology with metaphoric dimensions, that is, the state as asylum acting *in loco parentis*. This argument is directed by a heuristic application of the criteria of the "concept" of childhood—segregation, protection, dependence, and delayed responsibilities—which came to embrace those remaining categories of children who had escaped the benefits of the criteria: the poor, foreign, native, and handicapped. In order that the narrative not become a paean to progress, it emphasizes the ambiguities intrinsic to the rescue motive that came to restrain children even as they were rescued.

The colonial period has been neglected in the study of childhood, as indeed are many of the intellectual roots and historical influences that preceded mid-to late-nineteenth-century Canada. Although several comprehensive articles have been written on general relief during this period, they include little information about the treatment of children within such structures.[20] (There seems reason to suppose, however, that French-Canada has been more attentive to its colonial period. "*Les Petite-Sauvages*—The Children of Eighteenth Century New France," by Peter N. Moogk, makes for a refreshing diversion in a history weighted heavily in favor of the late nineteenth and early twentieth centuries.[21]) Although children were only part of a *general* pauper population, the shift in this perception demonstrated by an astounding flurry of specialized institution-building—for example orphan asylums from the late 1830s to the 1880s—is an instructive example not only of the growth of child-saving sentiment, but also of the practical dimensions of this sentiment with all its variety and confusion of humanitarian sensibilities and social control motives.[22] This flurry of asylum-building places the foremothers of later social reformers in the center of the earliest child-rescue efforts and makes for an important case study of female experience in institution-building and the creation of a female domain. It offers us one of Canada's earliest examples of "maternal feminism."[23]

There is a tendency to minimize the repressive aspects of social reforms, whose language is less overtly crude, as in the case of the debates around boarding-out and the children's aid societies, when compared with the language of the institutionalizing mode. When the Reverend W. H. Sedgewick of the London (Ontario) Children's Aid Society praised its work, he asserted that "a redeemed childhood was a redeemed generation," as if this belief was something quite new. In fact, he was saying no more than the 1857 Montreal Protestant Orphan Home annual report, which, while asserting that street arabs were "little social pests" from whose depredations society must be protected, believed that if separated from undesirable elements (parents and companions), they could be trained into becoming "useful members of society"; in brief, a redeemed childhood, a redeemed generation.[24]

Children's *institutions*, either a bright or a brooding symbol of the Whig dilemma, were there to impose order on the disorder found in the drunkenness along the waterfronts, the squalor and brutishness in the meanest streets, or the surly looks of the masses. Their promoters believed that children were contaminated if housed in public relief institutions, exposed to the "moans of the dying, the screams of parturition, the drivellings of the idiot, the ravings of the maniac and the jeers of the depraved."[25] As the Toronto *Daily Colonist*, August 4, 1858, glumly observed of the inmates in the city's new juvenile institution: "Suppose that these sixty children again are let loose upon society what a frightful increase of crime would be the result?" Boys and girls, "old in ways of deceit and tarnished by depravity,"[26] were to be rescued (separated and protected) from rudeness, blasphemy, and lewdness as well as from dirt, discomfort, and neglect.

The orphan asylum represented a new view of human development, and contributed to an expanded and more inclusive understanding of the concept of "childhood" as a specialized social category. A reemphasis emerged from a shaping or forming metaphor that stressed the institutional regimen as growth or gardening, one in which careful guidance and nurture were requisite for proper development of individual potential and the making of citizens—a redeemed childhood; a redeemed generation. The asylum, therefore, marked the beginning of specialization of rescue in contrast to the reliance on traditional institutional routines to transform a mass of unclassified paupers.

Although the lack of staff and scientific knowledge limited the effectiveness of the attempted resocialization within the children's institutions, the managers sought to inculcate a sense of dependence through psychological control, training, and indoctrination. The records—replete with runaways, manipulation, parental reclamation, and binding-out practices—negated much of the hard-won benefits of resocialization, while problems of transience (the "ins and outs") suggest that resocialization was not as effective as the official propaganda, eager to sustain public sympathy and support, claimed. Moreover, in light of the economic constraints, the problems of supply and demand, the failures of resocialization, the growing criticisms of a mode of caregiving already in disrepute in Britain and the United States, and the search for alternatives to counteract pauperism, the institution foundered. By the end of the nineteenth century the rhetoric was embracing a commitment to family models for resocializing children, no longer into useful employment, which the institution represented, but into participation in a family setting other than the child's natural one, if this was judged to be inadequate.

The Reverend Mr. Sedgewick's voice was one among many. "A redeemed childhood; a redeemed generation" justified the linking of child and family welfare, thus opening the door for systematic intervention into lower-class life while apparently showing the human face of social welfare. Although the view that children were a means of reforming their families had been voiced by early-nineteenth-century philanthropic societies and writers of moral tales for children, the rise of state guardianship under the aegis of the children's aid societies and provincial departments of neglected children and the passage of the Juvenile Delinquents Act (1908) gave a new legal sanction for family case work. The common assumption that protection of children routinely called for intervention into poor, immigrant, and working-class families showed the limits of even the most progressive of the second generation of child rescue.

Although *Discarding the Asylum* analyzes one aspect of pre-Confederation child rescue, that of institutional patterns and the transplantation of philosophical assumptions, especially from British models, two articles examine pre-Confederation family patterns. Jennifer S. H. Brown's "Children of the Early Fur Trades," along with Moogk's New France study, analyzes a social organization and view of children quite distinct from anything that followed. Brown's is more a study of family patterns than of children's lives, which uncovers fascinating documentary evidence about intermarriage and cohabitation (among the French, Scots, Indians, and Metis) in an environment more noted for its transience than its stability.[27] On the other hand, Moogk's piece provides a useful analysis of the term "childhood," as used in the French language of the time, as well the structures of the patriarchal family. He also examines practices of guardianship, foster parentage, adolescence, and formal education in ways that could well be emulated, if not precisely replicated, by Anglophone commentators.

Little has been done on the question of adoption and guardianship, yet institutional records are available from Anglophone Catholic child-saving efforts, including foundling hospitals and adoption procedures, which retained traditional and fluid characteristics much longer than their Protestant counterparts. Foundling hospitals require more extensive treatment than they have received, especially after a tantalizing but underdeveloped study of a later period by Leslie Savage, "Perspective on Illegitimacy: The Changing Role of the Sisters of Misercordia in Edmonton 1900–39." Savage examined an originally Francophone religious community transplanted to the Canadian West and the moral and institutional adaptations that occurred as a result of this experience.[28] Indeed, having examined

Protestant orphan asylums we have been waiting for some enterprising scholar to do a similar study of Anglophone Catholic institutions (as distinct from Francophone ones), whose custodial function was more flexible than that of their Protestant counterparts, according to our own evidence as well as the study by Bettina Bradbury, "The Fragmented Family" (1982), in which she analyzes the life cycle of working-class families in mid-nineteenth-century Montreal.[29] Given the number of caretakers in religious orders, the constancy of surveillance because of their "vocational" commitment, the ethnic diversity of the clienteles, the theological traditions of corporal "works of mercy," the large populations in the Catholic orphanages, and the more open-door policies compared with their Protestant counterparts, we would expect a data base that is distinct from the Protestant orphan homes. Quite apart from national studies, such as the John Bosco Homes and the work of St. Vincent de Paul, there are numerous opportunities for case studies. The Catholic experience in Canada has been virtually ignored.

If Catholic resources have not been tapped, equally mystifying is the dearth of analysis of the federal government's contribution to child welfare policy, especially since a division of child welfare was established in 1920 of the newly created Department of Health and headed until 1934 by Dr. Helen MacMurchy. This department promoted child and maternal health and hygiene by means of manuals ("The Little Blue Books") as well as by films, posters, and pamphlets and by coordinating the activities of provincial and municipal health departments. Although Suzann Buckley, "Ladies or Midwives? Efforts to Reduce Infant and Maternal Mortality" (1979), and Veronica Strong-Boag, "Intruders in the Nursery" (1982), noted these efforts, there is much that can be done with content analysis of advice literature generally, whether from magazines and the popular press or from government publications, such as "The Canadian Mother's Book" (1923), which confidently proclaimed the ideology of motherhood to complement the ideology of childhood with the words, "No national service is greater or better than the work of the Mother in her own home. The Mother is 'The First Servant of the State.' "[30] There is no reason why Bernard Wishy's or Christina Hardyment's quite different discussions on American and British child-rearing advice cannot provide models for similar explications in Canada.[31]

Child-saving usually is seen as those efforts related to children who received care outside their biological families—social outcasts, foundlings, institutional children, children at risk and in-care, young offenders—but as incarceration became outmoded, child-saving philosophies gave birth to efforts at family life intervention or to keeping of children within their families except *in extremis*. Therefore, child-saving is the foundation of later forms of child welfare. Here is another field, rich in sources and open to interpretation.[32]

Considering that so little has been produced in areas where child life was politicized and medicalized despite abundant primary sources, it is not surprising that even less work has been done on "children's experiences," that enigmatic and illusive recreation of the rhythms and sensibilities of children—the world of childhood. Neil Sutherland, one of the few scholars who has attempted to recover "children's voices," admits to the problems of filtering through the lenses of adult memory and perceptions as well as the methodological problems inherent in an emphasis on oral history.[33] Nevertheless, even while recognizing the methodological and disciplinary constraints, an innovative and ambitious project financed by the university and the Social Sciences and Humanities Research Council is under way at the University of British Columbia. To avoid being merely a journey into nostalgia or a miscarried flirtation with folklore (which is not to demean "folklore"), the project must creatively borrow from the sophisticated techniques of other disciplines to interpret its findings—ethnology, ethnomethodology, object relations psychology, sociological reference group theory, cultural anthropology, linguistic analysis, and studies of gender and material culture.[34]

The *private* world of childhood or the domestic life, including play, peers, siblings, family sentiments, chores, psychosocial arrangements, literature, rhymes, and games that most frequently cultivate it, is a challenging area of investigation. This private world relies on the creation of new categories of signification along with new methodologies, whereas the *public* world of childhood is more accessible to traditional historical methods. Yet even here there is little published: a history of children's work, particularly child labor (as understood in the context of former centuries), is in its embryonic stages. Recent articles by Lorna F. Hurl and John Bullen on child labor in late-nineteenth-century Ontario are a welcome addition to the few unpublished papers presented at the annual meetings of the Canadian Historical Association.[35] There is a seemingly limitless fund of sources waiting—boys' and girls' clubs, work-training schemes, Sunday schools, church organizations, girl guides, and boy scouts, to name only a few possibilities.[36] A study of these and similar agencies and organizations will bring alive again past rites of passage, those rhythms of inclusion or exclusion whose symbolic subtleties are in danger of being lost.

THE JUVENILE MIGRATION MOVEMENT

The juvenile migration movement between 1869 and 1930 has been a major theme in Canadian child studies history. The movement of sending unaccompanied children from Britain began on a modest scale. Benevolent gentlewomen such as Charlotte Alexander, Maria Rye, and Annie McPherson, some isolated poor law unions, and children's refuges and orphan asylums such as the Shaftesbury Ragged School Union, the Children's Friend Society, and the Society for the Permanent Support of Orphan and Destitute Children by Means of Apprenticeship in the Colonies participated.[37] All agreed that Canada represented the "home of happy childhood" and provided a "fairer chance" for pauper children than their inadequate family life and dead-end jobs. The Permanent Support Society noted that "any lot would be better than that which they appear to inherit" and that "any change of circumstances would ameliorate their condition."[38] After the trans-Atlantic voyage the children were placed out to be adopted, fostered, or indentured into agricultural and domestic service.

From such modest beginnings the stage was set for later state-assisted emigration schemes on a grander scale. Philanthropies in the United Kingdom such as the Thomas Barnardo Homes, the William Quarrier's Orphan Homes of Scotland, and the Thomas Bowman Stephenson's National Children's Homes sent older children to Canada partially in answer to the protestations at home and abroad with regard to the youth of some of the children previously sent.[39] Ironically, humanitarian demands and subsequent regulation (even legislation) assured that the migrant children—if they were to be sent at all—be older. This meant that they were invariably indentured rather than fostered and adopted and exploited as cheap labor. Because of the continued bad press that poor law children received, as well as reports of their ill treatment, the Local Government Board in London abandoned earlier schemes, and fewer children were transported by the boards of guardians.[40] Nevertheless, philanthropic agencies continued to send children from impoverished urban families, a practice that totaled approximately 80,000 children over a sixty-year span.

The Dominion response to the movement was mixed, and changed from an initial welcome to an increasing resistance as the numbers of children increased. Many, especially the eugenicists, saw the children as a "contaminating influence on native born Canadians," a view expressed in the *Montreal Gazette*, July 27, 1895; humanitarians saw them as unfortunate waifs and strays to be welcomed in a land of limitless opportunity; potential employers—farmers and their wives, or middle-class women—saw them as cheap labor without the nuisance factor of kinfolk or guardians to protect them; nativists and nationalists alike accused Britain of dumping unwanted surplus population on the colonies; trade unionists identified the children, particularly the older boys, as competitive future urban labor; and, finally, the emerging social work professionals saw the children as "competition" for homes that might have been made available to wards in the Children's Aid Societies but at the same time deploring the treatment given to the young Britons in these very homes. A prevailing sentiment seemed to be that the children, as the *Ottawa Citizen* in September 1869 noted, were "the physiological off scourings of the Old World dumped on our shores." Indeed, the *Montreal Gazette* had gone so far as to call them "the scum of Europe" and "little better than brutes," apparently agreeing with James C. Moyal, chief inspector of penitentiaries, who had described them in 1877 as "Cockney sneak thieves and pickpockets . . . pests fathered from the slums of St. Giles and the East End of London."[41]

The current fascination with this phenomenon might be explained at the popular and undergraduate level by the extraordinary nature of the exchange, the poignancy of individual stories, the drama of the collective ordeal, and its uniquely Canadian (and, to a lesser extent, Australian) experience. On the other hand its fascination for scholars can be attributed to several factors, including the interest in historical "mutes," which emerged in the 1960s. Not surprisingly, the descendants of a social category that had been seen as "a wholesale dumping of moral refuse on [Canada's] shores," representing the "lowest scum of the slums," had been in hiding for decades.[42] Therefore, the search for genealogical roots popularized in the mass culture proved a boon to oral historians who had shown little interest until the seventies in the rather opaque references to the immigrant children made in earlier histories. Apart from this, scholarly interest must be attributed to what is an embarrassment of riches with regard to sources. For example, the Public Archives of Canada alone contains numerous boxes of materials from child-savers who brought children across, such as Charlotte Alexander and Ellen Bilbrough, the child-saving agencies in Canada that participated in the schemes, such as the Middlemore, Marchmont, and Fairknowe receiving homes, as well as the bungling Montreal-based "British Immigration and Colonization Association."[43] Boxes of materials from groups who opposed the movement—the National Council of Women, the Trades and Labour Congress, the Canadian Council on Child Welfare, the Social Service Council of Canada, and the children's aid societies—are accessible.

Moreover, there are hundreds of pages of immigration documents to examine, including ship's manifests, which give the origins and ages of the children; reports of the federal inspector of child immigration, G. Bogue Smart; reports of medical officers; remarks on deportations and runaways; terms of indenture; the movements of children; infringements of compulsory school attendance; and parliamentary debates, commissions of inquiry, and detailed correspondence between British emigration homes and Canadian receiving homes. More primary sources can be mined in most provincial archives in light of the provincially supported various training schemes, including those under the Empire Settlement Act of 1922, which raised the children's ages to seventeen years for females and nineteen for males. As if all of this is not a surfeit of riches, the Canadian and British presses provide eloquent testimony to social attitudes, and the libraries and archives of Britain are replete with pertinent materials: the archives of such cities as Birmingham, Liverpool, Manchester, Bristol, Dublin, and Glasgow; the colonial office correspondence housed in the Public Record Office at Kew; and poor law records housed at the London City Council archives. Library collections such as the British Museum and Goldsmith's College contain government inquiries, printed materials, and hundreds of samples of imperialist and romantic child-saving literature. Ongoing organizations such as the Church Army, the Salvation Army, and the Barnardo Homes retain minute books, annual reports, and correspondence from philanthropists, émigrés, parents, and clergy, comments from the general public, and even letters from the children.

Juvenile immigration has been part of the general histories such as *Children in English-Canadian Society*, while two detailed chapters provide a linchpin to understanding the transition from child rescue to child welfare in *Discarding the Asylum*.[44] It has spawned its own specialized histories, which have not been placed in the broader context of child studies history. It is more commonly included in immigration history, drawing its interpretive base from the "dumping ground'' theories articulated by former colonial societies and dominant in imperial history[45] or in labor history. Joy Parr's reconstruction of a random sample of Barnardo children in *Labouring Children* (1980) interprets her data in the latter context.[46] The heart of her study is in a quantitative analysis of 997 dossiers of children migrated by Barnardo between 1882 and 1908. She identifies British evangelicals as the pawns of imperialist expansionism imposing their value system on the children and, in consequence, on Canada. Unfortunately this view is inclined to minimize the crudities and exploitations of the Canadian response. By ending her sample in 1908 Parr fails to address the significant changes that occur in the next decades. Nevertheless, Parr's study illumines much about indenture practices whose antecedents can be traced to a previous century, the likelihood of better treatment when the boarding-out *payment* system was used for apprentices (as with the Barnardo and Catholic ''home children''), and the social mobility for boys and girls placed in rural areas. In many ways the evidence she presents to substantiate her own interpretation can just as readily be used to substantiate the claims of the British societies that the youngest children adjusted best to their new lives, whereas older children found adjustment more painful.

By contrast Kenneth Bagnell's *The Little Immigrants* (1980) attempts a less ambitious, but more sympathetic reconstruction of the children's trauma.[47] Along with Gillian Wagner's biography of *Barnardo* (1979) and her *Children of the Empire* (1982)—British contributions—they present a balanced telling of the story.[48] If one is interested in an optimistic presentation of the events, Gail Corbett's effusions in *Barnardo Children in Canada* (1981) can qualify.[49] Its main use is heuristic in that the instructor can contrast this viewpoint with Parr's or Bagnell's, which tells the darker side of the story, thus demonstrating how the same historical evidences can be used to present either a revisionist or a pollyanna interpretation of past events. An all too often neglected contribution is Phyllis Harrison's *The Home Children* (1979) in which she edited and chronologically recorded a faithful and moving attempt to listen to the ''children's voices.''[50]

Despite the initial promise, there is a hiatus in current scholarship.[51] This is perplexing, given how much evidence there remains to be examined. If juvenile migration is rich in sources, it also is rich in connections. Several immediately come to mind. We think of how the subject lends itself to the subtleties and intellectual possibilities of psycho-history, but to our knowledge only one piece has attempted this approach.[52] As well there are connections to be developed between the movement and the ''Children West'' crusade initiated by Charles Loring Brace of the New York Children's Aid Society, especially in light of his acquaintance with Annie Macpherson, one of the pioneers in emigrating British children to Canada. Moreover, if not examined in splendid isolation as an exotic species of Canadian history, the movement can highlight a discussion of Canadian child labor, a topic that, despite Parr's study, remains undeveloped. Much remains to be done in relating the movement to contemporary social and philosophical views, including pseudopsychological and criminological theories, the eugenics movement, the impulse to professionalize, penological reforms, juvenile delinquency, and social organization.[53] The pertinence of religious attitudes and beliefs to the history of child studies is illustrated by Philip Greven, *The Protestant Temperament* (1977), and Edmund Morgan, *The Puritan Family* (1944). Neil Semple, "The Nurture and Admonition of the Lord: Nineteenth-Century Canadian Methodism's Response to 'Childhood' " (1981), and Parr, "Transplanting from the Dens of Inequity" (1979), are only beginnings.[54] Theological relations require deeper analysis, particularly the marriage of the evangelical "rescue motive" (represented in the Arminian breakthrough of the eighteenth century) and scientific knowledge. These two strands embraced progressive ideas on the prevention of social problems, and at the same time ultimately contributed to people being seen as "populations" and children, as national resources.

Rooke and Schnell interpret the juvenile migration movement as both a catalyst for and a reflection of the transforming patterns of child care that involved discernible shifts from philanthropic child rescue and public relief to charity organization followed by increasing state intervention into family life and dependent child life. They argue that the motives for the attack on the juvenile migrants were mixed—trade union opposition, humanitarian sensibilities, complicated middle-class reforms, and the growing professionalization of child welfare. They also contend that the motives cannot be appreciated without placing the debate against the discourse on "childhood" generally, the transplantation of experimental approaches and models dealing with the problems of child life, and the questions surrounding boarding-out.

Discarding the Asylum makes the connection between child emigration and boarding-out explicit and emphasizes that both positions were couched in similar rhetoric. In short, child emigration was the most extreme, yet logical consequence of the boarding-out debate. We recall a pertinent comment from the 1883 *Annual Report* of the Birmingham Emigration Home: "We would conclude by calling the emigration of pauper and criminal children merely an inexpensive system of boarding-out in Canada; it is a system of boarding-out without payment."[55] This discourse was made more potent by imperialist appeals such as that expressed by Arthur Chilton, cofounder of the Catholic Canadian Emigration Society: "We are merely transferring them from part of the Empire to another—from our own England where they have no prospects, to our own Canada where their prospects are as bright as the flame that glows on the maple leaf in the fall."[56] Boarding-out no less appealed to the idea of giving deprived children "a fair chance." In this case the belief that the venture was "twice blessed"—blessing the nation that gave and the nation that took—seemed a cruel joke on the children involved.

Whatever the whole story, it is patently obvious that selection procedures, aftercare arrangements, apprenticeship conditions, and indenture agreements of the young Britons were inadequately supervised by the British guardians who separated young children from their familiar haunts and familial memories in what Parr has described as a form of "philanthropic abduction." Certainly there is a sober reminder of their distress in the 1874 report of the Gutter Children's Home when it noted that "it is no small thing to make a girl, even if she is but five years old, forget the mother who bore her; and the work that can do this is certainly a thorough one." Perhaps "philanthropic *seduction*" can equally describe the situation, for neither can we overlook the fact that working-class parents used "separation" (from home or of siblings) as a family strategy.[57] Sadly, many parents, coerced by economic stress, gave permission for their children to go on that lonely trans-Atlantic voyage to make a new life in Canada. What some of these children felt about their going while siblings remained is told in *The Home Children*. What most of the children felt when they were separated in Canada from siblings and even from a twin can never really be told. And no immigrant child's situation was more invidious than for a girl such as Gladys Hunt, or Ada Francis, or Alice Brittnel—all young adolescents and known to have been either sexually molested or made pregnant.[58] Neither was Canada—its people and its government—entirely blameless in the exchange.

Finally, the juvenile migration movement is not a simple tale of dramatic Manichaean proportions with good overcoming evil and even less a story of "progress" culminating in a better state of affairs. Rather, it is a complex thread in Canadian history that weaves in and out of a much broader tapestry that warrants further investigation. Rooke and Schnell demonstrated that Charlotte Whitton's interest in advancing her career and expanding the influence of a *national* child welfare council was every bit as exploitive of the children as the farmers and women for whom they worked.[59] But it was Whitton and the emerging social work professionals who were able to secularize the discourse of child rescue formerly couched in humanitarian and even evangelical metaphors.

JUVENILE DELINQUENCY

The literature of the history of juvenile delinquency is spotty, with the main emphasis on the campaign for federal legislation and the role of Ontario child-savers in extending noninstitutional treatment of young offenders. There is no sustained historical study, and the major published sources are three chapters in Sutherland's *Children in English-Canadian Society* and a small collection of articles, some decidedly repetitive. In brief, the area suffers the same limitations of most aspects of child studies history.

The published stories are, with few exceptions, Whiggish and laudatory of juvenile court promoters and the early magistrates and staff. The leading Whig interpretation is offered by Sutherland.[60] Starting with the 1880s, Sutherland argues that although the aims of English-Canadians with regard to controlling criminal behavior changed little over the last two decades of the nineteenth century, "new conditions and theories sometimes produced substantial changes in methods." For English-Canadians in the 1880s the concerns were to defend society against the predations of criminal youth and to improve society. They acquired "a heightened sense both of childhood itself and of the importance of the family in rearing children." These new sensibilities compelled them to seek new means of caring for vagrant, orphaned, neglected, dependent, incorrigible, and delinquent children. Institutional means became increasingly suspect unless assimilating family life structure and claiming to rehabilitate.

In any case, child-savers all stressed specialized and separate provision for children. All commentators attach great importance to the work of the Royal Commission on the Prison and Reformatory System of Ontario and its 1891 *Report*.[61] In essence, the Commission straddles the issue of family home versus institutional care by recommending both. The Commission, however, set the stage for the nation's first children's aid society in Toronto in 1891. The campaign to establish the Toronto children's aid society was spearheaded by J. J. Kelso.

For Sutherland, efforts to establish industrial schools in Ontario represented the last gasp of all child-saving views that believed in the efficacy of institutions. The Royal Commission, in promoting separate and specialized treatment for children and youth, encouraged efforts for provincial legislation for dependent, neglected, and delinquent children and for federal legislation affecting the trial and disposition of juvenile delinquents. According to Sutherland, children's aid societies first emphasized prevention but by the turn of the century had moved to rehabilitation. In Ontario the "most effective example of home over institutional care for juvenile delinquents" was the decision aided by the efforts of Kelso and associates to close the Ontario Reformatory for Boys. Finally, the last stage of the campaign centered on the passage of federal legislation establishing juvenile courts.

Sutherland cites the 1908 Juvenile Delinquents Act "as a great triumph for the idea of family-centred care of problem children." Whatever the idea underlying the Act, juvenile courts and their successors, family courts, were, in most cases, extensions of magistrate or police courts. Thus, even assuming that family-centered care "became the Canadian norm," there is a need to ask what forms did the intervention take?

Sutherland notes that in 1921, approximately 1 percent of the under-sixteen population in Ontario was "subject to continued care and oversight." He also makes much of the character of the first generation of juvenile court magistrates (e.g., Emily Murphy of Edmonton, Helen Gregory MacGill of Vancouver, and J. Edward Starr of Toronto).[62] Although the ideas and arguments used to support the juvenile justice system are interesting and significant, historical events are best understood in light of their consequences. The few studies of the aftermath of the establishment of the courts (and usually in Toronto) demonstrate the tendency to deal with cases informally—"occurrences"—with all the resultant intrusion into lower-class family life. Even as late as 1969 the Minister of Justice, John Turner, was able to observe:

And so one may find two separate systems of family law—the family law of the rich, created, developed and administered by the courts, and the family law of the poor, as public law, administered largely through provincial or state or local non-juridical agencies.

These agencies are sometimes more concerned with minimizing the cost of relief than maximizing the rights and interests of the recipients.[63]

In an analysis of the Toronto Family Court, Dorothy B. Chunn found that between 1920 and 1945, the number of formal hearings ranged from a low of 2,168 in 1938 to a high of 4,726 in 1930, but that the number of occurrence interviews (i.e., nonformal hearings) grew from a low of 2,314 in 1924 to a high of 20,283 in 1945. Moreover, that beginning with the operation of the Toronto Family Court in 1929, informal dispositions average between 66 percent and 84.7 percent of all adults and children processed. The ideal of family-centered care and the inclination to use home rehabilitation may have become the norm, but so did massive public intervention into the lives of the poor.[64]

James G. Snell has offered a Whig interpretation of the courts of domestic relations by observing that seeing the occurrence interviews solely as a form of social control is "to ignore the responses of the 'clients' of the interviews—indeed of the individual courts and officials themselves—and thus potentially to misrepresent the development of family relations courts."[65] Our understanding of juvenile delinquency would be served immensely by studies of how the courts actually worked both historically and contemporaneously.

Sutherland places the responsibility for these circumstances, which are only vaguely referred to, on the demands of a more ordered society generally. For him, the courts and the associated services were substantially social reforms and the leading advocates, "the humane and sensible men and women who formed the first generation of juvenile court judges" and child-savers such as Kelso were powerful reformers.

The claim of a consensus on child-saving between 1880 and 1920 has been challenged by two studies of child-saving in Ontario. The older study is by Andrew Jones of the closing of the Ontario Reformatory for Boys at Penetanguishene in 1904.[66] Opened in 1859 as a reformatory prison for boys, the institution was reorganized as a reformatory for boys and substantial changes proposed for its operation in 1880. After reaching a record 263 inmates in 1882 its population gradually declined because of efforts to place boys as apprentices with farmers or to obtain pardons for those showing good behavior; thus between 1893 and 1902 approximately 60 percent of the inmates received early releases. The establishment of industrial schools originally intended for unmanageable children provided alternatives for neglected children. The schools also established basic tenets of child-saving belief: that all neglected children were potentially delinquents and that any evidence of parental neglect was sufficient cause for commitment.

Despite the excitement of the child-savers at the closing of Penetanguishene and Mercer Refuge for Girls in 1905, hard-core delinquents (children originally sent to the Reformatory and Refuge) were now committed to the industrial schools, further compounding the confusion of neglect and delinquency. Even the enthusiastic Kelso modified his position by advocating a reformatory for hardened older juveniles and for the establishment of new industrial schools, which, although on a lesser scale, continued the practice of remitting their inmates to foster homes or to farm households.

After 1904 child-savers directed their efforts at the establishment of a separate juvenile justice system with its own judges, detention facilities, and probation officers. Thus, although the number of institutionalized young people declined relative to the population, the child-savers created new means of controlling troublesome youth and eventually their families.

Although Andrew Jones' study raises some questions as to both the consensus and the role of institutions in late-nineteenth-century child-saving, Paul W. Bennett directly challenges Sutherland's consensus by asserting that in Ontario, the child welfare system for the period from 1883 to the 1920s was characterized by disagreement as well as consensus.[67] Bennett examines the industrial schools movement and its leaders within the context of Ontario child welfare reform. For its promoters, the first institutions, the Victoria Industrial School (1887), was a modern experiment in the humane treatment of children. The florid language of one of its founders, who described it as an English type of "boarding school for the poor . . . for boys who are unmanageable," is no more exceptional than Kelso's effusions. The founders, prominent Ontario politicians and professional men, wanted to create an institution based on the cottage or family system with thirty boys to a cottage under the supervision of surrogate parents in the form of a guard and matron. Their plans failed in the flood of change that occurred in Ontario's arrangements for dependent, neglected, and delinquent young people. The cottages soon contained as many as fifty boys, as the closing of Penetanguishene turned the Victoria Industrial School into a dumping ground for troublemakers, and it was by 1910 overrun with older juvenile delinquents. It was finally closed in 1934 with much of the same reputation of the earlier reformatories it had replaced.

Susan Houston has written on the origins of juvenile delinquency in mid-nineteenth-century Ontario with later attention to the ubiquitous Kelso.[68] In her dissertation and elsewhere Houston examines the creation of institutions that were proposed as surrogates "for the lower classes approximately analogous to middle-class family life." She argues that although theoretically the discussion assumed that there was a distinction between neglected and destitute children and criminal children, the reality was a distinction between potentially and actually criminal children. Houston framed the dilemma as one in which "a blameless child [was] nevertheless guilty." The distinction was based on the belief that although the child was innocent—blameless in Houston's terms—it was inexperienced and vulnerable to vicious influence and example. Consequently two central questions arose during the period: (1) When is a family not a family? and (2) When is a nonfamily a family? The first question was central to decisions about removing children from the families, and the second, to the possibility of institutional care for children who had left their families or who had been abandoned by them or removed from them. Houston claimed that the

"Homes" movement in Ontario of the 1850s and 1860s proved a relative failure partly because reformers were really interested in reformatories.

In two later studies, which focus on the period from the 1880s to the 1890s, Houston reconsiders the interaction of juvenile reform and those for whom it was intended.[69] Her interpretation of the Ontario industrial schools is quite at variance with both Sutherland and Bennett. For Houston, they were institutions that were used by boys and their families—in a perverse form of family strategy— as means of gaining training and subsistence. In short, they *were* boarding schools for the poor!

Jeffrey S. Leon individually[70] and with John Hagan[71] have produced several articles on Canadian juvenile justice that include historical background. Unfortunately the historical parts of the articles are repetitive. The most interesting— perhaps because it appeared in a Canadian law journal—is "The Development of Canadian Juvenile Justice: A Background for Reform" (1977). Leon argues that Canadian reformers mixed the protection *of* and the protection *from* children—the persistent theme of neglect and criminality—which led to the mixing of adjudication and disposition stages in which the trial itself was part of the treatment. Canadian juvenile justice was characterized by summary convictions and the systematic use of probation for rehabilitative purposes. Because the reformers viewed neglected children as potential criminals, they were eager to save the children from incarceration in both industrial schools and reformatories—in this Leon fully agrees with Sutherland—but neither did they want to return them to deficient home environments. Thus probation, with its intervention into family life, was emphasized. Children's aid societies, by actively working with children accused of crimes and frequently serving as juvenile court committees, simply gave concrete force to the assertion by the architect of the Juvenile Delinquents Act (1908), W. L. Scott, that all delinquents were neglected and that all neglected children not delinquent were only so by a matter of accident.

There is much left to be done in the history of Canadian juvenile justice. Except for Sutherland's chapters, there are no national surveys. Nearly all the studies are not just limited to Ontario but also to Toronto.[72] Also, given the connection in Ontario of the juvenile court movement and the children's aid societies, the role of Kelso is certainly overemphasized. Moreover, the tendency to end the studies in the early 1920s have deprived us of understanding the operation of the courts nationally as the first generation of pioneers were replaced by professional and perhaps career-minded judges.

NEEDS AND OPPORTUNITIES FOR STUDY

The migration of British children and youth under the auspices of voluntary societies has been well served by recent historical scholarship and, with the exception of the schemes established under the Empire Settlement Act in the interwar years, deserves to be followed up. On the other hand, the whole range of topics associated with the history of child studies is undeveloped.

Nineteenth-century children's institutions, especially those operated by the Catholic Church in English-Canada, need study. Although some records (e.g., those relating to industrial schools and other institutions for delinquents) were turned over to appropriate provincial offices, most have been retained by the sponsoring religious orders.

The major organizational challenge to these institutions, the children's aid societies, remains largely unstudied. The emphasis on the analysis of the movement's rhetoric and on its leading advocate, Kelso, has left us without a clear understanding of organizational practice and policy implementation. Both studies of major children's aid societies (e.g., Toronto or Ottawa) and provincial operations are needed.

Juvenile delinquency is another neglected theme. The events and ideas leading to the Juvenile Delinquents Act of 1908 have been reasonably covered; however, the first generation of magistrates remain shadowy figures, and the growth of juvenile justice under them remains unexplored. With few exceptions the operations of the courts after the first generation of judges have not been studied. Indeed, the shift from formal court appearances to occurrence interviews in Ontario, for example, calls for detailed inquiry into the day-to-day operations of juvenile and family courts.

Child labor is another terra incognita, with the only recent work on late-nineteenth-century Ontario. Given the great diversity of Canadian economic and social development, especially if one includes pre-Confederation Newfoundland, the issue of child labor promises significant insights in the political and cultural life of Canada's provinces and regions. A related topic that has received some attention is the transition from family and school to work and the problems of youth unemployment.

The whole area of recreation and social clubs for young people needs work. This would include the activities of churches, including Sunday schools and other voluntary agencies, to provide facilities and supervision for youth as well as municipal and provincial programs.

All areas of policy study—voluntary and governmental—need development. Even major organizations (e.g., the Canadian Council on Child Welfare) are without histories. Provincial and federal policies and departments serving children and their families remain unstudied. Although the federal government established a division of child welfare in the national Department of Health in 1920, federal efforts at child health and hygiene have been neglected. Provincial activities have fared no better. Most leading twentieth-century advocates of child welfare are without adequate biographies.

Day care, nursery schools, and other services for infants and young children do not exist in the literature. Nor are there scholarly studies of governmental policy relations to services for children and families.

Finally, Canadian participation in the social activities of international organizations—voluntary and governmental—is a promising area of investigation. Indeed, the placement of Canada as a North American nation with substantial, if rapidly declining, British and Commonwealth connections and including a legitimate and protected Francophone minority makes it an interesting focus of differing cultural and policial traditions.

In brief, the archival resources are adequate for the work, but the laborers are few and show little prospects of increase. The short supply of human resources is partly caused by the only recent development of mass graduate education in Canada and by the lack of private support for intellectual and cultural activities. Since the Report of the Royal Commission on National Development in the Arts, Letters and Sciences in 1951 the federal government has provided generous financial support for university research by faculty and graduate students.[73] This leaves Canadian historians of child studies at the mercies of government funding. Support by provincial governments is focused on current practical issues and restricted by official control over the dissemination of the results. Thus research and publication remain a largely individual enterprise, sustained by personal interest and whatever available institutional support.

NOTES

We acknowledge the help of Kathy Oliver, graduate assistant at the University of Calgary, in locating dissertations and published studies and in tracking down errant citations.

1. Ian Winchester, "Introduction—Illuminating Education," *Interchange* 17:2 (1986):3–8.

2. Alison Prentice, "The School Promoters: Education and Social Class in Mid-Nineteenth Century Upper Canada" (Ph.D. diss., University of Toronto, 1975); published as a monograph, *The School Promoters* (Toronto: McClelland & Stewart, 1977). Also Susan E. Houston, "The Impetus to Reform: Urban Crime, Poverty, and Ignorance in Ontario, 1850–1875" (Ph.D. diss., University of Toronto, 1974); Harvey T. Graff, "Literacy and Social Structure in the Nineteenth Century City" (Ph.D. diss., University of Toronto, 1975); and Ian E. Davey, "Educational Reform and the Working Class: School Attendance in Hamilton, Ontario 1851–1891" (Ph.D. diss., University of Toronto, 1975). Also see Terrence R. Morrison, "The Child and Urban Social Reform in Late Nineteenth Century Ontario" (Ph.D. diss., University of Toronto, 1971), which, although done under another adviser, demonstrated the bracing winds of the new social history at Toronto.

3. See, for example, the euphoric assessments in Chad Gaffield, "Going Back to School; Towards a Fresh Agenda for the History of Education," *Acadiensis* 15 (Spring 1986):169–190, and J. Donald Wilson, *An Imperfect Past: Education and Society in Canadian History* (Vancouver: Centre for the Study of Curriculum and Instruction, Faculty of Education, University of British Columbia, 1984).

4. Michael B. Katz, *The People of Hamilton, Canada West: Family and Class in a Mid-Nineteenth Century City* (Cambridge, Mass.: Harvard University Press, 1975).

5. The list of topics included in Melissa A. Smith, compiler, *A Survey of Sources for the History of Child Studies at the Rockefeller Archive Center 1988* (Pocantico Hills, North Tarrytown, N.Y.: Rockefeller Archives Center, 1988), adequately covers the interests of this review: adoptions and care of orphans, child development, child health

and hygiene, day care, family relations, family welfare and services, juvenile delinquency, parent education, recreation and social clubs, rural youth, and youth unemployment (p. 1). We would add child labor, imperial juvenile migration, native children, and religion to round out the list.

6. National Library of Canada, *Doctoral Research on Canada and Canadians, 1884–1983* (Ottawa: Supply and Services Canada, 1986).

7. William O'Neill, "Feminism as a Radical Ideology," in *Dissent: Explorations in the History of American Radicalism*, ed. Alfred F. Young (Dekalb: Northern Illinois University, 1968), pp. 275–300. Barbara Welter, "The Cult of True Womanhood 1820–1860," *American Quarterly* 18 (Summer 1966):151–174.

8. Wayne Roberts makes the connection between maternal feminism and childhood explicit in " 'Rocking the Cradle for the World': The New Woman and Maternal Feminism, Toronto 1877–1914," in *A Not Unreasonable Claim: Women and Reform in Canada 1880's–1920's*, ed. Linda Kealey (Toronto: The Woman's Press, 1979), pp. 15–46. Although many other articles in women's history intervene, it seems to be Veronica Strong-Boag who completes the chronological circle of this argument in "Intruders in the Nursery: Childcare Professionals Reshape the Years One to Five 1920–40," in *Childhood and Family in Canadian History*, ed. Joy Parr (Toronto: McClelland & Stewart, 1982), pp. 144–160.

9. T. R. Morrison, " 'Their Proper Sphere': Feminism, the Family and Child-Centred Social Reform in Ontario, 1875–1900," *Ontario History* 68 (March–June 1970):45–64, 65–74; and "Reform as Social Tracking: The Case of Industrial Education in Ontario 1870–1900," *The Journal of Educational Thought* 8 (August 1974):87–110.

10. Morrison, "Child and Urban Social Reform," p. 3.

11. Morrison, " 'Their Proper Sphere,' " pp. 97–98, 111.

12. Norah Lewis, "Physical Perfection for Spiritual Welfare; Health Care for the Urban Child, 1900–1939," in *Studies in Childhood History: A Canadian Perspective*, ed. Patricia T. Rooke and R. L. Schnell (Calgary: Detselig Enterprises, 1982), pp. 135–166. Also see Norah Lillian Lewis, "Advising the Parents: Child Rearing in British Columbia During the Inter-War Years" (Ed.D. diss., University of British Columbia, 1980). Related studies that appeared too late to be included in this survey include Cynthia Comacchio Abeele's " 'The Mothers of the Land Must Suffer': Child and Maternal Welfare in Rural and Outpost Ontario, 1920–1940," *Ontario History* 80 (September 1988): 183–205, and Theresa Marianne Rupke Richardson's "The Century of the Child: The Mental Hygiene Movement and Social Policy in the United States and Canada" (Ph.D. diss, University of British Columbia, 1987).

13. Neil Sutherland, *Children in English-Canadian Society: Framing the Twentieth-Century Consensus* (Toronto: University of Toronto Press, 1976), p. 21.

14. Ibid., p. 112. There is enough evidence to counteract this suggestion apart from the distance and discernment one must retain when purveying documents written in the third person by the historical actor making such claims for himself—something Kelso was prone to do.

15. Quoting the *Toronto Daily Star*, January 14, 1921, in Paul W. Bennett, "Turning 'Bad Boys' into 'Good Citizens': The Reforming Impulse of Toronto's Industrial Schools Movement 1883 to the 1920s," *Ontario History* 78 (September 1986):226.

16. For example, Ian Bain, "The Role of J. J. Kelso in Launching of the Child Welfare Movement in Ontario" (Master's thesis, University of Toronto, 1955); W. Baker, "The Place of Private Agencies in the Administration of Government Policy: The Ontario

Children's Aid System 1892–1965'' (Ph.D. diss., Queen's University, 1966); Russell Joliffe, "The History of the CAS of Toronto 1891–47" (Master's thesis, University of Toronto, 1950); Morrison, "Child and Urban Social Reform"; and Dean Ramsay, "The Development of Child Welfare Legislation in Ontario" (Master's thesis, University of Toronto, 1949).

17. Henry C. Klassen, "In Search of Neglected and Delinquent Children: The Calgary Children's Aid Society, 1909–1920," in *Town and City: Aspects of Western Canadian Urban Development*, ed., Alan F. J. Artibise (Regina: Canadian Plains Research Center, University of Regina, 1981), pp. 375–391. Also see Ann Margaret Angus, *Children's Aid Society of Vancouver, B.C. 1901–1951* (Vancouver: The Society, 1951). Roslyn Cluett has a dissertation on "The Ontario Children's Aid Societies, 1893–1935," under way at the University of Guelph. The dates span Kelso's tenure as superintendent of neglected and dependent children. Rebecca Coulter, " 'Not to Punish But to Reform': Juvenile Delinquency and Children's Protection Act in Alberta, 1909–1929," in Rooke and Schnell, eds., *Studies in Childhood History*, p. 171.

18. For a different assessment of Kelso, see Rooke and Schnell, *Discarding the Asylum: From Child Rescue to the Welfare State in English-Canada, 1800–1950* (Lanham: University Press of America, 1983), pp. 298–305.

19. This claim is made by Doug Whyte in a paper presented to the history department at Carleton University, January 23, 1978, "The Evolution of Federal Juvenile Immigration Policy 1894–20," p. 25. Even for juvenile immigration, it cannot be sustained (certainly not for the later Montreal-based British Immigration and Colonization Society) and less so if one simultaneously examines Canadian primary sources for children's aid societies, child welfare departments, and various children's agencies. This is not claiming either was any worse than the other; it is said to merely caution historians into making unsubstantiated cross-cultural comparisons!

20. For example, Allana G. Reid, "First Poor Relief System of Canada," *Canadian Historical Review* 27 (December 1946):424–431; Judith Fingard, "The Winter's Tale: The Seasonal Contours of Pre-Industrial Poverty in British North America 1815–60," *Canadian Historical Papers* (1974): 65–94, and "The Relief of the Unemployed Poor in Saint John, Halifax, and St. John's 1815–1860," *Acadiensis* 5 (Autumn 1975):32–53; G. E. Hart, "The Halifax Poor Man's Friend Society 1820–27," *Canadian Historical Review* 34 (June 1953):109–123; J. M. Whalen, "Social Welfare in New Brunswick 1784–1900," *Acadiensis* 2 (Autumn 1972):54–64; Brereton Greenhous, "Paupers and Poorhouses: The Development of Early Poor Relief in New Brunswick," *Social History/ Histoire Sociale* 1 (April 1968):103–126; and Stephen A. Speisman, "Munificent Parsons and Municipal Parsimony: Voluntary Against Public Poor Relief in Nineteenth Century Toronto," *Ontario History* 65 (1973):33–50. We voiced concern about the lack of interest in the intellectual roots of and historical precedents to the nineteenth century at the first Canadian History of Education Association Conference, 1980, in "The Institutional Society: Childhood, Family and Schooling," in *Approaches to Educational History*, ed. David C. Jones and others (Winnipeg: Faculty of Education, University of Manitoba, 1981), pp. 113–130.

21. Peter N. Moogk, "*Les Petits Sauvages*: The Children of Eighteenth-Century New France," in Parr, ed., *Childhood and Family*, pp. 7–13. Michael Katz and Ian E. Davey have written on midcentury family life in "Youth and Early Industrialization in a Canadian City," in which they test the hypothesis suggested by Edward Shorter (1975) that parent-child relations become more intense with the onset of industrialization in answer to Michael

Anderson's claim that they became more attenuated and weaker. Hamilton, Ontario, from 1850 to the 1880s, is their point of reference. See Edward Shorter, *The Making of the Modern Family* (New York: Basic Books, 1975), and Michael Anderson, *Family Structure in Nineteenth Century Lancashire* (Cambridge: Cambridge University Press, 1971). The article by Katz and Davey is in *Turning Points: Historical and Sociological Essays on the Family*, ed. John Demos and Sarane Spence Boocock (Chicago: University of Chicago Press, 1978), pp. 81–119.

22. Patricia T. Rooke and R. L. Schnell, "Childhood and Charity in Nineteenth Century British North America," *Social History/Histoire Sociale* 15 (Spring 1982):157–179, and "Guttersnipes and Charity Children: Nineteenth Century Child Rescue in the Atlantic Provinces," in Rooke and Schnell, eds., *Studies in Childhood History*, pp. 82–104.

23. Patricia T. Rooke and R. L. Schnell, "The Rise and Fall of the Protestant Orphans Asylum as Women's Domain 1850–1930," *Atlantis* 7 (Spring 1982):21–35.

24. London (Ontario) Children's Aid Society, *15th Annual Report* (1908), University of Western Ontario Archives, and Montreal POH, *Annual Report* (1857), Public Archives of Canada.

25. William Hattie, "Report of the Inspector of Humane Institutions, 1913–14," in Legislature of Nova Scotia, *Report on Public Charities*, 1914 (Halifax: King's Printer, 1914), pp. 8, 30, 50.

26. Halifax Industrial School, *Report* (1857), Public Archives of Nova Scotia.

27. Jennifer S. H. Brown, "Children of the Early Fur Trade," in Parr, ed., *Childhood and Family*, pp. 44–68.

28. Leslie Savage, "Perspectives on Illegitimacy: The Changing Role of the Sisters of Misercordia in Edmonton, 1900–39," in Rooke and Schnell, eds., *Studies in Childhood History*, pp. 105–133.

29. Bettina Bradbury, "The Fragmented Family: Family Strategies in the Face of Death, Illness, and Poverty, Montreal, 1860–1885, in Parr, ed., *Childhood and Family*, pp. 109–128.

30. See Strong-Boag, "Intruders in the Nursery"; Suzann Buckley, "Ladies or Midwives? Efforts to Reduce Infant and Maternal Mortality," in Kealey, ed., *A Not Unreasonable Claim*, pp. 131–150; and Sutherland, *Children in English-Canadian Society*, pp. 62–63, 75–76, 85, 229. *The Canadian Mothers Book* (Ottawa: Department of Health, 1923) was authored by Dr. Helen MacMurchy, the division's first chief. R. L. Schnell has examined the founding of the division and MacMurchy's leadership in "Female Separation and Institution-Building: Continuities and Discontinuities in Canadian Child Welfare 1913–1935," *International Review of History and Political Science* 25 (May 1988):14–41, and in "A Children's Bureau for Canada: The Origins of the Canadian Council on Child Welfare 1913–1921," in *The 'Benevolent State': The Growth of Welfare in Canada*, ed. Allen Moscovitch and Jim Albert (Toronto: Garamond Press, 1987), pp. 95–110, which discusses the Canadian Council on Child Welfare and its hopes to be an equivalent of the U.S. Children's Bureau; and "The Public Interest and the Social Market: An Experiment in Privatizing the Federal Child Welfare Division 1933–37," a paper presented to the Third National Conference on Provincial Social Welfare Policy, Banff, Alberta, April 1987; Diana Hodson's paper "To Diagnose and Prescribe: The Politics of the Provincial Survey and CWC Activity During the Depression," ibid. Also Tamara Hareven, "An Ambiguous Alliance. Some Aspects of American Influences in Canadian Social Welfare," *Social History/Histoire sociale* 3 (April 1969):82–98.

31. Bernard Wishy, *The Child and the Republic: The Dawn of Modern American Child Nurture* (Philadelphia: University of Pennsylvania Press, 1968), and Christina Hardyment, *Dream Babies; Child Care from Locke to Spock* (Oxford: Oxford University Press, 1984).

32. See Patricia T. Rooke and R. L. Schnell, "Child Welfare in English Canada 1920–48," *Social Service Review* 55 (September 1981):484–506, and " 'Making the Way More Comfortable': Charlotte Whitton's Child Welfare Career," *Journal of Canadian Studies* 17 (Winter 1983):33–45. A key organization is the Canadian Welfare Council. See Diana Hodson's "Child Welfare and Social Development: A History of the Canadian Welfare Council, 1920–1941," (Ph.D. diss., University of Calgary, forthcoming).

33. Two articles that have come out of the project are Neil Sutherland, " 'Listening to the Winds of Childhood': The Role of Memory in the History of Childhood," *Canadian History of Education Association Proceedings*, Winter 1988, pp. 5–29, and " Everyone Seemed Happy in Those Days': The Culture of Childhood in Vancouver Between the 1920s and the 1960s," *History of Education Review* (1986):37–51.

34. One of the most exciting uses of object-relations psychology with application to both gender studies and childhood history is Nancy Chodorow, *The Reproduction of Mothering* (Berkley: University of California Press, 1983).

35. Lorna F. Hurl, "Restricting Child Factory Labour in Late Nineteenth Century Ontario," *Labour/Le Travail* 21 (Spring 1988):87–121, and John Bullen, "Hidden Workers: Child Labour and the Family Economy in Late Nineteenth Century Urban Ontario," *Labour/Le Travail* 18 (Fall 1986):163–187. Also see Bullen's "Child Labour in Early Industrial Canada," (Ph.D. diss., University of Ottawa, 1989). Robert G. McIntosh has a dissertation on "Grotesque Faces and Figures: Child Labour in Mining Industries in Canada" under way at Carleton University.

36. Some examples are Margaret Prang, " 'The Girl God Would Have Me Be': The Canadian Girls in Training 1915–39," *Canadian Historical Review* 66 (1985):154–184; Patricia Dirks, "Beyond Family and School: An Analysis of the Changing Place of Protestant Churches in the Lives of Canada's Young 1900–1918," paper presented at the annual meeting of the Canadian Historical Association, Vancouver, B.C., June 1983. Also David Macleod, "A Live Vaccine: The YMCA and Male Adolescence in the United States and Canada 1870–1920," *Social History/Histoire Sociale* 11 (May 1978):5–25; Murray G. Ross, *The YMCA in Canada: The Chronicle of a Century* (Toronto: Ryerson Press, 1951); Leila Mitchell McKee, "Voluntary Youth Organizations in Toronto 1880–1930" (Ph.D. diss., York University, 1983); Diana Pederson, "On the Trail of the Great Quest: The YMCA and the Launching of Canadian Girls in Training 1909–21," paper presented at the Annual Meeting of the Canadian Historical Association, Ottawa, Ontario, 1982; and Veronica Strong-Boag, *The New Day Recalled: Lives of Girls and Women in English Canada 1919–39* (Toronto: Copp Clark Pitman, 1988), which is part of the University of British Columbia's Canadian Childhood History Project. Rebecca Coulter's "Teenagers in Edmonton, 1921–1931: Experiences of Gender and Class" (Ph.D. diss., University of Alberta, 1987), was anticipated by her "The Working Young of Edmonton 1921–31," in Parr, ed., *Childhood and Family*, pp. 143–159. See also John A. MacDonald, "Juvenile Training Schools and Juvenile Justice Policy in British Columbia," *Canadian Journal of Criminology* 20 (October 1978):418–436, and Diane L. Matters, "The Boys' Industrial School: Education for Juvenile Offenders," in *Schooling and Society in Twentieth Century British Columbia*, ed. J. Donald Wilson and David C. Jones (Calgary: Detselig Enterprises, 1980), pp. 53–70.

37. Scattered cases of early emigration schemes that prefigured what was to become

a "movement" are found in Toronto Boys' Home, *Ninth Annual Report* (Toronto: Thomas Cattell & Sons, 1869), p. 5: Toronto City Council Papers (April 1834–February 1837), and May 18, 1858, House of Industry Board Minute Book (1836–1858), City of Toronto Archives. See also "Destitute Children of the Metropolis" (London, 1830).

38. *Report of the Permanent Support Society . . .* [1831], Goldsmith's Library, University of London.

39. Other agencies included Birmingham Rescue Society, Catholic Emigration Society, Gutter Children's Homes, The Church of England Society of Waifs and Strays, Liverpool Catholic Children's Protection Society, Birkdale Farm School, Redhill Reformatory, Fegan's Homes, The Manchester and Salford Boys and Girls Refuge, and Liverpool Sheltering Homes. Industrial training ships such as the *Clio, Formidable, Cumberland,* and *Cornwell* supplied boys. Numerous female refuges and rescue societies sent girls.

40. Evidence that few in proportion to the total number came from the poor laws is found in "Final Report of the Select Standing Committee on Agriculture and Colonization," *Journals of the House of Commons 1896.*

41. Moyal objected to "exotics unsuited to the soil and moral atmosphere of the Dominion." See Superintendent of Dependent and Neglected Children, Ontario, *5th Annual Report,* Appendix, "Special Report on Immigration of British Children, 1897." The later admission of refugee Armenians and Jews, including children, was opposed by some of the same actors, including Charlotte Whitton, who had campaigned against the British children. See Irving Abella and Harold Troper, *None Is Too Many* (Toronto: Lester & Orpen Dennys, 1982).

42. See Dr. Barnardo's Homes, *Annual Report* (1885), p. 14, and *Labour Journal,* July 10, 1903.

43. British Immigration and Colonization Association Papers, MG28, I62, PAC, and Thomas E. Jordan, " 'Stay and Starve, or Go and Prosper!' Juvenile Emigration from Great Britain in the Nineteenth Century," *Social Science History* 9 (Spring 1985):145–165.

44. See p. 328 of Index for the many citations given immigrant children in Sutherland, *Children in English-Canadian Society,* and Rooke and Schnell, *Discarding the Asylum,* pp. 185–272. Andrew Jones and Leonard Rutman refer to Kelso's involvement throughout *In the Children's Aid: J. J. Kelso and Child Welfare in Ontario* (Toronto: University of Toronto Press, 1981).

45. Two examples of the "dumping ground" theory are H.G.M. Johnston, *British Emigration Policy 1815–30: Shovelling Out Paupers* (Oxford: Clarendon Press, 1972), and Edward Gibbon Wakefield's famous *A View of the Art of Colonization* (London: John W. Parker, 1894), especially p. 145. Australian historical scholarship is replete with this interpretation, which is scarcely surprising or indefensible in light of its beginnings as a penal outpost of the Empire.

46. Joy Parr, *Labouring Children* (London: Croom-Helm, 1980). A later movement of British children to Canada during World War II is chronicled by Geoffrey Bilson, *The Guest Children: The Story of the British Child Evacuees Sent to Canada During World War II* (Saskatoon: Fifth House, 1988).

47. Kenneth Bagnell, *The Little Immigrants* (Toronto: Macmillan, 1980).

48. Gillian Wagner, *Barnardo* (London: Weidenfeld & Nicolson, 1979), and *Children of the Empire* (London: Weidenfeld & Nicolson, 1982).

49. Gail H. Corbett, *Barnardo Children in Canada* (Peterborough: Woodland Publishing, 1981).

50. Phyllis Harrison, *The Home Children* (Winnipeg: Watson & Dwyer, 1979).

51. Several articles are worth noting: Wesley B. Turner, "Miss Rye's Children and the Ontario Press, 1875," *Ontario History* 68 (September 1976):169–204, and "Eighty Stout and Healthy Looking Girls," *Canada: An Historical Magazine* (1975):36–49; Leonard Rutman, "Importation of British Waifs into Canada: 1868–1916," *Child Welfare* 52 (March 1973):158–166; and Patricia T. Rooke and R. L. Schnell, "Imperial Philanthropy and Colonial Response: British Juvenile Emigration to Canada 1896–1930," *The Historian* 46 (November 1983):56–77. Also Morrison, "Child and Urban Social Reform," pp. 132–138.

52. Patricia T. Rooke and R. L. Schnell, "The King's Children' in English-Canada: A Psychohistorical Study of Abandonment, Rejection and Canadian Response to British Juvenile Immigrants," *Journal of Psychohistory* 8 (Spring 1981):387–420.

53. Although the scholarly books mentioned have all referred to any of or all these topics, much more can be done perhaps in the spirit of Ellen Ryerson, *The Best-Laid Plans: America's Juvenile Court Experiment* (New York: Hill & Wang, 1979).

54. Joy Parr, " 'Transplanting from Dens of Inequity': Theology and Child Emigration," in Kealey, ed., *A Not Unreasonable Claim*, pp. 169–184. Neil Semple's article is found in *Social History/Histoire sociale* 14 (May 1981):157–175. Also see Dirks, "Beyond Family and School." Sutherland, *English Children in Canadian Society*, discusses religion and the reform movement, pp. 236–237; Rooke and Schnell's *Discarding the Asylum*, the Arminian breakthrough, pp. 14–16; and Morrison, "Child and Urban Social Reform," applied Christianity.

55. In the City of Birmingham Archives.

56. Quoted in Rooke and Schnell, eds., *Discarding the Asylum*, pp. 216–217. Other "imperialistic" child-saving literature includes Annie MacPherson, *The Little London Arabs* (London: Morgan & Chase, 1870); Denis Crane, *John Bull's Surplus Children: A Plea for Giving Them a Fairer Chance* (London: H. Marshall, 1915); Thomas E. Sedgwick, *Lads for Empire* (London: P. S. King & Son, 1914); Joseph Forster, *Stay and Starve; or Go and Thrive* (Manchester: J. Heywood, 1884), and The Catholic Truth Society, *Our Waifs and Strays* (London: The Society, 1889). See also Patrick A. Dunae, "Making Good: The Canadian West in British Boys' Literature 1890–1914," *Prairie Forum* 4 (Fall 1979):165–182.

57. See Parr, *Labouring Children*, pp. 62–81, for an interesting discussion of the forms of "family strategy" involved. Also see Bradbury, "Fragmented Family." Anderson observes what he calls a "calculative mentality" among the working classes in *Family Structure in Nineteenth Century Lancashire*.

58. For the case of Ada Francis see *Saint John Star*, November 13, 1907; for the others see Harrison, *Home Children*, p. 188, and J. Obed Smith to Scott, December 13, 1904, RG 76 Vol. 100, File 13204, Pt. 2 and RG 76 Vol. 62, File 2869, PAC. One of the most appalling abuses of trust is found in records of the Middlemore Receiving Home, Halifax, which placed 4,000 children in Nova Scotia and New Brunswick between 1872 and 1915. Here the superintendent, J. Sterling King, victimized girls and subjected children to abuse over a period of years. RG 76 Vol. 62, File 2869, Pt. 1, and Vol. 63, PAC.

59. Patricia T. Rooke and R. L. Schnell, *No Bleeding Heart: Charlotte Whitton a Feminist on the Right* (Vancouver: University of British Columbia Press, 1987), pp. 67–82. Also see Schnell, "Female Separatism and Institution-Building," and "A Children's Bureau for Canada."

60. Sutherland, *Children in English-Canadian Society*, pp. 91–92.

61. *Report of the Commissioners Appointed to Enquire into the Prison and Reformatory System of Ontario, 1891* (Toronto: Warwick & Sons, 1891).

62. There are no critical studies of the pioneer generation of juvenile court magistrates. Two early women magistrates have at least hagiographies; see Elsie Gregory MacGill, *My Mother as Judge: A Biography of Helen Gregory MacGill* (Toronto: Peter Martin Associates, 1981; originally published by The Ryerson Press, 1955); Bryne Hope Sanders, *Emily Murphy, Crusader* (Toronto: Macmillan Co. of Canada, 1945); and Christine Mander, *Emily Murphy, Rebel* (Toronto: Simon & Pierre, 1985).

63. Canadian Press, December 2, 1969, Address to North American Judges Association.

64. Dorothy E. Chunn, "Family Courts and the Dependent Poor in Ontario, 1920–1945: Intended and Unintended Consequences of Reform," paper presented at the Annual Meeting of the Canadian Historical Association, Vancouver, June 1983. Also see her dissertation, "From Punishment to Doing Good: The Origins and Impact of Family Relations Courts in Ontario, 1888–1942" (Ph.D. diss., University of Toronto, 1986). For British Columbia, McDonald has examined the development of training (industrial) schools and juvenile justice policy to 1975 in "Juvenile Training Schools and Juvenile Justice in British Columbia," and Diane L. Matters, the first fifteen years of the Boys Industrial School in "The Boys' Industrial School: Education for Juvenile Offenders."

65. James G. Snell, "Courts of Domestic Relations: A Study of Early Twentieth Century Judicial Reform in Canada," *Windsor Yearbook of Access to Justice* 6 (1986):36–60.

66. Andrew Jones, " 'Closing Penetanguishene Reformatory': An Attempt to De-institutionalize Treatment of Juvenile Offenders in Early Twentieth-Century Ontario," *Ontario History* 70 (December 1978):227–244.

67. Bennett, " 'Turning "Bad Boys" into "Good Citizens,' " pp. 209–232.

68. Susan Houston, "The Impetus to Reform: Urban Crime, Poverty, and Ignorance in Ontario, 1850–1875." (Ph.D. diss., University of Toronto, 1974), and "Victorian Origins of Juvenile Delinquency: A Canadian Experience," *History of Education Quarterly* 12 (Fall 1972): 254–279.

69. Susan Houston, "Late Victorian Juvenile Reform: A Contribution to the Study of Educational History," in Jones and others, eds., *Approaches to Educational History*, pp. 7–23, and "The 'Waifs and Strays' of a Late Victorian City: Juvenile Delinquents in Toronto," in Parr, ed., *Childhood and Family*, pp. 129–142.

70. Jeffrey S. Leon, "The Development of Canadian Juvenile Justice: A Background for Reform," *Osgood Hall Law Journal* 15 (June 1977):71–107, and "New and Old Themes in Canadian Juvenile Justice: The Origins of Delinquency Legislation and the Prospects for Recognition of Children's Rights," *Interchange* 8:1–2 (1977–1978):151–175.

71. Jeffrey S. Leon and John Hagan, "Philosophy and Sociology of Crime Control: Canadian-American Comparisons," *Sociological Inquiry* 47:3–4 (1977):181–208, and "Rediscovering Delinquency: Social History, Political Ideology and the Sociology of Law," *American Sociological Review* 42 (August 1977):587–598.

72. For a study of Ontario that examines the pre-Confederation period and female offenders, see Robin M. Sandstrom, " 'Snakes and Snails and Puppy-dog Tails': The Neglected Question of Female Juvenile Offenders in Toronto in the 1840s," paper pre-

sented at the Annual Meeting of the Canadian Historical Association, Vancouver, June 1983.

73. Royal Commission on National Development in the Arts, Letters and Sciences, 1949–1951, *Report* (Ottawa: Edmond Cloutier, 1951).

REFERENCES

Abella, Irving, and Harold Troper. *None Is Too Many*. Toronto: Lister & Orpen Dennys, 1982.

Abeele, Cynthia Comacchio. " 'The Mothers of the Land Must Suffer,': Child and Maternal Welfare in Rural and Outpost Ontario, 1920–1940.'' *Ontario History* 80 (September 1988):183–205.

Anderson, Michael. *Family Structure in Nineteenth Century Lancashire*. Cambridge: Cambridge University Press, 1971.

Angus, Ann Margaret. *Children's Aid Society of Vancouver, B.C. 1901–1905*. Vancouver: The Society, 1951.

Bagnell, Kenneth. *The Little Immigrants*. Toronto: Macmillan, 1980.

Bain, Ian. "The Role of J. J. Kelso in Launching of the Child Welfare Movement in Ontario." Master's thesis, University of Toronto, 1955.

Baker, W. "The Place of Private Agencies in the Administration of Government Policy: The Ontario Children's Aid System 1892–1965." Ph.D. diss., Queen's University, 1966.

Barnardo's Homes, Dr. *Annual Report*. London: Barnardo's, 1885.

Bennett, Paul W. "Turning 'Bad Boys' into 'Good Citizens': The Reforming Impulse of Toronto's Industrial Schools Movement 1883 to the 1920s." *Ontario History* 78 (September 1986):209–232.

Bilson, Geoffrey. *The Guest Children: The Story of the British Child Evacuees Sent to Canada During World War II*. Saskatoon: Fifth House, 1988.

Bradbury, Bettina. "The Fragmented Family: Family Strategies in the Face of Death, Illness, Poverty, Montreal 1860–1885." In *Childhood and Family in Canadian History*, edited by Joy Parr. Toronto: McClelland & Stewart, 1982, pp. 109–128.

British Immigration and Colonization Association Papers. MG28,I62. Public Archives of Canada (PAC), Ottawa.

Brown, Jennifer S. H. "Children of the Early Fur Trades." In *Childhood and Family in Canadian History*, edited by Joy Parr. Toronto: McClelland & Stewart, 1982, pp. 44–68.

Buckley, Suzann. "Ladies or Midwives? Efforts to Reduce Infant and Maternal Mortality." In *A Not Unreasonable Claim*, edited by Linda Kealey. Toronto: The Woman's Press, 1979, pp. 131–150.

Bullen, John. "Hidden Workers: Child Labour and the Family Economy in Late Nineteenth Century Urban Ontario." *Labour/Le Travail* 18 (Fall 1986):163–187.

———. "Child Labour in Early Industrial Canada." Ph.D. diss., University of Ottawa, 1989.

Canada. *Journals of the House of Commons*. 1896. Report of the Select Standing Committee on Agriculture and Colonization, Appendix No.2.

———. Royal Commission on National Development in the Arts, Letters and Sciences. *Report*, 1949–1951. Ottawa: Edmond Cloutier, 1951.

The Catholic Truth Society. *Our Waifs and Strays*. London: The Society, 1889.

Chodorow, Nancy. *The Reproduction of Mothering*. Berkeley: University of California Press, 1983.

Chunn, Dorothy E. "Family Courts and the Dependent Poor in Ontario, 1920–1945: Intended and Unintended Consequences of Reform." Paper presented at the Annual Meeting of the Canadian Historical Association, Vancouver, June 1983.

———. "From Punishment to Doing Good: The Origins and Impact of Family Relations Courts in Ontario, 1888–1942." Ph.D. diss., University of Toronto, 1986.

Cluett, Roslyn. "The Ontario Children's Aid Societies, 1893–1935." Ph.D., in progress, University of Guelph.

Corbett, Gail H. *Barnardo Children in Canada*. Peterborough: Woodland Publishing, 1981.

Coulter, Rebecca. "Alberta's Department of Neglected Children, 1909–1929: A Case Study in Child Saving." Master's thesis, University of Alberta, 1977.

———. " 'Not to Punish But to Reform': Juvenile Delinquency and Children's Protection Act in Alberta, 1909–1929." In *Studies in Childhood History*, edited by Patricia T. Rooke and R. L. Schnell. Calgary: Detselig Enterprises, 1982, pp. 167–184.

———. "The Working Young of Edmonton 1921–31." In *Childhood and Family in Canadian History*, edited by Joy Parr. Toronto: McClelland & Stewart, 1982, pp. 143–159.

———. "Teenagers in Edmonton, 1921–1931: Experiences of Gender and Class." Ph.D. diss., University of Alberta, 1987.

Crane, Denis. *John Bull's Surplus Children: A Plea for Giving Them a Fairer Chance*. London: H. Marshall, 1915.

Davey, Ian E. "Educational Reform and the Working Class: School Attendance in Hamilton, Ontario, 1851–1891." Ph.D. diss., University of Toronto, 1975.

Dirks, Patricia. "Beyond Family and School: An Analysis of the Changing Place of Protestant Churches in the Lives of Canada's Young 1900–1918." Paper presented at the Annual Meeting of the Canadian Historical Association, Vancouver, June 1983.

Dunae, Patrick A. "Making Good: The Canadian West in British Boys' Literature 1890–1914." *Prairie Forum* 4 (Fall 1979):165–182.

Fingard, Judith. "The Winter's Tale: The Seasonal Contours of Pre-Industrial Poverty in British North America 1815–60." *Canadian Historical Association Papers* (1974):65–94.

———. "The Relief of the Unemployed Poor in Saint John, Halifax, and St. John's 1815–1860." *Acadiensis* 5 (Autumn 1975):32–53.

Forster, Joseph. *Stay and Starve; or Go and Thrive* Manchester: J. Heywood, 1884.

Gaffield, Chad. "Going Back to School: Towards a Fresh Agenda for the History of Education." *Acadiensis* 15 (Spring 1986):169–190.

Graff, Harvey T. "Literary and Social Structure in the Nineteenth Century City." Ph.D. diss., University of Toronto, 1975.

Greenhous, Brereton. "Paupers and Poorhouses: The Development of Early Poor Relief in New Brunswick." *Social History/Histoire sociale* 1 (April 1968):103–126.

Greven, Philip. *The Protestant Temperament*. New York: Alfred A. Knopf, 1977.

Hardyment, Christina. *Dream Babies: Child Care from Locke to Spock*. Oxford: Oxford University Press, 1984.

Hareven, Tamara. "An Ambiguous Alliance. Some Aspects of American Influences in Canadian Social Welfare." *Social History/Histoire sociale* 3 (April 1969):83–98.

Harrison, Phyllis. *The Home Children*. Winnipeg: Watson & Dwyer, 1979.

Hart, G. E. "The Halifax Poor Man's Friend Society 1820–27." *Canadian Historical Review* 34 (June 1953):109–123.

Hattie, William. "Report of the Inspector of Humane Institutions, 1913–14." In Legislature of Nova Scotia, *Report on Public Charities*. Halifax, 1914.

Hodson, Diana. "To Diagnose and Prescribe: The Politics of the Provincial Survey and CWC Activity During the Depression." Paper presented at the Third National Conference on Provincial Social Welfare Policy, Banff, Alberta, 1987.

———. "Child Welfare and Social Development: A History of the Canadian Welfare Council, 1920–1941." Ph.D. diss., University of Calgary, 1990.

Houston, Susan E. "The Impetus to Reform: Urban Crime, Poverty, and Ignorance in Ontario, 1850–1875." Ph.D. diss., University of Toronto, 1974.

———. "Late Victorian Juvenile Reform: A Contribution to the Study of Educational History." In *Approaches to Educational History*, edited by David C. Jones and others. Winnipeg: Faculty of Education, University of Manitoba, 1981, pp. 7–23.

———. "The 'Waifs and Strays' of a Late Victorian City: Juvenile Delinquents in Toronto." In *Childhood and Family in Canadian History*, edited by Joy Parr. Toronto: McClelland & Stewart, 1982, pp. 129–142.

Hurl, Lorna F. "Restricting Child Factory Labour in Late Nineteenth Century Ontario." *Labour/Le Travail* 21 (Spring 1988):87–121.

Johnston, H.G.M. *British Emigration Policy 1815–30: Shovelling Out Paupers*. Oxford: Clarendon Press, 1972.

Joliffe, Russell. "The History of the CAS of Toronto 1891–47." Master's thesis, University of Toronto, 1950.

Jones, Andrew. " 'Closing Penetanguishene Reformatory': An Attempt to De-institutionalize Treatment of Juvenile Offenders in Early Twentieth-Century Ontario." *Ontario History* 70 (December 1978):227–244.

Jones, Andrew, and Leonard Rutman. *In the Children's Aid: J. J. Kelso and Child Welfare in Ontario*. Toronto: University of Toronto Press, 1981.

Jordan, Thomas E. " 'Stay and Starve, or Go and Prosper!' Juvenile Emigration from Great Britain in the Nineteenth Century." *Social Science History* 9 (Spring 1985):145–165.

Katz, Michael B. *The Irony of Early School Reform: Educational Innovation in Mid-Nineteenth Century Massachusetts*. Cambridge, Mass.: Harvard University Press, 1968.

———. *The People of Hamilton, Canada West: Family and Class in a Mid-Nineteenth Century City*. Cambridge, Mass.: Harvard University Press, 1975.

Katz, Michael B., and Ian E. Davey. "Youth and Early Industrialization in a Canadian City." In *Turning Points: Historical and Sociological Essays on the Family*, edited by John Demos and Sarane Spence Boocock. Chicago: University of Chicago Press, 1978, pp. 81–119.

Klassen, Henry C. "In Search of Neglected and Delinquent Children: The Calgary Children's Aid Society, 1909–1920." In *Town and City: Aspects of Western Canadian Urban Development*, edited by Alan F. J. Artibise. Regina: Canadian Plains Research Centre, University of Regina, 1981, pp. 375–391.

Leon, Jeffrey S. "The Development of Canadian Juvenile Justice: A Background for Reform." *Osgoode Hall Law Journal* 15 (June 1977):71–107.

———. "New and Old Themes in Canadian Juvenile Justice: The Origins of Delinquency Legislation and the Prospects for Recognition of Children's Rights." *Interchange* 8:1–2 (1977–1978):151–175.

Leon, Jeffrey S., and John Hagan. "Philosophy and Sociology of Crime Control: Canadian-American Comparisons." *Sociolgial Inquiry* 47:3–4 (1977):181–208.

———. "Rediscovering Delinquency: Social History, Political Ideology and the Sociology of Law." *American Sociological Review* 42 (August 1977):587–598.

Lewis, Norah Lillian. "Advising the Parents: Child Rearing in British Columbia During the Inter-War Years." Ed.D. diss., University of British Columbia, 1980.

———. "Physical Perfection for Spiritual Welfare; Health Care for the Urban Child, 1900–1939." In *Studies in Childhood History: A Canadian Perspective*, edited by Patricia T. Rooke and R. L. Schnell. Calgary: Detselig Enterprises, 1982, pp. 135–166.

London (Ontario) Children's Aid Society. *15th Annual Report*. London: The Society, 1908.

MacDonald, John A. "Juvenile Training Schools and Juvenile Justice Policy in British Columbia." *Canadian Journal of Criminology* 20 (October 1978):418–436.

MacGill, Elsie Gregory. *My Mother as Judge: A Biography of Helen Gregory MacGill*. Toronto: Peler Martin Associates, 1981 (originally published by Ryerson Press, 1955).

McIntosh, Robert G. " 'Grotesque Faces and Figures': Child Labour and the Canadian Coalfields, 1820–1930." Ph.D. diss., in progress, Carleton University.

McKee, Leila Mitchell. "Voluntary Youth Organizations in Toronto 1880–1930." Ph.D. diss., York University, 1983.

Macleod, David. "A Live Vaccine: The YMCA and Male Adolescence in the United States and Canada 1870–1920." *Social History/Histoire Sociale* 11 (May 1978):5–25.

MacMurchy, Helen. *The Canadian Mothers Book*. Ottawa: Department of Health, 1923.

MacPherson, Annie. *The Little London Arabs*. London: Morgan & Chase, 1870.

Mander, Christine. *Emily Murphy, Rebel*. Toronto: Simon & Pierre, 1985.

Matters, Diane L. "The Boys' Industrial School: Education for Juvenile Offenders." In *Schooling and Society in Twentieth Century British Columbia*, edited by J. Donald Wilson and David C. Jones. Calgary: Detselig Enterprises, 1980, pp. 53–70.

Montreal Protestant Orphans Home. *Annual Report, 1857*. Montreal: The Home, 1857.

Moogk, Peter N. " '*Les Petite Sauvages*'—The Children of Eighteenth Century New France." In *Childhood and Family in Canadian History*, edited by Joy Parr. Toronto: McClelland & Stewart, 1982, pp. 17–43.

Morgan, Edmund J. *The Puritan Family: Religion and Domestic Relations in Seventeenth-Century New England*. Rev. ed. New York: Harper & Row, 1966 (originally published in 1944).

Morrison, Terrence R. " 'Their Proper Sphere.' Feminism, the Family and Child-Centred Social Reform in Ontario, 1875–1900." *Ontario History* 68 (March–June 1970):45–64, 65–74.

———. "The Child and Urban Social Reform in Late Nineteenth Century Ontario." Ph.D. diss., University of Toronto, 1971.

———. "Reform as Social Tracking: The Case of Industrial Education in Ontario 1870–1900." *The Journal of Educational Thought* 8 (August 1974):87–110.

National Library of Canada. *Doctoral Research on Canada and Canadians, 1884–1983*. Ottawa: Supply and Services Canada, 1986.

O'Neill, William. "Feminism as a Radical Ideology." In *Dissent: Explorations in the History of American Radicalism*, edited by Alfred F. Young. Dekalb: Northern Illinois University, 1968, pp. 275–300.

Ontario. *Report of the Commissioners Appointed to Enquire into the Prison and Reformatory System of Ontario, 1891*. Toronto: Warwick & Sons, 1891.

Parr, Joy. " 'Transplanting from Dens of Inequity': Theology and Child Emigration." In *A Not Unreasonable Claim*, edited by Linda Kealey. Toronto: The Woman's Press, 1979, pp. 169–184.

———. *Labouring Children*. London: Croom-Helm, 1980.

Pederson, Diana. "On the Trail of the Great Quest: The YMCA and the Launching of Canadian Girls in Training 1909–21." Paper presented at the Annual Meeting of the Canadian Historical Association, Ottawa, Ontario, 1982.

Platt, Anthony. *The Child Savers: The Invention of Delinquency*. Chicago: University of Chicago Press, 1969.

Prang, Margaret. " 'The Girl God Would Have Me Be': The Canadian Girls in Training 1915–39." *Canadian Historical Review* 66 (June 1985):154–184.

Prentice, Alison. "The School Promoters: Education and Social Class in Mid-Nineteenth Century Upper Canada." Ph.D. diss., University of Toronto, 1975.

———. *The School Promoters*. Toronto: McClellan & Stewart, 1977.

Ramsay, Dean. "The Development of Child Welfare Legislation in Ontario." Master's thesis, University of Toronto, 1949.

Reid, Allana G. "First Poor Relief System of Canada." *Canadian Historical Review* 27 (December 1946):424–431.

Richardson, Theresa Marianne Rupke. "The Century of the Child: The Mental Hygiene Movement and Social Policy in the United States and Canada. Ph.D. dissertation, University of British Columbia, 1987.

Roberts, Wayne. " 'Rocking the Cradle for the World': The New Woman and Maternal Feminism, Toronto 1877–1914." In *A Not Unreasonable Claim: Women and Reform in Canada 1880's–1920's*, edited by Linda Kealey. Toronto: The Woman's Press, 1979, pp. 15–46.

Rooke, Patricia L., and R. L. Schnell. "The Institutional Society: Childhood, Family and Schooling." In *Approaches to Educational History*, edited by David C. Jones and others. Winnipeg: Faculty of Education, University of Manitoba, 1981, pp. 113–130, 158–163.

———. "The 'King's Children' in English-Canada: A Psychohistorical Study of Abandonment, Rejection and Canadian Response to British Juvenile Immigrants." *Journal of Psychohistory* 8 (Spring 1981):387–420.

———. "Child Welfare in English Canada 1920–48." *Social Service Review* 55 (September 1981):484–506.

———. "Guttersnipes and Charity Children: Nineteenth Century Child Rescue in the Atlantic Provinces." In *Studies in Childhood History: A Canadian Perspective*, edited by Patricia T. Rooke and R. L. Schnell. Calgary: Detselig Enterprises, 1982, pp. 82–104.

———. "The Rise and Fall of the Protestant Orphans Asylum as Women's Domain 1850–1930." *Atlantis* 7 (Spring 1982):21–35.

————. "Childhood and Charity in Nineteenth Century British North America." *Social History/Histoire Sociale* 15 (May 1982):157–79.

————. *Discarding the Asylum: From Child Rescue to the Welfare State in English Canada, 1800–1950.* Lanham: University Press of America, 1983.

————. "Imperial Philanthropy and Colonial Response: British Juvenile Emigration to Canada 1896–1930." *The Historian* 46 (November 1983):56–77.

————. " 'Making the Way More Comfortable': Charlotte Whitton's Child Welfare Career." *Journal of Canadian Studies* 17 (Winter 1983):33–45.

————. *No Bleeding Heart: Charlotte Whitton a Feminist on the Right.* Vancouver: University of British Columbia, 1987.

Ross, Murray G. *The YMCA in Canada: The Chronicle of a Century.* Toronto: Ryerson Press, 1951.

Rutman, Leonard. "Importation of British Waifs into Canada: 1868–1916." *Child Welfare* 52 (March 1973):158–166.

Ryerson, Ellen. *The Best-Laid Plans: America's Juvenile Court Experiment.* New York: Hill & Wang, 1979.

Sanders, Bryne Hope. *Emily Murphy, Crusader.* Toronto: Macmillan Co. of Canada, 1945.

Sandstrom, Robin M. " 'Snakes and Snails and Puppy-dog Tails': The Neglected Question of Female Juvenile Offenders in Toronto in the 1840s." Paper presented at the Annual Meeting of the Canadian Historical Association, Vancouver, June 1983.

Savage, Leslie. "Perspectives on Illegitimacy: The Changing Role of the Sisters of Misercordia in Edmonton 1900–39." In *Studies in Childhood History: A Canadian Perspective*, edited by Patricia T. Rooke and R. L. Schnell. Calgary: Detselig Enterprises, 1982, pp. 105–133.

Schnell, R. L. "A Children's Bureau for Canada: The Origins of the Canadian Council on Child Welfare 1913–1921." In *'The Benevolent State': The Growth of Welfare in Canada*, edited by Allen Moscovitch and Jim Albert. Toronto: Garamond Press, 1987, pp. 95–110.

————. "The Public Interest and the Social Market: An Experiment in Privatizing the Federal Child Welfare Division 1933–37." Paper presented to the Third National Conference on Provincial Social Welfare Policy, Banuff, Alberta, 1987.

————. "Female Separation and Institution-Building: Continuities and Discontinuities in Canadian Child Welfare 1913–1935." *International Review of History and Political Science* 25 (May 1988):14–41.

Sedgwick, Thomas E. *Lads for Empire.* London: P. S. King & Son, 1914.

Semple, Neil. "The Nurture and Admonition of the Lord: Nineteenth Century Canadian Methodism's Response to 'Childhood.' " *Social History/Histoire sociale* 14 (May 1981):157–175.

Shorter, Edward. *The Making of the Modern Family.* New York: Basic Books, 1975.

Smith, Melissa A., comp. *A Survey of Sources for the History of Child Studies at the Rockefeller Archive Center 1988.* Pocantico Hills, North Tarrytown, N.Y.: Rockefeller Archive Center, 1988.

Snell, James G. "Courts of Domestic Relations: A Study of Early Twentieth Century Judicial Reform in Canada." *Windsor Yearbook of Access to Justice* 6 (1986):36–60.

Speisman, Stephen A. "Munificent Parsons and Municipal Parsimony: Voluntary Against

Public Poor Relief in Nineteenth Century Toronto.'' *Ontario History* 65 (1973):33–50.

Strong-Boag, Veronica. "Intruders in the Nursery: Childcare Professionals Reshape the Years One to Five 1920–40.'' In *Childhood and Family in Canadian History*, edited by Joy Parr. Toronto: McClelland & Stewart, 1982, pp. 144–160.

———. *The New Day Recalled: Lives of Girls and Women in English Canada 1919–39*. Toronto: Copp Clark Pitman, 1988.

Sutherland, Neil. *Children in English-Canadian Society: Framing the Twentieth-Century Consensus*. Toronto: University of Toronto Press, 1976.

———. " 'Everyone Seemed Happy in Those Days': The Culture of Childhood in Vancouver Between the 1920s and the 1960s.'' History of Education Review 15 (1986):37–51.

———. " 'Listening to the Winds of Childhood': The Role of Memory in History of Childhood.'' In *Canadian History of Education Association Proceedings* (Winter 1988):5–29.

Toronto Boys' Home. *Ninth Annual Report of the Committee of Management of the Boy's Home for the Training and Maintenance of Destitute Boys Not Convicted of Crime*. Toronto: Thomas Cattell & Sons, 1869.

Turner, Wesley B. "Eighty Stout and Healthy Looking Girls.'' *Canada: An Historical Magazine* 3 (1975):36–49.

———. "Miss Rye's Children and the Ontario Press, 1875.'' *Ontario History* 68 (September 1976):169–204.

Wagner, Gillian. *Barnardo*. London: Weidenfeld & Nicolson, 1979.

———. *Children of the Empire*. London: Weidenfeld & Nicolson, 1982.

Wakefield, Edward Gibbon. *A View of the Art of Colonization*. London: John W. Parker, 1894.

Welter, Barbara. "The Cult of True Womanhood 1820–1860.'' *American Quarterly* 18 (Summer 1966):151–174.

Whalen, J. M. "Social Welfare in New Brunswick 1784–1900.'' *Acadiensis* 2 (Autumn 1972):54–64.

Whyte, Doug. "The Evolution of Federal Juvenile Immigration Policy 1894–20.'' Paper presented to the history department at Carleton University, January 23, 1918, p. 21.

Wilson, J. Donald *An Imperfect Past: Education and Society in Canadian History*. Vancouver: Centre for the Study of Curriculum and Instruction, Faculty of Education, University of British Columbia, 1984.

Winchester, Ian. "Introduction—Illuminating Education.'' *Interchange* 17:2 (1986):3–8.

Wishy, Bernard. *The Child and the Republic: The Dawn of Modern American Child Nurture*. Philadelphia: University of Pennsylvania Press, 1968.

9

EAST AFRICA

Sara Harkness and Charles M. Super

East Africa, comprising Kenya, Uganda, and Tanzania, is a political entity whose creation was brought about by the British colonial presence during the first two-thirds of the current century and whose demise followed the competition and conflicts among those nations after their attainment of independence in the early 1960s. Despite the current estrangement of these three countries, there is much besides a shared colonial history to unite them as a cultural area relevant to the study of childhood. In this chapter we review the sources available for the study of childhood in East Africa, and sketch with broad strokes the predominant patterns that have been found in children's environments, child-rearing practices, and the outcomes of these for child development and health. In the process we briefly discuss some of the main theoretical issues relevant to childhood that have emerged from this research.

SOURCES

The recorded history of childhood in East Africa begins with the establishment of the British colonial presence soon after the turn of the twentieth century. Although a few Europeans had reported on their travels in this part of the world previously, the establishment of a British colonial organization was a tremendous impetus for understanding the way of life of the peoples under British administration. Partly, of course, the British presence provided indispensable support services for ethnographers interested in studying the heretofore unknown peoples of East Africa. Further, the British administration had a practical need to understand the ways of the people to establish and maintain political authority and to implement appropriate educational services, necessary in turn for training members of the growing new economy and governmental networks. Missionaries joined in this later effort, for they also needed to understand the religious customs and beliefs they were trying to change. One of the classic accounts of childhood in East Africa, O. F. Raum's *Chaga Childhood* (1940), was written by the son of missionaries among the Chaga, who became a student of anthropologist Bronislaw Malinowski at the University of London and eventually the head of the colonial department of education at the same university. Most of the more general ethnographic studies of other East African groups omitted study of childhood as, following the dominant anthropological mode of the times, they focused on rituals, beliefs, and social structure; yet even these discussed, at a minimum, customs surrounding marriage, childbirth, and the ceremonial transition to adulthood (e.g., Beidleman 1971; Peristiany 1939; Roscoe 1911, 1923; Winter n.d.).

An important product of the British educational efforts in East Africa was Africans with literacy skills for documenting their own societies. In relation to childhood, the published results have been few, but they provide a significant insider's perspective on customs and practices also noted by foreign observers. The most well known of these is *Facing Mount Kenya* (1938), an ethnography of the Kikuyu people of Kenya by another of Malinowski's students, Jomo Kenyatta, the man who later became Kenya's first president. Three more modest accounts by members of the first graduating class of the bachelor of education program at Makerere University, in Uganda, were gathered together and edited by their teacher, Lorene K. Fox, for publication as *East African Childhood* (1967).

Political repression and violence in Uganda and an anti-Western bias in socialist Tanzania have discouraged research by anthropologists in recent years. In contrast, Kenya became a major focus for anthropological studies of childhood under the auspices of the Child Development Research Unit (CDRU; later the Bureau of Educational Research), a joint endeavor between Harvard University and the University of Nairobi funded primarily by the Carnegie Corporation and initiated by John and Beatrice Whiting. The Whitings' previous project to study child rearing in six cultures (Whiting and Whiting 1975) had included a study of the Gusii of western Kenya, carried out by Robert A. LeVine and Barbara LeVine (now Lloyd) (1963). Under the auspices of the CDRU, field research on child rearing and child development was carried out in a dozen ethnic groups during the 1960s and 1970s by teams of American and Kenyan anthropologists and psychologists, including Kenyan research assistants, some of whom later continued their education in the United States. At the same time LeVine's new project in Gusii (R. LeVine and S. Levine 1988; S. LeVine 1979) and other anthropological research carried out independently during the same era (e.g., Goldschmidt 1976) have provided perhaps the most intensive documentation of childhood in non-Western settings currently available for any country in the world. Beatrice Whiting and Carolyn Edwards (1988) have recently used much of the field data collected through this work for a cross-cultural analysis of childhood, a particularly valuable resource, since it includes empirically based comparisons of behavior toward and by children in East Africa and elsewhere.

Extensive though this literature is, it is not the only resource for the study of childhood in East Africa. Demographic studies, particularly in Kenya, have been carried out since the early 1960s, and provide an important other dimension for the understanding of children's environments. As has been documented repeatedly, Kenya's rate of population growth owing to natural increase is among the highest in the world. Both the Kenya government and academic researchers interested in the dynamics of population change have sought not only to measure population trends in Kenya, but also to understand their causes (Dow and Werner 1983; Mburugu 1986). In addition, numerous studies of maternal and child health in East Africa are important for knowledge of the health experiences of children in this part of the world. This diverse body of work includes basic neonatology (Ebrahim 1969), studies of economic and familial risk factors for malnutrition and its consequences (Dixon, LeVine, and Brazelton 1982; Fleuret 1987), school health surveys (Berger and Salehe 1986), and traditional health practices in transition (O'Dempsey 1988).

HISTORICAL BACKGROUND

The history of East Africa, like sub-Saharan Africa in general, is one of constant culture change brought about by the interactions, both friendly and hostile, of different ethnic groups as they migrated across the lands in search of better grazing lands for their animals, more fertile soils for their crops, or simply new homesteads for their children. Using Greenberg's linguistic classification, historians of East Africa have identified three main groups in East Africa: the Cushites, who expanded into the area from northern origins in Ethiopia; the Nilotes; and the Bantus. Whereas the Cushitic-speaking peoples are believed to have been present in East Africa since before the Iron Age, the Nilotes and Bantus expanded rapidly into this area during the past two thousand years, absorbing many Cushitic culture traits in the process. The Nilotes, arriving from the west and north, have been predominantly pastoralists, whereas the Bantus, who are thought to have originated in the Congo area, are traditionally mainly agriculturalists. These two groups have interacted in turn, while subgroups within them formed and were transformed by interactions with other groups. As Sutton (1968, pp. 94–95) summarizes these processes, "the history of East Africa and of its component regions is not just a collection of histories of individual tribes or groups of tribes, but a story of fusion and interaction by which all tribes and groups have been constantly altered or even transformed."

The significant point of this history for the study of childhood in East Africa is that although accounts are specific to different ethnic groups, there are many more similarities than differences among them. There are exceptions to this general picture of cultural interaction: the coastal populations influenced by Arab culture, the few remaining hunter-gatherer groups living mainly in forested regions, and the non-African populations (mainly East Indian and European) have distinctive ways of life. In this chapter we are concerned with the "mainstream" East African cultures, the pastoralists and agriculturalists who have lived in the highlands and fertile grasslands of East Africa and shaped most of its cultural landscape up to the present.

THE ECOCULTURAL CONTEXT

The ecocultural context of childhood in East Africa is set, first, by its history and geography and, second, by the "maintenance systems," or socioeconomic organization, that derive from these (J.W.H. Whiting 1977). In contrast to West Africa, much of the land in East Africa enjoys a relatively temperate climate because of its elevation. This ecology has supported the development of pastoralism and simple hoe agriculture, the dominant forms of subsistence. Pastoralism has traditionally been accorded higher status in East Africa, both among ethnic groups and within them, so that pure pastoralists, such as some of the Masai, are greatly admired by other groups, such as the Kipsigis, that practice a mixed economy. Most groups in East Africa have both cattle (as well as smaller livestock) and agricultural fields. Within this system care of the cattle is traditionally delegated to the men and older boys, whereas agricultural work is the domain of the women and younger children. The relatively lower status of the women and younger children mirrors the pastoral/agricultural status differential.

Despite their lower status, women and children in East African societies are important as social and economic assets. Polygyny (in which a man may take several wives) is the culturally desired family form in virtually all groups, and wives are acquired through payment of bride-price, usually in the form of cattle and other livestock, to the bride's father. Once married, a wife's primary road to greater social status in her husband's extended family and the community is through childbearing, with high fertility (eight or more living children) the desired norm. Within this system men and women tend to lead fairly separate lives: even if they are not separated by the traditional demands of nomadic pastoralism, as in some groups, they work, eat, and sleep apart. This is particularly true of those households in which a man has more than one wife. In these each woman has her own hut for herself and her young children, and the husband visits each in turn. In many societies the husband maintains his own hut for entertaining his friends, and he may call one of his wives to join him for the night there.

The father, in this system, is a rather distant and authoritarian figure in the family, but authority does not extend much beyond the household. With the exception of the Ugandan kingdoms and some chiefly societies, most groups in East Africa have traditional authority systems based on the male-dominated kin groups. Descent, inheritance, and residence are through the male, such that families pass through stages of organization and renewal, with the "ideal" form consisting of the patriarch and his wives, his married sons and their wives and children, and his unmarried children. With the death of the patriarch ownership of land and cattle is divided among the sons through their mothers, with seniority given to the eldest son in some cases.

The environments of children within their own households are culturally structured along several dimensions that we have conceptualized together as the "developmental niche" (Harkness and Super 1983; Super and Harkness 1986). For a child at any given culturally defined developmental stage the niche consists of three major components: (1) the physical and social settings in which the child lives; (2) culturally regulated customs of child care and child rearing; and (3) the psychology of the caretakers, especially their beliefs about the nature of children and their values for family life. These three subsystems share the common function of mediating the individual's developmental experience within the larger culture, and hence there are systematic forces to bring them into harmony. On the other hand, each has a distinct set of relations to the history, economy, and social structure of the larger society, and thus they constitute somewhat independent routes of disequilibrium and change. Our description of childhood in East Africa concerns the relevant settings, customs, and beliefs that are frequently found there. In some cases focused research has demonstrated the developmental consequences of the culturally constructed experiences. Additionally, the informed observer can see how continuities in the themes and tasks of infancy and childhood define issues and assumptions for later periods of life, both traditionally and during the modern period of rapid culture change.

Childhood in East Africa is culturally defined as the period from birth until circumcision, a ritual transition for both boys and girls that involves genital surgery, social seclusion, and teaching. Groups that do not practice circumcision per se (e.g., the Luo of Kenya) have other, parallel ceremonies. Age at circumcision seems to have varied traditionally from the mid-twenties for young men of pastoralist groups to as young as seven or eight years of age for girls among the predominantly agricultural Gusii people (LeVine and LeVine 1963). Completion of the circumcision ceremonies for an individual can be the immediate precursor to marriage, especially for girls, or the beginning of a relatively free life-stage that we might characterize as "youth," during which individuals, especially boys, might be expected to carry out important responsibilities as warriors, but at the same time are accorded considerable social and sexual freedom with few domestic responsibilities. In this chapter we focus on the years before circumcision, starting with birth and including several culturally recognized stages of childhood.

BIRTH

Birth for children in East Africa traditionally took place at home, and this is still true for the great majority, especially in rural areas. Although traditional birth attendants are to be found in many communities, labor and delivery are customarily attended mainly by the mother's mother-in-law, her own mother, and other female relatives and neighbors. Men are barred from observation, although in some groups they may wait outside the hut. In cases of difficulty in labor men may be called on to apply emergency measures such as blowing into the mother's lungs, with the idea that this pressure from above will force the baby out. Women in Kokwet, a rural Kipsigis community, reported very short labors of about two hours, and many babies (especially for multiparous women) were born without any help from others (Harkness 1987). On the other hand, difficulty in labor leads to heightened intervention by others, focused around finding the fault (usually in the mother's past behavior) that has caused the difficulty. In Kokwet, for example, one mother who had a difficult labor was blamed by other women in attendance for having had sexual relations with her husband during the pregnancy, a culturally forbidden act. Similarly, the LeVines report that among the Gusii, a woman having difficulty in labor is reprimanded for her fears and urged to admit any adulterous relationships (LeVine and LeVine 1963, 135). Raum (1940) describes responses to difficulties in labor among the Chaga of Tanzania as follows:

In the frantic search for the "some one who has blundered," it is the woman herself who is first singled out. Frequently a quarrel she has had with her parents-in-law is unearthed. She has to ask their pardon by sending her necklace round to be spat at, and thus have the curse withdrawn. Or it may be said that the woman's hard-heartedness has offended an ancestral spirit, who retaliates by obstructing the birth. The husband, as mediator between living and dead, must reconcile him, and the libation offered is to break the spell. The husband himself may be blamed, especially if the placenta is retained. An occasion will be remembered when he scolded his father, and if the latter has since died a sacrifice has to be offered. (p. 84)

Extensive scarification of the vaginal area, owing to the female circumcision operation (involving removal of the clitoris and outer labia for many groups), makes parturition a great deal more painful for women than it would otherwise be, but women are expected to be stoic throughout, lest they shame themselves or even bring harm to the baby. Nevertheless, women are reported to be fearful of childbirth, especially the first time around (Harkness 1987; LeVine and LeVine 1963; Raum 1940).

Given the various circumstances of birth in East Africa, it is hardly surprising that perinatal mortality was very high and continues to be at least moderately high, and maternal mortality also was not uncommon. In addition, not all babies born alive were allowed to survive in traditional systems, although this situation has been altered under pressure from government prohibitions of infanticide. Raum (1940) discusses a number of circumstances leading to infanticide, centering around the elimination of infants who seemed abnormal in their delivery, their appearance, or their early development. Among the Kipsigis, babies born to uncircumcised (and therefore unmarried) mothers were traditionally killed at birth. Describing the Sebei in recent times, Goldschmidt (1976) states that the Sebei deny engaging in infanticide as a regular practice, but it is apparently not infrequent and there is no penalty against it, although a man may divorce his wife "if she has children three times and kills them each time" (p. 244). The birth of twins in East African groups was considered an extraordinary event perceived either as very unlucky (as among the Chaga [Raum 1940]) or as a special blessing requiring special attentions and precautionary rituals (among the Bakitara [Roscoe 1923]).

Customs of care after the successful birth of a child in East Africa are strikingly similar in many respects. The mother is supposed to rest in the seclusion of her hut—for four days after the birth of a boy or three days after the birth of a girl. During this time, and for the weeks following, she is cared for by her mother or mother-in-law or her cowives. Among the Kipsigis of Kokwet, the women had organized a neighborhood system of reciprocal help during the postpartum period, so that the new mother could rest while others gathered firewood, brought water from the river, cooked, and cared for her older children (Harkness 1987). In many groups the father is forbidden to see his wife or his new baby during this time, for fear that he might be tempted to break the postpartum sex taboo, or that he might unwittingly harm the vulnerable newborn by his very presence, or even that his own masculinity might be compromised by close contact with a baby. Parents do not always follow their own cultural prescriptions, however, as Joseph Lijembe (1967) describes in relation to accounts of his own birth, after two previous births of girls who died early:

According to Luyia custom, husbands must not be seen around at the time of delivery, though they are to be informed immediately by messenger of the sex of the infant. My father tells me, however, that being anxious to know the sex of his newborn baby, he lingered around the home during this birth, pretending to be doing some useful work, so that as soon as the attendants left the place he would find out at once. When he learned that his new baby was a boy, he admits, he could not help pushing the customary practice aside. . . . Thus, ignoring all the taboos of the tribe, my father was my first visitor, holding me in his arms with happiness, all the time thinking what lucky names he would give to his new-born son." (p. 2)

INFANCY

Although high fertility is the desired goal for all groups in East Africa, this is tempered by customs designed to protect the healthy development of the infant. Primary among these is the period of culturally mandated sexual abstinence, which seems to have varied from a year to two or more traditionally. This period was and is coterminous with breast-feeding, such that the mother would practice sexual abstinence to protect her ability to nurse the baby, but then would wean the baby as soon as she found herself pregnant again. In combination with abstinence, breast-feeding has been the main factor in the timing of births, with a two- to two-and-a-half-year interbirth interval most common. Birth intervals have become shorter among younger and less traditional mothers, as is discussed later. The traditional pattern is that the mother nurses her baby on demand, and uses nursing as a means to quiet a fussing baby. Frequent nursing during the night is facilitated by mother-child sleeping arrangements: mother and baby sleep in skin-to-skin contact with each other, and the mother is able to nurse the baby at night almost without waking up herself. Super and Harkness (1982) have documented the effects of this on infant sleep patterns among the Kipsigis: babies continue to wake at approximately three-hour intervals at night during at least the first eight months of life, in contrast to American babies, who learn to sleep through the night by four months of age. One interesting consequence of this set of practices, combined with others, such as the use of sibling caretakers (see below), is a different pattern of individual differences among babies that create stresses for the family system; in this case the baby who has difficulty sleeping through the night does not cause the level of distress in rural Africa that it does in metropolitan America. There may be, in addition, subtle consequences for the pattern of physical growth and health (Konner and Super 1988).

Although breast-feeding is universal for all groups in East Africa, supplementary feeding from birth also is the norm. Raum (1940) describes infant food supplements that include milk and butter, bananas and soda, and porridge that are premasticated and spit into the infant's mouth from the second day of life among the Chaga; and the LeVines (1963) report that Gusii newborns are fed a meal of juice from cooked pumpkin leaves and liquid porridge. A common practice is to pour a thin gruel into the baby's mouth from the side of the cupped hand, holding the baby's nose to force it to swallow. This form of feeding has been strongly discouraged by Western medical practitioners, who attribute many infant deaths to inhaling food into the lungs.

The health status of infants in traditional East African societies was and still is understandably fragile, and many customs recognize the vulnerability of this period. Among the Kipsigis of Kokwet, infants were protected from social contact with others, particularly strangers, men, or women who, perhaps through no fault of their own, were thought to have the "evil eye." Vulnerability was considered greatest during the first weeks and months after birth, but a child was not thought entirely free until after the first two years of life. The Gusii have more highly articulated theories of witchcraft that can harm babies through the supposed penetration of any small material objects (e.g., feathers or pieces of lint) through the delicate, light-colored infant skin; interestingly, they attribute the origin of these beliefs to the Kipsigis (LeVine and LeVine 1963). In all groups the shared joy of a new baby seems to be combined with apprehensions about its health and survival. J. Mutuka Nzioki (1967) describes a scene he witnessed as a young Kamba child after the birth of a baby in their neighborhood:

The women were drinking tea from mugs, and some of the big girls from small containers made from gourds. Any one could tell from the outside that something outstanding had occurred under the roof of that hut. I had never heard the village women talk so loudly, so happily and, above all in such a co-operative manner. They were all friends alike as they celebrated the arrival of a child. One villager, however, did not stay long to share in the chat. The village's witch, probably fearing that that anything wrong that happened would surely be attributed to her, slipped away without notice. (p. 87)

Infants in East Africa are under the charge of women. Fathers, having been excluded from the birth, remain aloof from their babies throughout the infancy period. Whiting and Edwards (1988) asked ethnographers of child life in five Kenyan communities to rate how often fathers would play with or entertain, hold, carry outside the house, care for, or take charge of the baby in the mother's absence: all rated fathers as ''rarely'' or ''never'' engaging in these activities. Whiting and Edwards relate this pattern to polygyny, mother-child sleeping arrangements, and other ways in which the lives of fathers are separated from those of their wives.

Although the pattern of little interaction between a father and his infant is widespread, reports vary on the affective tone of relations between parents and their infants or young children. Gray (1963, 66) comments on the agricultural, mostly monogamous Sonjo of Tanzania: ''Relations between parents and children are decorous and, in appearance at least, affectionate.'' Likewise, Gulliver (1955, 52), describing family life among the pastoralist Jie of Uganda:

The children grow up under the care of their mother, who, in Jieland as elsewhere, has a deep, natural affection for them and a great concern for their well-being. The pattern of affectionate ties established in childhood continues into the adult life of the sons. Gradually all the daughters leave the group, though established feelings persist even so; but *vis-a-vis* her sons a mother remains in close and constant contact with usually very real affection on both sides.

The Kilbrides (1974, 305), who specifically focused their ethnographic research on the development of social relations, report that ''adults and children are frequently seen smiling at and talking to infants to coax smiles from them.'' The conscious emphasis on social behavior, according to the Kilbrides (1974, 1975, 1983), is a reflection of status mobility in traditional and modern Ugandan society. Among the Kipsigis, who lack the cultural background of social hierarchy, Super and Harkness (1974) also noted considerable social play with infants by mothers and other family members. Observers of other Kenyan groups comment on the rapid responsiveness to infant crying, which reflects the independent belief that infants' needs should be met without delay (e.g., Munroe and Munroe 1971).

In contrast to this happy picture, Goldschmidt (1975) reports little affectionate interaction between Sebei infants and their mothers, who, with ''idle hands and absent eyes,'' sustain their infant's basic development but without engaging much satisfying emotional involvement. Similarly, Ainsworth (1967), in her classic study of Baganda infancy, reports that ''Ganda babies very rarely manifest any behavior pattern even closely resembling European affection'' (p. 344). The LeVines (1963) report that Gusii parents are not affectionately demonstrative with their infants and toddlers (although other relatives, such as grandparents or the sibling caretaker, often are), and Gusii mothers appear embarrassed when asked to talk and play with their infants seated in a face-to-face position (Keefer et al. 1977). R. LeVine has suggested that maternal emotional detachment during infancy is part of a larger complex of parental concern with survival in groups with high mortality, and that it ultimately plays a role in patterns of personality among agricultural African groups (LeVine 1973, 1974a, 1974b).

There remains considerable doubt about the empirical basis of these comparisons of mother-infant affection, primarily because of methodological shortcomings. The most striking problem is the probable inhibiting effect of the observer. Ainsworth (1967, 39), for example, points out that the structure of her observations "perhaps bore more resemblance to social visits than to scientific interviews," and it is easy to imagine that social play with the baby would have been considered by the mothers as secondary to entertaining the distinguished visitor and, in that context, rude. In addition, as the LeVines (1963, 145) point out for the Gusii, in societies where belief in jealous witchcraft and the "evil eye" is prevalent, maternal displays of affectionate attention to an infant in the presence of someone outside the family might be strongly muted. It also must be noted that the empirical data cited to support claims of relatively uninvolved interaction between infants and mothers are not always obviously different from similar data from Western countries, and in the absence of controlled comparisons it is difficult to be certain of the extent of group differences (see Super 1980, for a review). The weight of evidence at this point does suggest some difference in social interaction with infants—that is, who does how much of what, when— even among African groups with similar ecologies of infancy, but it also indicates broad universals in the deep pleasures of welcoming a responsive newcomer into the family.

In many East African groups infants are specifically encouraged in the attainment of motor skills, especially sitting and walking (but not, in most cases, prone behaviors such as crawling). The usual procedure for teaching sitting, to take a common example, involves propping up the infant in a circle of cloths or towels or placing the infant in a shallow hole. Both procedures give support to the lower back, and the infant is left in this position for several minutes, often while being encouraged with enthusiastic banter from the mother, grandmother, and siblings. Such training in the motor milestones of infancy have been reported in many groups, including the Baganda and Acholi of Uganda (Ainsworth 1967; Lijembe 1967, Ocitti 1973); the Luhyia (Fox 1967); the Gusii (LeVine and LeVine 1963); the Kamba (Sengoba 1978); the Pokot, Teso, Duruma, Boran, Luo, Kiga, and Kipsigis (Super 1976, 1981) of Kenya; and the Sukuma of Tanzania (Varkevisser 1973). Practice in walking and standing may occur on a daily basis over the several months before mastery, and progress is a common topic of conversation within the family. Even neighbors may be heard to greet the mother, passing at the river or near her fields, "What has he learned?" rather than "How is your baby?" Many rural East African mothers believe that deliberate instruction is important to the infant's proper development, and that without such training the child would be delayed, or even permanently impaired, in walking. In addition to specific tutoring in motor skills most rural infants receive considerable exercise of the trunk muscles from the traditional methods of being carried on the back or hip. This combination of deliberate practice and incidental exercise is thought to be responsible for the widely reported precocity of attainment of walking, sitting, and related milestones (but not of crawling and prone behaviors) by traditionally reared infants (see Super 1981, for a comprehensive review).

In contrast to the deliberate importance given to motor development in many East African groups, learning to talk often is not given priority, even in later infancy and early childhood. Among the Kipsigis and Luo, for example, mothers express the view that children learn to talk naturally from one another and do not require specific encouragement for normal development (Blount 1969, 1972; Harkness 1977; Harkness and Super 1982).

A striking element in the pattern of infant care and training throughout East Africa is the use of child caretakers, usually older female siblings of the infant. Roscoe (1923) recounts that among the Bakitara of Uganda, a nurse of the father's clan is assigned to take care of the baby soon after its birth, and the mother is only supposed to nurse it. Anna Apoko (1967) describes the use of child nurses among her native Luo:

As soon as a mother has given birth to her baby, if she does not have older children of her own, she looks around among her relatives for *lapidi*, a selected young child, preferably a girl from six to ten years old, to act as the baby's "nurse." During a recent vacation I met a woman who was once my classmate; she had come sixty-five miles from where she was living with her husband, back to her father's home, looking for *lapidi*. She found a little girl, five years old, who went back with her.

The very young baby, from one to three months old, is tied on *lapidi*'s back. *Lapidi*, carrying the baby in this way, goes with the mother to the field where she may be working for most of the day. If the baby wakes up from its sleep and begins to cry, the mother unties it from the child's back and breast-feeds it. By the time the baby is four months old, it may be left at home with *lapidi*, who again follows after the mother as soon as the baby is hungry and begins to cry. . . . Thus *lapidi* is the second mother to the baby; and there are some babies who are fonder of their *lapidi* than of their own mothers. (p. 51)

Child nurses are expected not only to carry the baby around, but also to play with it, sing lullabies to it, feed it porridge if the mother is unavailable, and help the baby in learning to talk and walk. Psychological processes of infant attachment to the mother, primarily studied in the Euro-American context, have been found to operate in a somewhat similar way for both mother and child caretaker in East Africa. This distinctive pattern has considerable theoretical value for refining basic developmental theory (e.g., Kermoian and Leiderman 1986). The baby's mother in this setting plays more of an "executive" role, supervising the work of her children, including care of the baby, while she herself carries on with her agricultural work and the many chores of the household. From the point of view of the baby, this system can work well as long as the mother is not too far away and the child caretaker is old enough to be somewhat responsible. If the fields are far away or the mother has other work, such as trading at far-off markets, the baby may be left for many hours with only a young child to attend to its needs.

Infancy in East Africa ends with weaning and the birth of the next child. These two events usually are related, as the mother customarily weans her child when she discovers that she is again pregnant. This event is supposed to be postponed by sexual abstinence, and Gray (1963) reports that among the Sonjo of Tanzania, the mother was not supposed to engage in sexual intercourse before weaning her previous child. More commonly the mother's next pregnancy puts an end to her nursing. Weaning practices are re orted to be abrupt and, by Western standards, rather harsh. The mother may smear bitter substances on her nipples, slap the child, or tell it "I don't want you" as it tries to nurse. The weanling also may be sent away to live with the grandparents or other relatives for awhile to forget about nursing. Although the child usually is about a year old when this happens, it may be considerably older if the mother has not become pregnant, as in the example recounted by Lijembe (1967, 3) of his Luhyia childhood:

I was still suckling my mother's breasts, I am told, at the age of three years. Then one day as I started to suckle I suddenly tasted an unusual bitterness. Startled, and whimpering, I was afraid of touching my mother's breasts ever again. Shortly after this, I was sent abruptly to my maternal uncle's home for a period of many months. When I came back, I found that my little sister, Mang'ong'o Alusa, had arrived."

EARLY CHILDHOOD

The birth of the next baby marks a difficult but, in East African culture, necessary transition from infancy to childhood. If there is no next baby because the mother has passed childbearing age, the youngest child is nursed longer, usually is pampered, and in some ways never grows up quite the way he or she should. The last-born is a "spoiled" child, and this fact may be used to explain his or her behavior even in adulthood. Because most families in East Africa are very large, seven out of eight children will be replaced by a younger sibling. When this happens the second-to-youngest child also is weaned from being carried on its mother's back, and no longer sleeps at her front. As described by Harkness and Super (1982), for Kipsigis culture, this transition is accompanied by changes in the young child's language environment: the child spends less time in the company of adults and more time with other children, is talked to less, and does less talking. This shift corresponds to a relative decline in the rate of language learning. The young child in this setting assumes a rather

marginal position in the family, no longer receiving the special attentions be-
stowed on babies but not yet able to participate effectively in the work of the
household. Harkness (1977) observed that children at this stage appeared shyer
and less sociable than children of the same age who were still the youngest
members of their families.

The father's involvement in the care and training of children aged 18 to 36
months (whom Whiting and Edwards, following Margaret Mead, call "knee-
children") is low, although greater than his interaction with infants (Whiting
and Edwards 1988): according to ethnographic reports from five communities
in Kenya, fathers "do not care for, carry, teach, or take charge of knee children
more than occasionally." Mothers, however, begin serious efforts to train their
children to be obedient and responsible, and to help with the work of the household, from this age. Whiting and Edwards (1988, 94–95) provide a cogent
summary of the style of mothering typical of their sub-Saharan samples that they
term the "training mother":

The training mothers in subSaharan Africa believe that responsibility and obedience can
and should be taught to young children. They begin teaching household, gardening, and
animal husbandry skills at a comparatively early age. The Negeca [a periurban community
of Kikuyu near Nairobi] mothers we interviewed are typical: they believe that they should
train a child to be a competent farmer, herdsman, and child nurse and that a child from
age 2 on should be assigned chores that increase in complexity and arduousness with
age. They punish their children for failure to perform these tasks responsibly or for
stubbornly refusing to do what their elders request of them. They allow much of their
children's learning to occur through observation and imitation; only occasionally do they
instruct them explicitly. Moreover, mothers seldom praise their children lest they become
proud, a trait that is unacceptable. They allow the major rewards for task performance
to be intrinsic.

Mothers' responses to their young children's dependency behavior seem to
vary among East African groups. Whereas the Gusii are reported to punish their
children severely for such behavior (LeVine and LeVine 1963), analysis of
mothers' responses to crying by two-year-olds in a Kipsigis community showed
a typical pattern of comforting they child by holding it and offering food before
disengaging to continue with other activities (Harkness and Super 1985a).

Parents in East Africa also may use fear to train their children to avoid real
dangers and to conform to desirable behavioral norms. In societies where witchcraft beliefs are well developed, toddlers may be taught not to accept food from
others (e.g., Raum 1940) lest they be poisoned, or to stop crying lest they be
thrown to the hyenas (LeVine and LeVine 1963). Apoko (1967) reports that
young children in her Acholi community become so frightened by their parents'
threats of harm that they refuse to go to bed on their own, and instead stay up
until they fall asleep in the midst of the adults' conversation. Of course, because
the children's sleeping place is in the midst of the family "kitchen," going to
bed early would, in any case, be difficult.

MIDDLE CHILDHOOD

Middle childhood in East Africa is a time for helping out with the work of the household, and intensive training for adult roles. Children, from the age they can carry out simple chores until they pass through the circumcision ceremonies, are a primary source of manpower to their parents: by the age of four to five years children in Kenyan communities are observed engaged in chores about a third of the time during the day, and this rises to around 50 percent for six-to ten-year-old children (Harkness and Super 1985a; Whiting and Edwards 1988, 68). Children's chores include virtually the whole range of activities necessary for household functioning: looking after the house, collecting firewood, gathering vegetables from the fields, shelling maize, making the fire, cooking and serving food, washing dishes and clothes, sweeping the house, and smearing the walls with a fresh mixture of mud and cow dung. Whereas girls are more apt to be assigned these chores, boys are more frequently sent to herd and tend the cows, oxen, sheep, and goats; both boys and girls help in gardening and farming tasks (Sieley 1975). In addition, as discussed previously, children this age (especially girls) are nurses for their infant siblings or other relatives. A Sebei mother interviewed by Goldschmidt (1976, 259) described the work of girls as follows:

When a mother goes away from home she may leave a girl of four or five years. She gives her a small gourd to fetch water in and tells her to sweep the house, bring firewood, collect vegetables, and look after the younger children. A few years later, when the girl is seven or eight, she will start to dig in the gardens. She will start to cook and make the fire by the time she is eight. She is taught to do exactly as her mother does, so that when her mother goes anywhere, she will return home to find the work done. If the mother finds the work improperly done, she only abuses the girl the first time, saying: "I hope that you have stomach pains and dysentery." Mothers are concerned that their daughters learn proper housekeeping so that their husbands will not beat them for neglecting their duties, and so it will not be said that they failed to learn proper behavior from their mother.

Boys and girls are differentially assigned to tasks in parallel with the adult division of labor between men and women, although children may be assigned to opposite-sex chores if there is no child of the appropriate age and sex available, with possible effects on social and personality development (Ember 1973). Kenyatta (1938) describes how Kikuyu fathers teach their boys to do agricultural work and to know about the plants and animals of the forest, while the mother likewise teaches her girls to tend the gardens and manage the homestead. Gray (1963, 64) recounts how young Sonjo boys "within a year or two of learning to walk" are put in charge of the goats at the house, and by the age of six or seven years are sent out to the goat camps with older boys and men to live. Girls, on the other hand, are mainly used as child nurses. The separation of boys and girls, in addition to having a practical basis, is motivated by a culturally shaped parental desire to bring up their boys and girls into psychologically and socially separate worlds. Thus Raum (1940, 131) reports that the Chaga father takes an interest in his sons from the age of seven or eight, when he removes them from the mother's tutelage, "imbuing them with a contempt for everything womanly." In contrast, "mother and daughter remain united for many more years in a co-operative association which is only dissolved at the girl's marriage."

The issue of how children's assigned activities influence their behavioral styles has been considered by Whiting and Edwards (1988). They find that although same-age boys and girls are similar to each other in their interactions with younger "knee children," girls act more like their mothers, and they attribute this to the fact that girls spend more time in the company of their mothers as well as more time caring for children who elicit this type of maternal behavior. Other research finds high levels of cooperation among both boys and girls from rural families, when presented with specially designed games (Munroe and Munroe 1977). This tendancy presumably reflects their socialization and learning in the traditional African environment.

For both boys and girls in East Africa the central theme in the chores of childhood is learning obedience and responsibility, a culturally mandated task that, as we have seen, begins in early childhood. The importance of obedience and responsibility in parental folk theories of child development is illustrated by Harkness and Super's research among the Kipsigis: most mothers did not think that they could judge their children's "personalities" until the children were old enough to be assigned a responsible chore, such as making tea over the fire or going to a local store to buy something for the mother, in contrast to a sample of American middle-class mothers, who thought that they could know a child's personality by the age of two or three, as soon as the child had learned to talk (Super and Harkness 1989). Further, the Kipsigis mothers rated children's "intelligence" in terms of being able to carry out household chores capably and without being supervised, although they also recognized a separate category of "intelligent in school." As one mother said:

For a girl who is *ng'om*, after eating she sweeps the house because she knows it should be done. Then she washes the dishes, looks for vegetables, and takes good care of the baby. When you come home, you feel pleased and say, "This child is *ng'om*." Another girl may not even clean her own dishes, but just go out and play, leaving the baby to cry. For a boy, if he is *ng'om*, he will watch the cows, and take them to the river without being told. He knows to separate the calves from the cows and he will fix the thorn fence when it is broken. The other boy will let the cows into the maize field and will be found playing while they eat the maize. (Super and Harkness 1986, 558).

As we have seen, parents in East Africa put a great deal of effort into training their children to be obedient and responsible through assigning them chores from an early age. When children disobey (or sometimes when the parents are displeased, whether justifiably or not) physical punishment is the cultural norm. Berg-Schlosser (1984), in a survey of reported methods of punishment by parents in seven ethnic groups of Kenya, finds that "severe physical punishment" (e.g., beating or "caning") is used by about 70 to 90 percent of parents, in contrast to other forms (mild physical punishment, deprivation of privileges, or verbal punishment) that are used by 10 percent or fewer of the respondents. This pattern should be seen in the broader context of authority relations within the household that are buttressed by physical punishment. Wife-beating is widespread in the East African cultures we have considered here. As recently as the 1970s the national congress of Kenya considered outlawing wife-beating and decided against it; members of congress, a virtually all-male group, reflected the general male view that wife-beating is a regrettable but necessary means of maintaining family discipline and order. More broadly, social relations are organized around differentiations of status that demand commensurate behavior. Kenyatta (1938, 106) provides a clear statement of this cultural value for his native Kikuyu:

Growing boys and girls learn that they have one thing to learn which sums up all the others, and that is the manners and deportment proper to their station in the community. They see that their happiness in the homestead, their popularity with their playmates, their present comforts and their future prospects depend on knowing their place, giving respect and obedience where is is due. Presumption, conceit and disobedience to those above them are grave offenses. The whole Kikuyu society is graded by age and the prestige which accompanies a status in age-grouping, and this is done in such a way that even small children are aware of it.

Thus older siblings (especially boys) may discipline younger ones, and parents seldom interfere with squabbles among children unless someone is hurt; in the words of Whiting and Edwards (1988, 188), this "sanctions the authority of older over younger siblings." Likewise, the mother may discipline her children by threatening to have their father beat them. In this context the father (especially in polygynous families) may be a rather distant and fearful figure to his children. Lijembe (1967, 16) recounts a vividly remembered episode of paternal wrath from his childhood in Luhyia:

I remember once as a young child returning from *isimba* [a sleeping place for youths] to find my mother crying outside the house. Out of sheer emotion I also started crying, thereby showing my sympathy for my mother. When my father emerged from the house, he tried to separate me from my mother who was then holding me firmly. He failed to separate us. As a result he slapped both of us in fury and ordered us to be away from his sight. Later that day we made off for my mother's house where we stayed for a period.

Despite the fear and pain of punishment, middle childhood in traditional East African societies also is a time for playing with peers, with considerably more freedom from parental monitoring than is possible in most Western middle-class homes. A great deal of play takes place in the context of work: groups of child nurses may gather together to play while taking care of their infant charges (sometimes to the detriment of the latter), while boys assigned to herding also may hunt birds, wrestle, or just rest together while observing the passing scene (Harkness and Super 1985b). A striking element in most ethnographic accounts of children's play in traditional East African groups is the predominance of imaginative play (e.g., Goldschmidt 1976; Kenyatta 1938; Raum 1940; Roscoe 1923). Children are reported to make their own toys and "props" to reenact their own versions of adult life. Roscoe (1923, 259–260) describes the make-believe games of Bakitara children aged five to six as they watched the calves: "They played at going out to war, fighting battles and capturing prisoners and cattle and bringing the spoils to the king; they married and built their kraals, observing taboos as their elders did; they bought, sold and exchanged cattle and tended them, healing them of various diseases." Raum's (1940) detailed observations of children's imaginative play among the Chaga lead him to a particularly interesting analysis: he argues that this kind of play is not so much "imitative" of adult life as it is a selective and creative child's-view reconstruction, based on the "scraps he is allowed to know about it" (Raum 1940, 256). Many children's games have features found worldwide, such as rhyming and hand play (Durojayie 1977). In contrast to accounts such as these, LeVine and LeVine (1963) report that they saw almost no examples of imaginative play among the Gusii children's play groups they observed. Children's imaginative play is not included in Whiting and Edwards' (1988) comparative analysis, and it is not clear whether such play is actually less prevalent in the more transitional societies included in their sample.

END OF CHILDHOOD

Childhood in East Africa ends with the ceremonies, often including circumcision, that mark the passage to adulthood or youth. For some children this transition comes very early: Nzioki (1967) reports, for example, that as a Kamba boy he was circumcised at age seven, whereupon he started attending school, an interesting reversal of the Western pattern of childhood transitions. Among the Gusii, also, circumcision is early (aged ten to twelve for boys and eight to nine for girls) and is followed by a period of youthful freedom that apparently presents some rather difficult issues for parents (LeVine and LeVine 1963). At the other extreme are groups such as the Sebei, the Sonjo, and the Kipsigis, in which male initiation ceremonies were traditionally held only every six to seven years, for young men in their late teens or early twenties. Young men thus initiated attained the status of warriors, and were not supposed to marry until they had filled the requisite number of years thus—as many as fourteen (or two initiation cycles later). For girls in these groups initiation was the prerequisite for marriage, so girls were not—and still are not—supposed to undergo the ceremonies until their elders judge them ready to assume the responsibilities of motherhood. Nevertheless, the circumcision ceremonies for children of whatever age mark the end of childhood chores, the beginning of new freedom of movement and behavior, and the attainment of a new level of respect by both parents and younger children. It is not surprising, then, that although the ceremonies involve considerable pain and health risks, especially for girls, they continue to be attractive cultural milestones of development for young people.

EAST AFRICAN CHILDHOOD IN CULTURAL TRANSITION

We have used the convenient "ethnographic present" to describe childhood in East Africa, but the picture we have presented is in the process of change, like childhood in all parts of the world (B. Whiting, 1977). In East Africa many forces act and interact to influence childhood: these include rapid population growth and urbanization, improvements in public health and the growth of schooling, greater access to knowledge of the "modern" world through mass media, more available transportation, and new sources of employment. The effects of these changes on children are both positive and negative. On the one hand, improvements in public health and medical care, and government prohibitions of infanticide, have led to greatly improved survival rates for children. Because parents in East Africa continue, for the most part, to desire many children, children nowadays tend to grow up in larger families than their parents did. Further, declines in the traditional means of spacing births without adoption of modern methods have led to a shortening of birth intervals. This may have negative implications for children's development in the early years, since infancy continues to be defined in terms of the birth of the next child (Harkness and Super 1987). Greeley (1988) has criticized population policy planners in Kenya for failing to make better use of the traditional means of birth spacing. Many societal changes, including the reduction of land for rural families and corresponding loss of family herds, have contributed to trends in marriage and child-bearing that include both later marriage for some and a much higher rate of teenage pregnancy and single motherhood (Worthman and Whiting 1987). With the growth of cities has come prostitution as a means of livelihood for young women newly arrived from the countryside with no resources (Dutto 1975). These women have become a significant factor in the spread of acquired immunodeficiency syndrome in Kenya as elsewhere in sub-Saharan Africa (Hudson et al. 1988).

Despite the large immigrations to urban areas, most Kenyans still define "home" as a piece of land in their own ethnic area. A common practice is for the wife and children to remain at the farm while the husband seeks work in the city to supplement the family income (Abbott 1976). These "divided homesteads" have been described by Weisner (1976, 1979), who finds in the urban niche a shift in the children's pattern of social behavior. Unfortunately the father's income too often is spent before he reaches home, and the mother is left to support the farm and her children on her own (Abbott and Klein 1979; S. LeVine 1979). Despite new opportunities for women to become educated and to work, the expectations and assumptions of many Kenyan males remain quite traditional. A woman who marries today has no guarantee, no matter what her qualifications, that her husband will not take another wife as well as appropriating her own earnings. In response to this situation many of the most educated Kenyan women are today choosing to raise families by themselves, without the threat of male domination.

These changes in the environments for childhood in East Africa reflect cultural continuities, for example in the traditional separation of men and women and the cultural primacy of childbearing. But at least some East African parents, under the influence of Western education, are attempting to make more fundamental changes, and in this they have recourse to the same kinds of cultural sources of knowledge that Western parents use—books on child rearing. For the parents as well as the children this is a complex and difficult process, as Lijembe (1967, 38) comments:

It isn't always easy for modern parents to change from the old ways. My wife and I, for example, are trying to bring up our children in line with what Western books on child-rearing and child-development advise. At the same time we wonder at the wisdom of thus trying to fit them into a life based on the Western culture when in actual fact a good proportion of their time as children will be lived with other children in the traditional Luyia society. This tends to create a feeling of insecurity in the parents—and perhaps in the children.

But he concludes on a more hopeful note (p. 41):

Careful application of Western methods of health and childcare, and critical retention of what is good in traditional methods, can help us modern parents to create a sense of balance in our children, enabling the future generation to work out, from the two cultures, a way of life more appropriate than either one of these.

REFERENCES

Abbott, S. 1976. Full-time farmers and week-end wives: An analysis of altering conjugal roles. *Journal of Marriage and the Family* 38(1):165–174.

Abbott, S., and R. Klein. 1979. Depression and anxiety among rural Kikuyu in Kenya. *Ethos* 7:161–188.

Ainsworth, M.D.S. 1967. *Infancy in Uganda: Infant care and the growth of love.* Baltimore, Md.: Johns Hopkins University Press.

Apoko, A. 1967. At home in the village: Growing up in Acholi. In *African childhood: Three versions*, edited by L. K. Fox. Nairobi: Oxford University Press, pp. 45–75.

Beidelman, T. O. 1971. *The Kaguru: A matrilineal people of East Africa.* New York: Holt, Rinehart and Winston.

Berg-Schlosser, D. 1984. *Tradition and change in Kenya.* Zurich: Ferdinand Schonigh.

Berger, I. B., and O. Salehe. Health status of primary school children in central Tanzania. *Journal of Tropical Pediatrics* 32(1):26–29.

Blount, B. G. 1969. Acquisition of language by Luo children. Ph.D. diss., University of California, Berkeley.

————. 1972. Parental speech and language acquisition: Some Luo and Samoan examples. *Anthropological Linguistics* 14:119–130.

Dixon, S. D., R. A. LeVine, and T. B. Brazelton. 1982. Malnutrition: A closer look at the problem in an East African village. *Developmental Medicine and Child Neurology* 24(5):670–685.

Dow, T. E., Jr., and L. H. Werner. 1983. Perceptions of family planning among rural Kenyan women. *Studies in Family Planning* 14(2):35–43.

Durojaiye, S. M. 1977. Children's traditional games and rhymes in three cultures. *Educational Research* 19(3):223–226.

Dutto, C. A. 1975. *Nyeri townsmen, Kenya*. Nairobi; East African Literature Bureau.

Ebrahim, G. J. 1969. *The newborn in tropical Africa*. Nairobi: East African Literature Bureau.

Edgerton, R. B. 1971. *The individual in cultural adaptation: A study of four East African peoples*. Berkeley: University of California Press.

Edwards, C. P. 1978. Social experience and moral judgment in Kenyan young adults. *Journal of Genetic Psychology* 133:19–29.

Ember, C. R. 1973. Feminine task assignment and the social behavior of boys. *Ethos* 1(4):424–439.

Fleuret, A. 1987. Agricultural development and child health in two Taita communities. *Urban Anthropology* 16(1):63–72.

Fox, L. K., ed. 1967. *East African childhood: Three versions*. Nairobi: Oxford University Press.

Goldschmidt, W. 1975. Absent eyes and idle hands: Socialization for low affect among the Sebei. *Ethos* 3:157–163.

————. 1976. *The culture and behavior of the Sebei*. Berkeley: University of California Press.

Gray, R. F. 1963. *The Sonjo of Tanganyika: An anthropological study of an irrigation-based society*. London: Oxford University Press.

Greeley, E. H. 1988. Planning for population change in Kenya: An anthropological perspective. In *Anthropology of development and change in East Africa*, edited by D. W. Brokensha and P. D. Little. Boulder, Colo.: Westview Press, pp. 201–216.

Gulliver, P. H. 1955. *The family herds: A study of two pastoral tribes in East Africa, the Jie and Turkana*. London: Routledge & Kegan Paul.

Harkness, S. 1977. Aspects of social environment and first language acquisition in rural Africa. In *Talking to children: Language input and acquisition*, edited by C. Snow and C. A. Ferguson. Cambridge: Cambridge University Press, pp. 309–316.

————. 1987. The cultural mediation of postpartum depression. *Medical Anthropology Quarterly* 1(2):194–209.

Harkness, S., and C. M. Super. 1982. Why African children are so hard to test. In *Cross-cultural research at issue*, edited by L. L. Alder. New York: Academic Press, pp. 145–152.

————. 1983. The cultural construction of child development: A framework for the socialization of affect. *Ethos* 11:221–231.

————. 1985a. Child-environment interactions in the socialization of affect. In *The socialization of emotions*, edited by M. Lewis and C. Saarni. New York: Plenum, pp. 21–36.

————. 1985b. The cultural context of gender segregation in children's peer groups. *Child Development* 56:219–224.

————. 1987. Fertility change, child survival, and child development: Observations on a rural Kenyan community. In *Child survival: Anthropological perspectives of the treatment and maltreatment of children*, edited by N. Scheper-Hughes. Boston: D. Reidel, pp. 59–70.

Hudson, C. P., et al. 1988. Risk factors for the spread of AIDS in rural Africa: Evidence from a comparative seroepidemiological survey of AIDS, hepatitis B, and syphilis in southwestern Uganda. *AIDS* 2(4):255–260.

Keefer, C. H., et al. 1977. A cross-cultural study of face to face interaction: Gusii infants and mothers. Paper presented at a meeting of the Society for Research in Child Development, New Orleans.

Kenyatta, J. 1938. *Facing Mount Kenya: The tribal life of the Gikuyu*. London: Secker & Warburg.

Kermonian, R., and P. H. Leiderman. 1986. Infant attachment to mother and child caretakers in an East African community. *International Journal of Behavioral Development* 9(4):455–569.

Kilbride, J. E., and P. L. Kilbride. 1975. Sitting and smiling behavior of Baganda infants: The influence of culturally constituted experience. *Journal of Cross-cultural Psychology* 6:88–107.

Kilbride, P. L., and J. E. Kilbride. 1974. Sociocultural factors and the early manifestation of sociability behavior among Baganda infants. *Ethos* 2:296–314.

————. 1983. Socialization for high positive affect between mother and infant among the Baganda of Uganda. *Ethos* 11(4):232–245.

Konner, M. J., and C. M. Super. 1987. Sudden infant death: An anthropological perspective. In *The role of culture in developmental disorder*, edited by C. M. Super. New York: Academic Press, pp. 95–109.

Laukaran, V. H. and B. Winikoff. 1985. Contraceptive use, amenorrhea, and breast-feeding in postpartum women. *Studies in Family Planning* 16(6):293–301.

LeVine, R. A. 1973. Patterns of personality in Africa. *Ethos* 1:123–152.

————. 1974a. Comment on the note by Super and Harkness. *Ethos* 2:382–386.

————. 1974b. Parental goals: A cross-cultural view. *Teachers College Record* 76:226–239.

LeVine, R. A., and B. B. LeVine. 1966. *Nyansongo: A Gusii community in Kenya*. Six Cultures Series, vol. 2. New York: John Wiley & Sons.

LeVine, R. A., and S. E. LeVine. 1988. Parental strategies of the Gusii of Kenya. *New Directions for Child Development* 40:27–35.

LeVine, S. 1979. *Mothers and wives: Gusii women of East Africa*. Chicago: University of Chicago Press.

Lijembe, J. A. 1967. The valley between: A Muluyia's story. In *East African childhood: Three versions*, edited by L. K. Fox. Nairobi: Oxford University Press, pp. 1–41.

Mburugu, E. K. 1986. Some notable patterns of fertility behavior in Africa. *International Sociology* 1(2):203–211.

Munroe, R. H., and R. L. Munroe. 1971. Household density and infant care in an East African society. *Journal of Social Psychology* 83:3–13.

Munroe, R. L., and R. H. Munroe. 1977. Cooperation and competition among East African and American children. *Journal of Social Psychology* 10(1):145–146.

Nzioki, J. M. 1967. *Thorns in the Grass: The Story of a Kamba Boy*. In *East African childhood: Three versions*, edited by L. K. Fox. Nairobi: Oxford University Press, pp. 79–137.

Obbo, C. 1980. *African women: Their struggle for economic independence*. London: Zed Press.

Ocitti, J. P. 1973. *African indigenous education: As practiced by the Acholi of Kenya*. Nairobi: East African Literature Bureau.

O'Dempsey, T. J. 1988. Traditional belief and practice among the Pokot people of Kenya with particular reference to mother and child health. 1. The Pokot people and their environment. *Annals of Tropical Paediatrics*. 8(2):49–60.

Peristiany, J. G. 1939. *The social institutions of the Kipsigis*. London: G. Routledge & Sons.

Raum, O. F. 1940. *Chaga Childhood: A description of indigenous education in an East Africa tribe*. London: Oxford University Press.

Richman, A. L., et al. 1988. Maternal behaviors to infants in five cultures. *New Directions for Child Development* 40:81–97.

Roscoe, J. 1911. *The Baganda: An account of their native customs and beliefs*. New York: Barnes & Noble.

———. 1923. *The Bakitara or Banyoro: The first part of the report of the Mackie ethnological expedition to Central Africa*. Cambridge: Cambridge University Press.

Sengoba, C.M.E.B. 1978. The effects of nutritional status on the psychomotor development of rural Kenyan infants. Ph.D. diss., University of Michigan.

Sieley, S. 1975. Environmental influences on the cognitive development of rural children: A study of a Kipsigis community in Western Kenya. Ph.D. diss., Harvard University.

Super, C. M. 1976. Environmental effects on motor development: The case of "African infant precocity." *Developmental Medicine and Child Neurology* 18:561–567.

———. (1980). Cognitive development: Looking across at growing up. *Anthropological Perspectives on Child Development*, edited by C. M. Super and S. Harkness. San Francisco: Jossey-Bass, pp. 59–69.

———. 1981. Behavioral development in infancy. In *Handbook of cross-cultural human development*, edited by R. H. Munroe, R. L. Munroe, and B. B. Whiting. New York: Garland STPM, pp . 181–270.

Super, C. M., and S. Harkness. 1974. Patterns of personality in Africa: A note from the field. *Ethos* 2:377–381.

———. 1982. The infant's niche in rural Kenya and metropolitan American. In *Cross-cultural research at issue*, edited by L. L. Adler. New York: Academic Press, pp. 145–152.

———. 1986. The developmental niche: A conceptualization at the interface of child and culture. *International Journal of Behavioral Development* 9:545–569.

———. 1989. Parental theories of children's intelligence and personality. Unpublished manuscript.

Sutton, J.E.G. 1968. The settlement of East Africa. In *Zamani: A Survey of East African History*, edited by B. A. Ogot. Narobi, Kenya: East African Publishing House, pp. 70–97.

Turnbull, C. M. 1972. *The mountain people*. New York: Simon & Schuster.

Varkevisser, D. M. 1973. *Socialization in a changing society: Sukuma childhood in rural* and urban *Mwanza, Tanzania*. Den Haag: Center for the Study of Education in Changing Societies.

Weisner, T. S. 1976. The structure of sociability: Urban migration and urban-rural ties in Kenya. *Urban Anthropology* 5(2):199–223.

―――. 1979. Urban-rural differences in sociable and disruptive behavior of Kenya children. *Ethnology* 18(2):153–172.

Whiting, B. B. 1977. Changing lifestyles in Kenya. *Daedalus* 106(2):211–225.

Whiting, B. B., and C. P. Edwards. 1988. *Children of different worlds: The formation of social behavior*. Cambridge, Mass.: Harvard University Press.

Whiting, B. B., and J.W.M. Whiting. *Children of six cultures: A psycho-cultural analysis*. Cambridge, Mass.: Harvard University Press.

Whiting, J.W.M. 1977. A model for psychocultural research. In *Culture and infancy: Variations in the human experience*, edited by P. H. Leiderman, S. R. Tulkin, and A. Rosenfeld. New York: Academic Press, pp. 29–48.

Winter, E. H. n.d. *Bwamba: A structural-functional analysis of a patrilineal society*. Cambridge: W. Heffer & Sons.

Worthman, C. M., and J.W.M. Whiting. 1987. Social change in adolescent sexual behavior, mate selection, and premarital pregnancy rates in a Kikuyu community. *Ethos* 15(2):145–165.

10

ENGLAND

Nupur Chaudhuri

With the rise of "new social history" in the 1960s the concept of childhood emerged as a subject for historical study. Childhood experience and the nurturing of children have proved to be important means of access to explore the dynamics of family life, and consequently family historians began to include children in their studies. Because conception, pregnancy, childbirth, nursing, and child care are the most important elements in the configuration of women's private lives, scholars of women's history focused on the roles of children in the analyses of women's private and working lives. Hence the development of the history of childhood can be traced to recent growths in family history and women's history. From the 1960s historians of childhood and scholars of women's history began determined efforts in reconstructing the lives of children and adolescents through the ages. This chapter summarizes the major themes that have been addressed in scholarly accounts on the history of childhood in England.

STAGES OF CHILDHOOD

In his book *Centuries of Childhood*, published in 1960, Philippe Ariès has noted that a distinction between childhood and adolescence was first made in the eighteenth century. Ariès' work became the landmark of scholarly investigations on family history in which the parent-children relationship constituted a major focus. Addressing the role of children in a familial framework, Ariès has maintained that the concept of childhood did not exist in the Middle Ages because parents were not concerned about the well-being of their children. He has claimed that although in the sixteenth century they had concerns about the children, adults were not aware of childhood as a separate state of adulthood. To Ariès, the modern view of childhood emerged in the eighteenth century.

An exponent of Ariès' theory in English is Lawrence Stone.[1] Stone claims that during the sixteenth and seventeenth centuries the English family changed from a predominantly kin-oriented to an essentially nuclear structure. In its early evolution the nuclear family became more patriarchal and authoritarian than the kin-oriented family.[2] The main argument of Stone's book, *The Family, Sex and Marriage in England 1500–1800*, is that between 1500 and 1800, the English family evolved through three successive stages. The earliest stage involved the open lineage family, with emphasis on kinship ties. The intermediate stage appeared in the early seventeenth century, and was characterized by the restricted patriarchal family. In the last stage, beginning in the late seventeenth century and developing rapidly in the eighteenth, came the intimate domesticated nuclear family, in which there was a greater intimacy between spouses and a tender and loving relationship between parents and children.[3] Since Ariès' pioneering work other historians have not only explored to verify his claim, but also addressed the question of the age when childhood ends and adolescence begins.[4]

Linda A. Pollock, Ralph A. Houlbrooke, and Barbara A. Hanawalt question the assertions of Ariès and others who shared similar views. In *Forgotten Children: Parent-Child Relations from 1500–1900* Pollock claims that Ariès' thesis rests on slender evidence. Basing her arguments on more than 400 British and American diaries and autobiographies dating from the late sixteenth to the early twentieth centuries, Pollock maintains that a concept of childhood was very much alive in the sixteenth century, during which time children were not subject to brutality, nor was the parent-child relationship formal.[5] Pollock's work by itself has advanced understanding on the history of childhood because the studies of diaries and autobiographies provide readers with an idea of actual childhood experience.

Houlbrooke supports Pollock's contention that a tie between parents and their young children was quite strong even before the eighteenth century.[6] Similarly, examining coroners' inquests, manorial court rolls, wills, popular advice books, church court records, and literary sources, Hanawalt concludes that "childhood was a recognized separate period in life" during the Middle Ages. She defends the notion that medieval parents were conscious of and attended to the needs of their children and insists that as the children grew up, "the parents continued to provide for them to the best of their abilities."[7]

Studies on apprentices, monastic novices, students, and ritualistic patterns of urban and rural youth groups have pointed toward the existence of a notion of adolescence in various European cultures between the fourteenth and seventeenth centuries.[8] Judith M. Bennett suggests that the transition from childhood to adolescence in the Middle Ages probably occurred between twelve and fourteen years of age.[9] Houlbrooke, analyzing records on educational matters and children's clothings, argues that between 1450 and 1700 childhood comprised two phases, one up to the age of seven and the other from seven to puberty.[10]

Focusing on the records of adolescent apprentices in the sixteenth century, Anne Yarbrough argues that "almost all entered service between the ages of 12 and 17, with the majority making the transition somewhere between the ages of 14 and 16." She further claims that the "beginning of apprenticeship entailed an abrupt shift from childhood to adolescence."[11] Susan Brigden contends that during the English Reformation, childhood ended at the age of fifteen, when a confirmation service was performed.[12]

John R. Gillis defines adolescence as "that segment of the life cycle which bridges childhood and adulthood."[13] Gillis maintains that before 1770, "youths" referred to those of ages from eight to the late twenties. Youths in preindustrial times left home at about age seven or eight to live as servants or apprentices in another household. Class-based categorization of youths began between 1770 and 1870.

The years from 1870 to 1900 were the period when adolescence became a distinct occasion in the lives of middle-class youths between fourteen and eighteen. But the concept of adolescence was not so nascent. Providing an excellent discussion on childhood and adolescence from the sixteenth century to the present, John Springhall, like Yarbrough, argues that in late Victorian and Edwardian Britain, "the initial experience of an adolescent in the works or in a factory was almost a 'rite of passage' between boyhood and adulthood."[14] Examining the Parliamentary Act: 1918 8 and 9 Geo.V., c. 39., which prohibited exemption from attendance at school between ages five and fourteen, Marjorie Cruishank and James Walvin conclude that fourteen was the upper age limit for childhood during the second decade of the twentieth century.[15]

CHILD MORTALITY AND CHILD NEGLECT

During the Middle Ages the rate of infant and child mortality was very high. For example, of the fifty-eight children under one year of age appearing in the coroners' inquests, 33 percent died in fires.[16] More than a fifth of all children born during the reign of Elizabeth I and about a quarter of those born under the Stuarts probably died before reaching their tenth birthday.[17] Infant mortality continued high throughout the nineteenth century. For example, of the 167,000 children in the age-group zero to five years old who died in England and Wales in 1860, 101,000 were one year old or less. In 1890 children less than one year old formed only 2.4 percent of the total population but accounted for nearly a quarter (131,000) of all deaths (562,000) that year.[18]

Hanawalt, analyzing accidental deaths of peasant children, concludes that the time of day and the season of the year of accidental deaths for one-year-old or younger babies in medieval England demonstrate that the babies were probably left unattended, as their parents were too busy with other chores to watch them. Hanawalt also has found enough evidence to show that parents did not like to leave their children alone, nor did the villagers approve a practice of leaving the children unattended. Hanawelt asserts that no grand scheme by the parents existed to neglect their own children.[19]

Houlbrooke argues that between 1400 and 1750, infant deaths were largely due to things beyond parental control or understandings, and that the existence of widespread culpable neglect has so far proved difficult to demonstrate. He claims that "it seems likely that in most places the great majority of children were cherished and as well cared for as the age's primitive understanding of hygiene and disease and the economic pressures upon families would allow."[20]

Barbara A. Kellum, however, finding that accidental deaths of infants were too many to be believable, suggests that infanticide was a cause of children's deaths. Depending much on evidence from literary sources, Kellum concludes that, besides economic pressures, "there was a possibility that a widespread infanticide component was present in the medieval personality."[21] But Hanawalt maintains that finding concrete evidence that infanticide was widespread in medieval England has proved impossible.[22]

Alan Macfarlane infers that a considerable number of bastard children must have been murdered at birth if there was need for an act passed in 1624 by James I "to prevent the murthering of bastard children."[23] Focusing on legal records from some English counties, Peter C. Hoffer and N.E.H. Hull maintain that official concerns about infanticide could be traced from about 1580 to 1803.[24]

Touched by infanticide of illegitimate children, Thomas Coram, a ship's captain, Massachusetts shipbuilder, and colonizer in Georgia, founded the London Foundling Hospital. In 1722 he established a nonprofit corporation to provide shelter for illegitimate children, many of whom he saw in London dock areas. In his petition to the Crown, Coram wrote that he hoped that by invoking the "example of France, Holland, and other Christian Countrys," he could provide for the indiscriminate admission of all such foundlings.[25]

Ruth K. McClure has discussed the management, finances, health, and education of orphans in Coram's foundling home, and has described eighteenth-century English society's "prejudice" against illegitimate children. Included in McClure's book are responses of those who received aid, minutes of governors' meetings that addressed incidents of forced separation of mothers and infants, accounts of orphans making inquiries about their parents, and records of feelings of runaway children who attempted to see their country nurses. McClure has stated that to stem the tide of applicants for the foundling home, the management in 1740 set the rules (which later proved ineffective) that a foundling had to be under two months old and free from venereal disease, scrofula, and leprosy; a woman wanting to put a child to hospital had to wait for the result of the medical examination.[26] McClure's analyses of the conditions for the foundlings are based on her study of the hospital archives.

Throughout the eighteenth century, policies for admission to the Foundling Hospital went through several changes. Discussing admission policies of the London Foundling Hospital, Bernd Weisbrod concludes that "the London Foundling Hospital provided the only 'legitimate' way of adoption available in early

Victorian London for those illegitimate children whose mothers had decided to give them up for good and for whom alternative forms of family care were not available.''[27] Examining coroners' reports on suspicious deaths and inquests, Lionel Rose has determined that the practice of infanticide continued during the nineteenth century. In 1869, for example, of the 3,979 inquests of subjects under one year old, 1,251, or nearly a third, were for babies who were "illegitimate or unknown.''[28]

As Anna Davin describes the case, middle-class reformers blamed working-class parents for this high rate of infant mortality. These reformers believed that because of their outside employment, working-class mothers neglected their children, causing the high infant mortality. These reformers also perceived working-class mothers as ignorant and incompetent in matters of infant care.[29] Carole Dyhouse shows how middle-class attitudes molded the policy and outlook of early infant welfare work.[30] In reality working-class parents tried to be responsible for their children. Drawing from statistical evidence and contents in nineteenth-century literature, Michael Anderson cogently demonstrates that most working-class mothers were affectionate and did what they saw as the best for their children while they were young. But, although they loved and appreciated their fathers, some children feared their fathers for being drunk and intolerant.[31]

ILLEGITIMACY

Misbegotten children have been the focus of several studies since the mid–1960s. Examining the baptism records of twenty-four English parishes between 1581 and 1810, in *The World We Have Lost* Peter Laslett establishes that the number of illegitimate children baptized was high between 1581 and 1630 and also between 1741 and 1810.[32] Christopher Durston points out that although the justices in a number of English counties were known to have made a special effort to uncover cases of bastardy and establish paternity, the data compiled by demographic historians not only failed to reveal any increase in the rate of illegitimate births or prenuptial pregnancy in the 1650s, but also established that the rates in the 1650s were lower than those in any other similar span of time in the seventeenth century.[33] Keith Wrightson concludes that the rate of bastardy did not really decline, arguing that the greater inadequacy of the registration system during these years was responsible for this apparent decline in bastardy rates.[34] In the introduction of *Bastardy and Its Comparative History* Laslett claims that age on marriage was inversely related to illegitimacy and maintains that illegitimacy had a strong geographical bias reflecting cultural traditions as expressed in courtship conventions.[35] The first part of this book contains eight essays on different aspects of illegitimacy in England and Scotland from the late sixteenth to the nineteenth century. Taking a statistical approach, N.F.R. Crafts endorses the hypotheses put forward by Laslett concerning illegitimacy before World War II. But Crafts adds that illegitimacy could be traced to increased employment opportunities for women.[36]

Like Laslett and Crafts, John R. Gillis claims that illegitimacy in nineteenth-century Britain varied by region, culture, and class. Gillis has analyzed 1,200 cases to show "that London illegitimacy was primarily, if not exclusively, a problem involving domestic servants."[37] This observation is not surprising in view of the fact that domestic service was certainly the largest profession for single women. Of London women with occupations who were recorded in the 1841 census, 51.3 percent worked as domestic servants, among whom 77 percent were under twenty.[38] Of the 1,200 female domestics who were studied by Gillis, 65.6 percent were successful in their applications to the London Foundling Hospital.[39]

In 1834 the House of Commons passed a Poor Law Amendment Act. The two sections of the Poor Law Amendment dealt with the bastardy clauses, which included a summary of the statutes governing chargeable bastards (illegitimate children whose parents were unable to support them), a description of the abuses arising from these statutes and administrative interpretations of them, and suggestions for reform. The proponents of this law believed that illegitimacy could be diminished by placing all the onus of self-control on women. Liability for the maintenance of an illegitimate child was placed on the mother, if single, and on her husband if she was married. In a lengthy discussion U.R.Q. Henrique shows why this part of the Poor Law was not passed by the Parliament.[40]

INFANT AND CHILD CARE

Swaddling and breast-feeding have come to symbolize the gulf between modern and premodern society. Literary evidence shows that as early as in the ninth century, babies wore swaddling clothes. The practice of swaddling apparently continued through the Middle Ages. After the baptism ceremony, which occurred soon after its birth, the baby would wear swaddling clothes, which were designed to maintain a womblike environment for the newborn. Some seventeenth-century evidence suggests that children were transferred from swaddling clothes to "coats" between one and three months after birth.[41]

Breast-feeding of babies had been long accepted as the safest and most sound means of nurturing babies, but the mode of breast-feeding and the emphasis of its use as nourishment changed through times. Hanawalt states that in the Middle Ages, upper-class women employed wet nurses, while the peasant women nursed their own babies except when the mother died or had no milk.[42] Houlbrooke writes that during the sixteenth and early seventeenth centuries, humanists, doctors, and both Catholic and Protestant reforming clerics advocated maternal breast-feeding. The custom of using wet nurses continued in Britain until about 1870. Taking their cue from their counterparts in England, English wives in the empire also used wet nurses. Because European wet nurses were not available, despite their racist contempt for indigenous women, these wives were forced to use local women as wet nurses.[43] After 1870 came a significant decline in wet nursing in Britain. Ann Roberts claims that public disquiet at a potential connection of wet nursing to infant mortality contributed to the campaign against wet nursing.[44] Theresa McBride maintains that the decline of wet nursing was due to the lack of finding nurses with high moral character and impeccable health to assuage middle-class parents' fears for their children.[45] The proliferation of baby food in the market during the 1860s perhaps contributed to the decline of the wet nursing.[46] Jane Lewis asserts that eugenic concern about the quality of racial stock was raised on the fertility behavior of upper- and middle-class women. She points out that attacks on middle-class women for "shirking" their "racial duty" were common well into the twentieth century. Both male and female doctors told adult women that motherhood combined the twin ideals of personal vocation and racial and national progress. Women who left infant-feeding to the care of a nurse were condemned for their selfishness.[47]

Studies of childrearing practiced by different families provide a good perspective on infant care by any group during a period. Records of the childhood of Ralph Josselin, a seventeenth-century clergyman, and of his relationship with his children serve as a source of information about how some clerical children were reared.[48] Analyzing the family life of the Verneys, Miriam Slater illustrates how seventeenth-century aristocratic families usually reared their children.[49] J. H. Plumb has claimed that in the eighteenth century, children of wealthy parents "had become luxury objects upon which their mothers and fathers were willing to spend larger and larger sums of money, not only for their education, but also for their entertainment and amusement." Plumb has added that because of this parental attitude, "children's world of the eighteenth century—at least for those born higher up the social scale than the labouring poor—changed dramatically."[50]

Nineteenth-century histories of English children cover a broad range of topics. Works of Marion Lochhead, F. Gordon Roe, and Pamela Horn provide the readers with a general view of English childhood during this period. Lochhead describes "the everyday life and background of Victorian children throughout the Queen's reign, beginning with the Royal childhood itself, and continuing through the successive early, mid, and late Victorian periods."[51] She devotes one chapter to working-class and poor children, whom she refers to as "Those Other Children." Roe describes the life-style of upper-middle-class families and their children.[52] Horn provides a good sketch of lives of children in rural areas.[53]

Unlike the works of Lochhead and Roe, who have focused mostly on the children of the propertied class, those of James Walvin and Thomas Jordan give special emphasis on both younger and older working-class and pauper children. Walvin's discussion of how children were taught to handle death is quite interesting. Because of high infant mortality, death became a recurrent theme in nineteenth-century children's literature. Walvin asserts that this literature was designed for children from prosperous homes, "where, because of the better material conditions, death was less common and was handled more discreetly." Because of crowded living conditions in the poorest areas of the cities, working-class children were forced to witness "the protracted and often painful process of death in their homes.''[54] Walvin advances a reader's understanding of roles of class and gender in molding the lives of children. Jordan surveys the environments of childhood and focuses on childhood experiences in the Victorian period. He has used both statistical analyses and anecdotal evidence gleaned from such Victorian observers as Henry Mayhew.[55] Emphasizing the importance of both class and gender differences, Jordan traces the developments in various matters related to Victorian children such as health, labor, learning, and sports in the context of changes produced by the development of urban industrial society.

Responsibilities and duties of English mothers of different periods have become the focus of many studies. Based on the writings of nineteenth-century upper-middle-class men and woman about their childhood, Priscilla Robertson concludes that English mothers tend to be cool and distant and fathers were tyrannical toward their children.[56] In his *The Rise and Fall of the British Nanny* Jonathon Gathorne-Hardy discusses the evolution of the nanny in the world of children from the fourteen century to World War II. He argues that despite employing nannies, mothers continued to play a dominant role in the upbringing of their children as late as the eighteenth century. This dominance of the mother is lessened in the following centuries. Based on oral interviews of the nannies and accounts recorded in autobiographies and biographies, Gathorne-Hardy claims that from 1850 to 1939, many upper- and upper-middle-class English mothers left the caring of their children to their nannies, many of whom provided their charges with love and discipline and controlled minute details of the children's lives. Because nannies came from working-class background, Gathorne-Hardy states that through nannies, many upper- and upper-middle-class children assimilated some lower-class behavior.[57]

Theresa McBride has argued that middle-class women were involved in child rearing more than was believed by Gathorne-Hardy or Robertson. Gathorne-Hardy and Robertson have based their arguments on experiences of upper-class children. Analyzing the income level of middle-class families, McBride concludes that because the ''middle class had to strain the family budget to employ a servant, they generally chose a young woman who could perform a variety of functions,'' which included child care. McBride further claims that ''in the middle-class household in which childrearing was divided between the mother and a single servant, most of the actual caring for the children was performed by the mother, while the servant would clean up after the children and help them to eat and dress.''[58] Steven Mintz maintains that around the early nineteenth century, middle-class women made motherhood a self-conscious vocation. Middle-class women were asserting increased responsibility over child rearing and control over domestic morals and manners.[59] M. Jean Peterson refutes Mintz's claim that child rearing was the actual focus of middle-class women's lives. Many of the upper-middle-class families Peterson examines in her books had nannies and governesses, but mothers and fathers also involved themselves directly and frequently in their children's lives. Despite this active involvement, Peterson asserts that these women did not show any evident commitment to the theoretical notion of the primacy of motherhood, nor did their day-to-day activities demonstrate that the relationship between the Victorian mother and the children was the central focus of a woman's life.[60]

CHILDREN'S EXPERIENCES USING ORAL HISTORIES AND MEMORIES

Until recently, much of our information on working-class children during the nineteenth and early twentieth centuries came from middle-class observers and reformers. Consequently their writings contain more information on middle-class values than on the actual life of the children. But recent studies, such as those of Stephen Humphries, Jeremy Searbrook, and Thea Thompson, have relied on oral interviews to understand working-class children's experiences during the late nineteenth and early twentieth centuries.

Humphries' *Holligans or Rebels? An Oral History of Working-Class Childhood and Youth, 1889–1939* is chiefly drawn from Paul and Thea Vigne's "Family Life and Work Experience Before 1918" collection at the University of Essex and from the Bristol People's Oral History Project. Through oral histories Humphries has reconstructed the lives of working-class children and juveniles, combining the evidence of memory with official documentation to describe roles that the state had assigned to adults who worked with children. Schoolteachers, policemen, probation officers, and the personnel of orphanages, reformatories, and borstals visibly expressed classist attitudes toward their charges. Humphries shows that almost all the behavior of the young was rational resistance to class oppression. In his discussions on schooling and classroom subversion Humphries asserts that "acts of disobedience, disorderly conduct and a reluctant and apathetic attitude towards learning" were important ways by which children held on to their self-respect and dignity. Humphries' work suffers from one weakness in an otherwise important contribution to the history of childhood. Describing all juvenile behavior as an important component in the movement of class struggle, the author ignores differences based on sex, age, and ethnic groups. Humphries describes racism that was directed against working-class Jews and young immigrants as "misdirected expression of class feeling and class hostility." He relates attacks by male gangs on working-class girls to "the desperate desire for personal dignity, self-assertion and escape experienced by many working-class youths when confronted by problems of poverty, monotonous labour and wartime conscription was diverted from potentially subversive inter-class conflict into socially divisive intra-class conflict." Humphries does not consider status and gender differences among the personalities he studied. His subjects of study range from paupers to skilled artisans. Despite these problems, his book is a good starting point for all future research in the field.[61] Searbook also has used oral history to find out the childhood experiences of the old. Based on interviews with both those over seventy and those under sixteen, this work demonstrates changing views of childhood by comparing the childhood experiences and the perceptions of familial relations of the older and the younger generations. Unlike Humphries' book, this work is gender-inclusive.[62] Thompson has carefully chosen for interview nine persons who represented a large cross section of English society in the Edwardian age. All were interviewed using the same set of questions. Their childhood experiences nicely illustrate the class, regional, and gender differences of the time.[63] Several recently published autobiographical accounts have served as important sources of information about children's family life. Mary Vivian Hughes was born in the 1870s in an upper-middle-class family. She mentioned that she had four brothers, and her mother trained her to wait on them. The family took outings to Kew and Richmond every Saturday. Occasionally Hughes went with her mother to Hyde Park, where they saw the Prince of Wales driving.[64] Robert Baltrop was born in a working-class family in Walthamstow in 1922. He described his neighborhood, where children had sores on their faces and some had growth disorders from malnutrition.[65] Maria Hull was born Maria Payne at Pool Village, Church Gresley in South Derbyshire, on May 21, 1881. She was one of seven children of Joseph Payne and Maria Whittaker. Her parents planned for her to leave school just before she was thirteen, and she went into domestic service for the weekly wage of one shilling.[66] Besides these publications, John Burnett, a social historian, has edited twenty-eight autobiographies that describe the writers' childhood, education, and home and family life from the 1820s to the 1920s.[67]

CHILDREN'S CONTRIBUTION TO THE ECONOMY

At various times and places children of the lower classes have been an important segment of the labor force. The history of childhood uncovers the complex nature of this economic role. In the Middle Ages peasant children, from the age of six, aided both parents in their work and contributed to the supplemental income of the household through fishing and gathering food. Both Bennett's and Hanawalt's works discuss in detail child labor in the Middle Ages.[68] A Royal Act of 1536 provided that all begging children over the age of five be put to service by local authorities. In the 1720s four-year-olds were employed in textile mills in Norwich, Colchester, and West Riding.[69] In the nineteenth century children worked long hours even from a very early age. In the 1850s and the 1860s children as young as seven were working in industries.[70] Pamela Horn claims, following the 1871 census data of Lancashire, that about one in four girls between ten and fifteen worked in cotton manufacture. She also maintains that in the 1870s, nearly one in three of Bedfordshire's girls in the age range between ten and fifteen were employed in straw plait trades, whereas about one in nine of the Buckinghamshire girls in the same age-group worked as pillow lacemakers.[71] In her novel *Lark Rise to Candleford* Flora Thompson provides in detail an account of the way in which young girls entered domestic service in one geographical area in the 1880s.[72] Like adults' lives, children's lives were touched by World War I. Children in rural areas were forced to leave school and help in farm work. Horn concludes that in many areas, school authorities let boys under twelve years of age leave school, provided they could earn adequate wages. She describes how children contributed to the war effort at the expense of their own schooling.[73]

CHILDREN'S LEGAL STATUS

Institutional policies related to the welfare of children are the focus of several scholarly studies. Ivy Pinchbeck and Margaret Hewitt provide a comprehensive picture of social attitudes toward the children and the treatment of children in England from the Tudor period to the Children's Act of 1948. An important value of these two-volume studies rests in their wealth of information about the formal provisions for children in need and at risk during the period. In addition, the authors show that through protective legislation in the nineteenth and twentieth centuries, children gained independent legal status.[74] Jean S. Haywood's study explores "the changing social patterns and ideas which lie behind the history of attention and care given to the deprived child," and examines nineteenth- and twentieth-century laws for children. In the third edition of her book she includes an analysis of the Children and Young Persons Act of 1963.[75] Like Pinchbeck and Hewitt and Haywood, James Walvin sees laws for the children as essentially protective. Analyzing legal systems and the life of street children in nineteenth-century England, Walvin gives customary interpretations of social policy. Similarly, subscribing a straightforward notion of progress, Thomas E. Jordan examines "the question of how progress in concern for children came about."

Marjorie Cruishank describes the living and working conditions of children in the rapidly industrializing cities in Lancashire (northwestern England) during the nineteenth century. She emphasizes how these developments affected children's health. She narrates passage of factory legislations and establishments of hospitals, dispensaries, and schools as the middle class became aware of young children who spent from dawn to dusk in unhealthy factories.[76]

Child abuse as a major social problem is not a recent development. In mid-nineteenth-century England cruelty in many forms toward children had attracted governmental concern. By 1870 many reform organizations attempted to extend legal protection for children, and thus tried to prevent child abuse cases. Acts in the 1870s on bastardy, birth registration, and infant life protection decreased parental control. These laws were succeeded by the more general Prevention of Cruelty to Children Act (1889, amended 1894), popularly known as the Children's Charter and the Children's Act of 1908. In *Child Abuse and Moral Reform in England* Behlmer analyzes how the London (later, National) Society for the Prevention of Cruelty to Children (NSPCC) tried to protect children from parental abuse by passing and enforcing national laws. Behlmer claims that the NSPCC was inspired by humanitarian concern for the health and safety of children. The NSPCC employed "cruelty men" (agents) to investigate reports of child abuse, usually among poor, and report them to the courts. Behlmer describes in detail how these agents were selected and trained by the society. Between 1889 and 1899, according to Behlmer, NSPCC assisted 109,364 boys and girls, 43 percent of whom were six years of age or under.[77]

The studies by Pinchbeck and Hewitt, Haywood, Walvin, Jordan, Cruishank, and Behlmer have created a general view that things got better for English children in the nineteenth and twentieth centuries as the state intervened more and more to define and protect children's rights. But recently this view has been challenged by Humphries. He argues that laws made by the middle class and enforced by the state were intended "to contain and control those elements within working-class youth culture that most threatened their continued domination."[78]

Poor and destitute children often were forced to join the professional beggars and criminals. The society did not have the resources to take care of all the children. But the cities were swelling with orphans who, like Oliver Twist, fell in with "kidsmen," such as "Fagin," who trained these children to be thieves.[79] Henry Mayhew provides us with anecdotal stories of criminal children.[80] Pinchbeck and Hewitt analyze different poor law acts that England passed to resolve the problems of juvenile delinquency between the sixteenth and eighteenth centuries.[81]

The rise of population and urban growth led to juvenile delinquency. Between 1787 and 1911 the number of British people increased more than 10 percent each decade. This growth of population led to the period of the most rapid urban expansion. By 1841 almost half the population of England and Wales lived in towns.[82] Many from the countryside came to town for employment, but because of limited opportunity, many of them soon joined the ranks of the unemployed and underemployed. Poverty forced many families to be beggars. Children of these vagrant beggar families often were initiated into the business of professional begging almost before they could walk. The street children, when they became a little older, tried every means to earn a living.

Kellow Chesney, J. J. Tobias, Steven Humphries, and Deborah Gorham have analyzed nineteenth-century juvenile delinquency. Chesney describes how beggar children became criminals and prostitutes.[83] Tobias examines in detail careers of some delinquent children.[84] Humphries, in his *Hooligans or Rebels?* includes a well-documented section on "larking about," dealing with the street and gang life of the period. Although orphans of both genders faced the same peril of poverty and risked being led into criminal life, girls were in additional danger of adopting the life of prostitutes. Poorly paid factory jobs or the lowest maid-of-all-work domestic employment was the only source of income for girls over the age of twelve. It was the dreariness of their lives that probably led many young girls into prostitution: the income and the excitement of the "gay" life must have seemed attractive. Discussing the movement to abolish child prostitution, Gorham shows that many late-Victorian middle-class social reformers did not want to bring any fundamental social change to improve the lot of these children.[85] Margaret May traces the evolution from eighteenth-century attitudes to the redefined concept of juvenile delinquency in the mid-nineteenth century. She explains that state recognition of reformatory and industrial schools in 1854 and 1857 for the first time acknowledged juvenile delinquency as a district social phenomenon and accepted responsibility not only for young offenders, but also for children who, although not in conflict with the law, required "care and protection." She further describes the impact of these laws on the pauper children.[86] Gillis describes the processes by which the idea of delinquency was transformed, laws changed, and police procedures altered between 1890 and 1914. He shows how adults involved with the new youth work transmitted their fears regarding youths' resistance, especially that of working-class youths, to legislators and law enforcement authorities, with the result that juvenile behavior previously dealt with in an informal way became the subject of prosecution.[87]

PRIVATE PHILANTHROPY AND SCHEMES FOR SOCIAL REFORM

Urban poverty reached a peak in early nineteenth-century English society. Various private and public organizations tried to solve this problem. The 1834 report of the Royal Commission on the Poor Laws recommended assistance to those who were totally dependent on public relief and those who spent the nights in workhouses.[88] The largest single group in the workhouses was the old; the second largest group was the children.[89] Although the English agreed that the environment of workhouses would be detrimental to a child, they argued about the means to remove a child from that environment. Lionel Rose explains that before the state became directly involved through legislation for destitute children, private philanthropic efforts assisted "street Arabs." Among these private efforts the Ragged Schools were the most well known. The Ragged School Union was formed in 1844. Using sheds or even railway arches, improvised schools were set up for these children; a meal and the possibility of night shelter were used as inducements to attend. But this attempt failed to stop the waifs from begging.[90]

Children aged between seven and fourteen years charged with vagrancy were sent to industrial schools. In 1861 there were nineteen industrial schools in England for the purpose of stopping these children from joining the criminal world. The industrial school population of Great Britain increased from 1,668 in 1864 to more than 22,000 in 1898. Kathleen Hessman describes how voluntary societies and individuals at the beginning rescued the children from the streets and sent them to industrial schools.[91] Rose writes that later on these schools' preventive work was largely credited by the Royal Commission on Reformatories and Industrial Schools in 1884 with breaking up the gangs of juvenile thieves and with reducing juvenile crime since the 1850s.[92] In 1853 Mary Carpenter, founder of a reformatory school, organized the first major conference on delinquency. J. Manton describes Mary Carpenter's work with the pauper children.[93]

Because it was too expensive for the state to maintain these children, some 80,000 English children were sent to Canada between 1869 and 1939. *Parliamentary Papers* related to emigration of pauper children (1875 and 1877) are the best source for official viewpoints. Dr. Barnardo, a philanthropist and child care expert, was one of the most influential figures in child emigration of the period. He had a juvenile mission in the East End, and established numerous children's homes and orphanages. Both Norman Wymer and Gillian Wagner have written biographies of Dr. Barnardo. These biographies also provide us information about the street children.[94] Jordan analyzes the motivations of the English authorities to send children to the colonies.[95] Edna Bradlow describes early unsuccessful attempts by the Children's Aid Society to place poor English children in South Africa.[96] Instead of focusing on the activities of emigration societies, both Gillian Wagner, and Philip Bean and Joy Melville describe child migration from the children's perspective.[97] The primary value of Bean and Melville's study rests on oral testimonies of adults who as children were sent by the emigration societies to Canada, Australia, New Zealand, and African colonies.

To keep the boys off the streets and engage them in some form of healthy activities, Springhall claims that in the second half of the nineteenth century, middle-class activists, social reformers, and clergy proposed to create boys' clubs. He describes that boys' club movements began on a large scale in England in the 1880s with the creation of a boys' club network and ultimately led to the founding of the Boys' Brigade.[98] Springhall also describes how the War Office wanted to incorporate the Boys' Brigade into a national cadet force to be administered by the Territorial Force Association.[99] Springhall's *Sure and Steadfast: A History of the Boys' Brigade, 1883–1983*, also is important for this topic.[100] Lillian Lewis Shiman describes how The Band of Hope, the best-known offspring of the temperance movement, worked with working-class children in training them to shun drinking. This organization mixed education with recreation. Interesting addresses by dynamic speakers and visual aids were used to get the movements' messages across to the children. As part of their assignments, the children marched in parades and performed at temperance concerts and other public functions.[101] Many middle-class boys found an acceptable outlet for their energy in the imperialistic and militaristic Boy Scouts. On scouting one should consult R.S.S. Baden-Powell's *Scouting for Boys: A Handbook of Instruction in Good Citizenship*.[102] In his article "The Boy Scouts, Class and Militarism in Relation to British Youth Movements, 1908–1930" Springhall discusses the class consciousness and militaristic attitude of the Boy Scouts.[103] By November 1909 the girls also had organized themselves as Girl Guides, and received training to attend the injured in case of war. R. Kerr's *The Story of the Girl Guides*[104] is a good source of information on this subject.

CHILDREN'S LITERATURE

In *Some Thoughts Concerning Education* (1690) Locke wrote that as soon as a child knows the alphabet, he should be led to read for pleasure. F.J.H. Darton has found that despite plenty of schoolbooks and guides for the training of the children, there were no books to entertain the English children before the seventeenth century. He further asserts that "children's books did not stand out by themselves as a clear but subordinate branch of English literature until the middle of the eighteenth century."[105] From Darton's work one concludes that a cyclical pattern of a continual alternation exists between moral stories to improve and uplift children, and books designed to be read for pleasure. Darton's bibliographic list shows that since the early eighteenth century, children were reading Mother Goose and Aesop's and Gay's fables.

J. Sloman shows that most children's books that appeared between 1749 and 1820, especially those written by Sarah Fielding, John Newby, Mrs. Sherwood, and Mrs. Trimmer, taught their readers that they had a role in society as children. Sloman further claims that the authors expected children to be agreeable, to be a source of diversion and entertainment, and to create an atmosphere of relaxation and delight.[106]

In 1800 the level of literacy, the contemporary felt, rose dramatically. Books for children and reading for the poor became closely linked.[107] Between 1790 and 1830 several organizations distributed reading matter to the poor. Among these organizations, The Religious Tract Society, founded in 1799, was the most influential, as it became the foremost nineteenth-century institutional publisher of children's fiction.[108] Margaret Nancy Cutt analyzes nineteenth-century evangelical fictions for children. She explains how some authors were primarily concerned with the spiritual salvation of the reader, whereas others attempted to make children aware of prevailing social injustice and evils.[109] Like Cutt, Jacqueline S. Bratton examines evangelical writings for children during the nineteenth century. She shows how these writings contributed to the psychological development of a child.

Gillian Avery examines children's books to show adults' attitude toward children from 1780 to 1900. Analyzing fictions on morals and pleasures, Avery explains the authors' prescriptions for children for ways of growing up properly. Avery points out that the authors of juvenile fiction developed class consciousness among their readers. To show how the authors of juvenile fiction denounced trade Avery wrote, "they made the children of newly rich tradesmen or manufacturers the villains of their stories. Undisciplined, indulged, they tempted the sons of gentry into gambling, into borrowing money, they could not repay."[110] Avery extends her analysis to 1950 in a later study. She shows how several public school stories, adventure novels, and weekly periodicals published in the late nineteenth and early twentieth centuries created a feeling of manliness in a British boy who was supposed to "stand his ground and knock the stuffing out of any dirty foreigner who dared oppose Old England and rouse his men to do the same."[111] One of the authors Avery describes is George Alfred Henty (1832–1902), who wrote historical adventure tales. His work has been examined by a number of historians, all of whom agree that his books reflected and reinforced imperial sentiments.[112] In his article "Tom Brown's Imperialist Sons" Louis James discusses how schoolboy adventure stories in penny periodicals contributed to the ethos of imperialism.[113] Patrick A. Dunae explores the attitudes of individual authors, editors, and publishers on empire as expressed at various times and in various publications during the Victorian and Edwardian period.[114] Examining the illustrations of *Chums*, a boys' periodical, from 1892 to 1914, Robert H. MacDonald shows that these illustrations developed and exploited the myth of empire.[115]

The last quarter of the nineteenth century saw a proliferation of the penny press, which published and sold certain boys' periodicals, known as "penny dreadfuls." Contemporary clergymen, journalists, and magistrates claimed that these periodicals encouraged antisocial attitudes and criminal behavior among the young. By focusing on the critical reaction to the penny dreadfuls, Dunae shows that the dreadfuls did not contribute to juvenile crimes. He also claims that the "spirit of boys' literature changed less between 1870 and 1900 than did conservative attitudes. As a result, juvenile fiction which one generation of critics had denounced as 'blood and thunder' came, in a slightly altered form, to be regarded by the next generation as wholesome and patriotic."[116]

With the mid-nineteenth century a separate body of girls' fiction came into being. These books were a medium for the reinforcement of social expectations and socially acceptable behavior. Judith Rowbothom surveys changing middle-class attitudes between 1840 and 1905 through the channel of the fiction aimed at the young girls of that class.[117] Popular fiction for girls represented them essentially as passive, domesticated, and decorative. Mary Cadogan and Patricia Craig discuss several of these stories in the context of their own time and indicate how these books are regarded now.[118] In 1880 The Religious Tract Society began to publish *The Girls' Own Paper*, and to celebrate the centennial of *The Girl's Own Paper (1880–1901)*, Wendy Forrester has edited and reprinted materials from this weekly journal in *Great Grandmama's Weekly*.[119] It contains important information on what girls were reading at that time.

After surveying the English, Irish, and Scottish children's books published in past seventy years, Frank Eyre concludes that a new emphasis has been placed on fantasy.[120] Analyzing juvenile fiction of the late nineteenth and twentieth centuries, Bob Dixon shows the roles sex, race, and class played in children's fiction.[121] Examining critics, writings of Enid Blyton, imperial adventures and fantasy, and religious books for children, Dixon concludes that ruling ideas on gender, class, and race have been promoted in these works.[122]

Examining English children's periodicals from 1751 to 1945, Kirsten Drotner argues that "juvenile magazines must be understood and interpreted as emotional interventions into the everyday lives of their readers." She notes that "the magazines and their development can be interpreted in relation to the different ways in which they are read by girls and boys, by working-class and middle-class children and adolescents." Usefully, Drotner has structured this work in such a way that changes in the juvenile magazines are correlated with changes facing the young.[123]

CHILDREN'S EDUCATION

Although much has been written on the education of children, histories of education in medieval England are few. Nicholas Orme and Jo Ann Hoeppner Moran, however, have provided us information on the medieval educational system. Orme examines the education of monarchs and aristocrats at home and in the schools and covers topics such as military education and athletics. Despite his emphasis on male children, he does touch on female children's education. Orme discusses the transition from French to Latin to English to classical Latin among the aristocracy as educational trends changed. He notes the changes in the curriculum and the methods of teaching and broadening of those childhood activities that the elite regarded as educational.[124] Studying 15,000 wills, Moran asserts that between 1340 and 1548 85 grammar schools and 245 elementary schools were established in the diocese of York.[125]

Grant McCraren concludes that during the Tudor period, both noble and nonnoble children worked as servants in households superordinate to their own. McCraren claims that through this system, noble children learned social skills that helped them for upward mobility. Toward the end of Tudor period, however, noble children remained at home with a tutor or were sent off to university for more formal education, while nonnoble children were still sent out to be servants.[126] Lawrence Stone also shows that during the late sixteenth and mid-seventeenth centuries upper- and middle-class parents sent their male children to board in or near a school of good reputation.[127]

Between the end of Elizabeth's rule and the publication of John Locke's *Some Thoughts Concerning Education* (1693) several Puritans wrote on education. C. John Sommerville has analyzed these writings and argues that "having failed to influence society from the top, through their contacts in the Church hierarchy and the court, the Puritans tried to influence it from below, in their children."[128] Sommerville further claims that the Puritans were the first to distinguish between education and indoctrination.[129]

The political and religious unrest of the seventeenth century motivated the upper and middle classes to establish social discipline among the poor through education, and they established numerous charity schools throughout Great Britain. M. J. Jones' *The Charity School Movement: A Study of Eighteenth Century Puritanism in Action* is still the best work on this topic. Jones shows how the upper and middle classes, being influenced by John Locke's theory of *tabula rasa*, believed that, through education, they would be able to discipline the minds of the poor. He further analyzes the roles the Church of England and private individuals played in establishing charity schools throughout the eighteenth century. He discusses the management and curricula of these schools.[130] Like Jones, Stone subscribes that "the rise of popular elementary education was very largely an incidental by-product of the struggle between Anglicans and Dissenters for the allegiance of the lower class."[131]

Claiming that "after Locke the education of the child increasingly becomes social rather than religious," J. H. Plumb describes the educational system for wealthy English children during the eighteenth century. Focusing on the advertisements published in provincial newspapers from the 1760s onward, Plumb claims that educational emphasis was overwhelmingly on commercial subjects for boys and social deportments for girls.[132]

Jonathon Gathorne-Hardy emphasizes that anyone who writes about England in the nineteenth or early twentieth century has to deal with class.[133] The sons of aristocracy and the upper middle class went to the public schools in the nineteenth and twentieth centuries.[134] Gathorne-Hardy shows that between 1824 and 1900 public schools for boys and girls became increasingly class conscious and snobbish.[135] Edward C. Mack, John Chandos, J. R. de S. Honey, and Rupert Wilkinson discuss English public school education. Mack analyzes the relation between contemporary ideas and the evolution of public schools between 1780 and 1860.[136] Chandos examines public school boys from 1800 to 1864 in "intimate and particular terms." He describes corporal punishment, the fagging system, and the curriculum.[137] Honey also addresses nearly the same questions in his *Tom Brown's Universe: The Development of the Victorian Public School.*[138] Wilkinson argues that public school–educated boys later in their lives held leadership roles both in Britain and in the empire.[139]

The rise of the public schools in the nineteenth century led to the rise of the preparatory schools. The history of English preparatory school was first done by Donald Leinster-Mackay. In his *The Rise of the English Prep School* Leinster-Mackay points out that the middle class and the newly prosperous class in early- and mid-nineteenth-century England wanted their children to have public school education. This parental aspiration encouraged the growth of the preparatory schools, which prepared boys between ages eight and thirteen for the public schools and the Royal Navy. He also analyzes the changes preparatory schools have gone through from the 1830s to the 1970s in terms of curricula and management.[140]

Josephine Kamm has been one of the first scholars to trace the history of female education in England from the Anglo-Saxon period to the early 1960s. Focusing mostly on upper-class and middle-class girls' education, Kamm shows the development of elementary, secondary, technical, and university education.[141] Besides Kamm, Carol Dyhouse, Deborah Gorham, and Joan N. Burstyn discuss upper- and middle-class girls' education in England in the nineteenth century. Dyhouse describes how upper-class, upper-middle-class, and middle-class girls were educated in the late Victorian and Edwardian periods. She maintains that at the early stage, upper-class and upper-middle-class girls and boys were educated by a governess at home. Then the girls often were sent for two or three years to a local day school. From about twelve or thirteen until about seventeen years of age they attended a select boarding school.[142] Gorham analyzes the objectives of middle-class parents for educating their daughters. She argues that the quality of girls' education in the early Victorian period varied widely from excellent to deplorable. She concludes that most middle-class girls were not educated in a way that would prepare them for gainful employment. Whether they were educated at home or in school, it was assumed that their future lay in a domestic setting.[143] Burstyn also focuses her discussion on middle-class girls' education. She asserts that education for middle-class girls was unsystematic for most of the century. Until the 1870s those who could afford it hired governesses or sent their daughters to small private schools. Some middle-class girls received only sporadic education, attending schools when they were not otherwise engaged. Schooling was considered a way for girls to obtain social rather than intellectual skills. Only the upper middle classes could afford governesses or boarding schools. Families with income ranging from 100 pounds to 300 pounds annually sent their daughters to small private day schools and, in some places, to the voluntary church schools.[144]

Before 1870 individuals, voluntary organizations, and philanthropic societies provided elementary education to the working-class children. Sunday schools (established from 1785 onward) created by philanthropic societies played a major role in the education of children. For the many children who had no access to dayschooling until late in the century Sunday school afforded an opportunity to learn to read. Attendance to a school was compulsory for children until the age of ten in 1876, the age of eleven in 1893, and the age of twelve in 1899, when schooling also had become free.

John Burnett, Phil Gardner, Thomas Walter Laqueur, D. G. Paz, Robert Colls, and Pamela Horn focus on the education of working-class children of the nineteenth and twentieth centuries. Sifting through the autobiographical writings of working-class men and women, Burnett argues that "the view long persisted that elementary and secondary education were quite distinct systems, appropriate for different social classes, not successive stages in a single process to which all children had a right."[145] Gardner claims that state intervention and regulations destroyed working-class private schooling. Working-class schools were scattered throughout the industrial cities and manufacturing towns of England.[146] Focusing on the educational census, Laqueur demonstrates that "from an enrollment in 1818 of some 630,000 children— about 6.5% of the population—the number of students on school registers grew by 1851 to over 2 million—or 13% of the population. There were 450,000 Sunday school scholars in 1818 and five times that number by mid-century."[147] Laqueur argues that state intervention in education, public funding of schools, and compulsory attendance made schooling a public policy. Parents who did not want public policy to determine the content or structure of their children's education "widely supported [a] network of small schools which grew up, like butchers' or bakers' shops, in response to community demand."[148]

For the education of working-class children between 1839 and 1849 the state's financial commitment grew from 30,000 pounds to 125,000 pounds, and a new department of state—the Education Committee of the Privy Council, with its bureaucratic establishment, the Education Department—was created to direct central policy. Paz states that after 1833, ministers themselves made education policy because they believed that the education question involved a religious dimension too delicate to be left to the bureaucrats.[149] Colls claims that the men who financed and brought education to the colliery children of Northumberland and Durham from the 1830s to the 1870s used education for social control. According to Colls, the new schooling policy broke down the traditional patterns of working-class self-education by a process of substitution and built up the new generation of pitmen's children.[150] Horn describes the experiences of English and Welsh working-class children in school during the late nineteenth and early twentieth centuries.[151]

Both Horn and Maria Hull describe schooling in rural areas. In addition to her discussion of education acts for rural children, Horn balances her discussion by incorporating experiences of rural children from diaries and reminiscences preserved at the Essex Record Office and the Museum of English Rural Life at Reading.[152] Sometimes less prosperous rural children went to "dame schools" where for few pennies a week children could be educated.[153] In her autobiographical writing Hull explains that although her elder brother and sister joined a dame school in Pool village, in 1879, when she herself was ready to go to school, the dame was dead, so Hull went to the national school in Derbyshire.[154] Between 1830 and 1870 England's political and economic problems crystallized, and a period of social reforms started, with education part of this reform movement. Discussing the education acts of the nineteenth century, Midwinter shows how they influenced the twentieth-century education system and helped English education in general.[155]

The Butler Education Act of 1944 opened the door for free secondary education for all children. A competitive examination was given to children at age eleven to separate the academically superior students, who were sent to grammar schools, from those less intellectually gifted students, who were sent to modern secondary schools. Harry Judge points out that by the 1960s, "class was a powerful determinant of the progress and success of those boys who were admitted to grammar schools."[156] The Labour party in 1964 somewhat eliminated this two-tier educational system and replaced it with comprehensive schools, providing a core curriculum for all students, at least until the fourth year. To promote this new educational policy new schools were built in labor-controlled counties, and many previously established grammar schools were asked to implement the new policy or else face the consequences of the loss of their public funding. This came to an end with the economic contractions and Conservative party victories of the late 1970s. Judge analyzes how England's financial problems during the 1970s and 1980s influenced the quality of children's education.

CHILDREN'S SPORTS

Analyses of children's recreational activities have been useful in reconstructing English societal values among different classes. Knowledge of children's sports in pre-Victorian period is obscure. Noting that dolls have long served as an important source of amusement for children, Elizabeth Godfrey comments on the existence of dolls at least since the reign of Elizabeth I.[157] Iona and Peter Opie's *Children's Game in Street and Playground* traces the traditional lineage of children's spontaneous play from the ancient times to the present and indicates the social significance of several games. There are many expository studies on children's games that address activities of children during the Victorian and Edwardian periods. James Walvin, J. A. Magnan, Pamela Horn, Paul Atkinson, and Kathleen E. McCrone have made major contributions to the understanding of the social implications of children's sports in the nineteenth and twentieth centuries.

In tracing the growth of physical fitness programs that were popular among upper- and upper-middle-class children, Atkinson notes that at the beginning of the nineteenth century, students of major boarding schools came from landed aristocracy and gentry. Their life-styles included a range of outdoor activities, such as hunting, fishing, and shooting, that were associated with the use and enjoyment of their land. By the second half of the nineteenth century a large number of students came from urban upper-middle-class families. Consequently team sports, such as cricket and football (soccer), replaced the field sports of the earlier generation. In the 1870s skating and lawn tennis became popular among girls. Hockey, lacrosse, rounders, and basketball were introduced in the 1890s. Track athletics, swimming, and rowing also were introduced and were seen as possible activities for girls.[158] Walvin discusses sports for Victorian and Edwardian upper- and middle-class girls. Victorian girls played with dolls and made dolls' clothes. Toward the end of the century upper- and middle-class girls began to play tennis, croquet, and golf and enjoyed cycling. Walvin maintains that children's games in rural areas were seasonal; for example, cricket was played only in summer.[159] *In a Child's World* Walvin includes a chapter on "playing" in which he describes how public schools and commercial interests shaped children's sports and games.[160] Horn describes the games rural children played in *Country Children*. She writes that during the 1880s and 1890s, the girls regularly organized dancing or rhyming games, and the boys spent their time tree-climbing, fishing, and fox-hunting.[161] Mangan focuses on athleticism in public schools in the Victorian and Edwardian periods. Placing athleticism in institutional and ideological perspectives, Mangan shows that athleticism served as a successful agent of socialization, social control, and social cohesion.[162] McCrone advances that games were introduced to girls' schools by the first generation of college-educated women, who had learned to appreciate sports at Oxford and Cambridge. McCrone claims that team sports and games were promoted in girls' public schools after restructuring of their curricula modeled on those in boys' schools.[163]

This brief survey of literature demonstrates that management of English children has been the focus of a large number of scholarly studies on the history of childhood in England. These studies provide the foundation to understand different configurations of adult attitudes toward children. A few studies examine childhood and English society from the children's point of view. Perspectives of the English social, political, and economic worlds in the eyes of the children and adolescents are comparatively sketchy. What also emerges from this survey is that a fertile field of research exists on the experiences of children who returned from the colonies in Asia and Africa.

NOTES

1. James Walvin, "Seen and Heard: Historians and the History of Childhood," Seventh Annual Phi Alpha Theta Distinguished Lecture on History (1987), p. 3.

2. Lawrence Stone, "The Rise of the Nuclear Family in Early Modern England," in *The Family in History*, ed. Charles E. Rosenberg (Philadelphia: University of Pennsylvania Press, 1975), pp. 36–45.

3. Lawrence Stone, *The Family, Sex and Marriage in England* (New York: Harper & Row, 1977).

4. Philippe Ariès, *Centuries of Children: A Social History of Family Life*, trans. Robert Baldick (New York: Alfred A. Knopf, 1962), pp. 25–30.

5. Linda A. Pollock, *Forgotten Children: Parent-Child Relations from 1500 to 1900* (Cambridge, paper back ed. 1983), pp. 262–271.

6. Ralph A. Houlbrooke, *The English Family, 1450–1700*, (London: Longman, 1984), pp. 134–138.

7. Barbara A. Hanawalt, *The Ties That Bound: Peasant Families in Medieval England* (New York: Oxford University Press, 1986), p. 187.

8. Bernard Capp, "English Youth Groups and the Pindar of Wakefield," *Past and Present*, August 1977, pp. 126–133; S. R. Smith, "The London Apprentices as Seventeenth Century Adolescents," *Past and Present*, November 1973, pp. 149–161, and "Religion and the Conception of Youth in Seventeenth Century England," *History of Childhood Quarterly* 2 (Spring 1975):493–516.

9. Judith M. Bennett, *Women in the Medieval English Countryside: Gender and Household in Brigstock Before the Plague* (New York: Oxford University Press, 1987), p. 67.

10. Houlbrooke, *English Family*, p. 150.

11. Anne Yarbrough, "Apprentices as Adolescents in Sixteenth Century Bristol," *Journal of Social History* 13 (Fall 1979):67–81.

12. Susan Brigden, "Youth and English Reformation," *Past and Present*, May 1982, p. 37.

13. John Gillis, *Youth and History: Tradition and Change in European Age Relations* (New York: Academic Press, 1974), pp. ix–xii.

14. John Springhall, *Coming of Age: Adolescence in Britain 1860–1960* (Dublin: Gill & Macmillan, 1987), pp. 1–37.

15. Marjorie Cruishank, *Children and Industry: Child-Health and Welfare in North-West Textile Towns During the Nineteenth Century* (Manchester: Manchester University Press, 1981), p. 175; James Walvin, *A Child's World: A Social History of English Childhood, 1800–1914* (Middlesex, Eng.: Penguin Books, 1982), p. 13.

16. Hanawalt, *Ties That Bound*, p. 175.

17. Houlbrooke, *English Family*, p. 136.

18. Lionel Rose, *The Massacre of the Innocents: Infanticide in Britain, 1800–1939* (London: Routledge & Kegan Paul, 1986), p. 7.

19. Hanawalt, *Ties That Bound*, pp. 171–178.

20. Houlbrooke, *English Family*, pp. 136–140.

21. Barbara A. Kellum, "Infanticide in England in the Later Middle Ages," *Journal of Psychohistory* 1 (Winter 1974):367.

22. Hanawalt, *Ties That Bound*, pp. 102–103.

23. Ibid., p. 102; Houlbrooke, *English Family*, p. 139; Alan Macfarlane, "Illegitimacy and Illegitimate in English History," in *Bastardy and Its Comparative History*, ed. Peter Laslett, Karla Oosterveen, and Richard M. Smith (London: Edward Arnold, 1980), p. 77.

24. Peter C. Hoffer and N.E.H. Hull, *Murdering Mothers: Infanticide in England and New England 1558–1803* (New York: New York University Press, 1984).

25. The petition is printed in R. H. Nichols and F. A. Wray's *The History of the Foundling Hospital* (London: Oxford University Press, 1935), p. 16.

26. Ruth R. McClure, *Coram's Children: The London Foundling Hospital in the Eighteenth Century* (New Haven, Conn.: Yale University Press, 1981).

27. Bernd Weisbrod, "How to Become a Good Foundling in Early Victorian London," *Social History* 10 (May 1985):207–208.

28. Rose, *Massacre of the Innocents*, p. 60.

29. Anna Davin, "Imperialism and the Cult of Motherhood," *History Workshop Journal*, Spring 1978, pp. 32–43.

30. Carole Dyhouse, "Working Class Mothers and Infant Mortality in England, 1895–1914," *Journal of Social History* 12 (Winter 1978):247–261, and *Feminism and Family in England, 1880–1939* (London: Basil Blackwell, 1989), pp. 84–88.

31. Michael Anderson, *Family Structure in Nineteenth Century Lancashire* (Cambridge, 1971), pp. 68–78.

32. Peter Laslett, *The World We Have Lost*, 2d ed. (London: Methuen, 1979), p. 142.

33. Christopher Durston, *The Family in the English Revolution* (London: Basil Blackwell, 1989), pp. 158–159; Peter Laslett, *Family Life and Illicit Love in Earlier Generations* (Cambridge, 1977), p. 125; P. Laslett, K. Oosterveen, and R. Smith, eds., *Bastardy and Its Comparative History* (London: Edward Arnold, 1980), p. 14.

34. Keith Wrightson, "The Nadir of English Illegitimacy in the Seventeenth Century," in Laslett et al., eds., *Bastardy*, pp. 176–192.

35. Laslett et al., eds., *Bastardy*, p. 40.

36. N.F.R. Crafts, "Illegitimacy in England and Wales in 1911," *Population Studies* 36 (July 1982):327–331.

37. John R. Gillis, "Servants, Sexual Relations and the Risk of Illegitimacy in London, 1801–1900," *Feminist Studies* 5 (Spring 1979):142–145.

38. *Parliamentary Papers*, 1844, XXVII, p. 51.

39. Gillis, "Illegitimacy in London," p. 144.

40. U.R.Q. Henrique, "Bastardy and the New Poor Law," *Past and Present*, July 1967, pp. 103–129.

41. Hanawalt, *Ties That Bound*, pp. 171–176; Houlbrooke, *English Family*, p. 132; Elizabeth Godfrey, *English Children in the Olden Time* (1907; reprint ed., Williamstown, Mass.: Corner House, 1980), pp. 2–3.

42. Hanawalt, *Ties That Bound*, pp. 178–179.

43. Nupur Chaudhuri, "Memsahibs and Motherhood in Nineteenth-Century Colonial India," *Victorian Studies* 31 (Summer 1988):529.

44. Ann Roberts, "Mothers and Babies: The Wetnurse and Her Employer in Mid-Nineteenth Century England," *Women's Studies* 3 (1976):289.

45. Theresa McBride, "As the Twig Is Bend: The Victorian Nanny," in *Victorian Family: Structure and Stresses*, ed. Anthony S. Wohl (New York: St. Martin's Press, 1978), p. 47.

46. Rose, *Massacre of the Innocents*, p. 11.

47. Jane Lewis, *Women in England 1870–1950* (Bloomington: Indiana University Press, 1984), pp. 98–101.

48. Alan Macfarlane, *The Family Life of Ralph Josselin: A Seventeenth Century Clergyman* (Cambridge, 1970).

49. Miriam Slater, *Family Life in the Seventeenth Century: The Verneys of Claydon House* (Boston: Routledge & Kegan Paul, 1984).

50. J. H. Plumb, "The New World of Children in Eighteenth-Century England," *Past and Present*, May 1975, pp. 90, 65.

51. Marion Lochhead, *Their First Ten Years: Victorian Childhood* (London: John Murray, 1956), p. xi.

52. F. Gordon Roe, *The Victorian Child* (London: Phoenix House, 1959).

53. Pamela Horn, *The Victorian Country Child* (Kineton: Hornwood Press, 1974).

54. Walvin, *Child's World*, pp. 43–44.

55. Thomas E. Jordan, *Victorian Childhood: Themes and Variations* (New York: State University of New York Press, 1987).

56. Priscilla Robertson, "Home As a Nest: Middle Class Childhood in Nineteenth-Century Europe," in *The History of Childhood*, ed. Lloyd de Mause (New York: Psychohistory Press, 1975), pp. 423–425.

57. Jonathon Gathorne-Hardy, *The Rise and Fall of the British Nanny* (London: Hodder & Stoughton, 1972), pp. 61, 88, 316.

58. McBride, "As the Twig Is Bent," pp. 48–51.

59. Steven Mintz, *A Prison of Expectations: The Family in Victorian Culture* (New York: New York University Press, 1983), p. 58.

60. M. Jeanne Peterson, *Family, Love and Work in the Lives of Victorian Gentlewomen* (Bloomington: Indiana University Press, 1989), pp. 103–104.

61. Stephen Humphries, *Hooligans or Rebels? An Oral History of Working-Class Childhood and Youth 1889–1939* (London: Basil Blackwell, 1981), pp. 70, 191–192, 197–198.

62. Jeremy Searbook, *Working-Class Childhood* (London: Victor Golancz, 1982).

63. Thea Thompson, *Edwardian Childhood* (London: Routledge & Kegan Paul, 1981).

64. M. V. Hughes, *A London Child of the 1870s* (1934; reprint ed., London: Oxford University Press, 1977).

65. Robert Barltrop, *My Mother's Calling Me: Growing Up in North East London Between the Year* (London Borough of Waltham Forest Libraries and Arts Department, n.d.).

66. Maria Hull, "A Derbyshire Schooling: 1884–1893," *History Workshop*, Spring 1988, pp. 166–170.

67. John Burnett, *Destiny Obscure: Autobiographies of Childhood, Education and Family from the 1820s to the 1920s* (Middlesex, Engl.: Allen Lane, 1982).

68. Hanawalt, *Ties That Bound*, ch. 10.

69. Houlbrooke, *English Family*, p. 154.

70. Anderson, *Family Structure*, p. 75.

71. Pamela Horn, "Child Workers in the Pillow Lace and Straw Plait Trades of Victorian Buckinghamshire and Bedfordshire," *Historical Journal* 17 (December 1974):779.

72. Flora Thompson, *Lark Rise to Candleford* (London: Oxford University Press, 1945), ch. 10.

73. Pamela Horn, *Rural Life in England in the First World War* (New York: St. Martin's Press, 1984), pp. 168, 181.

74. Ivy Pinchbeck and Margaret Hewitt, *Children in English Society*, 2 vols. (London: Routledge & Kegan Paul, 1969, 1973).

75. Jean S. Haywood, *Children in Care: The Development of the Service for the Deprived Children*, 3rd ed., rev. (London: Routledge & Kegan Paul, 1978).

76. Cruishank, *Children and Industry*.

77. George K. Behlmer, *Child Abuse and Moral Reform in England, 1870–1908* (Stanford, Calif.: Stanford University Press, 1982), pp. 162–170, 186.

78. Humphries, *Hooligans and Rebels*, p. 238.

79. Edna Bradlow, "The Children's Friend Society at the Cape of Good Hope," *Victorian Studies* 27 (Winter 1984):156.

80. Henry Mayhew, *London Labour and the London Poor* (1851; reprint ed., New York: Dover, 1968).

81. Ivy Pinchbeck and Margaret Hewitt, *Children in English Society: From Tudor Times to the Eighteenth Century*, vol. I (London: Routledge & Kegan Paul, 1969).

82. James Walvin, *Victorian Values* (Athens: University of Georgia Press, 1987), pp. 7–8; "Introduction: The Poor and the City, 1834–1914," in *The Poor and the City: The English Poor Law in Its Urban Context, 1834–1914*," ed. Michael E. Rose (Leicester: Leicester University Press, 1985), pp. 2–3.

83. Kellow Chesney, *The Victorian Underworld* (London: Maurice Temple Smith, 1970), pp. 196–228, 324–325.

84. J. J. Tobias, *Urban Crime in Victorian England* (New York: Schocken Books, 1972), ch. 5.

85. Deborah Gorham, "The 'Maiden Tribute of Modern Babylon' Re-examined: Child Prostitution and the Idea of Childhood in Late-Victorian England," *Victorian Studies* 21 (Spring 1978):378.

86. Margaret May, "Innocence and Experience: The Evolution of the Concept of Juvenile Delinquency in the Mid-Nineteenth Century," *Victorian Studies* 18 (September 1973):7–30.

87. John R. Gillis, "The Evolution of Juvenile Delinquency in England, 1890–1914," *Past and Present*, May 1975, pp. 96–126.

88. Michael E. Rose, "The Disappearing Pauper: Victorian Attitudes to the Relief of the Poor, in *In Search of Victorian Values: Aspects of Nineteenth-Century Thought and Society*, ed. Eric M. Sigsworth (Manchester: Manchester University Press, 1988), p. 57.

89. Walvin, Victorian Values, pp. 17, 21.

90. Lionel Rose, *"Rogues and Vagabonds": Vagrant Underworld in Britain, 1815–1985* (London: Routledge, 1988), p. 39.

91. Kathleen Hessman, *Evangelicals in Action: An Appraisal of Their Social Work in the Victorian Era* (London: Geoffrey Bless, 1962).

92. Rose, *"Rogues and Vagabonds,"* p. 131.

93. J. Manton, *Mary Carpenter and the Children of the Street* (London: Heinemann, 1977).

94. Norman Wymer, *Dr. Barnardo* (London: Longman, 1962); Gillian Wagner, *Barnardo* (London: Weidenfield & Nicholson, 1979).

95. Thomas E. Jordan, "Stay and Starve or Go and Prosper! Juvenile Emigration from Great Britain in the Nineteenth Century," *Social Science History* 9 (Spring 1985):146–151.

96. Bradlow, "Children's Friendly Society," pp. 155–177.

97. Gillian Wagner, *Children of the Empire* (London: Weidenfield & Nicholson, 1982); Philip Bean and Joy Melville, *Lost Children of the Empire: The Untold Story of Britain's Child Migrants* (London: Unwin Hyman, 1989).

98. John A. Springhall, *Coming of Age: Adolescence in Britain, 1860–1960* (Dublin: Gill & Macmillan, 1986), pp. 147–152.

99. John Springhall, *Youth, Empire and Society: British Youth Movements, 1883–1940* (London: Croom Helm, 1977), p. 29.

100. John A. Springhall, *Sure and Steadfast: A History of Boys' Brigade, 1883–1983* (Glasgow: Colins, 1983).

101. Lillian Lewis Shiman, "The Band of Hope Movement: Respectable Recreation for Working-Class Children," *Victorian Studies* 18 (September 1973):49–58.

102. R.S.S. Baden-Powell, *Scouting for Boys: A Handbook for Instruction in Good Citizenship* (1909; rev. ed., London: Scouts Association, 1963).

103. John Springhall, "The Boy Scouts, Class and Militarism in Relation to British Youth Movements, 1908–1930," *International Review of Social History* 16 (1971) Part 2:125–158.

104. R. Kerr, *The Story of Girl Guide* (London: Girl Guides' Association, 1933).

105. F. J. Harvey Darton, *Children's Books in England: Five Centuries of Social Life* (Cambridge: Cambridge University Press, 1932), p. 1.

106. J. Sloman, "Jane Eyre's Childhood and Popular Children's Literature," *Children's Literature: Journal of the Modern Language Association Seminar on Children's Literature and the Children's Literature Association*, 17 vols. to date (Philadelphia: Temple University Press, 1972–), 3:108.

107. Jacqueline S. Bratton, *The Impact of Victorian Children's Fiction* (London: Croom Helm, 1981), p. 31.

108. Ibid., p. 32.

109. Margaret Nancy Cutt, *Mi istering Angels: A Study of Nineteenth- Century Evangelical Writing for Children* (Wormley: Five Owl Press, 1979), p. 113.

110. Gillian Avery, *Nineteenth Century Children: Heroes and Heroines in English Children's Stories, 1780–1900* (London: Hodder & Stoughton, 1965), p. 195.

111. Gillian Avery, *Childhood's Pattern: A Study of the Heroes and Heroines of Children's Fiction, 1770–1950* (London: Hodder & Stoughton, 1975), pp. 197–198.

112. Robert A. Huttenback, "G. A. Henty and the Vision of Empire," *Encounter* 35 (1970):46–53; Mark Nadis, "G. A. Henty's Idea of India," *Victorian Studies* 8 (September 1964):49–58; A. P. Thornton, "G. A. Henty's British Empire," *Fortnightly Review* 175 (1954):97–101; Roy Turnbaugh, "Images of Empire: G. A. Henty and John Buchan," *Journal of Popular Culture* 9 (Winter 1975):734–741.

113. Louis James, "Tom Brown's Imperialist Sons," *Victorian Studies* 17 (Summer 1973):89–99.

114. Patrick A. Dunae, "Boys' Literature and the Idea of Empire," *Victorian Studies* 24 (Autumn 1980):105–121.

115. Robert H. MacDonald, "Signs from the Imperial Quarter: Illustrations in *Chums*, 1892–1914," *Children's Literature* 16 (1988):31.

116. Patrick A. Dunae, "Penny Dreadfuls: Late Nineteenth-Century Boys' Literature and Crime," *Victorian Studies* 22 (Winter 1979):134, 150.

117. Judith Rowbotham, *Good Girls Make Good Wives: Guidance for Girls in Victorian Fiction* (Oxford: Basil Blackwell, 1989).

118. Mary Cadogan and Patricia Craig, *You're a Brick Angela! A New Look at Girls' Fiction from 1839 to 1975* (London: Victor Gollancz, 1976), p. 10.

119. Wendy Forrester, *Great Grandmama's Weekly* (London: Guileford; London: Lutterworth Press, 1980).

120. Frank Eyre, *British Children's Books in the Twentieth Century* (New York: E. P. Dutton, 1973), pp. 19–20, 161–162.

121. Bob Dixon, *Catching Them Young: Sex, Race and Class in Children's Fiction* (London: Pluto Press, 1977).

122. Bob Dixon, *Catching Them Young: Political Ideas in Children's Fiction*, vol. 2 (London: Pluto Press, 1977), p. xv.

123. Kirsten Drotner, *English Children and Their Magazines, 1751–1945* (New Haven, Conn.: Yale University Press, 1988), pp. 4, 10.

124. Nicholas Orme, *From Childhood to Chivalry: The Education of the English Kings to Aristocracy 1066–1530.* (New York: Methuen, 1985).

125. Jo Ann Hoepner Moran, *The Growth of English Schooling, 1340–1548: Learning, Literacy and Laicization in Pre-Reformation York Diocese* (Princeton, N.J.: Princeton University Press, 1985).

126. Grant McCraren, "The Exchange of Children in Tudor England: An Anthropological Phenomenon in Historical Context," *Journal of Family History* 8 (Winter 1983):307.

127. Lawrence Stone, "The Educational Revolution in England, 1560–1640," *Past and Present*, July 1964, pp. 41–80.

128. C. John Sommerville, "English Puritans and Children: A Social-Cultural Explanation," *Journal of Psychohistory* 5 (Spring 1978):122.

129. C. John Sommerville, "The Distinction Between Indoctrination and Education in England, 1549–1719," *Journal of History of Ideas* 44 (July 1983):387–406.

130. M. G. Jones, *The Charity School Movement*, rev. ed. (Hamden, Conn.: Archon Books, 1964), pp. 4–5, 19, 73–109.

131. Lawrence Stone, "Literacy and Education in England, 1640–1900," *Past and Present*, February 1969, p. 81.

132. Plumb, "New World of Children," pp. 69–75.

133. Jonathon Gathorne-Hardy, *The Public School Phenomenon, 1597–1977* (London: Hodder & Stoughton, 1977), p. 21.

134. T. W. Bamford, "Thomas Arnold and the Victorian Idea of a Public School," in *The Victorian Public School: Studies in the Development of an Educational System*, ed. Brian Simon and Ian Bradley (Dublin: Gill & Macmillan, 1975), p. 61.

135. Gathorne-Hardy, *Public School Phenomenon*, pp. 228, 230–267.

136. Edward C. Mack, *Public Schools and British Opinion, 1780–1860* (New York: Columbia University Press, 1939).

137. John Chandos, *Boys Together: English Public Schools 1800–1864* (New Haven, Conn.: Yale University Press, 1984), p. 11.

138. J. R. de S. Honey, *Tom Brown's Universe: The Development of the Victorian Public School* (New York: Quadrangle, 1977).

139. Rupert Wilkinson, *The Prefects: British Leadership and the Public School Tradition: A Comparative Study in the Making of Rulers* (London: Oxford University Press, 1964), p. 100.

140. Donald Leinster-Mackay, *The Rise of the English Prep School* (London: Falmer Press, 1984), pp. xiv–xvi, 4–5.

141. Josephine Kamm, *Hope Deferred: Girls' Education in English History* (London: Methuen, 1965), and *Indicative Past: A Hundred Years of the Girls' Public Day School Trust* (London: Allen & Unwin, 1971).

142. Carol Dyhouse, *Girls Growing Up in Late Victorian and Edwardian England* (London: Routledge & Kegan Paul, 1981), pp. 40–42.

143. Deborah Gorham, *The Victorian Girl and the Feminine Ideal*(Bloomington: Indiana University Press, 1982), p. 24.

144. Joan N. Burstyn, *Victorian Education and the Ideal of Womanhood* (New Brunswick, N.J.: Rutgers University Press, 1984), pp. 22–24.

145. Burnett, *Destiny Obscure*, p. 170.

146. Phil Gardner, *The Lost Elementary Schools of Victorian England* (London: Croom Helm, 1984).

147. Thomas W. Laqueur, "Working-Class Demand and the Growth of English Elementary Education, 1750–1850," in *Schooling and Society: Studies in the History of Education*, ed. Lawrence Stone (Baltimore: Johns Hopkins University Press, 1976), p. 192.

148. Ibid., p. 202.

149. D. G. Paz, "Working-Class Education and the State, 1839–1849: The Source of Government Policy," *Journal of British Studies* 16 (Fall 1976):129, 150–151.

150. Robert Colls, "Oh Happy English Children! Coal, Class and Education in the North-East," *Past and Present*, November 1976, pp. 75, 96.

151. Pamela Horn, *The Victorian and Edwardian Schoolchild* (Glouster: Alan Sutton Publishing, 1989).

152. Pamela Horn, *Labouring Life in the Victorian Countryside* (Dublin: Gill & Macmillan, 1976), ch. 3.

153. D. P. Leinster-Mackay, "Dame Schools: A Need for Review," *British Journal of Educational Studies* 24 (February 1976):33–48; A.F.B. Roberts, "A New View of the Infant School Movement," *British Journal of Educational Studies* 20 (June 1972):154–164.

154. Hull, "Derbyshire Schooling," pp. 166–170.

155. Eric Midwinter, *Nineteenth Century Education* (London: Longman, 1970), pp. 19–20, 25–33.

156. Harry Judge, *A Generation of Schooling: English Secondary Schools Since 1944* (New York: Oxford University Press, 1984), pp. 46–47.

157. Elizabeth Godfrey, *English Children in the Olden Time* (1907; reprinted Williamstown, Mass.: Corner House, 1980), pp. 67–68.

158. Paul Atkinson, "Fitness, Feminism and Schooling," in *The Nineteenth-Century*

Woman: Her Cultural and Physical World, ed. Sara Delamont and Lorna Duffin (London: Croom Helm, 1978), pp. 93, 113.

159. James Walvin, "Children's Pleasure," in *Leisure in Britain, 1780–1939*, ed. John K. Walton and James Walvin (Manchester: Manchester University Press, 1983), pp. 230–232.

160. Walvin, *A Child's World*, pp. 78–100.

161. Horn, *Victorian Country Child*, pp. 150–151.

162. J. A. Mangan, *Athleticism in the Victorian and Edwardian Public School: The Emergence and Consolidation of an Educational Ideology* (Cambridge, 1981), p. 206.

163. Kathleen E. McCrone, "Play Up! Play Up! and Play the Game! Sport at the Late Victorian Girls' Public School," *Journal of British Studies* 23 (Spring 1984):113, 117.

REFERENCES

Anderson, Michael. *Family Structure in Nineteenth Century Lancashire*. Cambridge, 1971.

Ariès, Philippe. *Centuries of Children: A Social History of Family Life*. Translated by Robert Baldick. New York: Alfred A. Knopf, 1962.

Avery, Gillian. *Nineteenth Century Children: Heroes and Heroines in English Children's Stories, 1780–1900*. London: Hodder & Stoughton, 1965.

———. *Childhood's Pattern: A Study of Heroes and Heroines of Children's Fiction, 1770–1950*. London: Hodder & Stoughton, 1975.

Baden-Powell, R.S.S. *Scouting for Boys: A Handbook for Instruction in Good Citizenship*. 1909. Rev. ed., London: Scouts Association, 1963.

Barthrop, Robert. *My Mother's Calling Me: Growing Up in North East London Between the Year*. London Borough of Waltham Forest Libraries and Arts Department, n.d.

Bean, Philip, and Joy Melville. *Lost Children of the Empire: The Untold Story of Britain's Child Migrants*. London: Unwin Hyman, 1989.

Behlmer, George K. *Child Abuse and Moral Reform in England, 1870–1908*. Stanford, Calif.: Stanford University Press, 1982.

Bennett, Judith M. *Women in the Medieval English Countryside: Gender and Household in Brigstock Before the Plague*. New York: Oxford University Press, 1987.

Bradlow, Edna. "The Children's Friend Society at the Cape of Good Hope." *Victorian Studies* 27 (Winter 1984):155–177.

Bratton, Jacqueline S. *The Impact of Victorian Children's Fiction*. London: Croom Helm, 1981.

Brigden, Susan. "Youth and English Reformation." *Past and Present*, May 1982, pp. 37–67.

Burnett, John. *Destiny Obscure: Autobiographies of Childhood, Education and Family from the 1820s to the 1920s*. Middlesex, Engl.: Allen Lane, 1982.

Burstyn, Joan N. *Victorian Education and the Ideal of Womanhood*. New Brunswick, N.J.: Rutgers University Press, 1984.

Cadogan, Mary, and Patricia Craig. *You're a Brick Angela! A New Look at Girls' Fiction from 1839 to 1975*. London: Victor Gollancz, 1976.

Capp, Bernard. "English Youth Groups and the Pindar of Wakefield." *Past and Present*, August 1977, pp. 126–133.

Chandos, John. *Boys Together: English Public Schools 1800–1864*. New Haven, Conn.: Yale University Press, 1984.

Chaudhuri, Nupur. "Memsahibs and Motherhood in Nineteenth-Century Colonial India." *Victorian Studies* 31 (Summer 1988):517–535.

Chesney, Kellow. *The Victorian Underworld*. London: Maurice Temple Smith, 1970.

Colls, Robert. "Oh Happy English Children! Coal, Class and Education in the North-East." *Past and Present*, November 1976, pp. 75–99.

Crafts, N.F.R. "Illegitimacy in England and Wales in 1911." *Population Studies* 36 (July 1982):327–331.

Cruishank, Marjorie. *Children and Industry: Child-Health and Welfare in North-West Textile Towns During the Nineteenth Century*. Manchester: Manchester University Press, 1981.

Cutt, Margaret Nancy. *Ministering Angels: A Study of Nineteenth-Century Evangelical Writing for Children*. Wormley: Five Owl Press, 1979.

Darton, F. J. Harvey. *Children's Books in England: Five Centuries of Social Life*. Cambridge: Cambridge University Press, 1932.

Davin, Anna. "Imperialism and the Cult of Motherhood." *History Workshop Journal*, Spring 1978, pp. 9–65.

Delamont, Sara, and Lorna Duffin, eds. *The Nineteenth-Century Woman: Her Cultural and Physical World*. London: Croom Helm, 1978.

Dixon, Bob. *Catching Them Young: Sex, Race and Class in Children's Fiction*. Vol. 1. London: Pluto Press, 1977.

———. *Catching Them Young: Political Ideas in Children's Fiction*. Vol. 2. London: Pluto Press, 1977.

Drotner, Kirsten. *English Children and Their Magazines, 1751–1945*. New Haven, Conn.: Yale University Press, 1988.

Dunae, Patrick A. "Penny Dreadfuls: Late Nineteenth-Century Boys' Literature and Crime." *Victorian Studies* 22 (Winter 1979):133–150.

———. "Boys' Literature and the Idea of Empire." *Victorian Studies* 24 (Autumn 1980):105–121.

Durston, Christopher. *The Family in the English Revolution*. London: Basil Blackwell, 1989.

Dyhouse, Carole. "Working Class Mothers and Infant Mortality in England, 1895–1914." *Journal of Social History* 12 (Winter 1978):248–267.

———. *Girls Growing Up in Late Victorian and Edwardian England*. London: Routledge & Kegan Paul, 1981).

———. *Feminism and Family in England, 1880–1939*. London: Basil Blackwell, 1989.

Eyre, Frank. *British Children's Books in the Twentieth Century*. New York: E. P. Dutton, 1973.

Forrester, Wendy. *Great Grandmamma's Weekly*. London: Lutterworth Press, 1980.

Gardner, Phil. *The Lost Elementary Schools of Victorian England*. London: Croom Helm, 1984.

Gathorne-Hardy, Jonathon. *The Rise and Fall of the British Nanny*. London: Hodder & Stoughton, 1972.

———. *The Public School Phenomenon, 1597–1977*. London: Hodder & Stoughton, 1977.

Gillis John. *Youth and History: Tradition and Change in European Age Relations*. New York: Academic Press, 1974.

———. "The Evolution of Juvenile Delinquency in England, 1890–1914." *Past and Present*, May 1975, pp. 96–126.

———. "Servants, Sexual Relations and the Risk of Illegitimacy in London, 1801–1900." *Feminist Studies* 5 (Spring 1979):142–173.

Godfrey, Elizabeth. *English Children in the Olden Time*. 1907. Reprint. Williamstown, Mass.: Corner House, 1980.

Gorham, Deborah. "The 'Maiden Tribute of Modern Babylon' Re-examined: Child Prostitution and the Idea of Childhood in Late-Victorian England." *Victorian Studies* 21 (Spring 1978):353–379.

———. *The Victorian Girl and the Feminine Ideal*. Bloomington: Indiana University Press, 1982.

Hanawalt, Barbara A. *The Ties That Bound: Peasant Families in Medieval England*. New York: Oxford University Press, 1986.

Haywood, Jean S. *Children in Care: The Development of the Service for the Deprived Children*. 3rd ed., rev. London: Routledge & Kegan Paul, 1978.

Henrique, U.R.Q. "Bastardy and the New Poor Law." *Past and Present*, July 1967, pp. 103–129.

Hessman, Kathleen. *Evangelicals in Action: An Appraisal of Their Social Work in the Victorian Era*. London: Geoffrey Bless, 1962.

Hoffer, Peter C., and N.E.H. Hull. *Murdering Mothers: Infanticide in England and New England 1558–1803*. New York: New York University Press.

Honey, J. R. de S. *Tom Brown's Universe: The Development of the Victorian Public School*. New York: Quadrangle, 1977.

Horn, Pamela. *The Victorian Country Child*. Kineton: Hornwood Press, 1974.

———. "Child Workers in the Pillow Lace and Straw Plait Trades of Victorian Buckinghamshire and Bedfordshire." *Historical Journal* 17 (December 1974):779–796.

———. *Labouring Life in the Victorian Countryside*. Dublin: Gill & Macmillan, 1976.

———. *Rural Life in England in the First World War*. New York: St. Martin's Press, 1984.

Houlbrooke, Ralph A. *The English Family, 1450–1700*. London: Longman, 1984.

Hughes, M. V. *A London Child of the 1870s*. 1934. Reprint. London: Oxford University Press, 1977.

Hull, Maria. "A Derbyshire Schooling: 1884–1893." *History Workshop*, Spring 1988, pp. 166–170.

Humphries, Stephen. *Hooligans or Rebels? An Oral History of Working-Class Childhood and Youth 1889–1939*. London: Basil Blackwell, 1981.

Huttenback, Robert A. "G. A. Henty and the Vision of Empire." *Encounter* 35 (1970):46–53.

James, Louis. "Tom Brown's Imperialist Sons." *Victorian Studies* 17 (Autumn 1980):89–99.

Jones, M. G. *The Charity School Movement*. Rev. ed. Hamden, Conn.: Archon Books, 1964.

Jordan, Thomas E. "Stay and Starve or Go and Prosper! Juvenile Emigration from Great Britain in the Nineteenth Century." *Social Science History* 9 (Spring 1985):145–166.

———. *Victorian Childhood: Themes and Variations*. New York: State University of New York Press, 1987.

Judge, Harry. *A Generation of Schooling: English Secondary Schools Since 1944*. New York: Oxford University Press, 1984.

Kamm, Josephine. *Hope Deferred: Girls' Education in English History*. London: Mathuen, 1965.

Kellum, Barbara A. "Infanticide in England in the Later Middle Ages." *Journal of Psychohistory* 1 (Winter 1974):367–388.

Kerr, R. *The Story of Girl Guide*. London: Girl Guides' Association, 1933.

Laslett, Peter. *Family Life and Illicit Love in Earlier Generations*. Cambridge, 1977.

———. *The World We Have Lost*. 2nd rev. ed. London: Methuen, 1979.

Laslett, Peter, K. Oosterveen, R. Smith, eds. *Bastardy and Its Comparative History*. London: Edward Arnold, 1980.

Leinster-Mackay, D. P. "Dame Schools: A Need for Review." *British Journal of Educational Studies* 24 (February 1976):33–48.

———. *The Rise of the English Prep School*. London: Falmer Press, 1984.

Lewis, Jane. *Women in England 1870–1950*. Bloomington: Indiana University Press, 1984.

Lochhead, Marion. *Their First Ten Years: Victorian Childhood*. London: John Murray, 1956.

McBride, Theresa. "As the Twig Is Bent: The Victorian Nanny," in *Victorian Family: Structure and Stresses*, edited by Anthony S. Wohl. New York: St. Martin's Press, 1978.

McClure, Ruth R. *Coram's Children: The London Foundling Hospital in the Eighteenth Century*. New Haven, Conn.: Yale University Press, 1981.

McCraren, Grant. "The Exchange of Children in Tudor England: An Anthropological Phenomenon in Historical Context." *Journal of Family History* 8 (Winter 1983):303–313.

McCrone, Kathleen E. "Play Up! Play Up! and Play the Game! Sport at the Late Victorian Girls' Public School." *Journal of British Studies* 23 (Spring 1984):106–134.

MacDonald, Robert H. "Signs from the Imperial Quarter: Illustrations in *Chums*, 1892–1914," *Children's Literature*. 16 (1988): 30–39.

Macfarlane, Alan, "Illegitimacy and Illegitimate in English History." In *Bastardy and Its Comparative History*, edited by Peter Laslett, Karla Oosterveen, and Richard M. Smith. London: Edward Arnold, 1980.

Mack, Edward C. *Public Schools and British Opinion, 1780–1860*. New York: Columbia University Press, 1939.

Mangan, J. A. *Athleticism in the Victorian and Edwardian Public School: The Emergence and Consolidation of an Educational Ideology*. Cambridge: 1981.

Manton, J. *Mary Carpenter and the Children of the Street*. London: Heinemann, 1977.

May, Margaret. "Innocence and Experience: The Evolution of the Concept of Juvenile Delinquency in the Mid-Nineteenth Century." *Victorian Studies* 18 (September 1973):7–30.

Mayhew, Henry. *London Labour and the London Poor*. 1851. Reprint. New York: Dover, 1968.

Midwinter, Eric. *Nineteenth Century Education*. London: Longman, 1970.

Mintz, Steven. *A Prison of Expectations: The Family in Victorian Culture*. New York: New York University Press, 1983.

Moran, Jo Ann Hoepner. *The Growth of English Schooling, 1340–1548: Learning, Lit-*

eracy and Laicization in Pre-Reformation York Diocese. Princeton, N.J.: Princeton University Press, 1985.

Nadis, Mark. "G. A. Henty's Idea of India." *Victorian Studies* 8 (September 1964):49–58.

Nichols, R. H., and F. A. Wray. *The History of the Foundling Hospital*. London: Oxford University Press, 1935.

Orme, Nicholas. *From Childhood to Chivalry: The Education of the English Kings to Aristocracy 1066–1530*. New York: Methuen, 1985.

Parliamentary Papers, 1844, XXVII, p. 51.

Paz, D. G. "Working-Class Education and the State, 1839–1849: The Source of Government Policy." *Journal of British Studies* 16 (Fall 1976):129–152.

Peterson, M. Jeanne. *Family, Love and Work in the Lives of Victorian Gentlewomen*. Bloomington: Indiana University Press, 1989.

Pinchbeck, Ivy, and Margaret Hewitt. *Children in English Society*. 2 vols. London: Routledge & Kegan Paul, 1969, 1973.

Plumb, J. H. "The New World of Children in Eighteenth-Century England." *Past and Present*, May 1975, pp. 64–93.

Pollock, Linda A. *Forgotten Children: Parent-Child Relations from 1500 to 1900*. Cambridge: University Press, 1983.

Roberts, A.F.B. "A New View of the Infant School Movement." *British Journal of Educational Studies* 20 (June 1972):154–164.

Roberts, Ann. "Mothers and Babies: The Wetnurse and Her Employer in Mid-Nineteenth Century England." *Women's Studies* 3 (1976):289.

Robertson, Priscilla. "Home As a Nest: Middle Class Childhood in Nineteenth-Century Europe." In *The History of Childhood*, edited by Lloyd de Mause. New York, 1975.

Roe, F. Gordon. *The Victorian Child*. London: Phoenix House, 1959.

Rose, Lionel. *The Massacre of the Innocents: Infanticide in Britain, 1800–1939*. London: Routledge & Kegan Paul, 1986.

———. *"Rogues and Vagabonds": Vagrant Underworld in Britain, 1815–1985*. London: Routledge, 1988.

Rose, Michael E., ed. *The Poor and the City: The English Poor Law in Its Urban Context, 1834–1914*. Leicester: Leicester University Press, 1985.

Rowbotham, Judith. *Good Girls Make Good Wives: Guidance for Girls in Victorian Fiction*. Oxford: Basil Blackwell, 1989.

Searbook, Jeremy. *Working-Class Childhood*. London: Victor Golancz, 1982.

Shiman, Lillian Lewis. "The Band of Hope Movement: Respectable Recreation for Working-Class Children." *Victorian Studies* 18 (September 1973):49–74.

Sigsworth, Eric M., ed. *In Search of Victorian Values: Aspects of Nineteenth-Century Thought and Society*. Manchester: Manchester University Press, 1988.

Simon, Brian, and Ian Bradley, eds. *The Victorian Public School: Studies in the Development of an Educational System*. Dublin: Gill & Macmillan, 1975.

Slater, Miriam. *Family Life in the Seventeenth Century: The Verneys of Claydon House*. Boston: Routledge & Kegan Paul, 1984.

Sloman, J. "Jane Eyre's Childhood and Popular Children's Literature." *Children's Literature: Journal of the Modern Language Association Seminar on Children's Literature and the Children's Literature Association*. Vol. 3. Philadelphia: Temple University Press, 1972.

Smith, S. R. "The London Apprentices as Seventeenth Century Adolescents." *Past and Present*, November 1973, pp. 149–161.

———. "Religion and the Conception of Youth in Seventeenth Century England." *History of Childhood Quarterly* 2 (Spring 1975):493–516.

Sommerville, C. John. "The Distinction Between Indoctrination and Education in England, 1549–1719." *Journal of History of Ideas* 44 (July 1983):387–406.

Sommerville, C. John. "English Puritans and Children: A Social-Cultural Explanation." *Journal of Psychohistory* 6 (Summer 1978):113–137.

Springhall, John. *Youth, Empire and Society: British Youth Movements, 1883–1940*. London: Croom Helm, 1977.

———. *Sure and Steadfast: A History of Boys' Brigade, 1883–1983*. Glasgow: Colins, 1983.

———. *Coming of Age: Adolescence in Britain 1860–1960*. Dublin: Gill & Macmillan, 1986.

———. "The Boy Scouts, Class and Militarism in Relation to British Youth Movements, 1908–1930." *International Review of Social History* 16 (1971) Part 2:125–158.

Stone, Lawrence. "The Educational Revolution in England, 1560–1640." *Past and Present*, July 1964, pp. 41–80.

———. "Literacy and Education in England, 1640–1900." *Past and Present*, February 1969, p. 81.

———. "The Rise of the Nuclear Family in Early Modern England." In *The Family in History*, edited by Charles E. Rosenberg. Philadelphia: University of Pennsylvania Press, 1975.

———. *The Family, Sex and Marriage in England*. New York: Harper & Row, 1977.

———, ed. *Schooling and Society: Studies in the History of Education*. Baltimore: Johns Hopkins University Press, 1976.

Thompson, Flora. *Lark Rise to Candleford*. London: Oxford University Press, 1945.

Thompson, Thea. *Edwardian Childhood*. London: Routledge & Kegan Paul, 1981.

Thornton, A. P. "G. A. Henty's British Empire." *Fortnightly Review* 175 (1954):97–101.

Tobias, J. J. *Urban Crime in Victorian England*. New York: Schocken Books, 1972.

Turnbaugh, Roy. "Images of Empire: G. A. Henty and John Buchan." *Journal of Popular Culture* 9 (Winter 1975):734–741.

Wagner, Gillian. *Barnardo*. London: Weidenfield & Nicholson, 1979.

———. *Children of the Empire*. London: Weidenfield & Nicholson, 1982.

Walton, John K. and James Walvin, eds. *Leisure in Britain, 1780–1939*. Manchester: Manchester University Press, 1983.

Walvin, James. *A Child's World: A Social History of English Childhood, 1800–1914*. Middlesex, Engl.: Penguin Books, 1982.

———. "Seen and Heard: Historians and the History of Childhood." The Seventh Annual Phi Alpha Theta Distinguished Lecture on History, 1987.

———. *Victorian Values*. Athens: University of Georgia Press, 1987.

Weisbrod, Bernd. "How to Become a Good Foundling in Early Victorian London." *Social History* 10 (May 1985):193–209.

Wilkinson, Rupert. *The Prefects: British Leadership and the Public School Tradition: A Comparative Study in the Making of Rulers*. London: Oxford University Press, 1964.

Wohl, Anthony S. *The Victorian Family: Structure and Stresses*. New York: St. Martin's Press, 1978.

Wymer, Norman. *Dr. Barnardo*. London: Longman, 1962.

Yarbrough, Anne. "Apprentices as Adolescents in Sixteenth Century Bristol." *Journal of Social History* 13 (Fall 1979):67–81.

11

FRANCE

Linda Clark

Historians of France have recently shown special interest in the history of child-hood for at least three reasons. First, the pathbreaking book that launched sub-stantial international interest in the history of childhood, Philippe Ariès' *Centuries of Childhood (L'Enfant et la vie familiale sous l'ancien régime*, 1960; English translation, 1962), used much evidence from French sources.[1] Second, although Ariès worked outside the university and institutionalized research set-tings that house most French historians, his subject nicely complemented French social historians' strong interest in the study of previously neglected and often powerless groups. Finally, the tumultuous events in France in May 1968 that began with student protests at universities in the Paris region prompted historians alert to contemporary crises to pay new attention to the intertwined subjects of the history of education and the history of childhood and youth.

This survey of some of the major themes addressed in European and American historians' studies of French childhood begins with a brief review of Ariès' seminal work. It then notes how his arguments and chronological organization relate to other historians' treatments of childhood during the Old Regime and, more particularly, the modern period dating from the Revolution of 1789. One conclusion that should emerge from this survey is that Ariès' theses, despite being subjected to substantial criticism, remain central not only for historians of childhood, but also for historians of the family, women, demography, edu-cation, social welfare, and labor. Since the seventeenth century, changes in attitudes toward childhood have contributed to changes in the policies of public institutions concerned with children; and institutional changes have, in turn, affected as well as mirrored private individuals' attitudes toward childhood.

PHILIPPE ARIÈS AND HISTORIANS OF EARLY
MODERN FRANCE

Ariès intrigued mid-twentieth-century readers by arguing that parents of an earlier era—the Middle Ages—lacked the concern about children's physical and emotional welfare that was epitomized, for Americans, by Dr. Benjamin Spock's best-selling manual on child care or, for the French, by comparable treatises on *puériculture*.[2] Medieval parents seemed emotionally detached from infants and young children, partly because of the high probability that half of all children born would be dead by the age of four. Ariès also contended that most children who survived until age seven were then treated essentially as young adults who were expected to help their families by becoming apprentices or doing agricultural work. To support his conclusions, Ariès cited an absence of discussions of childhood in medieval texts—a void that was probably not so total as he suggested[3]—and also pictorial evidence showing children dressed in miniature versions of adult garb. Although many of his examples date from the fifteenth or sixteenth century, Ariès used them to generalize about earlier centuries.

Ariès' second phase in the history of childhood and, by extension, the family was a transitional one begun in the sixteenth and seventeenth centuries and marked by a new, typically feminine coddling of children as well as new emphases among social elites on the formal education of boys. The seventeenth-century educational "revolution" was due largely to the bourgeoisie, Ariès believed, because aristocrats often employed tutors and governesses. In Europe's new classrooms, typically staffed by clerics, youths of different ages did not mingle to the same extent as in medieval classes; and curricula were modified to suit children's abilities at different ages. Finally, Ariès saw the expansion of formal schooling as evidence of the absolutist state's intervention in a domain of the family, and he asserted his preference for the medieval world's less intrusive state.

By the late eighteenth century, concluded Ariès, the stage was set for generalizing modern concerns about child welfare and for a greater privatization of family life, as demonstrated by the new division of houses into more private rooms. Jean-Jacques Rousseau's famous treatise *Émile* (1762) was thus not a totally new approach to child rearing and education, but rather the most notable example of a new genre of treatises on childhood by pedagogues and medical doctors. Women's roles and self-perceptions also would be dramatically affected by the new emphasis on child care. Although other historians have criticized Ariès for neglecting evidence, blurring chronology, or overdramatizing contrasts between historical periods, even critics, such as Adrian Wilson, acknowledged that Ariès had successfully inserted childhood and the family into history and reached a public eager for historical perspectives on this subject.[4]

Ariès' impact on other students of French history can be seen in studies published during the 1970s, beginning with David Hunt's *Parents and Children in History* (1970). Using diaries, letters, and treatises on childhood, Hunt focused on seventeenth-century parental attitudes toward children. He tried to test evidence against the schema of Ariès and the developmental psychology of Erik Erikson. In general, Hunt confirmed Ariès' picture of neglect of infants, citing, in particular, the diary of the physician to the little prince who became Louis XIII to argue that if the most important child in France nearly starved to death in infancy, then many other infants would have fared little better.[5] Nourishing little Louis XIII was a problem because of wet nurses' inadequacies and efforts to feed him solid foods too soon. Among the upper classes the use of wet nurses had become prevalent, and was probably more common in France than elsewhere for such reasons as elite culture's distaste for a practice seen as animal-like and debilitating and husbands' desires to monopolize wives' time. Hunt's picture was not totally bleak, for he did see signs of parental love for young children. He also utilized Erikson's eight phases of individual psychological development to highlight certain conclusions about the impact of childhood experiences on adult personalities. Early problems with getting enough food helped to produce a nation of adults more likely to distrust than to trust others, Hunt suggested. Because neglect of infants was replaced by the regulating and disciplining of two-year-olds, especially through toilet training and whippings, adults so treated in childhood typically perpetuated cruel treatment when they had children. Adults' fondling of children's genitals also made children distrustful and contributed to later problems with sexual intimacy. Presumably parents who had difficulty during the first three phases of life (tagged by Freudians as the oral, anal, and genital) would not become the nurturing adults whose urge to "generativity" represented for Erikson the seventh of eight stages of life. Because some seventeenth-century parents expressed affection for children, Hunt did see confirmation of a basic psychobiological urge to generativity; but his depiction was much less positive than the revisionist book of Linda Pollock, who used English letters and diaries to challenge theses about earlier generations' wide-ranging neglect of children.[6]

Since the publication of Ariès' and Hunt's books other historians of early modern France have scrutinized such themes as fertility rates and infant mortality, the use of wet nurses, and the treatment of children by mothers, fathers, servants, and educators. Historical demographers' contribution has been to establish the universality of a pattern of children being born to the typical family every two years, maternal breast-feeding by nonelite women being an important factor in delaying the next conception. When a "typical" family welcomed five to eight infants no single child received special care.[7] During the eighteenth century more children born to Europe's leading families survived, and, in turn, a decline in upper-class fertility began. France was 100 years ahead of other countries in deliberately limiting births, its birthrate falling from 4.8 per married couple in 1740 to 4.3 in 1800 and to 3.4 in 1850.[8] S. Ryan Johansson attributes the declining birthrate to several parental concerns: recognition of the substantial costs of educating and launching children, the wish to avoid dividing family property too often, and the desire to lavish more attention on individual children.

The last point confirms Ariès' argument but is also one that other demographers do not want to overemphasize.[9]

Demographers' charting of family size over time was under way when Ariès introduced the history of childhood, and Ariès contended that new attitudes toward children were central to society's changing definitions of the family. During the seventeenth century there was no special label for the modern nuclear family composed of two parents and their offspring because, Robert Wheaton suggests, when life was precarious, people hesitated to define themselves separately from other close relatives. Jean-Louis Flandrin, in turn, found three connotations of the term family during the Old Regime. The oldest definition of it as an extended kinship group had, by the 1680s, been supplemented by the idea that it included only the closest relatives. By the mid-eighteenth century "family" also could mean a group living in a single dwelling, but this definition permitted including servants. To account for changing definitions of the family, other historians, such as James Traer, have added to Ariès' emphasis on a new view of childhood the importance of more individualistic attitudes toward love between spouses and also the Industrial Revolution's considerable impact on the family's relation to the workplace.[10]

While definitions of the family evolved, the French state clearly enhanced the power of the male head of the family. Sarah Hanley has recently noted how this development affected both children and women. A major legal landmark was a measure promulgated in 1556 by the Paris region's chief law court, which extended the "age of minority" from twenty to thirty for men and from seventeen to twenty-five for women and also permitted disinheriting those who married without parental consent. Significantly, the state embraced this measure at a time when the Catholic Church, through the Council of Trent, denied the necessity of parental consent to marriage. Possible penalties for marrying without parental consent became considerably more severe in 1578.[11]

Certainly the extension of paternal authority within the family neatly paralleled the extension of the absolutist state's powers, but, as Ariès observed, other institutions displayed new concerns about children. Not only the state's wish to control subjects from an early age, but also the Church's desire to maintain the faith after the sixteenth-century religious upheaval contributed to new ways of treating children differently than adults. The Church's emphasis on the importance of a formal marriage ceremony produced a major drop in the rate of illegitimate births, a rate that was much lower than England's and remained low until the mid-eighteenth century.[12] The French church of the Catholic Reformation (or Counter-Reformation) also hoped that its education of children would help it to influence adults. A new emphasis on the sacrament of the first communion as a special religious fete illustrated this ambition. Although the first communion had once been common for the very young, the First Lateran Council in 1215 had identified ages twelve to fourteen as the appropriate time for it because then a child reached the "age of reason." That detail about the "age of reason," like Natalie Davis' studies of older youth groups of the sixteenth century, does contradict Ariès' contention that traditional society did not consider children after age seven to be different from adults.[13] The first reference to the first communion becoming a special fete dates from 1593; the first detailed description of the fete, from 1616; and the first lengthy instructions for priests about the first communion, from 1666. In an important refinement of the popular view that children were animals to be tamed, some Counter-Reformation churchmen combined convictions about the taint of original sin on all humanity with the belief that children were more innocent than adults and so, through their piety, could positively influence parents. Well into the seventeenth century, however, some priests continued to have children confess as a group, instead of individually, like adults. The transforming of the first communion into a special event for the family and community began in urban areas and spread later to the countryside, finally becoming generalized after 1750.[14]

Children's informed participation in religious ceremonies required not only instruction in doctrine, but also the ability to read catechisms and the Bible. Historians of education have well established that both the Reformation and the Counter-Reformation stimulated the growth of formal schooling.[15] In regions of France where the two religious credos competed, schooling became particularly common for the masses as well as the elites. Governmental funding for schools lagged behind that of religious orders, although in 1698 Louis XIV's regime recognized the desirability of each parish's having a schoolmaster and schoolmistress. Lessons varied considerably by locale, but elementary schools (*petites écoles*) typically offered reading, arithmetic, and, to a lesser extent, writing. Girls received formal schooling and learned to write less often than boys, and girls' classes often spent considerable time on needlework. In a stimulating discussion of how and why pupils, especially girls, who learned to read did not always learn to write, François Furet and Jacques Ozouf note that some religious authorities feared that the ability to write would enable women to produce scandalous love letters or deviate in other ways from prescribed roles. The central point, however, of Furet and Ozouf in *Lire et écrire*, an important collection of essays on the relation between schooling and literacy, is that local economic considerations often were decisive in determining the availability of schooling. By the late eighteenth century, literacy rates were typically higher in northern and eastern urban areas, where commercial activities that required literacy were important. Men were more literate than women (29 percent in 1700 and 47 percent in 1800, as compared with 14 percent of women in 1700 and 27 percent in 1800), and peasants were less literate because schooling long seemed to have no economic value.[16]

If religious upheaval stimulated interest in literacy, so, too, within the limits found by Harvey Chisick, did the Enlightenment. Rousseau's *Émile* advocated a ''natural'' upbringing that would not force a child to tackle an activity or area of learning until he was ready. For mothers, Rousseau prescribed the breast-feeding of infants and more preoccupation with their children's daily lives. His focus on the child's development matched that of other late eighteenth-century pedagogues and medical doctors who wrote treatises defining in greater detail than previously the characteristics of children aged three to seven, a phase of life then labeled the "second childhood."[17]

Historians typically agree that *Émile* (1762) appeared at a time when French aristocratic and bourgeois families were devoting more care to young children. Upper-class women now sometimes breast-fed their infants, partly because doctors advised that this best ensured a child's survival and because of beliefs that a wet nurse's bad traits could be transmitted to a child through her milk. Many upper-class women, however, still hired wet nurses (perhaps more carefully than before), and so did many urban working-class families, including the great majority of Parisians in the 1780s.[18] In a provocative chapter on children and servants Cissie Fairchilds argues that the better treatment for upper-class children during the last decades of the Old Regime typically occurred after, rather than during, infancy. At that point mothers took more pains to see that servants who cared for offspring used appropriate behavior and language with them. Fairchilds concludes that changes in eighteenth-century child rearing indeed produced happier children because the first noticeable cluster of references to happy childhoods appears in the memoirs of nobles born during the last decades of the Old Regime. Because servants remained actively involved in caring for upper-class children, Fairchilds also speculates that the affection that some children felt for servants contributed to an upper-class attitudinal change that might have helped to prompt nobles to support social reform and even the Revolution of 1789.[19]

FROM THE REVOLUTION OF 1789 TO WORLD WAR I

Education

Some effects of the Revolution of 1789 on French children have been documented in James F. Traer's study of the Revolution's changes in laws affecting the family. In 1793 the egalitarian revolutionaries abolished primogeniture and stipulated that all but one-tenth of parental property be equally distributed among heirs, male and female. To free older children from parental tyranny, the Revolution abolished the infamous *lettres de cachet*, which had enabled fathers to imprison adult children. The age of legal majority was reduced to twenty-one for both men and women. Under Napoleon I's Civil Code of 1804 paternal authority was again strengthened, at the expense of the rights of children and women, but the egalitarian and individualistic thrust in inheritance law was modified rather than abolished.[20] In the long run children also would benefit from the Revolution's commitment to providing free primary education to all children, although in practice the Revolution fell far short of delivering universal schooling and, in some cases, even made schooling less available because of its attack on religious institutions.[21]

Under both the Revolution (1789–1799) and Napoleon I (1799–1814) the old nobility typically withdrew from public life, in some instances emigrating from

France. Not surprisingly, private life became more important to aristocratic families, and aristocratic parents became more attentive to children. Margaret Darrow has presented evidence for the intensification of aristocratic mothering, which, to some extent, simply continued trends begun in the 1760s. Darrow also notes that some aristocrats viewed the Revolution as a punishment for their class' failings and so believed that regenerating the family was necessary if they were ever to help regenerate France. The model of the "mother-educator" (*mère-éducatrice*), developed by both aristocratic and bourgeois women, subsequently exerted much influence on nineteenth-century elites, as Barbara Corrado Pope has shown. Marie-Françoise Lévy's study also demonstrates that because public authorities neglected the education of girls longer than that of boys, nineteenth-century mothers had relatively more responsibility for the education of girls.[22]

Although attitudes toward children were changing among the bourgeoisie and aristocracy by 1800, additional changes had to occur before French public and private treatment of children approximated the child-centeredness of the mid-twentieth-century Western world. Nonetheless, by 1867 the noted author and educator Ernest Legouvé observed that in some parts of society, children had become "Messieurs les enfants," around whom households centered, and within middle-class families he detected more paternal as well as maternal indulgence of children. In 1901 Count François de Nion forecast that the twentieth century would be "the century of children," and, like present-day historians, he saw this representing a culmination of tendencies dating from Louis XV's reign.[23] Significant changes during the nineteenth century in public policy as well as private life help account for Legouvé's and Nion's observations. Among the areas of public policy to be discussed here are the expansion of schooling and eventual institution of compulsory attendance; regulation of child labor; reforms affecting society's most unfortunate children, the abandoned; and new methods of punishing juvenile miscreants separately from adult criminals. The place of children's literature and toys in private life also is noted.

Historians of education have contributed much to the study of nineteenth-century childhood. Indeed, in 1979 Maurice Crubellier observed in his survey of French childhood and youth since 1800 that the only well-developed part of the field was the history of education.[24] A decade later Crubellier's comment remains valid, although historians of education have become sensitive to his contention that families and peers often have had more impact on children than formal schooling.

The eighteenth century's educational legacy was one of *petites écoles* (primary schools) for children of the people and secondary schools (*collèges*) for the more privileged. Roger Chartier, Marie-Madeleine Compère, and Dominique Julia, however, argue in a revisionist volume that Old Regime *collèges* were less elitist than previously believed because they found in a sampling of students' social origins that one-fifth came from prosperous peasant families and one-third from artisanal backgrounds.[25] Nonetheless, the basic social division between primary schools for the masses and secondary schools largely for elites remained prominent in French schooling until after World War II.[26] Napoleon I's government laid the foundations of a rigorous public secondary system, the nationally funded *lycées*, but left primary schooling largely in the hands of religious authorities. More primary schools did open during the Restoration of the Bourbon Monarchy (1814–1830), but the Guizot Law of 1833, the initiative of King Louis Philippe's education minister, is typically considered the "charter" of primary education. Under the Orleanist July Monarchy (1830–1848) the number of boys attending primary school rose from an official figure of 1,372,206 in 1829 to 2,176,079 in 1847, but girls' enrollment in 1847 (1,354,056) was still less than boys' enrollment in 1829. By the end of Napoleon III's Second Empire (1852–1870) most French children received some formal schooling, although, as Jean-Noël Luc has demonstrated, official statistics typically exaggerated attendance. Even when revised downward, enrollment statistics do support the contention of Furet and Ozouf and also Raymond Grew and Patrick Harrigan that popular demand for schooling and local funding for it preceded the national government's willingness to spend money to guarantee it to all citizens.[27] Only in 1881–1882 did education minister Jules Ferry and the Third Republic (1870–1940) make schooling compulsory for children aged six to thirteen and also direct that in public schools, education would be free and, in content, secular.

What prompted public authorities to spend more on education? Both Marxists and non-Marxists have suggested that the industrial bourgeoisie prompted state action to ensure a minimally educated work force for the new factories of the Industrial Revolution. Furet and Ozouf, however, show that in part of the highly industrialized Northeast, literacy levels actually dropped during the early decades of industrialization. A complementary and more satisfactory explanation stresses the shared interests of the state, social elites, and employers in using schools to inculcate disciplined habits and respect for existing authorities, especially after the Revolutions of 1830 and 1848.[28] Just as Ariès regretted the absolute monarchy's assault on individual autonomy, so Michel Foucault and disciples such as Jacques Donzelot see the nineteenth-century expansion of schools, prisons, and hospitals as an encroachment by new professional "experts" on individual freedoms.[29] Certainly the utility of schools for social control was recognized by François Guizot, minister for a government under which only 2.5 percent of adult males could vote, for in 1833 he termed primary schools a major support for "order and social stability."[30] A half century later the democratic Third Republic determined that its dependence on universal manhood suffrage required a literate electorate whose labors also would help the nation recover from the trauma of losing the Franco-Prussian War in 1871. Recognition of the citizenry's political clout and essential labor was combined with a program of primary instruction that stressed not only hard work, thrift, and devotion to duty, but also respect for authority, be it parental, pedagogical, or governmental. Education minister Ferry believed that a democracy's primary schools should provide some opportunity for social advancement, but he also expected that most pupils would become "workers" or farmers.[31] In short, the programs for nineteenth-century primary schools reveal as much about various regimes' wishes to mold children for their own political ends as about concern for children's welfare.

The mandating of compulsory school attendance until age thirteen also added a new rite of passage from childhood to adolescence and, for most youth, work. Indeed, the preparation of better primary pupils for the Republic's certificate of primary studies came to rival the Church's concomitant preparation of the young for the first communion. Most employers preferred that both the school's and the church's rites be completed before hiring a young worker. In traditional areas the first communion, the celebration of which peaked in popularity during the nineteenth century, often was also accompanied by a change in dress, as boys put on long pants and girls covered their hair with a bonnet.[32]

What did children actually learn in schools? Studies of textbooks and test questions supply a partial answer. Analyzing the content of the best-selling primary textbook of the Third Republic, G. Bruno's *Tour de la France par deux enfants* (1877), Aimé Dupuy and later Dominique Maingueneau found in the tale of two orphaned boys, who traveled through all French regions and encountered most types of workplaces, many exhortations to devotion to duty, even in the face of adversity. The younger boy, Julien, was a model student who learned all that he could in "the very best school," but at age thirteen this bright boy became a farmer. His older brother was already a locksmith. Thus male role models for primary school children typically encouraged contentment with humble lives rather than anticipation of American-style Horatio Alger stories of amassing fortunes.[33]

Textbooks helped to perpetuate not only social class divisions, but also familiar assumptions about gender roles. Awareness of this important point is relatively recent among educational historians, partly because of French historians' overriding concern with the relation between schooling and social mobility (or the lack thereof) for males. Indeed, Antoine Prost assumed in 1968, in the still standard survey of modern French educational history, that the Third Republic's primary schools for "children of the people" did not mirror the concern about gender roles evident in the secondary curriculum for middle-class girls. Prost's assumption has been challenged by two recent books, Laura Strumingher's *What Are Little Girls and Boys Made Of?*, largely an analysis of two textbooks from the Second Empire, and Linda L. Clark's *Schooling the Daughters of Marianne: Textbooks and the Socialization of Girls in Modern French Primary Schools.* Clark's review of nearly 200 Third Republic textbooks and a lesser number from later periods shows a preponderance of female role models whose lives were centered in the home and whose chief personality traits were sweetness and gentleness, self-abnegation and devotion to other family members' welfare, and uncomplaining acceptance of adversity. The nation's future housewives also were instructed to urge men to accept the existing social and political order and were warned that if men strayed too often from the home to the cafe, it was probably because of wives' bad personalities and deficient housekeeping skills. Textbooks reflected the social reality that most girls walked to school alone or with siblings, while bourgeois girls, going to a different school, were accompanied in public by a maid.[34] If girls worked before marriage, they, like their brothers, were led to anticipate humble occupations. Not surprisingly, then, a survey in 1877 of the occupational expectations of thirteen-year-old Parisian girls about to leave primary school revealed that a majority expected to become seamstresses; many also said that they had accepted their mothers' advice about a job.[35]

The rigidity of female role models notwithstanding, the Third Republic did make important contributions to female education. More primary schools became available to girls, and the first true public secondary schools for girls were created after 1880. The girls' *lycées*, along with more than sixty new departmental normal schools to train primary teachers, significantly expanded professional opportunities for young Frenchwomen. As Françoise Mayeur's standard history of girls' secondary schools demonstrates, the curriculum of the girls' *lycées* was not identical to that for boys because republicans initially assumed that girls' secondary schools would simply train the wives of France's elites.[36] Only in 1924 was the girls' *lycée* curriculum changed so that adolescent girls would have the same opportunities as boys to prepare for the secondary school diploma, the *baccalauréat*, that was required for university study. Only a small minority of male or female adolescents went to secondary schools, and it was not until the 1930s, in the wake of a post-World War I push to "democratize" French public education, that any significant increase occurred in the number of male secondary school students.[37]

Child Labor

Alongside the expansion of schooling and requirement of compulsory attendance is the history of children's labor and new laws to control that labor. A major recent study, Colin Heywood's *Childhood in Nineteenth-Century France: Work, Health and Education Among the "Classes Populaires,"* attempts to modify assumptions that nineteenth-century industrialization had a typically negative impact on children who worked in factories. Not only Ariès but also Olwen Hufton, in *The Poor of Eighteenth-Century France*, had emphasized that, traditionally, by age six or seven most rural and urban children worked to contribute to the family economy. Heywood concedes that the long and structured factory workday intensified some children's labor, but he cautions against exaggerating the contrast between factory labor and agricultural labor. Eugen Weber's study of the primitiveness and rigor of rural life in late-nineteenth-century France confirms that point, as does the fact that young men from certain rural areas were more often rejected for military service than young men from cities. Nonetheless, by the 1830s reformers from the upper classes were voicing concern about children working in factories, and in 1841 the normally laissez-faire regime of Louis Philippe passed the first law to regulate child labor, a measure that was also the first important legislative intervention in the workplace since the Revolution had abolished guilds in 1791. Although unevenly enforced by unpaid inspectors from business backgrounds, the law limited the work of children aged eight to twelve to eight hours a day, and to twelve hours a day for ages twelve to sixteen.[38]

A major concern of Heywood is analyzing factors other than regulatory legislation that ultimately contributed to the decline of child labor. Heywood argues that the cheapness of child labor, which attracted some employers, was offset by children's physical weakness and lack of special skills. The need for skilled and strong adult workers, governmental regulation, and the expansion of schooling thus led to an important drop in child labor during the second half of the nineteenth century. Whereas one-third to one-half of children aged ten to fourteen were in the work force in 1851, one-fifth were so engaged in 1896. By the latter date an 1874 law had improved enforcement of limits on age and working hours through the creation of a paid inspectorate, the age for compulsory schooling had been set at thirteen, and another factory law of 1892 had raised the minimum working age to thirteen. Legislation in 1900 placed a ten-hour limit on the working day of youth under eighteen and women. Nonetheless, one study of family incomes notes that the contribution of children's wages to family income actually rose from 10 percent in 1907 to 18.5 percent in 1914.[39]

The impact of the Industrial Revolution on the working class family and that family's treatment of its young is another theme in Heywood's book. Although the image of families torn asunder by long hours of factory labor was long promoted by reformers, both Marxist and non-Marxist, Heywood suggests that the Industrial Revolution often helped to keep families together by enabling several family members to work for one firm or within one town. Social historian Michelle Perrot also has called for replacing the negative picture of nineteenth-century working-class families with a more nuanced one.[40] Similarly, Lenard Berlanstein challenges the argument that the working-class family did not (and could not) emulate the middle classes' concern for children's welfare until the end of the nineteenth century. In a study of mid-century Parisian orphan boys Berlanstein shows that many of these boys were well cared for by foster families (and particularly by women), and he concludes that if orphans received such care, so, too, did other working-class children. Doubting that poor material living conditions automatically dictated a lack of affection within families, Berlanstein cites the enduring importance of preindustrial artisanal and communal traditions for Paris workers, and sees these checking the development of a highly demoralized proletariat. Yet he concedes in a longer study, *The Working People of Paris*, that the evidence concerning the quality of working-class family life is, at best, "ambiguous," and that the quality of working-class life was probably more often determined by economic deprivation and the requirement of disciplined work habits than by affection.[41]

Whatever the stability or instability of working-class families, social elites feared that working-class children were not learning proper habits and values from their families or from apprenticeships, now in decline, and so decided to found *patronages* to help working-class youth. The first *patronages* for boys were founded by Catholic laymen and clerics early in the nineteenth century, and similar organizations for girls existed by mid-century. Some *patronages* were organized for adolescent workers in specific industries, such as those for Parisian cabinetmakers, studied by Lee Shai Weissbach, or for artificial flower–makers, studied by Marilyn Boxer. In 1885, during the battle over the secularization of schools touched off by the Ferry Laws, the first secular *patronages* linked to the public schools were founded. As of 1913, nearly 3,000 secular *patronages* competed with more than 4,300 of the Catholic variety.[42]

Juvenile Delinquency

The July Monarchy, which provided important legislative landmarks for education and for regulation of child labor, also identified the problem of juvenile delinquency. As Patricia O'Brien observed, after each French Revolution—1789, 1830, 1848, 1871—guardians of public order took new interest in prisons and penal reform, and after 1830 concern about younger offenders mounted. Public officials and humanitarian reformers joined to insist that when minors under age sixteen were sentenced to a period of confinement, they ought to be physically separated from adults, just as female offenders should be separated from males. With the creation of juvenile sections of prisons, work farms (*colonies agricoles*), and other correctional houses, another phase of what Michelle Perrot terms the nineteenth-century "segregation of childhood" took place. By 1853 half of all institutionalized minors were in agricultural colonies, then usually under private direction, for rural labor was believed to be especially effective for rehabilitation. The century's peak in the number of minors brought to trial was reached in 1854, when 11,026 such cases were heard. In Paris at mid-century about 2 to 3 percent of all boys had some difficulty with the law each year. The number of minors in jail rose from 6,600 in 1852 to 9,900 in 1875 before starting to drop significantly during the 1880s. Four out of five young prisoners were male, usually jailed for theft.[43]

Under Napoleon I, fathers had regained the right to have children confined for "correction" for limited terms, and, concluded Bernard Schnapper, the French made more use of paternal correction than any other European power except Sardinia during the nineteenth century. Although those confined because of parental requests constituted only 2 percent of all juvenile prisoners in 1881, about 75 percent of them were females, usually confined by parents because of precocious sexual activity.[44]

The system for correcting juvenile offenders underwent important legal and structural modifications during the Third Republic. After 1875 the education of incarcerated youth became more systematic, and the state assumed a greater role in administering institutions for rehabilitation, thereby removing them from clerical control. As in England, opinion in France on the causes of juvenile delinquency also shifted during the century from explanations stressing evil and

poverty to those emphasizing psychological factors, including differences between adolescent and adult personalities. In 1906 the age of minority for correctional purposes was raised from sixteen to eighteen, and in 1912 separate
tribunals for juveniles and a new probationary system were put into place.[45]

Child Welfare Policies

Alongside the Third Republic's educational efforts for children and adolescents, including delinquents, were some significant measures to improve the care
of infants. Official statistics had long demonstrated that infants sent to wet nurses
were at least twice as likely to die as those breast-fed by their mothers. Lowering
the high infant mortality rate seemed more essential after the loss of the Franco-
Prussian War in 1871 because French leaders noted that the new Prussian-led
German Empire was far more populous than France. Thus dramatizing the issue
of "depopulation," the result of France's birthrate dropping sooner than that of
other European countries, was combined with efforts to save more of those born.
The Roussel Law of 1874 imposed important new controls on the wet-nursing
business by expanding governmental supervision of the wet nurses hired by
parents—either working mothers unable to care for infants or middle-class families unwilling to do so—and by public authorities responsible for orphans and
the abandoned. A scientific development, the pasteurization of milk, contributed
after the 1870s to the gradual demise of the wet-nursing business. In 1894 the
state stopped sending abandoned babies to wet nurses because bottle-feeding
permitted their care in foundling homes. As George Sussman notes, the cultural
acceptability of wet nursing, especially in urban areas, meant that whereas 10
percent of all French babies were placed with wet nurses between 1874 and
1914, at least 26 percent of babies born in the department of the Seine were so
placed, as were 15 percent of Seine infants between 1919 and 1928. Ultimately,
Sussman argues, the rising cost of hiring wet nurses prompted most families to
abandon the practice. Also significant for the demise of wet nursing was a
growing body of medical literature on *puériculture* and the influence of a new
generation of physicians specializing in pediatrics. Similar influences contributed
to the state's creation of maternity leaves for teachers and other government
employees and to the generalization of such leaves through a law of 1913.[46]

Another perspective on Third Republic reforms affecting children is provided
by Rachel G. Fuchs' important study of public policies toward abandoned children. A Napoleonic decree of 1811 had required all foundling hospitals to have
a *tour*, a combination of a revolving door and a container, where an infant might
be left. The *tour*'s defenders called it a humanitarian alternative to infanticide,
but critics argued that it promoted child abandonment. Around 1830 abandonment
peaked at about 5 percent of all births, and during the 1850s and 1860s *tours*
were removed to discourage abandonment. In the meantime the state had begun
sending abandoned children who survived with wet nurses to foster families
whom the state supervised until the abandoned were twelve or, after 1852,

twenty-one. The use of foster care rather than orphanages made French policy unique. After 1871 governmental concern about lowering infant mortality led to more policies to encourage mothers, wed and unwed, to keep their babies. From her study of the abandoned and their mothers Fuchs concludes that abandonment represented less a sign of widespread maternal indifference to children than a demonstration that economic necessity forced many poor, young, and unwed mothers to choose abandonment so that their babies might have a chance to survive. Changes in official and private philanthropic policies helped to revise the image of the unwed mother and her child from sinners and deviants to victims and also offered more material aid. In turn, fewer unwed mothers resorted to abandonment. Improvements in state supervision of those abandoned, combined with pasteurization, meant that by the 1890s, the mortality rate of abandoned infants was only slightly higher than that for other infants.[47]

Fuchs' conclusion that the Third Republic's treatment of abandoned children demonstrated that society now cared more about children is repeated in a related study of official policies toward child abuse. Before the 1880s only abortion and infanticide were recognized as child abuse. Infanticide was more often a rural than an urban phenomenon, whereas abortion was more typically resorted to by urban women.[48] Prosecutions for infanticide peaked around 1860, whereas prosecutions for abortion rose noticeably after 1900; in both instances prosecutors had difficulty obtaining convictions. The expansion of the definition of child abuse to include physical and emotional cruelty as well as parental drunkenness and debauchery was reflected in laws in 1889 and 1898 that enabled the state to take over the care of children judged to be "morally abandoned."[49]

Toys and Children's Literature

In addition to the many recent studies of public policies affecting childhood, research on the history of toys and children's literature has found evidence for more affection and concern for children. The Second Empire—the moment when parents increasingly used the familiar pronoun *tu* instead of the more formal *vous* when addressing children—also is an important chronological benchmark for great expansion in toy manufacturing and publishing children's literature other than textbooks.[50] The economic prosperity of the 1860s and a greater propensity to indulge children with gifts provided toy manufacturers and publishers with a market. Although much remains to be learned about the history of toys, some interesting points about the history of dolls indicate how such objects reveal changes in cultural values. Rousseau's reference to Sophie's doll in *Émile* treats it as something to interest little girls in adult fashion and flirtation, a not surprising observation when the typical doll looked like a woman. By the 1830s the *Journal des enfants* recognized the doll's instructional value and first printed patterns for doll clothes to interest girls in sewing. After 1850, according to Robert Capia, dolls more often resembled little girls or infants.[51] As nineteenth-century elites increasingly embraced a "domestic ideology" for women, it is not surprising that girls' toys, like textbooks, emphasized women's anticipated maternal roles. For boys, miniature trains became available in 1832, and both sexes could enjoy stuffed animals after the 1870s. New toys added pleasure to childhood, but Crubellier notes negatively that mere possession of a number of toys became a status symbol for children. Furthermore, many poor parents could not afford to buy toys. As late as 1910 to 1920 in rural Brittany, for example, few children received manufactured toys.[52]

Like dolls, children's literature of the 1860s was intended to educate as well as entertain. Although fairy tales for children dated from Perrault's seventeenth-century classics, Crubellier sees in children's books of the mid-nineteenth century another sign of greater separation of children from adults. In a critical assessment Isabelle Jan sees this literature largely as a product for integrating children into bourgeois society and, as such, one reason for the judgment that French children may still be more regimented than those in other developed countries. Esther Kanipe's treatment of Hetzel, one of the first major publishers of children's literature, similarly notes the centrality of middle-class characters. Kanipe agrees that this literature confirms children's important role in the family, but she also notes much emphasis on discipline, a sign of Hetzel's worry that women might spoil children.[53]

As children's books became more common, so did depictions of children in books written for adults. Over time, concluded both Catholic educator Jean Calvet in 1930 and sociologist Marie-José Chombart de Lauwe in 1971, these representations have moved away from the image of the child as a small adult (*un homme commencé*) to one showing the child as a being immersed in his or her own imaginative world. Calvet attributed this to psychologists' and educators' better understanding of children, whereas Chombart de Lauwe saw it as a wish to flee the Industrial Revolution. Whereas Rousseau treated childhood as a time of goodness and innocence, authors of the past century avoid the characterization of "good" or "bad" and stress instead what is different about childhood.[54]

The picture of nineteenth-century childhood that emerges from recent studies is one that reveals not only improvements in the treatment of children, but also, as Theodore Zeldin noted, ambiguity. Zeldin cites, in particular, the coexistence of new concern about children's welfare with an often unpleasant sternness. Concerning infancy, Perrot points to both the massive child abandonment and employment of wet nurses and the eventual improvement in methods of caring for babies. Progress was related, she believes, to the falling birthrate, which helped to make each child seem more important. Authors typically agree that life had improved for middle-class and upper-class children, but, as R. Lalou observes, the continuation of child labor, juvenile prostitution, and infanticide indicates that much was not yet modern for working-class children.[55]

FROM 1919 TO THE PRESENT

After 1919 interest in French children's welfare remained high among policymakers, for dismay about the loss of life in World War I and the continuing low birthrate intensified prewar concerns about depopulation. The legislature sought new incentives to maternity with a law of October 1919 providing special payments to some nursing mothers and free milk to others and with the creation in May 1920 of motherhood medals for married women with at least five children. A law of July 1920 forbade advertising contraceptives and stiffened the penalties for abortion. More emphasis on citizens' duty to have children appeared in schoolbooks, Clark notes, and instruction on infant care became required for primary school girls. Employers of large numbers of women workers were enjoined to enable them to nurse their infants during the workday, either at on-site *crèches* or through longer breaks. The paying of special allowances for children was begun by private employers and later taken up by the state, initially for public employees. The natalist propaganda notwithstanding, the French birth-rate in 1939, at the end of a decade of economic depression, was among the lowest in the world: 1.97 per married couple, as compared with 2.8 in 1900. Thus in 1939 the legislature enacted a Family Code that provided special allo-cations if mothers remained at home. After World War II family allowances were expanded substantially, and, as a result, could be as much as one-third of a working-class family's income.[56]

Also typical of the interwar period was the extension of the length of many children's economic and emotional dependence on parents beyond the age limits set for compulsory schooling or going to work. If the concept of adolescence was developed by late-nineteenth-century writers, its generalization occurred during the 1920s, as Zeldin notes in his comments on the "cult of the adoles-cent." In 1936 the socialist-led Popular Front government raised the compulsory schooling age from thirteen to fourteen. In the background, states John Talbott, was a reform movement, led by schoolteachers and political allies, that had publicized the school system's role in perpetuating social inequalities and de-manded the creation of a single public school system (*école unique*) and op-portunities for more children to remain in school after age fourteen. The goal of the *école unique* was to end barriers traditionally making it difficult for bright primary pupils to enter the secondary system of *lycées* and *collèges*, which had their own fee-paying elementary classes. At the end of the 1930s the primary system still had a separate group of "complementary courses" and "higher primary schools," which served the same age-group as the secondary schools, and also a network of departmental normal schools separate from the universities. The abolition of fees for public secondary schools during the late 1920s and early 1930s helped to expand secondary enrollments, but massive growth in secondary schooling did not occur until after 1950.[57]

Other signs of the prolongation of childhood and separate treatment of ado-lescence were the ending in 1935 of criminal penalties for minors guilty of vagrancy or prostitution and of fathers' rights to institutionalize minors for cor-rection, a practice already largely abandoned.[58] At a time when many ideologies fiercely competed for constituencies, an unprecedented number of organizations specifically for older children and youth were launched or expanded. These included scouting—which Protestants started in 1911 and Catholics emulated in 1920—religious associations, and political groupings.[59] In the meantime school textbooks' presentation of children's place in the family also had changed. Although the traditional emphasis on duties to parents remained, authors such as Léon Emery told pupils of the 1930s that the family had been democratized because the father could no longer legally behave like "an absolute monarch" toward his spouse and children.[60]

Since World War II major changes in educational policy made by the Fourth Republic (1944–1958) and the Fifth Republic (1958–) have continued to affect children's lives. The postwar economic recovery and eventual prosperity prompted more parents to demand secondary schools for their offspring, who were now more numerous because of the postwar baby boom. Between 1947 and 1968 secondary enrollments nearly quadrupled, and university enrollments soared by nearly 500 percent. In 1959 the compulsory schooling age was raised to sixteen for children entering primary school in that year, a measure that guaranteed further growth at the secondary level. Larger secondary enrollments in the 1950s and 1960s produced more diversity in the social origins of secondary pupils than previously. Nonetheless, social critics and such historians of education as Antoine Prost still see the public school system as perpetuating class divisions. Indeed, statistical data have shown that during the primary school years (reduced by the Fifth Republic from ages six to fourteen to ages six to eleven), far more children from working-class families had to repeat a primary grade than children of the upper and middle classes. In addition to dramatically increasing enrollments, the Fifth Republic during the 1960s and early 1970s produced another kind of "educational revolution," albeit one little noticed: the adoption of coeducation to replace the traditional separation of the sexes in primary and secondary schools.[61]

Since the late 1940s many parents have clearly perceived an important link between extended schooling and children's professional and economic futures. Indeed, that realization and families' desire to provide more for children are typically cited to explain the increase since the 1950s in married women's participation in the work force. Some critics, however, see families' rising valuation of schooling between 1950 and 1970 as a sign that parents want more time for themselves and so expect schools to take care of some educational functions previously assumed by parents.[62]

The problem with singling out only one reason for growing public respect for schools becomes apparent when the post–1945 history of rising enrollments in the écoles maternelles (nursery schools) is explained. Founded by the July Monarchy to provide care for poor children whose mothers worked, these schools continued during the Third Republic to be viewed primarily as places for the less socially fortunate. Since World War II, however, their enrollments have soared for at least two reasons: a recognition by all social classes that écoles *maternelles* provide excellent early childhood education, and a growth in married women's employment. In 1982 nearly all four-year-olds, 90 percent of three-year-olds, and a third of two-year-olds attended *écoles maternelles*.[63]

In contrast to French commentary from fifty to a hundred years ago that announced a new, happier era for children, some contemporary observers note signs of decline in the quality of children's experiences. This negative perspective cites perceived changes in parental attitudes and actions, changing social values, and a breakdown of authority within schools. Thus F. Lebrun notes, for example, that adults who previously advocated birth control as a way to allow more care for individual children now value it as a way to avoid the emotional and economic burdens of parenting. Before his death Ariès also was criticizing parental selfishness. Chombart de Lauwe observed in 1971 that literary depictions of the relationship between children and adults showed an increasing tendency for each group to become more critical of the other. A recent volume on French private life also views with alarm a near tripling of the divorce rate between 1960 and 1980.[64]

In 1980 Yvonne Knibiehler and Catherine Fouquet concluded their history of motherhood by observing that society, after exalting motherhood between the late eighteenth and mid-twentieth centuries, had now placed maternity "in question." French women, like American women, had reacted to the postwar baby boom and emphasis on "la mère au foyer" (the mother at home) by entering the work force and recognizing that ideas about the "maternal instinct," often cited to discourage mothers from working, were in fact societal constructions open to challenge. A new climate of opinion concerning the rights of women and individuals had resulted in the removal in 1967 of prohibitions against advertising contraceptives and in the legalization of abortion in 1975. In turn, the birthrate fell from a baby boom level of 2.9 per married couple in 1964 to 1.8 twenty years later.[65]

To Edward Shorter, a North American historian, such trends as rising divorce rates, women's work, and conflict between generations represented the arrival in France, as elsewhere, of the "postmodern family," a not unwelcome development, since, in his view, the modern nuclear family of the nineteenth century often stifled individual development. A revealing sign of families' growing tolerance for individual choices appears in the differing results of polls in 1938 and 1977, each asking whether parents ought to select children's careers: whereas 30 percent replied affirmatively in 1938, only 4.4 percent did so in 1977. Many French historians, such as Crubellier, however, speak of "crisis" within the family and are alarmed by generational conflict. Crubellier opines that the influence of parents and schools on youth has been surpassed by that of peers whose values often represent a "barbarian culture" derived from the ubiquitous mass media. Prost also cites peer and media influences as important reasons for the lack of motivation encountered in secondary and university students in the early 1980s. Nonetheless, Prost's chronicling of the education system's reduced influence since the 1960s is accompanied by a provocative comparative statement about the way that French and American schools may affect students' ability to think independently. Prost believes that American education appears to be liberal and open to change but is in fact more moralistic than French education, which seems to produce conformity but actually encourages more truly independent judgment.[66]

A picture of often troubled youth also emerges in Gérard Vincent's recent essay on French private life. Vincent notes the seriousness of teenage drug problems and the impact of peers on drug usage, but he tries for balance in a discussion of parent-child relations. Whatever the tensions between generations, a poll in 1983 showed a substantial majority of teenagers (75 percent) affirming the importance of respecting parents, with 80 percent also indicating that they were close to their mothers and 72 percent, to their fathers. The indications of closeness to the father may well reflect the results of more paternal participation in child rearing since the early 1970s, for in an earlier, 1975 poll 45 percent of children had stated that they felt closer to their mothers than to their fathers (to whom only 10 percent felt closer) and 48 percent actually expressed fear of their fathers (as compared with only 13 percent fearing their mothers). What today's children do reject is the longstanding parental tendency to use public ridicule to control their behavior. In the early 1950s Laurence Wylie had seen this as the method of control that French parents preferred to spanking. A poll in 1989 of 60,000 students aged ten to thirteen revealed, however, that 78 percent of them believed that parental spanking could be justified, but 94 percent disapproved of adults reprimanding them with public sarcasm.[67]

These polls, which say something about children's reactions to family life, also can serve to point out the largest single neglected area in existing histories of French childhood: the analysis of what children themselves experienced. Nothing comparable to Pollock's use of published autobiographies and memoirs or unpublished private papers to reconstruct English childhood before 1900 exists for France. Nonetheless, various studies suggest possibilities for undertaking such a project. Already in 1930 Calvet highlighted Romantic authors' treatment of their own childhoods as evidence of new societal interest in childhood. Recent works on the history of servants, Parisian working people, and education also contain references to memoirs that mention childhood.[68] The memoirs of working-class activist Jeanne Bouvier have been much cited to exemplify the place of work in nineteenth-century childhood and stern parental expectations concerning children's performance as workers. The journal of Caroline Brame has shed light on the childhood of nineteenth-century middle-class girls.[69] More also can be done with private papers already housed in libraries and archives and with papers still in private hands. In the meantime many studies of French public policies that affected children amply demonstrate that adults have been much preoccupied with their welfare during the past two centuries.

NOTES

1. Philippe Ariès, *Centuries of Childhood: A Social History of Family Life*, trans. Robert Baldick (New York: Alfred A. Knopf, 1962).

2. Geneviève Delaisi de Parseval and Suzanne Lallemand, *L'Art d'accommoder les bébés, 100 ans de recettes françaises de puériculture* (Paris: Editions du Seuil, 1980).

3. Urban T. Holmes, "Medieval Children," *Journal of Social History* 2 (1968):164–172.

4. Adrian Wilson, "The Infancy of the History of Childhood: An Appraisal of Philippe Ariès," *History and Theory* 19 (1980):132–153.

5. David Hunt, *Parents and Children in History: The Psychology of Family Life in Early Modern France* (New York: Harper Torchbooks, 1972). Hunt's assumption that Louis XIII's childhood was typical of the seventeenth century is criticized in Elisabeth Wirth Marvick, "The Character of Louis XIII: The Role of His Physician," *Journal of Interdisciplinary History* 4 (Winter 1974):347–374.

6. Linda A. Pollock, *Forgotten Children: Parent-Child Relations from 1500 to 1900* (Cambridge: Cambridge University Press, 1983).

7. Jean-Louis Flandrin, *Families in Former Times: Kinship, Household and Sexuality*, trans. Richard Southern (Cambridge: Cambridge University Press, 1979), p. 53.

8. Jean-Pierre Bardet and Jacques Dupâquier, "Contraception: les français les premiers, mais pourquoi?" *Communications* 44 (1986):3–6.

9. Ibid., pp. 14–15; S. Ryan Johansson, "Centuries of Childhood/Centuries of Parenting: Philippe Ariès and the Modernization of Privileged Infancy," *Journal of Family History* 12 (1987):355–362.

10. Robert Wheaton, "Introduction: Recent Trends in the Historical Study of the French Family," in *Family and Sexuality in French History*, ed. Robert Wheaton and Tamara K. Hareven (Philadelphia: University of Pennsylvania Press, 1980), pp. 6–9; Flandrin, *Families*, pp. 4–10; James F. Traer, *Marriage and the Family in Eighteenth-Century France* (Ithaca, N.Y.: Cornell University Press, 1980), pp. 17–18.

11. Sarah Hanley, "Family and State in Early Modern France: The Marriage Pact," in *Connecting Spheres: Women in the Western World, 1500 to the Present*, ed. Marilyn J. Boxer and Jean H. Quataert (New York: Oxford University Press, 1987), pp. 53–63.

12. Bardet and Dupâquier, "Contraception," p. 30; Flandrin, *Families*.

13. Jean Delumeau, "Présentation," in *La première communion, quatre siècles d'histoire*, ed. Jean Delumeau (Paris: Desclée de Brouwer, 1987), pp. 7–13; Natalie Zemon Davis, *Society and Culture in Early Modern France* (Stanford, Calif.: Stanford University Press), pp. 107–108.

14. Maryvonne Goubet-Mahé, "Le premier rituel de la première communion XVIᵉ-XVIIᵉ siècle," and Odile Robert, "Fonctionnement et enjeu d'une institution chrétienne au XVIIIᵉ siècle," in Delmuneau, ed., *La première communion*, pp. 52–67, 104–109.

15. Roger Chartier, Marie-Madeleine Compère, and Dominique Julia, *L'Education en France du XVIᵉ au XVIIIᵉ siècle* (Paris: Société d'édition d'enseignement supérieur, 1976), p. 3; François Furet and Jacques Ozouf, *Lire et écrire, l'alphabétisation des français de Calvin à Jules Ferry*, 2 vols. (Paris: Editions de Minuit, 1977), 1:72–73.

16. Furet and Ozouf, *Lire*, pp. 176–245; Jean Perrel, "Les Ecoles de Filles dans la France de l'ancien régime," in *The Making of Frenchmen: Current Directions in the History of Education in France, 1679–1979*, ed. Donald N. Baker and Patrick J. Harrigan (Waterloo, Ontario: Historical Reflections Press, 1980), pp. 75–83.

17. Harvey Chisick, *The Limits of Reform in the Enlightenment* (Princeton, N.J.: Princeton University Press, 1981); Barbara Corrado Pope, "The Influence of Rousseau's Ideology of Domesticity," in Boxer and Quataert, eds., *Connecting Spheres*, pp. 136–145; Jean-Noël Luc, " 'A trois ans, l'enfant devient interessant': la découverte médicale

de la seconde enfance (1750–1900)," *Revue d'histoire moderne et contemporaine* 36 (January-March 1989):83–112.

18. Maurice Crubellier, *L'Enfance et la jeunesse dans la société française, 1800–1950* (Paris: Armand Colin, 1979), p. 39; George D. Sussman, *Selling Mothers' Milk: The Wet-Nursing Business in France, 1715–1914* (Urbana: University of Illinois Press, 1982), p. 93; Cissie Fairchilds, *Domestic Enemies: Servants and Their Masters in Old Regime France* (Baltimore: Johns Hopkins University Press, 1984), p. 215.

19. Fairchilds, *Domestic Enemies*, pp. 193–228.

20. Traer, *Marriage and the Family*, pp. 137–190.

21. Emmet Kennedy and Marie-Laurence Netter, "Ecoles primaires sous le directoire," *Annales historiques de la révolution française* 53 (1981):3–38.

22. Margaret Darrow, "French Noblewomen and the New Domesticity, 1750–1850," *Feminist Studies* 5 (Spring 1979):41–65; Barbara Corrado Pope, "Maternal Education in France, 1815–1848," *Proceedings of the Western Society for French History* 3 (1976):368–377; Marie-Françoise Lévy, *De Mères en filles, l'éducation des françaises, 1850–1880* (Paris: Calmann-Lévy, 1984).

23. Ernest Legouvé, *Les Pères et les enfants au XIXe siècle, enfance et adolescence* (Paris: J. Hetzel, 1867), pp. 1–8; Comte François de Nion, "Le Siècle des enfants," *Fémina* 1 (February 1901):11.

24. Crubellier, *L'Enfance*, pp. 5–8.

25. Chartier, Compère, and Julia, *L'Education*.

26. Antoine Prost, *Histoire de l'enseignement en France, 1800–1967* (Paris: Armand Colin, 1968).

27. Linda L. Clark, *Schooling the Daughters of Marianne: Textbooks and the Socialization of Girls in Modern French Primary Schools* (Albany: State University of New York Press, 1984), pp. 8–11; Jean-Noël Luc, *La Statistique de l'enseignement primaire* (Paris: Economica, 1985); Furet and Ozouf, *Lire*; R. Grew, P. J. Harrigan, and J. B. Whitney, "La Scolarisation en France, 1829–1906," *Annales: Economies, sociétés, civilisations* 39 (January 1984):116–157.

28. R. D. Anderson, *Education in France, 1848–1870* (Oxford: Oxford University Press, 1975); Pierre Bourdieu and Jean-Claude Passeron, *Reproduction in Education, Society, and Culture*, trans. Richard Nice (Beverly Hills, Calif.: Sage, 1977); Furet and Ozouf, *Lire*; Françoise Mayeur, *De la Révolution à l'école républicaine (1789–1930)*, vol. 3 of *Histoire générale de l'enseignement et de l'éducation en France*, 4 vols., ed. Louis-Henry Parias (Paris: Nouvelle Librairie de France, 1981), p. 314.

29. Jacques Donzelot, *The Policing of Families*, trans. Robert Hurley (New York: Random House, 1979), pp. 48–95.

30. Mayeur, *De la Révolution*, p. 314.

31. "Jules Ferry" and "Morale et instruction civique," in *Nouveau dictionnaire de pédagogie*, 2 vols, ed. Ferdinand Buisson (Paris: Hachette, 1911), 1:613–615, 2:1352–1355; Prost, *Histoire*.

32. J. Mellot, "Rite de passage et fête familiale, rapprochements," and Delumeau, "Conclusion," in Delumeau, ed., *La première communion*, pp. 185–192, 313–314.

33. Aimé Dupuy, "Les Livres de lecture de G. Bruno," *Revue d'histoire économique et sociale* 31 (1953):128–151; Dominique Maingueneau, *Les Livres d'école de la république 1870–1914, discours et idéologie* (Paris: Le Sycomore, 1979); Clark, *Schooling*, p. 42.

34. Prost, *Histoire de l'enseignement*, p. 261; Laura S. Strumingher, *What Were Little*

Girls and Boys Made Of? Primary Education in Rural France, 1830–1880 (Albany: State University of New York Press, 1983); Clark, *Schooling*, pp. 20–80.

35. John W. Shaffer, "Family, Class, and Young Women's Occupational Expectations in Nineteenth-Century Paris," *Journal of Family History* 3 (1978):62–77.

36. Françoise Mayeur, *L'Enseignement secondaire des jeunes filles sous la troisième république* (Paris: Presses de la fondation nationale des sciences politiques, 1977).

37. John E. Talbott, *The Politics of Educational Reform in France, 1918–1940* (Princeton, N.J.: Princeton University Press, 1969); Jean-Pierre Briand, Jean-Michel Chapoulie, and Henri Péretz, "Les Conditions institutionnelles de la scolarisation secondaire des garçons entre 1920 et 1940," *Revue d'histoire moderne et contemporaine* 26 (1979):391–421.

38. Colin Heywood, *Childhood in Nineteenth-Century France: Work, Health and Education Among the "Classes Populaires"* (Cambridge: Cambridge University Press, 1988); Olwen Hufton, *The Poor of Eighteenth-Century France, 1750–1789* (Oxford: Clarendon Press, 1974); Eugen Weber, *Peasants into Frenchmen: The Modernization of Rural France, 1870–1914* (Stanford, Calif.: Stanford University Press, 1976).

39. Heywood, *Childhood*, pp. 84, 100, 265; Louise A. Tilly and Joan W. Scott, *Women, Work, and Family* (New York: Holt, Rinehart, & Winston, 1978), p. 185.

40. Heywood, *Childhood*, p. 187; Michelle Perrot, "Sur la ségrégation de l'enfance au dix-neuvième siècle," *La Psychiatrie de l'enfant* 25 (1982):180.

41. Tilly and Scott, *Women*, p. 59; Crubellier, *L'Enfance*, p. 31; Lenard Berlanstein, "Growing Up as Workers in Nineteenth-Century Paris: The Case of the Orphans of the Prince Imperial," *French Historical Studies* 11 (Fall 1980):551–576, and *The Working People of Paris, 1871–1914* (Baltimore: Johns Hopkins University Press, 1984), pp. 137–140.

42. Pierre Pierrard, *Enfants et jeunes ouvriers en France (XIXe–XXe) siècles* (Paris: Editions ouvrières, 1987), pp. 190–203; Lee Shai Weissbach, "*Oeuvre Industrielle, Oeuvre Morale*: The *Sociétés de Patronage* of Nineteenth-Century France," *French Historical Studies* 15 (Spring 1987):99–120; Marilyn J. Boxer, "Women in Industrial Homework: The Flowermakers of Paris in the Belle Epoque," *French Historical Studies* 12 (Spring 1982):408–412.

43. Patricia O'Brien, *The Promise of Punishment: Prisons in Nineteenth-Century France* (Princeton, N.J.: Princeton University Press, 1982), pp. 18, 110–147; Henri Gaillac, *Les Maisons de correction* (Paris: Editions Cujas, 1971); Perrot, "Sur la ségrégation"; Lenard Berlanstein, "Vagrants, Beggars, and Thieves: Delinquent Boys in Mid-Nineteenth-Century Paris," *Journal of Social History* 12 (1979):534.

44. Bernard Schnapper, "La Correction paternelle et le mouvement des idées au dix-neuvième siècle (1789–1935)," *Revue historique* (1980):319–349; O'Brien, *Promise of Punishment*, p. 117.

45. O'Brien, *Promise of Punishment*, pp. 147, 191–203; Perrot, "Sur la segrégation," p. 203; Schnapper, "La Correction," pp. 341–346.

46. Rachel G. Fuchs, *Abandoned Children: Foundlings and Child Welfare in Nineteenth-Century France* (Albany: State University of New York Press, 1984), p. 232; Sussman, *Selling Mothers' Milk*, pp. 161–181; Luc Boltanski, *Prime éducation et morale de classe* (Paris: Mouton, 1977); Mary Lynn McDougall, "Protecting Infants: The French Campaign for Maternity Leaves, 1890s–1913," *French Historical Studies* 13 (1983):79–105.

47. Fuchs, *Abandoned Children*.

48. Jacques Dupâquier, "Combien d'avortements en France avant 1914?" and Richard Lalou, "L'Infanticide devant les tribunaux français (1825–1910)," *Communications* 44 (1986):87–106, 175–200.

49. Rachel G. Fuchs, "Crimes Against Children in Nineteenth-Century France: Child Abuse," *Law and Human Behavior* 6 (1983):237–259.

50. Crubellier, *L'Enfance*, pp. 337–376; Legouvé, *Les Pères*, p. 5.

51. Crubellier, *L'Enfance*, p. 340; Martine Sonnet, Review of Elisabeth Chauveau et al., *Bleuette et les poupées dans les périodiques enfantins en France de 1768 à 1960* (Courbevoie: Centre d'étude et de recherche sur la poupée, 1984), *Histoire de l'éducation* 29 (January 1986):131–132; Robert Capia, *Les Poupées françaises* (Paris: Hachette, 1979), pp. 39–40.

52. Crubellier, *L'Enfance*, p. 347; Mayeur, *De la Révolution*, p. 204.

53. Crubellier, *L'Enfance*, pp. 352–357; Isabelle Jan, "Children's Literature and Bourgeois Society in France Since 1860," and Esther Kanipe, "Hetzel and the Bibliothèque d'Education et de Récréation," *Yale French Studies* 43 (1969):57–72, 73–84.

54. J. Calvet, *L'Enfant dans la littérature française*, 2 vols. (Paris: F. Lanore, 1930), 2:203–218; Marie-José Chombart de Lauwe, *Un monde autre: l'enfance de ses représentations à son mythe* (Paris: Payot, 1971), pp. 148, 412.

55. Theodore Zeldin, *France 1848–1945*, 2 vols. (Oxford: Clarendon Press, 1973, 1977), 1:315; Perrot, "Sur la segrégation," pp. 183–184, 204; Lalou, "L'Infanticide," p. 178.

56. Clark, *Schooling*, p. 83; Bardet and Dupâquier, "Contraception," p. 6; Angus McLaren, *Sexuality and Social Order: The Debate over the Fertility of Women and Workers in France, 1870–1920* (New York: Holmes & Meier, 1983), p. 181; Jane Jenson, "Both Friend and Foe: Women and State Welfare," in *Becoming Visible: Women in European History*, 2nd ed., ed. Renate Bridenthal, Claudia Koonz, and Susan Stuard (Boston: Houghton Mifflin, 1987), p. 543.

57. Zeldin, *France*, 1:334; Talbott, *Politics*.

58. Fuchs, "Crimes," p. 255; Schnapper, "La Correction," p. 348.

59. Gérard Cholvy, ed., *Mouvements de jeunesse chrétiens et juifs, sociabilité dans un cadre européen, 1799–1968* (Paris: Editions du Cerf, 1985).

60. Clark, *Schooling*, p. 88.

61. Antoine Prost, *L'Ecole et la famille dans une société en mutation (1930–1980)*, vol. 4 of *Histoire générale de l'enseignement et de l'éducation en France*, 4 vols., ed. Louis-Henri Parias (Paris: Nouvelle Librairie de France, 1981), pp. 164, 231, 367, 509.

62. Ibid., p. 147; Tilly and Scott, *Women*, p. 219.

63. Clark, *Schooling*, p. 162; Prost, *L'Ecole*, p. 89.

64. François Lebrun, "La Place de l'enfant dans la société française depuis le XVIe siècle," *Communications* 44 (1986):256; Philippe Ariès, "Two Successive Motivations for a Declining Birth Rate in the West," *Population and Development Review* 6 (1980):645–650; Chombart de Lauwe, *Un monde autre*, pp. 207, 217, 412; Antoine Prost and Gérard Vincent, eds., *De la première guerre mondiale à nos jours*, vol. 5 of *Histoire de la vie privée*, 5 vols., ed. Philippe Ariès and Georges Duby (Paris: Editions du Seuil, 1987), p. 97.

65. Yvonne Knibiehler and Cathérine Fouquet, *L'Histoire des mères du moyen âge à nos jours* (Paris: Editions Montalba, 1980), pp. 336–374; Bardet and Dupâquier, "Contraception," p. 10.

66. Edward Shorter, *The Making of the Modern Family* (New York: Basic Books,

1975), pp. 269–280; Prost, *L'Ecole*, p. 615; Prost and Vincent, *De la première guerre in Histoire*, p. 79; Crubellier, *L'Enfance*, pp. 370, 380–383.

67. Prost and Vincent, *De la première guerre*, pp. 269–271; Prost, *L'Ecole*, p. 124; Laurence Wylie, *Village in the Vaucluse*, 3d ed. (Cambridge, Mass.: Harvard University Press, 1974); *Le Monde* (Paris), June 25–26, 1989.

68. Calvet, *L'Enfant*, 1:75–117; Fairchilds, *Domestic Enemies*; Berlanstein, *Working People; Clark, Schooling; Mayeur, De la Révolution.*

69. Jeanne Bouvier, *Mes mémoires*, ed. Daniel Armogathe and Maïté Albistur (Paris: Maspéro, 1983); Tilly and Scott, *Women*, p. 113; Caroline Brame, *Le Journal intime de Caroline Brame* (Paris: Montalba, 1985); Lévy, *De mères.*

REFERENCES

Anderson, R. D. *Education in France, 1848–1870*. Oxford: Oxford University Press, 1975.

Ariès, Philippe. *Centuries of Childhood: A Social History of Family Life*. Translated by Robert Baldick. New York: Alfred A. Knopf, 1962.

———. "Two Successive Motivations for a Declining Birth Rate in the West." *Population and Development Review* 6 (1980):645–650.

Ariès, Philippe, and Georges Duby, eds. *Histoire de la vie privée*. 5 vols. Paris: Editions du Seuil, 1987. Vol. 4: *De la Révolution à la grande guerre*, edited by Michelle Perrot. Vol. 5: *De la première guerre mondiale à nos jours*, edited by Antoine Prost and Gérard Vincent.

Baker, Donald N., and Patrick J. Harrigan, eds. *The Making of Frenchmen: Current Directions in the History of Education, 1679–1979*. Waterloo, Ontario: Historical Reflections Press, 1980.

Bardet, Jean-Pierre, and Jacques Dupâquier. "Contraception: les Français les premiers, mais pourquoi?" *Communications* 44 (1986):3–33.

Berlanstein, Lenard. "Vagrants, Beggars, and Thieves: Delinquent Boys in Mid-Nineteenth Century Paris." *Journal of Social History* 12 (1979):531–552.

———. "Growing Up as Workers in Nineteenth-Century Paris: The Case of the Orphans of the Prince Imperial." *French Historical Studies* 11 (Fall 1980):551–576.

———. *The Working People of Paris, 1871–1914*. Baltimore: Johns Hopkins University Press, 1984.

Boltanski, Luc. *Prime éducation et morale de classe*. Paris: Mouton, 1977.

Bourdieu, Pierre, and Jean-Claude Passeron. *Reproduction in Education, Society, and Culture*. Translated by Richard Nice. Beverly Hills, Calif.: Sage, 1977.

Bouvier, Jeanne. *Mes mémoires*, edited by Daniel Armogathe and Maïté Albistur. Paris: Maspéro, 1983.

Boxer, Marilyn J. "Women in Industrial Homework: The Flowermakers of Paris in the Belle Epoque." *French Historical Studies* 12 (Spring 1982):401–423.

Boxer, Marilyn J., and Jean H. Quataert, eds. *Connecting Spheres: Women in the Western World, 1500 to the Present*. New York: Oxford University Press, 1987.

Brame, Caroline. *Le Journal intime de Caroline B*. Paris: Montalba, 1985.

Briand, Jean-Pierre, Jean-Michel Chapoulie, and Henri Péretz. "Les Conditions institutionnelles de la scolarisation secondaire des garçons entre 1920 et 1940." *Revue d'histoire moderne et contemporaine* 26 (1979):391–421.

Bridenthal, Renate, Claudia Koonz, and Susan Stuard, eds. *Becoming Visible: Women in European History*. 2nd ed. Boston: Houghton Mifflin, 1987.

Buisson, Ferdinand, ed. *Nouveau dictionnaire de pédagogie*. 2 vols. Paris: Hachette, 1911.

Calvet, J. *L'Enfant dans la littérature française*. 2 vols. Paris: F. Lanore, 1930.

Capia, Robert. *Les Poupées françaises*. Paris: Hachette, 1979.

Chartier, Roger, Marie-Madeleine Compère, and Dominique Julia. *L'Education en France du XVIe au XVIIIe siècle*. Paris: Société d'édition d'enseignement supérieur, 1976.

Chisick, Harvey. *The Limits of Reform in the Enlightenment*. Princeton, N.J.: Princeton University Press, 1981.

Cholvy, Gérard, ed. *Mouvements de jeunesse chrétiens et juifs, sociabilité dans un cadre européen, 1799–1968*. Paris: Editions du Cerf, 1985.

Chombart de Lauwe, Marie-José. *Un monde autre: l'enfance de ses représentations à son mythe*. Paris: Payot, 1971.

Clark, Linda L. *Schooling the Daughters of Marianne: Textbooks and the Socialization of Girls in Modern French Primary Schools*. Albany: State University of New York Press, 1984.

Crubellier, Maurice. *L'Enfance et la jeunesse dans la société française, 1800–1950*. Paris: Armand Colin, 1979.

Darrow, Margaret. "French Noblewomen and the New Domesticity, 1750–1850." *Feminist Studies* 5 (Spring 1979):41–65.

Davis, Natalie Zemon. *Society and Culture in Early Modern France*. Stanford, Calif.: Stanford University Press, 1975.

Delaisi de Parseval, Geneviève, and Suzanne Lallemand. *L'Art d'accommoder les bébés: 100 ans de recettes françaises de puériculture*. Paris: Editions du Seuil, 1980.

Delumeau, Jean, ed. *La première communion, quatre siècles d'histoire*. Paris: Desclée de Brouwer, 1987.

DeMause, Lloyd, ed. *The History of Childhood*. New York: Psychohistory Press, 1974; Harper Torchbooks, 1975.

Donzelot, Jacques. *The Policing of Families*. Translated by Robert Hurley. New York: Random House, 1979.

Dupâquier, Jacques. "Combien d'avortements en France avant 1914?" *Communications* 44 (1986):87–106.

Dupuy, Aimé. "Les Livres de lecture de G. Bruno." *Revue d'histoire économique et sociale* 31 (1953):128–151.

Fairchilds, Cissie. *Domestic Enemies: Servants and Their Masters in Old Regime France*. Baltimore: Johns Hopkins University Press, 1984.

Flandrin, Jean-Louis. *Families in Former Times: Kinship, Household and Sexuality*. Translated by Richard Southern. Cambridge: Cambridge University Press, 1979.

Fuchs, Rachel G. "Crimes Against Children in Nineteenth-Century France: Child Abuse." *Law and Human Behavior* 6 (1983):237–259.

———. *Abandoned Children: Foundlings and Child Welfare in Nineteenth-Century France*. Albany: State University of New York Press, 1984.

Furet, François, and Jacques Ozouf, eds. *Lire et écrire, l'alphabétisation des français de Calvin à Jules Ferry*. 2 vols. Paris: Editions de Minuit, 1977. Translation: *Reading and Writing: Literacy in France from Calvin to Jules Ferry*. Cambridge: Cambridge University Press, 1983.

Gaillac, Henri. *Les Maisons de correction*. Paris: Editions Cujas, 1971.

Grew, R., P. J. Harrigan, and J. B. Whitney. "La Scolarisation en France, 1829–1906."
  Annales: Economies, sociétés, civilisations 39 (January 1984):116–157.
Guillemard, Colette. *La Vie des enfants dans la France d'autrefois*. Paris: Christian de
  Bartillat, 1986.
Heywood, Colin. *Childhood in Nineteenth-Century France: Work, Health and Education
  Among the "Classes Populaires."* Cambridge: Cambridge University Press,
  1988.
Holmes, Urban T. "Medieval Children." *Journal of Social History* 2 (1968):164–172.
Hufton, Olwen. *The Poor of Eighteenth-Century France, 1750–1789*. Oxford: Clarendon
  Press, 1974.
Hunt, David. *Parents and Children in History: The Psychology of Family Life in Early
  Modern France*. New York: Basic Books, 1970; Harper Torchbook, 1972.
Jan, Isabelle. "Children's Literature and Bourgeois Society in France Since 1860." *Yale
  French Studies* 43 (1969):57–72.
Johansson, S. Ryan. "Centuries of Childhood/Centuries of Parenting: Philippe Ariès and
  the Modernization of Privileged Infancy." *Journal of Family History* 12
  (1987):343–365.
Kanipe, Esther S. "Hetzel and the Bibliothèque d'Education et de Récréation." *Yale
  French Studies* 43 (1969):73–84.
Kennedy, Emmet, and Marie Laurence Netter. "Ecoles primaires sous le directoire."
  Annales historiques de la révolution française 53 (1981):3–38.
Knibiehler, Yvonne, and Cathérine Fouquet. *L'Histoire des mères du moyen âge à nos
  jours*. Paris: Montalba, 1980.
Lalou, Richard. "L'Infanticide devant les tribunaux français (1825–1910)." *Communi-
  cations* 44 (1986):175–200.
Lebrun, François. "La Place de l'enfant dans la société française depuis le XVIᵉ siècle."
  Communications 44 (1986):247–257.
Legouvé, Ernest. *Les Pères et les enfants au XIXe siècle, enfance et adolescence*. Paris:
  J. Hetzel, 1867.
Lévy, Marie-Françoise. *De Mères en filles, l'éducation des françaises, 1850–1880*. Paris:
  Calmann-Lévy, 1984.
Luc, Jean-Noël. *La Statistique de l'enseignement primaire*. Paris: Economica, 1985.
———. " 'A trois ans, l'enfant devient intéressant': la découverte médicale de la seconde
  enfance (1750–1900)." *Revue d'histoire moderne et contemporaine* 36 (January-
  March 1989):83–112.
    McDougall, Mary Lynn. "Protecting Infants: The French Campaign for Maternity
    Leaves, 1890s–1913." *French Historical Studies* 13 (1983):79–105.
McLaren, Angus. *Sexuality and Social Order: The Debate over the Fertility of Women
  and Workers in France, 1870–1920*. New York: Holmes & Meier, 1983.
Maingueneau, Dominique. *Les Livres d'école de la république 1870–1914, discours et
  idéologie*. Paris: Le Sycomore, 1979.
Marvick, Elisabeth Wirth. "The Character of Louis XIII: The Role of His Physician."
  Journal of Interdisciplinary History 4 (Winter 1974):347–374.
Mayeur, Françoise. *L'Enseignement secondaire des jeunes filles sous la troisième ré-
  publique*. Paris: Presses de la fondation nationale des sciences politiques, 1977.
———. *L'Education des filles en France au dix-neuvième siècle*. Paris: Hachette, 1979.
Meyer, Philippe. *The Child and the State: The Intervention of the State in Family Life.*

Translated by Judith Ennew and Janet Lloyd. Cambridge: Cambridge University Press, 1983.

Moody, Joseph N. *French Education Since Napoleon*. Syracuse, N.Y.: Syracuse University Press, 1978.

Nion, Comte François de. "Le Siècle des enfants." *Fémina* 1 (February 1901):11.

O'Brien, Patricia. *The Promise of Punishment: Prisons in Nineteenth-Century France*. Princeton, N.J.: Princeton University Press, 1982.

Parias, Louis-Henry, ed. *Histoire générale de l'enseignement et de l'éducation en France*. 4 vols. Paris: Nouvelle Librairie de France, 1981. Vol. 2: *De Gutenberg aux lumières*, by François Lebrun, Marc Venard, and Jean Quéniart. Vol. 3: *De la Révolution à l'école républicaine (1789–1930)*, by Françoise Mayeur. Vol. 4: *L'Ecole et la famille dans une société en mutation (1930–1980)*, by Antoine Prost.

Perrot, Michelle. "Sur la segrégation de l'enfance au dix-neuvième siècle." *La Psychiatrie de l'enfant* 25 (1982):179–206.

Pierrard, Pierre. *Enfants et jeunes ouvriers en France (XIXᵉ–XXᵉ siècles)*. Paris: Editions ouvrières, 1987.

Pollock, Linda A. *Forgotten Children: Parent-Child Relations from 1500 to 1900*. Cambridge: Cambridge University Press, 1983.

Pope, Barbara Corrado. "Maternal Education in France, 1815–1848." *Proceedings of the Western Society for French History* 3 (1976):368–377.

Prost, Antoine. *Histoire de l'enseignement en France 1800–1967*. Paris: Armand Colin, 1968.

Schnapper, Bernard. "La Correction paternelle et le mouvement des idées au dix-neuvième siècle (1789–1935)." *Revue historique* (1980):319–349.

Shaffer, John W. "Family, Class, and Young Women's Occupational Expectations in Nineteenth-Century Paris." *Journal of Family History* 3 (1978):62–77.

Shorter, Edward. *The Making of the Modern Family*. New York: Basic Books, 1975.

Sonnet, Martine. Review of Elisabeth Chauveau et al., *Bleuette et les poupées dans les périodiques enfantins en France de 1768 à 1960* (Courbevoie: Centre d'étude et de recherche sur la poupée, 1984), in *Histoire de l'éducation* 29 (January 1986):131–132.

Strumingher, Laura S. *What Were Little Girls and Boys Made Of? Primary Education in Rural France, 1830–1880*. Albany: State University of New York Press, 1983.

Sussman, George D. *Selling Mothers' Milk: The Wet-Nursing Business in France, 1715–1914*. Urbana: University of Illinois Press, 1982.

Talbott, John E. *The Politics of Educational Reform in France, 1918–1940*. Princeton, N.J.: Princeton University Press, 1969.

Tilly, Louise A., and Joan W. Scott. *Women, Work, and Family*. New York: Holt, Rinehart, & Winston, 1978.

Tomlinson, Richard. "The 'Disappearance' of France, 1896–1940: French Politics and the Birth Rate." *Historical Journal* 28 (1985):405–415.

Traer, James F. *Marriage and the Family in Eighteenth-Century France*. Ithaca, N.Y.: Cornell University Press, 1980.

Weber, Eugen. *Peasants into Frenchmen: The Modernization of Rural France, 1870–1914*. Stanford, Calif.: Stanford University Press, 1976.

Weissbach, Lee Shai. "*Oeuvre Industrielle, Oeuvre Morale*: The *Sociétés de Patronage* of Nineteenth-Century France." *French Historical Studies* 15 (Spring 1987):99–120.

Wheaton, Robert, and Tamara K. Hareven, eds. *Family and Sexuality in French History.* Philadelphia: University of Pennsylvania Press, 1980.

Wilson, Adrian. "The Infancy of the History of Childhood: An Appraisal of Philippe Ariès." *History and Theory* 19 (1980):132–153.

Wylie, Laurence. *Village in the Vaucluse.* 3rd ed. Cambridge, Mass.: Harvard University Press, 1974.

Zeldin, Theodore. *France 1848–1945.* 2 vols. Oxford: Clarendon Press, 1973, 1977.

12

GERMANY

Mary Jo Maynes and Thomas Taylor

There has not been much room for children in Germany history. The expansion of the terrain of history that in the United States brought families, women, workers, and racial and ethnic minorities, as well as the young, onto the historical stage came later and in a different form in German history. Moreover, it has been less fully institutionalized there than in many other Western countries. Scholars who have written about recent historiography in Germany have noted what has been variously termed the "underdeveloped," "limited," or "marginal" character of social history, family history, demographic history, and women's history in Germany, and in particular in the Federal Republic.[1] Even now, with the belated flourishing in the German context of all these subfields, results of the new research have been slow in entering the mainstream and have yet to force a recasting of the dominant research traditions and problematics of German history. Furthermore, earlier connections established between the history of young people in Germany and the dominant historical questions in the field tended to isolate the history of childhood in Germany from the sociohistorical concerns that provided the impetus for the history of childhood elsewhere. German history may or may not be "peculiar," but German historiography certainly has been.[2]

The earliest forays into the history of childhood took on a retrospective problem of concern in analyses of other areas of modern German history. Starting with the driving question of twentieth-century Germany history—the origins of Nazism—historians who first looked at the role of childhood often were attempting to find evidence of a peculiarly German culture or psyche that might account for the national susceptibility to Hitler. Some historical explorations centered on the phase of youth and youth organizations in the epoch preceding the Nazi takeover. The pre–World War I youth movement known as the *Wandervogel*, with its links to the *Volkisch* traditions that fed into the Nazi ideology, became a focus of scholarship and a touchstone for understanding German character writ large. These organizations, hence German youth, were seen as stridently anti-modern, anti-urban, backward-looking, and anti-Semitic. Veterans of the *Wandervogel* emerged as natural recruits into Nazism in the 1920s. Another explanation centered on the particular sociopsychological experiences of the generation that came to maturity during World War I and provided the basis for the later Hitler electorate and Nazi party membership. German child-rearing practices also came under scrutiny and emerged as authoritarian, as the testimony of children's literature, for example, was brought to witness. The history of childhood and youth, in other words, was initially defined as an aspect of the rise of fascism.[3]

Despite its marginal and particularist start, the history of childhood in Germany is now not only flourishing, but pathbreaking. As in other areas of social history, there may have been in the history of childhood some advantages attached to "backwardness." Some of the most creative conceptualization of past childhood currently is being done by historians in Germany. In part at least, this creativity is linked with the previous isolation from the trends in childhood history characteristic of the French and Anglo-American research, and the embeddedness of much of the German research in somewhat different theoretical and historiographic traditions. First, the theoretical discussion that has framed much of the recent work on German childhood centers explicitly on the relation between social class formation and socialization, a dimension of childhood experience quite neglected in the masterworks that launched research into childhood in France, England, and the United States. Second, some of the particular problems that have been of concern to German historians have ultimately proved encouraging of the drawing of connections between the history of childhood and other areas of social and even political history. The children of the past, although previously kept in place more firmly in Germany than elsewhere, are poised to intrude noisily into German history.

This chapter explores those areas of the history of modern German childhood about which research has been especially rich and important. We begin with an examination of childhood in the preindustrial family economy and its transformation in the context of early capitalism and protoindustry. We then examine the creation of a new understanding of childhood and youth in the eighteenth and early nineteenth centuries and the connections between this new understanding and the social evolution of the middle classes. We then look at the evolution of a specifically proletarian childhood in the era of industrial capitalism, and especially after the mid-nineteenth century. The final section addresses the history of youth and transitions to adulthood, especially as these transitions were affected by new educational possibilities and changing patterns of intergenerational occupational determination toward the beginning of the twentieth century.

GERMAN CHILDHOOD IN THE ERA OF THE
FAMILY ECONOMY

Family image and rhetoric originating in nineteenth-century sociology, and reclaimed to some extent by the political right in the early twentieth century, held up the sturdy patriarchal peasant household—*das ganze Haus*—as a family model.[4] Headed by a strict but concerned *Hausvater*, seconded by the housekeeping enterprise of the *Hausmutter*, this household comprised not only the parents and their progeny, but also assorted kin and servants. The household was an enterprise providing its own subsistence and a commercial surplus. This image of the solid Germany family, created in the industrial era, was as much rhetorical fabrication as description. Sociohistorical research has produced a picture of early modern family life and childhood that is more complex and decidedly less benign.[5]

Certainly large peasant homesteads existed—more commonly in some regions than in others. Some areas of Bavaria, for example, or of northwestern Germany were characterized by systems of impartible inheritance, large homesteads, and multigenerational households in the early modern epoch. But these were pockets of peasant-household prosperity in the midst of regional varieties that encompassed, by the late seventeenth century, fully developed commercial agricultural estate economies (notably the *Gutsherrschaft* regime of the East-Elbian Germany) with their mixed populations of bound peasants, cottagers, and landless laborers; the tiny "handkerchief plots" of the southern Rhineland resulting from generations of overpopulation and subdivision; and the putting-out industrial villages of the river valleys and mountainous regions of western and central Germany. Preindustrial family life, and the lives of children in the family, can hardly be spoken of in terms of generalizations. Regional and social contours made for widely varying regimes on the threshold of the industrial revolution that affected how the massive historical changes of the eighteenth and nineteenth centuries were in turn experienced.

One of the few general statements that can be made is that during the era of the household economy that persisted in central Europe until at least the middle of the nineteenth century, and in some regions even later, the condition of children was strongly shaped by the family's status and labor requirements. Whether the nature of the family enterprise was agricultural production, industrial employment in an artisanal or putting-out system, or (as was increasingly common by the seventeenth century) some combination, children were expected to assume responsibility for contributing to work at a young age.[6] Some of the fullest accounts of the kinds of work children did emerge beginning in the late eighteenth century, a period when state authorities throughout much of central Europe were attempting to increase school attendance and encountered problems resulting from conflicting demands on the time of children. Thus one Badenese *Industrieschule* inspector wrote at the beginning of the nineteenth century:

Woodworking serves as an occupation for boys while girls drive the spindle. In the regions of viniculture, carrying night soil into the vineyards keeps boys busy on good winter days while girls spin at home. Where the woods are interspersed with fields, the girls occupy themselves in winter with women's work [i.e., the needle trades] for which the growing of flax and hemp provide a natural opportunity, while boys make benches, baskets and pots during the time when they are not taking care of the cattle and pigs.[7]

As participants in a family enterprise, children were incorporated fairly early into adult roles and were not regarded as having special needs. Socialization centered on the gradual and early introduction into the household economy and into the round of village social activities that punctuate the calendar year.[8] Nor were young children the object of much intensive parental care. What many would later consider as "natural" bonds between mother and child, producing the particular patterns of nurturance we now associate with mothering, were barely recognizable in many descriptions of German parenting in the preindustrial era.

Edward Shorter wrote one of the earliest studies on mothering that used central European evidence from the later eighteenth and early nineteenth centuries. Shorter argues that the neglect of children characterized preindustrial mothering and that this changed only when women made a dramatic, one-time, and fairly abrupt shift in their attitudes toward their children. This shift, he argues, was a by-product of the revolution in sentiment that Shorter associates with modern, market-oriented individualism.[9] Shorter's work was subsequently criticized for its overdrawn generalizations and ahistorical character—indifferent mothering is depicted as a universal and timeless "traditional" behavior. Subsequent research has altered this portrait in important ways. First, the medical reports that Shorter himself read rather uncritically have been interpreted as part of the reform effort of middle-class and state authorities aimed at creating a new relationship between parents and children as part of a larger disciplinary effort. These reports are valuable pieces of evidence, but they need to be read in this context. Furthermore, a close reading of them yields significant regional variations.[10]

The Bavarians, whose behavior has been at the center of a number of family-historical studies, were, as it turns out, something of an extreme. At least since the sixteenth or seventeenth century many Bavarian mothers had stopped nursing their children almost entirely and resorted instead to artificial means of feeding. In contrast with contemporaneous French (especially urban) mothers who could not or would not nurse and sent their *nourrissons* out to the country to wet nurses, the Bavarians' main resort was to *Mehlbrei* (flour and milk gruel), notorious in the medical reports for its unsanitary quality and inappropriateness for the infant digestive system. One early nineteenth-century doctor condemned common Southern Germany infant formulas that

consisted primarily of pap that more often resembles paste than food. It is made of milk and flour and under the right circumstances can even provide good nourishment. But it is usually so thick that it has to be forced into the child and only becomes digestible when mixed with saliva and stomach fluids. At its worst it is curdled and sour. People think it's never too early to give this pap to their children.[11]

The result of artificial feeding in Bavaria and other regions of southern Germany was elevated infant mortality, among the highest discovered by demographic historians anywhere in Europe. On the order of one out of three infants died before their first birthday as compared with one out of ten in the regions of lowest infant mortality.[12]

In part as a result of this heightened infant mortality and disinclination to breast-feed, Bavarian mothers became pregnant more frequently (their birth intervals were on the order of twenty-two to twenty-four months, in contrast with the thirty to thirty-three months characteristic in several northern Germany villages.[13]). These shorter intervals between births took its toll on both maternal and infant health and nurturance, and may well have contributed to the indifferent mothering commented on by many contemporary and disapproving observers in the late eighteenth and early nineteenth centuries.

Related evidence of a different sort has been presented by Regina Schulte as part of her research on rural women, especially maidservants, in Bavarian history. Schulte found that servants sometimes resorted to infanticide, which, she argues, was a largely accepted practice in the marginal regime of the Bavarian rural lower orders, although it clashed with state policy and was punished where discovered. This practice was no doubt rooted in a generalized indifference to the fate of certain newborns. According to Schulte,

the infanticide dossiers offer no approach to the feelings accompanying the death of the babies. They appear not to have existed. Most of the statements are full of indifference, coldness and callousness, but not perplexity. Even the statements of witnesses give the same impression . . . a seeming emotional muteness consequently gives the impression of a general impoverishment of feeling.[14]

Schulte points to the limits of the sources themselves to reveal emotion, but also to a tendency she detects to deny human identity to an infant who was destined not to survive. Schulte interprets infanticide as one variant of a complex of mothering practices that includes neglect and indifference as well as selective nurturance.

Historians thus take varying stands on this "bad mothering" ranging from the relativist account Schulte provides to the presentist condemnation by Shorter. More fruitful, it seems, have been the efforts to place this complex of child-rearing practices in a comparative perspective in an effort to tease out and understand the differing "rationalities" of childhood that prevailed in different regions and assess possible origins and implications. The recent work of historical demographer Arthur Imhof and of historian Christophe Duhamelle are intriguing in this respect. They posit within Germany a bipolar set of demographic regimes—the regime of wastefulness and the regime of conservation—as characteristic of southern and northern Germany, respectively.

In the South (more extreme in Bavaria but detectable in areas of Württemberg, Baden, and Austria as well) there prevailed higher fertility and mortality rates, shorter birth intervals, and indifferent nurture of infants and young children that amounted to a "disguised form of infanticide." In the North, especially the Frisian islands, but also more generally in Hesse, Prussia, Oldenburg, and elsewhere, lower rates of birth and death, longer birth intervals, and protracted breast-feeding were more usual. The effect of these two regimes was in one sense similar, a rough demographic homeostasis or population equilibrium that demographers have found characteristic of ancien régime Europe. But there is at least a suggestion that these alternative routes to homeostasis involved different mentalities about the meaning and preservation of life, patterns of investment in child care, and, presumably, impacts on personality of early childhood experiences.

Just what the origins and impact of these regimes were remain open to question. Duhamelle, following Imhof, postulates a southern fatalism rooted in the historical traumas of the early modern era. Certainly the suggestion is strong that fatalistic habits of infant and child nurturance (perhaps reinforced by alternative religious accounts of the fate of infants who died young) may have contributed to the cycle of neglect, death, and indifference that characterized parenting in Bavaria. But further accounts of the origins of regional variations await the disclosure of sources that take us out of the realm of speculation.[15]

Whatever their origins, these regimes of childhood were internally coherent, alternative rationalities, if mutually incompatible. Within these broad alternative regional demographic regimes the fate of children was very much affected by particular local circumstances, especially changing patterns of family and women's labor. Historical work has begun to delimit the family economic contours of regional child care regimes. Moreover, rather than seeing the "traditional" fatalism depicted by Shorter as a timeless past, much of the research suggests that the period of transition to capitalism, especially the protoindustrial epoch, may well have represented a deterioration of the condition of family life. The marginality of family economies and the paradoxical demographic regime in which "those whose material conditions of inherited possessions rendered them least capable of rearing large numbers of children nevertheless produced them" meant that more children were raised under poverty than had been the case in earlier epochs.[16] This poverty, coupled with the enhanced possibility for children to earn wages at a very young age in the protoindustrial household, may well have meant that work demands on children intensified in the early capitalist era in these milieus. In other words, research on the history of childhood suggests that the conditions of children may well have been deteriorating among the rural poor at precisely that point in time when in urban middle- and upper-class milieus children were the subject of increasing attention and protection.

THE DISCOVERY OF THE CHILD IN GERMANY

As is true everywhere else, the historiography of childhood in Germany has acknowledged Philippe Ariès, or at least Ariès' questions and claims.[17] The early modern "discovery" of the child that Ariès demonstrates in bourgeois milieus in Western Europe certainly did not elude the Germans, even if their discovery came characteristically "late" and through partially foreign channels. By the early eighteenth century, however, a middle-class public was, in some German towns, at least creating a distinct presence for itself through reading circles and theaters, through municipal associations and institutions, and through new life-styles. Boundaries between this stratum and the aristocracy, on the one hand, and the old urban *Kleinburgertüm* of artisans and shopkeepers, on the other, were drawn as much by distinctive patterns of child rearing as by distinctive ways of earning a livelihood.

The German middle-class public could read about new ideas concerning children along with new ideas about political arrangements or trade in the same publications. Important to both was the flourishing of the periodical press centered in the cities of northern and Rhineland Germany, and especially those early family magazines known as "moral weeklies." The largest in circulation of the perhaps 200 such publications was *Der Patriot*, published in Hamburg, but distributed to 5,000 individual and group subscribers throughout the German states. Among its aims was to counter what were presumed to be common child-rearing practices. The articles it printed called for close parental supervision of children, moral seriousness rather than casual attitudes toward children, and an education rooted in the emergent understanding of child development and aimed at the child's destined future, rather than schooling centered on memorization of dead languages. Children were neither toys nor ornaments: "Pride, vanity and boastfulness are the results of youthful education; the children are dressed and shined in an overly zealous manner and brought at an early age to behaviors inappropriate for children."[18] A similarly didactic discussion of child rearing in the 1740 edition of a Königsberg publication, *Der Einsiedler*, spelled out appropriate roles for mother and father. According to this article, the good wife nurses her own children (following the example of her *own* virtuous mother). Once they are weaned, she "takes care to watch them even more attentively, they are never without their mother, and she loves them far too tenderly to give them over for whole days or weeks into the hands of nursemaids. She knows that in the absence of parents, the children are neglected." After the fifth year she turns the sons over to the close attention of their father, and takes on her daughters' education by herself.[19]

At the service of parents conscious of their serious responsibilities vis-à-vis their children were not only the new periodicals, but also advice manuals, childrens' educational texts, and children's literature. Certainly the accounts in the prescriptive literature need to be read with caution. These were as much diatribes against presumed aristocratic decadence as they were prescriptions for reform. But it also is clear that accounts of childhoods contained in middle-class autobiographies of the epoch suggest that the prescriptions and the recollections echoed each other. According to the new prescriptions and practices, children were relegated to special places in the home, and demarcated from their elders by special clothing and special activities.[20] This physical and functional separation was symptomatic of an emotional demarcation, a kind of "distancing" between parents (as educators) and their children, that occurred even as parent-child relations intensified. The proximity of adults and children—in the same rooms or activities or apparel or beds as their elders—appeared in the eighteenth century as promiscuity. At the same time social intercourse with the lower orders, the children of the streets, was curtailed to avoid the corruption such contact would bring with it.[21] Proper children were circumscribed to the home, leaving it only for the occasional outing with their parents. Only those below the margins of respectability allowed their children the run of the street.

If the home was the ideal site of child rearing, boys at least required some academic preparations for their future careers. Accompanying the redefinition of childhood was a new concern with pedagogy and a critique of existing educational institutions. Educational experiments, the most famous, if not successful, of which was probably the *Philanthropin* founded in Dessau in 1774, attempted to put into practice the new principles. But the *Realschulen*, trade schools, business schools, and the like all date to this era, and share a critique of classical erudition devoid of moral or practical grounding.

Behind this array of new institutions and practices lay the aim to raise sons who were self-disciplined, emotionally controlled, strongly aware of the boundaries between themselves and others, individualistic, and morally upstanding. Daughters were raised to be willing and able to take on the serious moral, emotional, and managerial responsibilities of organizing a household and raising children but without having the ambition to aspire beyond its walls. Although not without contradictions, this assertive reorientation of socialization practices in the urban upper middle classes can be understood as an essential aspect of the formation of the *Bürgertum* itself. Its existence and success as a class depended on ambitious career men, professionals, and entrepreneurs whose aspirations and values flowed naturally from their upbringing and on women who would be the kinds of mothers this upbringing demanded.

As these patterns established themselves among the urban middle classes they began to assume a hegemonic character as well. Increasingly, a "proper" childhood came to be envisioned in these new terms. One aspect of class relations in the early industrial epoch was the effort to extend certain features of bourgeois child-rearing patterns to the urban and rural masses. This effort occurred on two fronts at least. Already mentioned was the medical front. Doctors intervened in child-rearing practices that they regarded as outmoded, damaging, or unenlightened, and the records of their encounters with the lower orders provide us with, for example, the observations about infant feeding practices cited earlier. The second front was the school. Behind school reform was the suspicion that family life was a deficient basis for moral upbringing among the lower orders. The only hope lay in getting the children of the people into school early and keeping them there during more of their childhood.

Central European states involved themselves precociously in the reform and extension of elementary schooling.[22] The first reform wave had already occurred during the Reformation, and because of the distinctive relation between state and church that the Reformation created in the German states, schools were never without a political dimension thereafter.[23] Still, most historians argue that active state intervention in popular schooling began in the last third of the eighteenth century and was signaled by the passage of the Prussian *Landschulre-glement* and its subsequent imitation in other German states. By the turn of the nineteenth century these regulations were being enforced in at least some regions of Prussia, in the states of the Southwest, and perhaps other areas as well.

Certainly it can be argued that the schooling provided in these schools was aimed simultaneously at social engineering and discipline. State authorities envisioned curricula specified to the future occupational destinies of the pupils—peasant, artisan, or *Gebildete*. Indeed, state authorities had first been directly involved in institutions of a specialized and highly vocational nature for training state officials and army officers. Some of the late-eighteenth-century initiatives, such as *Industrieschulen* and sewing schools, were directly related to mercantilist policies designed to boost protoindustrial production.[24] Virtually all were designed to limit the social ambitions of their pupils even as they extended the reach of elementary skills.[25] For peasant children in the country schools minimal literacy and familiarity with the tenets of religion were deemed sufficient, and the program was compatible with a family economy that still rested heavily on child labor. Urban school systems could be more complex affairs, but they, too, were designed to provide appropriate numbers of hours of schooling and levels of skill for more diverse urban clientele that ranged from the very poor to the comfortable shopkeeper. (The aristocracy and upper bourgeoisie relied on home education almost exclusively for its daughters and until secondary school age for its sons as well.)[26] The schools were perhaps the most important institutions that brought middle-class understandings of childhood to bear on lower-class families, but outside the classroom the world of the child of the popular classes followed a very different historical trajectory.

CHILDHOOD UNDER INDUSTRIAL CAPITALISM

Through a history at odds with the bourgeois experience the proletarian child also was created as a central part of the process of class formation in the nineteenth century. The East German historian Jurgen Küczynski was probably the first to attend to this development. He argued that the new requirements of an industrial work force held implications for working-class childhood. In contrast with the work habits characteristic of the protoindustrial sector, industrial workers had to be rational, disciplined, and highly productive. The logic of capital called for intensive exploitation (getting the most from each worker) rather than extensive exploitation (pulling more laborers into production). Shifting labor requirements, so Kuczynski's argument went, affected policies regarding the socialization of future workers. Not only did there emerge a new emphasis on schooling, but the characteristic school of the industrial capitalist era emphasized basic skills rather than the vocational training that had been taught in the *Industrieschulen*.[27]

Kuczynski's interpretation certainly overstates the role of economic requirements in schooling processes. After all, employers in the new factories as often as not preferred to employ children rather than see them in school. State and local government authorities often found themselves in conflict with both employers and working-class parents in their efforts to enforce obligatory schooling.

In another vein, the dynamics of working-class socialization can only be fully understood through reference to the changing family economy of the emergent working classes. Thanks to an astonishing proliferation of research on the German working-class family that has succeeded Kuczynski's pioneering efforts, we can begin to relate the history of working-class childhood.[28]

Put most simply, research suggests that working-class families were unable to fulfill the requirements of "proper" childhood as spelled out in the new post-Enlightenment norms. This impossibility stemmed from several sources: first, economic marginality and demographic vulnerability precluded the kind of parenting—and especially mothering—that the norm prescribed; second, continued reliance on the labor of children for family survival meant that children continued to be integrated into adult activities (and in this working-class children were not unlike the children of peasants and rural laborers); finally, the material surroundings in which bourgeois childhood developed, such as private space and specialized reading material and equipment, were beyond imagining in the crowded tenements of German *Grossstädte*.[29]

The demographic parameters that shaped working-class life and distinguished it from the typical middle-class life course also held obvious implications for the history of childhood. In the realm of mortality, class differentials persisted and ever widened in the context of overall decline throughout the nineteenth century. Reinhard Spree has shown that in many industrial cities of Germany, the class character of neighborhoods was reflected in prevailing levels of mortality, especially infant mortality. In Berlin, for example, in 1886, infant mortality (including stillbirths) reached 381 per thousand in the working-class district of Wedding, whereas it was 202 per thousand in wealthy Friedrichstadt. Levels of infant mortality also varied predictably with the occupation of father or mother. In 1880 public officials' infants died at the rate of 180 per thousand, a level that dropped to 153 per thousand by the turn of the century. Among servants the rate was 299 per thousand in 1880, and it stilled hovered above 300 even in 1900.[30]

Parental mortality also is significant, and here, too, class differentials apparently widened before they diminished in the early twentieth century.[31] Mortality statistics suggest, in short, that children in urban working-class families were more likely to die young than children in other urban classes or rural children, and they were likely to lose one or the other parent before reaching adulthood.

Fertility patterns also reflected class boundaries. During the late-nineteenth-century fertility decline, not all classes adopted family limitation at the same pace. Among couples who married in 1905—well after the transition to lower fertility had begun—professionals had, on the average, 3.21 children; teachers, 3.04; white-collar employees, 3.39; and workers, 4.67.[32] A high fertility strategy clearly persisted longer among workers than in other sectors. This can be seen as evidence of a dynamic not dissimilar to that which produced the high fertility in agrarian and protoindustrial settings. Urban working-class children could not be as fully employed as putting-out workers or peasant children, but inadequacy of parental incomes and the characteristics of working-class earning patterns over the family life cycle pressed young people into the labor force early. In addition, workers held attitudes about contraception that may have contributed to these differentials.

Evidence about working-class family budgets suggests that many families were unable to survive on the earnings of a single male breadwinner even at the end of the nineteenth century. Wages were still quite low in many industries (construction, for example), and even where they were higher, work often was irregular or seasonal. Male wages usually diminished with age, setting in motion an increased reliance on children's earnings as they matured.[33] Furthermore, levels of temporary migration or permanent abandonment by male workers meant that the presence of the husband-father was not to be counted on. (Annual out-migration peaked in 1880 at nearly 5 percent of the entire German population. Internal migration also was heavy. Of the population living in Berlin in 1907, only 40 percent had been born there.[34])

The historical evidence attests to the significance of the earnings of mothers and children throughout the period of industrialization. A 1907 survey suggested that even at this late date, workers' households reportedly relied on the earnings of wives and children for between 8 and 15 percent of their total income. More than half of the family income was spent on food. (In contrast, among teachers and middle-level officials, less than 2 percent of the total household income came from the earnings of wives and children.) Moreover, other forms of testimony, such as surveys of homework, autobiographies, and oral histories, attest to the virtually universal employment of working-class mothers in wage work, and suggest that budget reports may well have understated the persistence of married women's wage labor.[35]

This persistence of children's and mothers' work even after the full enforcement of mandatory school attendance resulted in what Marguerite Flecken and others have referred to as a *Doppelbelastung* of children that mimicked the double burdening of working-class mothers. Children were pressured to work whenever they weren't attending school. The lengthening of the schoolday and the enforcement of more frequent attendance meant that children's paid work had to be squeezed into their few spare hours. Mothers, in turn, had to divide their time between paid work and housework. Research on married women's work such as that done by Rosemary Beier suggests that psychic costs inherent in the working-class family economy: mothers took in work at home so as to be able to attend to their children, but the pace of work they needed to maintain meant that their children appeared as a constant source of annoyance and interruption. When the children worked by her side the mother was cast in the role of disciplinarian, for family earnings could be measured in proportion to diligence and persistence at the task of each worker.[36]

Working-class childhood and working-class mothering belied dominant norms. This dichotomy between the childhood of the bourgeois ideal and working-class reality did not escape the attention of proletarian children. Autobiographical accounts repeatedly contrast memories of their sorry existence as children and the prevailing images of "golden" childhood years that were supposed to be the most carefree of their lives. They peered into the shopwindows, saw the well-dressed children in the park or in the homes they worked in. The contrast came especially close to home for those children whose jobs as nursemaid allowed them to witness firsthand the life of the children who lived out the myth, or for those others who spent many hours of painstaking and poorly paid labor to make dolls and carved animals to provide amusement for the children of the upper classes. Indeed, the experience of "never having had a childhood" emerged in many working-class autobiographies as a political outcry and a deeply personal form of critique of the costs of social inequality.[37]

The history of working-class childhood in Imperial Germany can hardly be separated from the political culture in which it was enmeshed. So much of the evidence on which historians of the family rely, so many of the accounts of growing up working class, were formulated in the spirit of social commentary or critique. The evolution of a specifically socialist subculture, which included prescriptions for family life, was part of the process that finally created the claim to childhood for typical working-class children. Certainly by the 1890s the stabler and better-paid sectors of the manual labor force—those very sectors that were so important in the socialist and trade union movements—could create a family life that allowed for childhood. In some ways, despite its radicalism on other fronts, socialists recreated the patriarchal norms and family models of the dominant culture.[38] Despite right-wing fears that industrialization and social democracy were bound to destroy the family, what many workers aspired toward was the possibility of enough income and leisure to make family life possible. The decades between 1890 and 1930 saw the widening of this possibility. Certainly the emerging working-class childhood was not *the* childhood of the dominant myth. Working-class children still mostly went to work right out of the *Volksschule* and still felt the weight of poverty. But a specifically working-class version of childhood, centered on the streets and in the school as well as in homes, a childhood with its own costumes and reading material, its peculiar practices and customs, was well in place in working-class quarters of cities and suburbs by the turn of the century.[39]

YOUTH AND THE TRANSITION TO ADULTHOOD

As childhood became more closely defined and broadly institutionalized in nineteenth-century Germany so did the successive stage in the life cycle—youth.

In preindustrial Germany the differences between childhood and youth had not been so clearly defined. Work, as we have seen, could begin quite young at home or in domestic service. With the commencement of full- or part-time labor began an indefinite period of semidependency in which the young boy or girl lived in a kind of half-grown status, no longer a child but something less than an adult. Confirmation, at about age fourteen, was an important symbolic transition between the life of a child and youth, but only with marriage did the period of semidependency end and adulthood begin.[40]

As, near the end of the nineteenth century, stricter enforcement of child labor and mandatory schooling laws ensured that most children remained in school until the age of fourteen, the transition between childhood and youth became more clearly marked. During this same era, beginning in the last decades of the nineteenth century, psychologists and educators began to articulate theories of psychosexual and cognitive development that further specified the passage from childhood to youth.[41] Although these definitions of youth were couched in universal terms, in fact they most closely reflected the experiences of middle-class male youth in Wilhemine Germany. (Many of the earliest studies of the group that would eventually be called adolescents were based on the experiences of secondary-school pupils.) As was true of childhood, the notions and experiences of youth were class- and gender-bound.[42]

For working-class families industrialization brought changes in patterns of youthful residence and economic dependency, which are crucial determinants of the transition from childhood to adulthood. In areas where industry developed the availability of local work meant that often children could live at home for longer periods of time. When they did so, however, their enhanced ability to earn wages meant that they gained a measure of independence from their parents unknown in times past, although they still seemed to have been expected to turn over most of their wages to their parents.[43] Even in areas where agriculture remained dominant, the possibility of migrating to find industrial work provided an attractive alternative to the prospect of waiting to inherit the family plot.

Just how these new possibilities affected family dynamics is open to question. A study by Heilwig Schomerus, for example, suggests that these changes in residency and economic dependency spurred by industrialization in a factory town heightened generational conflicts.[44] As youth become more independent within the family structure, and geographical and cultural distances between generations widened, tensions between the generations grew. On the other hand, Andreas Gestrich, in his study of youth in the Württemberg village of Ohmenhausen, concluded the opposite. While acknowledging that industrialization changed the economic relation of parent and child, he found that this change did not increase parent-child antagonisms. Preindustrial patterns of youthful subservience to parental and community authority persisted until at least World War I. Furthermore, in this case, the possibilities of nearby factory employment made possible the survival of a half-peasant economy in the village and the preservation of its "traditional" youth culture.[45]

In these working-class and peasant milieus, "youth" began with the last day of elementary school and ended with marriage. For more than 90 percent of the population schooling never extended past the legally defined school-leaving age of thirteen or fourteen. Certainly secondary school remained beyond the means or the inclination of all but an exceptionally few working-class children. In fact, many historians have argued, secondary schooling became less available for working-class and rural youth as the century progressed. Margret Kraul, Peter Koppenhöeffer, Hartmut Kaelble, and Detlev Muëller, in separate studies on the evolution of the *Gymnasium* (classic secondary school), all contend that whereas these institutions had been relatively open in the early part of the century, by the foundation of the Second Empire (1871) changes in curricula, cost, and career-tracking effectively restricted access to them to the elite middle class.[46] As social prestige and career advancement became more closely tied to educational attainment, these reforms froze lower- and working-class children into their socioeconomic niche.[47]

But if most studies agree in pointing to the limited availability of secondary education, there is, nevertheless, some evidence to suggest that schooling did really matter for certain marginal social classes. Fritz Ringer, James Albisetti, and Konrad Jarausch, for example, note that although the educational reforms of the nineteenth century did little to aid the upward mobility of working-class children, the establishment and expansion of less classically oriented schools and the enhancement of girls' secondary education did mark the beginning of an era of increased, albeit limited, social mobility for the lower stratas of the middle-class and for middle-class girls.[48] As Jarausch observes, however, less work has been done on the social history of modern schools and on girls' schools, and therefore more conclusive analysis of social opportunity and these reforms must await this work.[49]

For the growing, if still select, numbers of young people who did continue on in their paths to professional or bureaucratic careers, the demands of secondary schooling, university study, and postuniversity training necessitated that they remain out of the work force and dependent on their parents or relatives for support for extended periods of time. In the late nineteenth and early twentieth centuries the flood of applicants to professional and bureaucratic positions that rising secondary and university enrollments produced, added even more years of waiting before a job could be found.[50] Secondary-school teacher trainees, for example, could not expect to begin a full-time career during this period until they were almost thirty-five. Aspiring lawyers, engineers, government officials, doctors, and pastors found their lot hardly more promising. As they had no income, coresidency with their parents remained a necessity for many students and trainees during this seemingly interminable wait for independence. Marriage, because it was dependent on financial security, had to be put off as well.[51] Some young men, such as Max Weber, found themselves returning to the nest after years of relative independence; the burden of this return to an almost childlike dependence on parents often was intolerable.

The relatively early entrance into work and financial independence for work-ing-class children in Imperial Germany stood in sharp contrast to this lengthy period of dependency that characterized the transition from childhood to adult-hood for many middle-class boys and an increasing proportion of middle-class girls. Paralleling these divergent experiences of working-class and middle-class youth was the emergence of class-bound youth cultures and identities. Problems of suicide, psychosexual torment, and generational conflict that became asso-ciated with adolescence reflected the lengthy moratorium of middle-class youth. Working-class children, because they became independent much sooner, often were considered immune from these storms and stresses of prolonged depend-ency.[52] Organizations such as the *Wandervogel*, a middle-class youth hiking society, were established in the 1890s by concerned parents and teachers to combat the problems of middle-class youth.[53] Working-class youth groups, es-pecially those founded by the Social Democratic party around the turn of the century, often focused on issues of wages and workplace conditions, reflecting the different concerns of young laborers.[54] Even as there was no single history of childhood in Germany, so, too, does inquiry into the conditions and expe-riences of youth reveal important sociohistorical variations.

CONCLUSIONS

The literature on the history of childhood in Germany—in all its phases from infancy through the transition to adulthood—is a rich and suggestive one. No single theme can characterize it in its diversity, but it is worth returning to important leitmotivs that recur through much of it. The chronological, regional, class, and gender variations that have marked perceptions and experiences of children, as well as the institutions surrounding childhood in German history, emphasize the social construction of personality. Socialization practices are rooted in more general social relations and their transformation over time, but can serve to either reinforce or undermine them. Moreover, even if the pertinent boundaries of specific socialization practices turn out to be regional rather than national, or class-cultural rather than geographical, the close study of childhood in its German variants has suggested connections between alternative family rationalities and adult personality, behavior, and attitudes. The promise for his-torical understanding is immense: not a return to old cliches about national character, certainly, but a more nuanced understanding about the historical roots and the long-term consequences of child-rearing practices as these are felt over the life course, over the generations, and over the course of history.

NOTES

We thank Matt Søbek and Birgitte Soland for their help in the research for this article.

1. For a discussion of pertinent developments in German historiography, see G. Iggers, *New Directions in European Historiography* (Middletown, 1975); R. Lee, ''The

German Family: A Critical Survey of the Current State of Historical Research," in *The German Family. Essays on the Social History of the Family in Nineteenth- and Twentieth-Century Germany*, ed. R. Evans and W. R. Lee (London, 1981); G. Eley, "Memories of Underdevelopment: Social History in Germany," *Social History* 2 (1977):785–791. On historical demography in particular, see A. Imhof, *Einführung in die Historische Demographie* (Munich, 1977).

2. D. Blackbourn and G. Eley's *The Peculiarities of German History* (Oxford, 1984) addresses the leitmotiv of German "peculiarity" (the so-called *Sonderweg* thesis) that characterizes much of the historical writing about Germany since the Nazi era. Their powerful critique on various dominant formulations of the German past centers on the relations between social and political evolution. Nevertheless, studies of family and socialization also remain marginal to their critique.

3. These early studies of German youth include W. Laqueur, *Young Germany. A History of the German Youth Movement* (New York, 1962); P. Loewenberg, "The Psychohistorical Origins of the Nazi Youth Cohort," *American Historical Review* 76 (1971):1457–1502. The first comparative sociohistorical treatment in English of German youth was J. Gillis, *Youth and History. Tradition and Change in European Age Relations, 1770–Present* (New York, 1975). For a full bibliography see A. Esler, *The Generation Gap in Society and History. A Select Bibliography* (Monticello, Ill., 1984). Refer to the last section of the essay for a discussion of German youth history.

4. For a discussion of nineteenth-century family sociology, and especially the work of Wilhelm Riehl, see M. Mitterauer and R. Sieder, *The European Family* (Chicago, 1982), pp. 24ff., and R. J. Evans, "Politics and the Family: Social Democracy and the Working-Class Family in Theory and Practice before 1914," in Evans and Lee, eds., *German Family*.

5. For an introduction to the history of the German family in the preindustrial era see Mitterauer and Sieder, *European Family*; L. Berkner, "The Stem Family and the Developmental Cycle of the Peasant Household. An Eighteenth-century Austrian Example," *American Historical Review* 77 (1972):398–430; E. Shorter, *The Making of the Modern Family* (New York, 1975); I. Weber-Kellermann, *Die deutsche Familie. Versuch einer Sozialgeschichte* (Frankfurt, 1974); T. Hubbard, *Familiengeschichte. Materielen zur deutschen Familie seit dem Ende des 18. Jahrhunderts* (Munich, 1983). For bibliographic guidance see G. Soliday et al., eds., *History of the Family and Kinship. A Select International Bibliography* (New York, 1980), and U. Herrmann, S. Rentfle, and L. Roth, eds., *Bibliographie zur Geschichte der Kindheit, Jugend und Familie* (Munich, 1980).

6. On child rearing in different social milieus see, in addition to the general family histories cited above, edited by J. Schlumbohm, *Kinderstuben. Wie Kinder zu Bauern, Bürgern, Aristokraten wurden, 1700–1850* (Munich, 1983).

7. M. J. Maynes, *Schooling for the People. Comparative Local Studies of Schooling History in France and Germany, 1750–1850* (New York, 1985), p. 110. For similar examples from other regions of Germany see Schlumbohm, *Kinderstuben*, pp. 62ff.

8. As elsewhere in Europe, village youth played a special role in the organization of village social life. See Gillis, *Youth and History*, and H. Medick, "Village Spinning Bees: Sexual Culture and Free Time Among Rural Youth in Early Modern Germany," in *Interest and Emotion. Essays on the Study of Family and Kinship*, ed. H. Medick and D. W. Sabean (Cambridge, 1984). A. Gestrich, *Traditionelle Jugundkultur und Industrialisierung. Sozialgeschicte der Jugend in einer ländlichen Arbeitergemeinde Württem-*

bergs, 1800–1920 (Göttingen, 1986), traces village youth culture through the early twentieth century.

9. Shorter, *Making of the Modern Family*, ch. 5.

10. For a discussion of these reports see H. Teuteberg and A. Bernard, "Wandel der Kindernahrung in der Zeit der Industrialisierung," in *Fabrik. Familie. Feierabend. Beiträge zur Sozialgeschichte des Alltags im Industriezeitalter*, ed. J. Reulecke and W. Weber (Wuppertal, 1978), and C. Duhamelle, "Les deux Allemagnes de l'enfance," *Institut d'histoire economique et sociale. Université de Paris I. Récherches et travaux* 16 (January 1987):9–51.

11. Cited in Teuteberg and Bernhard, "Wandel der Kindernahrung," pp. 193–194.

12. For regional variation in infant mortality see Schlumbohm, *Kinderstuben*, pp. 33ff., and Duhamelle, "Les deux Allemagnes de l'enfance," as well as J. Knodel, "Natural Fertility in Pre-Industrial Germany," *Population Studies* 32 (1978):481–510.

13. J. Knodel, "From Natural Fertility to Family Limitation: The Onset of Fertility Transition in a Sample of German Villages," *Demography* 16 (1979):493–521.

14. R. Schulte, "Infanticide in Rural Bavaria in the Nineteenth Century," in Medick and Sabean, eds., *Interest and Emotion*, p. 92. See also O. Ulbricht, "Infanticide in Eighteenth-century Germany," in *The German Underworld*, ed. R. J. Evans (London, 1988).

15. Duhamelle, "Les deux Allemagnes," pp. 22ff.

16. From Hans Medick, "The Proto-industrial Family Economy: The Structural Function of Household and Family During the Transition from Peasant Society to Industrial Capitalism," *Social History* 3 (1976):291–315. See also W. R. Lee, "Family and 'Modernisation': The Peasant Family and Social Change in Nineteenth-century Bavaria," in Evans and Lee, eds., *German Family*; D. Sabean, "Small Peasant Agriculture in Germany at the Beginning of the Nineteenth Century: Changing Work Patterns," *Peasant Studies* 7 (1978):218–224; A. Imhof, "Women, Family and Death: Excess Mortality of Women of Childbearing Age in Four Communities in Nineteenth-century Germany," in Evans and Lee, eds., *German Family*.

17. The pathbreaking study by Philippe Ariès, translated into English in 1962 as *Centuries of Childhood*, appeared in German in 1975. J. Schlumbohm noted, however, that as early as 1956, an important Dutch study of the history of childhood by Jan Hendrick van den Berg appeared with far less fanfare and was translated into German in 1960. Only now, with a revived interest in the history of socialization and especially in the interpretations of the Dutch sociologist Norbert Elias, in this "pre-history" recalled. See Schlumbohm's "Geschichte der Kindheit—Fragen und Kontroversen," *Geschichtsdidaktik* 4 (1983):305–315.

18. Quoted in G. Stecher, *Die Erziehungsbestrebungen der deutschen Moralischen Wochenschriften* (Leipzig, 1914), p. 98. See also A. Brown, "On Education: John Locke, Christian Wolff, and the 'Moral Weeklies,' " *University of California Publications in Modern Philology* 36 (1952):153.

19. Quoted in Schlumbohm, *Kinderstuben*, p. 319.

20. On the history of children's literature see A. C. Baumgartner and H. Pleticha, *ABC und Abenteuer: Texte und Dokumente zur Geschichte des deutschen Kinder- und Jugendbuches* (Munich, 1985). For cultural artifacts surrounding childhood see I. Weber-Kellermann, *Die Kindheit. Kleidung und Wohnung, Arbeit und Spiel* (Frankfurt, 1979).

21. This interpretation is presented in J. Schlumbohm, "Traditional Collectivity and 'Modern' Individuality: Some Questions and Suggestions for the Historical Study of

Socialization. The Examples of the German Lower and Upper Bourgeoisies Around 1800,'' *Social History* 5 (1980):71–103, and D. Elschenbroich, *Kinder werden nicht geboren. Studien zur Entstehung der Kindheit* (Frankfurt/M., 1977).

22. On the general history of elementary schooling in central Europe see Maynes, *Schooling for the People*, and *Schooling in Western Europe. A Social History* (Albany, 1985); D. K. Müller, *Sozialstrucktur und Schulsystem. Aspekte zum Strukturwandel des Schulwesens im 19. Jahrhundert* (Göttingen, 1977); P. Lundgreen, *Sozialgeschichte der deutschen Schule im Überblick* (Göttingen, 1980–1981), and R. Bölling, *Sozialgeschichte der deutsche Lehrer. Ein Überblick von 1800 bis zur Gegenwart* (Göttingen, 1983). For aspects of dominant pedagogical theory and state organization see G. Petrat, *Schulunterricht. Seine Sozialgeschichte in Deutschland 1750 bis 1850* (Munich, 1979); M. Heinemann, *Schule im Vorfeld der Verwaltung: die Entwicklung der preussischen Unterrichtsverwaltung von 1771–1800* (Göttingen, 1974); and A. Leschinsky and P. M. Roeder, *Schule im historischen Prozess* (Stuttgart, 1976).

23. See G. Strauss, *Luther's House of Learning. Indoctrination of the Young in the German Reformation* (Baltimore, 1978), and M. J. Maynes, "The Virtues of Archaism: The Political Economy of Schooling in Europe, 1750–1850," *Comparative Studies in Society and History* 21 (1979):611–625.

24. On early state intervention in schooling see, for example, H. Titze, *Die Politisierung der Erziehung* (Frankfurt, 1973); A. Leschinsky and P. M. Roeder, *Schule im historischen Prozess. Zum Wechselverhältnis von institutioneller Erziehung und gesellschaftlicher Entwicklung* (Stuttgart, 1976), and K. Hartmann, F. Nyssen, and H. Waldeyer, eds., *Schule und Staat im 18. und 19. Jahrhundert* (Frankfurt, 1973).

25. See Maynes, *Schooling for the People*, especially ch. 8. The concluding section of this chapter treats studies of schooling and social mobility in the later nineteenth century.

26. On girls' education see Schlumbohm, *Kinderstuben*; J. Schneider, "Enlightened Reforms and Bavarian Girls' Education," and J. Jacobi-Dittrich, "Growing Up Female in the Nineteenth Century," in *German Women in the Nineteenth Century*, ed. J. Fout (New York, 1984); I. Weber-Kellermann, *Frauenleben im 19. Jahrhundert* (Munich, 1983), and I. Brehmer, J. Jacobi-Dittrich, E. Kleinau, and A. Kuhn, eds., *Frauen in der Geschichte IV. "Wissen heisst leben . . ." Beiträge zur Bildungsgeschichte von Frauen im 18. und 19. Jahrhundert* (Düsseldorf, 1983).

27. J. Kuczynski, *Studien zur Geschichte der Lage des arbeitenden Kinder in Deutschland von 1700 bis zur Gegenwart* (Berlin, 1968).

28. Some of the recent books, and collections containing articles on the working-class family of the nineteenth century include W. Conze and Ulrich Engelhardt, *Arbeiter im Industrialisierungsprozess* (Stuttgart, 1979); P. Borscheid and H. J. Teuteberg, eds., *Ehe, Liebe, Tod. Zum Wandel der Familie, der Geschlechts- und Generationsbeziehungen in der Neuzeit* (Münster, 1983); R. Beier, *Frauenarbeit und Frauenalltag. Heimarbeiterinnen in der Berliner Bekleidungsindustrie, 1880–1914* (Frankfurt, 1983); Evans and Lee, eds., *German Family*; M. Flecken, *Arbeiterkinder im 19. Jahrhundert. Eine sozialgeschichtliche Untersuchung ihrer Lebenswelt* (Weinheim, 1981); J. Reulecke and W. Weber, eds., *Fabrik. Familie. Feierabend. Beiträge zur Sozialgeschichte des Alltags im Industriezeitalter* (Wuppertal, 1978), and K. Saul et al., eds., *Arbeiterfamilien im Kaiserreich. Materielen zur Sozialgeschichte in Deutschland, 1871–1914* (Düsseldorf, 1982).

29. This argument is most fully elaborated in Flecken, *Arbeiterkinder*.

30. R. Spree, *Soziale Ungleichheit vor Krankheit und Tod* (Göttingen, 1981), pp. 170–171.

31. Ibid., pp. 46–49.

32. Ibid., *Soziale Ungleichheit*, p. 180.

33. The family life cycle in working-class occupations is discussed in H. Schomerus, "The Family Life-Cycle: A Study of Factory Workers in Nineteenth-century Württemberg," in Evans and Lee, eds., *German Family*, and M. Haines, *Fertility and Occupation* (New York, 1979).

34. G. Hohorst, J. Kocka, and G. A. Ritter, eds., *Sozialgeschichtliches Arbeitsbuch. Band II, Materialen zur Statistik des Kaisserreichs 1870–1914* (Munich, 1978), pp. 38–40.

35. Surveys cited in Hohorst et al., *Arbeitsbuch*, pp. 109ff. See also Flecken, *Arbeiterkinder*; Beier, *Frauenarbeit*; B. Franzoi, *At the Very Least She Pays the Rent* (Westport, Conn.: 1985); R. Dasey, "Women's Work and the Family: Women Garment Workers in Berlin and Hamburg Before the First World War," in Evans and Lee, eds., *German Family* (London, 1981).

36. Beier, *Frauenarbeit*, pp. 96ff., and Flecken, *Arbeiterkinder*, pp. 32ff.

37. See Flecken, *Arbeiterkinder*, and M. J. Maynes, "The Contours of Childhood: Demography, Strategy and Mythology of Childhood in French and German Lower-Class Autobiographies," in Gillis, Levine, and Tilly, eds., *The European Experience of Fertility Decline, 1850–1970* (London, 1991).

38. For two somewhat different accounts of German socialism and the family see R. J. Evans, "Politics and the Family: Social Democracy and the Working-Class Family in Theory and Practice Before 1914," in Evans and Lee, eds., *German Family*, and H. Niggemann, *Emanzipation zwischen Sozialismus und Feminismus* (Wuppertal, 1981).

39. See, for example, Gestrich, *Traditionelle Jugendkultur*; E. Rosenhaft, "Organizing the 'Lumpenproletariat': Cliques and Communists in Berlin During the Weimar Republic," in *The German Working Class, 1890–1933*, ed. R. J. Evans (London, 1982), and I. Behnken and J. Zinnecker, "Vom Strassenkind zum verhäuslichten Kind. Zur Modernisierung städtischer Kindheit 1900–1980," *Sozialwissenschaftliche Informationen* 16 (1987):87–96.

40. Until recently little attention has been paid to the evolution of youth as a phase of the life cycle and to the meaning of specific terms used to describe this period. Gillis' *Youth and History* was a pioneering work in this regard. Recent noteworthy contributions include Gestrich's *Traditionelle Jugendkultur*, G. Roth's *Die Erfindung der Jugendlichen* (Munich, 1982), and M. Mitterauer's "Gesindedienst und Jugendphase im europäischen Vergleich," *Geschichte und Gesellschaft* 11 (1985):177–204.

41. Despite their place at the forefront of child psychology, Germans did not establish a specific psychology of youth until the publication of A. Cramer's *Puberty and School* in 1910. Wilhelm Rein's *Encyclopedic Guide to Pedagogy*, written in 1895, dealt only with the psychology of children until the end of their elementary school years (the so-called *Flegeljahre*). For studies of adolescence in Wilhelmine Germany see Robert Paul Newmann, "Masturbation, Madness and the Modern Concepts of Childhood and Adolescence," *Journal of Social History* 8 (1975):1–28; Sterling Fishman, "Sex, Suicide and the Discovery of the German Adolescent," *History of Education Quarterly* 10 (1970):170–188; Roth, *Die Erfindung des Jugendlichen*; and Gillis, *Youth and History*.

42. Tom Taylor, "The Crisis of Youth in Wilhelmine Germany" (Ph.D. diss., University of Minnesota, 1988).

43. As with child labor in the preindustrial period, precious little has been done to define the impact of these changes in production on the transition from childhood to adulthood. Rudolf Braun's *Industrialisierung und Volksleben* (Erlenbach-Zurich, 1960) is still useful in this regard, as is Gillis' *Youth and History*. D. Crew's *A Town in the Ruhr: A Social History of Bochum 1860–1914* (New York, 1979) is indispensable for an understanding of the impact of industrialization on child labor, as are H. Schomerus, *Die Arbeiter der Maschinenfabrik Esslingen. Forschungen zur Lage der Arbeiterschaft des 19. Jahrhunderts* (Stuttgart, 1977), and Gestrich, *Traditionelle Jugendkultur*.

44. Schomerus, *Die Arbeiter.*

45. Gestrich, *Traditionelle Jugendkultur.*

46. Peter Koppenhöfer, *Bildung und Auslese. Untersuchungen zur sozialen Herkunft der höheren Schüler Badens, 1834/36–1890* (Weinheim, 1980); Margaret Kraul, *Gymnasium und Gesellschaft in Vormärz. Neuhumanistische Einheitsschule, städtische Gesellschaft und soziale Herkunft der Schüler* (Göttingen, 1980); Müller, *Sozialstruktur und Schulsystem.* David Crew also found little upward mobility through education in his study of Bochum, *Town in the Ruhr.* Hartmut Kaelble, focusing on the economic aspects of this transition, notes that in the early nineteenth century, scholarships and charity often made it possible for talented, yet poor children to go to secondary school. The mid-nineteenth century, in contrast, became an era of competitive opportunities in which scholarships diminished and, correspondingly, so did educational access. See his book, *Social Mobility in the Nineteenth and Twentieth Centuries: Europe and America in Comparative Perspective* (Leamington Spa, N.H., 1985), esp. 56–76.

47. Recent work by Peter Lundgreen suggests that despite the increasing importance of formal education for career allocation in the nineteenth century, it was only in the twentieth century that education replaced social origin as the main indicator of status attainment. See P. Lundgreen, "Educational Opportunity and Status Attainment: Two Different Cities in Nineteenth-Century Germany" (paper presented to *German Studies Association Conference*, St. Louis, October 1987). Lundgreen's paper is part of a larger work on education and social opportunity that he has written with M. Kraul and K. Ditt, *Bildungschancen und soziale Mobilität in der Städtischen Gesellschaft des 19. Jahrhunderts* (Göttingen, 1988).

48. These arguments are reviewed in two recent summaries of the debates on the relation between social mobility and educational opportunity: D. Müller, F. Ringer, and B. Simon, eds., *The Rise of the Modern Educational System: Structural Change and Social Reproduction, 1870–1920* (Cambridge, 1987), and K. Jarausch, "The Old 'New' History of Education': A German Reconsideration," *History of Education Quarterly* 26 (Summer 1986):225–241.

49. Jarausch, "Old 'New History of Education,' " p. 231. For women's education see James Albisetti, "Could Separate Be Equal? Helene Lange and Women's Education in Imperial Germany," *History of Education Quarterly* 22 (Fall 1982):301–317. Albisetti's fuller treatment of women's secondary education in Imperial Germany should be appearing soon. The discussion of the relation between education and social mobility also benefits from the appearance of a three-volume series of data handbooks on the history of German education at the elementary, secondary, and university levels currently being compiled by the QUARKI research consortium in Germany. See Jarausch, "Old 'New History of Education,' " p. 228.

50. This "excess of educated men" in Germany, as Lenore O'Boyle referred to it, has been a cyclic phenomena in modern German history. In fact, much of the recent

historical investigation into the problem of overproduction of academics in Germany has resulted from current concerns over these issues. L. O'Boyle, "The Problem of an Excess of Educated Men in Western Europe, 1800–1850," *Journal of Modern History* 4:42 (December 1970):471–495. See also H. Titze, "Die zyklische Überproduktion von Akademikern im 19. und 20. Jahrhundert," *Geschichte und Gesellschaft* 10 (1984):92–121.

51. In the United States, by way of comparison, most professional men had completed their education, started a career, and married by their mid-twenties. T. Taylor, "The Transition to Adulthood in Comparative Perspective: Professional Males in Germany and the United States at the Turn of the Century," *Journal of Social History* 21 (Summer 1988):635–658.

52. Taylor, "Crisis of Youth in Wilhelmine Germany." See also J. Albisetti, *Secondary School Reform in Imperial Germany* (Princeton, N.J., 1983).

53. The *Wandervogel* has been seen as a protest movement, started by middle-class secondary students in opposition to their elders. This interpretation is largely based on observations by an early member and historian of the group, Hans Blüher, author of *Wandervogel: Geschichte eine Jugendbewegung*, Part I *Heimat und Aufgang* (Berlin-Tempelhof, 1912). Two recent studies by German sociologists have contradicted Blüher's claim, arguing that intergenerational cooperation rather than conflict was typical in the *Wandervogel*. Parents and teachers used these organizations to enlist the support of middle-class youth in the struggles against Social Democracy. See U. Aufmuth, *Die deutsche Wandervogelbewegung unter soziologischen Aspekt* (Göttingen, 1979), and O. Neuloh and W. Zilius, *Die Wandervögel: eine emperisch-soziologische Untersuchung der frühen deutschen Jugendbewegung* (Göttingen, 1982).

54. Unfortunately much less has been done on working-class youth organizations than their middle-class counterparts. A useful introduction is Alex Hall, "Youth in Rebellion: The Beginnings of the Socialist Youth Movement, 1904–1914," in R. J. Evans, ed., *Society and Politics in Wilhelmine Germany* (London, 1978).

REFERENCES

Albisetti, James C. "Could Separate Be Equal? Helene Lange and Women's Education in Imperial Germany." *History of Education Quarterly* 22 (Fall 1982):301–317.

———. *Secondary School Reform in Imperial Germany*. Princeton, 1983.

Allen, Ann Taylor. "Gardens of Children, Gardens of God: Kindergartens and Day-Care Centers in Nineteenth-Century Germany." *Journal of Social History* 19 (1986):433–450.

Ariès, Philippe. *Centuries of Childhood. A Social History of Family Life*. New York, 1962.

Aufmuth, Ulrich. *Die deutsche Wandervogelbewegung unter soziologischen Aspekt*. Göttingen, 1979.

Baumgartner, A. C., and Heinrich Pleticha, eds. *ABC und Abenteuer: Texte und Dokumente zur Geschichte des deutschen Kinder-und Jugendbuches*. Vols. 1–2. Munich, 1985.

Behnken, Imbke, and Jürgen Zinnecker. "Vom Strassenkind zum verhäuslichten Kind. Zur Modernisierung städtischer Kindheit, 1900–1980." *Sozialwissenschaftliche Informationen* 16 (1987):87–96.

Beier, Rosemarie. *Frauenarbeit und Frauenalltag. Heimarbeiterinnen in der Berliner Bekleidungsindustrie, 1880–1914*. Frankfurt, 1983.

Berkner, L. "The Stem Family and the Developmental Cycle of the Peasant Household. An Eighteenth-Century Example," *American Historical Review* 77 (1972):398–430.

Blackbourn, David, and Geoff Eley. *The Peculiarities of German History.* Oxford, 1984.

Bölling, Rainer. *Sozialgeschichte der deutschen Lehrer. Ein Überblick von 1800 bis zur Gegenwart.* Göttingen, 1983.

———. "Schule, Staat und Gesellschaft in Deutschland. Neuere Literatur zur Sozialgeschichte der Bildung im 19. und 20. Jahrhundert." *Archiv fur Sozialgeschichte* 25 (1985):670–686.

Borscheid, Peter, and Hans Jürgen Teuteberg, eds. *Ehe, Liebe, Tod. Zum Wandel der Familie, der Geschlechts- und Generationsbeziehungen in der Neuzeit.* Münster, 1983.

Brehmer, Ilse, J. Jacobi-Dittrich, E. Kleinau, and A. Kuhn, eds. *Frauen in der Geschichte IV. "Wissen heisst leben . . ." Beiträge zur Bildungsgeschichte von Frauen im 18. und 19. Jahrhundert.* Düsseldorf, 1983.

Bulst, N., et al., eds. *Familien zwischen Tradition u. Moderne. Studien zur Geschichte der Familie in Deutschland u. Frankreich vom 16. bis zum 20. Jahrhundert.* Göttingen, 1981.

Conze, Werner, and Ulrich Engelhardt, eds. *Arbeiter im Industrialisierungsprozess.* Stuttgart, 1979.

Crew, David F. *A Town in the Ruhr: A Social History of Bochum 1860–1914.* New York, 1979.

Dasey, Robyn. "Women's Work and the Family: Women Garment Workers in Berlin and Hamburg Before the First World War." In *The German Family. Essays on the Social History of the Family in Nineteenth- and Twentieth-Century Germany,* edited by Richard J. Evans and W. R. Lee. London, 1981.

Dittrich-Jacobi, Juliana. "Growing Up Female in the Nineteenth Century." In *German Women in the Nineteenth Century,* edited by J. Fout. New York, 1984.

Duhamelle, Christophe. "Les deux Allemagnes de l'enfance." *Institut d'histoire économique et sociale. Université de Paris I. Recherches et travaux* 16 (January 1987):9–51.

Eley, Geoff. "Memories of Underdevelopment: Social History in Germany." *Social History* 2 (1977):785–791.

Elschenbroich, Donata. *Kinder werden nicht geboren. Studien zur Entstehung der Kindheit.* Frankfurt/M., 1977.

Esler, Anthony. *The Generation Gap in Society and History. A Select Bibliography.* Monticello, Ill., 1984.

Evans, Richard J. "Politics and the Family: Social Democracy and the Working-Class Family in Theory and Practice Before 1914." In *The German Family. Essays on the Social History of the Family in Nineteenth- and Twentieth-Century Germany,* edited by R. J. Evans and W. R. Lee. London, 1981.

Fischer, W., J. Krengel, and J. Wietog. *Sozialgeschichtliches Arbeitsbuch. Band I, Materialen zur Statistik des Deutschen Bundes 1815–1870.* Munich, 1982.

Fishman, Sterling. "Suicide, Sex and the Discovery of the German Adolescent." *History of Education Quarterly* 10 (1970):170–188.

Flecken, Margarete. *Arbeiterkinder im 19. Jahrhundert. Eine sozialgeschichtliche Untersuchung ihrer Lebenswelt.* Weinheim, 1981.

Franzoi, Barbara. *At the Very Least She Pays the Rent.* Westport, Conn., 1985.

Friedrich, G. *Die Volksschule im Württemberg im 19. Jahrhundert*. Weinheim, 1978.

Gestrich, Andreas. *Traditionelle Jugendkultur und Industrialisierung. Sozialgeschichte der Jugend in einer ländlichen Arbeitergemeinde Württembergs, 1800–1920*. Göttingen, 1986.

Gillis, John R. *Youth and History. Tradition and Change in European Age Relations, 1770–Present*. New York, 1981.

Haines, Michael. *Fertility and Occupation*. New York, 1979.

Hall, Alex. "Youth in Rebellion: The Beginnings of the Socialist Youth Movement, 1904–1914." In *Society and Politics in Wilhelmine Germany*, edited by Richard J. Evans. London, 1978.

Hardach, Gerd, and Irene Hardach-Pinke. *Deutsche Kindheiten. Autobiographische Zeugnisse, 1700–1950*. Kronberg, 1978.

Heinemann, Manfred. *Schule im Vorfeld der Verwaltung: die Entwicklung der preussischen Unterrichtsverwaltung von 1771–1800*. Göttingen, 1974.

———. "Economic Foundations for the Development of Schools in Prussia." In *L'offre d'école. Elements pour une étude comparée des politiques educatives au XIXe siècle*, edited by W. Frijhoff. Paris, 1983.

Herrlitz, Hans-Georg, Wulf Hopf, and Hartmut Titze. *Deutsche Schulgeschichte von 1800 bis zur Gegenwart. Eine Einführung*. Königstein, 1981.

Herrmann, Ulrich. "Pädagogische Anthropologie und die "Entdeckung" des Kindes im Zeitalter der Aufklärung—Kindheit und Jugendalter im Werk Joachim Heinrich Campes." In *Die Bildung des Bürgers. Die Formierung der bürgerlichen Gesellschaft und die Gebildeten im 18. Jahrhundert*, edited by Ulrich Herrmann. Weinheim, 1982.

———. *Schule und Gesellschaft im 19. Jahrhundert*. Weinheim, 1977.

Herrmann, Ulrich, Susanne Rentfle, and Lutz Roth. *Bibliographie zur Geschichte der Kindheit, Jugend und Familie*. Munich, 1980.

Hohorst, G., J. Kocka, and G. A. Ritter, eds. *Sozialgeschichtliches Arbeitsbuch. Band II, Materialen zur Statistik des Kaiserreichs 1870–1914*. Munich, 1978.

Hubbard, Thomas. *Familiengeschichte. Materielen zur Geschichte der Familie seit dem Ende des 18. Jahrhunderts*. Munich, 1983.

Iggers, George. *New Directions in European Historiography*. Middletown, Conn., 1975.

Imhof, Arthur E. *Einführung in die historische Demographie*. Munich, 1977.

———. *Die gewonnenen Jahre*. Munich, 1981.

———. "Women, Family and Death: Excess Mortality of Women in Childbearing Age in Four Communities in Nineteenth-Century Germany." In *The German Family. Essays on the Social History of the Family in Nineteenth- and Twentieth-Century Germany*, edited by R. J. Evans and W. R. Lee. London, 1981.

Jackson, James H. "Overcrowding and Family Life: Working-Class Families and the Housing Crisis in Late Nineteenth-Century Duisberg." In *The German Family. Essays on the Social History of the Family in Nineteenth- and Twentieth-Century Germany*, edited by Richard J. Evans and W. R. Lee. London, 1981.

Jacobi-Dittrich, J. "Growing Up Female in the Nineteenth Century." In *German Women in the Nineteenth Century*, edited by John Fout. New York, 1984.

Jarausch, Konrad. "The Old 'New History of Education': A German Reconsideration." *History of Education Quarterly* 26 (Summer 1986):225–241.

Kaelble, Hartmut. *Social Mobility in the Nineteenth and Twentieth Centuries: Europe and America in Comparative Perspective*. Leamington Spa, N.H., 1985.

Knodel, John. "Natural Fertility in Pre-Industrial Germany." *Population Studies* 32 (1978):481–510.

———. "From Natural Fertility to Family Limitation: The Onset of Fertility Transition in a Sample of German Villages." *Demography* 16 (1979):493–521.

Köllmann, Wolfgang. "Aus dem Alltag der Unterschichten in der Vor- und Frühindustrialisierungsphase." In *Fabrik. Familie. Feierabend. Beiträge zur Sozialgeschichte des Alltas im Industriezeitalter*, edited by Jürgen Reulecke and Wolfhard Weber. Wuppertal, 1978.

Koppenhöffer, Peter. *Bildung und Auslese. Untersuchungen zur sozialen Herkunft der höheren Schüler Badens, 1834/36–1890.* Weinheim, 1980.

Kraul, Margaret. *Gymnasium und Gesellschaft im Vormärz. Neuhumanistische Einheitsschule, städtische Gesellschaft und soziale Herkunft der Schüler.* Göttingen, 1980.

Kuczynski, Jurgen. *Die Geschichte der Lage der Arbeiter unter dem Kapitalismus*, Vol. 19. *Studien zur Geschichte der Lage des arbeitenden Kindes in Deutschland von 1700 bis zur Gegenwart.* Berlin, 1968.

Laqueur, Walter. *Young Germany. A History of the German Youth Movement.* New York, 1962.

Lee, Robert. "Family and 'Modernisation': The Peasant Family and Social Change in Nineteenth-Century Bavaria." In *The German Family. Essays on the Social History of the Family in Nineteenth- and Twentieth-Century Germany*, edited by Richard J. Evans and W. R. Lee. London, 1981.

———. "The German Family: A Critical Survey of the Current State of Historical Research." In *The German Family. Essays on the Social History of the Family ion Nineteenth- and Twentieth-Century Germany*, edited by R. Evans and W. R. Lee. London, 1981.

Leschinsky, Achim, and Peter Martin Roeder. *Schule im historischem Prozess. Zum Wechselverhältnis von institutioneller Erziehung und gesellschaftlicher Entwicklung.* Stuttgart, 1976.

Loewenberg, Peter. "The Psychohistorical Origins of the Nazi Youth Cohort." *American Historical Review* 76 (1971):1457–1502.

Lundgreen, Peter. "Bildung und Besitz—Einheit oder Inkongruenz in der europäischen Sozialgeschichte." *Geschichte und Gesellschaft* 7 (1981):262–275.

———. *Sozialgeschichte der deutschen Schule im Überblick.* Göttingen, 1980–1981.

———. "Educational Opportunity and Status Attainment: Two Different Cities in Nineteeth-Century Germany." Paper presented to the German Studies Association Conference, St. Louis, October 1987.

Lundgreen, Peter, Margaret Kraul, and Karl Ditt. *Bildungschancen und soziale Mobilität in der städtischen Gesellschaft des 19. Jahrhunderts.* Göttingen, 1988.

Maynes, Mary Jo. "The Virtues of Archaism: The Political Economy of Schooling in Europe, 1750–1850." *Comparative Studies in Society and History* 21 (1979):611–625.

———. *Schooling in Western Europe: A Social History.* Albany, 1985.

———. *Schooling for the People. Comparative Local Studies of Schooling History in France and Germany, 1750–1850.* New York, 1985.

———. "The Contours of Childhood: Demography, Strategy and Mythology of Childhood in French and German Lower-Class Autobiographies." To appear in a book in progress by the European Fertility Decline Group entitled *Starting to Stop. Class, Gender and Politics in the European Fertility Decline.*

Medick, Hans. "The Proto-industrial Family Economy: The Structural Function of Household and Family During the Transition from Peasant Society to Industrial Capitalism." *Social History* 3 (1976):291–315.

———. "Village Spinning Bees: Sexual Culture and Free Time Among Rural Youth in Early Modern Germany." In *Interest and Emotion. Essays on the Study of Family and Kinship*, edited by Hans Medick and David W. Sabean. Cambridge, 1984.

Meyer, Folkert. *Schule der Untertanen. Lehrer und Politik in Preussen, 1848–1900.* Hamburg, 1976.

Mitterauer, Michael. "Gesindedienst und Jugendphase im europäischen Vergleich." *Geschichte und Gesellschaft* 11 (1985):177–204.

Mitterauer, Michael, and Reinhard Sieder. *The European Family.* Chicago, 1982.

Muchow, Hans. *Sexualreife und Sozialstruktur der Jugend.* Reinbek bei Hamburg, 1959.

Müller, Detlef K. *Sozialstruktur und Schulsystem: Aspekte zum Strukturwandel des Schulwesens im 19. Jahrhundert.* Göttingen, 1977.

Müller, Detlef K., Fritz Ringer, and Brian Simon, eds. *The Rise of the Modern Educational System: Structural Change and Social Reproduction, 1870–1920.* Cambridge, 1987.

Mutschler, Susanne. *Landliche Kindheit in Lebenserinnerungen. Familien- und Kinderleben in einem württembergischen Arbeiterbauerndorf an der Wende vom 19. zum 20. Jahrhundert.* Tübingen, 1985.

Neuloh, Otto, and Wilhelm Zilius. *Die Wandervogel: eine empirisch-soziologische Untersuchung der frühen deutschen Jugendbewegung.* Göttingen, 1982.

Neumann, Frank. "La reforme scolaire francaise des années 1880 jugée par la social-democratie contemporaine de langue allemande." In *L'offre d'école. Elements pour une étude comparée des politiques educatives au XIXe siècle*, edited by W. Frijhoff. Paris, 1983.

Newman, Robert Paul. "Masturbation, Madness and the Modern Concepts of Childhood and Adolescence." *Journal of Social History* 8 (1975):1–28.

Niggemann, Heinz. *Emanzipation zwischen Sozialismus und Feminismus.* Wuppertal, 1981.

O'Boyle, Lenore. "The Problem of an Excess of Educated Men in Western Europe, 1800–1850." *Journal of Modern History* 4 (December 1970):471–495.

Petrat, Gerhard. *Schulunterricht. Seine Sozialgeschichte in Deutschland 1750 bis 1850.* Munich, 1979.

Reulecke, Jürgen. "Von der Dorfschule zum Schulsystem." In *Fabrik. Familie. Feierabend. Beiträge zur Sozialgeschichte des Alltags im Industriezeitalter*, edited by Jürgen Reulecke and Wolfhard Weber. Wuppertal, 1978.

Ringer, Fritz. *Education and Society in Modern Europe.* Bloomington, 1979.

Rosenhaft, Eva. "Organizing the 'Lumpenproletariat': Cliques and Communists in Berlin During the Weimar Republic." In *The German Working Class, 1890–1933*, edited by R. J. Evans. London, 1982.

Roth, L. *Die Erfindung des Jugendlichen.* Munich, 1982.

Sabean, David. "Small Peasant Agriculture in Germany at the Beginning of the Nineteenth Century: Changing Work Patterns." *Peasant Studies* 7 (1978):218–224.

Saul, K. "Der Kampf um die Jugend zwischen Volksscule und Kaserne." *Militargeschichtliche Mitteilungen* 1 (1971):97–143.

———. "Der Traum von einer besseren Welt. Anfänge einer sozialistischen Kinderliteratur im kaiserlichen Deutschland." *Journal für Geschichte* 1 (1979):2–11.

Saul, Klaus, et al., eds. *Arbeiterfamilien im Kaiserreich. Materielen zur Sozialgeschichte in Deutschland, 1871–1914.* Düsseldorf, 1982.

Schlumbohm, Jürgen. "Traditional Collectivity and 'Modern' Individuality: Some Questions and Suggestions for the Historical Study of Socialization. The Examples of the German Lower and Upper Bourgeoisies Around 1800." *Social History* 5 (1980):71–103.

———. "Geschichte der Kindheit—Fragen und Kontroversen." *Geschichtsdidatik* 8 (1983):305–315.

———, ed. *Kinderstuben. Wie Kinder zu Bauern, Bürgern, Aristokraten wurden, 1700–1850.* Munich, 1983.

Schneider, Joanne. "Enlightened Reforms and Bavarian Girls' Education." In *German Women in the Nineteenth Century*, edited by John Fout. New York, 1984.

Schomerus, Heilweg. *Die Arbeiter der Maschinenfabrik Esslingen. Forschungen zur Lage der Arbeiterschaft des 19. Jahrhunderts.* Stuttgart, 1977.

———. "The Family Life-Cycle: A Study of Factory Workers in Nineteenth-Century Württemberg." In *The German Family. Essays on the Social History of the Family in the Nineteenth- and Twentieth-Century Germany*, edited by Richard J. Evans and W. R. Lee. London, 1981.

Schulte, Regina. "Infanticide in Rural Bavaria in the Nineteenth Century." In *Interest and Emotion. Essays on the Study of Family and Kinship*, edited by Hans Medick and David W. Sabean. Cambridge, 1984.

Shorter, Edward. *The Making of the Modern Family.* New York, 1975.

Soliday, Gerald, et al., eds. *History of the Family and Kinship. A Select International Bibliography.* New York, 1980.

Spree, Reinhard. *Soziale Ungleichheit vor Krankheit und Tod.* Göttingen, 1982.

Taylor, Tom. "The Crisis of Youth in Wilhelmine Germany." Ph.D. diss., University of Minnesota, 1988.

———. "The Transition to Adulthood in Comparative Perspective: Professional Males in Germany and the United States at the Turn of the Century." *Journal of Social History* 21 (Summer 1988):635–658.

Tenfelde, Klaus. "Bildung uns sozialer Aufstieg im Ruhrbergbau vor 1914." In *Arbeiter im Industrialisierungsprozess*, edited by Werner Conze and Ulrich Engelhardt. Stuttgart, 1979.

———. "Grossstadtjugend in Deutschland vor 1914: eine historisch-demographische Annäherung." *Vierteljahresschrift für Sozial-und Wirtschaftsgeschichte* 69 (1982):182–218.

Teuteberg, Hans Jürgen, and Annegret Bernhard. "Wandel der Kindernahrung in der Zeit der Industrialisierung." In *Fabrik. Familie. Feierabend. Beiträge zur Sozialgeschichte des Alltags im Industriezeitalter*, edited by Jürgen Reulecke and Wolfhard Weber. Wuppertal, 1978.

Titze, Hartmut. *Die Politisierung der Erziehung.* Frankfurt, 1973.

———. "Die zyklische Überproduktion von Akademikern im 19. und 20. Jahrhundert." *Geschichte und Gesellschaft* 10 (1984):92–121.

Weber-Kellermann, I. *Die deutsche Familie. Versuch einer Sozialgeschichte.* Frankfurt, 1974.

———. *Die Kindheit. Kleidung und Wohnung, Arbeit und Spiel.* Frankfurt, 1979.

————. *Frauenleben im Neunzehnten Jahrhundert*. Munich, 1983.

Wegehaupt, Heinz. *Alte deutsche Kinderbucher. Bibliographie 1851–1900. Zugleich Bestandsverzeichnis der Kinder- und Jugendbuchabteilung der Deutschen Staatsbibliothek zu Berlin*. Stuttgart, 1985.

13

ISRAEL*

Selwyn Troen and Walter Ackerman

The history of childhood in Israel properly begins in the second half of the nineteenth century. Although the establishment of the state of Israel in 1948 brought significant changes to the framework in which children grew up, the continuities in the fundamental pattern were even more important. European Jewry's rising interest in returning to Zion or in assisting those who chose to live there brought about far-reaching demographic, cultural, and ideological changes in Jewish Palestine that permanently affected all social institutions. An early focus of change was the education of the young. This was necessarily so, since the modern influx of Jews was intended to alter the character of Palestinian society and to revolutionize Jewish culture. In this future-oriented outlook it became essential to prepare children for the society that was to be. The sensitivities to the relation between schooling and society were therefore acute, and educational institutions and informal but explicitly educational settings such as youth movements were consciously intended to foster the desired transformation in the child as a key instrument in the larger goal of social change.

The scenarios of change were many, and reflected the intentions and objectives of the various subcommunities or political groupings within the Jewish community. It is appropriate to understand that the diversity in childhood reflected the reality that the population was fragmented and that one cannot identify one archetypal history of childhood. In Palestine, and later in Israel, there was a multiplicity of experiences or the history of *childhoods*. Although such diversity

*This chapter is confined to describing and analyzing childhood within the Jewish communities of Palestine and Israel. Including a discussion of the Arab population—in its Muslim, Druse, and Christian subdivisions—is beyond the possible scope of this chapter.

may well be expected in the Ottoman period, when the Turkish authorities abdicated responsibility to all groups that cared to take the initiative, the social and political history of Palestine as well as the state of Israel has witnessed the maintenance of community divisions based on cultural, ideological, and religious factions. The state system that emerged in the 1950s mitigated the inherent and deep-rooted variety that had developed in the previous century, but did not abolish it.

During the Ottoman period there was no governmental support for education. Jewish and other non-Muslim social institutions were based on the Ottoman system of the millet—a governmental religious subdivision of non-Muslim inhabitants that was the basis for Ottoman administration. This system encouraged community fragmentation and autonomy based on religious lines. Each millet was self-contained, and had its own institutions as well as the power to tax to support them. In the case of Palestine, which was based on this system, the intrusion of nationalist movements at the end of the nineteenth century only strengthened the existing divisions in society. Thus at the turn of the century there had developed two populations: an Arab-speaking society consisting of Christians and Muslims, and a Jewish society that spoke Hebrew and a variety of other languages. Each of these groups maintained their own schools, although neither population had a unified school system.[1]

Although there was an overriding universality in community of belief and practice among Palestinian Jewry and traditional Jews abroad, closer inspection shows that the Palestinian community was a mosaic of religious subcommunities defined further by language, ethnic, and cultural differences that had important implications for the organization of institutions and patterns of socialization. There were Oriental Jews from countries as diverse as Yemen, Morocco, and Kurdistan, each with their own traditions and dialects. The European Jewish community was similarly subdivided into groups deriving from particular locales and owing allegiance to various religious authorities. It was through these subdivisions that synagogues, religious courts, and schools were organized. Particularly the development of the *Kolelim*, religious and social groupings based on place of origin, fragmented the community. There was no sense of a unified Palestinian Jewish community. Education of children reflected the separation between communities and was designed to maintain these divisions.

TRADITIONAL EDUCATION

The community of traditional Jews in Palestine was viewed by their brethren abroad as an elite community dedicated to the holy work of prayer and study, conforming to the dictates of religious law, and subscribing to a world view derived from an interpretation of Holy Writ. Moreover, they were a population closer to the ideas of the medieval world rather than the modern and unaffected by the currents that were transforming Jewish life in Western Europe and beginning to make inroads even in Eastern Europe. The consequence for children of these religious communities was that they were placed in narrow, traditional frameworks that encouraged the perpetuation of existing subdivisions. Their training was entirely religious instruction with no preparation for vocations or for general or liberal learning. Children were born in a closed universe and expected to perpetuate it.

Rabbinic tradition teaches that as soon as a boy child begins to talk, his father is obligated to speak to him in Hebrew, the Holy Tongue, and to teach him Torah. A father who neglects this injunction is likened to one who "has buried his son." Instruction begins with two verses—"Moses charged us with the teaching, it is the heritage of the congregation of Jacob" (Deut. 33:4); "You must love the Lord your God with all your heart and with all your soul and with all your might" (Deut. 6:4). As the child grows he is to be taught additional verses. At the age of six or seven, depending on his growth and development, he is to be taken to a teacher for the beginning of formal instruction (Baba Batra: 21a). Just as the father is enjoined first to teach his son and then to provide him with a teacher, so he himself is required to engage in study all the days of his life.

The day a child first attended school became a moment of celebration framed in ritual. Among Ashkenazi Jews of medieval Europe and later centuries, as in Jewish communities all over the world, the initiation of a youngster into a regimen of formal learning resonated with reminders of the theophany at Sinai and the eternal covenant between God and Israel, his chosen people.[2] The details of the ceremony were intended to "impress themselves on the child forever." Once in school—either a private *Heder* (literally, a "room" where instruction takes place, usually in the house of the teacher) for those children whose families could afford the fees or a *Talmud Torah* (the communal school for the poor) maintained by the community for the poor—the youngster followed a curriculum prescribed centuries before. He was first taught *Ivri*—nonsense reading of Hebrew—and introduced to the prayerbook. Even though males under the age of thirteen are neither obligated to the thrice-daily regimen of prayer nor counted in the quorum of ten required for public prayer, the ability to read the prayers and follow the order of the service provided entry into the world of adults and subsequent participation in the religious life of the community.

The initial phase of instruction was followed by the study of the Pentateuch in the original. Here, as earlier, instruction was completely oral; writing was not taught at any level. The language of instruction was the vernacular of the Jewish community, such as Yiddish in the case of Eastern European Jews. The order of learning followed the annual cycle of the weekly portion of the Torah read each sabbath in the synagogue. The Pentateuch, however, was only the first stage, and even a thorough knowledge of the text was not considered a significant achievement. As quickly as possible—even though the material often was beyond their understanding—youngsters were introduced to Talmud (the "oral law" formulated from rabbinic exegesis of the Pentateuch, which is the basis of Jewish law). Although most boys remained in school until the age of thirteen, the higher levels of learning, conducted in a Yeshiva, were reserved for the intellectually able. A folk saying captures the elitism of the process: ''A thousand people enter Scripture; out of them come one hundred who enter the Mishnah [first subdivision of the Talmud]; of these ten enter the Gemara [second section of the Talmud]; and one emerges.''

Class size in the *Heder* varied, depending on circumstance. Rabbinic dictum sets a limit on the number of pupils permitted one teacher: twenty-five children learn with one teacher; if their number increases beyond that and does not exceed forty, the teacher is to be given an assistant. Two teachers are required if the number exceeds forty.[3] Communal records indicate that in some places, serious efforts were made to maintain this standard.

There are no reliable statistics regarding attendance and enrollment rates. Perhaps more important than mere numbers, however accurate they may be, was the widespread belief that everyone should go to school. As early as the first century the historian Josephus Flavius (c. 38 and after 100 C.E.) wrote: ''Our principal care of all is this, to educate our children well . . . '' to ensure '' that they might be nourished up in the laws from their infancy, and might neither transgress them, nor have any pretence for their ignorance of them.''[4] Folk ideas and stories of more recent times maintain this image: children without schooling are depicted either as orphans inexplicably left to themselves or as having grown up in isolated rural areas far removed from teachers and schools.

Schooling was deeply embedded in the fabric of an organic community. The elders of the community conducted periodic examinations, intended to assess the achievements of *Talmud Torah* pupils. In many homes the father of the family practiced the custom of reviewing the weekly portion together with those of his children still in school. The child saw all about him concrete expressions of what he was taught: punctilious observance at home, a rhythm of life set by the calendar of sabbath and holidays, adult study groups in the synagogue, and communal institutions and practices that were rooted in rabbinic tradition. The fit between community, home, and school was extraordinarily close.

At the same time it is important to note that traditional Jewish education, with its exclusive concentration on the texts of Holy Writ, barely recognized the imperatives of childhood. Although skilled teachers sometimes might have used methods calculated to capture a child's attention and arouse his interest, general practice, whether in the *Heder, Talmud Torah,* or the Yeshiva, ''brought pupils directly into the cultural world of adults. The contents of teachings were chosen by the standards of that culture; no attention was paid to the intellectual abilities of children and no consideration given to their unique interests, needs, and experiences. Children were viewed as 'adults in miniature' and there was no doubt that matters which were central to adult life should also constitute the spiritual fare of the young.''[5]

Criticism was never lacking: the inadequacies of teachers, woeful physical conditions, a frozen curriculum that encouraged rote learning or barren intellectual gymnastics, and the absence of secular subjects even when these might have contributed to an understanding of the text. Despite all this, voiced in different times and places, the pattern of schooling outlined above was maintained in Jewish communities around the world well into the nineteenth century. Indeed, it obtains even today among ultra-Orthodox Jews.

The conception that guided the practice of traditional Jewish education is no less important than the details of the curriculum and the method of instruction. It assumed that the child is rational, educable, and capable of continuous moral and intellectual development. A child is a gift of God; he also is a creature of man. As such he is subject to the push and pull of instincts and appetite and requires training and guidance. "The rod and reproof give wisdom; but a child left to himself causeth shame to his mother" (Prov. 29:15). Properly taught from his very early years, the child will take his place in the congregation of Israel and in his observance of God's law fulfill the ultimate purpose of life.

Although Judaism teaches that man is of this world, the process of education described here is peculiarly beyond time and place. Even though learning was intended to provide a map for the religious life, the present was considered an exile of trial that bridged between a distant past—days of national independence and godly beneficence—and the promised coming of the age of the Messiah. Modern Jewish education has moved away from the textual focus of its forerunner. It is, however, more than an expansion of the curriculum to include secular subjects and a concern for the interests and abilities of the child. The changes bespeak the belief that children should be brought into history and taught to live in the present.

HARBINGERS OF CHANGE

This system of socialization was challenged in Europe as well as in Palestine as inroads were made on traditional Jewish life by modern European thought and society. The first significant force for change in the Palestinian Jewish community came through European Jewish philanthropy and then through the Zionist movement.

Philanthropy

Change was not welcomed by Orthodox Jewry. The first attempt to establish a vocational school for boys in Jerusalem in 1856 was viewed as a threat: "We see in the house of Israel something terrible. . . . There are in the city of God some men who want to build a school to teach the youth of Israel to write and speak the language of the land. . . . We well know through experience how bitter the end will be! Science will become the fundamental teaching and the Torah will be put in the background. It will be the cause of the desertion of the Torah and the impiety of Israel."[6] Similar foreboding greeted the founding in 1864 of the Evelina de Rothschild School for Girls in Jerusalem. Nevertheless, by 1885, the school numbered 160 and by World War I grew to 450 pupils, who, in addition to religious studies, learned "Hebrew, French, needlework and embroidery."[7]

Far more important than individual efforts were those supported by Jewish organizations in France and Germany. The most important were those of the Alliance Israëlite Universelle, which developed a network of schools for boys and girls throughout the country. The emphasis was on vocational education, and the instruction was in Hebrew, Arabic, and French. The capstone of the system was the Mikveh Israel agricultural school established in 1870. By 1912 there were a total of 2,000 students in Alliance schools in the major towns and in some of the agricultural colonies. These schools were viewed by both critics and supporters as exporters of French values, and thereby an expression of French cultural imperialism. Zionists, in particular, took issue, since the Alliance did not emphasize Palestine as the locus for immigration and the prime hope for the future of the Jewish people. They faulted the Alliance for treating Palestine no differently than Morocco, the Balkan states, and wherever else the organization was active.[8]

The same criticism was applied to Ezra, the network of schools founded by the Hilfsverein der Deutschen Juden. Between 1901 and 1913 Ezra established a network of twenty-seven schools, including a teacher's training seminary, a high school, elementary schools, and even kindergartens. The emphasis on preparing for a practical vocation led in 1913 to the establishment of the Technion, which would become Israel's leading university for engineering and many related sciences. This most ambitious program, endowed by the largesse of German Jewry even as the Alliance was supported by their French brethren, sought to export the best in the cultural values of the fatherland and was another expression of cultural imperialism. Nevertheless, these interventions and exports were the first significant steps in breaking the monopoly of traditional patterns of learning and making alternatives available for Jewish children in Palestine.[9]

Zionist Revolutions

A more far-reaching transformation was achieved by Zionists. Meeting in Basel, Switzerland, in 1897, the First Zionist Congress defined the goal of Zionism as the establishment of "a home for the Jewish people in Palestine secured by public law." Moreover, the platform of this Congress heralded fundamental changes in the population of Palestine by calling for "the programmatic encouragement of the settlement of Palestine with Jewish agricultural workers, labourers and those pursuing other trades" and "the strengthening of Jewish self-awareness and national consciousness."[10] The name and purpose of this newly organized Jewish national movement reflect a mix of the ancient and the contemporary. The term Zionism draws its resonance from the messianic strain in traditional Judaism; the vision of a sovereign state rests on modern ideas of nationhood and self-determination. This combination has shaped the contours of childhood for generations of children educated in Zionist schools.

Nationalist sentiment in the modern sense of that idea had begun to express itself, even if somewhat inchoately, in Eastern Europe some years before Theodor Herzl, the charismatic Viennese journalist, convened the First Zionist Congress. The devastating pogroms of 1881–1882, supported and abetted by the government, dashed whatever hopes Russian Jews might have harbored for a liberalization of czarist policy and an improvement in their social and economic condition. The *Hibbat Zion* ("Love of Zion") movement promoted the establishment of Jewish agricultural colonies in Palestine and lent its name and support to efforts designed to develop a new type of education. The *Heder ha'Metukan* (the reformed *Heder*), no less than the immigrant pioneer to Palestine, became both a symbol and an expression of the new national spirit. Children who attended these schools, never more than a small minority, were treated to an experience quite different from that provided by the traditional *Heder*. Clean, airy classrooms, a graded curriculum of modern subjects, nature study and hikes—all expressions of a new concern for the child and his needs—and above all Hebrew, both as an object of study and as the language of instruction, marked the beginning of a new era in Jewish education. Indeed, teachers in these new schools, the products of the *Heder* and the Yeshiva who by their own efforts had acquired a knowledge of then current educational theory and practice in Central and Western Europe, referred to their efforts as "Hebrew" education. The new designation came to signal a break with the past and the centrality of Hebrew, rather than Yiddish, in the national renaissance.

The importance of education to the Zionist endeavor was most completely formulated by Ahad Ha'am (Asher Ginsberg, 1856–1927), the father of "spiritual Zionism." Although not unmindful of the tenuous existence of Jews buffeted by a cruel anti-Semitism, he tirelessly insisted that the future of the Jewish people depended first and foremost on a regeneration of the spirit of Judaism; the physical survival of the Jews, in his view, was contingent on their desire and ability to develop and maintain a form of group life rooted in their cultural tradition and national experience, and therefore different from that of other nations. He assigned the school a place of critical importance in the long and arduous process of national metamorphosis. Its purpose was to teach "the child to know his people and the land of his forefathers . . . to educate our young children so that they will know the Hebrew language, the history of Israel and its Torah . . . to lead them to a love of the national heritage . . . the land of Israel and its settlement, the Torah of Israel, its language and wisdom, the memory of our forefathers and their history . . . to educate the [new] generation we require." The achievement of these objectives demanded a curriculum that afforded pride of place to the Hebrew language and its literature both because of the power of language in the shaping of personality and because Hebrew was essential to an understanding of the nation's literature, the storehouse of its culture. The Hebrew language and its literature, more than anything else, would "tie [children] with bonds of love and reverence to their people and its land and . . . awaken in them the desire to dedicate themselves to the service of their people and to contribute to the national rebirth.''[11]

These ideas were known to participants in *Asefat Hamorim* ("Teachers Assembly"), the first teachers' organization in Palestine, which met ten times between 1892 and 1895 before becoming defunct. The teachers, from both the towns and the new agricultural settlements, set themselves the task of defining goals for Hebrew schools, determining their structure, developing a common curriculum, devising methods of instruction, and choosing and writing textbooks. Their discussions reflect an urgent sense of national mission and a fierce devotion to the Hebrew language. The practical problem of teaching in a language as yet lacking a modern vocabulary colors the treatment of such issues as the balance between specifically Jewish subjects and more universal studies, the place of traditional texts, religion in the schools, and the implication of rural and urban settings. The course of study that resulted from these meetings tells us little about what the schools actually did; it does, however, give us an idea of what the teachers thought children *ought* to know. By the end of the first four years of the elementary schools, pupils were expected to have learned all the Five Books of Moses and sizable portions of Prophets and Writings, all world history from the earliest times until the present, basic ideas in nature study, selections from Hebrew literature, arithmetic operations and the beginning of geometry, and some Gemara and Mishnah. These exaggerated demands stand at some distance from the repeated references in the minutes of the meetings to the needs, interests, and abilities of the child.[12]

Subsequent efforts at curriculum development, directed first by organizations of teachers and then by the education department of the Zionist Executive in Jerusalem acting as the representative of the Jewish people during the period of the British rule in Palestine (1917–1948), resulted in a more realistic, if not less overloaded, program of study. The curriculum published in 1923 drew on the experience of almost three decades of Zionist education to chart the work of elementary schools in the new circumstances created by the commitment of the Balfour Declaration (1917) to the "establishment in Palestine of a national home for the Jewish people." The basic elements of this curriculum remain in place, even if with different emphasis, until this very day. Guided by the goal of "inculcating a pure Hebrew spirit in the hearts of pupils," the eight-year program suggested a mix of several broad subject matter categories: basic skill subjects; Jewish studies with special attention to Hebrew, Bible, Hebrew literature; social studies, which emphasized the Jewish experience, geography of the "homeland," and "learning about neighboring countries" and "those aspects of general history connected to Jewish history; arithmetic, general science, and nature study."[13]

Tripartite Zionist Education

Organized networks of Zionist-sponsored education date from 1914 when a group of Hebrew educators rebelled against an attempt by the Hilfsverein to make German the language of the Technion that was being built in Haifa. They formed the *Vaad Hahinuch* (Board of Education), which soon comprised twelve schools. At the beginning of the British mandate the board included forty schools, and grew within the first year to ninety-four schools from kindergartens to teacher-training schools with a total enrollment of more than 10,000. With the boom in Jewish immigration that occurred in the 1920s in the aftermath of the Balfour Declaration, this network reached more than 21,000 pupils by 1930. The great majority of these were in the lower grades with only 1,500 or 7 percent, in the high schools. Schooling was, then, primarily for preadolescent children.[14]

A major institution was the kindergarten, which actually included both pre-school and nursery ages. It became a center of educational activity very broadly construed. Kindergartens served as centers for health care and imparted instruction in hygiene; they released mothers for employment outside the home; and they very often introduced children to the Hebrew language, a most important function in an immigrant society in which Hebrew was not yet the language of the parents. The same language instruction function was continued through all levels of schooling. By the elementary grades the Hebrew Bible and Jewish history came to have a prominent role as the socially absorptive functions of the schools kept pace with the development of the child's educational capacity. As important as was Hebrew and the inculcation of the developing national culture, the schools at the higher levels introduced English and Arabic, although the former was always more important, reflecting the cultural orientation both of the parents and of the authorities.

Although there was much in common in the networks of schools that grew up during the period of the mandate, there also were essential differences that reflected the by now established pattern of fragmentation into discrete communities. There developed three trends based on the orientation of leading political parties: the General, the Mizrachi, and the Labour. Each trend was responsible to a special committee that superintended the appointment of teachers and approved the curriculum. As a consequence, different schooling and childhoods were maintained. Despite the fact that under the British mandate education was not compulsory, these separate initiatives produced opportunities and an environment that provided for nearly universal elementary education, so that schooling of some sort was the common experience of all who grew up in Jewish Palestine.[15]

The "General" trend attracted the most children, comprising about 60 percent in 1930 and still maintaining a little more than half at the time of independence. Its schools were coeducational and fundamentally secular. In a statement of purpose before a British commission of inquiry the aim of the General trend was "to give its pupils a National Zionist education combined with the progressive ideals of humanity." Despite a secular orientation, the Old Testament occupied a central place in the curriculum, since it was considered the basis of Jewish literature, history, and thought, and in some schools prayers and customs were taught as part of a perceived obligation to expose children to Jewish tradition. Sometimes children were even invited to wear traditional head coverings when engaged in studying prayers, although there was no explicit attempt to inculcate religious ideas or practices, which were left for the home.

The next largest group were the Mizrachi schools, which in 1930 comprised about one-third of the children and declined slightly to one-fourth at the end of the mandate. Here, in keeping with the expectations of the community that sponsored these institutions, religious practices were incorporated into the culture of the school, exemplified by requiring boys to wear the traditional scull cap. Similarly, boys and girls were separated, in keeping with an anticipation of the different roles prescribed for them by tradition and the demands of maintaining modesty in relations between the sexes. The curriculum, which sought a synthesis between the traditional religious studies and a modern European course of study, required that these children spend more time in school than those in the secular trends. Special emphasis was placed on learning Talmud, the ancient rabbinic discussions elaborating the Law as given in the Torah. Teachers were expected to be observant Jews themselves, and there was little or no premium placed on familiarity with modern educational techniques and theories. Like the General schools, these schools were designed to prepare the young to become participating members of a modern, Jewish society in Palestine.

Labour schools were initially the smallest component, growing from about 10 percent in 1930 to 25 percent in 1948. Although treating the Bible and the acquisition of Hebrew as essential to understanding the national culture, they emphasized preparing the young for life within the context of Labour Zionism. In the words of M. A. Beigel, who in 1923 founded the first Labour school, Beit ha-Hinukh (The House of Education): "It is our aim to educate children for the creation of a unified Hebraic labor society which will realize in Palestine the ideals of justice, equality, brotherly love, and peace."[16] In keeping with the motto of *Beit ha-Hinukh*, "Labour and Learn," preparation for practical work became an essential part of the curriculum. Schools in the agricultural settlements required work in the fields, and even those located in cities had agricultural plots for imparting the experience of working the land and teaching scientific principles. In keeping with the ideological roots of Labour Zionism the schools endeavored to inculcate such "progressive" ideas as a "children's community," social responsibility through "mutual aid," and the supreme responsibility of the individual for active "pioneering." In keeping with an ethos that encouraged communal democracy and governance a noncoercive environment was encouraged in which the teacher was expected to be less an authority figure than a sympathetic counselor or model of exemplary behavior. The agenda of Labour schools required keeping children in school for more hours than in the General schools. In addition, it was expected that children would devote a significant portion of their extracurricular time to participation in the youth movements associated with Labour Zionism, thereby reinforcing and putting into practice what they had been taught in the schools.[17]

Because the voluntarily maintained and largely autonomous Jewish school system had separated into three independent educational networks that were attached and even controlled by political parties with different approaches to Judaism and to Zionism, there was considerable difference in the amount of time devoted to each subject cluster. Mizrachi schools allocated almost 50 percent of their time to traditional Jewish studies; Labour schools, committed to the ideals of socialism and cooperative living in agricultural settlements or kibbutzim, devoted close to a quarter of their programs to agriculture, handicrafts, and nature study; General schools, the most conventional of all, allotted about one-third of the total instructional time to Hebrew language and literature and Bible. The politics and ideology that guided the school determined specific content and the meaning attached to it.[18]

A description of the curriculum, the detail of its subject matter categories and divisions of time, does not adequately capture the spirit that informed the work of schools in the period between the end of World War I and the establishment of the state of Israel in 1948. Zionist ideology, from its earliest days and through the catastrophic events of the Holocaust, set itself the task of creating a new type of Jew, "a young person who . . . is conscious of himself both as a human and as a Jew and . . . who has rid himself of that painful split between his Jewishness and other aspects of his life."[19] In contrast to their less fortunate fellows raised in the debilitative circumstances of Exile, young people growing up in the geography of the homeland, which resonated with the sights and symbols of Jewish sovereignty, were envisioned as physically strong and brave as well as free of the moral ambiguities forced on the Jew struggling for survival in a hostile environment. Above all, youth in Zion were imbued with the will to rebel against the circumstances that denied self-determination and national ful-fillment. The complicated fabric of transvaluation rejected the centuries-old ideal of the learned and pious Jew in favor of the heroic *Halutz* (pioneer), who with a rifle in one hand and a plow guided by the other was ready to sacrifice himself for the common good.[20]

The experience of childhood was framed by an atmosphere colored by a sense of the doom impending in Europe and charged with the imperative of absorbing successive waves of immigrants, reclaiming the land, building new social and economic institutions, and struggling against an increasingly unyielding man-datory power. The school was a laboratory for the invention of a new, usable past. The seemingly simple act of speaking and learning in Hebrew assumed historical importance; the adoption of the Sephardic pronunciation of Middle Eastern Jewry widened the break with custom. In the secular Labour and General schools Bible was taught as a record of human endeavor rather than as a divine statement, and prophetic protest was used to frame the vision of a new and more just social order. History was learned as the inevitable unfolding of the Zionist imperative. Holiday celebrations, so important a part of schooling and now observed in the place of their origins, emphasized national and agricultural motifs at the expense of the religious; in some cases, for instance, "nation" was substituted for "God" in the lyrics of traditional holiday melodies. Hikes and excursions to every part of the country were an integral part of the school experience and impressed the connection between land and people. Latter-day critics, including graduates of the schools looking back, find the curriculum narrow and unmindful of what it had rejected, excessively nationalistic, and oppressingly indifferent to individual needs and interests.[21]

INNOVATION IN NEW FRAMEWORKS

Despite the innovations in curriculum content and the commitment to informal educational activities, most schools adhered to fairly traditional patterns of form and structure. Labour-trend schools, especially those influenced by *Beit ha-Hinukh*, and the schools of the burgeoning kibbutz movement were exceptions to this rule. In both cases those responsible for creating these schools were profoundly influenced by the child-centered and progressive educational philosophies of Central European educators like Bernnfeld, Kirschensteiner, and Wyneken and the thought of John Dewey and Freud. The prospectus of *Beit ha-Hinukh* declared that

our school has no set curriculum. . . . If a normal child is capable during the first three years of his life of learning a language through play, we are sure he can acquire the knowledge necessary for his development and the cultural needs of the generation through his own free and independent efforts. In our school the pupil has absolute freedom in all that is connected to acquiring knowledge. Our teachers are always ready to help the child who asks for help. The child will instinctively ask for what he lacks.[22]

In the kibbutzim innovative approaches to schooling were intended to foster the development of a self-governing children's society that would prepare youngsters for their adult roles as members of the commune. Although there were differences of detail from place to place, there was general agreement regarding guiding principles: learning required the active involvement of pupils; attention should be paid to the abilities and interests of the individual pupil; the program of the school should provide opportunity for both individual and group work; a theme-centered curriculum was preferable to a course of study divided into discrete subjects; grades and diplomas should be eliminated; schooling was not to be isolated from the life of the kibbutz; and the class group also was a "social" group that encompassed all aspects of the children's lives. These principles are evident in a daily schedule that included work in one of the branches of the kibbutz, time for independent study, group discussions, formal class time, free time, and visiting with parents at the end of the day.[23]

Child-rearing techniques in the kibbutz were born of a mix of the theoretical and the practical: children living apart from parents, a practice abandoned by many kibbutzim in recent years, was justified not only by reference to psychological theory and the principles of life in a commune, but also by the need to free mothers to take their places in the work schedule. Some practices just grew out of circumstance:

The custom of boys and girls showering together did not come about as a result of some educational concern based on theory. It just grew out of what had been taken for granted when the children were very young. The children grew and no one thought to raise the question of separating them at a particular age. They had showered together since age three. . . . The fact that the practice existed was the starting point of our discussion and debates.[24]

The kibbutz experience is perhaps the best known instance of using the total environment to shape the new person required by Zionism. There are, however, two additional phenomena that bear mention: the youth movement, which influenced young people beyond the confines of the formal classroom, and the youth village, which, like the kibbutz, incorporated schooling within a larger nurturing and socializing environment.

YOUTH MOVEMENTS

Outside school as well as the home Jewish children spent much time in another educational setting—the youth movement. An importation of pioneers who came in the first years of the century, youth movements provided a framework that had great influence in shaping the young well into the second decade of the state. Greatly influenced by the example of the German Wandervogel and the English Scouts, Jewish youth at the turn of the century in Central and Eastern Europe organized their own youth movements. Deriving from the organization of adults who were redefining Jewish interests and identity in a changing society, youth usually were organized by political organizations. A partial list conveys the range and variety: *Dror* (Freedom) was organized as an offshoot of Labor Zionists; *Hashomer Hatzair* (the Young Guardian) was developed by a left-wing socialist-Zionist party, as was *Tzeirei Zion* (The Youth of Zion); *Gordonia* (after A. D. Gordon, the Zionist theoretician who celebrated Jewish labor in the return to Zion) was less to the left than *Hashomer Hatzair*; *Maccabi Hatzair* (the young Maccabi) was a middle-class organization; *Bnei Akiva* (named after the famed rabbi who led a revolt against the Romans) and *Hashomer Hadati* (the Religious Guardian) were spawned by religious Zionist parties; and *Betar* (contains a double meaning: the name of the last citadel to fall to the Romans in A.D. 135 or an acronym for "the covenant of Trumpeldor," the hero martyred in defense of early Zionist pioneers) had the right-wing orientation of Revisionist Zionism. There also were offshoots of European-founded students' associations such as the *Blau Weiss* (Blue and White), which emulated the German Wandervogel that excluded Jews, or *Kadimah* ("Eastward" or "Forward"), which originated as a Jewish fraternity in response to the anti-Semitic student organizations at the University of Vienna. The successful transfer to Palestine of many of these groups contributed to the social, political, and religious fragmentation found in the schools. In effect, miniature closed universes were created for the young with the anticipation that they would continue to function within similarly discrete political and social groupings in adult life.[25]

Divided into "nests" (*ken*) and "tribes" (*shvatim*), or subgroups with similar nomenclature, youth movements had branches throughout the country in towns, cities, and agricultural settlements. They were divided as well into levels with a curriculum designed to prepare each age-group for Zionist fulfillment. Between ages twelve and fourteen, emphasis was placed on character development through discussion of central figures in Zionist thought and colonization. There also was considerable organized physical activity to develop the body as well as the mind and personality. For those aged fifteen to sixteen and then seventeen to eighteen, elaboration of knowledge of Zionist history and the current needs and objectives of Jews living in Zion were deepened through study and discussion. Considerable effort was expended in ensuring that the young came to know their country as it was and as it had been by hiking extensively throughout the ancestral homeland.

After six years of meeting up to two afternoons per week, listening to lectures, reading assigned materials, participating in debates, working during the summers in kibbutzim, and hiking in every part of the country, it was expected that the young would identify with one another, their people, and their land and be prepared to devote themselves to collective, national goals. Inculcated with a sense of mission that became the experience of Jewish youth who grew up in Palestine during the mandate and during the early years of the state, childhood in Zion was a life of activity and commitment. In fact, "graduates" of these youth movements have provided a large proportion of Israel's political, military, cultural, economic, and intellectual elite.

Youth movements, then, were a complement to the formal education imparted in the various Zionist trends that worked toward the same results. Like the schools, they sought to refashion Jewish youth into a new personality typified by the qualities associated with the "sabra" (a native-born, Palestinian/Israeli Jew). Perhaps the most manifest consequence of these efforts are the sixty-six kibbutzim that were founded by various youth movements between 1930 and 1949 alone.[26]

YOUTH VILLAGES

As in other immigrant societies, social frameworks were damaged by uprooting and transplantation. This was particularly and poignantly characteristic of Zionist society into which from Nazi Europe and the Middle East poured literally tens of thousands of children without families or with families unable to care for their young in the new surroundings. As a consequence significant numbers of Israelis spent their early years in either publicly supported or privately sponsored residential institutions outside the family. Although extrafamilial domiciling of the young exists in many societies, the proportions probably were larger in Zionist society from the early 1930s through the first two decades of the state. Even today 18 percent of all children between the ages of thirteen and seventeen are in residential settings away from their families. Many children lived and studied in established institutions such as yeshivoth and residential schools for military or vocational preparation. The massive influx of refugee populations, including children, created special needs and new institutions.

The most important innovation was the youth village of the Youth Aliyah organization. Established in Germany as a response to the growth of anti-Semitism, Youth Aliyah assisted Jewish children facing hardship and persecution. The first sponsors sought to transfer children to Palestine where they might find a healthier as well as a safer life. In 1932 the first group of twelve arrived at Ben Shemen youth village, and it was expected that ultimately they would be integrated into kibbutzim. With the ascension of Hitler to power in January 1933, a group of German Jews organized the Juedische Jugendhilfe in cooperation with German Jewish youth movements to broaden the scope of its rescue activities. Shortly thereafter Youth Aliyah became a major project of the international Zionist Organization. By the outbreak of World War II more than 5,000 children had been removed to Palestine, of whom nearly nine-tenths were from Germany and Austria. Of the 15,000 more who were sent to Western European countries, 10,000 went to Britain, ironically because of the unwillingness of the British to issue certificates permitting entry to Palestine. Although the war virtually stopped these rescue operations, more than 15,000 children from all over Europe, largely survivors of the Holocaust, were brought to Palestine between 1945 and 1948. Over the next two decades Youth Aliyah became responsible for an additional 93,500 wards. About 80 percent of these either came as refugees from Arab countries in Africa and Asia or were born in Israel to parents who came from these areas.[27]

Youth villages were especially sensitive to currents of progressive education. An early influence was that of Gustav Wyneken's Freie Shulgenmeinde, which had exponents in Zionist circles even before World War I. Throughout, the villages were rooted in the principles of self-government and self-labor and became symbols of the national renaissance. Youth Aliyah developed two primary instruments for dealing with children: the youth community (*Hevrat Noar*) and the counselor or youth leader (*madrich*—literally, guide). The youth community comprised up to forty young people who stayed together from two to four years until the age of seventeen or eighteen when they would normally enter army service. The group was self-contained with much autonomy and usually was attached to a larger, permanent body, whether a kibbutz or an educational settlement such as a youth village. Typically, children would spend four hours a day in field work or in a workshop, four hours in study, and additional programmed time in communal or group activity. Supervising the children were the youth leader and house mother (*metapelet*—literally, one who takes care). Together they handled personal, emotional, educational, and social problems. Initially the youth leaders were temporary volunteers, but later they became professionals, attending special seminars established for their training. As the flow of immigrant children without parents was reduced, these institutions were assigned the role of nurturing and educating Israeli-born children from problem backgrounds. Altogether, such institutions have benefited from high social approval in a society that is very much family-oriented. It is understood that they arose out of special historic circumstances, and Israelis have perceived them as an efficient and wholesome means of coping with society's unfortunate children.

Those responsible for bringing up children from a multitude of backgrounds, many of whom had been traumatically separated from parents and familiar surroundings, were sorely tested and challenged. In addition to the normal needs that could be expected in such circumstances, there were many psychological problems that required attention. Not a few of the shapers of contemporary child and youth psychiatry spent the early part of their professional careers within the frameworks established to cope with these displaced children or addressed their special problems. Their studies constitute an important contribution to the literature of child and youth development.[28]

By the end of the mandate only the extreme Orthodox institutions, particularly those run by the Agudat Israel, remained beyond the pale. Regarding Hebrew as a holy tongue not to be profaned by common use, they maintained instruction in Yiddish. Remaining steadfast in viewing education as preparation for religious life, they offered nearly no secular instruction or vocational preparation aside from arithmetic in some schools. Here, the pre-Zionist and the anti-Zionist community endeavored to prepare their young for perpetuation of a traditional, closed religious community.

The tripartite Zionist system and the philanthropic and ultra-Orthodox schools reflected the political and cultural diversity of the Jewish community in the prestate period and pointed to the continuing fragmentation of Jewish communal life and the mosaic of subcultures that constituted it. Although the great majority of children grew up in institutions and settings that increasingly shared a common culture based on the Hebrew language and a vision of the past and future of the Jewish people in Palestine, there was still a considerable distance to traverse before achieving the kind of homogeneity a modern state could attempt to achieve or impose. At the conclusion of the mandate one could still speak of the history of childhoods. The question remained whether the creation of a state would or could change this.

AFTER INDEPENDENCE

Expanding the Schools' Mandate and Population

The establishment of the state of Israel in 1948 did not immediately meld the different societies of children in the country. Background, experience, and ideology continued to separate four major groupings: children of the ultra-Orthodox, whose religious convictions denied the legitimacy of the new state; the native-born—in rural and urban settings—whose parents had been actively involved in the struggle for independence; survivors of the Holocaust—with and without parents and families—who arrived from the displaced persons camps in Europe; and the tens of thousands newly arrived from the Arab countries of North Africa and Asia. The experience of schooling, for all its differences from place to place, may have been the only thing they shared in common. Indeed, schools, along with the army, were looked to as the agencies most capable of bridging the gap between these disparate groups.

Schools in Israel at the time, not unlike those in other countries newly arrived at independence or in countries where immigration caused significant demographic change, faced challenges not ordinarily encountered in long-established, stable, and homogeneous societies. In a climate charged by hostile neighbors and an ever-present threat of war the new state had to deal first with an explosive growth in the number of school-age children. In the twenty-year period from 1948–1949 to 1969–1970 the number of pupils, from kindergarten through secondary school, increased from 129,688 to 715,249. During the same period the number of schools jumped from 1,274 to 5,290; the number of teaching posts increased almost sevenfold—from 6,283 to 42,324.[29]

In addition to providing facilities, materials, and personnel the emerging state system was expected to transmit the values and symbols of a civil culture capable of uniting all sectors of the population, forge identification with the state, and inculcate respect for its authority. The generation of children born and raised in statehood was to be different from its predecessors, who, at best, had been taught to be wary of government and, in the case of the mandatory power, even to rebel against established authority. Ben-Gurion, Israel's first prime minister, stated the problem in characteristically blunt terms: "The majority of the Jews who were naturalized here between the world wars came from countries where they did not consider themselves citizens and looked upon the law as something external which was to be circumvented. This became habit during the days of the Mandate."[30] In the case of children of families from traditional Islamic societies loyalty to the abstract idea of a state demanded a civic consciousness broader than that formed by the boundaries of the tightly knit kinship system that shaped allegiance for their parents.

No less important a task for the schools was that of providing their pupils with the knowledge and experiences that would contribute to their definition of themselves. Even though the founders of the state had by and large rejected traditional Judaism, their education and experience as children and young adults in the organic Jewish communities of Eastern Europe marked them as Jews, both in their own eyes and in the view of others. The children of the Jewish colony in Palestine and then of Israel, both overwhelmingly secular, were exposed to teaching and practice that negated the achievements of the Diaspora and celebrated a nationalism rooted in the land. They were thought to be disconnected from the historic Jewish experience, from Jews in other parts of the world, and from the rites and ceremonies that distinguish Jews and Judaism from other peoples and cultures. Concern over the "Jewishness" of Israeli children led to demands for the development of school programs calculated to heighten the "Jewish consciousness" of pupils and to imbue them with an appreciation of those things that Jews everywhere shared in common.[31]

In addition, the destruction of European Jewry resulted in the loss of a population resource that had provided trained manpower ever since the beginnings of modern Jewish settlement in Palestine. The requirements of a rapidly growing modern state lent special importance to schooling as the instrument for providing a skilled citizenry essential to the proper functioning of both the private and the public sectors of the society.

The traditional Jewish respect for learning and the needs cited here serve as background to the passage of the Compulsory Schooling Law of 1949. The law provided for the free and compulsory education of all children from the ages of five to fourteen and of adolescents aged fourteen to seventeen who had not completed eight years of elementary school. The nine years of schooling included a year of kindergarten for five-year-olds. Adolescents who had not completed elementary school were required by law to attend classes for "working youth," usually held in the afternoon and evening. At the end of the decade of the seventies free and compulsory education was extended to age fifteen and completion of the tenth grade. By the middle of the sixties 95 percent of the children in the six-to-fourteen age group were enrolled in school.

Steady growth also characterized programs outside the reach of compulsory education. In 1983, 99 percent of all children aged three to four were in preschool. The statistics of school-holding power are perhaps even more telling. Of all pupils entering the first grade in the school year 1957–1958, 82.7 percent reached the eighth grade and only 32.2 percent completed a four-year high school; for the cohort that began school in 1967–1968 the comparable figures are 95.5 percent and 55.9 percent. School retention through twelve grades rose dramatically to 74 percent with the next year's cohort, 1968–1969, owing to the elimination of tuition during the 1970s.[32]

Integration Through Schooling

The growth of the student population was most impressive, given the circumstances of the new state. Between 1948 and 1952, as a consequence of massive immigration, the number of children in schools tripled, as did the population of the country. As many as 1,000 new places had to be found each week. The fact that new students came from a bewildering variety of backgrounds posed a challenge to those concerned with encouraging social cohesion. The problem was compounded by the divisiveness inherent in the "trend" system that came increasingly to be recognized as a threat to national unity. A partial solution to this problem was found in the enactment of the State Education Act of 1953.

With the establishment of the state, the relative weight of the different trends changed substantially. The new immigrants favored the Labour trend, making it for this short period the largest, with 43.4 percent of the student population as opposed to 27.1 percent in the General, 19.1 percent in the Mizrachi, and but 2.1 percent in the Agudah or ultra-Orthodox schools.[33] This rise of Labour gave vent to a prolonged and acrimonious debate that culminated in legislation abolishing the trends in favor of a more homogeneous state system. In particular, there was fear that because Labour became Israel's dominant political party, it would work to the prejudice of the other trends and that children would be coerced into Labour schools. These fears were in part based on Ben-Gurion's preaching in the prestate period that it must be the goal of Labour Zionism to transform Zionist society by using all available cultural and educational institutions. The crisis that erupted in 1950 over the alleged coercion of children of immigrant Yemenites, who were traditional and religious Jews, into the growing Labour trend occasioned the crisis that was to be resolved in 1953 only through national legislation abolishing the trend system. The tenor of the criticism leveled against Labour is captured by an inflammatory leaflet distributed by Yeshiva students in the immigration camps: "The evil instructors and clerks are forcing you to turn your children, of the holy seed, over to the Devil, who will train them to abandon the ways of the righteous and become part of the unclean life in Israel."[34]

The new law endeavored to blend the objectives of the three trends with an omnibus declaration: "The object of State Education is to base elementary education in the State on the values of Jewish culture and the achievements of science, on love of the Homeland and loyalty to the State and the Jewish people, on practice of agricultural work and handicraft, on *halutzi* (pioneering) training, and on striving for a society built on freedom, equality, tolerance, mutual assistance, and love of mankind."[35] Ben-Gurion, who forcefully backed this legislation even at the expense of diminishing the role of the Labour schools that were connected to his own party, stressed two aspects concerning the education of children that he thought were unique. First, he commented that the call for the inculcation of loyalty from the young to the state was a special need in the new state: "For two thousand years we had had no sense of statehood and the mere proclamation of a State does not remedy the situation." Moreover, he commented that "loyalty requires much cultivation, in Israel more than in any other new country, because Israel is not only the State of its inhabitants but of tens of thousands of Jews still dispersed throughout the world." The diversity of the population, the continuance of the exile, and the very tradition of statelessness in exile made it necessary to at once reaffirm ties with those who remained behind even as new bonds were being forged to the new political entity that had been created. Second, he stressed the need to inculcate pioneering by making the young aware "of the historic mission and a dedication to its service, unconditionally and unflinchingly, in spite of difficulty and danger."[36] There were significant attempts to impress both messages on children through formal subject matter as well as song, symbols, ceremonies, and other informal means.

Shortly after the passage of the State Education Act the Ministry of Education and Culture produced a curriculum intended to guide all the state schools, religious and secular alike. The new curriculum, the first such comprehensive effort since the early twenties, attempted to respond to the new circumstances created by the establishment of the state. In defending the idea of a single curriculum for all schools Professor Ben Zion Dinur, a distinguished historian and then minister of education and culture, gave voice to the complicated problems involved in the arduous process of *Mizug Galuyot* (integration of the exiles):

It is self-evident that there can be only one curriculum for all our schools, for the model school in Haifa and for the school in an immigrant settlement. We have no intention of establishing schools on two levels; that approach is totally unacceptable. I am convinced that all our children everywhere are capable of coping with this curriculum. Our goal, our ideal, should be to achieve the intellectual and cultural equality of all our children.[37]

Equality of Opportunity Through Schooling

Minister Dinur's position on the curriculum, even though far from gaining acceptance in all quarters, was only one expression of the idea of equality of educational opportunity for all children that informed the policy of the ministry, the capstone of a highly centralized system, in the early years of the state. Sometimes that posture conflicted with the equally important need, especially urgent in a country poor in natural resources, of fostering the development of an intellectual elite trained to assume positions of leadership. The tension between divergent needs and intentions affected the growth and development of the educational system and colored the experience of children attending its schools.

Given the intent to provide a common curriculum, the culture of the schools provided little space for the customs and traditions of children of non-Western background. The atmosphere was set by the values of Zionist ideology, the practices of Eastern Europe Jewry, and the demands of modernity. Immigrant children of different backgrounds were expected to assimilate to the patterns of behavior and modes of thought of the veteran settlers of the host society. Schools must have seemed like foreign territory to many children. A new language, a different conception of time, and unfamiliar patterns of discipline—among other skills and values—required that they live in two worlds at the same time, that of school and that of their families.

The realization that large numbers of these children, especially those of non-Western background, were unable to cope with the academic demands of the regular school program led to a variety of means calculated to compensate for the cognitive deprivations of early childhood. Pupils designated as culturally disadvantaged (*teunei tipuach* or *needing care* in Hebrew) were afforded the opportunity of additional instruction within the framework of an extended school day; nursery and kindergarten programs for three- and four-year-olds sought to provide preparation for the regular preschool, which began with five-year-olds; patterns of remedial instruction were developed for pupils in grades two through five; schoolwide homogeneous groups for instruction in Hebrew language, mathematics, and English were instituted in the seventh and eighth grades; in addition, enrichment programs, special instructional materials, and new methods of language teaching were introduced throughout the school system.

The net effect of these efforts was more a reflection of good intent and high purpose than a solution to the problem. Although an increasing number of disadvantaged children were able to manage successfully and to continue their studies on both secondary and collegiate levels, a disturbingly large percentage remained incapable of mastering the skills and techniques required for postelementary education and economic self-sufficiency in a technological society. An analysis of the results of the 1966 survey (*Seker*), an examination administered to all eighth-grade students during the last year of the elementary school to determine secondary school placement, disclosed that whereas 75 percent of the students of European and Western parentage achieved passing scores, two-thirds of the children of Eastern or Asian/African communities failed the examination. Depressingly similar statistics can be cited for every index of school achievement: dropout and continuation rates, part-time or full-time postelementary studies, attendance at day and evening high schools, enrollment in academic or vocational secondary schools, and university registration. The slowly but steadily growing number of children of non-Western origins who learned to cope with the demands of school and subsequently moved on to higher levels of training and education seemed only to highlight the problems of the larger numbers who lagged behind.

The constant search for new and effective ways of dealing with a widening educational gap that threatened to perpetuate the existence of a "Second Israel" led in 1966 to the appointment of a special parliamentary committee. The mandate of the committee, outlined by Zalman Aranne, then minister of education and culture, was to devise ways and means by which schools of all kinds and on all levels could become more responsive to the needs of the country; to propose solutions to the pressing problems of an increasing dropout rate; to suggest procedures that would enable schools to respond to the needs of a variegated population and bridge the gap between the various sectors of the community; and to determine what was required to enhance the "national and social" education of the younger generation.

The major recommendations of the committee were structural reorganization of schools into a six-year/three-year/three-year pattern, and extension of the period of schooling by making education compulsory for the fourteen- to sixteen-year-old age group by 1975. This report sparked intense and often acrimonious public debate. Positions for and against the proposals reflected a deeply held commitment to education and an almost naive belief in the power of schooling. Consensus as to the need for a bold and dramatic reform did not, however, produce agreement as to the specific means required to guarantee all children equality of life-chance. Nevertheless, as finally approved by the government and enacted by the Knesset, the report emphasized the importance of the proposed regional middle school and the comprehensive high school as the loci of efforts to integrate pupils of different economic, ethnic, and social backgrounds.

The plan for the middle school as designed by the Ministry of Education and Culture, acting under the influence of the Coleman Report, was calculated to change the nature of the school experience of children. Initially, there was an attempt at homogenizing experience. By the ninth grade the "common subjects" constituted but 25 percent of the curriculum. At this point a student's record and counseling services determine his placement in one of three tracks: one leading to completing the prerequisites for university admission in a variety of fields from agriculture, technology, science, social sciences, humanities, or medicine; studies that lead to the completion of high school or a vocational school; and termination of studies at the conclusion of the ninth grade. In short, tracking takes place.[38]

The streaming that begins in the ninth grade and significantly affects a young-ster's future becomes more apparent in the statistics of high school enrollment. In the 1986–1987 school year, out of 191,519 pupils attending 516 secondary schools, 86,813 (45 percent) were registered in academic high schools; 91,720 (48 percent) in vocational schools; 7,683 (4 percent) in agricultural schools; and 8,303 (4 percent) in continuation classes.[39]

Whatever their background or socioeconomic status, once children are in school they encounter a fairly standardized or rigid organizational structure. No matter the degree of individual attention accorded children, they find their place in school primarily as members of a class. The idea of the class in Israeli schools transcends the purely administrative function of grouping children for the con-venience of control. "Belonging to a class" is a means of impressing the Zionist values of collectivism and cooperative endeavor on the child. Class units often are maintained intact over several grades. Extended trips to all parts of the country and annual stints of community service strengthen the connections between classmates. The fact that elementary schools are by and large neighborhood schools and that neighborhoods are still important in Israel makes the class a significant factor in the life of the child outside of school as well. It is the basis of informal associations in the street, the organization of youth groups, and the many other activities that occupy children.

Associated with the idea of the class, and thus part of growing up in the country, is another important feature of Israeli schools—the *mechanech*. In some respects the *mechanech* (educator), as distinguished from *ha'moreh* (teacher), may be likened to the homeroom teacher in American schools. His or her func-tions for the class, however, extend far beyond the merely administrative. For the child, the *mechanech*, who also is a regular classroom teacher, is a counselor, advocate, and "friend." Pupils meet with the *mechanech* in a weekly "social" or "educational hour." This is a period devoted to discussing current events, school policy, class problems, and other items of concern and interest. Pupils also may come to him or her with personal problems. In junior high and high school youngsters may expect the *mechanech* to "represent" them before subject matter teachers and the school administration. They also know that on occasion the *mechanech* may visit their homes to discuss school-related issues with their parents. The *mechanech* accompanies the class on trips, distributes report cards, and performs other tasks that make him or her a central figure of the child's life in school. The role is perhaps best described as a mechanism of caring—for every class there is at least one adult who is available to every pupil in a truly personal way. In this sense, through the class and the *mechanech* the schools have adapted and institutionalized the society of children and the function of the *madrich* or youth leader that was developed in the youth villages.[40]

Although not eliminating socioeconomic differences, the programs, policies, interventions, and innovations of the Ministry of Education and Culture have produced significant results. These have been brought about by early intervention in the education of the child, experiments in teaching methods and curricula, and changes in the structure of schools and their programs. For example, the expenditure of thought, effort, and money, including the waiving of high school tuition in the early 1980s, has brought all children aged four and most of those aged three into day-care centers and nursery schools. Almost universal elementary school attendance has been followed by a marked increase in secondary school enrollments, so that currently two-thirds of the seventeen-year-olds in the country complete twelve years of schooling. Among youngsters of Asian/African background two-thirds graduated from vocational schools; the same percentage of graduates of Western background completed academic high schools. At the end of the 1960s only 6 percent of Asian/African high school graduates passed the matriculation examination, a condition for university entrance, as compared with 33 percent of those of European or American parentage. By the early 1980s the rate of success of the former had risen to 15 percent, whereas that of the latter remained substantially the same.[41] In sum, four decades of concerted national effort have contributed to bridging the social and ethnic gap and encouraging equality of opportunity for the country's children.

CONCLUSION

The creation of the state substantially affected some aspects of childhood but hardly influenced others. The forging of a citizenry that was committed to the development of the new nation and loyal to it necessarily became a primary goal in Israel even as it is among a multitude of other new states. The massive and sudden introduction in the country's early years of diverse cultures from war-scarred Europe and from African and Asian countries made the realization of national integration complicated and difficult, if all the more important. In this context the education of children became an object of great public concern. The result was the establishment of institutions and programs that fostered a commonality of experience for the nation's young. These included ensuring that Hebrew become the common language; that a shared historical tradition and appropriate political and social values be inculcated; and that knowledge and love of the new homeland be imparted. These efforts produced tangible results. The great majority of children have grown up identifying with Israeli society and have been loyal to it. In these ways much of what Zionist educators had tried to accomplish in the decades before the establishment of the state has been realized in the decades since independence.

As against these forces for integration and homogenization there have been powerful centrifugal and differentiating forces that have contributed to the maintenance of discrete childhoods. Ethnic differences did not disappear and, in fact, have even enjoyed a measure of official sanction and support. More important, class differences, a cause for social separation nearly everywhere, may actually be growing as Israel becomes wealthier and the once powerful and leveling socialist ideology suffers probably irreversible decline.

Probably more important than class and ethnicity, religion has remained the most important differentiator in the Israeli experience. The fact that the state education system supports non-Zionist, ultra-Orthodox institutions as well as religious-Zionist and secular-Zionist ones has served to preserve the social fissures that have existed since the Ottoman period. In this way the state actually protects and maintains divisions.

Although Zionism intended to shape Jewish experience in the modern world by creating a new kind of Jew, it never attempted to impose its program on traditional Jews. Its success in persuading them to adopt its vision has been limited even within the Zionist state. The consequence has been not only the survival of very traditional communities but, owing to the largesse of the state, their efflorescence. The bewildering multiplicity of traditional, religious-centered subcommunities that characterized pre-Zionist Palestine has persisted even as the rest of Jewish society has become increasingly modern and probably similar to other societies in the Western world. Indeed, the gap between religious and secular Jewish childhoods may even be greater now than a century ago. Nevertheless, given the diversity of origins among the country's population and the range of problems the state has had to face, including frequent wars, the creation of a common framework for the young has remained a powerful commitment and a guiding principle in shaping the institutions that nurture and educate the great majority of Israel's children.

NOTES

1. Esco Foundation for Palestine, *Palestine; A Study of Jewish, Arab, and British Policies* (New Haven, Conn.: Yale University Press, 1947), pp. 463ff.

2. The term Ashkenazi designates the relatively compact area of Jewish settlement in northwest Europe originally on the banks of the Rhine. It denotes a cultural complex that spread from this early center in France and Germany to Poland and Lithuania and assumed characteristics different from those of the Sephardi Jews originally centered in Spain.

3. Maimonides, *Hilchot Talmud Torah*, 2:5.

4. William Whiston. *The Works of Flavius Josephus*, vol. 2. (Philadelphia: J. P. Lippincott, 1888), pp. 478, 516.

5. Aaron Kleinberger, *Ha'Machshava ha'Pedagogit shel ha'Maharal m'Prague* (The Educational Thought of the Maharal of Prague) (Jerusalem: Hebrew University, 1962), p. 30. A more complete treatment of traditional Jewish education may be found in Isadore Fishman, *The History of Jewish Education in Central Europe from the End of the Sixteenth*

Century to the End of the Eighteenth Century (London: Goldston, 1949); Emanuel Gamoran, *Changing Conceptions in Jewish Education* (New York: Macmillan, 1924), chs. 3–5; Louis Ginzburg, "The Jewish Primary School," in *Students, Scholars and Saints* (Philadelphia: Jewish Publication Society, 1928); Shmaryahu Levin, *Children in Exile*, trans. Maurice Samuel (New York: Harcourt, Brace, 1929).

6. Quote from Nima Hirschensohn, "The Intellectual Development of Palestine," reprinted from *The Maccabaean Magazine*, August-October, 1912, pp. 5–6.

7. Kurt Grunwald, "Jewish Schools Under Foreign Flags in Ottoman Palestine," in *Studies of Palestine During the Ottoman Period*, ed. Moseh Ma'Oz (Jerusalem: Magnes, 1975), p. 171.

8. Norman Bentwich, *Jewish Schools in Palestine* (New York: Federation of American Zionists, 1912).

9. On Ezra see Moshe Rinott, *Hevrat ha'Ezra li'Yehudei Germania; b'Yit6zirah u'Vemaavak* (Hilfsverein der Deutschen Juden—Creation and Struggle) (Jerusalem: 1971); for the Alliance see A. Chouraqui, *L'alliance israélite universelle et la renaissance juive contemporaire, 1860–1960* (Paris, 1965).

10. Walter Lacquer, *A History of Zionism* (New York: Holt, Rinehart & Winston, 1972), p. 106.

11. A good introduction to the life and thought of Ahad Ha'am may be found in Leon Simon, *Ahad Ha'am* (Philadelphia: Jewish Publication Society, 1961).

12. For a detailed treatment of the Teachers' Assembly see Shlomo Carmi, *T'lamim Rishonim b'Hinuch ha'lvri* (Beginnings of Hebrew Education) (Jerusalem: Maas, 1986). See also Walter Ackerman, "Religion in the Schools of Eretz Yisrael: 1904–1914," *Studies in Zionism* 6:1 (1985): 1–13.

13. Rieger Eliezer, *Ha'Chinuch Ha'lvri b'Eretz Yisrael* (Hebrew Education in Eretz Yisrael) (Tel-Aviv: Dvir, 1940), 2:113–115. For a summary description of Jewish education in Palestine between the two world wars see Randolph Braham, *Israel: A Modern Educational System* (Washington, D.C.: Government Printing Office, 1966). See also Joseph Bentwich, *Education in Israel* (Philadelphia: Jewish Publication Society, 1965).

14. *The Jewish Schools of Palestine* (Jerusalem: Waad Leumi of the Knesset Yisrael, 1932), pp. 11ff.

15. Ibid., pp. 5–10. There are excellent statistics in the various reports of the Jewish Agency as well as the Mandatory Period. All the various international commissions to study the Arab-Jewish dispute over Palestine had sections describing Palestinian society, including the Arab and Jewish educational systems.

16. Quoted in Noah Nardi, *Education in Palestine* (Washington, D.C.: ZOA, 1945), p. 250, n. 138.

17. Judith Wolf, *Selected Aspects in the Development of Public Education in Palestine, 1920–1946* (Ph.D. diss., Boston College, 1981), pp. 256–262.

18. Mitchell Cohen, *Zion and State; Nation, Class and the Shaping of Modern Israel* (Oxford: Basil Blackwell, 1987), pp. 234ff.

19. Ahad Ha'am, "Ha'Gymnasium Ha'lvri b'Yafo" (The Hebrew Gymnasium in Jaffa), p. 416.

20. Marc Rosenstein, *Ha'Yehudi He'Hadash: ha'Zikah b'Mesoret ha'Yehudi b'Chinuch ha'Tichoni ha'Klali b'Eretz Yisrael me'Reshita v'ad Kum ha'Medina* (The New Jew; the Place of Jewish Tradition in General Zionist Education from Its Beginning Until the Establishment of the State) (Ph.D. diss., Hebrew University of Jerusalem, 1985).

21. Jonathan Shapiro, *Ilit l'Lo Hemshaich* (An Elite Without Successors) (Tel-Aviv: Sifriat Poalim, 1984); see also Ruth Feerer, *Sochanim shel ha'Chinuch ha'Zioni* (Agents of Zionist Education) (Tel-Aviv: Sifriat Hapoalim, 1985).

22. Shimon Reshef, *Chinuch Chadash b'Eretz Yisrael* (Progressive Education in Eretz Yisrael) (Tel-Aviv: Sifriat Poalim, 1985), p. 91.

23. Reuben Porat, *Ha'Yachid v'ha'Yachad: Toldot Beit ha'Sefer ha'Kibbutzi* (Together But on Our Own: The Creation of Schools in the Kibbutz Movement) (Tel-Aviv: Ha'Kibbutz ha'Meuchad, 1987), p. 85.

24. Ibid., p. 53.

25. See Hans Kohn, "Youth Movements," in *The Encyclopedia of the Social Sciences* (New York: Macmillan, 1935); Shlomo Bardin, *Pioneer Youth in Palestine* (New York: Bloch Publishing, 1932); Max Mader and Yehuda Riemer, *Youth Movements Past and Present* (Tel Aviv: Ichud Habonim, 1964). For a consistent and excellent source in English on German Jewish youth movements but applicable to the whole subject, especially since most articles deal with the transfer of the movements to Palestine, see the *Year Book* of the Leo Baeck Institute, London.

26. See J. Peres, "Youth and Youth Movements in Israel," *Jewish Journal of Sociology* 5:1 (1962): 94–110; Orit Ichilov, "Youth Movements in Israel as Agents for Transition to Adulthood," *Jewish Journal of Sociology* 19 (1977): 21–32; Rina Shapira and Eva Etzioni, "Identity in Israeli Youth Groups," *Jewish Journal of Sociology* 12:2 (1970): 165–179. Rina Shapira and Rachel Peleg, "From Blue Shirt to White Collar," *Forum* 38 (Summer 1980): 127–140; and Yonathan Shapiro, "Jewish Youth Movements in Eretz-Israel and the Elite," *The Jerusalem Quarterly* 36 (Summer 1985): 17–30.

27. For children in the kibbutz see Bruno Bettelheim, *Children of the Dream* (New York: Macmillan, 1969); A. I. Rabin, *Growing Up in the Kibbutz* (New York: Springer, 1965); Melford E. Spiro, *Kibbutz; Venture in Utopia* (Cambridge, Mass.: Harvard University Press, 1956); Dan Leon, *The Kibbutz, a New Way of Life* (Oxford: Pergamon Press, 1969).

28. Among those involved with uprooted Jewish children during the Holocaust and through the early years of the state were Bruno Bettelheim, Gerald Caplan, and Fred Stone. For a sampling of the place of Israeli youth in the international literature see E. James Anthony and Colette Chiland, *The Child in His Family: Children and Their Parents in a Changing World* (New York: Wiley, 1978), foreword by Erik H. Erikson; and Gerald Caplan, *Emotional Problems of Early Childhood* (New York: Basic Books, 1955).

29. *Shnaton Statisti L'Yisrael* (Israel's Statistical Yearbook) (Jerusalem: Central Office of Statistics, 1970), 21: 543–545.

30. As quoted in Haim Roth, *Al Chinuch ha'Ezrach* (On the Education of the Citizen) (Jerusalem: Hebrew University/Magnes Press, 1950), p. 9.

31. B. Ben-Yehuda, *L'Mahuta shel ha'Toda'ah ha'Yehudit* (The Essence of Jewish Consciousness) (Jerusalem: Ministry of Education and Culture, 1966).

32. Walter Ackerman, Arye Carmon, and David Zucker, eds., *Chinuch b'Hevra Mithavah; ha'Maarechet ha'Yisraelit* (Education in an Evolving Society; Schooling in Israel) (Jerusalem: Van Leer Foundation/Ha'Kibbutz ha'Meuchad, 1985), 2:911.

33. Aharon Kleinberger, *Society, Schools and Progress in Israel* (Oxford: Pergamon Press, 1969), p. 121.

34. David Ben-Gurion, *Israel; Personal History* (Tel-Aviv: Sabra Books, 1972), p. 386.

35. Ibid., p. 407.

36. Ibid., p. 407–408.

37. Ben-Zion Dinur, *Arachim v'Drachim* (Values and Means) (Tel-Aviv: Urim, 1958), p. 129.

38. For a more detailed account of the Reform and the debate that accompanied its introduction see Walter Ackerman, "Reforming Israeli Education," in *Israel Social Structure and Change*, ed. Michael Curtis and Mordecahi Chertoff (New Brunswick, N.J.: Transaction Books, 1973), pp. 397–408.

39. *Mosdot Chinuch* (Educational Institutions), no. 170 from *Monthly Statistics*, no. 11, 1987.

40. David Gordon and Walter Ackerman, "The *Mechanech*: Role Function and Myth in Israeli Secondary Schools," *Comparative Education Review*, 28:1 (February 1984): 105–115.

41. Chaim Adler, "Ha'Chinuch ha'Yehudi b'Medinat Yisrael; Hebyt Sociologie," (Education in the State of Israel; A Sociological Perspective), *Yahadut Zemanenu* (Contemporary Jewry) 4 (1988).

REFERENCES

There is a large and constantly growing literature relating to the history of children in Israel that can be found in Hebrew and European languages, especially English. This research has appeared in scholarly journals of all the disciplines impinging on education. The best place to begin is with ERIC (Educational Resources Information Center).

Historical scholarship is overwhelmingly directed toward children in institutions, particularly the schools. This is an appropriate reflection of the emphases of the Zionist movement, which since its earliest days assigned prime importance to education and allocated scarce resources accordingly. This focus has dictated the direction and contents of this chapter, since many topics that would normally fall under the history of childhood have yet to be treated in the scholarly literature. The notes of this chapter contain many references to key issues. The following is a select bibliography, largely containing additional items. Aside from two overviews in Hebrew, the bibliography is devoted to listing studies in English that should be generally accessible.

Hebrew

Ackerman, Walter, Arye Carmon, and David Zucker, eds. *Chinuch b'Hevra Mithavah; ha'Maarechet ha'Yisraelit* (Education in an Evolving Society; Schooling in Israel). Jerusalem: Van Leer Foundation/Ha'Kibbutz ha'Meuchad, 1985. Also in German translation: *Erziehung in Israel*. Stuttgart: Klett Cotta, 1982.

Elboim-Dror, Rachel. *Ha'Chinuch ha'Ivri b'Eretz Yisrael* (Hebrew Education in Eretz Israel). Jerusalem: Yad Ben-Zvi, 1986. 2 vols.

English

A wealth of information as well as analysis is located in the numerous official reports generated from the early years of the British mandate by Jewish and British agencies as well as various international commissions. Among the British documentation, the various

White Papers and United Nations reports describing social conditions are most valuable. Regular reports published by the Jewish agency are similarly useful. For example:

Anglo-American Committee of Inquiry on Palestine. *Report*. London and Washington: 1946.

Great Britain. *Palestine: Report on Immigration, Land Settlement and Development*, by John Hope Simpson. Comd. 3686. London: 1927.

————. *Palestine Royal Commission Report*. Cmd. 5479. London: 1937.

Jewish Agency for Palestine. *Statistical Handbook of Jewish Palestine*, edited by A. Gertz. Jerusalem: 1947.

Palestine. Department of Education. *Annual Report*. Prepared from the 1920s to 1947.

Vaad Leumi. Executive. *Memorandum Submitted to the Commission of Inquiry into the Jewish Education System*. Jerusalem: 1945.

Selected General Bibliography

Arieli, Mordechai. *Israel Residential Schools as People Processing Institutions*. Tel-Aviv: Ramot, 1983.

Bentwich, Joseph S. *Education in Israel*. Philadelphia: Jewish Publication Society, 1965.

Bentwich, Norman. *Jewish Schools in Palestine*. New York: Federation of American Zionists, 1912.

Braham, Randolph L. *Israel: A Modern Education System*. Washington, D.C.: Department of Health, Education and Welfare, 1966.

Eisenstadt, S. N. *The Absorption of Immigrants*. London: Routledge & Kegan Paul, 1954.

————. *The Transformation of Israeli Society*. London: Weidenfeld & Nicolson, 1985.

Enright, Sharon, and John Shulz. *Impressions of Education in Israel: A Report of Educational Staff Seminar Study Mission*. Washington, D.C.: George Washington University Institute of Educational Leadership, 1976.

Esco Foundation for Palestine. *Palestine: A Study of Jewish, Arab, and British Policies*. New Haven, Conn.: Yale University Press, 1947. 2 vols.

Kleinberger, Aharon. *Society, Schools and Progress in Israel*. Oxford: Pergamon Press, 1969.

Minkovich, Abraham, Dan Davis, and Joseph Bashi. *An Evaluation Study of Israeli Elementary Schools*. Jerusalem: Van Leer Foundation, 1977.

Shoneveld, J. *The Bible in Israeli Education*. Amsterdam: Van Gorcum, 1976.

Smilansky, Moshe. *The Gifted Disadvantaged: A Ten Year Longitudinal Study of Compensatory Education in Israel*. London: Gordon & Breach, 1979.

14

ITALY

Mary Gibson

In 1980 Marcello Flores lamented in a review article on the history of childhood that "for this topic, the traditional gulf that separates studies in Italian social history from similar French and Anglo-American ones is even more accentuated."[1] Unlike the more advanced historiography of these latter nations, he continued, researchers in Italy tended to portray children as appendages to the history of adults or institutions. Although the number of works that shed light on the history of childhood in modern Italy has grown enormously since 1980, Flores' observation is still pertinent. Insight into the lives of children in the Italian past must be gleaned, for the most part, from works primarily focused on related but different topics such as the family, charity organizations, and schools. Even studies that apparently deal directly with children, such as those on fascist youth groups, emphasize the ideology and leadership of adults rather than the experience of their charges.

Several historiographical trends explain the emphasis in Italian research on adults and institutions to the neglect of children as the protagonists of their own story. One is the strong tradition of family history that has focused on the economic and social foundations of family structures and strategies. In this context inheritance patterns, for example, are analyzed from the point of view of parents making decisions to perpetuate their patrimony rather than that of their children, living out the economic, social, and psychological consequences of these decisions. Second, studies of foundling homes, nursery schools, and orphanages reflect an interest in the history of charity and welfare and the transition of these institutions from private or religious foundations to organs of the state. These studies tend to subordinate the daily lives of young inmates to the analysis of patrons of these institutions and their philosophy of amelioration. Third, the point of view of children often is peripheral to studies of education or child labor, whose focus is the centralization and increase of state power after unification in 1861. The theory behind the new legislation of united Italy, rather than its actual effects on the lives of children, dominates these studies.

Two new historiographical trends promise to shift the focus to children, although each has sometimes continued to privilege the perspective of adults. An anthropological or ethnographic emphasis on the everyday activities of all members of society has had great impact on the historiography of early modern Italy, and is finally encouraging modern Italian historians to switch their focus from ideological and institutional to actual experience.[2] A vibrant new women's history also is experimenting with innovative approaches to the past with an emphasis on gender differences between the lives of girls and boys.[3]

This chapter reviews the literature on childhood, ideas about childhood, and institutions for children in Italy from the late eighteenth century to World War II. I rejected 1861 as the beginning date, even though it marks Italy's birth as a politically united nation. Other fundamental processes, such as demographic growth, the end of primogeniture and other feudal practices, the development of manufacturing, and the increasing importance of the bourgeoisie, began with the Napoleonic occupation of Italy in the 1790s, and sometimes preceded it. Even political trends, such as the centralization and secularization of charity, date from the late eighteenth century. Thus the seven sections of the chapter cover the period of "modern Italy" and follow the life cycle of the child from birth to adulthood.

NATIVITY AND MORTALITY

Carlo M. Cipolla still provides the best historical overview of the rates of birth and infant mortality in his brief article titled "Four Centuries of Italian Demographic Development," published in 1965.[4] He provides a series of tables that define the major demographic trends for Italy as a whole. According to Cipolla, the Italian population began to expand after 1660 because of the disappearance of the plague and other sources of "extraordinary" mortality, such as epidemics and famine. The rise in the crude birthrate was not significant until after 1820, and even then it was small in annual terms. The accumulated impact of these small increments left the birthrate at 36.9 per thousand during the decade 1871–1880, which constituted a rather high figure for a nation already densely populated in the Renaissance. Decline in fertility, typical of the "demographic transition" in Western Europe, began only around 1890, and proceeded much more quickly in the more industrialized and urbanized North of Italy than in the agricultural South.

According to Cippola, infant mortality was high before 1870, fluctuating between 200 and 300 per 1,000 in mid-century. After 1870 the rate declined precipitously from 215 in 1871–1880 to 160 in 1901–1910, 104 in 1931–1940, and 58 in 1951–1955. Interestingly, northern and southern Italy experienced similar rates of overall decrease in infant mortality between 1871 and 1955; because the birthrate was still high in the South, Cipolla characterizes that region as still involved in the demographic transition as late as the 1950s. He attributes the initial decline in infant death to improved hygiene and progress in medicine rather than economic factors, since cyclical depressions characterized Italy during the last three decades of the nineteenth century.

Another excellent source of national statistics on fertility is Massimo Livi Bacci's contribution to the series on the European demographic transition commissioned by Princeton University's Office of Population Research.[5] Titled *A History of Italian Fertility During the Last Two Centuries*, it argues that the decline of fertility in late-nineteenth-century Italy began with the wealthy, more educated urban population before spreading to other social groups. According to Livi Bacci's model of the demographic transition, "innovation, imitation, or diffusion are the technical means through which the behavior of the privileged groups is accepted by the rest of the population."[6] Livi Bacci also notes that the traditional pattern of family size, with the wealthy having more children than the poor, was temporarily broken when the upper classes began to adopt birth control. From the late nineteenth century to World War II an "aberrant" situation existed in which an inverse relation existed between income and fertility. Since World War II Livi Bacci sees the normal, traditional pattern reasserting itself.

Since Cipolla and Livi Bacci, studies have begun to trace the many regional variations in the decline of fertility typical of Italy's emergence as a modern, industrialized state. For example, Giorgio Gattei, in his article "Sul comportamento amoroso dei bolognesi: Le nascite dall'unità al fascismo," establishes that births in Bologna fell to the "modern" rate of 30 per 1,000 by 1870, almost a half-century before the peninsula as a whole.[7] Gattei attributes this low birthrate mainly to the widespread use of coitus interruptus, a practice in which married couples persisted even during Mussolini's natalist campaign of the 1920s and 1930s. Jane and Peter Schneider also found the use of coitus interruptus, or "reverse gear" as the peasants called it, in a small Sicilian town at the other end of the nation.[8] In this agricultural area only the *civili*—the class of landowners, wealthy merchants, and professionals—began consciously to limit their families before World War I. They were followed by the artisans in the 1920s and finally the peasants after World War II.

Although Italy lagged behind other Western European nations in its adoption of birth control, it nevertheless successfully replicated the transition to low fertility in the face of opposition from many groups. Although contraception was legal until the fascist era, the Catholic Church consistently condemned birth control as a sin. More surprisingly, the developing profession of gynecologists warned against contraception in the late nineteenth and early twentieth centuries, according to Rosanna De Longis.[9] In her article " 'In difesa della donna e della razza' " De Longis cites physicians who opposed coitus interruptus for causing nervous maladies in women, who could enjoy physical and psychological health only by fulfilling their maternal role. Feminists remained, for the most part, silent on this controversial topic. In a companion article titled "La guerra tra il pane e l'amore" Susanna Bucci argues that even the leaders of the Italian Socialist party tended to ignore issues of "private life." When they did address the birthrate they prescribed revolution rather than birth control as the solution to poverty and the problems of the working classes.[10] The small and embattled ranks of the Malthusians consisted of two groups, according to De Longis: bourgeois moderates, who warned against the impoverishment of lower-class families burdened with many children, and libertarian anarchists, who championed birth control as a corollary of free love.

Abortion, another method of birth control, has received little attention from nineteenth-century historians, perhaps because the subject remained taboo in public discourse until its loud condemnation by the fascist dictatorship. Interestingly, until World War I neither church nor state considered all abortions illegal. In 1917, however, the new Code of Canon Law prescribed excommunication for all parties involved in any abortion. The fascist regime incorporated its opposition to abortion by defining it a crime against "the integrity and health of the race" in the Rocco Criminal Code of 1930. In her article, "Un aspect de la politique demographique de l'Italie fasciste: La répression de l'avortement" Denise Destragiache documents the failure of the fascists to stop the practice of abortion.[11] Even the official statistics, which greatly underestimated the incidence of abortion, attest to its steady rise during the 1930s. Despite repressive campaigns by police to arrest women for abortion, Destragiache finds that many judges used legal subterfuges to avoid applying the law rigorously. Many defendants saw their cases dropped or the punishment reduced to short prison terms. Mussolini's own judiciary, therefore, undercut the dictator's ferocious battle against abortion.

Luisa Passerini also has attempted to reconstruct the reality of abortion in fascist Italy by relying not only on trial records of abortion prosecutions, but also on interviews with working-class women.[12] She agrees with Destragiache that abortion was widespread and growing as a means of birth control in the 1920s and 1930s. Despite surveillance by fascist police, women were willing to undergo abortions when they and their husbands could not afford another child, when women's health was endangered, or when they considered themselves too old to bear more children. Passarini sees abortion as typical of urban, married women who received information about it from their colleagues, neighbors, and local midwives; in contrast, rural women continued to resort to infanticide and abandonment to get rid of unwanted offspring. She also suggests that changes in political regimes had little effect on women's conviction that they had the right to control their own reproductive behavior, since several informants were otherwise patriotic and loyal to Mussolini. They also remained good Catholics, receiving light penalties and apparent understanding from their confessors. More research is needed to see how far back these attitudes can be traced.

Demographers and historians are beginning to examine the causes and patterns of not only fertility, but also child mortality typical of the demographic transition. Athos Bellettini and Alessandra Samoggia utilize extensive parish records, typical of Italian towns before unification, to trace the deaths of all infants in a village near Bologna from the sixteenth through the nineteenth centuries ("Premières recherches sur les tendances de longue période de la mortalité infantile dans la campagne de Bologne [XVIIe-XIXe siècle"]).[13] Within this long span the only significant decrease occurred in the early nineteenth century, "caused—we must believe—by a general improvement in health and diet."[14] The authors found a consistent improvement in the health of infants managing to survive the first few days of life, although large numbers continued to die immediately after birth. From the middle of the eighteenth century mortality dropped most noticeably for children over the age of five.

Although Bellettini and Samoggia warn against generalizing from the data on one small town, their final observation fits with the findings of Antonio Bellacicco and Maurizio Maravelle, who studied regional differences in infant mortality during the century after Italian unification ("Sulle oscillazioni fondamentali della mortalità infantile a livello regionale dal 1863 al 1961").[15] They found two peaks of child mortality, one at ages two to three in all regions of Italy and another at ages five to six in the underdeveloped regions. Together, the two articles suggest that older children have profited most from economic development.

Finally, Agopik Manoukian provides an invaluable statistical appendix to his important collection of essays, *I vincoli familiari in Italia: Dal secolo XI al secolo XX*.[16] Following a useful introduction to the available sources, a series of tables offer a wealth of data on demographic trends from 1861 to 1981, including rates of births and infant mortality. Also of interest is his table on the median number of children per family, which fell from 4.72 in the decade 1861–1870 to 3.89 by World War I, 2.73 by World War II, and 1.89 by 1981. As Manoukian offers no analysis of this trend, future historians must weigh both the material and the psychological effects of diminishing family size on the life experiences of children in all regions of Italy.

INFANTICIDE AND ABANDONMENT

In the absence of effective methods of birth control and abortion some parents fell back on infanticide or abandonment to rid themselves or their families of unwanted babies. Little has been written on infanticide in modern Italy, possibly because it decreased with industrialization and urbanization. Infanticide never disappeared, however, and Maria Pia Casarini has examined criminal court records for infanticide in two articles. In "Maternità e infanticidio a Bologna: Fonti e linee di ricerca," she found that most of the thirteen cases prosecuted between 1816 and 1823 in Bologna resulted in light sentences or absolution.[17] Although infanticide was legally equivalent to homicide or parricide, judges accepted a host of attenuating circumstances: the preservation of an unmarried woman's honor, the youth or inexperience of the defendant, the lack of assistance while giving birth, or the baptism of the child before death. Rather than punishing infanticide severely, officials of the Papal States, which governed Bologna in this period, put more energy into preventing the crime by active police surveillance over midwives and single women migrating from the countryside, especially servants. In her subsequent article ("Il buon matrimonio: Tre casi di infanticidio nell'800") Casarini explores three typical cases of infanticide to suggest a profile of female defendants.[18] Contrary to the medical and legal literature of the early nineteenth century, women who committed infanticide were not deviant "denatured mothers," but single women living in their families and pregnant by their fiancés but not yet able to marry. They did not reject motherhood, but only prenuptial pregnancy, which hindered their future marriages and integration into the community as legal wives and mothers.

From the Renaissance to the mid-nineteenth century abandonment increased and gradually replaced infanticide as the fate of unwanted children. A large bibliography already exists on foundlings and institutions for their care, so that, as David Kertzer has written, "this is perhaps the most exciting current research topic in family history in Italy."[19] In 1974 Mariagrazia Gorni and Laura Pellegrini pioneered work on the subject with their book *Un problema di storia sociale: L'infanzia abbandonata in Italia nel secolo XIX.*[20] It offers an excellent survey on the national level of institutions for abandoned children, statistics on foundlings, wet nursing, and laws on children in late-nineteenth-century Italy. Gorni and Pellegrini establish the main issues taken up by later studies: the large and increasing number of foundlings in the nineteenth century; the growing proportion of legitimate children among the abandoned; the gradual abolition after 1867 of the *ruota*, or turnstyle, which allowed parents to anonymously leave their children at foundling homes; and the unhealthy conditions within these institutions, leading to high infant mortality. Their material offers insights into the experiences of children admitted to the foundling homes. For example, some were reclaimed after months or years by their parents, who had pinned an identifying note, medal, or saint's picture on their swaddling clothes when left at the *ruota*. Others were nursed by their own mothers, who had sought employment at the foundling home to receive wages for raising their own children. Still others were sent to rural wet nurses, who often kept the children after weaning to raise as future workers. Peasants preferred boys to girls, since the latter required dowries for marriage. Girls, therefore, tended to remain longer in foundling homes, some of which provided dowries or placement in domestic service for older girls.

Franco della Peruta, the dean of social historians in Italy, gave further legitimacy to the subject of child abandonment when he included it in his pathbreaking article "Infanzia e famiglia nella prima metà dell'Ottocento," published in 1979.[21] Treating an earlier period than Gorni and Pellegrini, he places the growing interest in the plight of poor children within the larger context of the debate on pauperism in early nineteenth-century Italy. With a wealth of statistics he establishes the massive rise in abandonment throughout all regions of Italy in this period as well as the extremely high mortality rates within foundling homes.

This death rate, which sometimes reached 70 percent, drew public attention to the phenomenon of abandonment. Reformers began to label it the "massacre of the innocents" or "legal infanticide."[22] They were especially concerned that the percentage of legitimate children among foundlings was rising. The middle classes attributed this trend to the need of urban poor women to work for wages and the belief among the working classes that they had the "right" to consign their offspring to charity institutions, at least during the difficult period of nursing.

Other historians of eighteenth- and nineteenth-century Italy have begun to fill out the general picture sketched by Gorni, Pellegrini, and Della Peruta by focusing on specific cities or regions. With the exception of Rome (DiGiorgio) and Naples (De Rosa) most local studies have dealt with northern cities and towns: Turin (Doriguzzi), Milan (Hunecke), Brescia (Onger), Verona (Cappelletto), Chiavari near Genoa (Bianchi Tonizzi), Ravenna (Bolognesi and Giovanni), and Florence (Corsini).[23] Because some of the material in these studies is repetitive, I have organized my discussion around central topics of common interest to these authors.

The majority of these studies treat the eighteenth century, which saw an explosion of child abandonment during its last few decades.[24] Abandonment was facilitated by the *ruota*, a revolving compartment within the door of an institution that allowed parents to leave their children without being seen from the inside. The *ruota* dated back to the seventeenth century in some cases, so it does not completely explain the upturn in abandonment in the 1770s and 1780s. Most authors agree that the rise in illegitimacy and the increasing unwillingness of both ecclesiastical and state courts to prosecute fathers of illegitimate children led to the dependence by unwed mothers on the *ruota*. Single women, who had earlier been sanctioned to demand financial support, if not marriage, from the fathers of their children, now found themselves alone and unprotected. The introduction of the Napoleonic Code in most regions of Italy in the 1790s reinforced this trend toward placing blame only on the mother of illegitimate offspring by making paternity suits illegal. Official vocabulary enshrined the transition of illegitimate children from their former status as recognized members of the community to embarrassing and hidden products of sin by replacing the seventeenth-century term "natural children" with the modern "children of unknown parents."

By the mid-nineteenth century legitimate children began to account for the continued expansion in the number of foundlings.[25] In Milan, for example, an average of seven children came through the *ruota* each night, 75 percent of which were legitimate. Middle-class reformers took alarm, blaming working-class mothers for their lack of maternal feelings. They denied that the families of legitimate foundlings were impoverished, but claimed that such families simply refused to lower their standard of living to keep their babies. Most historians seem to have accepted this second argument, although Onger, in his study of Brescia, limits its applicability to the period after 1850, when conditions of working-class life did improve. Such outrage led to campaigns to eliminate the

ruota and thus the anonymity of abandonment. In fact, once admission to foundling homes required the public presence of a parent, abandonment dropped
precipitously in the late nineteenth century.

Many authors question whether parents felt affection for their abandoned
children, and lament the difficulty of addressing this issue through institutional
records. Most note that a good proportion of foundlings carried notes, religious
medallions, or some other sign of identification; both Cappelletto and Onger
include photographs of such objects. Doriguzzi found that more than half the
babies admitted to the Central Hospital of San Giovanni in Turin were accompanied by letters giving the baby's name, date of baptism, reason for abandonment, and promise to return in the future. She hypothesizes that this group was
made up of legitimate infants of working-class or artisan families, whereas
foundlings without identification were illegitimate children of poor, single mothers. Unmarried women may have had little feeling for their offspring and certainly
no desire to retrieve them from San Giovanni. In examining the same question
for Verona, Cappelletto surmises that the increasing intervention of mediators
between mothers and foundling homes—priests, local administrators, and midwives—may have served to cushion the pain of separation for women, since
these mediators took care of admission.

Finally, these articles on regional institutions for abandoned children provide
some information about life within them. Infant mortality was high, especially
for illegitimate babies who had been born under the least favorable circumstances.[26] Babies sent out to rural wet nurses survived at a higher rate than those
kept in institutions, where, as DiGiorgio reports, babies might be crowded sixty-
eight to a room and six to a cradle. Although rates of abandonment did not seem
to have varied by sex, boys were more likely to be adopted as apprentices or
farmhands. Girls tended to grow up in institutions, which they left if married
or hired as domestic servants by their early twenties. Some remained for life.

INSTITUTIONS OF ASSISTANCE AND DISCIPLINE

A further array of institutions complemented the foundling homes for the
purpose of either decreasing the high rate of child abandonment or taking care
of orphans and other "deviant" children once they had survived infancy. To
discourage child abandonment, bourgeois reformers urged the establishment of
nursery schools to take care of the legitimate children of working parents. Della
Peruta initiated research on nursery schools, analyzing them as part of the growing
philanthropic concern with poverty in the early nineteenth century.[27] He notes
that the spread of nursery schools was mainly limited to the northern provinces
of Italy, with little success in the South, where education in general was less
valued.

In two articles Christina Sideri has explored more closely the movement to
establish nursery schools in Milan. In "Asili infantili di carità: Aspetti della
fondazione di un'opera pia milanese" she traces the struggle between church

and state to control these institutions whose function was not initially clear.[28] The Church defined them as schools as part of its effort to retain and enlarge its traditional control over lower education. The state, on the other hand, insisted on the purely charitable nature of the nurseries so that they not become competitors to the growth of public elementary schools.

Statistics show that the working classes of nineteenth-century Milan did need nursery schools; after the first was founded in 1836 seven more followed in the next eight years. Between 1836 and 1856 the number of children served by the nurseries per year rose from 1,000 to 1,422, while 25 percent of the applicants were turned away for lack of space. In "Le origini degli asili infantili" Sideri describes the routine that governed the life of children in the nurseries.[29] They were to arrive punctually with a parent, equipped with bread and a handkerchief, for a stay of eight to twelve hours. The school provided free soup, eaten by the pupils standing up at a long table. All wore "uniform little frocks," and were separated by age and sometimes sex. Activities included instruction, play, walking, prayers, and singing, punctuated by visits from private, upper-class benefactors of the institutions. Although the nurseries were marked by discipline, obedience, and a rigid organization of the day, they were a vast improvement over the few previous schools run by *donnicciuole* (simple women), where children sat immobile all day awaiting the return of their parents.

Yet the nurseries did not accept children under two and one-half years of age, necessitating the establishment of "shelters" (*ricoveri*) for smaller babies, both those still nursing (*di latte*) and those already weaned (*di pane*). Della Peruta dates the first shelter in Milan to 1850, which, like the nurseries, accepted only legitimate children of working-class mothers.[30] Staffed by wet nurses and doctors, the shelters had cribs, games, and a garden in which babies could sleep and play free from their swaddling clothes. Although reformers were dismayed at the high utilization of the shelters by women who did piecework at home rather than in factories, they were pleased at the large number of babies admitted, the low rates of disease and mortality among them, and the apparent drop in the abandonment of legitimate children.

Besides foundling homes and nursery schools the eighteenth and nineteenth centuries saw the establishment or expansion of a variety of other institutions for older children and adolescents. The institutionalization of youth was not new, since most Renaissance cities had supported "conservatories" for girls whose honor was endangered by poverty or the death of a parent. The Enlightenment encouraged not only a new wave of humanitarian ventures, but also the assignment of different types of "deviants" to separate and specialized institutions. According to Carlo Simoni in his article " 'Dal consorzio uman proscritti, infelici, derelitti': Discoli e traviate a Brescia nel secondo Ottocento," not only were children separated from adults, but also boys from girls.[31] Delinquent boys were referred to as *discoli*, idle scamps with a propensity for theft. Girls, on the other hand, were labeled *traviate*, or prostitutes, showing that their deviance was defined as primarily sexual.

As yet, little research has been done on the male segment of the young "dangerous classes." In "La 'Generala' o 'penitenziario dei giovani discoli' di Torino, 1840–1877" Luisa Marucco charts the founding of an agricultural reformatory for boys near Turin in 1845.[32] Mixed with adults in a workhouse until this date, young delinquents now had their own institution, called "La Generala," to restore them to moral and physical health through hard work, therapeutic fresh air, and religious instruction. Interestingly, only a minority of the inmates were sentenced to "La Generala" by the courts; some had been sent at the request of their parents and the majority by local administrators at the advice of police. Marcella Rossi describes the growth of police powers over youth in her article "Discoli e vagabondi in Liguria nella prima metà del secolo XIX."[33] Focusing on the fear of vagabondage and theft in the wake of the revolutions of the late eighteenth and early nineteenth centuries, she describes the concern of the middle classes to reform and reinsert young, male delinquents into society. In the years preceding Italian unification she notes the evolution of reforming ideas from an exclusive reliance on work to a recognition of the need for education of the lower classes in institutions such as "La Generala."

The literature on institutions for girls is vaster and richer, perhaps because it has built on an already existing historiographical trend for early modern Italy.[34] The title of the article by Daniela Maldini, "Donne sole, 'figlie raminghe,' 'convertite' e 'forzate': Aspetti assistenziali nella Torino di fine Ottocento," gives an idea of the variety of labels assigned "deviant" girls and the corresponding institutions in Turin.[35] *Donne sole*, or respectable orphans, for example, were interned in "retreats" (*ritiri*) for protection of their honor until arriving at the age of marriage. Military orphans who "had a certificate of good conduct, were single, and were serious" as well as born of a legitimate, Catholic marriage were sent to their own institution. "Figlie raminghe," or homeless girls of the lower classes, were not eligible for the retreats housing honorable, well-to-do women, but were taught skills such as lacemaking at separate asylums. Finally, two separate institutions took in "convertite" and "forzate," women who had already "fallen" into prostitution. While forming a hierarchy depending on the economic and moral attributes of their inmates, all these institutions, according to Maldini, were "factories of humility," teaching the female virtues of obedience, silence, devotion, and total submission.[36]

Angela Groppi emphasizes the ambiguous nature of institutions meant to both assist and punish women in her analysis of the Monastero di Buon Pastore (Monastery of the Good Shepard) in nineteenth-century Rome ("Una gestione collettiva di equilibri emozionali e materiali: La reclusione delle donne nella Roma dell'Ottocento").[37] Like "La Generala" for boys in Turin, the "Buon Pastore" accepted girls at the insistence of their parents, police, or the courts, blurring the line between disobedient and delinquent youth. It also took in victims of rape, battering, and adultery at the request of girls themselves. Whether sinner or victim, inmates sought to repair their honor, the most important female attribute, through pious reclusion in a respected institution. By the mid-nineteenth century Groppi notes change and decay in the "Buon Pastore," which, by continuing to stress motherhood as the only future for its inmates, lost contact with the new industrialized society, in which women needed a skill to survive.

The most ambitious work to date on reformatories for girls is Annarita Buttafuoco's analysis of the *Asilo Mariuccia*, an asylum founded in 1902 in Milan by a feminist organization, the Unione Femminile (*Le Mariuccine: Storia di un'istituzione laica, l'Asilo Mariuccia*).[38] Buttafuoco explores not only the institutional experiences of its inmates, but also their former lives as children growing up in poor families. According to the asylum's records, 70 percent of the girls admitted between 1902 and 1922 had been victims of rape or incest or came from families marked by incest. Thus Buttafuoco sees the lower-class family at the turn of the century as the locus of violence and instability for children. Many of the inmates had practiced prostitution or at least were accustomed to the promiscuity of relatives and friends. Although the Unione Femminile tried to carry out its progressive philosophy of molding its charges into modern— that is, economically and psychologically independent—women, the relation between the bourgeois directors and the working-class girls was riddled by ambiguities. The girls did not prove to be "malleable subjects," able and willing to forget their experiences on the streets to conform to the model of innocent and decorous "daughters" demanded by their bourgeois "mothers."

EDUCATION

Compared with the rather recent historiographical trend toward studying charitable institutions for children, the development of public schooling has long received scholarly attention in Italy. I will, therefore, focus on the more recent and innovative contributions. Even these studies tend to focus on educational laws and pedagogy formulated by adults rather than on the actual classroom experience of children. They do, however, clearly trace changing ideas about the nature of childhood and offer a solid base for further research into the actual effects of these ideas on children's lives.

Dina Bertoni-Jovine offers a general introduction to the educational policies of united Italy in her book *La scuola italiana dal 1870 ai giorni nostri*.[39] She traces the extension of education from the elite to the popular classes in relation to the development of political parties and trade unions of the left. More useful for the English-language reader is Edward Tannenbaum's clear and insightful chapter on "Education" in the volume *Modern Italy: A Topical History Since 1861*, which he coedited. In this essay he discusses the changes in educational policy enshrined in the Casati Law of 1859, the Gentile Reform of 1923, and finally the piecemeal revisions of the postwar era.[40] In a less optimistic analysis than that of Bertoni-Jovine, Tannenbaum argues that Italy's schools have always been bourgeois and elitist, stressing the classics and humanities at the expense of science and technology. The requirement of Latin for admission to the universities is symptomatic of this traditionalist policy. Thus the school system has never served the needs of the lower classes, as reflected in the high illiteracy and low attendance rates of the nineteenth century, the continued tracking of children destined for university as early as the fifth grade, and the student revolts of 1968–1969. Written in 1973, the article evinced pessimism for any substantial change in the future.

Two recent works have looked more closely at Bertoni-Jovine's theme of the spread of education to the working classes in the nineteenth century. In a collection of essays edited by Tina Tomasi titled *Scuola e società nel socialismo riformista (1891–1926): Battaglie per l'istruzione popolare e dibattito sulla "questione femminile"* various authors have analyzed the pedagogical theories of the new socialist party founded in 1892, especially those expressed in the journal *Critica Sociale*.[41] In "Socialisti e cattolici di fronte al problema della refezione scolastica all fine dell'800'' Stefano Pivato takes up the important topic of the church-state struggle over education, in this case the state being defended by the socialists.[42] Socialists insisted that the public schools provide food and clothing to poor children to encourage their attendance. Catholics, on the other hand, recommended the traditional avenue of private charity for meeting such needs, warning that the socialist policy would lead to radicalism and revolt. Pivato argues that the Church was afraid that the provision of free meals and clothing in the public schools would drain children away from the private Catholic system of education.

Feminist historians have produced the most innovative work on nineteenth-century education by exploring the variety of meanings that "education" had for girls. In her pioneering three-part article "La donna nella scuola dall'unità d'Italia a oggi: Leggi, pregiudizi, lotte e prospettive" Simonetta Ulivieri provided a chronological framework for more recent research.[43] Not until the Casati Law of 1859 did the Italian state mandate elementary education for girls, although it eschewed coeducation. The curriculum for girls emphasized "female skills" (*lavori donneschi*), that is housekeeping. For most of the nineteenth century the only public high schools open to girls were the "normal" schools of teacher training. These were less rigorous than those for boys, since women were prohibited from teaching at the elite *licei*, the college preparatory schools for boys. As Ulivieri remarks, "this created a vicious circle in which women instructed women who would be teaching children, always within the limits of a reduced and less challenging program."[44] Women began to take degrees at Italian universities after they were opened to both sexes in 1874, although entrance to the professions was difficult or impossible.

Throughout the nineteenth century the only available secondary education for girls outside the normal schools was provided by private "colleges." Administered most often by the Church and open only to the daughters of the wealthy, these colleges were much more concerned with protecting their students' morality than with developing their minds, according to Silvia Franchini in her article "L'istruzione femminile in Italia dopo l'Unità: Percorsi di una ricerca sugli educandati pubblici di elite."[45] On the model of the cloister, these colleges discouraged contact between students and the outside world, including their families. Even visits home were frowned on, and all correspondence was censored. In a subsequent article ("Educande, privilegi del censo e matrimonio nell'Italia dell'Ottocento") Franchini argues that unlike the normal schools, the elite colleges continued throughout the nineteenth century to prepare their charges only for marriage rather than a profession.[46] This preparation consisted of teaching the *arts d'agrement*, such as dance, music, drawing, and comportment, as well as "female skills," such as the elaborate embroidery necessary to complete an upper-class trousseau. Most important, the colleges consistently combated any sign of independence, teaching students "to renounce liberty and personal preferences in order to carry out their social mission for the good of the family."[47]

The most recent contribution to the historiography of women's education has been a collection of essays edited by Simonetta Soldani titled *L'educazione delle donne: Scuole e modelli di vita femminile nell'Italia dell'Ottocento*. Because limited space precludes a review of all these interesting articles, I will focus on Soldani's contribution, "The Book and the Skein of Yarn" ("Il libro e la matassa: Scuole per 'lavori donneschi' nell'Italia da costruire").[48] For Soldani the book and the skein of yarn represent the "double instruction" typical of education for nineteenth-century women that most often took place not in public schools, but in institutes attached to workshops and factories. Thus more education did exist for nineteenth-century women than has yet been recognized, but education linked to work. In this sense the refuges and conservatories for deviant girls also were schools and perhaps provided the model for the myriad of institutes teaching "female skills" that sprang up in the nineteenth century to provide workers for the manufacturing economy. Although the curriculum at these schools was not academic, it did encourage literacy, and therefore must be included in the history of education. A companion volume, edited by Ilaria Porcini, catalogues an exhibit of written and material documents on women's education in the nineteenth century.[49] The photograph on the cover, a schoolgirl's sampler, illustrates Soldani's thesis that education and work were closely related. The sampler is embroidered in the capital letters of the alphabet used for monographing linens; it lacks an "H," since no Italian name begins with that letter. Thus girls learned the alphabet, but only an abbreviated one, to perform "women's skills."

Education during the fascist regime from 1922 to 1945 also has drawn scholarly attention perhaps because of the centrality of youth to Mussolini's vision of the new regime. His propaganda boasted of the youthful, dynamic, and active nature of fascism compared with the tired, outworn ideologies of nineteenth-century liberalism and socialism. In addition, he promised to create a "new man" of fascism, a task that obviously necessitated the inculcation of the appropriate values into children from a young age. One instrument for implementing this fascist "revolution" was the school system, from elementary through university levels.

Historians have debated the success of Mussolini's educational policy in "fascistizing" Italian youth between the wars. Tannenbaum, for example, concludes that "teen-age students in the late 1930s were more likely to be Fascist-oriented than not," although the humanistic tradition of the elite *licei* may have mitigated this tendency for the minority of adolescents attending them.[50] Michel Ostenc, in his *L'éducation en Italie pendant le fascisme*, is a bit more skeptical.[51] Although admitting that students were attracted to Mussolini himself (the *Duce*) and the nationalist fervor of his regime, Ostenc believes that "Fascist education was a . . . failure in that the Duce was not able to create the [new] man of Mussolini."[52] Richard Woolf also argues that the fascitization of Italian youth was limited, since Catholic influence in Italian schools increased during the dictatorship, especially after the Concordat of 1929 between church and state ("Catholicism, Fascism and Italian Education from the Riforma Gentile to the Carta della Scuola, 1922–1939").[53]

The difficulty in evaluating fascist education arises partially from the conflicts within the party itself about proper pedagogy. Although Mussolini called the early Gentile reform of 1923 the "most fascist of reforms," most historians agree that it represented only a restoration of the outmoded curriculum of the nineteenth century based on the classics and philosophy. The party admitted as much by continually "retouching" the law to make it less elitist and more useful for producing ideologically indoctrinated students. Yet as schools came under direct control of the party in the 1930s, disagreements remained between Mussolini and Giuseppe Bottai, self-styled fascist intellectual and minister of national education from 1936 to 1943. For Mussolini the aim of fascist pedagogy was to create youth "critically disposed to fight and die for that which was designated as good for the nation," in the words of Tina Tomasi in her *Idealismo e fascismo nella scuola italiana*.[54] Mussolini, who expected to designate that which was patriotic, called this "the virile and military education." Bottai, on the other hand, argued that youth should participate in the continual revision and renewal of fascism by being educated to debate and critique rather than passively submit to orders from above.[55] Bottai was not apolitical like Gentile, however, and his *Carta di Scuola* (School Regulations), issued in 1939, required censorship of textbooks, loyalty oaths for teachers, and political indoctrination of students, through the new media of radio and film as well as traditional books and lectures.[56]

YOUTH GROUPS

The literature on youth groups is not as extensive as that on schools perhaps because the developed only in the twentieth century, for the most part after World War I. Research has so far focused on the two rivals for the allegiance of youth in the interwar period, the Catholic Church and the fascist party. Although the earliest Catholic youth group, *Gioventù Cattolica*, dated back to 1905, Italian youth showed little enthusiasm for meeting with others of their own age until the founding of the Catholic Scouts in 1916. Modeled on the Anglo-American Boy Scouts, the Catholic Scouts combined an emphasis on physical exercise and military games with religious training. Throughout the 1920s and 1930s the Church vied with fascism to attract and socialize youth in its own principles. Unable to quash the power of the Church, Mussolini sanctioned the continuation of Catholic youth groups in the Lateran Accords of 1929, leaving them the only legal alternative to fascist youth organizations.

Although scouting was reserved for boys, two recent articles have explored a Catholic organization for girls, the *Gioventù Femminile*. Primarily devoted to the adoration of the Sacred Heart of Jesus, this group was founded in 1918 for young, single women. According to Paola Di Cori in "Rosso e bianco: La devozione al Sacro Cuore di Gesù nel primo dopoguerra," members combined a strong interior religiosity with a busy schedule of activities to spread their message.[57] Part of this message concerned the role of women: "The Gioventù Femminile wished to show women a third alternative to lay and socialist feminism which was confessional, firmly opposed to female emancipation, and characterized by a militancy within the structure of the Church and under the control of the ecclesiastical hierarchy."[58] In an analysis of the periodicals issued by Gioventù Femminile, Michela De Giorgio also found a preoccupation with reasserting the traditional virtues of women, such as patience, renunciation, and control of the passions ("Metodi e tempi di un'educazione sentimentale: La Gioventù Femminile Cattolica Italiana negli anni venti").[59] Yet both authors point out the novelty for women of meeting and organizing outside the home, activities that ironically resembled those of their enemies, the feminists.

Like Catholic youth organizations, the fascist Opera Nazionale Balilla (ONB) strove to inculcate a traditional message through a radically new tactic: detaching children from their parents for organized activity each week. Carmen Betti offers a complete history of the ONB in her book *L'Opera Nazionale Balilla e l'educazione fascista*.[60] Building on the early spontaneous organizations of fascist students, the ONB developed in the 1920s as a parallel institution to the schools for the indoctrination of youth by the regime. Promising to provide all children with "a spiritual as well as a material uniform," the ONB became increasingly focused on military exercises, such as marching in formation. In such a climate the sections for boys were always privileged over those of girls, who, as Tracy Koon points out, were allowed only to participate in a " 'doll drill,' passing in review holding dolls 'in the correct manner of a mother holding a baby' " (*Believe, Obey, Fight: Political Socialization of Youth in Fascist Italy, 1922–1943*).[61] The gender differentiation in fascist socialization is only one of the themes in Koon's thorough analysis of Mussolini's youth policy, complemented by a series of useful statistical tables.

Renamed the Gioventù Italiana del Littorio (GIL) in 1937 and brought directly under party control, the organization's motto remained, "Believe, obey, fight." In "La jeunesse italienne et le fascisme à la vielle di la seconde guerre mondiale," Ostenc assesses the success of the GIL in attracting the allegiance of youth to the regime by the late 1930s.[62] He notes growing tension between the party and the more educated youth, who turned the yearly *Lictoriales*, or debating conferences, into a "scandal" by publicly criticizing the immobility, bureaucratization, and censorship within fascism. Although Ostenc finds little conscious antifascism among youth before World War II, he believes that this "malaise" of youth presented an unsolvable problem for the party.

CHILD LABOR

The field of labor history is highly developed in Italy, but few scholars have focused specifically on the work of children. Several recent studies, however, have tried to measure the impact of work on the quality of life of children in the era of industrialization. Armando Pavan, in his article "I fanciulli nelle manifatture del bresciano: Inchiesta autriache della prima metà del secolo XIX," describes the first child labor legislation issued by the Austrian rulers of Lombardy before unification.[63] Issued in 1843, this law was quite progressive by Italian standards, and forbade any work for children under nine years of age; night work for those between nine and twelve; more than ten hours of work for the same age-group and twelve hours for those between twelve and fourteen; corporal punishment; and mixing of the sexes in factories. Despite glowing reports on the widespread application of the law by provincial authorities, Pavan expresses skepticism, noting that many industrialists received "dispensations" from various provisions of the law.

In a provocative article titled "Childhood and Industrialization in Italy" Kertzer challenges historians to reconsider their traditional assumptions about the evil of child labor in the nascent factories of the nineteenth century.[64] On the basis of data from Casalecchio di Reno, a sharecropping village outside Bologna, Kertzer argues that the establishment of a local textile mill strengthened family unity by promoting coresidency of children and parents. Rather than passing their childhood as apprentices and servants in the houses of relatives or strangers, children of peasant families now had the opportunity to live at home with their parents while working in manufacturing. Without denying the "dreadful conditions of factory labor" for children, Kertzer reminds us that children's work was almost universal and probably unpleasant in the earlier agricultural era, and warns against "an overly romantic portrait of childhood in pre-industrial times."[65]

Angiolina Arrù argues for the importance of the variable of sex when generalizing about urban domestic service in nineteenth-century Italy ("Protezione e legittimazione: Come si usa il mestiere di serva nell'800").[66] Using Rome as an example, Arru plots the feminization of domestic service as men began to find employment in other sectors of the economy. Tending to be young migrants from the countryside who remained in service for ever longer periods of their lives, female servants formed a distinct social group marked by prolonged celibacy. Arrù argues that despite low wages, domestic service offered something to young women not needed by men: the protection and moral patronage of an honorable and wealthy family.

Besides farming, manufacturing, and domestic service a variety of other, more marginal, and sometimes illegal, occupations attracted youth. Prostitution, for example, offered an alternative for teenage girls to unemployment or the low wages, long hours, and moral surveillance typical of most types of female work. In *Prostitution and the State in Italy, 1860–1915*, Mary Gibson explains how the Italian state legalized and regulated prostitution after unification; legal prostitutes had to register with police and undergo biweekly vaginal examinations for venereal disease.[67] Although prostitution laws prohibited police from registering girls under sixteen before 1888 and under twenty-one after that, arrest records and data from hospitals for venereal disease attest to the practice of prostitution at younger ages, especially in the South. The Italian government also legislated against the employment of children in "strolling professions," such as peddling, and playing music on the streets, by a law of 1873. In "I mercanti di fanciulli nelle Campagne e la tratta dei minori: Una realtà sociale dell'Italia fra '800 '900" Mario Ferrari explains that children in such professions were the target of illegal merchants, who bought them from their families and sent the "slaves" to work in foreign countries such as France, Germany, England, and the United States.[68] Despite the law, these merchants enlarged their trade by the turn of the twentieth century by supplying Italian children to foreign factories.

FAMILY LIFE

The recent development of a rich historiography in Italian family history has produced few studies focused primarily on children. A host of historians— including Alberto Mario Banti, Alberto Caracciolo, Mariuccia Giacomini, Giuseppina Laurita, Donald Pitkin, Carlo Poni, Franco Ramella, and Gian Albino Testa—have indirectly shed light on the experience of growing up in the modern Italian family through their discussion of household structure and patterns of inheritance.[69] Histories of family law, such as Paolo Ungari's excellent *Storia del diritto della famiglia in Italia*, outline the formal legal perimeters within which parents made decisions about their offspring.[70] Yet we currently know more about the attitudes of institutions of charity toward children under their care than those of eighteenth-, nineteenth-, and twentieth-century parents.

One exception to this generalization is the masterful work by Marzio Barbagli, *Sotto lo stesso tetto: Mutamenti della famiglia in Italia dal XV al XX secolo.*[71] Focusing on northern and central Italy, he summarizes and extends recent research on the types of family structure within which children spent their early years. He notes the long tradition in Italian cities of the nuclear family, reaching back to the fourteenth and fifteenth centuries among artisans and the working class. Extended families, composed of several generations of siblings and their spouses living under one roof, typified urban elites and the peasantry, especially sharecroppers. In the late eighteenth and early nineteenth centuries this pattern began to break down as all groups increasingly converged on the model of the

nuclear family. This trend was accelerated by the abolition of primogeniture
during the Napoleonic occupation, forcing families to split their patrimony among
all male heirs. But most innovative in Barbagli's study is his discussion of the
changing relations between parents and children from that of distance and discipline to intimacy and affection. Relying on letters written by children of the
aristocracy to their parents, he traces the revolutionary shifts in the form of
address used by children from the stilted and submissive "Lei" to the formal
"Voi" to the democratic "tu." Noting in addition the proliferation of pet names
and nicknames within families, Barbagli argues that at the beginning of the
nineteenth century, the aristocracy made the transition from the "authoritarian"
to the "intimate" family, a process followed later by the middle and lower
classes.

Employment or marriage signaled the end of childhood; we have discussed
the first, so we now turn to the second. Parents had great if not complete control
over both the age of marriage of their children and the size of their inheritance
or dowry. Based on marriage contracts registered in Florence between 1808 and
1812, Giovanni Gozzini finds the average age of marriage for sons to have been
30.8 years against 25.9 for daughters ("Matrimonio e mobilità sociale nella
Firenze di primo Ottocento").[72] In her article on the second half of the nineteenth
century, "Variabilità del celibato e dell'età al matrimonio in Italia nella seconda
metà del XIX secolo," Rosella Rettaroli produces similar statistics for Italy in
general: twenty-seven years of age for men and twenty-three to twenty-four for
women.[73] These figures had changed little from the seventeenth century, and
applied to both northern and southern regions of Italy. Rates of marriage did
rise significantly in the South at the turn of the twentieth century, a striking
development that Rettaroli attributes to the disruptive effects of heavy emigration
to Northern Europe and the New World.

Only a few scholars have turned their attention to dowries, a topic that has
produced a wealth of data for medieval and early modern Italy.[74] Although
dowries began to disappear in the nineteenth century, the rate and geographical
configuration of this change are as yet unknown. Guiseppe Moricola has supplied
a piece of this puzzle in his study of dotal contracts in the city of Avellino from
1840 to 1885 ("Sui contratti dotali della borghese avellinese [1840–1885]").[75]
He traces the liberalization in dotal law from the Napoleonic Code, which de-
moted the husband from being the owner to the administrator of his wife's dowry,
to the Italian Civil Code of 1865, which abolished the requirement that parents
dower their daughters. Within this framework he found that the lower classes
began to dispense with dowries by the 1880s, leaving the custom most widespread
among the bourgeoisie. Within the middle class, daughters of the same family
received equal amounts of money and property.

Jane Schneider has found that Sicilian girls of all classes have continued to
bring dowries to their marriages, even after World War II.[76] In her fascinating
article "Trousseau as Treasure: Some Contradictions of Late Nineteenth-Century
Change in Sicily" she questions why embroidered linens replaced handmade

cloth as the staple of lower- and middle-class trousseaus in the late nineteenth century. The answer is complex, combining the availability of machine-made cloth, the emulation of the aristocracy, and the need to keep adolescent girls busy within the home to preserve their honor. Finally, the trousseau in fact constituted a "treasure" or type of insurance policy for the newly married couple, since handmade embroidery commanded a high price and could be sold in times of economic crisis.

CONCLUSION

Future research on the history of childhood in modern Italy can build on some strengths and must repair some weaknesses. Italian historiography can boast a strong grounding in demography, pedagogy, and the family in relation to economics. Rather than being lopsided in favor of studies of boys, the literature has already recognized the different and equally important experience of girls. Yet children's point of view remains elusive. As Pavan has suggested, it is time for Italian historians to ask the following questions: "What happened to children? What did that majority who managed to survive do during their few years [of childhood]? In sum, how did they act and why?" He goes on to compare children with other marginal groups in the past who were not understood and "often punished because they were guilty of being themselves."[77] Italian historians must go beyond the analysis of ideas and institutions constructed by adults to uncover the hidden experience of children in modern Italy.

NOTES

1. Marcello Flores, "Infanzia e società borghese nella recente storiografia," *Movimento operaio e socialista* 4 (1980):497–506.

2. For example, see the excellent collection of essays by Christiane Klapisch-Zuber, *Women, Family and Ritual in Renaissance Italy*, trans. Lydia G. Cochrane (Chicago: University of Chicago Press, 1985). The historical journal *Quaderni storici* has been a leader in publishing articles influenced by anthropological theory.

3. See the journals *Memoria* and *Nuova Donnawomanfemme* for trends in Italian women's history.

4. Carlo Cipolla, "Four Centuries of Italian Demographic Development," in *Population in History: Essays in Historical Demography*, ed. D. V. Glass and D.E.C. Eversley (London: Edward Arnold, 1965), pp. 570–587.

5. Massimo Livi Bacci, *A History of Italian Fertility During the Last Two Centuries* (Princeton, N.J.: Princeton University Press, 1977), translated into Italian as *Donna, fecondità, e figli: Due secoli di storia demografica italiana* (Bologna: Il Mulino, 1980).

6. Livi Bacci, *History of Italian Fertility*, p. 287.

7. Giorgio Gattei, "Per una storia del comportamento amoroso dei Bolognesi: Le nascite dall'unità al fascismo," *Società e storia* 9 (1980):613–639.

8. Jane Schneider and Peter Schneider, "Demographic Transitions in a Sicilian Rural Town," *Journal of Family History* 9 (Fall 1984):245–272.

9. Rosanna De Longis, " 'In difesa della donna e della razza'," *Nuova Donnawomanfemme* 19–20 (Winter–Spring 1982):149–177.

10. Susanna Bucci, "La guerra tra il pane e l'amore," *Nuova Donnawomanfemme* 19–20 (Winter–Spring) 1982):178–189.

11. Denise Destragiache, "Un aspect de la politique démographique de l'Italie fasciste: La répression de l'avortement," *Mélanges de l'École francaise de Rome* 92, pt. 2 (1980):691–735.

12. Luisa Passerini, "Donne operaie e aborto nella Torino fascista," *Italia contemporanea* 151–152 (September 1983):83–109.

13. Athos Bellettini and Alessandra Samoggia, "Premières recherches sur les tendances de longue période de la mortalité infantile dans la campagne de Bologne (XVIIe–XIXe)," *Genus* 38 (January–June 1982):1–25.

14. Ibid., p. 24.

15. Antonio Bellacicco and Maurizio Maravelle, "Sulle oscillazioni fondamentali della mortalità infantile, a livello regionale, dal 1863 al 1961," *Genus* 20 (1974):203–223.

16. Agopik Manoukian, "La rappresentazione statistica dei vincoli familiari," in *I vincoli familiari in Italia: Dal secolo XI al secolo XX*, ed. A. Manoukian (Bologna: Il Mulino, 1983), pp. 437–447.

17. Maria Pia Casarini, "Maternità e infanticidio a Bologna: Fonti e linee di ricerca," *Quaderni storici* 49 (April 1982):275–284.

18. Maria Pia Casarini, "Il buon matrimonio: Tre casi di infanticidio nell'800," *Memoria* 7 (September 1983):27–36.

19. David J. Kertzer and Carolyn Brettell, "Advances in Italian and Iberian Family History," *Journal of Family History* 12 (1987):101. This article provides an excellent introduction to the major historiographical debates and bibliography in Italian family history.

20. Mariagrazia Gorni and Laura Pellegrini, *Un problema di storia sociale: L'infanzia abbandonata in Italia nel secolo XIX* (Florence: Nuova Italia, 1974).

21. Franco Della Peruta, "Infanzia e famiglia nella prima metà dell'Ottocento," *Studi storici* 20 (1979):473–491. This article was reprinted in Manoukian, ed., *I vincoli familiari*, pp. 375–392.

22. Ibid., p. 478.

23. Giorgio Di Giorgio, "Gli esposti dell'ospedale del Santo Spirito nella seconda metà del Settecento," *Storia e politica* 21 (September 1982): 480–517; Gabriele De Rosa, "L'emarginazione sociale in Calabria nel XVIII secolo: Il problema degli esposti," *Ricerche di storia sociale e religiosa* 13 (January–June 1978): 5–29; Franca Doriguzzi, "I messagi dell'abbandono: Bambini esposti a Torino nell '700," *Quaderni storici* 53 (1983):445–468; Volker Hunecke, "Problemi della demografia milanese dopo l'unità: La chiusura della ruota e il 'crollo' della nascita," *Storia urbana* 2 (May–August 1978):81–90; Sergio Onger, *L'infanzia negata: Storia dell'assistenza agli abbandonati e indigenti a Brescia nell'Ottocento* (Brescia: AIED, 1985); Giovanna Cappelletto, "Infanzia abbandonata e ruoli di mediazione sociale nella Verona del Settecento," *Quaderni storici* 53 (August 1983):421–468; M. Elisabetta Bianchi Tonizzi, "Esposti e balie in Liguria tra Otto e Novecento: Il Caso di Chiavari," *Movimento operaio e socialista* 6 (1983):7–31; Dante Bolognesi and Carla Giovannini, "Gli esposti a Ravenna fra '700 e '800," in *Città e controllo sociale in Italia tra XVIII e XIX secolo*, ed. Ercole Sori (Milan: Franco Angeli, 1982), pp. 307–328; and Carlo Corsini, "Materiali per lo studio della famiglia in Toscana nei secoli XVII–XIX: Gli esposti," *Quaderni storici* 33 (September–December

1976):998–1052. A book-length study by Hunecke appeared after the completion of this article: *I trovatelli di Milano: Bambini esposti e famiglie espositrici dal XVII al XIX secolo*.

24. See Corsini and Cappelletto. In Ravenna abandonment did not begin to rise until the first decades of the eighteenth century, according to Bolognesi and Giovannini.

25. See Hunecke and Onger.

26. See De Rosa, Di Giorgio, and Onger.

27. Della Peruta, "Infanzia e famiglia."

28. Cristina Sideri, "Asili infantili di carità: Aspetti della fondazione di un'opera pia milanese," *Il Risorgimento* (It) 34 (June 1982):98–119.

29. Cristina Sideri, "Le origini degli asili infantili e l'esperienza milanese," *Studi bresciani* 14 (May–August 1984):7–18.

30. Della Peruta, "Infanzia e famiglia."

31. Carlo Simoni, " 'Dal consorzio uman proscritti infelici, derelitti': Discoli e traviate a Brescia nel secondo Ottocento," *Studi bresciani* 14 (May–August 1984):37–57.

32. Luisa Marucco, "La 'Generala' o 'Penitenziario dei giovani discoli'di Torino, 1840–1877: Alcune relazioni mediche sui giovani reclusi," in Sori, ed., *Città e controllo sociale*, pp. 501–514.

33. Marcella Rossi, "Discoli e vagabondi in Liguria nelle prima metà del secolo XIX," *Movimento operaio e socialista* 6 (1983):33–51.

34. See, for example, Luisa Ciammitti, "Conservatori femminili a Bologna e organizzazione del lavoro," Quaderni storici 14 (May–August 1979):760–764; Luisa Ciammitti, "Quanto costa essere normali: La dote nel Conservatorio femminile di Santa Maria del Baraccano (1630–1680)," *Quaderni storici* 53 (August 1983):469–497; Sherrill Cohen, "Convertite e malmaritate: Donne 'irregolari' e ordini religiosi nella Firenze rinascimentale," *Memoria* 5 (November 1982):46–63; and Lucia Ferrante, "L'onore ritrovato: Donne nella Casa del Soccorso di San Paolo a Bologna (sec. XVI–XVII)," *Quaderni storici* 53 (August 1983):499–527.

35. Daniela Maldini, "Donne sole, 'figlie raminghe,' 'convertite' e 'forzate': Aspetti assistenziali nella Torino di fine Ottocento," *Il Risorgimento* (It) 33 (June 1981):115–138.

36. Ibid., p. 121.

37. Angela Groppi, "Una gestione collettiva di equilibri emozionali e materiali: La reclusione delle donne nella Roma dell'Ottocento," in *Ragnatele di rapporti: Patronage e reti di relazione nella storia delle donne*, ed. Lucia Ferrance (Turin: Rosenberg & Sellier, 1988), pp. 130––147.

38. Annarita Buttafuoco, *Le Mariuccine: Storia di un'istituzione laica, l'Asilo Mariuccia* (Milan: Franco Angeli, 1985).

39. Dina Bertoni-Jovine, *La scuola italiana dal 1870 ai giorni nostri*, 2nd ed. (Rome: Riuniti, 1967). More recent works on specific regions of Italy include Gaetano Bonetta, *Istruzione e società nella Sicilia dell'Ottocento* (Palermo: Sellerio, 1981); Stefano Pivato, *Pane e grammatica: L'istruzione elementare in Romagna alla fine dell'Ottocento* (Milan: Franco Angeli, 1983); Simonetta Ulivieri, *Gonfalonieri, maestri e scolari in Val di Cornia* (Milan: Franco Angeli, 1985).

40. Edward R. Tannenbaum, "Education," in *Modern Italy: A Topical History Since 1861*, ed. Edward R. Tannenbaum and Emiliana Noether (New York: New York University Press, 1974), pp. 231–253. The Casati Law, originally promulgated in the kingdom of Piedmont, became Italian law after unification in 1861.

41. Tina Tomasi, ed., *Scuola e società nel socialismo riformista (1891–1926): Battaglie per l'istruzione popolare e dibattito sulla "questione femminile"* (Florence: Sansoni, 1982).

42. Stefano Pivato, "Socialisti e cattolici di fronte al problema della refezione scolastica all fine dall'800," *Movimento operaio e socialista* 6 (1983):109–116.

43. Simonetta Ulivieri, "La donna nella scuola dall'unità d'Italia a oggi: Leggi, pregiudizi, lotte e prospettive," *Nuova Donnawomanfemme* 2 (January–March 1977):20–47; 3 (April–June 1977):115–140; 4 (July–September 1977):81–105.

44. Ibid., 2:42.

45. Silvia Franchini, "L'istruzione femminile in Italia dopo l'Unità: Percorsi di una ricerca sugli educandati pubblici di elite," *Passato e presente* 10 (January–April 1986):53–94.

46. Silvia Franchini, "Educande, privilegi dal censo e matrimonio nell'Italia dell'Ottocento," *Memoria* 23 (1988):51–68.

47. Ibid., p. 60.

48. Simonetta Soldani, "Il libro e la matassa: Scuole per 'lavori donneschi' nell'Italia da costruire," in *L'educazione delle donne: Scuole e modelli di vita femminile nell'Italia dell'Ottocento*, ed. Simonetta Soldani (Milan: Franco Angeli, 1989), pp. 87–129. The volume contains the proceedings of a conference held in Siena in 1987.

49. Ilaria Porciani, ed., *Le donne a scuola: L'educazione femminile nell'Italia dell'Ottocento* (Florence: "Il Sedicesimo," 1987). This is a catalogue of an exhibition held February–April 26, 1987, in Siena in conjunction with the conference described in the note above.

50. Tannenbaum, "Education," p. 244.

51. Michel Ostenc, *L'éducation en Italie pendant le fascisme* (Paris: Publications de la Sorbonne, 1980).

52. Ibid., p. 379.

53. Richard J. Woolf, "Catholicism, Fascism and Italian Education from the Riforma Gentile to the Carta della Scuola, 1922–1939," *History of Education Quarterly* 20 (1980):3–26. On church-state relations concerning youth see also Albert C. O'Brien, "Italian Youth in Conflict: Catholic Action and Fascist Italy, 1929–1931," *Catholic Historical Review* 68 (1982):625–635.

54. Tina Tomasi, *Idealismo e fascismo nella scuola italiana* (Florence: Nuova Italia, 1969), p. 129.

55. This argument comes from Paolo Nello, "Mussolini e Bottai: Due modi diversi di concepire l'educazione della gioventù," *Storia contemporanea* 8 (June 1977):335–366. On Bottai's educational philosophy see also Rino Gentili, *Giuseppe Bottai e la riforma fascista della scuola* (Florence: Nuova Italia, 1979).

56. Teresa Maria Mazzatosta includes a useful chart comparing the Gentile Reform and the *Carta di Scuola* in her book *Il regime fascista tra educazione e propaganda 1935–1943* (Bologna: Cappelli, 1978), p. 156.

57. Paola Di Cori, "Rosso e Bianco: La devozione al sacro cuore di Gesù nel primo dopoguerra," *Memoria* 5 (1982):82–107.

58. Ibid., pp. 103–104.

59. Michela De Giorgio, "Metodi e tempi di un'educazione sentimentale: La Gioventù Femminile Cattolica Italiana negli anni venti," *Nuova Donnawomanfemme* 10–11 (January–June 1979):126–145.

60. Carmen Betti, *L'Opera Nazionale Ballila e l'educazione fascista* (Florence: Nuova

Italia, 1984). The ONB provided an umbrella administration for a variety of youth groups: the Balilla, for boys aged eight to fourteen; the Avanguardisti, for boys aged fourteen to eighteen; the Piccole italiane, for girls aged eight to fourteen; and the Gruppi giovanili, for girls aged fourteen to eighteen.

61. Tracy Koon, *Believe, Obey, Fight: Political Socialization of Youth in Fascist Italy, 1922–1943* (Chapel Hill: University of North Carolina Press, 1985), p. 97.

62. Ostenc, "La jeunesse italienne et le fascisme à la veille de la seconde guerre mondiale," *Revue d'histoire de la deuxième guerre mondiale* 94 (April 1974):47–64.

63. Armando Pavan, "I fanciulli nelle manifatture del bresciano: Inchieste austriache della prima metà del secolo XIX," *Studi bresciani* 14 (May–August 1984):19–35.

64. David I. Kertzer, "Childhood and Industrialization in Italy," *Anthropological Quarterly* 60 (October 1987):152–159.

65. Ibid., pp. 153, 157.

66. Angiolina Arrù, "Protezione e legittimazione: Come si usa il mestiere di serva nell'800," in Ferrante et al., eds., *Ragnatele di rapporti*, pp. 381–416.

67. Mary Gibson, *Prostitution and the State in Italy, 1860–1915* (New Brunswick, N.J.: Rutgers University Press, 1986).

68. Mario Enrico Ferrari, "I mercanti di fanciulli nelle campagne e la tratta dei minori, una realtà sociale dell'Italia fra '800 e '900," *Movimento operaio e socialista* 6 (1983):87–108.

69. Alberto Mario Banti, "Strategie matrimoniali e stratificazione nobiliare: Il caso di Piacenza (XIX secolo)," *Quaderni storici* 64 (April 1987):153–174; Alberto Caracciolo, *L'Albero dei Belloni: Una dinastia di mercanti del Settecento* (Bologna: Il Mulino, 1987); Mariuccia Giacomini, *Sposi a Belmonte nel Settecento: Famiglia e matrimonio in un borgo rurale calabrese* (Milan: Giuffrè, 1981); Giuseppina Laurita, "Comportamenti matrimoniali e mobilità sociale a Napoli," *Quaderni storici* 56 (August 1984):433–465; Donald S. Pitkin, *The House That Giacomo Built: History of an Italian Family, 1898–1978* (New York: Cambridge University Press, 1985); Carlo Poni, "La famiglia contadina e il podere in Emilia Romagna," in Manoukian, ed., *I vincoli familiari*, Franco Ramella, "Famiglia, terre e salario in una communità tessile dell'Ottocento," in Manoukian, ed., *I vincoli familgliari*, pp. 265–287; Gian Albino Testa, "La strategia di una famiglia imprenditoriale fra Otto e Novecento," in Manoukian, ed., *I vincoli familiari*, pp. 393–408. This list is not exhaustive.

70. Paolo Ungari, *Il diritto di famiglia in Italia (1796–1942)* (Bologna: Il Mulino, 1970).

71. Marzio Barbagli, *Sotto lo stesso tetto: Mutamenti della famiglia in Italia del XV al XX secolo* (Bologna: Il Mulino, 1984).

72. Giovanni Gozzini, "Matrimonio e mobilità sociale nella Firenze di primo Ottocento," *Quaderni storici* 57 (December 1984):907–939.

73. Rosella Rettaroli, "Variabilità del celibato e dell'età al matrimonio in Italia nella seconda metà del XIX secolo," *Memoria* 23 (1988):69–90.

74. See, for example, Stanley Chojnacki, "Dowries and Kinsmen in Early Renaissance Venice," *Journal of Interdisciplinary History* 4 (1975):571–600; Diane Owen Hughes, "From Brideprice to Dowry in Mediterranean Europe," *Journal of Family History* 3 (Fall 1978):262–296; and Anthony Molho, "Investimenti nel monte delle doti di Firenze: Un'analisi sociale e geografica," *Quaderni storici* 61 (April 1986):147–170.

75. Giuseppe Moricola, "Sui contratti dotali della borghesia avellinese (1840–1885)," *Quaderni storici* 56 (August 1984):467–491.

76. Jane Schneider, "Trousseau as Treasure: Some Contradictions of Late Nineteenth-Century Change in Sicily," in *Beyond the Myths of Culture: Essays in Cultural Materialism*, ed. Eric B. Ross (New York: Academic Press, 1980), pp. 323–356; it has been reprinted in Marion A. Kaplan, ed., *The Marriage Bargain: Women and Dowries in European History*. Vol. 10 of *Women and History* (New York: Institute for Research in History and Haworth Press, 1985), pp. 81–119.

77. Pavan, "I fanciulli nelle manifatture," pp. 19–20.

REFERENCES

Arru, Angiolina. "Protezione e legittimazione: Come si usa il mestiere di serva nell'800." In *Ragnatele di rapporti: Patronage e reti di relazioni nella storia delle donne*, edited by Lucia Ferrante et al. Turin: Rosenberg & Sellier, 1988, pp. 381–416.

Banti, Alberto Mario. "Strategie matrimoniali e stratificazione nobiliare: Il caso di Piacenza (XIX secolo)." *Quaderni storici* 64 (April 1987):153–174.

Barbagli, Marzio. *Sotto lo stesso tetto: Mutamenti della famiglia in Italia dal XV al XX secolo*. Bologna: Il Mulino, 1984.

Bellacicco, Antonio and Maurizio Maravelle. "Sulle oscillazioni fondamentali della mortalità infantile a livello regionale, dal 1863 al 1961." *Genus* 20 (1974):203–223.

Bellettini, Athos, and Alessandra Samoggia. "Premières recherches sur les tendances de longue période de la mortalité infantile dans la campagne de Bologne (XVIIe–XIXe siecle)." *Genus* 38 (January–June 1982):1–25.

Bertoni-Jovine, Dina. *La scuola italiana dal 1870 ai giorni nostri*. 2nd ed. Rome: Riuniti, 1967.

Betti, Carmen. *L'Opera Nazionale Balilla e l'educazione fascista*. Florence: Nuova Italia, 1984.

Bianchi Tonizzi, M. Elisabetta. "Esposti e balie in Liguria tra Otto e Novecento: Il caso di Chiavari." *Movimento operaio e socialista* 6 (1983):7–31.

Bolognesi, Dante, and Carla Giovannini. "Gli esposti a Ravenna fra '700 e '800." In *Città e controllo sociale in Italia tra XVIII e XIX secolo*, edited by Ercole Sori. Milan: Franco Angeli, 1982, pp. 307–328.

Bonetta, Gaetano. *Istruzione e società nella Sicilia dell'Ottocento*. Palermo: Sellerio, 1981.

Bucci, Susanna. "La guerra tra il pane e l'amore." *Nuova Donnawomanfemme* 19–20 (Winter–Spring 1982):178–189.

Buttafuoco, Annarita. *Le Mariuccine: Storia di un'istituzione laica l'Asilo Mariuccia*. Milan: Franco Angeli, 1985.

Cappelletto, Giovanna. "Infanzia abbandonata e ruoli di mediazione sociale nella Verona del Settecento." *Quaderni storici* 53 (August 1983): 421–468.

Caracciolo, Alberto. *L'Albero dei Belloni: Una dinastia di mercanti del Settecento*. Bologna: Il Mulino, 1987.

Casarini, Maria Pia. "Maternità e infanticidio a Bologna: Fonti e linee di ricerca." *Quaderni storici* 49 (April 1982):275–284.

———. "Il buon matrimonio: Tre casi di infanticidio nell'800." *Memoria* 7 (September 1983):27–36.

Chojnacki, Stanley. "Dowries and Kinsmen in Early Renaissance Venice." *Journal of Interdisciplinary History* 4 (1975):571–600.

Ciammitti, Luisa. "Conservatori femminili a Bologna e organizzazione del lavoro." *Quaderni storici* 14 (May–August 1979):760–764.

———. "Quanto costa essere normali: La dote nel Conservatorio femminile di Santa Maria del Baraccano (1630–1680)." *Quaderni storici* 53 (August 1983):469–497.

Cipolla, Carlo. "Four Centuries of Italian Demographic Development." In *Population in History: Essays in Historical Demography*, edited by D. V. Glass and D.E.C. Eversley. London: Edward Arnold, 1965, pp. 570–587.

Cohen, Sherrill. "Convertite e malmaritate: Donne 'irregolari' e ordini religiosi nella Firenze rinascimentale." *Memoria* 5 (November 1982):46–63.

Corsini, Carlo. "Materiali per lo studio della famiglia in Toscana nei secoli XVII–XIX: Gli esposti." *Quaderni storici* 33 (September–December 1976):998–1052.

De Giorgio, Michela. "Metodi e tempi di un'educazione sentimentale: La Gioventù Femminile Cattolica Italiana negli anni venti." *Nuova Donnawomanfemme* 10–11 (January–June 1979):126–145.

Della Peruta, Franco. "Infanzia e famiglia nella prima metà dell'Ottocento." *Studi storici* 20 (1979):473–491.

De Longis, Rosanna. "In difesa della donna e della razza." *Nuova Donnawomanfemme* 19–20 (Winter–Spring 1982):149–177.

De Rosa, Gabriele. "L'emarginazione sociale in Calabria nel XVIII secolo: Il problema degli esposti." *Richerche di storia sociale e religiosa* 13 (January–June 1978):5–29.

Destragiache, Denise. "Un aspect de la politique démographique de l'Italie fasciste: La répression de l'avortement." *Mélanges de l'École francaise de Rome* 92, pt. 2 (1980):691–735.

Di Cori, Paola. "Rosso e Bianco: La devozione al sacro cuore di Gesù nel primo dopoguerra." *Memoria* 5 (1982):82–107.

Di Giorgio, Giorgio. "Gli esposti dell'ospedale del Santo Spirito nella seconda metà del Settecento." *Storia e politica* 21 (September 1982):480–517.

Doriguzzi, Franca. "I messaggi dell'abbandono: Bambini esposti a Torino nell'700." *Quaderni storici* 53 (1983):445–468.

Ferrante, Lucia. "L'onore ritrovato: Donne nella Casa del soccorso di San Paolo a Bologna (sec. XVI–XVII)." *Quaderni storici* 53 (August 1983):499–527.

Ferrari, Mario Enrico. "I mercanti di fanciulli nelle campagne e la tratta dei minori: Una realtà sociale dell'Italia fra '800 e '900." *Movimento operaio e socialista* 6 (1983):87–108.

Flores, Marcello. "Infanzia e società borghese nella recente storiografia." *Movimento operaio e socialista* 4 (1980):497–506.

Franchini, Silvia. "L'istruzione femminile in Italia dopo l'Unità: Percorsi di una ricerca sugli educandati pubblici di elite." *Passato e presente* 10 (January–April 1986):53–94.

———. "Educande, privilegi del censo e matrimonio nell'Italia dell'Ottocento." *Memoria* 23 (1988):51–68.

Gattei, Giorgio. "Per una storia del comportamento amoroso dei Bolognesi: Le nascite dall'unità al fascismo." *Società e storia* 9 (1980):613–639.

Gentili, Rino. *Giuseppe Bottai e la riforma fascista della scuola*. Florence: Nuova Italia, 1979.

Giacomini, Mariuccia. *Sposi a Belmonte nel Settecento: Famiglia e matrimonio in un borgo rurale calabrese*. Milan: A Giuffrè, 1981.

Gibson, Mary. *Prostitution and the State in Italy, 1860–1915.* New Brunswick, N.J.: Rutgers University Press, 1986.

Gorni, Mariagrazia, and Laura Pellegrini. *Un problema di storia sociale: L'infanzia abbandonata in Italia nel secolo XIX.* Florence: Nuova Italia, 1974.

Gozzini, Giovanni. "Matrimonio e mobilità sociale nella Firenze di primo Ottocento." *Quaderni storici* 57 (December 1984):907–939.

Groppi, Angela. "Una gestione collettiva di equilibri emozionali e materiali: La reclusione delle donne nella Roma dell'Ottocento." In *Ragnatele di rapporti: Patronage e reti di relazioni nella storia delle donne,* edited by Lucia Ferrante et al. Turin: Rosenberg & Sellier, 1988, pp. 130–147.

Hughes, Diane Owen. "From Brideprice to Dowry in Mediterranean Europe." *Journal of Family History* 3 (Fall 1978):262–296.

Hunecke, Volker. "Problemi della demografia milanese dopo l'unità: La chiusura della ruota e il 'crollo' della nascita." *Storia urbana* 2 (May–August 1978):81–90.

———. *I trovatelli di Milano: Bambini esposti e famiglie espositrici dal XVII al XIX secolo.* Bologna: Il Mulino, 1989.

Kertzer, David I. "Childhood and Industrialization in Italy." *Anthropological Quarterly* 60 (October 1987):152–159.

Kertzer, David I., and Carolyn Brettell. "Advances in Italian and Iberian Family History." *Journal of Family History* 12 (1987):87–120.

Klapisch-Zuber, Christiane. *Women, Family, and Ritual in Renaissance Italy,* translated by Lydia G. Cochrane. Chicago: University of Chicago Press, 1985.

Koon, Tracy H. *Believe, Obey, Fight: Political Socialization of Youth in Fascist Italy, 1922–1943.* Chapel Hill: University of North Carolina Press, 1985.

Laurita, Giuseppina. "Comportamenti matrimoniali e mobilità sociale a Napoli." *Quaderni storici* 56 (August 1984):433–465.

Livi Bacci, Massimo. *Donna, fecondità, e figli: Due secoli di storia demografica italiana.* Bologna: Il Mulino, 1980.

Maldini, Daniela. "Donne sole, 'figlie raminghe,' 'convertite' e 'forzate': Aspetti assistenziali nella Torino di fine Ottocento." *Il Risorgimento* (It) 33 (June 1981):115–138.

Manoukian, Agopik. "La rappresentazione statistica dei vincoli familiari." In *I vincoli familiari in Italia: Dal secolo XI al secolo XX,* edited by Agopik Manoukian. Bologna: Il Mulino, 1983, pp. 437–447.

Marucco, Luisa. "La 'Generala' o 'Penitenziario dei giovani discoli' di Torino, 1840–1877: Alcune relazioni mediche sui giovani reclusi." In *Città e controllo sociale in Italia tra XVIII e XIX secolo,* edited by Ercole Sori. Milan: Franco Angeli, 1982, pp. 501–515.

Mazzatosta, Teresa Maria. *Il regime fascista tra educazione e propaganda (1935–1943).* Bologna: Cappelli, 1978.

Molho, Anthony. "Investimenti nel monte delle doti di Firenze: Un'analisi sociale e geografica." *Quaderni storici* 61 (April 1986):147–170.

Moricola, Giuseppe. "Sui contratti dotali della borghesia avellinese (1840–1885)." *Quaderni storici* 56 (August 1984):467–491.

Nello, Paolo. "Mussolini e Bottai: Due modi diversi di concepire l'educazione della gioventù." *Storia contemporanea* 8 (June 1977):335–366.

O'Brien, Albert C. "Italian Youth in Conflict: Catholic Action and Fascist Italy, 1929–1931." *Catholic Historical Review* 68 (1982):625–635.

Onger, Sergio. *L'infanzia negata: Storia dell'assistenza agli abbandonati e indigenti a Brescia nell'Ottocento*. Brescia: AIED, 1985.

Ostenc, Michel. "La jeunesse italienne et le fascisme à la veille de la seconde guerre mondiale." *Revue d'histoire de la deuxième guerre mondiale* 94 (April 1974):47–64.

―――. *L'éducation en Italie pendant le fascisme*. Paris: Publications de la Sorbonne, 1980.

Passerini, Luisa. "Donne operaie e aborto nella Torino fascista." *Italia contemporanea* 151–152 (September 1983):83–109.

Pavan, Armando. "I fanciulli nelle manifatture del bresciano: Inchieste austriache della prima metà del secolo XIX." *Studi bresciani* 14 (May–August 1984):19–35.

Pitkin, Donald S. *The House That Giacomo Built: History of an Italian Family, 1898–1978*. New York: Cambridge University Press, 1985.

Pivato, Stefano. *Pane e grammatica: L'istruzione elementare in Romagna alla fine dell'Ottocento*. Milan: Franco Angeli, 1983.

―――. "Socialisti e cattolici di fronte al problema della refezione scolastica all fine dell'800." *Movimento operaio e socialista* 6 (1983):109–116.

Poni, Carlo. "La famiglia contadina e il podere in Emilia Romagna." In *I vincoli familiari in Italia: Dal secolo XI al secolo XX*, edited by Agopik Manoukian. Bologna: Il Mulino, 1983, pp. 289–311.

Porciani, Ilaria, ed. *Le donne a scuola: L'educazione femminile nell'Italia dell'Ottocento (Mostra documentaria e iconografica)*. Florence: "Il Sedicesimo," 1987.

Ramella, Franco. "Famiglia, terra e salario in una communità tessile dell'Ottocento." In *I vincoli famigliari in Italia: Dal secolo XI al secolo XX*, edited by Agopik Manoukian. Bologna: Il Mulino, 1983, pp. 265–287.

Rettaroli, Rosella. "Variabilità del celibato e dell'età al matrimonio in Italia nella seconda metà del XIX secolo." *Memoria* 23 (1988):69–90.

Rossi, Marcella. "Discoli e vagabondi in Liguria nella prima metà del secolo XIX." *Movimento operaio e socialista* 6 (1983):33–51.

Schneider, Jane. "Trousseau as Treasure: Some Contradictions of Late Nineteenth-Century Change in Sicily." In *Beyond the Myths of Culture: Essays in Cultural Materialism*, edited by Eric B. Ross. New York: Academic Press, 1980, pp. 323–356.

Schneider, Jane, and Peter Schneider. "Demographic Transitions in a Sicilian Town." *Journal of Family History* 9 (1984):245–272.

Sideri, Cristina. "Asili infantili di carità: Aspetti della fondazione di un'opera pia milanese." *Il Risorgimento* (It) 34 (June 1982):98–119.

―――. "Le origini degli asili infantili e l'esperienza milanese." *Studi bresciani* 14 (May–August 1984):7–18.

Simoni, Carlo. " 'Dal consorzio uman proscritti, infelici, derelitti': Discoli e traviate a Brescia nel secondo Ottocento." *Studi bresciani* 14 (1984):37–57.

Soldani, Simonetta. "Il libro e la matassa: Scuole per 'lavori donneschi' nell'Italia da costruire." In *L'educazione delle donne: Scuole e modelli di vita femminile nell'Italia dell'Ottocento*, edited by Simonetta Soldani. Milan: Franco Angeli, 1989, pp. 87–129.

Tannenbaum, Edward R. "Education." In *Modern Italy: A Topical History Since 1861*, edited by Edward R. Tannenbaum and Emiliana P. Noether. New York: New York University Press, 1974, pp. 231–253.

Testa, Gian Albino. "La strategia di una famiglia imprenditoriale fra Otto e Novecento." In *I vincoli familiari in Italia: Dal secolo XI a secolo XX*, edited by Agopik Manoukian. Bologna: Il Mulino, 1983, pp. 393–408.

Tomasi, Tina. *Idealismo e fascismo nella scuola italiana*. Florence: Nuova Italia, 1969.

———, ed. *Scuola e società nel socialismo riformista (1891–1926): Battaglie per l'istruzione popolare e dibattito sulla 'questione femminile'*. Florence: Sansoni, 1982.

Ulvieri, Simonetta. "La donna nella scuola dall'unità d'Italia a oggi: Leggi, pregiudizi, lotte e prospettive." *Nuova Donnawomanfemme* 3 pts. (1977):20–47; 3:115–140; 4:81–105.

———. *Gonfalonieri, maestri e scolari in Val di Cornia*. Milan: Franco Angeli, 1985.

Ungari, Paolo. *Il diritto di famiglia in Italia (1796–1942)*. Bologna: Il Mulino, 1970.

Woolf, Richard J. "Catholicism, Fascism and Italian Education from the Riforma Gentile to the Carta della Scuola, 1922–1939." *History of Education Quarterly* 20 (1980):3–26.

15

JAPAN

Kathleen S. Uno

Silver, gold, and precious stone,
What are they in comparison
With a daughter and son?

—Eighth-century poem[1]

According to an old Japanese saying, "Children are treasures."[2] Examination of modern Japanese folk beliefs, literary works, child-rearing advice, and child-rearing practices suggests that Japanese have long regarded children as precious. It seems unlikely, however, that Japanese parents invariably showed solicitude in rearing their children over the past three centuries. This chapter considers the extent to which Japanese attitudes and behaviors toward children matched the ideals of folk wisdom by exploring children's experiences in households and other institutions from the early modern (1600–1867) to the pre–World War II (modern or prewar) (1868–1945) and postwar (or contemporary) periods (1946–).[3]

To do justice to this quest, one must look beyond the limited literature on the history of Japanese children available in English,[4] for two reasons. First, Western historical studies on children in Japan currently are lacking. Second, the current approaches in social sciences this literature are of limited utility for historical studies. The concepts of shame[5] and later of psychological dependence (called *amae* by some researchers)[6] have predominated in works by Western social scientists that treat postwar Japanese childhood and family life. The former has subsequently been questioned by U.S. and Japanese social scientists.[7] In addition, although much historical evidence suggests that caregivers and child-rearing goals have shifted since the early modern period, neither concept can cope satisfactorily with change over time.[8] As existing Western concepts may be best suited to analysis of children in the twentieth century, I have adopted an empirical approach, exploring the themes of children as treasures at length before offering several tentative generalizations regarding children in modern Japanese history at the end of the chapter.

Space constraints prevent inclusion of a section treating childhood as a stage of life, although defining childhood is an important and interesting problem. For purposes of this chapter, my definition of childhood is a loose one, including both infancy and the late teens to early twenties. Thus later I touch on aspects of childhood ranging from infant care and youth culture. As we shall see, childhood has varied greatly since the early modern era. For example, if childhood is defined as economic dependence on the family of origin, youngsters indentured as servants at ages four to seven in the early modern period would not fit the category "children." Or if formation of a family of procreation is a criterion of adulthood, then in the same period, non-inheriting children and servants who were not allowed to marry never became full-fledged adults.[9]

The study of children in Japanese history is a relatively new research area. Although research is most advanced regarding children and children's institutions in postwar Japan, examination of childhood in the early modern and prewar eras reveals long-term trends affecting children and conceptions of childhood that greatly illuminate Japanese childhood in the present. Further studies will not only enrich our understanding of Japanese society in the past and present, but equally important, they also will contribute to the development of comparative family studies and social history, especially children's and women's history.

CHILDREN IN HOUSEHOLDS

The structure and goals of the Japanese household (the *ie*) help to account for the saying, "Children are treasures."[10] The household constituted a residential, legal, affective, economic, and ritual unit for its members, although the extent to which propertyless early modern and prewar Japanese held the *ie* as an ideal deserves further study.[11] *Ie* structure resembled that of a stem family, for a large household might have married couples of two or more generations and their unmarried offspring as well as servants.[12] Above, all the *ie* required a successor to marry and bring forth the next household, who would in turn produce a successor to preserve the household name, honor, status, and occupation.[13] Customs and laws of the early modern and prewar eras placed a premium on household continuity rather than satisfaction of individual desires and interests.

Household structure and goals exerted great influence on attitudes toward children, child-rearing practices, and the length of childhood as a stage of life. Most important was the fact that only one child plus spouse and offspring were linked to the future of the household. The child could be male or female, for considerable variation in succession practices existed from the early modern period until promulgation of the Meiji Civil Code in 1898. In some regions of

Japan the oldest son remained to become the next househead. In other areas the youngest son or the husband of the oldest daughter succeeded to the headship.[14] To preserve household property and livelihood, unitary inheritance by the successor was widely practiced.[15] Noninheriting children left the household as apprentices, adoptees, spouses, or servants, or remained as unmarried adult dependents in their natal household. The Japanese saying ''The sibling is the beginning of the stranger'' reflects the fact that *ie* residents constituted a more significant social group than blood relations.[16] Entering members such as spouses and long-term servants proved their worth to the household after years of hard work, while memories of kin who departed the local community faded with the passage of time.

As household resources were limited and household survival was by no means assured, adults tended to allocate a larger share of resources to the child who would remain as successor. In the early modern (and prewar) periods the future successor or the daughter whose husband would become the adopted successor tended to receive better food and clothing than the other children. From adults' point of view, expenditures on clothing and food for children who would depart for another household wasted *ie* resources.[17] Of course, practice did not always match prescriptions. Setting aside household considerations, one or more adults might dote on a noninheriting child because of cleverness, docility, or resemblance to a departed loved one.

Yet succession involved more than coddling the future successor or the daughter who would marry the incoming heir. Valuing household prosperity over individuals' happiness and security, senior members were willing to bypass natural children of the house for an unrelated, adopted successor. Determination to maintain *ie* social and economic status motivated prosperous merchants to disinherit inept or profligate sons and to instead name able clerks as successors, marrying them to natural and adopted daughters.[18]

In the prewar era the *ie* continued to be the dominant form of household, although the new, assertive central government attempted to eliminate class and regional diversity in succession, and inheritance practices in the Civil Code of 1898.[19] The household entered members in the household register (*koseki*) at a local government office. The law gave the head the unilateral right to list illegitimate children, obliging his wife to take responsibility for their upbringing. The head had the power to determine the residence of all household members, to approve the marriages of men under age thirty and women under age twenty-five, and to expel (*kandoo*) disobedient members. Barring incorrigibility or serious disability, succession passed to the oldest son under the new laws. Adoption practices and concubinage were not affected by the new laws, but concern over Japan's image in the eyes of the West led lawmakers to omit explicit references to the latter practice in the code.[20]

From the early twentieth century the state attempted to establish the early modern household as a bulwark against political unrest. The authority of the household head became linked to imperial authority in the ideology of the ''family-state'' (*kazoku kokka*) or emperor system (*tennoo seido*). Ordinary citizens, including children, were to demonstrate their loyalty to the emperor (*chuu*) by practicing filial piety (*koo*).[21] Yet state efforts to prevent ordinary citizens from organizing labor unions and political associations took place at a time when economic and social changes had begun to undercut the viability of the *ie*. After 1890 urbanization, new employment opportunities, and the diffusion of alternative visions of family life eroded *ie* values and the househead's authority. The home lives of migrants to the city escaped the direct supervision of employers and village elders. Young men and women imbued with Western notions of individualism, romantic love, social responsibility, or religion began to question the value of sacrificing individual plans to benefit the *ie*. Furthermore, access to new occupations helped youths to break free of *ie* constraints.

In the early twentieth century the growth of a new urban middle class gave rise to a novel style of family life.[22] In the households of wage and salaried workers children could not become successors to the household enterprise. Adult members' authority diminished as direct control over their children's future livelihood disappeared. As economic change and Western influences buffeted the prewar *ie*, calls for changes in family law surfaced. Nonetheless, the government steadfastly refused to revise the civil code, for *ie* values were central to the prewar political ideology.

After World War II the occupation authorities forced the Japanese to abolish the *ie*, a wellspring of militarism and authoritarianism in the American view.[23] Despite promulgation of a new constitution (1946) and civil code (1947), the old notion of the corporate household continued to influence Japanese attitudes and behavior toward children during the postwar era. For example, the tendency for family life to be child-centered rather than couple-centered (or companionate) is a legacy of the prewar past. Yet as youths born in the postwar era came of age in the 1980s, the influence of *ie* values further diminished.[24] This tendency is reinforced by demographic trends: the rise of the nuclear family, the decline in coresident relatives and servants, and the falling birthrate, all of which enhance parent-child contact by reducing the number of adults in the household.

HOUSEHOLD DIVISION OF LABOR: DEMOGRAPHY, CHILD-REARING, AND CHILDREN'S WORK

Historical demographic research suggests the contours of children's home life, providing valuable insights given the current dearth of other early modern sources. Analyses of household registers shed light on fertility, infant and child mortality, spacing of siblings, age at first marriage, age differences between spouses, household size, and household composition for scattered localities.[25] The treatment here focuses primarily on the implications of household composition and size for child rearing and children's work from the early modern to the contemporary eras, for combined with literary evidence, these characteristics illuminate responsibility for child rearing and children's participation in household activities.[26]

Possibilities for interaction between children and adults varied according to household size and composition. Estimates of mean household size in early modern Japan converge at about five members per household after the mid-eighteenth century,[27] not a large size considering that the stem family formed the core of the *ie* and that servants also lived in households.[28] Small household size often meant that just two or three children lived at home.[29] With only a few children present parents could have lavished attention on their offspring, but biographical and literary evidence suggest that parents did not necessarily assume the major role in rearing their own children. When living with older in-laws a mother tended to have weak authority over child rearing and little responsibility as caregiver for infants or socialization of children. The senior householders were particularly reluctant to entrust the rearing of the heir to the mother, a newcomer to the household who did not know its customs and might not have its best interests at heart.[30] On the other hand, the proximity of work and family life allowed male household members such as fathers, brothers, uncles, and grandfathers to participate in the physical care and socialization of children. In particular, the head's responsibility for household continuity often led to involvement in the upbringing of his successor.[31]

One can discern two early modern patterns of child care, reflecting the differing composition of ordinary and wealthy households, which persisted into the prewar period. Poorer households tended to be smaller, possibly with only one adult member.[32] When older members, including mothers, were preoccupied with gaining a livelihood older siblings (as young as age four), a grandparent (if present), or others who could contribute little to household subsistence took care of infants and toddlers. If all were busy working to subsist, no one watched the youngest householder.[33] In prosperous households, which tended to be larger and more diverse, coresident grandparents, unmarried uncles and aunts, older siblings, and servants of various types and ages as well as parents and siblings were possible caregivers for children. Boy apprentices, child baby-sitters (*komori*), or other hired help tended infants for part of the day, but in very rich households specialized servants such as wet nurses and governesses might care for newborns and older children day and night.

The juxtaposition of work and family life facilitated children's participation in both domestic and productive labor, as did small household size. Rich households that could afford to hire many servants did not need to rely on their children's labor, but ordinary and poor households invariably did. Except in the wealthiest families, children helped with domestic chores such as housecleaning, wood-gathering, cooking, and baby-sitting. They also contributed to the household livelihood by weeding, harvesting, plaiting ropes, gathering grass to fertilize crops, making handicrafts for sale, or hiring out as servants or laborers on a daily basis or for longer periods.[34]

Differential participation in domestic and productive work meant that childhood as a stage of life varied considerably by class. Poorer children tended to experience work and economic independence from their natal households early in life, whereas rich youngsters enjoyed a longer period of economic dependence and a more leisurely life-style. Yet children of wealthy households, too, might be placed out to another household as servants or apprentices. While in service, girls learned self-control, etiquette, and household management to prepare them for virilocal marriage; boys gained occupational skills. Adults recognized that children might learn better in the households of strangers, who would be less inclined to spoil them.[35]

In the prewar era, most urban and rural households, productive and domestic work still took place under one roof, allowing those who worked at home to engage in childrearing and other domestic tasks as before.[36] The need of poor and ordinary households to employ the labor of able-bodied adults and children remained roughly constant, for household size,[37] and the proportion of families on the land, and farm technology changed slowly.[38] In the long run, however, the government's compulsory education policy interfered with the customary household division of labor, especially the allocation of child care tasks and the use of children's labor. Households that sent children to school lost the labor of sibling, apprentice, and child baby-sitters as well as other young servants and workers for much of the day for four to six years.

The loss of children's labor began to undermine the pattern of shared caregiving by household members just at the time that prewar demographic and economic changes began to foster a new pattern of child rearing among the new wage-earning classes, especially the new urban middle class. For urban wage and salaried workers domestic and work life took place in separate spaces. Those working outside the home (principally fathers) became unable to help with child care or other domestic activities during the long hours they were away from home.[39] Nor could school-aged children of wage employees baby-sit while they attended school during the daytime. With wage workers and students absent, by default mothers were left at home with children under age six.[40] The emerging pattern of mother as sole caregiver for children at home became increasingly important, despite the small size of the new wage-earning class, for some of its members wielded considerable influence in society as teachers, professors, civil servants, managers, engineers, and journalists. Magazines, books, public lectures, and school curricula began to treat the role of mothers, rather than mothers-in-law, in rearing children and managing the household according to new, enlightened methods.

In the postwar era sweeping demographic as well as economic changes have altered the possibilities for interaction between adults and children in households. Long-term trends toward smaller household size, simpler household composition, and wage labor have tended to increase parental responsibility for child rearing, especially that of mothers, and have diminished the role of other household members in the care and education of children.[41] Urban mothers in salaried households rear children single-handedly, for male wage earners spend nearly all day away from home, and the household now tends to be a two-generation family, without in-laws, servants, or other relatives. Furthermore, even if in-laws are present, the abolition of the *ie* as a legal entity and the postwar emphasis on democratic social and political values have reduced the older generation's authority over children.

Shrinking household size also means that significant numbers of children have no siblings.[42] An only child does not compete with brothers or sisters for parental attention; one child is less likely to strain material and emotional household resources. In addition, labor-saving devices such as washing machines and pre-pared foods have enabled many Japanese mothers to devote less time to household chores and more time to child rearing. This is particularly true for middle-class women, whose husbands' earnings enable them to be full-time homemakers, but not so true for wives of farmers and small shopkeepers. The intensity of bonds between full-time mothers and their children has led some teachers, psycholo-gists, and social critics to complain about overprotective mothers, absent fathers, and spoiled children who have difficulty getting along with their classmates.[43]

Urbanization also has affected children's lives and attitudes toward child rear-ing. Postwar urbanization proceeded at an astonishing pace between 1955 and 1975.[44] By 1970, 46.1 percent of Japan's population had concentrated in the three great cities of Tokyo, Osaka, and Nagoya.[45] In the crowded cities and suburbs there are few large open spaces in which children can play. Some social observers fret that lack of exercise will result in weak, uncoordinated future citizens.

Because the proportion of farm mothers has sharply declined in the postwar era, urban rather than rural child-rearing practices and problems have come to receive the lion's share of public attention.[46] Although there is little evidence that farm women feel guilty about having less time to devote to child rearing than the wives of urban salaried workers, the issues that dominate discussions of family problems on national television and printed media are mainly those of urban middle-class families. School refusal syndrome, bullying, violence against teachers, entrance examination stress, selection of afterschool examination prep-aration schools, and *mazakon* ("mother complex") have emerged almost exclu-sively in urban settings.[47] For example, the "mother complex," the problem of young men who depend excessively on their mothers, is not dysfunctional for a farm or urban small enterprise successor, who is expected to make decisions about his work in consultation with his parents, but it can greatly hamper the work efficiency of an employee in a nonfamilial enterprise.

CHILD-REARING ATTITUDES AND PRACTICES

At times Japanese treatment of children and attitudes toward them may seem to bely the saying "Children are treasures," for until the postwar period *ie* values dictated that children be reared as the keys to the future of households rather than to prepare them to make their own way as individuals in the world. Children, however, were not equally cherished; most adults regarded the child destined to stay in the household as the successor or the wife of the successor as more precious than the other children. In fact, adults prized household survival more than the survival of individual children. For the sake of the household Japanese parents and grandparents were willing to adopt a successor and disown their own dull or dissolute natural offspring. Children perceived as harming *ie* interests might be aborted or killed at birth. With the postwar demise of the *ie* and the decline of enterprise households attitudes toward children have shifted away from such a utilitarian view. Yet, perhaps surprisingly, despite changes in who cares for children at home, child-rearing practices, save the use of physical punishments, have apparently changed little from the early modern and prewar periods.

Early modern adults assumed that young children's minds and characters were malleable. Accordingly, they usually attempted to train children to serve the *ie* from an early age. The saying "Like three, like a hundred" reflected popular belief that habits and attitudes instilled in toddlers would last a lifetime.[48] Thus child-rearing advice manuals instructed parents to provide proper moral guidance and vocational training to children aged six or even younger.[49] The practice of womb education (*taikyoo*) further demonstrates belief in the malleability of children's character during the early stages of life. Mothers who practiced womb education tried to avoid extreme emotional states such as anger or excitement, and extraordinary physical exertions, fearing negative effects on the development of the child's character.[50]

The folk saying "Until seven among the gods" had relevance for child-training methods. It commonly believed that the young child's soul was loosely bound to the body, and that a severe shock, including a sudden noise, could cause the infant's death by dislodging the spirit from the body. This implied that young children required gentle care, although some caregivers may have failed to treat infants gently.[51] The basics of infant care included carrying, feeding, and toilet training. The caregiver—whether mother, sibling, child baby-sitter, apprentice, nanny, or grandparent—strapped the baby on her or his back with its head facing in the same direction as the caregiver's. The infant was unstrapped to nurse on demand at the mother's or wet nurse's breast, but feeding could be delayed when the mother was working at an important task.[52]

As for education at home, early modern adults encouraged very young and older children to learn social and vocational skills by imitating good models. They used patient persuasion, cajoling, moral lecturing, and silent example to train children, but also resorted to harsher means, such as scolding, physical punishment, confinement in dark storehouses or cages, locking children out of the house, and, for extremely intractable children, moxa cauterization (burning dried vegetable powder on the child's skin).[53] Although the latter three punishments might seem to contradict the regard for children as treasures, they reflected adults' determination to instill in children willingness to obey their seniors and to think of household before self. Despite preference for rather gentle methods overall, early modern child-rearing advice pamphlets warned parents, especially mothers, against displaying too much affection for children. An excess of sentiment could lead to overindulgence and lax discipline, resulting in a spoiled, willful child who refused to subordinate personal desires to *ie* interests.[54] The absence of a romantic view of the mother-child bond is striking.

Ie interests took precedence over the life of a newborn when a household could not spare the resources for its upbringing, although infanticide, too, may seem inconsistent with the professed view of children as treasures.[55] Mothers and midwives "returned" unwanted children to the gods at birth, although offerings and prayers to statues of gods and buddhas suggest that the lives of the "returned" infants were not held in light regard.[56] In cities and the countryside pregnant women sought to prevent births by visiting abortionists or drinking medicines believed to induce miscarriages.[57]

In the prewar period Japanese attitudes toward children and child rearing exhibited both continuity and change. The persistence of *ie* household organization ensured that childhood experiences and attitudes toward children would remain uneven. And beliefs in the malleability, innocence, and purity of young children and the importance of early training, too, persisted even into the postwar period. Convinced of children's impressionability, adults, especially those in enterprise households, continued to teach social and vocational skills at home from children's earliest years. Still, over time, educational institutions assumed a greater role in the care and socialization of prewar children. After 1890, following an early flirtation with liberal education to develop the maximum potential of individuals, state goals of instilling loyalty to emperor and service to empire in children became the central purpose of education. Both prewar household members and the state tended to regard children as members of a social unit rather than as individuals; nonetheless, household and state goals for children conflicted at times, as when the government conscripted villagers' sons for military service.

During the prewar era Japanese came in contact with Western ideas, including conceptions of childhood and parent-child relations. Japanese views of childhood and child rearing, especially among the educated elite, were reshaped to some extent by assimilation of Western ideas. During the 1870s advice to elite women to nurse and rear their children themselves instead of hiring wet nurses and governesses constitutes an early example of Western influence.[58] In the 1880s Ueki Emori argued that the collective values of the *ie* oppressed children, and called for new family values that would allow people greater choice over their own destinies.[59] In the early twentieth century Western ideas introduced by educators, child welfare experts, intellectuals, and feminists, including the writings of Ellen Key, Swedish author of *Century of the Child*, sparked lively debates concerning the social role of mothers and the pros and cons of mothers' pensions.[60] Overall, Western influences promoted individualism in contrast to *ie* collectivism, and maternal responsibility rather than diffuse sharing of child-rearing tasks among kin and nonkin household members. Yet it is difficult to assess how broadly and how quickly the new ideas spread to the lower classes.[61]

Since the end of World War II child-rearing goals have shifted from training children to serve household and empire to preparing children for smooth and willing participation in smaller collectives such as family, schoolmates, work group, and company, a different sort of contribution to the social order and the national weal. Faith in young children's malleability persists,[62] but now mothers and schools, rather than older household and community members, are the primary socializers of children.[63] Today mothers are extolled as the most suitable caregivers for children. Yet the association of maternal care with healthy infant development is weaker than that articulated in countries where early childhood experts subscribe to Freudian psychology. While mothers are regarded as the best caregivers for children, and mothers who slight child rearing for work or other activities outside the home draw criticism, they are not accused of inflicting fundamental, irreparable distortion of their offspring's emotional development. Although paid baby-sitters are virtually unheard of, local and national funds flow to private as well as public day-care centers; such support is possible because the separation of preschoolers from the mothers is not perceived as the root of irremediable psychological damage.

By and large, a rather romantic view of children as cute, dependent, and needing much tender care has become prevalent in urban Japan today, in contrast to the earlier utilitarian conceptions of children as successors to the household enterprise, subjects of the emperor, or contributors to empire that prevailed in the early modern and prewar eras. Children over age six are perceived as dependents and consumers, rather than as household workers; adults assume that children require prolonged, attentive nurturing by their mothers. Despite abolition of the *ie*, children have remained central to family life, but in a less compelling manner than before the war.Children are recipients of affection and their achievements can enhance family status, but they are not needed as successors in the households of wage and salary earners.[64] Today one reads much about urban new middle-class mothers who seek to shore up family prestige and gain vicarious fulfillment in life by managing their children's educational and career achievements. On the other hand, some mothers (and fathers) permit their children to freely choose their own path in life. One might argue that in contrast to the past, when children were encouraged to obey their elders in household and community to gain a living and a place in society, today's children acquire more varied social and vocational skills that they learn in a greater range of settings from a greater variety of teachers, for they must belong to many diverse social groups— family, schools, company, community, and nation, and perhaps clubs, political organizations, and trade associations as well, to participate fully in society.

Today child-training methods are still rather lenient, as a rule. American observers have marveled at the patience of Japanese mothers. Early modern methods of child rearing such as strapping the child on the back for long hours, cosleeping, patient persuasion, and toilet training utilizing the child's natural elimination rhythms persist in Japan today. Today withholding of affection, persuasion, and bribes are the main means of inducing cooperation of children, even very young ones, but use of physical punishment seems to have declined.[65]

CHILDREN'S INSTITUTIONS

In contrast to the virtual absence of specialized welfare facilities, schools of many kinds serving the major social classes abounded by the end of the early modern era. Domainal and private academies served the upper classes; temple schools (*terakoya*) served children of less prosperous families. Warrior boys, especially the son succeeding to his father's position, received educations at academies established by feudal lords. Children of prosperous warrior, merchant, and peasant households studied at home with tutors, but some also attended Confucian, native learning (*kokugaku*), Shingaku, and Dutch or other Western studies academies.[66]

Although ordinary children gained most social and occupational skills at home, temple schools teaching the "3 R's" to commoner children multiplied toward the end of the period, especially in cities and nearby commercially advanced rural districts. Sons of merchants needed to be able to calculate sums, read circulars, and record inventories; daughters also profited from learning such skills. As wives, they assisted the business, sometimes assuming the headship if the husband died during the successor's minority. In villages where literacy functioned as a mark of social status, local elites frowned on the teaching of letters to poorer peasants. Nonetheless, temple schools flourished in many rural regions, for literacy enabled the growing number of farmers engaged in cash cropping and the sale of rural handicrafts to keep agricultural diaries and to study agricultural handbooks.[67] Most rural and urban children who did not attend school acquired social and vocational knowledge from adult householders and villagers, but in some rural communities youngsters between the ages of seven and thirteen to fifteen learned the ways of the village from children's groups (*kodomo kumi*) and above age fifteen they might continue to gain social and work skills in male and female youth groups.[68]

In the prewar era schools competed with household and community groups as sites of moral and occupational training. The government established a nationwide system of schools and four years of compulsory education for both sexes in 1872.[69] By 1910 elementary school enrollment rates had risen from 43 percent to 97 percent,[70] and a variety of secondary and postsecondary institutions flourished.[71] Yet adult householders continued to impart social and vocational skills to children. Furthermore, households did not readily relinquish their claim to children's labor. After the razing and burning of schools during the 1850s ceased, parents still kept children home from school when the household enterprise needed additional workers.[72]

The proliferation of educational institutions, including preschool facilities, has continued during the postwar era.[73] Today most children acquire work skills at vocational high schools, higher technical schools, colleges, and the workplace, not at home. Rising educational aspirations in the contemporary era have elevated the afterschool preparatory academy (*juku*) to a prominent place in the galaxy of postwar children's institutions, especially for junior and senior high school children.[74] In addition, sports clubs as well as teachers and schools offering enrichment lessons in piano, dance, swimming, and English have mushroomed.[75]

Government officials in some domains founded facilities and programs to succor orphans and children born to poor families after 1780; however, the programs aimed at stabilizing revenues by maintaining sufficient cultivators on the land, rather than guaranteeing the child's right to live. There was little need for specialized institutions to rear orphaned and abandoned children, for households of all classes took in abandoned children as adopted successors and prosperous households absorbed them as workers.[76]

During the late nineteenth and early twentieth centuries orphanages, reformatories, day nurseries, day-care centers, paupers' schools, afterschool programs, playgrounds, health clinics, milk depots, children's employment exchanges, and counseling centers sprang up, mainly in the cities. Almost all these children's institutions were established under private auspices, as the government preferred to invest in economic and military development rather than in health and welfare facilities.[77] The government did, however, issue several ordinances of quite limited scope, the Foundling Law (1871, rev. 1873), the Relief Law (Kyuugo hoo, 1874) furnishing token amounts of assistance to needy children, and the Reformatory Law (Kanka hoo, 1900) providing for rehabilitation of delinquent children.[78] These established a meager framework for child protection until depression (1927) and war (1931) fostered passage of new legislation such as the Poor Relief Law (1929), the Prevention of Cruelty to Children Law (1933), the Minors' Reformatory Law (1933), the Maternal and Child Protection Law (1937), and the National Eugenics Law (1940). Although the 1929 relief law reflected increased state willingness to assume responsibility for assistance to the needy, and the 1937 law provided financial assistance to poor mothers for the rearing of their children, the goal of the wartime legislation was to ensure an adequate supply of high-quality manpower for industrial and military needs, rather than to improve the lives of children as individuals. Thus the Eugenics Law provided for sterilization of carriers of hereditary defects and abortion of imperfect fetuses.[79]

Welfare institutions for children have continued to proliferate since the end of World War II. Several child welfare issues emerged during the postwar period. In the chaotic postsurrender years homeless and delinquent children and orphans required immediate assistance. Longer-range goals included (a) improvement of the health of infants and mothers through reduction of the high parturition and infant mortality rates and improvement of health and child development facilities, and (b) improvement of maternal and child welfare through financial assistance, better housing environments, and other measures. Although poor children, delinquents, and physically and mentally challenged children have received special attention, considerable effort has been directed at ordinary children through the national network of mother and child advice centers, mother and child health clinics, and day-care centers established under the Child Welfare Law (Jidoo fukushi hoo, 1947), the Maternal and Child Welfare Law (Boshi fukushi hoo, 1964) and the Maternal and Child Health Law (Boshi hoken hoo, 1965) after the postwar economic recovery was well under way.[80] Thanks to these new institutions, the infant mortality rate fell from 76.7 per thousand in 1947 to about 18.5 and 5.5 per thousand in 1965 and 1980, respectively, and life expectancy rose from 42.6 years for men and 51.1 for women in 1947 to 67.7 for men and 72.9 for women in 1965.[81] Overall, children's chances of growing up in good health have greatly improved in the postwar era.

CONCLUSION

To what extent have adults perceived children as treasures and treated them as such during Japan's modern era? Overall, the evidence presented here suggests that neither attitudes nor behavior toward children has remained static during the past three centuries. Techniques of care such as carrying on the caregiver's back, cosleeping, and indulgence toward very young children seem to have exhibited greater continuity than childhood as a stage of life, attitudes toward children as household or family members, and treatment of children at home and in institutions.

Attitudes toward children have shifted with the decline of the early modern enterprise household (*ie*). In particular, the growth of employment for wages at large-scale economic organizations since the 1890s encouraged new attitudes toward children. In households that did not depend on a single child to become the next househead adults became freer to cherish all children rather than the successor alone. Paradoxically, as children have become less essential to the household, more children per family have become precious to adults. Yet as household members began to relinquish their grip on children during the prewar era, the state exerted an unprecedented claim on children as keys to the future growth and strength of the empire. Since 1945, however, children are no longer bound to serve household or state.

In the postwar era treatment of children in households has become more egalitarian, owing to changing laws and values as well as the further decline of the early modern household as an economic entity. Adults have become less inclined to shower affection and material goods on the successor at the expense of noninheriting children. The treatment of children has changed in another way. Since the early modern period nonfamilial institutions have come to play a much greater role in the care and socialization of children. Postwar children spend many hours each day away from parents and other household members. Besides regular schools, afterschool academies (*juku*), clubs, movies, and other forms of entertainment outside the home socialize and educate children, and diverse influences ranging from television, magazines, comic books, and radio reach inside the home to help shape children's goals and values. Finally, the experience of childhood as a stage of life has become more uniform. In the early modern era poor children departed their natal households as servants or apprentices at ages four to ten; in 1980, 90 percent of children finished high school, with 58 percent opting to continue vocational or college education after graduation.[82] On the whole, postwar children live as economically dependent students with their parents until they begin work after high school, junior college, higher technical schools, or university graduation.[83]

This study has drawn on the existing literature to explore the history of childhood and child rearing in modern Japan; it should be obvious, however, that more research is needed in many important areas.[84] What should appear on an agenda for future research? There is a pressing need for studies concerning the children in early modern and prewar history. Here the greatest need is for investigation of class differences in children's experiences and adult attitudes and behavior. The greatest lacunae are the lack of research on child-rearing practices of early modern peasants, artisans, and merchants and of prewar working-class and enterprise households. For the postwar era more attention to urban lower-class and current rural attitudes and child rearing is needed. Generalizations based on detailed studies of class and local variations will surely have greater validity. Second, it may prove profitable to pursue the main theme in studies by Japanese historians and educational historians—that the discovery of childhood accompanied the economic, political, and social changes they refer to as "modernization" or "the rise of capitalism."

Fortunately since the late 1970s rising interest in the social history of children, women, and the family; increased anxiety over youth and family problems; and renewed interest in qualitative sociology (*seikatsu shi*) have stimulated Japanese scholars to produce new works of interest to children's historians.[85] As popular and scholarly interest in children's, women's, and social history in general show no signs of flagging in Japan, in the near future we can look forward to additional new monographs and general works that will form the basis for more comprehensive Western studies of Japanese children in history.

NOTES

I warmly thank Yasuko Ichibangase, Kyuuichi Yoshida, Kazuyo Yamamoto, Kuni Nakajima, Takeo Shishido, Hiroshi Urabe, Ryuutaroo Kinoshita, Chizu Teshi, Motoko Oota, Hiroko Hara, Kaoru Tachi, Yoshiko Miyake, Masako Ohtomo, Miharu Nishimura, Keiko Katoda, Michiko Mabashi, Keiko Kawai, and Kiyoko Tani, as well as Teruko Inoue, Kazuko Tanaka, Mitsue Yoneda, Gerry Harcourt, Janet Golden, Per Gjerde, and N. Ray Hiner for their encouragement and assistance during the initial stages of research for this chapter. In addition, I am grateful to the Japan Foundation and American Association of University Women for financial support for the research and to William Cutler III, Peter Gran, Lynn Wiener, Gary Leupp and Dorinne Kondo for comments regarding previous versions.

1. Quoted in Takayuki Namae, "Child Welfare Work in Japan," in *Standards of Child Welfare*, ed. William L. Chenery and Ella A. Merritt (Washington, D.C.: Children's Bureau, U.S. Department of Labor, 1919; rpt., New York: Arno Press, 1974), p. 326. See also Masami Yamazumi and Kazue Nakae, *Kosodate no sho* (Tokyo: Heibonsha, 1976), 1:3.

2. Yamazumi and Nakae, *Kosodate no sho*, 1:8; Hiroshi Wagatsuma and Hiroko Hara, *Shitsuke* (Tokyo: Koobundoo, 1974), pp. 11–15.

3. In Japanese the terms Edo or Tokugawa *jidai* (or *kinsei*) denote the early modern period; *kindai*, the prewar period; and *sengo* (or *gendai*), the postwar period. The prewar period also is referred to as the modern period, but then in this chapter, "modern" refers to the period 1600–present. Imperial reigns in the prewar and postwar periods are Meiji (1868–1912), Taisho (1912–1926), Showa (1926–1989), and Heisei (1989–).

4. Exceptions are Hiroshi Wagatsuma, "Some Aspects of the Contemporary Japanese Family: Once Confucian, Now Fatherless?" in *The Family*, ed. Alice Rossi, Jerome Kagan, and Tamara K. Hareven (New York: W. W. Norton, 1977), pp. 181–210; Kathleen Uno, "Day Care and Family Life in Industrializing Japan, 1868–1926," (Ph.D. diss., University of California, Berkeley, 1987). The latter discusses changes in the care and education of children from the nineteenth to the early twentieth centuries. In German see Hiroko Hara and Mieko Minagawa, "Japanische Kindheit Seit 1600," in *Zur Sozialgeschichte der Kinderheit*, ed Jochen Marten and August Nitschke (Munich: Verlag Karl Alber Freiburg, 1986), pp. 113–189, or "Japanese Childhood Since 1600," the unpublished English translation of the chapter. For a survey of the field of Japanese family studies see Susan Orpett Long, *Family Change and the Life Course*, Cornell East Asia Papers No. 44 (Ithaca, N.Y.: Cornell University Japan-China Program, 1987).

5. For a characterization of Japan as a culture of shame rather than guilt and an analysis of the role of shame in child rearing see Ruth Benedict, *Chrysanthemum and the Sword* (Boston: Houghton Mifflin, 1946), pp. 195–227, 253–296.

6. Takie S. Lebra, *Patterns of Japanese Behavior* (Honolulu: University of Hawaii Press, 1976), pp. 50–66,137–155; Takeo Doi, *The Anatomy of Dependence* (New York: Kodansha International, 1973); Ezra Vogel, *Japan's New Middle Class: The Salary Man and His Family in a Tokyo Suburb* (Berkeley: University of California Press, 1963), pp. 227–252; Merry White, *The Japanese Educational Challenge* (New York: Free Press, 1987), pp. 20–42.

7. George De Vos, *Socialization for Achievement* (Berkeley: University of California Press, 1973); Wagatsuma and Hara, *Shitsuke*, pp. 91–95, 162–179.

8. Regarding the major approaches of Japanese scholarship, see the conclusion of this chapter.

9. Chizuko Ueno, "The Position of Japanese Women Reconsidered," *Current Anthropology* 28 (1987):575. The age of majority in postwar Japan is twenty.

10. I refer to the *ie* as "household" rather than "family," following Chie Nakane, *Kinship and Economic Organization in Rural Japan* (London: Athlone Press, 1967); Jane Bachnik, "Recruitment Strategies for Household Succession: Rethinking Japanese Household Organization," *Man* 18 (1983):160–182; Matthews Hamabata, *For Love and Power: Family Business in Tokyo* (Ithaca, N.Y.: Cornell University Press, 1990), especially pp. 33–41; Dorinne Kondo, *Crafting Selves: Work, Identity, and the Politics of Meaning in a Japanese Factory* (Chicago: University of Chicago Press, 1990), especially pp. 121–141; Takie S. Lebra, *Japanese Women: Constraint and Fulfillment* (Honolulu: University of Hawaii Press, 1984), indicates alternative views, pp. 20–21. Occasionally I have used

"family" in discussing the *ie* as an affective unit or "house." Although one may refer to the household residential unit as "family" after enactment of the 1947 Civil Code, I have used the term "household," for conceptions of childhood, child rearing, and children's futures shaped by the *ie* lingered after its formal abolition.

11. The diffusion of *ie* values among commoners during the early modern period requires further research. On the one hand, Fumie Kumagai, "Modernization and the Family in Japan," *Journal of Family History* 11 (1986):375, asserts that *ie* consciousness did not penetrate propertyless rural and urban commoners during the early modern period. The special treatment Toshio Takai's father accorded his first-born son, however, suggests that by the early twentieth century, propertyless male househeads as well wished for successors. Toshio Takai, *Watashi no jokoo aishi* (Tokyo: Soodo bunka, 1980), p. 809. Although poor households lacked property to pass to an heir, they possessed a place in the village and a reputation to maintain, and ancestors for which rites needed to be performed.

12. Regarding servants' membership, see Kumagai, "Modernization and the Family," p. 373. For numbers of servants per household in the early modern period, see Akira Hayami and Nobuko Uchida, "Size of Household in a Japanese County Throughout the Tokugawa Era," in *Household and Family in Past Time: Comparative History in the Size of the Domestic Group Over the Last Three Centuries*, ed. Peter Laslett (Cambridge: Cambridge University Press, 1972), pp. 503–505. Also note that between 1671 and 1870 only 25 to 30.5 percent of households in the rural communities they studied had three or more generations present (p. 504). According to Susan B. Hanley, "Family and Fertility in Four Tokugawa Villages," in *Family and Population in East Asian History*, ed. Susan B. Hanley and Arthur P. Wolf (Stanford, Calif.: Stanford University Press, 1985), 58.6 to 65.4 percent of villagers lived in elementary families (p. 210). For one ward of the metropolis of Osaka, Robert J. Smith reports 48.7 percent of families residing in elementary households and 26.8 percent residing in stem households. "Transformations of Commoner Households in Tennooji-mura, 1757–1858," in Hanley and Wolf, eds., *Family and Population in East Asian History*, p. 255. Regarding urban class differences, see note 32.

13. Even propertyless Buddhist believers wanted to have descendants to perform rites assisting the journey of the spirit (*hotoke*) after death. Adherents of the native religion (Shinto) made offering to the deceased's spirit (*kami*) to dissuade it from exerting malevolent influence on the world of the living.

14. Harumi Befu, *Japan: An Anthropological Introduction* (San Francisco: Chandler Publishing Co., 1971), p. 41; Ryoosuke Ishii, *Nihon soozoku hoo shi* (Tokyo: Soobunsha, 1980). In a few regions more than one son and spouse remained in the household; however, only one child became househead (i.e., Nakane, *Kinship and Economic Organization*, pp. 8–16). In addition, succession practices varied widely from ostensible norms. For example, a later-born son could displace the firstborn as heir, and adopted sons could be named successor instead of natural sons. Susan B. Hanley and Kozo Yamamura, *Economic and Demographic Change in Preindustrial Japan, 1600–1868* (Princeton, N.J.: Princeton University Press, 1977), pp. 250–252. In the early modern period this was more easily accomplished by peasant and merchant households, for unlike those of warriors, their successors were not subject to the feudal lord's approval. To some this flexibility suggests that early modern Japanese prized household continuity over maintenance of a specific household form. Robert J. Smith, "The Domestic Cycle in Selected Commoner Families in Urban Japan: 1757–1858," *Journal of Family History* 3 (1978):223–224.

15. For exceptions, see Akira Hayami, "The Myth of Primogeniture and Impartible Inheritance in Tokugawa Japan," *Journal of Family History* 8 (1983):3–29. See also note 14.

16. Nakane, *Kinship and Economic Organization*, p. 7.

17. For example, see Lebra, *Japanese Women*, pp. 40–41. Higher education for children also validated household status in general and fostered alliances with like households. In the prewar period parents were willing to invest in the education of a noninheriting son to ease his departure for employment elsewhere; the education of a daughter facilitated her marriage into a household or the entry of an adopted son from a prominent family as her husband. Kathleen Uno, "Family Strategy in Late Tokugawa and Early Meiji Japan" (unpublished paper, 1979), pp. 52–72; Lebra, *Japanese Women*, pp. 52–54.

18. Regarding merchants, see Takashi Nakano, *Shooka doozokudan no kenkyuu* (Tokyo: Miraisha, 1964); Yoshio Nakano, *Osaka choonin soozoku no kenkyuu* (Kyoto: Sagano shoin,1976). As for farmers in the prewar era, "one representative national sample of farm households, for example, revealed that over three generations prior to 1948 a son other than the eldest had in fact succeeded in about 25 percent of all the relevant cases." John C. Pelzel, "Japanese Kinship: A Comparison," in *Family and Kinship in Chinese Society*, ed. Maurice Freedman (Stanford, Calif.: Stanford University Press, 1970), p. 231; cf. notes 14 and 15.

19. In 1914 the new middle class (wage and salaried professional workers) constituted 29 percent of Tokyo's 2.5 million residents, but accounted for only 4.3, 4.8 and 4.5 percent of the population as a whole in 1909, 1920, and 1930, respectively. Tooru Arichi, *Nihon no oyako nihyakunen* (Tokyo: Shinchoosha, 1986), pp. 83–84; Tadashi Fukutake, *The Japanese Social Structure: Its Evolution in the Modern Century* (Tokyo: University of Tokyo Press, 1982), p. 58.

20. See J. E. Becker, trans., *The Principles and Practice of the Civil Code of Japan* (London: Butterworth, 1921), pp. 525–788; R. P. Dore, *City Life in Japan* (Berkeley: University of California Press, 1958), pp. 97–98, 100–103.

21. See Kiyomi Morioka, "The Appearance of 'Ancestor Religion' in Modern Japan: The Years of Transition from the Meiji to the Taisho Periods," *Japanese Journal of Religion* 4:2–3 (June–September 1977):183–212. Daikichi Irokawa, *The Culture of the Meiji Period* (Princeton, N.J.: Princeton University Press, 1985), pp. 245–309; Carol Gluck, *Japan's Modern Myths* (Princeton, N.J.: Princeton University Press, 1985), pp. 187–188.

22. See note 19 above.

23. Kurt Steiner, "Postwar Changes in the Japanese Civil Code," *Washington Law Review* 25:3 (August 1950):286–312.

24. These changes are treated in greater detail in the next section.

25. Regarding the nature and quality of the early modern sources, see L. L. Cornell and Akira Hayami, "The *Shuumon Aratame Choo*: Japan's Population Registers," *Journal of Family History* 11 (1986):314–329; Thomas C. Smith, *Nakahara: Family Farming and Population in a Japanese Village, 1717–1830* (Stanford, Calif.: Stanford University Press, 1977), pp. 15–32; Long, *Family Change*, pp. 19–21.

26. Infanticide and abortion are treated in the next section. For a discussion of fertility in English, see Hanley, "Family and Fertility," and Akira Hayami, "Rural Migration and Fertility in Tokugawa Japan: The Village of Nishijo, 1773–1868," in Hanley and Wolf, eds., *Family and Population*, pp. 122–132; Yooichiroo Sasaki, "Urban Migration and Fertility in Tokugawa Japan: The City of Takayama, 1773–1871," in Hanley and

Wolf, eds., *Family and Population*, pp. 139, 143, among others. Fertility and mortality are treated in T. C. Smith, *Nakahara*, pp. 46–85; Hanley and Yamamura, *Economic and Demographic Change*, pp. 199–334; Dana Morris and Thomas C. Smith, "Fertility and Mortality in an Outcaste Village in Japan, 1750–1869," in Hanley and Wolf, eds., *Family and Population*, pp. 229–246. Issues of migration, marriage, and succession to headship are important for understanding the life course of older children. Regarding these see Hayami, "Rural Migration" and "Myth of Primogeniture"; T. C. Smith, *Nakahara*, pp. 107–156; Hanley and Yamamura, *Economic and Demographic Change*, pp. 254–255, 300; Mark Fruin, "Farm Family Migration: The Case of Echizen in the Nineteenth Century," *Keio Economic Studies* 10:2 (1973):37–46; Susan B. Hanley, "Migration and Economic Change in Okayama During the Tokugawa Period," *Keio Economic Studies* 10:2 (1973):19–35; L. L. Cornell, "Retirement, Inheritance, and Intergenerational Conflict in Preindustrial Japan," *Journal of Family History* 8 (1983):55–69; Kanji Masaoka, "Role Transitions and Their Timing in the Peasant Life Course During the Late Tokugawa Period, 1825–1869," *Journal of Family History* 11 (1986):429–432, analyze succession patterns.

27. For rural communities, see Hayami and Uchida, "Size of Household," pp. 473–515, esp. 490, 505; Chie Nakane, "An Interpretation of the Size and Structure of the Household in Japan Over Three Centuries," in Laslett, ed., *Household and Family*, pp. 519–520; Hanley, "Family and Fertility," pp. 202–210, esp. 203–204; T. C. Smith, *Nakahara*, pp. 35–37. Hayami and Uchida also discuss falling household size in 100 communities, 1701–1850. For cities see Nakane, "Interpretation," p. 520; Robert J. Smith, "Small Families, Small Households, and Residential Instability: Town and City in 'Pre-Modern' Japan," in Laslett, ed., *Household and Family*, pp. 445–455; Kozo Yamamura, "Samurai Income and Demographic Change: The Genealogies of Tokugawa Bannermen," in Hanley and Wolf, eds., *Family and Population*, pp. 67–71, 341, notes 9–10.

28. For percentages of rural households containing servants and household size minus resident kin and servants see Hayami and Uchida, "Size of Household," pp. 503–505.

29. Ibid., pp. 499–500. Hayami and Uchida list the number of unmarried children residing at home in four rural districts from 1671 to 1870. After 1701 the number ranged between 1.29 and 1.91, whereas before 1700 in one district it ran as high as 2.80.

30. Uno, "Day Care," pp. 18–60; Wagatsuma, "Contemporary Japanese Family," p. 198; Lebra, *Japanese Women*, pp. 178–179.

31. For additional information and references on socialization see the section on children's institutions. Kathleen Uno considers the role of men and boys in child rearing in greater detail in "Day Care" and "Women and Changes in the Household Division of Labor," in *Recreating Japanese Women, 1600–1945*, ed. Gail Lee Bernstein (Berkeley: University of California Press, 1991), pp. 22–51.

32. In one ward of Osaka, 1757–1858, average household size of property owners was 4.39 persons, whereas for tenants it was 3.45. As for structure, 39.2 to 41.7 percent of propertied households and 53.2 to 60.1 percent of tenant households were elementary in form, and 30.9 to 35.2 percent of owners and 20.7 to 22.6 percent of tenants lived in stem families. R. J. Smith, "Transformations," pp. 255, 263; R. J. Smith, "Small Families," p. 238. Regarding urban warriors, see K. Yamamura, "Samurai Income," pp. 68, 70. Regarding class differences in rural household size see T. C. Smith, *Nakahara*, pp. 74–76; Hanley and Yamamura, *Economic and Demographic Change*, p. 286; Hanley, "Family and Fertility," pp. 273–278.

33. Rural mothers in some regions placed babies in cradles (*ejigo*) at the edge of fields while they worked. Wagatsuma and Hara, *Shitsuke*, pp. 41–56. T. C. Smith argues that Nakahara villagers deliberately spaced first and second births far apart so that older children could tend younger siblings. T. C. Smith, *Nakahara*, p. 79–81.

34. See Uno, "Day Care," pp. 30–37.

35. In Japanese this was called *shitsuke hookoo* (upbringing service). For the early modern period, regarding peasants, see Atsuko Nagashima, "Bakumatsu nooson josei no koodo no jiyuu to kaji roodoo," in *Ronshuu kinsei joseishi*, ed. Kinsei joseishi kenkyuukai (Tokyo: Yoshikawa koobunkan, 1986), pp. 151–154, 155–157; regarding merchants see Robert Leutner, *Shikitei Sanba and the Comic Tradition in Edo Fiction* (Cambridge, Mass.: Harvard University Press, 1985), pp. 183–185; Edward McClellan, *Woman in the Crested Kimono* (New Haven, Conn.: Yale University Press, 1983), pp. 24–31. For the prewar period see Lebra, *Japanese Women*, pp. 42–50, 60–65.

36. See note 14 above. In 1909 employees constituted 14.2 percent of Japan's population; the proportion rose to 27.5 percent in 1920 and 40.2 percent in 1930. Fukutake, *Japanese Social Structure*, p. 58.

37. Accurate statistics are lacking for the first fifty years of the prewar era. See Irene Taeuber, *The Population of Japan* (Princeton, N.J.: Princeton University Press, 1958); Hiroshi Ohbuchi, "Demographic Transition in the Process of Industrialization," in *Japanese Industrialization and Its Social Consequences*, ed. Hugh Patrick (Berkeley: University of California Press, 1976), pp. 330–333. Akira Hayami, "Another *Fossa Magna*: Proportion Marrying and Age at Marriage in Late Nineteenth-Century Japan," *Journal of Family History* 12 (1987):60–61, is less pessimistic. Rural mean household size (MHS) was 4.99 persons in 1920, whereas urban MHS was 4.47; overall (rural and urban areas combined) MHS was 4.89. By 1940 MHSs were respectively, 5.25, 4.62, and 5.00. Nakane, "Interpretations," pp. 531–532. It is likely that the increase in household size in 1940 resulted from government pronatalist policies during the Pacific War (1931–1945).

38. Thomas C. Smith, *The Agrarian Origins of Modern Japan* (Stanford: Stanford University Press, 1959), pp. 208–213.

39. The reasons for exclusion of married women from the wage labor force are important to an understanding of changes in who cared for children during industrialization; however, this important issue has not yet received the attention its deserves from either Western or Japanese scholars.

40. Children have begun school at age six since the founding of the national educational system in 1872.

41. In 1955 MHS was 5.31 persons in rural areas, 4.73 in urban areas, and 4.97 overall. In 1965 MHS was 4.48 in rural areas, 3.86 in urban areas, and 4.05 overall. Nakane, "Interpretations," p. 528. By 1930 MHS had shrunk still further to 3.33. Fukutake, *Japanese Social Structure*, p. 124. Between 1955 and 1980 the proportion of nuclear households rose from 59.6 to 63.3 percent, whereas other forms of kin-linked households fell from 36.5 to 20.7 percent. In contrast, the percentage of one-person households rose from 3.4 to 15.8. Fukutake, *Japanese Social Structure*, p. 124.

42. In 1983 the "total fertility rate" (presumably the number of children ever born) of Japanese women was 1.80, in contrast to a rate of 4.3 in the 1940s. Kumagai, "Modernization and the Family," p. 376. Regarding contraception see Samuel Coleman, *Japanese Family Planning: Traditional Birth Control in a Modern Urban Culture* (Princeton: Princeton University Press, 1982).

43. Regarding postwar motherhood see note 59. The following give critical scrutiny to postwar parenting: Arichi, *Nihon no oyako nihyakunen*, pp. 242–249; Doi, *Anatomy of Dependence*, pp. 150–163; Kinko Sato, "Is Your Mother Nice to You?" *Japan Echo* 9 (Special Issue 1982):33–40; Wagatsuma, "Contemporary Japanese Family," pp. 181–210.

44. In 1950, 37.5 percent of the Japanese population lived in urban areas; by 1975 the proportion had risen to 75.9 percent. (Cf. 1930, when 76 percent of the Japanese population lived in 24.1 urban areas.) Tokue Shibata, "Urbanization in Japan," *Bulletin of Concerned Asian Scholars* 11:1 (January–March 1979):45.

45. Fukutake, *Japanese Social Structure*, p. 100.

46. The percentage of the population engaged in agriculture was 38.5 in 1955, 23.0 in 1960, and 19.3 in 1965. Nakane, "Interpretations," p. 528. The proportions of the working population engaged in self-employment and upaid family labor have fallen, respectively, from 23.9 and 30.3 percent in 1955 to 17.2 and 10.9 percent in 1980. Fukutake, *Japanese Social Structure*, p. 89.

47. See Arichi, *Nihon no oyako nihyakunen*, pp. 208–231, 240, 248–259; Mamoru Tsukada, "A Factual Overview of Japanese and American Education," in *Educational Policies in Crisis*, ed. William K. Cummings (New York: Praeger, 1986), pp. 104–110; Ikuo Amano, "Educational Crisis in Japan," in Cummings, ed., *Educational Policies*, pp. 23–43; Thomas Rohlen, *Japan's High Schools* (Berkeley: University of California Press, 1983), pp. 111–141, 271–305, 327–334; Tokumitsu Mitsumasa, "The Morose Children," *Japan Quarterly* 26 (Nos. 1–3 1979):75–84.

48. Yamazumi and Nakae, *Kosodate no sho*, 1:8.

49. Yoshiaki Yamamura, "The Child in Japanese Society," in *Child Development and Education in Japan*, ed. Harold Stevenson, Hiroshi Azuma, and Kenji Hakuta (New York: Freeman Press, 1986), pp. 30–31; Hideo Kojima, "Child Rearing Concepts as a Belief-Value System of the Society and the Individual," in Stevenson et al., eds., *Child Development*, pp. 42–45; Yamazumi and Nakae, *Kosodate no sho*, vols. 1 and 2.

50. Kathleen Uno, "Good Wives, Wise Mothers in Early Twentieth Century Japan"(unpublished paper, 1988), pp. 5–6; Yamazumi and Nakae, *Kosodate no sho*, 1:22–25, 44.

51. Y. Yamamura, "The Child," pp. 32, 33, 35–36; Wagatsuma and Hara, *Shitsuke*, pp. 11–19; Yoshiharu Iijima, "Folk Culture and the Limnality of Children," *Current Anthropology* 28 (1987):S41–S48.

52. McClellan, *Woman in Crested Kimono*, pp. 22–25, 41–48, 52–54; Leutner, *Shikitei Sanba*, pp. 150–153, 173–177, 180–185, esp. 191; Kojima, "Child Rearing Concepts,"pp. 43–46; Uno, "Day Care," pp. 15–42; Gail Lee Bernstein, *Japanese Marxist: A Portrait of Kawakami Hajime 1879–1946* (Cambridge, Mass.: Harvard University Press, 1976), p. 6; Hyman Kublin, *Asian Revolutionary: The Life of Sen Katayama* (Princeton, N.J.: Princeton University Press, 1964), pp. 11–17. Modern techniques are treated in Robert J. Smith and Ella Lury Wiswell, *The Women of Suye Mura* (Chicago: University of Chicago Press, 1984), esp. pp. 202–253, and Benedict, *Chrysanthemum and the Sword*, pp. 253–296. Regarding postwar mothering see note 6.

53. Leutner, *Shikitei Sanba*, pp. 150–153; Kokichi Katsu, *Musui's Story: The Autobiography of a Tokugawa Samurai*, trans. Teruko Craig (Tucson: University of Arizona Press, 1988), pp. 9–44, 61–69.

54. Uno, "Good Wives," pp. 2–7; Kojima, "Child Rearing Concepts," p. 46; Yamazumi and Nakae, *Kosodate no sho*, 1:87–93, 178–202; 2:3–89.

55. See Hanley and Yamamura, *Economic and Demographic Change*, pp. 233–244, 313–317; T. C. Smith, *Nakahara*, pp. 59–85. According to the former, inability to provide for another child and desire to reduce embarrassment because of late childbearing and extramarital pregnancies were reasons for infanticide. Political authorities opposed infanticide for the practical reason that a decline in the number of peasants would bring about a fall in revenue from the primary tax on rice. Bonsen Takahashi, *Datai mabiki no kenkyuu* (Tokyo: Chuuoo shakai jigyoo kyookai shakai jigyoo kenkyuuio, 1937), treats anti-infanticide policies in depth.

56. Narimitsu Matsudaira, "The Concept of *Tamashii* in Japan," in *Studies in Japanese Folklore*, ed. Richard M. Dorson (Bloomington: Indiana University Press, 1963), p. 186; Wagatsuma and Hara, *Shitsuke*, pp. 11–15; and Anne Page Brooks, "*Mizuko kuyoo* and Japanese Buddhism," *Japanese Journal of Religious Studies* 8:3–4 (September–December 1981):119–147, discuss the infant's spirit.

57. Hanley and Yamamura, *Economic and Demographic Change*, pp. 233–235; Takahashi, *Datai mabiki no kenkyuu*, pp. 9–46.

58. Yasuko Ichibangase, Jun Izumi, Nobuko Ogawa, and Takeo Shishido, *Nihon no hoiku* (Tokyo: Domesu shuppan, 1962), p. 15.

59. Kaoru Yokosuka, ed., *Jidoo kan no tenkai, Kindai Nihon kyooiku ronshuu* (Tokyo: Kokudosha, 1969), pp. 37–57. See also Carmen Blacker, *The Japanese Enlightenment* (Cambridge: Cambridge University Press, 1964), pp. 67–79.

60. Hiroshi Urabe, Takeo Shishido, and Yuuichi Murayama, *Hoiku no rekishi* (Tokyo: Aoki shoboo, 1981), p. 42.

61. Smith and Wiswell, *Women of Suye Mura*, esp. pp. 202–253; Uno, "Day Care," chs. 3 to 5.

62. Hence the willingness of postwar parents to expose children to a variety of early childhood learning experiences ranging from kindergarten attendance to preschool enrichment lessons to sessions at home teaching letters and numbers.

63. Regarding postwar mothers' role see Lebra, *Japanese Women*, pp. 158–216; Lebra, *Patterns*, pp. 137–155; Harumi Befu, "The Social and Cultural Background of Child Development in Japan and the United States," in Stevenson et al., eds., *Child Development and Education*, pp. 14–18; Suzanne Vogel, "Professional Housewife: The Career of Urban Middle Class Japanese Women," *Japan Interpreter* 12 (Winter 1978):16–43; Anne Imamura, *Urban Japanese Housewives: At Home and in the Community* (Honolulu: University of Hawaii Press, 1987), pp. 19–23, 69–80; Merry White, "The Virtue of Japanese Mothers: Cultural Definitions of Women's Lives," *Daedalus* 116:3 (Summer 1987): 149–163. Cf. Mariko Fujita, "It's All Mother's Fault: Childcare and the Socialization of Working Mothers in Japan," *Journal of Japanese Studies* 15 (1989):67–92.

64. Despite the legal demise of the *ie*, wealthy enterprise households still seek a successor to occupation, status, and name.

65. Joy Hendry, *Becoming Japanese: The World of the Pre-School Child* (Honolulu: University of Hawaii Press, 1986), pp. 47–177; White, *Japanese Educational Challenge*, pp. 20–49, 95–109; David Plath, "Who Sleeps by Whom? Parent-Child Involvement in Urban Japanese Families," in *Japanese Culture and Behavior*, ed. Takie S. Lebra and William P. Lebra (Honolulu: University of Hawaii Press, 1974), pp. 277–312. Paradoxically, children gave low marks to their mothers' performances in one 1979 survey. Sato, "Is Your Mother Nice to You?" pp. 33–40.

66. In English see Herbert Passin, *Society and Education in Japan* (New York: Columbia University Press Teachers College Press, 1965; rpt. New York: Kodansha, 1982),

pp. 11–61, 163–204; Ronald P. Dore, *Education in Tokugawa Japan* (Berkeley: University of California Press, 1965); Richard Rubinger, *Private Academies of the Tokugawa Period* (Princeton, N.J.: Princeton University Press, 1982); Tetsuo Najita, *Visions of Virtue: The Kaitokudoo Merchant Academy of Osaka* (Chicago: University of Chicago Press, 1987). Autobiographies and biographies that shed light on early modern educational experiences include McClellan, *Woman in the Crested Kimono*; Katsu, *Musui's Story*; Etsu Sugimoto, *A Daughter of the Samurai* (New York: Doubleday Doran Co., 1935); Yukichi Fukuzawa, *The Autobiography of Fukuzawa Yukichi*, trans. Eiichii Kiyooka (New York: Columbia University Press, 1960); Haruko Matsukata Reischauer, *Samurai and Silk* (Cambridge, Mass.: Harvard University Press, 1985). In Japanese see Tomitaroo Karasawa, *Gakusei no rekishi* (Tokyo: Soobunsha, 1955); *Nihon kindai kyooiku hyakunen shi*, 10 vols. (Tokyo: Kokuritsu kyooiku kenkyuujo, 1974), among the multitude of significant works.

67. Regarding commoners' education and temple schools see Dore, *Education in Tokugawa Japan*, pp. 214–290; Passin, *Society and Education*, pp. 27–37; T. C. Smith, *Nakahara*, pp. 109, 115–116, treats agricultural writings.

68. Wagatsuma and Hara, *Shitsuke*, pp. 57–63; Iijima, pp. S44–S45; Yuki Ootoo, *Kodomo no minzokugaku: ichinin mae ni sodateru* (Tokyo: Soodo bunka, 1982), pp. 172–184; Hendry, *Becoming Japanese*, p. 60. In many areas children's groups also had ritual functions in local festivals. Youth and girls' groups (*wakamonogumi, musumegumi*) carried out socialization of young men and women from age fifteen into the twenties and sometimes thirties in some villages; see Richard Varner, "The Organized Peasant: The *Wakamonogumi* in the Edo Period," *Monumenta Nipponica* 32 (1977):459–483; Ueno, "The Position of Japanese Women," p. S78; Kiyoko Segawa, *Wakamono to musume o meguru minzoku* (Tokyo: Miraisha, 1972).

69. Passin has discussed the prewar system and translated relevant documents. *Society and Education*, pp. 62–160, 205–269. See also Edward Beauchamp, ed. *Learning to Be Japanese: Selected Readings on Japanese Society and Education* (Hamden, Conn.: Linnet Books, 1978), pp. 6–180; Richard Rubinger, "Education: From One Room to One System," in *Japan in Transition: From Tokugawa to Meiji*, ed. Marius B. Jansen and Gilbert Rozman (Princeton, N.J.: Princeton University Press, 1986), pp. 195–230. Four years of compulsory education were required before 1907, six years thereafter until 1947, and nine years since 1947. Passin, *Society and Education*, pp. 73, 108.

70. Tokiomi Kaigo, *Japanese Education: Its Past and Present* (Tokyo: Kokusai bunka shinkokai, 1965), pp. 65–66.

71. Ibid., pp. 76–115; Tadahiko Inagaki, "School of Education: Its History and Contemporary Status," in Stevenson et al., *Child Development and Education*, pp. 72–95. Regarding higher school culture and student life see Early Kinmonth, *The Self-Made Man in Meiji Japanese Thought* (Berkeley: University of California Press, 1981); Irwin Scheiner. *Christian Converts and Social Protest in Meiji Japan* (Berkeley: University of California Press, 1971), pp. 15–99; Roka Tokutomi, *Footprints in the Snow* (Rutland, Vt.: Tuttle, 1970), a novel; Yoshitake Oka, "Generational Conflict After the Russo-Japanese War," in *Conflict in Modern Japanese History: The Neglected Tradition*, ed. Tetsuo Najita and J. Victor Koschmann (Princeton, N.J.: Princeton University Press, 1982), pp. 197–225; Donald Roden, *Schooldays in Imperial Japan: A Study in the Culture of a New Elite* (Berkeley: University of California Press, 1980); Henry D. Smith III, *Japan's First Student Radicals* (Cambridge, Mass.: Harvard University Press, 1972).

72. Katsufumi Tanaka, "Ie de hataraku kodomo," in *Fukoku kyooheika no kodomo*,

ed. Arata Naka, vol. 5 of *Nihon kodomo no rekishi* (Tokyo: Daiichi hooki, 1978), p. 245; Kooji Kashima, *Taishoo no Shitayakko* (Tokyo: Seiaboo, 1977), pp. 82–83.

73. Inagaki, "School of Education," pp. 75–92; Rohlen, *Japan's High Schools*, pp. 45–76; Beauchamp, *Learning to Be Japanese*, pp. 180–297; U.S. Department of Education, *Japanese Education Today* (Washington, D.C.: Government Printing Office, 1987), pp. 5–14, 21–56; (Japan) Ministry of Education, Science, and Culture, *Education in Japan: A Brief Outline* (Tokyo: The Ministry, 1986). More specialized books treating aspects of postwar education include White, *Japanese Educational Challenge*; Cummings, *Educational Policies*; Benjamin Duke, *The Japanese School: Lessons for Industrial America* (New York: Praeger, 1986); William K. Cummings, *Education and Equality in Japan* (Princeton, N.J.: Princeton University Press, 1980); Donald Thurston, *Teachers and Politics in Japan* (Princeton, N.J.: Princeton University Press, 1973). Regarding preschool institutions see Early Childhood Education Association of Japan, ed., *Early Childhood Education and Care in Japan* (Tokyo: Child Honsha, 1979); Joseph Tobin, David Y. H. Wu, and Dana H. Davidson, *Preschool in Three Cultures: Japan, China and the United States* (New Haven, Conn.: Yale University Press,1989); and articles in *Journal of Japanese Studies* 15:1 (Winter 1989): Sarane Spence Boocock, "Controlled Diversity: An Overview of the Japanese Preschool System," pp. 41–66; Catherine C. Lewis, "From Indulgence to Internalization: Social Control in the Early Years," pp. 139–157; Lois Peak, "Learning to Become Part of the Group: The Japanese Child's Transition to Preschool Life," pp. 93–124; and Toshiyuki Sano, "Methods of Social Control and Socialization in Japanese Day-Care Centers," pp. 125–138. See also Catherine C. Lewis, "Cooperation and Control in Japanese Nursery Schools," *Comparative Education Review* 28 (1984):69–84.

74. Inagaki, "School of Education," pp. 82–83, 86; U.S. Department of Education, *Japanese Education Today*, pp. 11–14; White, *Japanese Educational Challenge*, pp. 76–78, 145–151. Regarding youth culture see Rohlen, *Japan's High Schools*, esp. pp. 271–305; Cummings, *Educational Policies*, pp. 34–63, 215–218, 226–234; and White, *Japanese Educational Challenge*, pp. 134–162, esp. pp. 151–162.

75. White on enrichment lessons, *Japanese Educational Challenge*, p. 76. For the early modern period see Leutner, *Shikitei Sanba*, p. 183; Dore, *Education in Tokugawa Japan*, pp. 269–270. For the prewar period, see Lebra, *Japanese Women*, pp. 58–60.

76. Taizoo Miyoshi, "Philanthropy in Japan," in *Fifty Years of New Japan*, ed. Shigenobu Okuma (New York: E. P. Dutton, 1909), 1:104–105; Takahashi, *Datai mabiki no kenkyuu*, pp. 121–170, 197–282; Yamazumi and Nakae, *Kosodate no sho*, 1:34–42.

77. Kyuuichi Yoshida, *Nihon shakai jigyoo no rekishi* (Tokyo: Keisoo shoboo, 1981), esp. pp. 99–170; Kyuuichi Yoshida, *Gendai shakai jigyoo shi kenkyuu* (Tokyo: Keisoo shoboo, 1979), pp. 64–121, 246–252, 302–333, 341–345 (or 1–401); Shaikai fukushi choosa kenkyuukai, ed., *Senzen Nihon no shakai jigyoo choosa* (Tokyo: Keisoo shoboo, 1983).

78. The Foundling Law provided that three and a half bushels of rice should be given to an abandoned child until age fifteen (after 1873 until age thirteen). The poor law provided that orphaned children as well as children with no relatives under age seventy or over age fifteen would receive three and a half bushels of rice per year. The Reformatory Law provided that each prefecture should establish reform schools for children under eighteen years old. Namae, "Child Welfare Work in Japan," pp. 321–324. The Factory Law of 1911 contained easily evaded provisions concerning child labor. Ronald P. Dore,

"The Modernizer as a Special Case: Japanese Factory Legislation, 1882–1911," *Comparative Studies in Society and History* 11 (1969):438.

79. Tetsu Tsukamoto, Hiroshi Urabe, Tatsuzoo Ootsuka, and Seiichi Kookoo, eds., *Shakai fukushi jigyoo jiten* (Kyoto: Minerva shoboo, 1966), pp. 26–29, 260. Some discussion of the prewar eugenics law appears in Sandra Buckley, "Body Politics: Abortion Law Reform," in *Modernization and Beyond: The Japanese Trajectory*, ed. Gavan McCormack and Yoshio Sugimoto (New York: Cambridge University Press, 1988), pp. 205–217.

80. The postwar changes in child welfare laws are discussed in Yoshida, *Gendai*, pp. 412–421, 432–472, 510–526, 547–557; Hiroshi Urabe, *Nihon no jidoo mondai* (Tokyo: Shinju shuppan, 1977), pp. 102–122, 183–196, 206–225. For a qualitative description of women's encounters with the clinics and advice centers see Lebra, *Japanese Women*, pp. 211–213; Buckley presents a more critical view of the functions of the clinics, pp. 214–216. See also Early Childhood Education Association of Japan, ed., *Early Childhood Education and Care In Japan* (Tokyo: Child Honsha, 1979).

81. Japan Family Life Study Association, *Family Life in Japan 1967* (Tokyo: Nihon katei seikatsu mondai kenkyuu kyookai, 1968); UNICEF, *The State of the World's Children* (New York: Oxford University Press, 1988), p. 40. In 1980 life expectancy had climbed to 73.3 years for men and 78.8 for women. Fukutake, *Japanese Social Structure*, p. 204.

82. Rohlen, *Japan's High Schools*, pp. 82–84. In 1984, 29.6 percent of high school graduates entered university, college, or junior college programs, while 25 percent chose vocational training programs; 39.8 percent entered the labor force. U.S. Department of Education, *Japanese Education Today*, p. 78. A graph showing U.S. and secondary and higher education school enrollment rates, 1950–1982 appears in Tsukada, "Factual Overview," p. 98.

83. U.S. Department of Education, *Japanese Education Today*, p. 78; Morikazu Ushiogi, "Transition from School to Work: The Japanese Case," in Cummings, ed., *Educational Policies*, pp. 197–209. Because of low starting salaries, young employees often continue to live at home until marriage.

84. Not only Western scholars, but Japanese researchers as well feel a need for additional research. Although a number of works by folklorists and historians of education (i.e., see Shootaroo Sakurai, *Nihon jidoo seikatsu shi* [Tokyo: Nikko shoin 1941]; Kunio Yanagita, *Bunrui jidoo goi [Tokyo: Tokyodoo shuppansha, 1949]*; Yuki Ootoo, *Ko Yarai* [Tokyo: Mikuni shoboo, 1944]; and Ken Ishikawa, *Waga kuni ni okeru jidoo kan no hattatsu* [Tokyo: Shinreisha, 1949]) Yokosuka, ed., *Jidoo Kan no tenkai*, pp. 1–33, especially p. 19, had previously been published, in 1971 Kuni Nakajima lamented that comprehensive Japanese studies of the history of childhood were missing. Kuni Nakajima, "Kodomo no seikatsu shi: kenkyuu no genjoo," in *Jidoo fukushi: Nihon no genjoo to mohdaiten*, ed. Nihon joshi daigaku bungakubu shakai fukushi gakka kenkyuushitsu (Tokyo: Kasei kyooikusha, 1971), pp. 311–312, 319–324. Fifteen years later Arichi voiced a similar complaint. Arichi, *Nihon no oyako nihyakunen*, p. 80.

85. Yamazumi, Arichi, and Nakae, *Kosodate no sho*, 1:3–50; Kooji Yokosuka, *Kosodate no shakaishi* (Tokyo: Keisoo Shoboo, 1986); Koonosuke Fujimoto, *Kikikaki Meijo no kodomo: asobi to kurashi* (Tokyo: Honpoo shoseki, 1986).

REFERENCES

Amano, Ikuo. "Educational Crisis in Japan." In *Educational Policies in Crisis*, edited by William K. Cummings. New York: Praeger, 1986, pp. 23–43.

Arichi, Tooru. *Nihon no oyako nihyakunen*. Tokyo: Shinchoosha, 1986.

Bachnik, Jane. "Recruitment Strategies for Household Succession: Rethinking Japanese Household Organization." *Man* 18 (1983):160–182.

Beauchamp, Edward, ed. *Learning to Be Japanese: Selected Readings on Japanese Society and Education*. Hamden, Conn.: Linnet Books, 1978.

Befu, Harumi. *Japan: An Anthropological Introduction*. San Francisco: Chandler Publishing Co., 1971.

Benedict, Ruth. *Chrysanthemum and the Sword*. Boston: Houghton Mifflin, 1946.

Bernstein, Gail Lee. *Japanese Marxist: A Portrait of Kawakami Hajime 1879–1946*. Cambridge, Mass.: Harvard University Press, 1976.

Blacker, Carmen. *The Japanese Enlightenment*. Cambridge: Cambridge University Press, 1964.

Boocock, Sarane Spence. "Controlled Diversity: An Overview of the Japanese Preschool System," *Journal of Japanese Studies* 15 (1989):41–66.

Brooks, Ann Page. "*Mizuko kuyoo* and Japanese Buddhism." *Japanese Journal of Religious Studies* 8:3–4 (September–December 1981):119–147.

Buckley, Sandra. "Body Politics: Abortion Law Reform." in *Modernization and Beyond: The Japanese Trajectory*, edited by Gavan McCormack and Yoshio Sugimoto. New York: Cambridge University Press, 1988, pp. 205–217.

Coleman, Samuel. *Japanese Family Planning: Traditional Birth Control in a Modern Urban Culture*. Princeton, N.J: Princeton University Press, 1982.

Cornell, L. L. "Retirement, Inheritance, and Intergenerational Conflict in Preindustrial Japan." *Journal of Family History* 8 (1983):55–69.

Cornell, L. L., and Akira Hayami. "The *Shuumon Aratame Choo*: Japan's Population Registers." *Journal of Family History* 11 (1986):314–329.

Cummings, William K. *Education and Equality in Japan*. Princeton, N.J.: Princeton University Press, 1980.

Cummings, William K., ed. *Educational Policies in Crisis*. New York: Praeger, 1986.

de Becker, J. E. *The Principles and Practice of the Civil Code of Japan*. London: Butterworth, 1921.

De Vos, George. *Socialization for Achievement*. Berkeley: University of California Press, 1973.

Doi, Takeo. *The Anatomy of Dependence*. New York: Kodansha International, 1973.

Dore, Ronald P. *City of Life in Japan*. Berkeley: University of California Press, 1958.

———. *Education in Tokugawa Japan*. Berkeley: University of California Press, 1965.

———. "The Modernizer as a Special Case: Japanese Factory Legislation, 1882–1911." *Comparative Studies in Society and History* 11 (1969):433–450.

Duke, Benjamin. *The Japanese School: Lessons for Industrial America*. New York: Praeger, 1986.

Early Childhood Education Association of Japan, ed. *Early Childhood Education and Care in Japan*. Tokyo: Child Honsha, 1979.

Fruin, Mark. "Farm Family Migration: The Case of Echizen in the Nineteenth Century." *Keio Economic Studies* 10:2 (1973):37–46.

Fujimoto, Koonosuke. *Kikikaki Meiji no Kodomo: asobi to kurashi*. Tokyo: Honpoo shoseki, 1986.

Fukutake, Tadashi. *The Japanese Social Structure: Its Evolution in the Modern Century*. Tokyo: University of Tokyo Press, 1982.

Fukuzawa, Yukichi. *The Autobiography of Fukuzawa Yukichi*, trans. by Eiichi Kiyooka. New York: Columbia University Press, 1960.

Gluck, Carol. *Japan's Modern Myths*. Princeton, N.J.: Princeton University Press, 1985.

Hamabata, Matthews. *For Love and Power: Family Business in Tokyo*. Ithaca, N.Y.: Cornell University Press, 1990.

Hanley, Susan B. "Migration and Economic Change in Okayama During the Tokugawa Period." *Keio Economic Studies* 10:2 (1973):19–35.

———. "Family and Fertility in Four Tokugawa Villages." In *Family and Population in East Asian History*, edited by Susan B. Hanley and Arthur P. Wolf. Stanford, Calif.: Stanford University Press, 1985, pp. 196–228.

Hanley, Susan B., and Kozo Yamamura. *Economic and Demographic Change in Preindustrial Japan, 1600–1868*. Princeton, N.J.: Princeton University Press,1977.

Hara, Hiroko, and Mieko Minagawa. "Japanische Kindheit Seit 1600." In *Zur Sozialgeschite der Kinderheit*, edited by Jochen Marten and August Nitschke. Munich: Verlag Karl Alber Freiburg, 1986, pp. 113–189.

Hayami, Akira. "The Myth of Primogeniture and Impartible Inheritance in Tokugawa Japan." *Journal of Family History* 8 (1983):3–29.

———. "Rural Migration and Fertility in Tokugawa Japan: The Village of Nishijo, 1773–1868." In *Family and Population in East Asia*, edited by Susan B. Hanley and Arthur P. Wolf. Stanford, Calif.: Stanford University Press, 1985, pp. 122–132.

———. "Another *Fossa Magna*: Proportion Marrying and Age at Marriage in Late Nineteenth-Century Japan." *Journal of Family History* 12 (1987):57–72.

Hayami, Akira, and Nobuko Uchida. "Size of Household in a Japanese County Throughout the Tokugawa Era." In *Household and Family in Past Time: Comparative History in the Size of the Domestic Group Over the Last Three Centuries*, edited by Peter Laslett. Cambridge: Cambridge University Press, 1972, pp. 473–516.

Hendry, Joy. *Becoming Japanese: The World of the Pre-School Child*. Honolulu: University of Hawaii Press, 1986.

Ichibangase, Yasuko, Jun Izumi, Nobuko Ogawa, and Takeo Shishido. *Nihon no hoiku*. Tokyo: Domesu shuppan, 1962.

Iijima, Yoshiharu. "Folk Culture and the Limnality of Children." *Current Anthropology* 28 (1987):S41–S48.

Inagaki, Tadahiko. "School Education: Its History and Contemporary Status." In *Child Development and Education in Japan*, edited by Harold Stevenson, Hiroshi Azuma, and Kenji Hakuta. New York: Freeman Press, 1986, pp. 72–95.

Irokawa, Daikichi. *The Culture of the Meiji Period*. Princeton, N.J.: Princeton University Press, 1985.

Ishii, Ryoosuke. *Nihoon soozoku hoo shi*. Tokyo: Soobunsha, 1980.

Ishikawa, Ken. *Waga kuni ni okeru jidoo kan no hattatsu*. Tokyo: Shinreisha, 1949.

(Japan) Ministry of Education, Science, and Culture. *Education in Japan: A Brief Outline*. Tokyo: The Ministry, 1986.

Japan Family Life Study Association. *Family Life in Japan 1967*. Tokyo: Nihon katei seikatsu mondai kenkyuu kyookai, 1968.

Kaigo, Tokiomi. *Japanese Education: Its Past and Present*. Tokyo: Kokusai bunka shinkokai, 1965.

Karasawa, Tomitaroo. *Gakusei no rekishi*. Tokyo: Soobunsha, 1955.

Katsu, Kokichi. *Musui's Story: The Autobiography of a Tokugawa Samurai*. trans. by Teruko Craig. Tucson: University of Arizona Press, 1988.

Kinmonth, Earl. *The Self-Made Man in Meiji Japanese Thought*. Berkeley: University of California Press, 1981.

Kondo, Dorinne. *Crafting Selves: Work, Identity, and the Politics of Meaning in a Japanese Factory*. Chicago: University of Chicago Press, 1990.

Kojima, Hideo. "Child Rearing Concepts as a Belief-Value System of the Society and the Individual." In *Child Development and Education in Japan*, edited by Harold Stevenson, Hiroshi Azuma, and Kenji Hakuta. New York: Freeman Press, 1986, pp. 39–54.

Kublin, Hyman. *Asian Revolutionary: The Life of Sen Katayama*. Princeton, N.J.: Princeton University Press, 1964.

Kumagai, Fumie. "Modernization and the Family in Japan." *Journal of Family History* 11 (1986):371–382.

Lebra, Takie S. *Patterns of Japanese Behavior*. Honolulu: University of Hawaii Press, 1976.

———. *Japanese Women: Constraint and Fulfillment*. Honolulu: University of Hawaii Press, 1984.

Lebra, Takie S., and William P. Lebra, eds. *Japanese Culture and Behavior*. Honolulu: University of Hawaii Press, 1974.

Leutner, Robert. *Shikitei Sanba and the Comic Tradition in Edo Fiction*. Cambridge, Mass.: Harvard University Press, 1985.

Lewis, Catherine C. "Cooperation and Control in Japanese Nursery Schools," *Comparative Education Review* 28 (1984):69–84.

———. "From Indulgence to Internalization: Social Control in the Early Years," *Journal of Japanese Studies* 15 (1989):139–157.

Long, Susan Orpett. *Family Change and the Life Course*, Cornell East Asia Papers No. 44. Ithaca, N.Y.: Cornell University Japan-China Program, 1987.

McClellan, Edward. *Woman in the Crested Kimono*. New Haven, Conn.: Yale University Press, 1983.

Masaoka, Kanji. "Role Transitions and Their Timing in the Peasant Life Course During the Late Tokugawa Period, 1825–1869." *Journal of Family History* 11 (1986):429–432.

Matsudaira, Narimitsu. "The Concept of *Tamashii* in Japan." In *Studies in Japanese Folklore*, edited by Richard M. Dorson. Bloomington: Indiana University Press, 1963, pp. 181–197.

Mitsumasa, Tokumitsu. "The Morose Children." *Japan Quarterly* 26 (Nos. 1–3, 1979):75–84.

Miyoshi, Taizoo. "Philanthropy in Japan." In *Fifty Years of New Japan*, edited by Shigenobu Okuma. Vol. 1. New York: E. P. Dutton, 1909.

Morioka, Kiyomi. "The Appearance of 'Ancestor Religion' in Modern Japan: The Years of Transition from the Meiji to the Taisho Periods." *Japanese Journal of Religion* 4:2–3 (June–September 1977):183–212.

Morris, Dana, and Thomas C. Smith. "Fertility and Mortality in an Outcaste Village in Japan, 1750–1869." In *Family and Population in East Asia*, edited by Susan B. Hanley and Arthur P. Wolf. Stanford, Calif.: Stanford University Press, 1985, pp. 229–246.

Nagashima, Atsuko. "Bakumatsu nooson josei no koodo no jiyuu to kaji roodoo." In *Ronshuu kinsei joseishi*, edited by Kinsei joseishi kenkyuukai. Tokyo: Yoshikawa koobunkan, 1986, pp. 139–173.

Najita, Tetsuo. *Visions of Virtue: The Kaitokudoo Merchant Academy of Osaka*. Chicago: University of Chicago Press, 1987.

Naka, Arata, ed. *Fukoku kyooheika no kodomo*. Vol. 5 of *Nihon kodomo no rekishi*. Tokyo: Daiichi hooki, 1978.

Nakajima, Kuni. "Kodomo no seikatsu shi: kenkyuu no genjoo." In *Jidoo fukushi: Nihon no genjoo to mondaiten*, edited by Nihon joshi daigaku bungakubu shakai fukushi gakka kenkyuushitsu. Tokyo: Kasei kyooikusha, 1971, pp. 311–324.

Nakane, Chie. *Kinship and Economic Organization in Rural Japan*. London: Athlone Press, 1967.

———. "An Interpretation of the Size and Structure of the Household in Japan Over Three Centuries." In *Household and Family in Past Time: Comparative History in the Size of the Domestic Group Over the Last Three Centuries*, edited by Peter Laslett. Cambridge: Cambridge University Press, 1972, pp. 517–543.

Nakano, Takashi. *Shooka doozokudan no kenkyuu*. Tokyo: Miraisha, 1964.

Nakano, Yoshio. *Osaka choonin soozoku no kenkyuu*. Kyoto: Sagano shoin, 1976.

Namae, Takayuki. "Child Welfare Work in Japan." In *Standards of Child Welfare*, edited by William L. Chenery and Ella A. Merritt. Washington, D.C.: Children's Bureau, U.S. Department of Labor, 1919; rpt., New York: Arno Press, 1974, pp. 326–344.

Nihon kindai kyooiku hyakunen shi. 10 vols. Tokyo: Kokuritsu kyooiku kenkyuujo, 1974.

Ohbuchi, Hiroshi. "Demographic Transition in the Process of Industrialization." In *Japanese Industrialization and Its Social Consequences*, edited by Hugh Patrick. Berkeley: University of California Press, 1976, pp. 329–361.

Oka, Yoshitake. "Generational Conflict After the Russo-Japanese War." In *Conflict in Modern Japanese History: The Neglected Tradition*, edited by Tetsuo Najita and J. Victor Koschmann. Princeton, N.J.: Princeton University Press, 1982, pp. 197–225.

Ootoo, Yuki. *Ko yarai*. Tokyo: Mikuni shoboo, 1944.

———. *Kodomo no minzokugaku: ichininmae ni sodateru*. Tokyo: Soodo bunka, 1982.

Passin, Herbert. *Society and Education in Japan*. New York: Columbia University Teachers College Press,1965; rpt. New York: Kodansha, 1982.

Peak, Lois. "Learning to Become Part of the Group: The Japanese Child's Transition to Preschool Life," *Journal of Japanese Studies* 15 (1989):93–124.

Pelzel, John C. "Japanese Kinship: A Comparison." In *Family and Kinship in Chinese Society*, edited by Maurice Freedman. Stanford, Calif.: Stanford University Press, 1970, pp. 227–248.

Plath, David. "Who Sleeps by Whom? Parent-Child Involvement in Urban Japanese Families." In *Japanese Culture and Behavior*, edited by Takie S. Lebra and William P. Lebra. Honolulu: University of Hawaii Press, 1974, pp. 277–312.

Reischauer, Haruko Matsukata. *Samurai and Silk*. Cambridge, Mass.: Harvard University Press, 1985.

Roden, Donald. *Schooldays in Imperial Japan: A Study in the Culture of a New Elite*. Berkeley: University of California Press, 1980.

Rohlen, Thomas. *Japan's High Schools*. Berkeley: University of California Press, 1983.

Rubinger, Richard. *Private Academies of the Tokugawa Period*. Princeton, N.J.: Princeton University Press, 1982.

———. "Education: From One Room to One System." In *Japan in Transition: From*

Tokugawa to Meiji, edited by Marius B. Jansen and Gilbert Rozman. Princeton, N.J.: Princeton University Press, 1986, pp. 195–230.

Sakurai, Shotaroo. *Nihon jidoo seikatsu shi*. Tokyo: Nikkoo Shoin, 1941.

Sasaki, Yooichiroo. "Urban Migration and Fertility in Tokugawa Japan: The City of Takayama, 1773–1871." In *Family and Population in East Asia*, edited by Susan B. Hanley and Arthur P. Wolf. Stanford, Calif.: Stanford University Press, 1985, pp. 133–153.

Sano, Toshiyuki. "Methods of Social Control and Socialization in Japanese Day-Care Centers," *Journal of Japanese Studies* 15 (1989):125–138.

Sato, Kinko. "Is Your Mother Nice to You?" *Japan Echo* 9 (Special Issue 1982):33–40.

Scheiner, Irwin. *Christian Converts and Social Protest in Meiji Japan*. Berkeley: University of California Press, 1971.

Segawa, Kiyoko. *Wakamono to musume o meguru minzoku*. Tokyo: Miraisha, 1972.

Shaikai fukushi choosa kenkyuukai, ed. *Senzen Nihon no shakai jigyoo choosa*. Tokyo: Keisoo shoboo, 1983.

Shibata, Tokue. "Urbanization in Japan." *Bulletin of Concerned Asian Scholars* 11:1 (January–March 1979):44–57.

Smith, Henry D., III. *Japan's First Student Radicals*. Cambridge, Mass.: Harvard University Press, 1972.

Smith, Robert J. "Small Families, Small Households, and Residential Instability: Town and City in 'Pre-Modern' Japan." In *Household and Family in Past Time: Comparative History in the Size of the Domestic Group Over the Last Three Centuries*, edited by Peter Laslett. Cambridge: Cambridge University Press, 1972, pp. 445–471.

Smith, Robert J. "The Domestic Cycle in Selected Commoner Families in Urban Japan: 1757–1858." *Journal of Family History* 3 (1978):219–235.

Smith, Robert J. "Transformations of Commoner Households in Tennooji-mura, 1757–1858." In *Family and Population in East Asian History*, edited by Susan B. Hanley and Arthur P. Wolf. Stanford, Calif.: Stanford University Press, 1985, pp. 247–276.

Smith, Thomas C. *The Agrarian Origins of Modern Japan*. Stanford, Calif.: Stanford University Press, 1959.

Smith, Thomas C. *Nakahara: Family Farming and Population in a Japanese Village, 1717–1830*. Stanford, Calif.: Stanford University Press, 1977.

Steiner, Kurt. "Postwar Changes in the Japanese Civil Code." *Washington Law Review* 25:3 (August 1950):286–312.

Sugimoto, Etsu. *A Daughter of the Samurai*. New York: Doubleday Doran Co., 1935.

Taeuber, Irene B. *The Population of Japan*. Princeton, N.J.: Princeton University Press, 1958.

Takahashi, Bonsen. *Datai mabiki no kenkyuu*. Tokyo: Chuuoo shakai jigyoo kyookai shakai jigyoo kenkyuujo, 1937.

Takai, Toshio. *Watashi no jokoo aishi*. Tokyo: Soodo bunka, 1980.

Thurston, Donald. *Teachers and Politics in Japan*. Princeton, N.J.: Princeton University Press, 1973.

Tobin, Joseph, David Y. H. Wu, and Dana H. Davidson. *Preschool in Three Cultures: Japan, China and the United States*. New Haven, Conn.: Yale University Press, 1989.

Tokutomi, Roka. *Footprints in the Snow*. Rutland, Vt.: Tuttle, 1970.

Tsukada, Mamoru. "A Factual Overview of Japanese and American Education." In *Educational Policies in Crisis*, edited by William K. Cummings. New York: Praeger, 1986, pp. 104–110.

Tsukamoto, Tetsu, Hiroshi Urabe, Tatsuzoo Ootsuka, and Seiichi Kookoo, eds. *Shakai fukushi jigyoo jiten*. Kyoto: Minerva shoboo, 1966.

UNICEF. *The State of the World's Children*. New York: Oxford University Press, 1988.

Ueno, Chizuko. "The Position of Japanese Women Reconsidered," *Current Anthropology* 28 (1987):S75–S84.

Uno, Kathleen. "Family Strategy in Late Tokugawa and Early Meiji Japan." Unpublished paper, 1979.

———. "Day Care and Family Life in Industrializing Japan, 1868–1926." Ph.D. diss., University of California, Berkeley, 1987.

———. "Good Wives, Wise Mothers in Early Twentieth-Century Japan." Unpublished paper, 1988.

———. "Women and Changes in the Household Division of Labor." In *Recreating Japanese Women*, edited by Gail Lee Bernstein. Berkeley: University of California Press, 1991, pp. 22–51.

Urabe, Hiroshi. *Nihon no jidoo mondai*. Tokyo: Shinju shuppan, 1977.

U.S. Department of Education. *Japanese Education Today*. Washington, D.C.: Government Printing Office, 1987.

Ushiogi, Monkazu. "Transition from School to Work: The Japanese Case." In *Educational Policies in Crisis*, edited by William K. Cummings. New York: Praeger, 1986, pp. 197–209.

Varner, Richard. "The Organized Peasant: The *Wakamonogumi* in the Edo Period," *Monumenta Nipponica* 32 (1977):459–483.

Vogel, Ezra. *Japan's New Middle Class: The Salary Man and His Family in a Tokyo Suburb*. Berkeley: University of California Press, 1963.

Vogel, Suzanne. "Professional Housewife: The Career of Urban Middle Class Japanese Women." *Japan Interpreter* 12:1 (Winter 1978):16–43.

Wagatsuma, Hiroshi. "Some Aspects of the Contemporary Japanese Family: Once Confucian, Now Fatherless?" In *The Family*, edited by Alice Rossi, Jerome Kagan, and Tamara K. Hareven. New York: W. W. Norton, 1977, pp. 181–210.

Wagatsuma, Hiroshi, and Hiroko Hara. *Shitsuke*. Tokyo: Koobundoo, 1974.

White, Merry. *The Japanese Educational Challenge*. New York: Free Press, 1987.

White, Merry. "The Virtue of Japanese Mothers: Cultural Definitions of Women's Lives." *Daedalus* 116:3 (Summer 1987):149–163.

Yamamura, Kozo. "Samurai Income and Demographic Change: The Genealogies of Tokugawa Bannermen." In *Family and Population in East Asia*, edited by Susan B. Hanley and Arthur P. Wolf. Stanford, Calif.: Stanford University Press, 1985, pp. 62–80.

Yamamura, Yoshiaki. "The Child in Japanese Society." In *Child Development and Education in Japan*, edited by Harold Stevenson, Hiroshi Azuma, and Kenji Hakuta. New York: Freeman Press, 1986, pp. 28–38.

Yamazumi, Masami, and Kazue Nakae. *Kosodate no sho*. Vol. 1. Tokyo: Heibonsha, 1976.

Yanagita, Kunio. *Bunrui jidoo goi*. Tokyo: Tokyodoo shuppansha, 1949.

Yokosuka, Kaoru, ed. *Jidoo kan no tenkai, Kindai Nihon kyooiku ronshuu*. Tokyo: Kokudosha, 1969.

Yokosuka, Kooji. *Kosodate no shakaishi*. Tokyo: Keisoo Shoboo, 1986.

Yoshida, Kyuuichi. *Gendai shakai jigyoo shi kenkyuu*. Tokyo: Keisoo shoboo, 1979.

———. *Nihon shakai jigyoo no rekishi*. Tokyo: Keisoo shoboo, 1981.

16

MEXICO

Asunción Lavrin

Few attempts have been made to explore in depth the experience of Mexican children in the past, either as subjects of historical study or as members of families and society. The memory of childhood has been assimilated to that of education or welfare, and the works that have dealt with children in this manner have used an institutional approach in which they have remained ancillary rather than the centerpiece of the research. The possibilities of writing a different type of history by raising other types of questions exist, however.

Mexican history is rich in documentation and complex in its evolution. A mosaic of indigenous cultures had a long evolution before the arrival of the Spanish conquerors. The physical and cultural superposition of European patterns over established populations from the sixteenth through the eighteenth centuries generated a distinct colonial experience that helped to give the area a long period of acculturation to Western values and institutions while retaining significant elements of its indigenous heritage. After breaking ties with Spain in 1821 Mexico sought further definition of its identity as a nation in a process characterized by challenges to tradition and a search for stability. As the first western hemisphere nation to experience a political revolution in the twentieth century, it has attempted to institutionalize—stabilize—that drastic attempt to change its own past by creating a rather homogeneous political system that its leaders have claimed to be the best medium to serve the social needs of its people. An ethnic quasi-homogeneity has been achieved through a slow process of miscegenation (*mestizaje*) that began with the conquest and has resulted in a proud recognition of their being a people of Indian-Spanish ancestry, partaking of the cultural heritage of both, but with a unique cultural approach to life.

This background is important to an inquiry into the history of Mexico's children. Children have been central to Mexicans at several points when its population has depended on reproduction and childhood to recover from the demographic stress. Such was the case in the late sixteenth and early seventeenth centuries, when Mexico (then called New Spain) suffered a severe demographic slump.[1] In the early nineteenth and twentieth centuries the wars of independence and the political revolution beginning in 1910 took several million lives. A vigorous demographic growth that began in the 1940s and reached its peak in the 1960s has contributed to shape a "young" Mexico. In 1963, 45.7 percent of an estimated 18.4 million inhabitants were children under fourteen years of age. In the early 1980s, 55 percent of the population was under twenty years of age.[2] An inquiry into the history of Mexican childhood, therefore, is a desirable agenda, given the importance that the renewal of generations and the nursing of the young had in bringing the nation back from several crises.

The definition of childhood itself is one of the premises of any study of this topic. The Spanish legal system in use in Mexico through the end of the nineteenth century defined the family with greater accuracy than it did childhood. Children were wards of their fathers in an eminently patriarchal society that granted women rights over their children only under exceptional circumstances such as in default of a natural or appointed male relative or in cases of children born out of wedlock and under the care of their mothers.[3] Because the presence or absence of children was crucial in the process of inheritance of property and status, a bilateral property division ensured that both parents had vested interests in the protection of the offspring. The law also ensured an initial equity between the sexes by stipulating that male and female children had to inherit equally. Yet certain legal mechanisms allowed preferential treatment to favored children in the allocation of specified cores of properties. The premises of Spanish family law remained largely unchanged until the late nineteenth century, and were not significantly revised until the 1960s.

The definition of childhood was not exclusively a legal matter. The ages at which a child could take communion and began to confess were important landmarks in the process of growth, as they assigned children increasing spiritual and moral responsibilities. Civil and canon law began to close the doors of childhood at twelve for girls and fourteen for boys, when they could legally agree to marry, initiate religious life, or issue a will. Puberty was hardly acknowledged.

We have more information on the experience of childhood for native American children in the early sixteenth century than for their Spanish counterparts. The religious indoctrination carried out by the early missionaries explains this situation. The friars in charge of evangelizing the new world sought information about the conquered peoples with the ability of contemporary anthropologists and learned much about all the stages of their life cycles. These sources describe societies conscious of the period of childhood as one of learning and preparation for the tasks of adulthood, and furnish a general picture of the methods of raising children in which class divisions in the native societies were reinforced through apprenticeship in special schools and religious training.[4]

Children participated actively in religious conversion and adaptation to a new cultural system. The Church targeted children as the most promising element for evangelization, educating them in the new faith and in the new culture in schools founded after the conquest. The religious zeal burnt high for several decades before bureaucratization and increasing jealousy from the Spanish population led to the decline of these institutions. As a result, historians have learned much about sixteenth-century pedagogical methods and the expectations of humanist educators facing a new race and a new social reality, and the performance of the students.[5]

Unfortunately Indian children become more elusive as historical subjects as time passed, and a near enigma toward the close of the sixteenth century. On the other hand, information on Spanish and mixed-blood children becomes more accessible as colonialism matured. Among the institutional sources we may count on for yielding information, the most important are notarial materials such as wills, apprenticeship contracts, sales and manumissions of slaves, the administrative books of schools and charitable institutions, and some judicial and ecclesiastical records. The possibilities of recovering children's past using judicial and legal records are hinted at by a recent investigation on rape using the criminal records of the city of Guadalajara.[6] Wills were more often used by those with some property, but we find wills among people with few belongings. They are a potential source of information on children—legitimate, illegitimate, and adopted—and the allocation of family resources among them.

Although these sources are by no means abundant, they allow us to establish some preliminary parameters. Class, race, and gender shaped the experience of childhood in the colonial period and throughout the late nineteenth century, since independence did not radically alter the social or cultural makeup of Mexican society. We know that there were significant differences in the childhood of an African slave, a rural Indian, an urban mixed-blood, and an upper-class white child, even though we still do not have precise details to characterize their experience.

Infant and child care were of great concern among all peoples, but not all practiced the same methods to nurse, clothe, and educate their children. Indian or black nurses were used by some upper-class women, despite condemnation by ecclesiastical and educational authorities. Other elements in the physical care of infants and children yet to be established may be gathered in medical and, later, pediatric treatises, educational manuals, and advice to mothers, which become increasingly available as the popular and feminine press began to develop in Mexico in the nineteenth century.[7]

Treatises on male and female education are useful for establishing models of behavior, defining the cultural perception of childhood, and tracing its European roots.[8] The extent to which educational treatises were applied to the education of the less endowed is open to question and research. Education of the masses was not the state's objective, and the church had several educational levels designed to suit the needs of people's status in society. Most of the educational treatises of the sixteenth and seventeenth centuries were written for the upper classes, and tended to establish a methodology of advice for genteel life. This situation began to change in the mid-eighteenth century as a result of the Enlightenment and the promotion of a secular spirit in education, and gained momentum and eventual endorsement after the mid-nineteenth century. Reflecting this evolution we begin to find educational materials addressing the needs and goals of the urban middle class, combining the practical and moral education shared by the home and the school. Historians may explore these sources to trace the development of a different educational mentality and a changing perception of childhood. Doubtless many cultural and social values persisted. The difference between male and female educational goals characteristic of the sixteenth and seventeenth centuries lingered through the late eighteenth century and beyond. Yet the Enlightenment began to emphasize the need to redress the neglect of girls as potentially productive members of society.[9]

Although more difficult to analyze, religious works used for catechizing children and biographies of members of the church also are sources for the study of models of behavior and education. A recent study of the images of childhood in religious literature is an example of how formal sources may be used to begin building an archetype of childhood that, although far removed from common behavior, served as pedagogical tools.[10]

Prescriptive sources are important to assess the establishment of roles, but they need to be compensated by an analysis of actual forms of behavior. Information on educational institutions and pedagogical treatises reveal only a slice of childhood. Noninstitutional sources are the key to learning about the issues of childhood and child rearing. This methodology poses significant difficulties for the colonial and republican periods. Lacking individual sources of information such as autobiographies and letters, historians will have to undertake a careful and painstaking analysis of those ecclesiastical, notarial, judicial, and criminal records mentioned above to unveil the daily experience of childhood.

The handful of solid works written to the present show that the educational goals of all schools was the containment of children's natural impulses and their training for the responsibilities of adulthood, either academically or through "practical" instruction. Children were neither vessels of latent wickedness nor glorified sources of joy and purity. They were potential adults whose development into duty-bound and God-fearing people seemed to have been the most important concern of those who cared about them. These objectives are reflected in the paintings of the period, which show children mostly dressed up as miniature adults. Only late-eighteenth-century pictures present children informally dressed in the environment of home and family.

Episcopal visits and the administrative documents generated by diocesan administration are yielding the few glimpses we now have of childhood and family life beyond the institutional framework. Ecclesiastical records, such as baptismal, marriage, and death records, are the only demographic information before the mid-eighteenth century, when the first state censuses began to be taken. Demographic and family studies are, as yet, at an early stage of development to sustain much confidence in characterizing the contours of the home in which children grew up. We know that members of the upper class tended to marry later than members of the lower classes, but women, as a gender, married earlier than in Europe, regardless of class or ethnic affiliation. The family was conceived as a nuclear unity, but both upper- and lower-class urban people throughout Mexican history have resorted to extended family networking or even multiple-family dwellings for economic survival or to strengthen familial and economic ties.[11]

Infant and child mortality did not become subjects of statistical concern until the late nineteenth century, and few authors have shown any concern with this topic as a potential subject of historical research. The connections among epidemics, agricultural crises, and child abandonment in an indigenous community have been the object of only one study during two periods in the middle colonial years, a subject that may be profitably researched for society as a whole.[12] This survey has found a significant correlation between the number of abandoned children, periods of economic crisis or disease, and the adoption of children as potential workers. Whereas a study of child abandonment may be seen as a result of external social and economic factors, the manner whereby any society copes with the problem reveals changing attitudes about childhood and child care. The foundation of charity institutions by religious and lay people to shelter and protect abandoned children dates back to the sixteenth century, and was one response to the problem of abandoned childhood not taken over by the state until the mid-nineteenth century.[13] Although several early orphanages for infants and children were in existence before the eighteenth century, some of them foundered for lack of support. Beneficence and charity were synonyms, and depended on the alms of the rich as well as on the patronage of the church. The history of these institutions has only received partial and summary treatment, and because some of the available studies date back to the nineteenth century, a monographic treatment of any of them would be a desirable research topic.[14]

Child abandonment and adoption are somewhat connected with widespread out-of-wedlock births throughout Mexican history, an important demographic and cultural phenomenon that should receive further consideration in the future. Much more data are needed to establish firm patterns for all Mexico throughout several centuries, but it seems that although children began to be born outside marriage since the sixteenth century, the percentage increased significantly throughout the seventeenth century. Race mixture was part of this development, but it cannot be singled out as its main cause. Although mixed-bloods and slaves were more frequently born out of wedlock than members of other ethnic and economic groups, the incidence among whites increased during the mid-colonial years.[15] Data registered in national censuses after independence indicate that children born out of wedlock became a fixed feature of Mexican society for several centuries. The incidence of such births began to decline around the mid-twentieth century.[16] Such data have more than a demographic value. Out-of-wedlock births generated a special social situation for children. The lack of parental protection put them in a vulnerable situation, and made them subject to labor exploitation, disease, and emotional distress. Informal adoption was widespread, however, and it seemed to have partially readdressed child abandonment. Whether adoption was a compensating social mechanism to cover up the contradictory values of double standards of morality or simply an imperative imposed by a sexual and demographic imbalance is a subject that needs discussion and clarification, especially since informal adoption seemed to have ceased in the nineteenth century. The accessibility of parochial registers throughout Mexico makes the possibility of researching this intriguing topic relatively easy and highly desirable.

RESEARCH IN THE MODERN PERIOD

Thematically and chronologically, the possibilities of research expand significantly after the second half of the nineteenth century. The increasing role of the state in the provision of educational and welfare services accounts for a body of official sources and statistical materials that the researcher can follow up to the present. Mexico did not escape the Western shift to a more child-oriented society in which the government took a growing interest in shaping the future of its population as an asset to development. The education, health, and labor of children, and the legal and judiciary reforms affecting them, are important research topics from the second half of the century to the present. The role of the state in defining policies, initiating reforms, and executing programs is important in a centralized state such as Mexico. Despite its nominal federal political system, the nucleus of governmental policies still is in the federal capital. As a result, much of what we know or will learn later refers to Mexico City or its surrounding core area, leaving wide gaps of information about the states and geographically distant areas. To compensate for this imbalance, state and municipal records should be used to fill up lacunae of information in areas beyond the geographical-administrative center.[17]

Considering that in 1821 illiteracy was practically universal in Mexico, the significance of education becomes obvious. Educational problems in Mexico could not be solved until the nation reached a modicum of political stability, however. Torn by political and ideological factions, the loss of its northern territories from Texas to California, an internal civil war, and the creation of a puppet empire, its final national identity was not achieved until the late 1860s. Despite the chaotic condition of the nation during its first decades of independence, historians have been able to underline the government's efforts to change the nature of education beginning in the 1830s.[18] Such efforts became more systematized once the nation began building its educational system.[19] Reports from the secretariat of education issued regularly since the 1860s through the present provide important quantitative and qualitative information on the plans for developing a primary and secondary school system.[20]

Official records need to be thoroughly analyzed however, if we are to go beyond the boundaries of a mere history of education. Such records represent important generational perceptions of childhood and its needs, and we should treat them as more than mere sources of factual information about school-building. The success of any effort to rescue a true history of childhood from these sources depends on a concerted effort to move away from the current analysis of education as a political tool of the state, or as the expression of the educational ideology of different ministers and educators, although the latter remains an important part of the picture.[21] What is needed is a deconstruction of the educational materials generated by the official system to reach an understanding of how Mexicans have viewed childhood, the formal and informal means used to shape individuality and sociability in the child, the difficulties faced by educators, parents, and bureaucrats in achieving that undertaking, and the role of education as a tool to form a new type of citizen. For example, an analysis of the theoretical framework of the educational system after the Mexican revolution began in 1910 suggests that it pursued the eradication of the privileges and inequities created by economic, geographical, and ethnic factors. Underneath the structural apparatus was the perception that childhood was a medium for the achievement of a national hope for restructuring the social system. This type of analysis and this particular concept should be pursued in future studies.

Between 1860 and 1940 Mexico enjoyed a stellar series of educational secretaries (such as Gabino Barreda, Joaquín Baranda, Justo Sierra, José Vasconcelos, and Narciso Bassols), whose writings and educational reforms have been analyzed from an intellectual, political, and even educational point of view. Yet the child envisioned by Barreda was not the child of Bassols. Not only a political revolution had taken place, but also a complex institutional infrastructure was beginning to be set into place in the 1930s. It sought to ensure a more efficient and thorough enforcement of the government's educational policies, which at that time began taking a definite turn to the left and assigning children a new role in the future of the nation. As one researcher has stated, "the conflicts endangering the most the endurance of revolutionary administrations were originated by educational policies."[22] Materials specifically oriented toward children and with a significant infusion of politics are available for the 1930s and 1940s. A subsequent turn in the political base of education in 1946 returned it to a democratic concept of the world and human relations. The state continued to reserve for itself the right to design the educational content and philosophy of the nation, and reinforced this role in the 1960s by the free distribution of primary reading texts. The message delivered to the children was one of sacrifice, selflessness, and assumption of responsibilities as an individual.

Textbooks and presidential messages can be used to discover the patterns of individual and social values surrounding childhood and to analyze the archetypes of childhood projected for national consumption. Historians need to further analyze such material and assess their value as tools for the manipulation of childhood at a national level.[23] Although acknowledging the great influence of the Mexican government on the socialization of children, Rafael Segovia states that by 1980, the state had given up its revolutionary dreams of being the fundamental socializing agent of the Mexican child. Yet, after many years of active leadership in the national education, his opinion is that the government has succeeded in significantly "politicizing" childhood, creating a positive perception of revolutionary events among children of workers, for example, and predisposing others to participation in politics.[24]

Although most official statements do not make gender differentiations, people continue to hold different attitudes about the education of boys and girls that betray deeply rooted assumptions about gender roles. Many public primary schools operated on a sex-segregated basis in the large urban centers until the mid-1940s. We must not assume that gender loses relevance in the study of contemporary Mexican childhood. In fact, we must look for gender stereotypes in all areas of public education, mass communication media, and reading materials to learn how gender typologies develop.

Institutional and state policies, however, are not the only tools for unearthing the meaning of educational changes taking place since the 1850s. Despite the slow increase of literacy and its uneven results, the pedagogical literature offers two important paths for the investigation of childhood: the technical literature on the education of children for educators and the reading materials for children. The first opens the doors to the methodology of teaching, which, in itself, permits an analysis of the archetypes of childhood pursued in different periods. The concern of the Mexican government to preserve the distinctive character of some of its indigenous groups has led to the creation of a special department within the secretariat of education devoted to the education of Indian children and the preservation of ethnic identity and bilinguality.[25]

On the other hand, reading materials for children allow the analysis of the creative efforts that pedagogues, writers, and artists put into the production of learning and recreational materials for learning. Encyclopedias, books, and newspapers for children have been published in Mexico since the mid-nineteenth century.[26] The value of comparing colonial and nineteenth- and twentieth-century texts is obvious to historians. These sources shift the researchers' attention from educational plans and politicians' speeches to the more pragmatic subject of what and how to teach children, but focus on the tools for instruction rather than the pedagogical theory.

The dialectic of norm and practice that historians of other areas have already explored should be incorporated into the history of Mexican childhood. A primary example of the value of examining texts written for children is reflected in the choice of topics and the illustrations used. Since the 1930s fostering nationalism has become a target of Mexican education, regardless of changes in the political ideology. The result of this policy is reflected in the homogenization of national textbooks and a uniform view of the nation and its history. Interesting nuances can be observed in this trend. For example, there is an increased sensitivity to the national phenotype, as illustrated by the pictures used in the books. Nonetheless, the market is still flooded with a large number of children's books translated from other languages and dealing with other cultures. This suggests the possibility of studying their competition with nationalistic themes, and the degree of penetration of foreign cultures through the mass media, which should include television programs for children.[27]

Although the study of children's education has a potentially large array of sources, child labor is at the opposite extreme. A topic in great need of further research, it is unlikely to develop very fast because of the difficulty in gathering materials. Colonial records attest to the training of poor urban boys in useful crafts. This tradition of pragmatic education for the poor was to remain a valid one through the twentieth century. Through several centuries the norm was to end childhood as soon as the child was able to help the family. Such reinforcement of class differences through training could be further understood by more research.

National censuses have acknowledged the reality of a working childhood by beginning to assess the economically active population at the age of twelve.[28] The incorporation of rural children into the labor force is difficult to trace and document before the nineteenth century, although it was commented on by observers such as ecclesiastics in their diocesan visits.[29] Getting rural children to attend school throughout the year and not simply when agricultural and familial demands waned posed a constant challenge to the Mexican state as yet not totally superceded.

The magnitude of the problem of unaccounted child labor in the nation should have encouraged research of the subject. Yet child labor has not been historically well documented in Mexico and remains a topic open to any kind of probing. Turn-of-the-century photographs help to identify children as street and market sellers, and establish a linkage with the thousands of children currently so employed in Mexico.[30] The 1917 Constitution, the most important attempt to restructure Mexican society in the twentieth century, had little to say about children. In addition to forbidding their labor before the age of twelve, it attempted to restrict it to six hours a day for those under age sixteen. At the same time it legislated a minimum of five hours of education a day for children under fifteen. Such inconsistencies were made irrelevant by the lack of enforcement. An increased concern with child welfare in the 1930s resulted in legislation restricting child labor in factories and self-employed occupations, such as a bootblack. Nonetheless, the extraordinary growth of the population since 1940 to the present and the increasing rural-urban migration in the past thirty years have created strong economic pressures on poor urban families that have been resolved by a resurgence of child labor.

The International Year of the Child (1969) revealed the almost absolute lack of national information on child labor. The Department of Labor had undertaken a few studies of a sample of children working as packers and stevedores helping to unload merchandise in urban markets to test the enforcement of protective legislation. As other Latin American nations, Mexico has been mostly concerned with the legislative and formal aspects of child labor. The social needs of children in the informal sector of the economy are subject to no legislation, and therefore have escaped state surveillance and research attention. The only recent study of children in the informal sector was carried out in 1979 by a team of sociologists sponsored by the Department of Labor. Data attempting to establish the number of minors working in Mexico or in Mexico City were highly speculative, but suggested that between 200,000 and 400,000 children were working in 1979.[31] This study covered children who worked independently in the federal district, half of whom were between twelve and sixteen years of age. It revealed that nearly half the 1,000 children surveyed were simply street sellers who were compelled to engage in this activity to help the family budget and who had an average of slightly over two years of experience.[32] Young children who accompany their mothers to work in the streets were not represented, and have not been the object of any study.

The elusiveness of employment in the informal sector poses a great challenge to those interested in investigating the historical roots of child labor in Mexico. The existence of information on children employed in private industries may be detected by combing through reports submitted to the Department of Labor. Scavenging newspapers, the recent national and household censuses, and photographic archives may prove fruitful in the recovery of materials. That such a scarcity of information exists on such an important topic is in itself significant.

Less difficult to access and to research is the topic of child welfare and health. The sources for its study are mostly institutional and medical. As public institutions were created under the auspices of the state, records were created and preserved. Such records are available through the National Archives of the Nation, and allow a chronological reconstruction of institutions dedicated to child health and the mapping of changes in the philosophies of welfare. Although the state had assumed the responsibility of beneficence since the mid-nineteenth century, the political interests of the government through 1910 were not oriented toward the provision of a social infrastructure. Beneficence was a gloss on the national surface. The revolutionary years were less propitious than ever for welfare or beneficence. Only in the late 1920s, as Mexico returned to administrative stability, could beneficence receive some attention. At that point nineteenth-century structures were still in place, despite cosmetic changes in names.[33]

Welfare and health programs became intimately bound after the 1920s. During this decade Latin American nations began to design and put into effect public health projects as the result of increasing social pressure from labor groups, the attraction of eugenic concepts among the professional middle class, and the activities of new political leaders who lent their support to health programs to gain the backing of an expanding voting population. By the mid–1920s the revolutionary government of Mexico, still under considerable political pressure resulting from internal power struggles, initiated a social program of health for expectant mothers and infants and children (prenatal and postnatal *puericultura*). A lay association, the National Association for the Protection of Childhood (*Asociación Nacional de Protección a la Infancia*) was founded in 1924 to begin implementing the new policies. The First and Second Mexican Congress of the Child (1923 and 1925) drew desirable objectives in child care and the setting up of a network of service institutions that remained as blueprints for many years.[34]

The development of a philosophy and practice of child care implied a redefinition of the nature of children's needs and the role the state would assume in planning their future. From the plans of the 1920s the Mexican nation passed to the establishment of a mixed system of private and public assistance in the 1930s. The foundations of a state-controlled health and welfare system began precisely in this decade. If there was to be a commitment to social change, plans had to comprise children, argued those who advocated such changes.[35] In the 1930s several governmental secretariats shared different services to children, curtailing the possibilities of an effective central policy.[36] After World War II Mexico began to reverse the charitable spirit that permeated its protective institutions and developed a service-oriented system of child welfare. For example, the state began founding child-care centers for the children of state employees, and putting them under the responsibility of the secretariat of health and assistance.[37]

The nuances of the changes in national policies are expressed in the creation of institutions such as the secretariat of public assistance (1937), which in 1943 became the secretariat of public health and public assistance, and the national Institute for the Protection of Childhood (*Instituto Nacional de Protección a la Infancia*), founded in 1961 and restructured in 1974. The Mexican Institution for Assistance to Childhood (*Institución Mexicana de Asistencia a la Niñez*, 1968) and the Institute for the Protection of Childhood were put under one administration known as Integral Development for the Family (*Desarrollo Integral de la Familia*) in 1977. The records of these various agencies will allow future researchers to delineate the philosophy of child welfare and its implementation, subjects that remain to be mapped out.[38]

The Mexican evolution in social services to children was consonant with that of other Latin American nations, which by 1965 also were aided in their efforts to face the problems of their children by organizations such as the Inter American Institute of the Child, an agency of the Organization of the American States, and UNICEF.[39] By the mid–1960s Mexico experienced its highest population peak, and it was forced to consider the many implications of such a demographic explosion. Although some international organizations considered the problems of childhood as part of development, the provision of services to an increasing number of children began to tax the economic possibilities of the Mexican state.[40] Its ideological commitment to equality of access and services for its young population eventually drove Mexico to adopt a national population policy of family planning in 1974. As one of the first Latin American states to endorse such a policy, Mexico had made considerable changes in less than fifty years, moving from a timid policy of child and family protection to an assertive standing on both. While aiming at providing services, it definitely opted for an open acknowledgment that the quality of childhood was more desirable than its quantity. This does not mean, however, that the nation is closer to achieving a modicum of fair protection for its children. Far from it, the stringent economic conditions of Mexico today make childhood a wrenching experience for a large number. Having embarked on an official policy of population planning since the mid–1970s, Mexico offers the possibility of studying attitudes about the desirability of children, the spacing of their births, the division of responsibility toward their education, among others. Such data, although recent, are not ancillary to the history of childhood, and they should help to determine the contours of parenting among the current generation of Mexicans.[41]

Health and nutritional problems beacon as an important area for research, even though they may have to be focused on fairly recent times. Information on both subjects for the 1930s and onward is available in the publications of professional associations such as the Mexican Association for Child Care and UNICEF.[42] The records and publications of the secretariat of public health and public assistance, and current research by biometricians and demographers could help to trace the physical and physiological profile of Mexican children in the recent past.[43] Complementary to these sources are those official publications that popularize the concepts of health and works devoted to the education of parents and teachers through the intermediary figure of the doctors.[44]

In the countryside and among indigenous groups anthropological research has contributed to a small pool of information on childhood. By exploring the meaning of daily activities, rituals, and kinship, anthropologists have provided insightful, important, and sometimes the only available commentaries on pregnancy, childbirth, child care, and the integration of the child into the family as well as the community.[45]

These suggestions for research indicate that the status of children in society has changed significantly, as have the perceptions of their legal dependency and their juridical personality. The most important reform to the former concept in the twentieth century has been the extension of *patria potestad* to the mother. But whereas family legislation redefined the boundaries of parental power over children, other legal minds focused more sharply on the children themselves. The first Tribunal for Minors was established in 1928. The ideological premises of the several Pan-American Congresses on the Child served as a base for the promotion of reform in penal legislation affecting minors, a subject that began to be vigorously promoted in the early 1930s. Several studies of child delinquency in that period supported the doctrine that the state had the obligation to recognize the differences between child and adult transgressions. Critics of the system identified the most common causes for children's crime, acknowledged the neglect of this issue by the Mexican state, and promoted the adoption of the novel concept of the rights of children.[46] An institutional dimension may be added to the study of the concept of crime in childhood by studying the system of "correctional'' schools established in the nineteenth century and the changes—or lack thereof—in these institutions throughout the twentieth century. In fact, child criminality and rehabilitation remain uncharted waters in Mexican history.

The twentieth-century migration of Mexicans to the United States has triggered a new curiosity about the performance of Mexican-American children in the North American environment, vis-à-vis children of other ethnic groups. Many of those studies have begun as doctoral dissertations in departments of education across the United States, and represent a new field of interest and research.[47]

Finally, a country rich in iconographic materials emanating from religious sources should provide astute researchers an opportunity to explore the changing patterns in the visual memory of childhood. The Spaniards brought a religion in which the figure of Jesus as a child was paramount. The iconographic and devotional study of the infant Jesus and the mother-child relationship of the numerous paintings and sculptures produced for churches throughout the history of the Mexican nation could be topics attractive to mentalité history.[48] Portraiture began to develop in the nineteenth century, whereas the twentieth century has been rich in murals and paintings that express personal and social visions of a society experiencing important changes.[49] Following childhood visually would give art and social historians a new territory for exploration. On the other hand, literature has produced few novels based on childhood, but the theme could be pursued in works otherwise more comprehensive in scope.[50]

This survey covers only several key aspects of childhood in Mexico. Many of the topics here defined and discussed could bear further branching for research purposes. The most important task for the present is to encourage historians of Mexico to regard the history of childhood as worthy of attention and further research. Its cultivation could only enrich our understanding of Mexican society.

NOTES

1. The demographic catastrophe experienced in the Americas in the sixteenth and early seventeenth centuries hit Mexico hard. Although experts disagree on the number of people who perished, the net result is that this area of the New World lost at least half its population in the sixteenth century. See William M. Denevan, ed., *The Native Population of the Americas in 1492* (Madison: University of Wisconsin Press, 1976), for further bibliographical information.

2. Maria Antonieta Montaño Sánchez, *Creación de un Instituto Nacional de Protección Integral del Menor* (Mexico: n.p., 1964), p. 50; *Las razones y las obras. Gobierno de Miguel de La Madrid. Crónica del Sexenio 1982–1988* (Mexico: Fondo de Cultura Económica, 1988), pp. 322–323.

3. *Los códigos españoles. Concordados y anotados*, 12 vols. (Madrid: Imprenta de M. Rivadeneira, 1874–1951). All the important medieval legislation, such as *Siete Partidas* and the *Leyes de Toro*, that applied to colonial Spanish America is in this collection.

4. Bernardino de Sahagún, *Historia de las cosas de Nueva España*. 3 vols. (Mexico: Editorial Porrúa, 1956); Toribio de Motolinía, *Historia de los indios de Nueva España* (Mexico: Chávez Hayhoe, 1941). The latter has been translated into English by Elizabeth

A. Foster as *History of the Indians of New Spain* (Berkeley, Calif.: The Cortés Society, 1950). For information on childbirth practices see Thelma D. Sullivan, trans. "Pregnancy, Childbirth, and the Deification of the Women Who Died in Childbirth," in *Estudios de Cultura Nahuatl* (Mexico: Universidad Nacional Autónoma de Mexico, 1966), pp. 63–96. See also Florencio García Cisneros and Rafael Llerena, *Maternity in Pre-Columbian Art* (Salamanca: Gráficas Ortega, 1970). Child sacrifice, practiced among Mayas and Aztecs, posed a sharp contrast to the religious values of the cult of Jesus as a child, a favorite subject of Roman Catholicism. This topic could be further probed.

5. José María Kobayashi, *La educación como conquista* (Mexico: El Colegio de Mexico, 1974); Elisa Luque Alcaide, *La educación en Nueva España en el Siglo XVIII* (Sevilla: Consejo Superior de Investigaciones Científicas, 1970).

6. Carmen Castañeda, "La memoria de las niñas violadas," in *Segundo Simposio de Historia de las Mentalidades: La memoria y el olvido* (Mexico: Instituto Nacional de Antropología e Historia, 1985), pp. 107–116.

7. José Joaquín Fernández de Lizardi, *La Quijotita y su prima* (Mexico: Editorial Porrúa, 1967). A good example of midwifery and the raising of children is Damián Carbón, *Libro de las comadres* (Mallozca: Bernardo de Canzolca, 1541). Instruction on infant care is given in Josefa Amar y Borbón, *Discurso sobre la educación física y moral de las mujeres* (Madrid: B. Cano, 1790). Nineteenth- and twentieth-century pediatric sources are abundant, and should be tapped for historical research.

8. Juan Luis Vives, *Instrucción de la mujer cristiana* (Buenos Aires: Espasa-Calpe, 1940); Martín de Córdoba, *Jardín de nobles doncellas*, Colección Joyas Bibliográficas (Madrid, 1953); Antonio de Guevara, *Reloj de príncipes y Libro de Marco Aurelio* (Madrid: Signo, 1936).

9. José Joaquín Fernández de Lizardi, *El Periquillo Sarniento*, 2 vols. (Madrid: Editorial Nacional, 1976), and *La Quijotita y su prima*, as in note 7. These sociopedagogical novels published in the first quarter of the nineteenth century are excellent sources for the analysis of the current ideas of childhood and education. See also the essays by Juan Wenceslao Sánchez de la Barquera in *Semanario Económico de Mexico*, November–December 1810. A number of magazines for women were founded throughout the nineteenth century. Although their purpose was not specifically educational, they may be profitably scanned for materials on female childhood and women's education. For a list of these journals and information on the education of women before 1857 see Silvia M. Arrom, *The Women of Mexico City, 1790–1857* (Stanford, Calif.: Stanford University Press, 1985), p. 365, and ch. 1; Jane Herrick, "Periodicals for Women in Mexico During the Nineteenth Century," *The Americas* 14:2 (1957) 135–144; Johanna S. R. Mendelson, "The Feminine Press: The View of Women in the Colonial Journals of Spanish America, 1790–1810," in *Latin American Women: Historical Perspectives*, ed. Asunción Lavrin (Westport, Conn.: Greenwood Press, 1978), pp. 198–218; María del Carmen Castañeda, *La educación en Guadalajara durante la colonia, 1552–1821* (Mexico: El Colegio de Mexico, 1984); Gloria Carreño, *El colegio de Santa Rosa de Santa María de Valladolid, 1743–1810* (Morelia: Universidad de San Nicolás, 1979); Pilar Foz y Foz, *La revolución pedagógica en Nueva España: 1754–1820. María Ignacia Azlor y Echevers y los Colegios de la Enseñanza.* 2 vols. (Madrid: Instituto Gonzalo Fernández de Oviedo, 1981); Pilar Gonzalbo Azpuru, *Las mujeres en la Nueva España. Educación y vida cotidiana* (Mexico: El Colegia de Mexico, 1987).

10. Using religious biographies, a researcher has recently analyzed the colonial stereotypes of the childhood of religious personalities. See Cristina Ruiz Martínez, "La

memoria sobre la niñez y el estereotipo del niño santo,'' in *Segundo Simposio de Historia de las Mentalidades: La memoria y el olvido* (Mexico: Instituto Nacional de Antropología e Historia, 1985), pp. 117–124; Anne Staples, "El catecismo como libro de texto" (paper presented at the Sixth Conference of Mexican and United States Historians, Chicago, September 1981). This work deals with the nineteenth century. As an example of religious catechism, see Jerónimo de Rosales, *Catón christiano y catecismo de la doctrina christiana para la educación y buena crianza de los niños y muy provechoso para personas de todos estados* (Mexico: Imprenta Nueva de la Biblioteca Mexicana, 1761). Because the analysis of religious literature also can be carried out with contemporary materials, researchers should not overlook the possibility of studying the connections between past and present objectives. See *Historia sagrada para los niños* (Mexico: Fernández Editores, 1986); *El amigo de la niñez. Publicación Semanal Salesiana* (Mexico: Francisco E. Erdey, 1918–1967).

11. Thomas Calvo, "The Warmth of the Hearth," in *Sexuality and Marriage in Colonial Latin America*, ed. Asunción Lavrin (Lincoln: University of Nebraska, 1989), pp. 287–312.

12. Elsa Malvido, "El abandono de los hijos: Una forma de control del tamaño de la familia y del trabajo indígena. Tula (1683–1730), *Historia Mexicana* 24:4 (April–June 1980):521–561.

13. Martiniano Alfaro, *Reseña histórica del antiguo hospicio de Mexico* (Mexico: Imprenta del Gobierno Federal, 1906); Josefina Muriel, "La protección del niño en Nueva España," in *Coloquios*, Reunión Hispano-Mexicana de Historia (Santa María de la Rábida, Huelga, 1980); Juan de Dios Peza, *La beneficencia en Mexico* (Mexico: Imprenta da Francisco Díaz de León, 1881); Pilar Gonzalbo Aizpuru, "La casa de niños expósitos de la ciudad de Mexico: una fundación del siglo XVIII," *Historia Mexicana* 31:3 (January–March 1982);409–430.

14. Josefina Muriel, *Hospitales de la Nueva España*. 2 vols. (Mexico: Editorial Jus, 1955); Rómulo Velasco Ceballos, *El niño mexicano ante la caridad y el estado* (Mexico: Beneficencia Publica en el D. F., 1935). By the same author see a bibliography for researching welfare institutions, *Fichas bibliográficas sobre Asistencia en Mexico* (Mexico, 1943); Pablo Lorenzo Laguarta, *Historia de la beneficencia española en Mexico* (Mexico, 1955). See also a turn-of-the-century dissertation, Albert Judson Steelman, *Charities for Children in the City of Mexico* (Chicago: E. M. Steelman, 1907); Joaquín García Izcabalceta wrote a report, posthumously printed, of public beneficence reflecting their state in the 1860s. See Joaquín García Izcabalceta, *Informe sobre los establecimientos de beneficencia y corrección de esta capital* (Mexico, 1907); Alfaro, *Reseña histórica del antiguo hospicio de Mexico*; A. Robles Gil, *Album commemorativo de la inauguración del Hospicio de Niños* (Mexico, 1905). Colonial materials with information on children in several institutions, their rules, and administration are available in several archival collections. The Archivo de la Secretaría de Salubridad y Asistencia and the archives of the Archbishopric of Mexico, for example, shelter the papers of the home for abandoned children Señor San José founded in 1767.

15. Calvo, "Warmth of the Hearth."

16. The yearly statistic for 1930 reported that between 1925 and 1927, Mexico had 236,723 out-of-wedlock against 244,020 legitimate births. Reported in *Revista Mexicana de Puericultura* 8:85 (January 1938):129. Consensual unions did not begin to decline until the 1940s. See Moisés González Navarro, *Población y sociedad en Mexico (1900–1970)* (Mexico: UNAM, 1974), pp. 79–145.

17. The use of municipal administrative, judicial, and educational records could shed much light on socioeconomic issues. For a recent example of the use of such records in developing the topic of education see Dorothy Tanck de Estrada, "Las escuelas lancasterianas en la ciudad de Mexico: 1822–1842," *Historia Mexicana* 22:4 (April–June) 1973:494–513. The recent movement toward the decentralization of education reinforces the notion of studying this subject at a local level.

18. Dorothy Tanck de Estrada, *La educación ilustrada, 1786–1836* (Mexico: El Colegio de Mexico, 1977). *Reglamento para la Compañia Lancasteriana de Mexico* (Mexico: Imprenta de Vicente García Torres, 1869); Mary Kay Vaughan, "Primary Schooling in the City of Puebla, 1821–1860," *The Hispanic American Historical Review* 67:1 (February 1987):39–62.

19. Alejandro Martínez Jiménez, "La educación elemental en el porfiriato," *Historia Mexicana* 22:4 (April–June 1974):514–552; Ernesto Meneses, *Tendencias educativas oficiales en Mexico, 1821–1911. La problemática de la educación mexicana en el siglo XIX y principios del siglo XX*. 2 vols. Vol. 1 (Mexico: Editorial Porrúa, 1938); vol. 2 (Mexico: Centro de Estudios Educativos, 1986).

20. The secretariat's name has changed throughout times, and the titles for these bulletins have changed slightly. See Secretaría de Instrucción Pública y Bellas Artes, *Boletín de Instrucción pública* (1903–1913). Between 1917 and 1921 it was known as Departamento Universitario y de Bellas Artes. After 1921 it became Secretaría de Educación Pública. See also *Boletín de la Secretaría de Educación Pública* (1922–1931); *Anuarios escolares* (1910–1911); Secretaría de Educación Pública, *Memoria* (dating back to 1924), and *Folletín Estadístico, Noticia estadística sobre la educación pública de Mexico*, 1925–1928, and *Anuario de estadística educativa*, 1947–. The Dirección General de Estadística Educativa publishes *Estadística educativa*. See also state sources such as *Educación* (Mérida, Yucatán: Departamento de Educación Pública, 1940–194?), and the journal edited by Xalapa, Veracruz, 1953– by the same name. For a complete list of journals on education see Ernesto Meneses, *Tendencias educativas oficiales en Mexico, 1821–1911*.

21. See, for exazmple, José Bravo Ugarte, *La educación en Mexico*; Carlos Alvear Acevedo, *La educación y la ley. Legislación mexicana en materia educativa el Mexico independiente* (Mexico: Editorial Jus, 1963); Fernando Solana et al., *Historia de la educación en Mexico* (Mexico: Secretaría de Educación Pública, 1981); Josefina Vázquez, *Nacionalismo y educación en Mexico* (Mexico: El Colegio de Mexico, 1975); Mary K. Vaughan, "Women, Class and Education in Mexico, 1880–1928," *Latin American Perspectives* 4:1–2 (1977):135–152, and *The State, Education, and Social Class in Mexico, 1880–1920* (DeKalb: Northern Illinois University Press, 1982).

22. Rafael Segovia, *La politización del niño mexicano* (Mexico: El Colegio de Mexico, 1975), p. 2.

23. Secretaría de Educación Pública, *La escuela y la guerra. Deberes que se imponen para el maestro, la maestra, el niño y la niña en la escuela, en el hogar, en el taller, en la ciudad y en el campo* (Mexico: Cuadernos del Niño, 1942); David Vivas Romero, *El niño proletario. Libro de lectura para el segundo año de educación primaria* (Mexico: Pluma y Lápiz, 1942). The secretariat of education created a national commission for the distribution of free school texts in 1959. Important debate on the homogenization of such texts have taken place in the recent past.

24. Segovia, *La politización*, passim.

25. Consultation of regional and national journals on education should help the un-

derstanding of the pedagogical objectives of the nation and the states. See, for example, Sociedad Mexicana de Pedagogía, *Revista Mexicana de Educación*, 1940–; *Revista Jaliscience de Educación* (Guadalajara: Departamento Cultural del Estado de Jalisco, 195–); Universidad Pedagógica Nacional, *Pedagogía*, 1984–); *Plan de estudios y programa de educación pre-escolar indígena* (Mexico: Secretaría de Educación Pública, 1987); *Manual para el fortalecimiento de la educación indígena bilingue-bicultural* (Mexico: Secretaría de Educación Pública, 1987).

26. *Biblioteca del Niño Mexicano* (Mexico: Mauxxi Hnos, 1899–1902); *El Correo de los Niños* (1877–1880). The more modern vintage of child literature offers a rich field for investigation to the interdisciplinary researcher. The wealth of materials precludes full coverage, but the following titles suggest the routes. Among the newspapers for children, see *Chapulín: la Revista del Niño Mexicano* (1942–1947), and *Semillita: Para la educadora y el niño* (1944–19??), printed by the department for pre-primary education. Noteworthy are those titles published by the National Council for the development of Education (Consejo Nacional de Fomento Educativo, or CONAFE). This council has series on child literature, ecological education, and methodological aids for teaching. Sample titles are *Como me lo contaron te lo cuento* (folklore literature), *¿Que hacer con la basura?* (garbage disposal), and *Como aprendemos matemáticas* (on learning mathematics). The private sector also publishes a vast array of titles. "Distribuidora Patria," for example, is a cooperative of editorials specializing in children's literature. They publish and distribute books on science and fiction, in translation or originally written in Spanish. For an emphasis on readings based on the national experience see the "Colección Piñata," from "Editorial Patria," with titles based on Mexican traditions and Mexican society. See also Manuel Velázquez Andrade, *Fermin: un libro para niños mexicanos* (Mexico: Primera Editora, 1986). A recent newcomer among newspapers for children is *Chispa* (1980–).

27. As an example of foreign children's literature, see the extensive catalog of Walt Disney titles edited by Editorial Cumbre and Fernández Editores, in Mexico City.

28. See *Estadística sobre la mujer: Inventario* (Mexico: Secretaría de Programación y Presupuesto, 1980). This source has data for 1969 and allows a comparison between working boys and girls between ages twelve and fifteen in several cities.

29. For an example see *Cuestionario de Don Antonio Bergoza y Jordán, Obispo de Antequera, a los señores curas de la diócesis (1802–1803)*. 2 vols. (Oaxaca: Gobierno del Estado de Oaxaca, 1948). The reports of the rural priests underlined the lack of interest of the indigenous population in that area in sending their children to school or learning Spanish.

30. Photographic documentation is possible thanks to excellent photographic archives in the National Archives of the Nation, Mexico City, and in the National Institute of Anthropology and History.

31. Alfonso Solórzano, *Estudio de mil casos de niños dedicados al comercio ambulante y los servicios en la ciudad de México* (Mexico: Secretaría del Trabajo y Previsión Social, 1979), pp. 26–30.

32. Ibid., see Table 2. This author drew a meaningful profile of the children's workers by breaking the data by sex, occupation, motivation for work, etc.

33. Only two reports on the activities of the Direction of Beneficence were written before 1935. See Juan Abadiano, *Memoria de Beneficencia* (Mexico, 1877), and *Memorias de la Junta Directiva de la Beneficencia Pública en el Distrito Federal* (Mexico, 1934). In 1931 the National Association for the Protection of Childhood brought women

into the patronage of a national vehicle for child welfare. This association depended on the Department of Public Beneficence.

34. *Memorias del Segundo Congreso Mexicano del Niño* (Mexico: Secretaría de Educación Pública, 1925); *Boletín de la Junta Federal de Protección de la Infancia* (Mexico: Secretaría de Educación Pública, 1925). The latter source lists all existing institutions for child protection and outlines the policies of the government for the future.

35. See Alfonso G. Alarcón, "Como debe organizarse en Mexico la asistencia social infantil," *Revista Mexicana de Puericultura* 7:79 (July 1937):269–275; Jesús Parra Muñoz, *El hijo del campesino y la legislación agraria* (Mexico: UNAM, 1957). This work advocated welfare plans for rural children.

36. In 1928–1929 there was a National Association for the Protection of Childhood (Asociación Nacional de Protección a la Infancia). The Department of Public Health took over the provision of counseling and services through a service of Infant Hygiene. In 1937 a department of social assistance to children was created and put under the secretariat of government (Asistencia Social Infantil). See *Diario Oficial* 102:40 (June 1937).

37. All *guarderías infantiles* do not depend on this institution. Some are under the budget of other federal or state institutions. For a description of several types of children's institutions in the capital see Mariá Luisa Rodríguez Sala, *Instituciones de protección a la infancia en el distrito federal* (Mexico: Instituto de Investigaciones Sociales, 1956).

38. *Instituto Nacional de Protección a la Infancia* (Mexico: INPI, 1964); Alicia Flores Villaseñor, *Escuela "Casa Amiga No. 5"* (Mexico: UNAM, 1962); María Antonieta Montaño Sánchez, *Creación de un Instituto de Protección Integral del Menor* (Mexico: n.p., 1964), p. 46. The Institute for the Protection of Minors provides breakfasts to primary school children and a broad net of health and child care services to help reduce problems of malnutrition. See also the *Bulletin* of the Dirección de Asistencia Materno-Infantil (1960–), a quarterly published by the department for the protection of mothers and children.

39. *Indicators in the Situation of Children in Latin America and the Caribbean* (Santiago de Chile: UNICEF, 1979); Instituto Interamericano del Niño, *Resumen de actividades, 1965–68* (Montevideo: Impresora Ligu, S.A., 1969; *Children and Youth in National Development in Latin America* (Santiago de Chile: UNICEF, 1965); United Nation Children's Fund, Regional Office for the Americas, *Situación de la infancia en America Latina y el Caribe* (Santiago de Chile: UNICEF-Editorial Universitaria, 1979). Another source for detecting national and continental concerns about health, education, and other problems of childhood are the Pan-American Congresses on the Child. See *Congresos Panamericanos del Niño, 1916–1963. Ordenación sitemática de sus recomendaciones* (Montevideo: Instituto Interamericano del Niño, 1965).

40. *Children and Youth in National Development in Latin American Conference* (Santiago de Chile: UNICEF, 1965). Mexico is used as one of the case studies.

41. Among the first studies on this topic and useful for the historian is María del Carmen Elú de Leñero, *¿Hacia donde va la mujer mexicana?* (Mexico: Instituto Mexicano de Estudios Sociales, 1969). For the adoption of responsible parenthood see Frederick C. Turner, *Responsible Parenthood: The Politics of Mexico's New Population Policies* (Washington, D.C.: American Enterprise Institute for Policy Research, 1974); Luis Leñero Otero, *Valores ideológicos y las políticas de población en Mexico* (Mexico: Editorial Edicol, 1979); Raul Benítez and Julieta Quilondrán, *La fecundidad rural en Mexico* (Mexico: El Colegio de Mexico and UNAM, 1983).

42. See *Revista Mexicana de Puericultura* (1930–1941); UNICEF, *Boletín Informativo de la Oficina Regional para America Latina*.

43. The *Memorias*, or annual reports, of the secretariat of welfare and assistance date back to 1937. See also *Incidencia de la mortalidad infantil en los Estados Unidos Mexicanos, 1940–1975* (Mexico: Secretaría de Programación y Presupuesto, 1981); Irma O. García y García, "Algunos factores asociados a la mortalidad infantil en Mexico," *Demografía y Economía* 17:3 (1983):289–320. Infant mortality has declined significantly since 1940 from 126 per thousand in 1940 to 60 per thousand in 1978. This article provides important information on infant care and practices; Robert M. Molina and J. H. Himes, "Patterns of Childhood Mortality and Growth Status in a Rural Zapotec Community," *Annals of Human Biology* 5:6 (November 1978):517–531; Johanna Faulhaber, *El crecimiento en un grupo de niños mexicanos* (Mexico: Instituto Nacional de Antropología e Historia, 1961); Francis Johnston et al., "An Analysis of Environmental Variables and Factors Associated with Growth Failure in a Mexican Village," *Human Biology* 54:4 (December 1980):627–637; Arnoldo de la Loza Saldívar, "Evaluación de los programas de salud para la niñez en Mexico," *Salud Pública de Mexico* 22:6 (November–December 1980):631–654.

44. Julio Manuel Torroella, *Pediatría para padres responsables* (Mexico: Editorial Patria, 198?; *Cuide a sus hijos* (Mexico: ISSTE, n.d.); (ISSTE, Institute for Security and Services for State Employees); *Como enfrentar los problemas de aprendizaje en los niños* (Mexico: La Prensa Médica Mexicana, n.d.). Articles on the care of children in popular women's magazines can be studied to assess the "popularization" of child care and the quality of such information against the pediatric literature of professional journals.

45. See, for example, Mary Lindsay Elmendorf, *Nine Maya Women: A Village Faces Change* (New York: Schenkman, 1976). For attitudes on reproduction and parenthood in an Oaxacan village see Carole H. Browner, "The Politics of Reproduction in a Mexican Village," *Signs: Journal of Women in Culture and Society* 11:4 (1986):710–724.

46. Mercedes Pena y Galindo. *Protección del menor en Mexico* (thesis) (Mexico: UNAM, 1935); Dolores Bedolla Rivera, *Proyecto de Código para menores* (thesis) (Mexico: UNAM, 1939); Guadalupe Soler Astorga, *Necesidad de una legislación especial de protección a la infancia* (thesis) (Mexico: UNAM, 1949).

47. I am grateful to Dr. Guadalupe Jiménez for calling my attention to this topic. She identified many titles of dissertations for me. Among them are Dianne Liles Griswold, "An Assessment of the Child-rearing Information Needs and Attitudes of Anglo, Black, and Mexican American Mothers" (Ph.D. diss., Arizona State University, Tempe, 1975); Marilyn Ray Brawner, "Factors in the School Completion Rates of Mexican-American Children in Racine, Wisconsin" (Ph.D. diss., University of Iowa, 1971); Lisa F. K. Barclary, "The Comparative Efficacies of Spanish-English Instruction with Mexican-American Head Start Children" (Ph.D. diss., Stanford University, 1969); Ronald P. Rohner et al., "Perceived Parental Acceptance-Rejection and Personality Organization Among Mexican and American Elementary School Children," *Behavioral Science Research, Journal of Comparative Studies* 15:1 (1980):23–39.

48. Such a study could follow the orientation of Jacques Lafaye's cultural study of the Virgin of Guadalupe. See Jacques Lafaye, *Quetzalcoatl and Guadalupe, The Formation of Mexican National Consciousness: 1513–1813* (Chicago: University of Chicago Press, 1974).

49. *Siempre niños. Sus imágenes en la historia de Mexico* (Mexico: Secretaría de Educación Pública, 1985). This catalogue of an exhibit of children in art illustrated the

possibility of using art to reconstruct history. The exhibit comprised paintings, toys, children's furniture, and photographs from the pre-Hispanic period to the present. I thank Dr. Barbara Tannenbaum for calling my attention to the catalogue.

50. Alonso Avila, *Niño Jalapeño. Novela de la niñez mexicana* (Mexico: Costa-Amic, 1965); Andrés Iduarte, *Niño: Child of the Mexican Revolution* (New York: Praeger, 1971).

REFERENCES

A. M. *Carta sobre la educación del bello sexo, por una señora americana.* Mexico: Tipografía de Rafael y Villa, 1851.

Abadiano, Juan. *Memoria de Beneficencia.* Mexico, 1877.

Alarcón, Alfonso G. "Como debe organizarse en Mexico la asistencia social infantil." *Revista Mexicana de Puericultura* 7:79 (July 1937):269–275.

Alfaro, Martiniano. *Reseña histórica del antiguo hospicio de Mexico.* Mexico: Imprenta del Gobierno Federal, 1906.

Alvear Acevedo, Carlos. *La educación y la ley. Legislación mexicana en materia educativa el Mexico independiente.* Mexico: Editorial Jus, 1963.

Amar y Borbón, Josefa. *Discurso sobre la educación física y moral de las mujeres.* Madrid: B. Cano, 1790.

El amigo do la niñez. Publicación Semanal Salesiana. Mexico: Francisco E. Erdey, 1918–1967.

Anuarios escolares, 1910–1911.

Arrom, Silvia M. *The Women of Mexico City. 1790–1857.* Stanford, Calif.: Stanford University Press, 1985.

Avila, Alonso. *Niño Jalapeño. Novela de la niñez mexicana.* Mexico: Costa-Amic, 1965.

Barclary, Lisa F. K. "The Comparative Efficacies of Spanish-English Instruction with Mexican-American Head Start Children." Ph.D. diss., Stanford University, 1969.

Bedolla Rivera, Dolores. "Proyecto de Código para Menores." Master's thesis. Mexico: UNAM, 1939.

Benítez, Raúl, and Julieta Quilondrán. *La fecundidad rural en Mexico.* Mexico: El Colegio de Mexico and UNAM, 1983.

Biblioteca del Niño Mexicano. Mexico: Mauxxi Hnos, 1899–1902.

Boletín de la Secretaría de Educación Pública. 1922–1931.

Boletín de la Junta Federal de Protección de la Infancia. Mexico: Secretaría de Educación Pública, 1925.

Brawner, Marilyn Ray. "Factors in the School Completion Rates of Mexican-American Children in Racine, Wisconsin." Ph.D. diss., University of Iowa, 1971.

Bravo Ugarte, José. *La educación en Mexico.* Mexico: Editorial Jus, 1966.

Browner, Carole H. "The Politics of Reproduction in a Mexican Village." *Signs: Journal of Women in Culture and Society* 11:4 (1986):710–724.

Calvo, Thomas. "The Warmth of the Hearth." In *Sexuality and Marriage in Colonial Latin America*, edited by Asunción Lavrin. Lincoln: University of Nebraska Press, 1989, pp. 287–312.

Carbón, Damián. *Libro de las comadres.* Mallozca: Bernardo de Canzolca, 1541.

Carreño, Gloria. *El colegio de Santa Rosa de Santa María de Valladolid, 1743–1810.* Morelia: Universidad de San Nicolás, 1979.

Castañeda, María del Carmen. *La educación en Guadalajara durante la colonia, 1552–1821*. Mexico: El Colegio de Mexico, 1984.

Castañeda, Carmen. "La memoria de las niñas violadas." *In Segundo Simposio de Historia de las Mentalidades: La memoria y el olvido*. Mexico: Instituto Nacional de Antropología e Historia, 1985, pp. 107–116.

Chapulín: la Revista del Niño Mexicano. 1942–1947.

Children and Youth in National Development in Latin America. Santiago de Chile: UNICEF, 1965.

Como enfrentar los problemas de aprendizaje en los niños. Mexico: La Prensa Médica Mexicana, n.d.

Congresos Panamericanos del Niño, 1916–1963. Ordenación sistemática de sus recomendaciones. Montevideo: Instituto Interamericano del Niño, 1965.

Constituciones del Colegio de San Ignacio de Loyola de Mexico. Mexico: Juan Antonio Lozano, 1753.

Córdoba, Martín de. *Jardín de nobles doncellas*. Colección Joyas Bibliográficas. Madrid, 1953.

Cuestionario de Don Antonio Bergoza y Jordán. Obispo de Antequera, a los señores curas de la diócesis (1802–1803). 2 vols. Oaxaca: Gobierno del Estado de Oaxaca, 1984.

Cuide a sus hijos. Mexico: Institute for Security and Services for State Employees (ISSTE), n.d.

Denevan, William M. ed. *The Native Population of the Americas in 1492*. Madison: University of Wisconsin Press, 1976.

Departamento de Educación Pública., Mérida. *Educación*. 1940–194?.

Dirección de Asistencia Materno-Infantil. *Bulletin*. 1960– .

Dirección General de Estadística Educativa. *Estadística educativa. El Correo de los Niños*. 1877–1880.

Elmendorf, Mary Lindsay. *Nine Maya Women: A Village Faces Change*. New York: Schenkman, 1976.

Elú de Leñero, María del Carmen. *¿Hacia donde va la mujer mexicana?* Mexico: Instituto Mexicano de Estudios Sociales, 1969.

Faulhaber, Johanna. *El crecimiento en un grupo de niños mexicanos*. Mexico: Instituto Nacional de Antropología e Historia, 1961.

Fernández de Lizardi, José Joaquín. *La Quijotita y su prima*. Mexico: Editorial Porrúa, 1967.

———. *El Periquillo Sarniento*. 2 vols. Madrid: Editorial Nacional, 1976.

Flores Villaseñor, Alicia. *Escuela "Casa Amiga No. 5."* Mexico: UNAM, 1962.

Foz y Foz, Pilar. *La revolución pedagógica en Nueva España: 1754–1820. María Ignacia Azlor y Echevers y los Colegios de la Enseñanza*. 2 vols. Madrid: Instituto Gonzalo Fernández de Oviedo, 1981.

Galindo y Villa, Jesús. *La educación de la mujer mexicana a través del siglo XIX*. Mexico: Imprenta del Gobierno Federal, 1901.

García Cisneros, Florencio, and Rafael Llerena. *Maternity in Pre-Columbian Art*. Salamanca: Gráficas Ortega, 1970.

García y García, Irma O. "Algunos factores asociados a la mortalidad infantil en Mexico." *Demografía y Economía* 17:3 (1983):289–320.

García Izcabalceta, Joaquín. *Informe sobre los establecimientos de beneficencia y corrección de esta capital*. Mexico, 1907.

García Icazbalceta, Joaquín. *El colegio de niñas de Mexico*. Mexico: Imprenta V. Agueros, 1896.

Gonzalbo Aizpuru, Pilar. "La casa de niños expósitos de la ciudad de Mexico: una fundación del siglo XVIII." *Historia Mexicana* 31:3 (January–March 1982):409–430.

———. *Las mujeres en la Nueva España. Educación y vida cotidiana*. Mexico: El Colegio de Mexico, 1987.

González Navarro, Moisés. *Población y sociedad en Mexico (1900–1970)*. Mexico: UNAM, 1974.

Griswold, Dianne Liles. "An Assessment of the Child-rearing Information Needs and Attitudes of Anglo, Black, and Mexican American Mothers." Ph.D. diss., Arizona State University, Tempe, 1975.

Guevara, Antonio de. *Reloj de príncipes y Libro de Marco Aurelio*. Madrid: Signo, 1936.

Herrick, Jane. "Periodicals for Women in Mexico During the Nineteenth Century." *The Americas* 14:2 (1957):135–144.

Historia sagrada para los niños. Mexico: Fernández Editores, 1986.

Iduarte, Andrés. *Niño: Child of the Mexican Revolution*. New York: Praeger, 1971.

Incidencia de la mortalidad infantil en los Estados Unidos Mexicanos, 1940–1975. Mexico: Secretaría de Programación y Presupuesto, 1981.

Indicators in the Situation of Children in Latin America and the Caribbean. Santiago de Chile: UNICEF, 1979.

Instituto Interamericano del Niño, *Resumen de actividades, 1965–1968*. Montevideo: Impresora Ligu, S.A., 1969.

Irma O. García y García. "Algunos factores asociados con la mortalidad infantil en Mexico." *Demografía y Economía* 7:3 (1983):289–320.

Johnston, Francis, et al. "An Analysis of Environmental Variables and Factors Associated with Growth Failure in a Mexican Village." *Human Biology* 54:4 (December 1980):627–637.

Kobayashi, José María. *La educación como conquista*. Mexico: El Colegio de Mexico, 1974.

Lafaye, Jacques. "Une lettre inédite du XVI è siècle relative aux Colleges des Indiens de la Compagnie de Jésus en Nouvelle Espagne," *Etudes Latino-Americains* (Aix-en Provence) 2 (1964):512.

Laguarta, Pablo Lorenzo. *Historia de la beneficencia española en Mexico*. Mexico, 1955.

Leñero Otero, Luis. *Valores ideológicos y las políticas de población en Mexico*. Mexico: Editorial Edicol, 1979.

Los códigos españoles. Concordados y anotados. 12 vols. Madrid: Imprenta de M. Rivadeneira, 1874–1951.

Loza Saldívar, Arnoldo de la. "Evaluación de los programas de salud para la niñez en Mexico." *Salud Pública de Mexico* 22:6 (November–December 1980):631–654.

Luque Alcaide, Elisa. *La educación en Nueva España en el Siglo XVIII*. Sevilla: Consejo Superior de Investigaciones Científicas, 1970.

Malvido, Elsa. "El abandono de los hijos: Una forma de control del tamaño de la familia y del trabajo indígena. Tula (1683–1730)." *Historia Mexicana* 24:4 (April–June 1980):521–561.

Manual para el fortalecimiento de la educación indígena bilingue-bicultural. Mexico: Secretaría de Educación Pública, 1987.

Martínez Jiménez, Alejandro. "La educación elemental en el porfiriato." *Historia Mexicana* 22:4 (April–June 1974):514–552.

Memorias del Segundo Congreso Mexicano del Niño. Mexico: Secretaría de Educación Pública, 1925.

Memorias de la Junta Directiva de la Beneficencia Pública en el Distrito Federal. Mexico, 1934.

Mendelson, Johanna S. R. "The Feminine Press: The View of Women in the Colonial Journals of Spanish America, 1790–1810." In *Latin American Women: Historical Perspectives*, edited by Asunción Lavrin. Westport, Conn.: Greenwood Press, 1978, pp. 198–218.

Meneses, Ernesto. *Tendencias educativas oficiales en Mexico, 1821–1911. La problemática de la educación mexicana en el siglo XIX y principios del siglo XX.* 2 vols. Vol. 1 Mexico: Editorial Porrúa, 1983; Vol. 2 Mexico: Centro de estudios Educativos, 1986.

Molina, Robert M., and J. H. Himes, "Patterns of Childhood Mortality and Growth Status in a Rural Zapotec Community." *Annals of Human Biology* 5:6 (November 1978):517–531.

Montaño Sánchez, Maria Antonieta. *Creación de un Instituto Nacional de Protección Integral del Menor.* Mexico: n.p., 1964.

Motolinía, Toribio de. *Historia de los indios de Nueva España.* Mexico: Chávez Hayhoe, 1941. Translated into English by Elizabeth A. Foster as *History of the Indians of New Spain.* Berkeley: The Cortés Society, 1950.

Muriel, Josefina. *Hospitales de la Nueva España.* 2 vols. Mexico: Editorial Jus, 1955.

———. *Las indias caciques de Corpus Christi.* Mexico: UNAM, 1963.

———. "La protección del niño en Nueva España." In *Coloquios.* Reunión Hispano-Mexicana de Historia. Santa María de la Rábida, Huelga, 1980.

Núñez de Miranda, Antonio. *Cartilla de la doctrina religiosa por uno de la Compañia de Jesús para dos niñas, hijas espirituales suyas, que se crían para monjas y desean serlos con toda perfección.* Mexico: Imprenta de Juan José Guillena Carrascoso, 1696.

O'Gorman, Edmundo. "La enseñanza primaria en la Nueva España." *Boletín del Archivo General de la Nación* 11:2 (April–June 1940):247–302.

Obregón, Gonzalo. *El Real Colegio de San Ignacio de Mexico (Las Vizcaínas).* Mexico: El Colegio de Mexico, 1949.

Olavarría y Ferrari, Enrique de. *El Real Colegio de San Ignacio de Loyola, vulgarmente conocido "de las Vizcaínas," en la actualidad Colegio de la Paz.* Mexico: Imprenta de F. Díaz de León, 1889.

Parra Muñoz, Jesús. *El hijo del campesino y la legislación agraria.* Mexico: UNAM, 1957.

Pena y Galindo, Mercedes. "Protección del menor en Mexico." Master's thesis. Mexico: UNAM, 1935.

Peza, Juan de Dios. *La beneficencia en Mexico.* Mexico: Imprenta de Francisco Díaz de León, 1881.

Plan de estudios y programa de educación pre-escolar indígena. Mexico: Secretaría de Educación Pública, 1987.

Reglamento para la Compañia Lancasteriana de Mexico. Mexico: Imprenta de Vicente García Torres, 1869.

Revista Mexicana de Puericultura. 1930–1941.

Revista Jaliscience de Educación. Guadalajara: Departamento Cultura del Estado de Jalisco, 195–.

Robles Gil, A. *Album commemorativo de la inauguración del Hospicio de Niños*. Mexico, 1905.

Rodríguez Sala, Maria Luisa. *Instituciones de protección a la infancia en el distrito federal*. Mexico: Instituto de Investigaciones Sociales, 1956.

Rohner, Ronald P., et al. "Perceived Parental Acceptance-Rejection and Personality Organization Among Mexican and American Elementary School Children." *Behavioral Science Research, Journal of Comparative Studies* 15:1 (1980):23–39.

Rosales, Jerónimo de. *Catón christiano y catecismo de la doctrina christiana para la educación y buena crianza de los niños y muy provechoso para personas de todos estados*. Mexico: Imprenta Nueva de la Biblioteca Mexicana, 1761.

Ruiz Martínez, Cristina. "La memoria sobre la niñez y el estereotipo del niño santo." In *Segundo Simposio de Historia de la Mentalidades: La memoria y el olvido*. Mexico: Instituto Nacional de Antropología e Historia, 1985, pp. 117–124.

Sahagún, Bernardino de. *Historia de las cosas de Nueva España*. 3 vols. Mexico: Editorial Porrúa, 1956.

Sánchez de la Barquera, Juan Wenceslao. *Semanario Económico de Mexico*, November–December 1810.

Secretaría de Educación Pública. *La escuela y la guerra. Deberes que se imponen para el maestro, la maestra, el niño y la niña en la escuela, en el hogar, en el taller, en la ciudad y en el campo*. Mexico: Cuadernos del Niño, 1942.

———. *Memoria*. 1924–.

———. *Noticia estadística sobre la educación pública de Mexico*, 1925–1928.

———. *Folletín Estadístico*.

———. *Anuario de estadística educativa*. 1947–.

———. *La educación pública en Mexico, 1964–1970*. Mexico: Secretaría de Educación Pública, 1970.

Secretaría de Instrucción Pública y Bellas Artes. *Boletín de Instrucción pública*. 1903–1913.

Segovia, Rafael. *La politización del niño mexicano*. Mexico: El Colegio de Mexico, 1975.

Semillita: Para la educadora y el niño. 1944–19??.

Siempre niños. Sus imágenes en la historia de Mexico. Mexico: Secretaría de Educación Pública, 1985.

Sociedad Mexicana de Pedagogía, *Revista Mexicana de Educación*. 1940–.

Solana, Fernando, et al. *Historia de la educación en Mexico*. Mexico: Secretaría de Educación Pública, 1981.

Soler Astorga, Guadalupe. "Necesidad de una legislación especial de protección a la infancia." Master's thesis. Mexico: UNAM, 1949.

Solórzano, Alfonso. *Estudio de mil casos de niños dedicados al comercio ambulante y los servicios en la ciudad de Mexico*. Mexico: Secretaría del Trabajo y Previsión Social, 1979.

Staples, Ann. "El catecismo como libro de texto." Paper presented at the Sixth Conference of Mexican and United States Historians, Chicago, September 1981.

Steelman, Albert Judson. *Charities for Children in the City of Mexico*. Chicago: E. M. Steelman, 1907.

Sullivan, Thelma D., trans. "Pregnancy, Childbirth, and the Deification of the Women

Who Died in Childbirth.'' In *Estudios de Cultura Nahuatl*. Mexico: Universidad Nacional Autónoma de Mexico, 1966, pp. 63–96.

Tanck de Estrada, Dorothy. ''Las escuelas lancasterianas en la ciudad de Mexico: 1822–1842.'' *Historia Mexicana* 22:4 (April–June 1973):494–513.

———. *La educación ilustrada, 1786–1836*. Mexico: El Colegio de Mexico, 1977.

Torre Villar, Ernesto de la. ''Notas para una historia de la instrucción pública en Puebla de los Angeles.'' *Estudios Americanos*. 1952–1953.

Torroella, Julio Manuel. *Pediatría para padres responsables*. Mexico: Editorial Patria, 198?

Turner, Frederick C. *Responsible Parenthood: The Politics of Mexico's New Population Policies*. Washington, D.C.: American Enterprise Institute for Policy Research, 1974.

UNICEF. *Boletín Informativo de la Oficina Regional para America Latina*. United Nations Children's Fund, Regional Office for the Americas, *Situación de la infancia en America Latina y el Caribe*. Santiago de Chile: UNICEF-Editorial Universitaria, 1979.

Universidad Pedagógica Nacional, *Pedagogía*. 1984–.

Vaughan, Mary Kay. ''Women, Class and Education in Mexico, 1880–1928.'' *Latin American Perspectives* 4:1–2 (1977):135–152.

———. *The State, Education, and Social Class in Mexico, 1880–1920*. Dekalb: Northern Illinois University Press, 1982.

———. ''Primary Schooling in the City of Puebla, 1821–1860.'' *The Hispanic American Historical Review* 67:1 (February 1987):39–62.

Vázquez, Josefina. *Nacionalismo y educación en Mexico*. Mexico: El Colegio de Mexico, 1975.

Velasco Ceballos, Rómulo. *El niño mexicano ante la caridad y el estado*. Mexico: Beneficencia Publica en el D.F., 1935.

———. *Fichas bibliográficas sobre Asistencia en Mexico*. Mexico, 1943.

Velázquez Andrade, Manuel. *Fermin: un libro para niños mexicanos*. Mexico: Primera Editora, 1986.

Vivas Romero, David. *El niño proletario. Libro de lectura para el segundo año de educación primaria*. Mexico: Pluma y Lápiz, 1942.

Vives, Juan Luis. *Instrucción de la mujer cristiana*. Buenos Aires: Espasa–Calpe, 1940.

17

MUSLIM MIDDLE EAST

Elizabeth Fernea

The recent interest in social history has resulted in a new appreciation for the processes by which cultures create their own social constructs of reality. Childhood is one such construct, and in the Middle East it is fair to say that after centuries of relative stability, the construct has been transformed in this century, and continues to change ever more rapidly.

The idea of childhood, the place of the child, the duties of the child: these are basic and important issues in the Middle East and have been since recorded history in the area, about 3000 B.C. They continue to be important issues today, but the context within which children are born and reared has changed. To understand how this has happened, we must look first at the cultural ideal of the place of the child, as expressed by people who live in the area, by religious leaders, and by ethnographers and sociologists who are both inside and outside the culture. The cultural ideal, we shall see, is expressed through images derived from scholarly work and ethnographic observation at different periods of history, images that are necessarily partial and fragmented. The cultural ideal in the past varied according to class and religious affiliation, as well as geographical area and rural or urban residence. Still, some common elements cut across those lines, and it is on these common elements that the first part of the chapter focuses.

The second part of the chapter concerns the rapid change that began at the end of the eighteenth century, with the European colonial invasion, and continued at a rapid pace through the first half of the twentieth century. My husband and I first began to do research in the area in 1956. By the summer of 1988, when I returned on a three-month Fulbright study grant, changes were apparent in all aspects of society, including the realm of childhood and socialization. Children under the age of fifteen today constitute more than 40 percent of the population in the majority of the countries of the Middle East. The needs of this burgeoning segment of the population can no longer be met by their families alone, as was the case in the past. Rather, the nation states have assumed an unprecedented role in taking care of children, a burden that poorer countries find hard to bear. But it is not merely an economic issue. As Dr. Mohammed Shoufani, of the ministry of education office in Marrakech, Morocco, stated in an interview during June 1988:

Children are the most important and the most complicated people in our society today, pulled as they are between two worlds, that of their illiterate, unambitious, resigned parents and that of their "modern" educated, highly aspiring peers. At a time when old absolutes are crumbling and old values are disregarded, what are young people to do? They are endangered because they are, in terms of value at least, at sea. And the government is left with the responsibility of making this new life more meaningful.

It is to this new, complex, contemporary generation of young people that the final third of the chapter is addressed.

It is worth noting here that childhood and family patterns of the Middle East are, in many ways, similar across religious and ethnic lines. But some significant differences also obtain: the ban on divorce in Christian groups, in contrast to Jewish and Muslim groups, means that the world of the child, as well as that of the adult, is not the same. In this chapter I have chosen to focus on childhood in the Muslim context, since 90 percent of the area's population is Muslim. The economic and political changes now in progress have affected and continue to affect all people in the area.

THE CULTURAL IDEAL

In the Middle East the child is seen as the crucial generational link in the family unit, the key to its continuation, the living person that ties the present to the past and to the future. Parents in the area seem to have had, until recently, few doubts about child-rearing practices, or about the goals of parents, children, and the family unit. In the United States the received wisdom about child-rearing practices in the twentieth century has varied widely between permissive and restrictive norms and has been promulgated by "experts" outside the family home. In contrast, child rearing and the concept of childhood in the Middle East were, until recently, based on widely accepted assumptions about the structure of society and the functions of people of all ages within that society.

In the predominantly agrarian societies of the past the primary social unit in the Middle East was the extended family, which might range in size from 20 to 200 persons, related on both sides of the marital connection. Within this kin group each child received identity, affection, discipline, role models, and economic and social support, ideally from birth to death; in exchange the family required conformity and loyalty from all members, beginning in early childhood.[1] The crucial test of allegiance came at the time of marriage, when the man or woman either acceded to or rebelled against the wishes of the family in preparing to extend the family unit into another generation. For marriage in the system was not "officially" perceived as an emotional attachment between individuals (although this might develop later), but as an economic and social contract between two family groups, a contract that was to benefit both.[2] Although marriage was a crucial step in tying individual members to the group, it was the birth of children that conferred full adult status on both the man and the woman. Only after the birth of children were the newly married man and woman considered full members of their particular family unit and adult members of the wider society.

Such attitudes toward marriage and children are found among Jewish and Christian groups, but within Islam they are intensified. "When a man has children he has fulfilled half of his religion, so let him fear God for the remaining half," states one of the hadith, or sayings of the prophet Muhammad.[3] Children, then, have always been valued in Middle Eastern traditions, not only for economic and political but also for religious reasons.

The Judaic, Christian, and Muslim family systems are patrilineal; that is, the reckoning of one's descent, and of kin group membership passes to one through the male line on the father's side. A girl is a member of her father's family, but unlike her brother, she cannot pass that membership on to her children. In the Islamic tradition male and female descendants of the same father inherit from him, and continue to carry his name throughout their lives. A daughter never takes her husband's surname, for example, but retains, like a son, the name of the father. If divorce or the death of a spouse should occur, both men and women have the customary right to return to their father's household, where, theory and practice hold, they may expect themselves to be cared for; a woman should always enjoy the protection of a husband or male relative, according to the traditional Islamic view.[4]

The patrilineal system is hierarchically organized with the oldest male ideally holding publicly accepted authority over his descendants. The oldest male, whether father or son, is the primary economic provider for the group, and the head of that group and controller of its economic resources, including the labor of its members, as long as he lives, a situation attested to with bitterness or affection by both men and women, depending on personal experience.[5] Without issue, and particularly male issue, the kin group as traditionally constituted clearly cannot continue. Hence great pressure is placed on newly married couples to produce sons, who can carry the name and take over the burdens of work for the family. Daughters also are important, to help mothers and grandmothers and as potential brides for men within the kin group, but sons are of primary importance. Marriage between paternal cousins or other more distant kinsmen has long been viewed with favor among Arab peoples, but such marriages are far from being the general rule today. A man has custody of his children, since they are of his patrilineage. Thus a man who divorces or who is widowed will take his children to his natal home, where his female relatives will care for them. This varies in practice, depending on class, economic circumstances, and personal affection. Sometimes families may be too poor to support a divorced daughter or their son and his children; other, wealthy families of a divorced wife, on the other hand, will negotiate with the husband to obtain partial custody of the children.

This patrilineal system has existed in broad outline in the Near East for at least 5,000 years, having come into existence with the development of agriculture and the forms of property ownership and labor that such a source of subsistence favors.[6] It was in the seventh century A.D. that Islam altered the system somewhat, first, by giving women legal status as people, rather than as property; second, by banning infanticide, or the exposure of unwanted children, and especially female children; and third, by prescribing that the father's inheritance should be shared by both sons and daughters; according to Islamic law, daughters were to receive half a brother's share.[7] Although the child does not have the same legal rights as an adult under Islamic law, he or she theoretically can inherit from both mother and father. Specific instructions about the care of the child, sometimes expanding on tenets expressed in Judaism and Christianity, are found in the hadith, such as "Cherish your children. Treat children with a view to inculcate self-respect in them. Verily a man teaching his child manners is better for him than giving one bushel of grain in alms."[8] During the Islamic medieval period from A.D. 900 to 1200, several treatises were written on the method of raising a child.[9]

Little of this material from the Middle East found its way into the West until the recent interest in childhood as an historical construct led to research on the subject. Long-held animosity toward Islam as a Christian heresy contributed to the lack of Western interest in Muslim child rearing and socialization and other aspects of Muslim life. Only after World War II did Western social scientists begin to work on this subject in the Middle East.

The small body of literature available in English on the socialization of children in the area varies in emphasis and in scope of research. Hilma Granqvist lived in the house of a European missionary in Artas, a small Palestinian village; Terry Prothro conducted a longitudinal survey of child-rearing practices in several Lebanese towns; Hamed Ammar undertook in-depth research into coming of age in Silwa, an Upper Egyptian village where he himself had grown up. Judith Williams did an ethnographic study of the Lebanese mountain community of Haouch El-Hakim. Susan Dorsky, in *Women of Amran*, adds some further recent details from Yemen.[10]

From these works some general patterns emerge, which are confirmed by our own ethnographic observations in Iraq (1956–1958), Egypt (1959–1965), and Morocco (1971–1972, 1976). Early indulgence of babies and demand breast-feeding are widely shared throughout the region plus a great deal of affectionate behavior toward the baby, primarily from the mother, but also from the father, older siblings, and other relatives. The Qu'ran endorses this.[11] In Morocco a baby is carried in a sling on its mother's back; in Egypt toddlers in the countryside ride astride their mothers' shoulders. Physical closeness and indulgence are combined with early toilet-training, before the age of one year; either long-term breast-feeding or abrupt weaning may occur, depending on when the next child is born into the family. The arrival of a new sibling usually signals the end of the period of indulgence for the older child.

Banishment from the mother's breast also means the beginning of socialization into specific gender roles and cultural values and the division of a child's labor according to sex and age. The prophet Muhammed is reported to have said, "Be gentle to your children the first seven years and in the following seven be firm,"[12] but in practice, discipline (*adab*) began long before the age of seven. Girls as young as four or five were expected to share responsibility for a younger sibling; young boys at the same age also would be given responsibilities. In rural areas this might mean caring for animals; in urban areas the boy would be asked to run errands or help in a family business. Such expectations are still common.

Socialization for other important societal norms of behavior began almost as soon as a child was conscious of others. These included respect for food, religion, and the kin group, hospitality to guests, and, above all, respect for and obedience to the authority of the father. Hospitality to guests was expressed by young children in many ways, such as politely greeting visitors to the house and learning to wait patiently while guests ate first.[13] The young child was taught the names and relationships of members of his or her kin group, and most preschoolers could recite their genealogies on both sides, going back five or more generations.[14] Religion involved a respect for food as well as learning to pray and understand religious duties as Muslims. Boys ordinarily were not taken to the mosque for Friday prayers until the age of puberty; girls seldom went to the mosque, nor do they commonly go there today. Children are not required to fast during the holy month of Ramadan, but some chose to do so, for a few days at least, in imitation of their parents. According to Hamed Ammar, a good child was one who is *mu'addab(a)* (i.e., polite, and disciplined in and conforming to the values of the group). A child was said to be without *agl*, or reason, and the goal of child rearing was to instill and develop the reason that is seen to be necessary for successful adult life in the society. Punishment included spanking or beating, as well as teasing and shaming before peers and before other members of the family.[15] The type of punishment varied from group to group. Some parents argued that corporal punishment was not condoned by the Koran; but most were in full accord with the "spare the rod and spoil the child" approach favored in some Western times and places.

Ritual events in the life of the child also played a part in socialization. Primary among these were ceremonies that surrounded birth and naming; circumcision, for all boys and for some girls; graduation from Koranic school, particularly for boys; and marriage.

Naming ceremonies are remarkably similar across a large part of the area.

Granqvist does not record a formal naming ceremony for the child in Artas, the village in Palestine where she worked, but other Palestinian informants testify to the presence of such a ceremony; Westermarck notes it in Morocco, both among the Berber tribes of the mountains and among the Arabs of the towns.[16] Like the Egyptian ceremony described by Ammar, and more recently by El Guindi, it is called *sebua*, from the Arabic word for the seventh day after birth, and is marked by sacrifice of an ox or a sheep and the gathering of the kin group for a feast.[17] Naming ceremonies are not found in Turkey, however, perhaps reflecting the different historical origins of the Turkish people. Between the ages of three and six all Muslim boys were circumcised. This was an important event in a boy's life, with religious ramifications, as in Judaism and Christianity, although it is not specifically required in the Qu'ran. Circumcision marked the change from babyhood to boyhood, the public noting of the acceptance of male identity, and was accompanied, like the naming ceremony, by feasting, sacrifice, and a family gathering. E. W. Lane notes the elaborate circumcision ceremony for a rich Egyptian merchant's son in the mid-nineteenth century, when the child, wearing white, was paraded through the streets of the neighborhood on a white horse.[18]

The circumcision of girls (clitorodectomy) was not universal and has no religious justification; the Koran does not mention it. According to Ammar, "the circumcision of girls has never had the universality of that of the boys; the religious authority behind it is very weak and could be rejected, and even its practice is not universal throughout the Moslem world at present." The practice occurs mainly along the Nile, among Christian and Muslim groups from Egypt to Somalia and Kenya, but not in North Africa, or Turkey and only incidentally in other parts of the Muslim world. When practiced, the ritual is attended only by female relatives, but was perceived as acceptance by the girl of *her* female identity, and as a necessary preparation for marriage.[19] Girls in North Africa had a different rite of passage, an ear-piercing ceremony, held when the child was four or five years old. Women family members gathered to feast and celebrate the child's assumption of female identity. This was made symbolically clear by the white veil the child wore, like a bridal veil, and the gifts of gold, similar to those given the bride by the female members of her family.[20]

Religious socialization took place not only in the home (for boys and girls) and in the mosque (for boys), but also in the Koranic school, or *kuttab*. A knowledge of the Koran was deemed necessary for a child's religious development, just as knowledge of the Bible and the Torah was deemed necessary for a Christian or Jewish child. Most parents, even the poorest, tried to send their sons, and sometimes their daughters, to a kuttab for some period of time. Successful completion of the course of study at the kuttab, involving memorization of the entire Koran, was an occasion for family gathering and celebration, which also might include the city neighborhood or, in rural areas, the entire village.[21] Boys traditionally spent more time in Koranic schools than girls, but there were exceptions. Rich parents often hired Koranic tutors for their daughters at home. Daughters of poor families had a more difficult time.[22]

Socialization of the child took place primarily within the home, and the father and mother were ultimately responsible for their offspring. Grandparents, aunts, uncles, and cousins also were expected to participate in a child's rearing and usually did so by acting as disciplinarians if parents were seen to be neglecting the child's progress toward becoming *mu'addab(a)* or by acting as affectionate, supportive figures if parents were seen as being too harsh. This participation varied according to class. In the homes of the elite, servants and nannies, often poor relatives, helped to socialize the children. In both rural and urban areas neighbors became involved in the child's socialization, as did the Koranic school-teachers. Thus many adults were participants in the discipline and development of the child, reinforcing one another and providing alternate role models and sources of support for the child as it grew to maturity.

In this idealized picture outlined above there is little evidence of the idea of "carefree childhood" or indeed of childhood as an important stage in itself. According to Ammar, "in adult eyes, the period of childhood is a nuisance. . . . The process of growing up is envisaged as a way of disciplining the child to conform to the adults' standards."[23] This does not mean that children did not play, but that play was child's business; for adults the emphasis was on the serious business of preparing children for their roles in the world of adulthood. In this system, then, "childhood" was not seen as a specific, bounded time period, and adolescence, as perceived in Western modern thought, scarcely existed. One moved from babyhood through childhood to puberty, and adulthood. Adult privileges and social status were assumed with marriage and childbearing, but adult economic responsibilities might begin at any age past infancy, an attitude not very different from that depicted by Charles Dickens in the novels of Victorian England.

Marriage, which took place after puberty, marked the end of childhood and the assumption of adult responsibility for the beginning of another family group, with its own children to socialize. Marriage was the significant moment when family honor was tested, a concept that might be defined as the reputation of the group for morality, courage, religiosity, and hospitality.

Honor was defined differently for boys and girls: a boy's honor, *sharaf*, concerned all the issues above, as did that of the girl, but for the girl, honor had a further, crucial meaning. A girl's honor, or *'ard*, is defined as her chastity before marriage and her sexual fidelity after marriage. A man's honor, once lost, can be regained. A woman's honor, once lost, can never be regained. The woman, therefore, had a greater burden of honor to protect, and was said to carry the honor of the group with her. Any breath of gossip impugning a girl's sexual behavior was cause for her to be severely punished and could result in her death. No such restriction was placed on boys. For a girl the intention to protect her honor was stated by modest behavior and by wearing modest dress.

Carried to its extreme in some contexts, it meant the wearing of the veil by girls after the age of puberty and seclusion of women after marriage.

The concept of honor is found in societies around the Mediterranean basin, including Greece, Spain, and Italy, as well as in nomadic Arab societies far from the Mediterranean. So-called honor and shame societies stress the responsibility and the reputation of the group, and the maintenance of a public image, free from dishonor. The moment of testing "honor" came at the climax of the marriage ceremony, the consummation. A man's honor and that of his family required him to be virile enough to consummate the marriage; a woman's honor and that of her family required that she be a virgin at marriage. To provide evidence of that virginity a blood-stained sheet, which family members traditionally publicly displayed, was offered as tangible proof that the groom's honor and the bride's honor were intact. Children were present at weddings from their earliest years, so these tests of honor were made clear through observation and example and through admonition and discussion of honor by parents, grandparents, siblings, and cousins. "Honorable," as opposed to "shameful," behavior was one of the strongest values for which male and particularly female children were socialized. Parental admonitions categorized much of children's behavior as either honorable (good) or dishonorable (bad).[24]

An Islamic family implied the possibility of polygyny, as the prophet Muhammed states that a man was allowed to take up to four legal wives, provided he could provide for them equally. In practice, the number of polygynous households was small, but the possibility that the father might take another wife was always present. Little evidence exists of the effects of polygyny on children, but occasional memoirs indicate that it was not always an easy lot.[25] Much depended on the stress or lack of stress on the issue in individual households, a matter of great variation.

In sum, the cultural ideal in the past contained several elements: the primacy of the group over its individual members; the importance of children, especially sons, to continue and maintain the group; the values of honor, morality, religiosity, generosity, hospitality, respect for parents, especially the father, and responsibility for their care in old age; strong masculine and feminine identity and the primacy of male over female in terms of authority; the division of labor by sex and age; and the idea of *adab* to develop a child who was *mu'addab(a)*, who would become an adult who was honorable and conformed to the norms of the group. The group was hierarchical, with adult males at the top. Religious ideology reinforced this ideal. This cultural construct was ideologically based on traditional idealism and religious dogma as well as on recognition of the pragmatic "fit" of this set of expectations and ideals to the economic, political, and social conditions of the preindustrial urban and rural areas of the Middle East. The social system it reflects was not based on equality and was not always just, but it fulfilled the needs of the people within the region for many centuries. The family unit remained the basic unit of support and control during the centuries that the Middle East was a loose confederation of large and small groups—

families, clans, tribes, religious and ethnic communities—within territories and empires. This began to change at the end of the eighteenth century with the invasion of the area by Western European colonial powers, followed by independence and the development of modern nation states.

HISTORICAL CHANGE: COLONIALISM AND AFTER

Napoleon invaded Egypt in 1798, a date that marks the beginning of the colonial period in the Middle East. For 150 years, until the end of the Algerian revolution in 1962, Western Europeans ruled the Middle East, bringing new ideas and technology, but also disrupting existing economic systems and attempting to change social patterns. Much recent literature deals with the political and economic effects of the colonial incursion,[26] but less has been written about the effects of Western European rule on people's daily lives.[27] By its very nature Western rule meant a devaluation of all aspects of the traditional society: language, technology, arts, religion (Islam was called the "stagnant hand of the past"), and family structure. Rule by powerful foreigners who were non-Muslims led to self-doubt and some reevaluation at the intellectual level of Middle Eastern society.[28] These included works on improving the position of women.[29] Although such works may have influenced some members of the society's elite to reconsider family patterns, few such doubts seem to have touched the rest of the society, if the ethnographic studies cited above are any indication. Further, although the colonial rulers took over the legal system as it affected criminal and commercial enterprises, religious affairs and family law usually were left to the local populations. Indeed, as the colonial presence became more pervasive and intrusive, the family (and thus the rearing of children) became the last relatively independent refuge of Middle East people under colonial rule. Fathers, denied a political role in public affairs, turned to the family to reassert their authority. (This was true not only in the Middle East, but also in other parts of the world affected by European colonialism and imperialism.)[30] Therefore, one could argue that although the Western European presence may have influenced a few people to change or at least reconsider long-held norms, in general colonialism intensified traditional family patterns, particularly those involving the differentials of gender identity and the protection of women, and the preservation of family honor. (For example, the all-enveloping *djellaba* with hood and half face veil was not worn in Morocco until after the French invasion in 1912. The djellaba first appears in illustrated books about 1914.)[31]

As opposition to the colonial presence grew and movements for self-determination gained momentum, the family became a center of resistance. Because the family was seen as the base of society, the survival of the society depended on the survival of the family group. In the independence movement across the area, from Morocco to Sudan, all members of the family group participated, children as well as parents, men as well as women.[32]

At the same time the family was being touted as the center of the society, some groups within that society argued for a need to "modernize" the family, to change family law so that men and women were more equal, and that children, too, might have legal rights. This meant that when independence came, the family's future was visualized in contradictory terms. When the new independent governments took power between 1948 and 1962 their manifestos included promises of free public education, land reform, political reform, industrialization, revival of devalued language, culture and arts, and reform of family law. The family would continue to be the basis on which the new independent states would be constructed, but what kind of family? One that conformed to the ideas of the past, or one that took from both Western and Eastern traditions?[33] This is the context within which today's children in the Middle East must be viewed.

THE PRESENT: CHANGES IN PRACTICES, SHIFTING IDEALS

The children now coming of age are the first generation to be born and grow up since independence from colonial rule, and therefore the first generation to perceive themselves as citizens of nation states, rather than primarily as members of tribes, or lineages. This is the first generation to take for granted and expect free secular education; the first to grow up with raised expectations for the future; the first to grow up with television and its implication for the widespread representation of other cultures, values, and consumer products; the first to grow up in a vastly changed class system, as the old aristocracy has declined and a middle class slowly emerges; and the first to grow up under economic conditions very different from those of their parents.

The Middle East is no longer an isolated segment of a larger empire, or a colonial possession, but a group of nation states within the larger interdependent world economic system. Nearly half the population is under fifteen years of age. It is no longer predominantly rural and agricultural, as it was only thirty years ago. More than half the people in the area now live in cities and earn their living in service and industrial jobs. Cash-cropping has replaced subsistence agriculture, and the area is marked by new mobility and different levels of unemployment and inflation. At the same time, development of oil resources in the Gulf and the construction of industries in almost every country have resulted in the creation of new jobs, although not all in the country or area of traditional residence. Thus the new phenomenon of international labor migration on a large scale has emerged, labor migration from the Arab world to Europe and the United States and between countries within the Arab world itself. Turkish workers are in Europe, as are Moroccans, Algerians, and Tunisians. Egyptian and Yemeni workers are in Saudi Arabia, Iraq, Libya, and Kuwait. So older residence patterns of family units have been broken.[34]

The high cost of living has meant that women as well as men must go outside the home to work if the family is to survive. Upper-middle-class and middle-class women seek professional opportunities,[35] but the majority are poor women who work out of necessity.[36] The entry of women into the paid labor force outside the home is one of the most profound changes in the area, with clear effects on child rearing and on children. Class differences affect this process. Rich families can still afford servants, and in oil-wealthy countries children are being raised by imported nannies and governesses, but for the new middle class, servants are as rare as in the past. Poor families may pool local kin or neighbors to care for younger children, but many are left alone and the demand for government-sponsored child-care centers is growing. Some centers are already present in Libya, Egypt, and Morocco, for example, but not enough to meet the need. Persistent conflict in Iraq, Iran, Lebanon, and the West Bank also has disrupted residence and family units.[37]

Accordingly, the sites of socialization of the child are shifting, as are the agents of socialization. The larger family unit is shrinking as it becomes spatially dispersed between city and village and within growing urban centers, so more socialization takes place within the nuclear family than among other kin. Labor migration, the subsequent absence of fathers, and mothers working outside the home have created millions of new kinds of households. Women-headed households are viewed as temporary arrangements, but fathers may be away for years. The child also is still socialized within a neighborhood, but the neighborhood has changed. Families, both rich and poor, moving from country to city, find themselves among strangers, whether in upper-middle-class villas and apartment houses or in the squatter settlements of major cities like Cairo, Casablanca, Tunis, Damascus, Baghdad, and Istanbul. Although the Koranic school remains a place of socialization and currently is experiencing a resurgence, as we shall see, it has been eclipsed in overall importance by the secular schools that have opened since the 1950s.[38]

New sites of socialization include the work force and the media. Child labor is said to have declined across the area, but many teenagers have gone to work in factories and shops, and among very poor families children's labor is still needed for survival. Because many of the new public schools are so overcrowded that they operate on two shifts, children may attend school for half a day and work the other half, contributing their wages to the family income. Reliable statistics on such labor are hard to find, but partial work, especially within the family unit, is seldom counted in official surveys, nor is women's piecework or informal income-generating work done in the home by both women and children. The presence of children and teenagers in the work force outside the home may mean the establishment of new social ties and new role models, yet the child's income goes back to the family head, and therefore tends to reinforce the power of adults over their children's lives.[39]

The media and the secular school seem far more challenging to traditional behavior. The school in particular represents the possibility of social mobility. Education has always been given high value in the Arab world, and the Koran states, "Educate your children for tomorrow." The implications of the secular school as a force for change may be measured by the strong early opposition to women's education in conservative countries like Saudi Arabia. Today all nations in the area devote a major part of their budget and energy to education of both men and women: Morocco's educational budget in 1988 was a *third* of its national income;[40] Saudi Arabia, after a slow start, is spending millions on education, although women are still educated separately from men.[41] In the secular school the child meets children from outside the family unit and the neighborhood, and also during long periods of its early life is exposed to both male and female teachers, role models with different values and aspirations from its parents. Further, as education extends childhood past puberty and marriage takes place later, adolescence is emerging as a recognized period in the life cycle.[42]

The media has begun to play a far greater role in everyday life. Book publishing has expanded, the publishing of literature written expressly for children is a new and thriving industry, and the Cairo annual book fair is one of the largest in the world. New magazines, including special magazines for children, appear in many countries. *Al-Sageer*, published in Kuwait, is sent throughout the world. Editors report that they receive 100 letters a day from children.[43] Every country has at least one government-owned television corporation. Turkey is about to launch a third channel, and latest statistics indicate that 70 percent of all Egyptian families have television in their homes. Although the government controls programming, viewers are still treated to a variety of programs from overseas (American programs like *Dallas*, *Dynasty*, and *Roots* and the Monte Carlo show from France) as well as news from around the world, locally produced soap operas, cultural revivals, religious sermons, public service announcements about such topics as family planning and health care, and tutoring sessions in mathematics and Arabic for children in primary classes.

Commercials for consumer products are beginning to appear on television in Egypt and Turkey, and children in the Middle East, like children in America, are now being urged to desire a far greater range of material possessions than their parents, and are developing aspirations that often are hard to fulfill under present-day economic circumstances. The new sites for socialization and the new agents of socialization mean that children's lives are changing and that some tensions between parents and grandparents' values and desires and those expressed by the children are appearing. Egyptian psychologists and sociologists are beginning to write about the loss of values, the rise of materialism, and the "fraying" of the family system, the basic unit of this 5,000-year-old society.[44] Not only has the kin group stretched, or diminished, but also the foundation of the unit, the authority of the father, is being challenged and threatened.

The current challenge to the authority of the father is noted by many scholars, but it is seen as beginning much earlier, with the erosion of men's public authority under colonial rule. As the economic base has changed and the cost of living has skyrocketed, men can no longer fulfill their traditional responsibilities of supporting and controlling a large group of family and kin or even their immediate families. Labor migration has further diminished that authority, as fathers have been absent from their families for long periods of time. The total number of migrant workers, men and women, is unknown, but it is estimated that by 1979, 3 million men from Egypt alone were working abroad.[45] These men, the well-trained artisans of their nation, tended to be in their twenties and thirties, at the peak of their abilities. They also were fathers of young children, and therefore not present in the family during an important formative period in their children's lives. Research in Turkey indicated that in such situations, "the boy does not get either positive or negative reinforcement from the father."[46] Egyptian researchers record hostility toward absent fathers and a lack of affective ties between the fathers and the children when the fathers do return.[47]

Hind Abu Seoud, an Egyptian sociologist, has suggested that the new women-headed households have increased women's self-esteem and self-reliance, and have given them important new status as authority figures with their children.[48] Deniz Kandiyoti did not find this to be true in Turkey, where, she points out, men who become labor migrants simply turn over their authority to a male surrogate, father, brother, uncle, or even an older son; these men maintain male authority, even cashing the remittance checks that are sent home and doling out allowances to the wives.[49] This also was the case in Old Nubia, where labor migration has been important for half a century. The Turkish case may be different, partly because of different perceptions of the place of wives in the kin group; in the Arab situation, as stated above, women remain members of their natal families all their lives, whereas in Turkey women after marriage tend to be seen as members of their husbands' families.

The situation is far from static, however. Families are responding to the labor migration situation in different ways. In the 1980s Turkish workers began to bring their families to Europe to stay, as did some Tunisian and Algerian workers. Statistics are incomplete, but the presence in German and French cities of entire neighborhoods populated by guest workers is illustrated by the prosperous food markets, the *halal* butchers, and specialty shops that feature Middle Eastern products. Yemeni and Egyptian workers in the Gulf still tend to migrate alone and to return every two or three years for holidays. The labor migration situation is beginning to change once more, as many industries and oil development projects are cutting back, both in Europe and in the Gulf, and consequently large numbers of guest workers either are going back home to stay or are caught between two worlds. Children of guest workers who have lived abroad find it hard to readjust in the country of origin. Guest workers who return to their families after many years find that local attitudes have changed in their absence, and living and working conditions are unfamiliar and often unacceptable or unaccepting.

Dr. Adil M. Al-Madani, a member of a group of Egyptian psychiatrists working with families in Cairo and in rural areas, reports that family therapy with "returned" fathers, struggling to remake the family pattern, indicates that the disruption has been serious, particularly among children. The tradition of the authoritarian father cannot be quickly broken, he argues. The child does not immediately replace a male authority figure and role model with a female model, and hence may become confused. Boys suffer the most in this situation, he states; girls, for obvious reasons, do not have as many problems, since their traditional role model, their mother, is not only present, but has gained in authority.[50]

The most dramatic evidence of children superseding the authority of the father and taking matters into their own hands is the 1987 uprising, or *intifada*, on the Israeli-occupied West Bank and Gaza Strip, which continues to the time of this writing. Here young Palestinian boys and girls, some as young as six, have literally changed the course of world politics. The "children of the stones," as they are called, are said to be reacting to the parental inability to accomplish any change in the stalemated Israeli-Palestinian conflict.[51]

Similar cases of the disregard of traditional male authority are seen in Lebanon, where the civil war has dragged on since 1976, partly, it is said, continued by teenage boys, often without fathers, who have grown up largely unsocialized to any behavior other than that of participating in armed militia activity.[52] In the recent Iran-Iraq war young Iranian teenagers were reported to have volunteered for army service in obedience to parental and religious dictum, in this instance showing not only respect for tradition, but also forging a new link between the father's authority, religious belief, and the nation state.

As the family unit is stretched and disrupted in many Middle Eastern countries, the central government of the nation state is beginning to assume some of the responsibilities formerly the prerogative of the family unit: education, employment, child and family counseling, and the care of orphans, the elderly, the insane, the handicapped, and the retarded. New institutions to care for the insane, the handicapped, the retarded, and orphans are emerging in Middle Eastern countries. In Egypt homes for the elderly, considered shameful only a generation ago, have begun to operate.[53] The issue of the elderly is a particularly sensitive one, for the responsibility of children to care for their parents has until now been considered sacrosanct, one of the most basic duties of younger members of the traditional family unit. As the parents' ability to survive alone is threatened by changing economic traditions, they tend to try and intensify the child's sense of duty toward them, often through religious training, for Islam emphasizes the responsibility of children toward their parents. Parents feel threatened not only by economic forces beyond their control, but also by what they view as the rise of alien (Western) attitudes. These are perceived as setting the individual's desires above those of the group, and therefore reducing the strength of their children's sense of duty toward their parents' needs. In addition, government family-planning programs help to restrict the size of the family unit, and government military training programs require most young men to serve at least two years in the nations' armies. Hence the government itself has become directly involved in the production and utilization of children.

Even on issues as private and basic as family honor and shame, the government has become involved. While codes of family honor are being challenged from a multitude of sources, published newspaper articles report that "crimes of honor" have increased, the murder of runaway daughters and sisters being the most common of these. According to Dr. Mohammed Mohieddin, Cairo sociologist, family-related crimes in Egypt increased from 0.5 to 10 percent between 1978 and 1988.[54] The government legal system finds itself in the anomalous position of indicting perpetrators of private family "punishments" that were once societally approved. One also may wonder whether a relatively larger urban population and a more rigorous reporting of crime may not have contributed to the rise in these figures.

The rise in the number of orphans noted by official sources and the relaxation of policies toward adoption signal another basic change in attitude. Traditional patrilineal ideology forbade premarital sex by women, and therefore, supposedly no illegitimate children were born. Clearly the reality was always somewhat different, but such children could be adopted into different branches of the family unit, and even given to childless couples by sympathetic midwives and doctors, with little or no public notice.[55] Why a public recognition of these children now? The struggle for independence in many countries (Algeria, 1954–1962) and natural disasters (the Agadir earthquake, Morocco), for example, created thousands of homeless children who were not illegitimate, in the strict sense of the word, but who were without kin and whose needs had to be met to satisfy *national* honor. Today the dispersion of the extended family unit has reduced opportunities for informal adoption, so central governments have responded in two ways: organizing more orphanages and changing adoption procedures. In 1962 in Cairo the only way one could adopt a child was for a man to go to court and swear that he was the biological father of the child to be adopted. By 1988 in Morocco adoption of any Muslim child was legally possible by other *Muslims*, male or female. Egypt is experimenting with family-style cottage orphanages, supervised by parental surrogates or foster parents. Morocco's Centre de Maternite, in Rabat, modeled after Western institutions, was begun in 1914 by French nuns. The Centre, one of several orphanages, was rebuilt and expanded in 1974 by the Moroccan government, and the king's sister, Princess Lalla Mariam, is its patroness. In the summer of 1988, 120 babies aged from a few days to three years were housed in this orphanage alone, and nurses explained that almost all the children would be adopted within six months. Girls are adopted more easily than boys, they stated, perhaps an indication of the persistence of the traditional view of a girl as servant in the household and a boy as carrier of the father's name and his inheritor.[56]

Koranic verses urging kindness to orphans and those bereft of family have been taken as the basis for new interpretations of religious writings.[57] King Hassan of Morocco has recently asked the nation's ulema, or religious specialists, to prepare fetwas, or legal opinions, somewhat like papal encyclicals on subjects such as illegitimate children, requirements for adoption, parental duties toward children, and children's duties toward parents.[58]

The current revivals of interest in religion, what local people call the "revivification" of religion by Muslim as well as Christian and Jewish groups, may be partially viewed as a reaction to the widespread but unevenly distributed

economic changes and to consumerism and materialism within the society. It is
thus a positive attempt to reassert identity and older values, including the ideology
of the traditional Islamic family in opposition to alien Western modes of life.

For Western observers the conservative social cast of much of the religious
revival, particularly the emphasis on modest dress and the importance placed on
mothers staying home with children rather than working outside the home, has
obscured the many constructive efforts by religious groups to not only ameliorate
social problems, but also to develop material benefits for the members of their
congregations. In Egypt, Islamic groups have provided investment opportunities
with fewer restrictions than those of other banking institutions. The Muslim
Women's Association offers interest-free loans to young women attending universities, and supervised living arrangements for women students far from the
family residence. Welfare associations, both formal and informal, proliferate
under religious auspices.[59]

In some countries, rather than totally rejecting secular schools and trying to
replace them with religious schools, religious organizations are attempting to
combine the two educational programs, or at least to supplement one with the
other. Morocco continues to license Koranic schools, but mostly at the preschool
or kindergarten level. Successful completion of this abbreviated two-year Koranic
instruction is recommended for children before they apply to the free government
secular schools. In Libya and Turkey religion has been added to the secular
curriculum of all public schools. In Egypt religious groups have opened and are
operating private religious schools for Muslims, just as Christian and Jewish
groups have done in Egypt for their own congregations. The new Muslim schools
include the government-prescribed school curriculum (science, mathematics,
language, literature, and social science) within a religious curriculum, so that
graduates can compete successfully in the governmentally administered examinations that are important in determining a child's future higher education. The
dedication of the teachers in these religious schools plus the small classes assure
those children whose parents can pay the substantial tuition fees a higher-quality
education than can be obtained in the overcrowded government schools.

But for a variety of reasons not all citizens view religious schools as an
unlimited good. Some see them as elitist. In Turkey, many Islamic schools are
financed through mosque organizations, and may or may not include subjects
other than religious studies. They are the subject of national dispute about not
only the quality of education they represent, but also the type of indoctrination
a child receives in such religious schools. Some of these institutions are boarding
schools, which remove the child from parental guidance and from most contact
with the outside world, including television broadcasts.[60]

Health care is another area in which Muslim religious groups have taken the
initiative, once more supplementing central government health clinics. Dr. Zahira
Abdine, director of the Giza children's hospital and herself a pious Muslim, has
spearheaded the effort to organize volunteers to provide much-needed basic health
care. Children and mothers are the principal patients at the free weekly clinics,

held throughout Cairo in the major mosques and staffed by men and women medical students.[61]

Religious organizations and government ministries are not the only elements of the society that are attempting to deal with the changing problems of children. Dr. Hassan al-Ibrahim, noted Kuwaiti educator, launched the Institute for the Advancement of the Arab Child in 1980, which sponsors research, publications, seminars, and educational videos on the subject of children throughout the region. The Arab Board for Child Development is a newly formed arm of the Arab League, conceived at a 1987 meeting on the future of the Arab world. Prince Bandar of Saudi Arabia is the president, and Suzanne Mubarak, wife of President Hosny Mubarak of Egypt, the vice-president. Egypt established its own High Council for Motherhood and Childhood in 1988 as an umbrella organization to deal with children's problems at all levels of society.

CONCLUSION

The children of the Muslim Middle East are growing up in a society vastly different from that of their parents and grandparents. The isolated communities described in the literature of the 1950s and 1960s, the villages and market towns of Palestine, Lebanon, Egypt, and Iraq no longer exist in forms that would be recognizable to the researchers of that period.

Since the beginning of the colonial period, and more swiftly with the struggle for independence and the formation of distinct nation states, the area has been in the grip of change far greater in pace and scope than ever before experienced. The move from rural to urban areas, the entry of the area into the interdependent world political-economic system, the contact with universal mass communications, the persistence of pockets of fierce local conflict, widespread labor migration, and the entry of women into the paid labor force outside the home all have, to some degree and in various ways, undermined the importance of the basic social unit of the area: the larger family group. This in turn has placed in question many of the basic beliefs of the society, including those associated with allegiance to the family and obedience to the father. Family authority is further weakened by the growing power of the central government in its assumption of some of the duties once performed by that family unit. Tension is evident at all levels: between parents and children, parents and grandparents, husbands and wives, and groups representing different approaches to the relationships within the family.

The traditional family, however, is not dying out, as many analysts have speculated. But it is changing, adapting to new needs and helping its members survive in a difficult economic time. Although the larger kin group may be more or less dispersed, some of the signs of unity remain. The rituals of childhood—naming, circumcision, graduation from school, marriage—continue but in somewhat different form. Naming ceremonies are still widespread among all economic groups, but boys' circumcision ceremonies are becoming less frequent in some areas as this operation becomes a routine part of hospital deliveries. Circumcision of girls is declining even in rural areas.[62]

Family ceremonies now respond to events set not only by the family unit, but also by the requirements of the larger social world. Graduation from Koranic school, although still an important rite of passage in some families, has been superseded by graduation from secondary school. When the student who has successfully passed his or her baccalaureate examination, the key to further achievement in the society, finds his or her name published in the national newspapers, the entire family honors the new graduate with a feast reminiscent of older celebrations. In all Middle Eastern countries a young man's rite of passage to adulthood is two years' compulsory military service, usually in an area of the country far from home. Once he has completed his military service he is free to marry and start a profession. In Turkey the entire village or neighborhood turns out to see the boy off on his bus journey into adulthood. Puberty no longer marks the end of childhood and the beginning of adulthood; an intervening stage, the construct known in the West as adolescence, is beginning to be documented.[63] Marriage, the final ritual that marks the beginning of adulthood, is occurring later. Engagements are lasting longer, and the choice of a marriage partner is becoming a matter of negotiation between children and parents, rather than the choice of parents alone.

In this urbanizing-industrial society class is becoming increasingly important as the gaps between the rich, the new middle class, and the poor widen, and the old signs of social status—birth and religious affiliation—are being replaced by educational achievement and the accumulation of wealth. The lives of children reflect this: those whose parents have some means are able to take advantage of the new educational and health opportunities, to move into newer jobs and become part of the middle- and upper-middle-class system, often referred to as the Western "modern" sector of the economy. Other children whose parents are struggling with crushing economic problems must help to maximize, through family group efforts, the minimal resources at their disposal. Although cooperative values of such families are admired, their material conditions are deplored by governmental pronouncement and frequent media attention.

Today children and teenagers also may be seen as exerting political force, not only in the West Bank and Lebanon, but throughout the area. Growing up to expect that a better life is their right, reading newspapers, and being exposed to international media on a regular basis, they put pressure on national leaders to achieve stated goals. Most Moroccans would agree with the government official who stated that "children and their problems and aspirations are the nightmare of the King." Here in the United States, as our population ages, it is difficult to conceive of the explosive possibilities of such a new youth-centered society, its aspirations often thwarted, its expectations unfulfilled.

The family of tomorrow in the Arab world may be smaller and less male-dominated, its child-rearing practices more varied, according to new class divisions and income differences, but the child is still perceived as the family's and society's crucial link between the past and the present; the future of the child is seen as crucial not only to the future of the family unit, but to the future of the entire nation state. In her monumental three-volume "Les Representations de l'Enfant dans La Societé Marocaine" (1988) Dr. Aisha Belarbi states that parents and teachers continue to characterize children as "creatures lacking *agl* or reason and needing discipline." Children in the same study, asked to characterize themselves, said, "I'm just a person aged so-and-so. I'm a person."[64] These young "persons" still see themselves as members of families and as citizens of nation states. But they see themselves primarily, it seems, as "persons" who will form the next generation and make more choices of their own. They constitute the overwhelming majority of today's population in the Middle East.

NOTES

1. See Halim Barakat, "The Arab Family and the Challenge of Social Transformation," and Safia K. Mohsen, "New Images Old Reflections: New Voices of Change," in *Women and the Family in the Middle East: New Voices of Change*, ed. Elizabeth Warnock Fernea (Austin: University of Texas Press, 1985), pp. 27–48, 56–71; and Andrea Rugh, *The Family in Contemporary Egypt* (Syracuse: Syracuse University Press, 1984).

2. Romantic attachments were important, although not always within marriages. See Arabic poetry, both classical and modern, and the new ethnographic literature on poetry in everyday life. Cf. *Desert Tracings: Six Classic Arabic Odes*, trans. Michael Sells (Middletown, Conn.: Wesleyan University Press, 1989); S. K. Jayyusi, ed., *Modern Arabic Poetry* (New York: Columbia University Press, 1987); Lila Abu-Lughod, *Veiled Sentiments* (Berkeley: University of California Press, 1986); and Roger Joseph and Terri Brint Joseph, *The Rose and the Thorn* (Tucson: University of Arizona Press, 1982).

3. Ghazi Ahmad, *Sayings of Muhammad* (Lahore: S. H. Muhammad Ashraf, 1968), p. 21.

4. In contrast, according to Hindu tradition, a bride leaves her natal family and becomes part of her husband's family. Her own natal family has no further legal tie or responsibility for her.

5. See, for example, the following novels and memoirs: Driss Chraibi, *Heirs to the Past* (London: Heinemann, 1971); Aziz Nesin, *Istanbul Boy* (Austin: University of Texas Press, 1977); and Najib Mahfuz, "The Mistake," in *Bayna al-Qasrayn* in *Middle Eastern Muslim Women Speak*, ed. Elizabeth Warnock Fernea and Basima Qattan Bezirgan (Austin: University of Texas Press, 1977, 1984).

6. See, for example, Samuel Noah Kramer, *The Sumerians* (Chicago: University of Chicago Press, 1963); and Gerda Lerner, *The Creation of Patriarchy* (Oxford: Oxford University Press, 1986).

7. *The Meaning of the Glorious Koran: An Explanatory Translation*, trans. Mohammad Marmaduke Pickthall (New York: New English Library, 1953). Sura IV, v. 11.

8. Inamullah Khan, *Maxims of Mohummud* (Karachi: Umma Publishing House, 1965), p. 41.

9. Ibn Miskawayh, *Tahdhib al-akhlag*; Al-Ghazali, *Ya Ayyuha al-Walad*.

10. Edwin T. Prothro, *Child Rearing in Lebanon* (Cambridge, Mass.: Harvard University Press, 1961); Hamed Ammar, *Growing Up in an Egyptian Village* (London: Routledge Kegan Paul, 1954); Hilma Grandqvist, *Birth and Childhood Among the Arabs; Child Problems Among the Arabs* (Helsingfors: Soderstom & Co., 1947, 1950); Judith R. Williams, *The Youth of Haouch El-Hakim, Lebanese Village* (Cambridge, Mass.: Harvard University Press, 1968); and Susan Dorsky, *Women of Amran* (Salt Lake City: University of Utah Press, 1986).

11. Qu'ran; Sura II, v. 233.

12. Quoted by a Nubian man in John G. Kennedy, *Struggle for Change in a Nubian Community* (Palo Alto, Calif.: Mayfield Publishing Co., 1977), p. 75.

13. On numerous occasions in Egyptian Nubia in 1962 I witnessed two- and three-year-old children sitting quietly while I and my restless American children of the same age were served tea, dates, and popcorn.

14. See Elizabeth W. Fernea, *Guests of the Sheik: An Ethnography of an Iraqi Village* (New York: Doubleday, 1965), p. 190.

15. Ammar, *Growing Up in an Egyptian Village*, pp. 125–127, 139.

16. E. A. Westermarck, *Ritual and Belief in Morocco* (New York: University Books, 1968), 2:386–395.

17. Ammar, *Growing Up in an Egyptian Village*, pp. 91–93; also Fadwa El-Guindi, *Sebua* (London: Ethnographic Film, 1987).

18. E. W. Lane, *Manners and Customs of the Modern Egyptians*. (London: J. M. Dent & Sons, 1860), pp. 89, 512–513.

19. Ammar, *Growing Up in an Egyptian Village*, pp. 110–121.

20. E. W. Fernea, research in Morocco; also see *Some Women of Marrakech*, PBS version of Granada Television London (Ethnographic Film, 1982).

21. Ammar, *Growing Up in an Egyptian Village*, pp. 206–210.

22. Umm Kulthum, excerpts from *The Umm Kulthum Nobody Knows*, in Fernea and Bezirgan, eds., *Middle Eastern Muslim Women Speak*, pp. 139–140.

23. Ammar, *Growing Up in an Egyptian Village*, p. 126.

24. See J. G. Peristiany, ed., *Honor and Shame: The Values of Mediterranean Society* (London: Weidenfield & Nicolson, 1965), particularly Ahmed Abou-Zeid, "Honor and Shame Among the Bedouin of Egypt"; Abu-Lughod, *Veiled Sentiments*; Julian Pitt-Rivers, *The Fate of Schechem: Or the Politics of Sex* (London: Cambridge University Press, 1977); see also Elizabeth W. Fernea and Robert Fernea, "A Look Behind the Veil," in *Anthropology 80/81* (Guilford, Conn.: Dushkin Publishing Co., 1981).

25. Halide E. Adivar, excerpts from "Memoirs," in Fernea and Bezirgan, eds., *Middle Eastern Muslim Women Speak*, p. 75.

26. W. Roger Louis, *The British Empire in the Middle East 1945–1951* (New York: Oxford University Press, 1984); William Cleveland, *Islam Against the West: Shahib Arslan and the Campaign for Islamic Nationalism* (Austin: University of Texas Press, 1985); Bernard Lewis, *The Middle East and the West* (New York: Harper & Row, 1964); Vanessa Maher, *Women and Property in Morocco* (London: Cambridge University Press, 1974).

27. Amal Rassam, "The Colonial Mirror: Reflections on the Politics of Sex in Morocco," and Alf Heggoy, "Cultural Disrespect: European and Algerian Views on Women in Colonial and Independent Algeria" (unpublished papers).

28. See John J. Donohue and John L. Esposito, eds., *Islam in Transition: Muslim Perspectives* (Oxford: Oxford University Press, 1982), especially Sayyid Jamal al-Din

al-Afghani, "An Islamic Response to Imperialism" and "Islamic Solidarity"; Shayk Muhammad Abduh, "Islam, Reason and Civilization"; Sir Sayyid Ahmad Khan, "India and English Government," "Islam: The Religion of Reason and Nature"; and Chiragh Ali, "Islam and Change."

29. Qasim Amin, excerpts in Mona Mikhail, *Images of Arab Women* (Washington, D.C.: Three Continents Press, 1979); see also Aziza Al-Hibri ed., *Women in Islam* (London: Pergamon Press, 1982).

30. Gail Minault, *Women and Political Participation in India and Pakistan* (Columbia, Mo.: South Asia Books, 1982).

31. Kenneth Brown, personal communication.

32. Frantz Fanon, *A Dying Colonialism* (New York: Grove Press, 1965); see also "Interviews with Jamilah Buhrayd, Legendary Algerian Hero," in Fernea and Bezirgan, eds., *Middle Eastern Muslim Women Speak*, pp. 263–266; Carolyn Fluehr-Lobban, "The Woman's Movement in the Sudan and Its Impact on Sudanese Law and Politics," Ahfad University College Symposium, 1979; Afaf Lutfi al-Sayyid Marsot, "The Revolutionary Gentlewoman in Egypt" in *Women in the Muslim World*, ed. Lois Beck and Nikki Keddie (Cambridge, Mass.: Harvard University Press, 1978); Richard Antoun, "On the Modesty of Women in Arab Muslim Villages: A Study in the Accommodation of Tradition," *American Anthropologist* 70 (1968):671–697.

33. Fadela M'rabet, excerpts from "Les Algeriennes," in Fernea and Bezirgan, eds., *Middle Eastern Muslim Women Speak*, pp. 319–358.

34. World Population Trends and Policies, UN Monitoring Report, 1981; J. K. Galbraith, *The Nature of Mass Poverty* (Cambridge, Mass.: Harvard University Press, 1979); Malcolm Kerr and Sayed al Yasin, eds., *Rich and Poor States in the Middle East: Egypt and the New Arab Order* (Boulder, Colo.: Westview Press, 1982).

35. Earl Sullivan, *Women in Egyptian Public Life* (Syracuse: Syracuse University Press, 1986).

36. Barbara L. Ibrahim, "Cairo's Factory Women," in Fernea, ed., *Women and the Family in the Middle East*; See also Barbara L. Ibrahim, "Family Strategies: A Perspective of Women's Entry to the Labour Force in Egypt," in *Arab Society*, ed. Nicholas Hopkins and Saad Eddin Ibrahim (Cairo: American University in Cairo Press, 1985); Mona Hammam, "Egypt's Women Workers," in *MERIP* 82 (November 1979).

37. Rosemary Sayigh, *Palestinians: From Peasants to Revolutionaries: A People's History* (London: Zed Press, 1979).

38. In all the Arab states between 1970 and 1985 alone the number of students in primary schools doubled and the number of students in universities quadrupled, from 12,602,000 to 23,796,000 and from 444,000 to 1,784,000, respectively. Figures from UNESCO Report of Meeting of Senior Education Officials in the Arab States, Amman, June 22–26, 1987.

39. See *The Impact of Economic Adjustment Policies on the Vulnerable Families and Children in Egypt*, a report prepared for the Third World Forum, Middle East Office and the United Nations Children's Fund, Egypt, 1987; also see Nawal al-Messiri, "Umalat al-Atfal fi al-Madina" (Paper delivered at a Conference on Child Labor, Cairo, 1987).

40. Driss Ouawisha, vice rector, Meknes University, Morocco, personal communication.

41. Nagat Al-Sanabary, "Continuity and Change in Women's Education in the Arab States," in Fernea, ed., *Women and the Family in the Middle East*, pp. 93–110.

42. See Susan Schaefer Davis and Douglas A. Davis, *Adolescence in a Moroccan Town* (New Brunswick, N.J.: Rutgers University Press, 1989).

43. Interviews with editors of *Al-Sageer*, in Kuwait at newspaper office, June 1988.

44. Mohammad Mohieddin, Adil M. Al-Madini, and Nabil Al-Zahar, interviews in Cairo, summer 1988.

45. Saad Eddin Ibrahim, "Oil, Migration, and the New Social Order," in Kerr and Yasin, eds., *Rich and Poor States in the Middle East*.

46. Anthropologist Jenny White, personal communication.

47. See note 45.

48. Hind Abou-Seuod Khattab and Syada Greiss El Daeif, "Impact of Male Labor Migration on the Structure of the Family and the Roles of Women," *The Population Council*, West Asia and North Africa Region, 2, Egypt, 1982.

49. Deniz Kandiyoti, "Sex Role and Social Change: A Comparative Appraisal of Turkey's Women," *Signs* 3 (1977):57–73.

50. Al-Madani, interview.

51. *Children of the Stones* (Washington, D.C.: ADC, 1989).

52. Jennifer Bryce and Hautune K. Armenian, eds., *In Wartime: The State of Children in Lebanon* (Beirut: American University Press, 1986); Maroun Baghdadi and Nayla Freige, "The Kalashnikov Generation" in Fernea, ed., *Women and the Family in the Middle East*, pp. 169–182.

53. Andrea Rugh, "Orphanages and Homes for the Aged in Egypt: Contradiction or Affirmation in a Family Oriented Society," *International Journal of Sociology of the Family* 11 (1981):203–233.

54. Moheiddin, interview.

55. Mary Allison, "Memoirs of a Missionary Doctor in Kuwait" (unpublished manuscript).

56. Interview, Centre de la Maternité, Rabat, Morocco, June 1988.

57. Qu'ran; Sura II, v. 177; Sura IV, v. 127.

58. "Le Code des Droits de L'enfant en Islam," *Le Matin du Sahara*, Rabat, Morocco, April 26, 1988.

59. Ibrahim, "Oil, Migration, and the New Social Order."

60. Anthropologist Jenny White, personal communication.

61. Interviews and visits to hospitals and clinics in 1981, 1988.

62. Unpublished papers presented at conference on "Changing Status of Sudanese Women," Ahfad University, Omdurmam, Sudan, 1979; see also proceedings of Seminar on "Bodily Mutilation of Young Females," Cairo, Egypt, Cairo Family Planning Association, 1979.

63. Davis and Davis, *Adolescence in a Moroccan Town*.

64. Aisha Belarbi, *Les Representations de l'Enfant dans la Societé Marocaine*. Thèse pour le Doctorat d'Etat Université Paris V, René Descartes; Sciences Humaines, unpublished Ph.D. diss., Sorbonne, 1988.

REFERENCES

Abu-Lughod, Lila. *Veiled Sentiments*. Berkeley: University of California Press, 1986.

Ahmad, Ghazi. *Sayings of Muhammad*. Lahore: S. H. Muhammad Ashraf, 1968.

Al-Hibri, Aziza. *Women in Islam*. London: Pergamon Press, 1982.

Ammar, Hamed. *Growing Up in an Egyptian Village*. London: Routledge & Kegan Paul, 1954.

Antoun, Richard. "On the Modesty of Women in Arab Muslim Villages: A Study in the Accommodation of Traditions." *American Anthropologist* 70 (1968).

Beck, Lois, and Nikki Keddie, eds. *Women in the Muslim World*. Cambridge, Mass.: Harvard University Press, 1978.

Belarbi, Aisha. *Less Representations de l'Enfant dans la Societé Marocaine*. Thèse pour le Doctorat d'Etat Université Paris V, René Descartes; Sciences Humaines, unpublished Ph.D. diss., Sorbonne, 1988.

Bryce, Jennifer, and Hautune K. Armenian, eds. *In Wartime: The State of Children in Lebanon*. Beirut: American University Press, 1986.

Chraibi, Driss. *Heirs to the Past*. London: Heinemann, 1971.

Cleveland, William. *Islam Against the West: Shahib Arslan and the Campaign for Islamic Nationalism*. Austin: University of Texas Press, 1985.

"Le Code des Droits de L'enfant en Islam." *Le matin du Sahara*. Rabat, Morocco, April 26, 1988.

Davis, Susan Schaefer, and Douglas A. Davis. *Adolescence in a Moroccan Town*. New Brunswick, N.J.: Rutgers University Press, 1989.

Donohue, John J., and John L. Esposito, eds. *Islam in Transition: Muslim Perspectives*. Oxford: Oxford University Press, 1982.

Dorsky, Susan. *Women of Amran*. Salt Lake City: University of Utah Press, 1986.

El-Guindi, Fadwa. *Sebua*. London: Ethnographic Film, 1987.

Fanon, Frantz. *A Dying Colonialism*. New York: Grove Press, 1965.

Fernea, Elizabeth Warnock. *Guests of the Sheik: An Ethnography of an Iraqi Village*. New York: Doubleday, 1965.

———, ed. *Women and the Family in the Middle East: New Voices of Change*. Austin: University of Texas Press, 1985.

Fernea, Elizabeth Warnock, and Basima Qattan Bezirgan, eds. *Middle Eastern Muslim Women Speak*. Austin: University of Texas Press, 1977.

Fernea, Elizabeth Warnock, and Robert Fernea. "A Look Behind the Veil." *Annual Edition Anthropology 80/81*. Guilford, Conn.: Dushkin Publishing Co., 1981.

Galbraith, John G. *The Nature of Mass Poverty*. Cambridge, Mass.: Harvard University Press, 1979.

Grandqvist, Hilma. *Birth and Childhood Among the Arabs*. Helsingfors: Söderstrom & Co., 1947.

Hammam, Mona. "Egypt's Women Workers." *MERIP* 82 (November 1979).

Hopkins, Nicholas, and Ibrahim Saad Eddin, eds. *Arab Society*. Cairo: American University in Cairo Press, 1985.

Jayyusi, S. K., ed. *Modern Arabic Poetry*. New York: Columbia University Press, 1987.

Joseph, Roger, and Terri Brint Joseph. *The Rose and the Thorn*. Tucson: University of Arizona Press, 1982.

Kandiyoti, Deniz. "Sex Roles and Social Change: A Comparative Appraisal of Turkey's Women." *Signs* (1977).

Khan, Inamullah. *Maxims of Mohummud*. Karachi: Umma Publishing House, 1965.

Khattab, Hind Abou-Seoud, and Syada Greisa El Daeif. "Impact of Male Labour Migration on the Structure of the Family and the Roles of Women." *The Population Council*, West Asia and North Africa Region, 2, Egypt, 1982.

Kennedy, John G. *Struggle for Change in a Nubian Community*. Palo Alto, Calif.: Mayfield Publishing Co., 1977.

Kerr, Malcolm, and Sayed al Yassin, eds. *Rich and Poor States in the Middle East: The New Arab Social Order*. Boulder, Colo.: Westview Press, 1982.

Kramer, Samuel Noah. *The Sumerians*. Chicago: University of Chicago Press, 1963.

Lane, E. W. *Manners and Customs of the Modern Egyptians*. London: J. M. Dent & Sons, 1860.

Lerner, Gerda. *The Creation of Patriarchy*. Oxford: Oxford University Press, 1986.

Lewis, Bernard. *The Middle East and the West*. New York: Harper & Row, 1964.

Louis, W. Roger. *The British Empire in the Middle East 1945–1951*. New York: Oxford University Press, 1984.

Maher, Vanessa. *Women and Property in Morocco*. London: Cambridge University Press, 1974.

Mikhail, Mona. *Images of Arab Women*. Washington, D.C.: Three Continents Press, 1979.

Minault, Gail. *Women and Political Participation in India and Pakistan*. Columbia, Mo.: South Asia Books, 1982.

Nesin, Aziz. *Istanbul Boy*. Austin: University of Texas, 1977.

Peristiany, John, ed. *Honor and Shame: The Values of Mediterranean Society*. London: Weidenfield & Nicolson, 1965.

Pickthall, Mohammad Marmaduke, trans. *The Meaning of the Glorious Koran: An Explanatory Translation*. New York: New English Library, 1953.

Pitt-Rivers, Julian. *The Fate of Schechem: Or the Politics of Sex*. London: Cambridge University Press, 1977.

Prothro, Edwin T. *Child Rearing in the Lebanon*. Cambridge, Mass.: Harvard University Press, 1961.

Rugh, Andrea. "Orphanages and Homes for the Aged in Egypt: Contradiction or Affirmation in a Family Oriented Society." *International Journal of Sociology of the Family* 11 (1981).

————. *The Family in Contemporary Egypt*. Syracuse: Syracuse University Press, 1984.

Sayigh, Rosemary. *Palestinians: From Peasants to Revolutionaries: A People's History*. London: Zed Press, 1979.

Sells, Michael, trans. *Desert Tracings: Six Classic Arabic Odes*. Middletown, Conn.: Wesleyan University Press, 1989.

Some Women of Marrakech. PBS Version of Granada Television (London) Ethnographic Film, 1982.

Sullivan, Earl. *Women in Egyptian Public Life*. Syracuse: Syracuse University Press, 1986.

Williams, Judith R. *The Youth of Haouch El-Harimi, a Lebanese Village*. Cambridge, Mass.: Harvard University Press, 1968.

Westermarck, E. A. *Ritual and Belief in Morocco*. New York: University Books, 1968.

18

RUSSIA AND THE USSR

David L. Ransel

Russia has no history of childhood. Neither Russians themselves nor foreigners who study them have turned their attention to the subject of children in any but a cursory manner. Even so, it is clear that the notion of childhood has undergone important changes in the course of modern Russian history, and indeed the construction of that notion has been in dispute among Russians themselves since at least the late seventeenth century. In speaking of Russia one must keep in mind the enormous cultural divide between the small educated elite and the rest of society throughout the modern era. The emergence of different ways of thinking about childhood occurs at different times in the two contexts.

In view of the dearth of research by Soviet scholars on the history of childhood my commentary focuses primarily on Western scholarly work on Russian childhood, accompanied by some observations from my own research on abandoned children and peasant children. I should nevertheless point out that several of the great Russian writers of the modern era were intensely interested in childhood and explored it in their works. Sergei Aksakov's *Family Chronicle*, Leo Tolstoy's *Childhood*, Feodor Dostoevsky's investigations of this theme in *Diary of a Writer*, Elizaveta Vodovozova's *A Russian Childhood*, and Maxim Gorky's *My Childhood* are some of the better known treatments of the issue. Although space does not permit an analysis of these books here, these and other works of fiction will provide an important body of sources when the history of Russian childhood is someday written.[1]

Childhood as an intellectual construct appeared relatively late in Russia as one of many elements in Russia's Westernization. This process began in the late seventeenth and early eighteenth centuries. It is in this period that we see the first attempts to establish institutions for the salvation of unwanted children and the first literary works recognizing that children had a manner of perceiving and apprehending the world around them that was different from that of adults.

The position of children before that time, in the eras known as medieval and Muscovite Russia, is poorly known.[2] The surviving legal record would suggest that children were not much valued, since public law afforded them no protection. Children enjoyed only the protection furnished by their own families. It is true that, just as in the West at the same time, constraints on killing children were expressed in church law, but close examination of these statutes makes clear that although the church no doubt wanted to protect children, its principal purpose was to deter the use of infanticide as a birth control measure or a means of concealing illicit sexual relations. Other than this sanction against killing infants the law did little to protect children from assaults by their parents. As late as the mid-seventeenth century Russian law explicitly forbade capital punishment for parents who murdered their children.[3] Early Russian legislation also allowed children to be sold into slavery. In the case of needy families this method of disposing of children was evidently regarded as perfectly reasonable and acceptable. Finally, among certain categories of slaves (slaves accounted for 8 to 10 percent of the population of Muscovite Russia), female infanticide may have been common.[4]

As in other European countries in early modern times the loss of life among children in Russia was high. Although precise figures are lacking for the premodern period, mortality could not have been much different from the rates of approximately 50 percent by age five that was the average for central Russia as recently as 100 years ago. The resulting expectation of the loss of many children was recognized and rationalized in the leading handbook on family and domestic life, the *Household Manual* (Domostroi) of the sixteenth century. The manual consoled parents with the idea, shared by some other European peoples, that dead children served as innocent emissaries who would intercede on behalf of their families before the throne of God.[5] Even the large number of children lost must therefore have been regarded as an asset because of the important role they could play in the heavens. This notion was part of what must have been a well-developed set of coping mechanisms that made the high death rates of children emotionally bearable.

The *Household Manual* also gave guidance on child rearing, advice that amounted to the "plain dumb rod," in the words of the famous Russian historian of the late imperial period, Vasilii Kliuchevskii. Children were to be saved by brutal indoctrination to parental will reinforced by religious authority. "If you care about your son," the manual advised, "do not spare the rod; if you have a daughter, strike terror into her" (although with the proviso not to harm her good looks when thrashing her). Kliuchevskii adopted an ambivalent attitude about these and the many similar admonitions in the manual, for he did not want to believe that these principles reflected the actual practice of child rearing in old Russia. He could not believe that parents could simply brutalize their children. To the extent that such measures were applied, Kliucheuskii contended that the parents looked on them as a kind of behavioral hygiene, as in the admonition "If you love your son, punish him when he is young, for he will not die from your rod, but will become the healthier for it, and by beating his body you will be saving his soul." Kliucheuskii believed that loving parents were sure to feel more pain than they inflicted in having to whip their children. So, despite the lack of legal constraints and the official encouragement of corporal punishment, love of parents for their children, in Kliuchevskii's view, served as a check on the brutality of established norms.[6]

These few ruminations by Kliuchevskii constitute most of what has been said about the private world of childhood in early Russia.

The first evidence of governmental concern for child welfare appeared in 1682 in a proposal for the organization of care facilities for the housing and education of homeless children. Practical steps came a few years later with the opening of a home for unwanted children in the city of Novgorod under the auspices of the local bishop. The famous reforming ruler, Peter the Great (reigned 1689–1725), learned of this effort and undertook to subsidize and expand it, the purpose being to save valuable human resources to staff the growing armed forces and industries of the new Russia that Peter was building.[7]

Peter also ended a distinction made in the previous century between punishments for killing a legitimate or illegitimate child. The killing of an illegitimate child had been a capital offense (the legislators' intent being, again, to discourage illicit sexual unions), whereas the murder of one's own child was treated as little more than a misdemeanor. In his military articles of 1716 Peter made the killing of any infant child punishable by death, for he cared less about illegitimacy than about losing population resources. Yet, while serving this purpose, Peter did not want to undermine parental authority. He therefore replaced the distinction between legitimate and illegitimate children with a distinction between infants and older children. In editing the draft of the article in the military code calling for death in the case of child murder Peter added in his own hand after the word "child" the qualifier "in infancy." Courts interpreted the article to mean that if a man accidentally killed his child (or his wife, for that matter) in the course of disciplining him or her, the homicide was not a capital offense.

So, we see still in the early eighteenth century, under a reformist emperor, an affirmation of the ferocious early Russian norms sustaining parental and especially patriarchal authority. The state nevertheless intervened to protect infant life through a broader definition of child murders carrying the death penalty and through its subsidization of care for unwanted children.

At about the same time, the compilers of Slavic primers were beginning to make a distinction between editions intended for adult training and newer models directed at children. The first of the new models came to Muscovy with a scholar, Simeon Polotskii, who had studied at the Kievan Academy in the Ukraine, an excellent school whose curriculum had been shaped by the influence of Jesuit scholastics. Polotskii's primer, produced in 1679, added to the traditional format a number of innovations designed for the young pupil, such as a variety of typefaces, especially large block type, illustrations, and introductory comments directed at youth. If Polotskii's contribution was more formal than substantive, one of his students, a monk by the name of Karion Istomin, went much further. In the 1690s Istomin created a radically new primer that included graphic design and the word-object and sentence methods of teaching reading. His work is a delight to read even today. He directly associated entire words with pictures of the objects they stood for, placing the word next to the picture. He even showed each letter in the shape of human beings forming it in the style we know from the television program "Sesame Street," as if he expected his pupils to learn the letters by acting them out in this way. His book taught reading not through the then common method of learning constructs of syllables, but through a system of phonics associated with whole words. These methods, which he apparently worked out largely by himself, did not come into common practice in the West for 200 more years. Istomin's work revealed with great clarity his understanding that children occupied a different mental world, perceived their surroundings differently from adults, and had special educational needs. He has justly been named "the first Russian children's writer."[8]

It has to be noted, however, that Istomin was one of those rare geniuses who was too far ahead of his time to exert a major impact. The prevailing methods of teaching literacy in Russia were those of the Ukrainian scholastics, and when in the early eighteenth century the government issued large editions of its own civil primer, Istomin's innovations were not included. The alphabet was updated and a variety of typefaces were used, but the traditional alphabetic system of reading was retained.

Istomin was not and could not have been an entirely isolated individual, and his understanding of childhood, out of step though it was, signaled a broader awareness among Russia's educated elite of the differentness of youth. For example, the new civil primer was published together with an etiquette book, *The Honorable Mirror of Youth*, which detailed proper behavior in relations between children and adults.[9] The *Mirror* was a Western import, and much of its advice, which was mostly concerned with decorum, proper speech, and the like, dated back to the *De civilitate morum* of Erasmus, but still, its translation and publication in Russia demonstrated the government's desire to enter an arena previously left to family and church and, in doing so, to define in accordance with Western notions an official view of the place of children. These "discoveries of childhood" in the fields of education and manners, along with their parallels in the field of child welfare, represented a new appreciation of the lives of young people, at least among the best educated members of Russian society.

At first the new ideas affected only the nobility. Peter the Great, who was both the product of Russia's Westernization and its most ardent promoter, demanded that the male children of the nobility suffer a Western education and master the rudiments of reading, writing, and arithmetic. Until they could pass basic tests in these subjects they were forbidden to marry. Equally important, the failure to attain an education blocked a young noble's access to jobs carrying official rank, which was an essential mark of status. So education quickly became a fundamental value for the Russian nobility.

If the content of child training changed, the methods for a long time remained those expressed in a seventeenth-century Russian couplet:

> The rod sharpens the mind
> And activates the memory.

In other words, the *Household Manual* of old, with its stress on instilling fear in children as the surest means to their well-being and salvation, was clearly still an important guide for many people. A well-known industrialist and social critic of Peter I's time, Ivan Pososhkov, advised his son that if he was going to send his son to school to study, he should "not allow him the slightest freedom and keep him in great fear."[10]

Pososhkov's contemporary, the historian and engineer Vasilii Tatishchev, wrote in a similar vein that children (a term that he applied to youngsters up to age twelve) were "stubborn and will not obey anyone except out of fear of punishment; a child is truculent . . . and fickle, remaining neither friendly nor angry for very long."[11] Yet Tatishchev's general approach was much different from Pososhkov's. Although Tatishchev did not approve of unreasonable behavior in children and thought that it had to be rooted out, he had a refined understanding of child development and recognized that children passed through a number of growth stages, each of which required an appropriate method of teaching. As Max Okenfuss has pointed out, what could only be inferred about Karion Istomin's understanding of children's minds from his exceptional primer is explicit in the writings of Tatishchev. He composed instructions for teachers, in which he outlined methods that worked best for each childhood age-group, and unlike Pososhkov and many others of his time, Tatishchev recognized positive aspects of the child's mind, noting that the natural curiosity of children and their good memories should be capitalized on in furthering their education.

Tatishchev was a man of the early enlightenment, and although he believed that children had to be disciplined, he did not recommend the kind of brutal punishment that was common in the education of many young nobles. For example, a famous memoirist of the mid-eighteenth century, Andrei Bolotov, reported that the German who was hired to teach him mathematics and foreign languages at home once beat him 200 times with a switch, and yet he dared not tell his father about the incident.[12] Several other personal memoirs from the period tell of the frequent application of corporal punishment to children by teachers in schools or by private tutors.[13]

Not until the 1760s, and then among only a few writers, did a more thoughtful approach to child rearing appear. Empress Catherine II and her chief adviser on educational policy, Ivan Betskoi, were among the first to express such ideas.

Their projects and decrees for the establishment of schools and foundling homes were based on the ideas of Locke, Commenius, Fénelon, and Rousseau. Betskoi's handbook for the care and rearing of young children, which the government published in several large editions, stood in sharp contrast to the child-care culture of the day. It spoke out against the common Russian practices of swaddling, feeding babies solid food, and corporal punishment for children. Children required freedom, fresh air, and play to develop, advised Betskoi, and their training should be accomplished by exemplary play, walks in nature, and loving care, rather than by rote learning enforced with the rod. Betskoi did eventually allow corporal punishment in extreme cases but usually used deprivation of freedom and food to control misbehavior.

The enlightenment stress on freedom and naturalness in handling children was accompanied in Betskoi's educational projects with a strict internment regime, for he was thoroughly imbued with sense-impressionist psychology and the notion that a child's mind was at birth a tabula rasa. Betskoi established a number of schools, including the first Russian school for women, a reformed cadet academy, a commercial college, and foundling home schools. The institutions were in the two capital cities and did not, therefore, exert a wide influence. According to his program, children began school at age six or seven (in the case of foundlings even earlier) and, except for vacations, did not return to their families until late teenage, when they would be fully formed by the enlightened training of the institution and untainted by the vices of normal Russian family life. The democratic strain in enlightenment thought about children failed to appear in Betskoi's projects, which conformed instead to the hierarchical structure of Russian society. Children were to receive the training appropriate to their station in life; nobles were taught one set of skills, townspeople another, and the non-privileged simply enough to permit them to be efficient servants for their "betters."[14]

A handful of other writers of the late eighteenth century took Western enlightenment thought and developed its more democratic side, although they were not in a position to realize their ideas in institutions of upbringing and education. Nikolai Novikov, one of the first Russians to operate an independent publishing business and to organize private charitable endeavors, considered children to be creatures with their own peculiar emotional makeup and experiential faculties. He edited and published the first Russian periodical of readings for children. These readings and his own theoretical tracts showed that he thought of children not as objects of parental will or of state authority (as in Betskoi's schemes), but as people possessing rights of their own. A child, he wrote, "has the same rights as you and I, the only difference being that a child requires greater outside assistance than we do."[15] Novikov's contemporary, the philosopher and political dissident Aleksandr Radishchev, went even further in denying parental dominance and according independent rights to children. In his instruction to his son he told him to abandon any thought that he was subject to his father's authority. "You are in no way obligated to me. Neither in reason and even less so in law, do I wish to seek the cement for our union. It must have its foundation in your heart."[16] But the notion that children were not bound in obedience to those who brought them into the world was not shared by many others in Russia at this time. If more people now understood that children had a peculiar developmental pattern, children were nevertheless still thought to be in need of strict subordination to those who, by God's will, were given the authority to shape and control their behavior.

Although scholars agree that a new kind of education became a fundamental value for Russian nobles in the eighteenth century, they disagree on the essential character of noble upbringing and especially the effects of the change in education. More than twenty years ago in a pathbreaking psychological study of the Russian nobility, Marc Raeff argued that the childhood and education of Russian nobles in the eighteenth and early nineteenth centuries alienated them from both their provincial roots and the autocratic government, and so created fertile ground for the growth of a revolutionary intelligentsia. Children of the nobility grew up on sleepy provincial estates and were nurtured by serf nurses and "uncles." Fathers often were away on government service, and mothers were too preoccupied or ignorant to participate in training the children, Raeff wrote. As a consequence, the sons lived in anarchy, enjoying but also lording over their serf supervisors and playmates. From about age seven the noble boys were torn from this freedom and subjected to a harsh school regimen either at home under the charge of a foreign teacher or seminarian or, more commonly, at an ecclesiastical or garrison school in town. From this time on the boys returned home only for vacations, moving from school to a long period of military or governmental administrative service, including frequent relocation. According to Raeff, the Russian nobleman, divorced from his home and unable to strike roots elsewhere, became alienated from his native land and formed bonds instead with peers, who shared his experience of education and state service.

The education received by the nobleman was not native, but Western. Instead of preparing him to deal with the reality of serf Russia, contended Raeff, Western education turned the nobleman against the government, whose growing bureaucratic administration not only protected the reality of serfdom and oppression, but also interposed itself between the nobleman and an idealized earlier personal connection with the autocrat that the nobleman liked to believe he and his forebears had enjoyed. At the same time, the noble's Western education furnished him with a number of abstract, not to say utopian, notions about how he might end Russia's ignorance and slavery and turn it into a country he could be proud of. In Raeff's view the childhood and education of the nobleman cut him off from his native roots at the bottom and from the tsarist father at the top while providing him with a critical model for radically altering the first and overthrowing the second. The revolutionary intelligentsia of the nineteenth century was born.[17]

Raeff's conception came under attack immediately by Michael Confino. Confino argued that Raeff was using the term "alienation" under a definition proper to conditions of a highly mobile twentieth-century American capitalist society and that its application to eighteenth-century Russia was anachronistic. Moreover, even if the conceptualization could be accepted, the description of the life of Russian nobles was inaccurate. They did not lose an attachment to their childhood home and, as their memoirs attest, continued during service to take responsibility for their family lands and to remember them fondly. At the end of service they returned home to manage their estates and live out their days there.

Confino also corrected Raeff's picture of the anarchic childhood of noblemen and traumatic break with it at the time they began formal education. Fathers were not absent most of the time, at least not after 1762, when the tsarist government released nobles from the requirement of service. The majority of noblemen, Confino wrote, thereafter served only ten or fifteen years, beginning in their teens, and returned home to manage their estates at ages twenty-five to thirty. They were on hand much of the time to supervise their children's upbringing. Even when fathers were away in service the image of the father remained; his power and his authority were not questioned. The role of rank and service in the life of the young noble was strongly reinforced in all his training and experience, so that there could be no confusion about his place in the world and no unresolvable tension between the freedom of his early childhood and the rigors of school and military service. Confino pointed out that if anyone had thought to ask the son of a noble what he wanted to be when he grew up, the child would scarcely have shown any confusion or responded, as children often do today, "I don't know." The question would have seemed pointless; the child knew exactly who he was and what he had to be when he grew up.[18]

Neither Raeff nor Confino had much to say about the childhood of girls, even though women played an important role in the revolutionary intelligentsia, the social group whose origins these scholars sought to explain. More attention to the childhood of both sexes was given in a dissertation by Jessica Tovrov that treated the nobility during the first half of the nineteenth century.[19] She emphasized the similarities in the early upbringing of boys and girls. Children of both sexes were placed in the care of nannies and allowed a good deal of freedom. From the parents' point of view early childhood was largely a matter of physical development. The thinking of educated Russians was heavily tinged with rationalism, and they could see little point in working with children until the children could begin to reason. Most educated grown-ups did not understand childish behavior as different or age-appropriate; non-adult conduct in children was simply viewed as wrong or inferior and, in this sense, punishable. As a rule, parents did not become involved with young children, but remained remote and were perceived less as companions than as models for the roles young people would one day have to occupy. Accordingly, children developed emotional bonds with their nannies and playmates (who were almost invariably members of their immediate or extended family). Again, as in Raeff's account, age seven or eight formed the break with early childhood. At this time boys had to leave the care of women and begin training under the tutelage of men for their role of state service and family leadership. A girl moved to the supervision of her mother or a governess. In both cases great stress was placed on training for a role. Personal development or self-enrichment had little place in Russian upbringing. The society was organized on the principles of strict hierarchy and authority, and behavior was strongly role-governed. Children, therefore, had to learn to subordinate individual needs to the demands of the roles for which they were being prepared.

In the second half of the nineteenth century this view of childhood began to be replaced among a narrow stratum of Western-educated Russians with the notion of childhood as a unique period of innocence. A former openness about sexuality, intimacy, and adult issues in the presence of children moved toward a more protective orientation. Separate play and sleeping arrangements for boys and girls became more common, as did parental involvement in early child rearing.

These changes paralleled a shift to the idea of marriage for love among the same social stratum. In short, the emotional side of life began to be taken more seriously.[20] One of the first places this new attitude could be seen was in the mothering practices of educated women living in frustrating forced marriages with men who were not their equals intellectually or emotionally. In examining the childhoods of women in the revolutionary movement of the 1860s and 1870s Barbara Engel found that the mothers of these women aspired to a life of greater freedom and personal development but were trapped in confining marriages of the old type. In reaction they broke with the old ways of child rearing and nurtured in their girls aspirations for lives of freedom and social commitment.[21]

Another kind of psychohistorical interpretation of Russian childhood was offered in the 1970s by Patrick P. Dunn. In a blend of Lloyd deMause's evolutionary scheme and Erik Erikson's child development model Dunn portrayed upper-class Russian childhood as a mixture of neglect and repression. The early years of childhood were marked by neglect and even hostility on the part of the parents, according to Dunn. In guiding their children Russian parents used "power-assertive discipline rather then warmth, understanding, and love-oriented disciplinary techniques."[22] Erikson's schema was used by Dunn to analyze the importance in the Russian context of the development of the child's sense of autonomy, a quality on which Russian experience had not placed a very high value and which was therefore repressed by Russian discipline. Dunn noted the slavish relations of children to parents and did not accept the usual explanation that parents blocked the autonomy of their children so as to conform them to the restricted autonomy that adults could exercise. He suggested more complicated mechanisms, arguing that the exaggerated deference of children to parents could be "a reaction formation in the service of the ego's repression of the impulse for autonomy,'' or, perhaps more intelligibly, that adult despotism was a compensatory, rechanneled expression of the original impulse for autonomy that had been repressed.[23]

Not everyone in Russia was quiescent and deferential. Dunn found the explanation for the revolutionary spirit in Russia to lie in the nonnormative behavior of some parents, who brought their children up in an atmosphere of love and concern that permitted the children to fully develop their sense of personal autonomy. Lenin's father, for example, was said to have "taught his children the art of the game of chess and constantly played with his sons." Finding similarly loving childhoods in the biographies of some other dissidents and revolutionaries, Dunn hypothesized that these autonomous individuals could not be happy in their society, and therefore devoted themselves to its destruction. This curious explanation of the Russian revolution has something in common with Raeff's depiction of alienation among the nobility of the eighteenth and early nineteenth centuries, and it is vulnerable to the same criticisms regarding the imposition of an analytical framework that does not take account of the peculiarities of Russian culture and an overinterpretation of source materials. It also should be mentioned that Dunn's study, unlike Raeff's, has a thin source base from which it frequently floats upward into pure theoretical speculation.

Much the same can be said about Erik Erikson's own attempt to explain Russian childhood in his fascinating study "The Legend of Maxim Gorky's Youth."[24] Gorky, by the way, is one revolutionary figure Patrick Dunn neglects to mention, and with good reason, since Gorky's childhood was hardly a story of a loving and supportive relationship with his parents or their stand-ins. Erikson's work is much better than Dunn's because of his awareness of the differentness of Russia: the role of multiple mothering and the powerful collective myths that shape the Russians' view of themselves and their world. Erikson's insight into the Russian personality is thoughtful and productive, but in relying largely on a single biography for his text he does not provide anything like a history of Russian childhood.

The most important and well grounded of the psychological studies of Russian childhood is the work of Richard Wortman. He is engaged in a major study of the imperial family, focusing on relations between individual family members and, more important, on the emotional bonds between rulers and ruled as they are symbolized and reinforced in ceremonial display and public rhetoric. Wortman's first publication on this theme was titled "The Russian Empress as Mother," a study that traced shifts in this mothering role from the incorporation of stern "masculine" values in the early nineteenth century to a more affective, "feminized" imperial upbringing toward the end of the period of tsarist rule.[25] He analyzed the mixture of traditional Russian upbringing and the evolving models of child psychosocial development imported from the West with Western-born empresses and assessed the influence of these patterns of child rearing on the personalities and political effectiveness of the rulers. Wortman's work gains in power because of its thorough grounding in a wealth of source material that draws on a wide range of personal memoirs, descriptions of court and public ceremonial, and newspaper and magazine reports of the contacts between the ruler and the people. Although his study begins with the imperial family, its importance is much broader because of the symbolic significance of the ruling family and the strong predisposition in Russian culture to understand authority in personal terms and to represent it in highly affective parent-child metaphors. The *American Historical Review* recently featured another segment of Wortman's work, "Rule by Sentiment: Alexander II's Journeys Through the Russian Empire," which concentrates on the youth of this reforming emperor.[26] The entire project is scheduled to appear soon in book form.

For the vast majority of Russians childhood remained until the late nineteenth century bound to the demands of the brutal need for survival. This was true for the merchant class and the clergy just as much as it was for the peasants. Life itself was a desperate gamble. As mentioned earlier, even in the last decades of the nineteenth century mortality of children to age five in central Russia was more than 50 percent. In some townships of Moscow province, areas that had better access to health information and services than most other parts of the country, the survival of males to recruitment age (twenty-one years) was only about 30 percent. In other words, parents could not count on their children's survival, and as a result, they may not have given much thought to the meaning of childhood and its significance for later life. Because merchants and clergy formed only a tiny fraction of the population of tsarist Russia, and the majority of them lived little better than the average peasant, a look at peasant childhood will give a sense of the experience of the non-privileged orders as a whole.

Judging from ethnographic accounts, the peasant attitude toward children was practical. Children were necessary to keep the household economy going and to provide support for the parents in their dotage. Yet children also were extra mouths to feed, and too many of them all at once could sink a young family. Looking at the high mortality, one is inclined to believe that peasants may have engaged consciously or unconsciously in a kind of differential child-care regime that would give them some assurance of survival of the most viable of their children while neglecting others. Many Russian doctors regarded peasant child-care practices as abusive, even murderous. When they asked peasants why they did not take better care of their children, they received the reply that it was God's will that the children died, and that no one could feed all the children that were born. One of the chief causes of infant death was the early use of solid food and consequent disruption of the child's digestive system, leading to weaning diarrheas and dehydration, and so, what looked to doctors as abuse may have been the peasants' effort to do more, not less, than they should have in trying in the only way they knew how to nourish their babies fully.[27]

It is believed that, as in most other cultures, Russian parents preferred boys to girls, at least until the nineteenth century. The knowledge of the preference for boys comes largely from proverbs, sayings, and reports by ethnographers of the reaction of peasant parents to the birth of a boy or a girl. More recently some confirming quantitative evidence has appeared. Richard Hellie did counts of slave populations in the seventeenth century that revealed large imbalances in the sex ratios in favor of males, data that he has interpreted as evidence of female infanticide. It should be pointed out that Hellie has no direct corroborative evidence for his conclusions, and early-eighteenth-century population counts do not reveal strong imbalances in sex ratios nationally. Still, there can be little doubt that in the slave populations he refers to, females were not valuable. In my own work on Russian foundlings I was able to recover the sex ratios for abandoned children from the middle eighteenth century to the end of the tsarist era, a count that showed a strong preference for the abandonment of girl babies in the late eighteenth century. This preference attenuated over the next 100 years, and by the 1870s sex no longer seemed to play a part in the decision to abandon a child.[28] This measure is drawn from a subset of the population in more desperate circumstances than others, and cannot therefore be taken as altogether typical (even though as many as one-third of the abandoning parents apparently were married).

Peasants continued even after this period, according to ethnographic accounts, to express more joy at the birth of a boy than of a girl. This was related to the Russian custom of girls marrying out. A boy, when he grew up, was likely to stay on in his natal household or in its immediate vicinity and contribute to the farm operation of his family, whereas girls married out and became labor power for another family. So the rearing of a girl was an investment ultimately in another family's well-being, a thought expressed in the Russian saying: "Feed my parents and I repay a debt; bring up my boys and I make a loan; but provide for a daughter and I throw money out the window."[29] But in the nineteenth century the growth of cottage industry, and the key role that females played in it from a young age, increased the value of girls to their natal families. Their contribution to the household's commercial economy may be important in explaining two shifts in peasant demographic behavior in the first half of the nineteenth century: the decreasing imbalance in the sex ratios of abandoned children and the increasing age at first marriage of all women.

I should add that not everyone in the peasant family preferred a boy to a girl. Peasant mothers, by most accounts, were happy if the first surviving child was a girl, for the mother would then have a helpmate to assist her in the domestic chores and in looking after the children who were to follow.

Other than these few impressions derived largely from demographic data, it is hard to recover notions peasants had about children. Attitudes toward young children in particular were so little articulated that one can easily get the almost certainly mistaken feeling that peasants did not think much about their children. Folklore studies may help to give more balance to our picture by providing insights into peasant attitudes.

Lullabies, in particular, offer glimpses of the feelings of mothers toward their children, even if the songs are largely projections of the mothers' hopes and fears. Some of the songs contained fantasies of wealth and happiness for the children, as in the following:

You'll grow up great—
And walk in gold,
Clothed in purest silver.[30]

But more often lullabies described a future filled with the toil typical of peasant life. Lullabies speak of laboring, plowing the fields, felling trees, catching fish, and going out into the world beyond the village to find work. Mothers also sang of the hard future that awaited their children:

You'll do much walking barefoot,
And have your fill of hunger.[31]

Peasants often spoke of their children as replacements or substitutes for the parents, and they understood the critical connection between the survival of some of their children and the continuation of their household and some assurance of care in their old age. "I rock my son in hopes that he will replace me; I rock my daughter in hopes of a son-in-law" went another lullaby.

Russian folktales are filled with images of children. Here the emphasis often is on the dangers of childhood, especially for girls. For example, wicked step-mothers focus their persecution on stepdaughters rather than, as in Western fairy tales, on both sexes. Could this, again, be a reflection of the differential valuation of the sexes? Much more work needs to be done on the images of children in peasant lore. Here is a rich field for research into the history of childhood in Russia. Russian folklorists have collected large bodies of data but have not, so far as I know, tried to understand their materials from the perspective of the history of childhood.[32]

To return to accounts by doctors and ethnographers, one receives the impression from them that peasant children grew up with a minimum of supervision. Those who survived, once they reached the age of seven or eight, became integrated into the family economy, first as baby-sitters (even before age seven) and then as shepherds. As they became older, the jobs of boys and girls differentiated into the expected adult roles, and by age sixteen the youngsters had taken on nearly the full burden of work appropriate to their sex. Before that time their tasks were combined with play. While shepherding, for example, the children would gather in groups for song and games or even mischief directed against the property of the villagers and the landlord. As they moved into teenage, groups of boys and girls blended work occasions with parties and flirtations.

A Russian anthropologist, Ol'ga Semenova, who spent a long time observing peasants of central Russia in the late nineteenth century, seeing their hard life at close quarters, the easy mixing of adults and children, and the early integration of the children into farm work, seemed to assume that these conditions in some sense cut short childhood for peasants.

It is not uncommon that a ten-year- old reasons like an adult. This is chiefly due to the uncomplicated nature of peasant life and to the participation of the child in almost all work and in all activities of peasant life, in which everything is out in the open. Adults are not restrained by the presence of children from speaking about anything they like, getting drunk, or fighting.[33]

Because children experience hunger and see every day the brutality that is part of their surroundings, they quickly learn the value of things and understand that might makes right, wrote Semenova. She added that a child's attitude toward the authorities and toward doctors and folk healers was the same as that of adults. "Children do not have their own special way of thinking about these people." The children perceive them just as the adults do: as powerful but in some sense incomprehensible actors.

At another point Semenova commented that about the only difference in peasant thinking between the child's and the adult's conception of the world is the important role of parental authority in the child's life and the great dependence that a child feels in regard to the parents. She also conceded that the natural world appeared scarier to children and the supernatural more real, although not a great deal more so, as peasant adults also harbored many irrational fears connected with changelings, witches, goblins, and the like. She drew distinctions less sharply between the child and adult outlooks of peasants than between the attitudes of peasant children and those of children of educated parents. For example, she stressed the "childish" aspects of adult peasant belief (superstition, magic) and the adult aspects of peasant childhood (hunger, brutality, labor, exposure to adult sex), and so collapsed the one into the other. In this respect Semenova's analysis reveals a strong residue of the nobility's paternalistic view of the common people, which was an important element of the rationalizations underlying the serf system that lasted in Russia until the 1860s.

The new view of childhood, which Semenova allowed only to the children of the educated urban dweller, can be found in her implied contrasts with the peasant world. "Little Ivans [peasant children] are very keenly aware of their dependence on their parents. Our children are no less dependent . . . but because they are well-fed, they feel it less." And again, "peasant children with drunken and abusive parents naturally are very frightened children of the kind that we do not have." A childhood protected from the world and separated from exposure to adult responsibilities and behavior was a luxury of the educated class. And by the same token, childhood was not something with its own peculiar rules and developmental patterns, but was, in Semenova's view, something contingent and required a special set of conditions for its achievement. Indeed, the shortest segment of her study of the life of the peasant "Ivan" is the description of childhood, a story largely of punishment and neglect.

Peasant life was not unchanging. A major new study of peasant schools in late-nineteenth-century Russia reveals the rapidly increasing contact of the village with educated urban society and the accompanying powerful striving of many peasants toward education for themselves and their children.[34] These experiences were inevitably associated with the growth of new ideas about the role of childhood and its phases of development. These matters, however, await further study.

After the Revolution of 1917 and the seizure of power by the Bolsheviks, ideas about childhood and the reality of life for most children of the country could scarcely have been farther apart. Leading Bolshevik feminists attacked the entire established context for childhood, including the prerevolutionary schools and the family. The leading Bolshevik feminist, Aleksandra Kollontai, fulminated against the domestic slavery of women and the corrupting influence of the "bourgeois family." Another female leader, Lilina, the head of the Petrograd Education Department, declared in 1918 that

we must exempt children from the pernicious influence of the family. We have to take account of every child, we candidly say that we must nationalize them. From the first days of their life they will be under the beneficial influence of communistic kindergartens and schools. Here they shall grow up as real Communists. Our practical problem is to compel mothers to hand over their children to the Soviet government.[35]

Schemes were projected for communal living arrangements and the near total institutionalization of upbringing, which was to become the preserve of trained specialists. The principal object of the feminists was to free women from household drudgery and the tyranny of husbands. Crucial to this goal was the economic independence of women. The idea was to free them to contribute to society by participating side by side with men in productive labor and Communist party activity. The proposals for the care and training of children were subordinate to this other aim and were not especially well thought out.

Central to the socialist understanding of children was environmentalism, and hence the stress on removing them from the corrupting influence of institutions tied to the old order. Beyond this notion the new leaders had little to go on except vague ideas about the need for inculcating values of collectivism and the solidarity of working people throughout the Soviet Republic and the world. The Soviet government and the party were the first to confront the problem of what a socialist childhood should consist of, what the method and content of a socialist upbringing should be. There were no models. The 1920s became a period of experimentation. A wide variety of methods and models were tried, including many child-centered approaches to upbringing and school, without any of the schemes gaining wide support or becoming the basis of a national policy.[36]

Much more urgent matters of child survival and the integration of large numbers of former rural dwellers into urban life soon overrode the hopes of those seeking fresh approaches to child rearing. The war, revolution, and civil strife had left millions of children orphaned and homeless. Precise figures are not available, but in the first years of the 1920s as many as 6 or 7 million children were apparently wandering the country without supervision or visible means of support. They lived in lean-tos and empty barrels on the edges of towns and railyards, and they survived as best they could by panhandling, robbery, and prostitution. Large numbers did not survive, however, and succumbed to disease, hunger, and violence.[37] The plight of these homeless children roused the sympathy and engaged the efforts of educational reformers with a more traditional bent, most prominent of whom was Anton Makarenko, a schoolteacher in the Ukraine who, with government assistance, opened a series of institutions for the care and rehabilitation of the homeless children. He combined the approaches of "tough love" with fierce group dependence, conformity, and solidarity in a successful program for educating and integrating the children (who had been living as a kind of criminal underclass) into Soviet society as productive citizens. Makarenko at first labored in obscurity, but toward the end of the 1920s, when the political line running from the regimentation of the civil war through the battles for leadership of the party and state at mid-decade to the ascendance of Stalin and his program of forced industrialization intersected with Makarenko's development of collectivist methods of child rearing, his ideas gained national prominence and formed the basis for much of Soviet educational thinking under Stalin's regime and beyond.[38]

The industrialization drive and collectivization of agriculture was accompanied by a massive influx of peasants to the cities and a ruralization of urban life and values, including attitudes toward children and family life. The government, too, not wishing to transfer funds from industry to child care, encouraged a return to traditional methods of child rearing. This amounted to placing the full burden on the family and, especially, the mother, who in many cases also was expected to work at wage labor. These changes doomed the experimentation of the 1920s and turned childhood back toward the peasant model in which older siblings or grandparents had responsibility for child rearing and much of the time children were left to grow up on their own. The child-centered family that had been developing among the long-settled urban workers in white collar and skilled craft jobs was for a time overwhelmed by the inundation of village people and their child-rearing practices.[39] Only after World War II did the shift come again toward the modern child-centered family, a process that was fed by many events, including devastating population losses, rapid increases in education levels, and a reversal of cultural influence from ruralization of the cities to urbanization of the villages.

NOTES

1. A recent work has, however, introduced Soviet readers to the issues and methods of the history of childhood as practiced in the West. See I. S. Kon, *Rebenok i obshchestvo (istoriko-etnograficheskaia perspektiva)* (Moscow, 1988). Unfortunately, Kon includes very little about childhood in Russia.

2. We should know more soon through Daniel Kaiser's nearly completed study of the family in early Russia.

3. For review of the legal evidence on children in medieval Russia, see Szeftel, "Le statut juridique de l'enfant en Russie avant Pierre le Grand," *Recueils de la société Jean Bodin pour l'histoire comparative des institutions*, 36:2 (Brussels, 1976): 635–656; on illegitimacy and infanticide, see Ransel, *Mothers of Misery: Child Abandonment in Russia* (Princeton, N.J., 1988), pp. 9–19.

4. Richard Hellie, *Slavery in Russia, 1450–1725* (Chicago, 1982), pp. 442–459.

5. *Domostroi sil'vestrovskogo izvoda*, ed. I. Glazunov, 2nd ed. (St. Petersburg, 1902), pp. 16–17.

6. V. O. Kliuchevskii, "Dva vospitaniia," *Russkaia mysl'*, 14:3 (1893), pp. 88–89. Quotes from this article and from *Domostroi*, p. 17.

7. Ransel, *Mothers of Misery*, pp. 23–29; for the background to charitable activity generally, see Adele Lindenmyer, "Public Poor Relief and Private Charity in Late Imperial Russia," Ph.D. dissertation (Princeton University, 1980), pp. 13–56.

8. So named by the Soviet scholar A. P. Babushkina, *Istoriia russkoi detskoi literatury* (Moscow, 1948), p. 40, as cited in Max J. Okenfuss, *The Discovery of Childhood in Russia: The Evidence of the Slavic Primer* (Newtonville, Mass., 1980), p. 22. I am indebted to Okenfuss's book for the information in this chapter on primers and the *Mirror*.

9. Okenfuss, *Discovery of Childhood*, pp. 22–35, 45–48.

10. I. T. Pososhkov, *Zaveshchanie otecheskoe* (St. Petersburg, 1893), p. 44.

11. V. N. Tatishchev, "Razgovor dvukh priiatelei o pol'ze nauki i uchilishchakh," in *Izbrannye proizvedeniia* (Leningrad, 1979), p. 67.

12. A. T. Bolotov, *Zhizn' i prikliucheniia Andreia Bolotova, opisannoe samim im*, 3 vols. (St. Petersburg, 1871), 1:66–68.

13. See examples cited in P. M. Maikov, *Ivan Ivanovich Betskoi: Opyt ego biografii* (St. Petersburg, 1904), p. 473; and in L. N. Semenova, *Ocherki istorii byta i kul'turnoi zhizni Rossii pervaia polovina XVIII v.* (Leningrad, 1982), pp. 97–98.

14. The best general account is P. M. Maikov, *Ivan Ivanovich Betskoi: Opyt ego biografii* (St. Petersburg, 1904); but see also Kliuchevskii, "Dva vospitaniia," for an assessment of the institutions.

15. *Ocherki istorii shkol i pedagogicheskoi mysli narodov SSSR XVIII v.–pervaia polovina XIX v.*, edited by M. F. Shabaeva (Moscow, 1973), p. 171.

16. A. N. Radishchev, *Izbrannye filosoficheskie i obshchestvenno-politicheskie proizvedeniia* (Moscow, 1952), p. 108.

17. Marc Raeff, *Origins of the Russian Intelligentsia: The Eighteenth-Century Nobility* (New York, 1966), especially chapters 4 and 5.

18. Michael Confino, "A propos de la noblesse russe au XVIIIᵉ siècle," *Annales E.S.C.* 22:6 (Nov.—Dec. 1967): 1186–1193.

19. Tovrov, "Action and Affect in the Russian Noble Family from the Late Eighteenth Century through the Reform Period," Ph.D. dissertation (University of Chicago, 1980), published in Garland series on Modern European History as *The Russian Noble Family: Structure and Change* (New York, 1987).

20. All this according to Tovrov, *The Russian Noble Family: Structure and Change*, pp. 146–183, 348–381.

21. Barbara Alpern Engel, *Mothers and Daughters: Women of the Intelligentsia in Nineteenth-Century Russia* (Cambridge, 1983), pp. 11–53.

22. Dunn, " 'That Enemy Is the Baby': Childhood in Imperial Russia," *The History of Childhood*, edited by Lloyd de Mause (New York, 1974), p. 393.

23. Dunn, " 'That Enemy Is the Baby,' " pp. 397–398.

24. Chapter 10 of his *Childhood and Society*, 2nd ed. (New York, 1963).

25. Richard Wortman, "The Russian Empress as Mother," in *The Family in Imperial Russia: New Lines of Historical Research*, edited by David L. Ransel (Urbana, 1978), pp. 60–74.

26. Richard Wortman, "Rule by Sentiment: Alexander II's Journeys through the Russian Empire," *American Historical Review*, 95 (June 1990): 745–771.

27. This is a problem that I am currently working on with a comparative analysis. See "Child Care Cultures in the Russian Empire," *Russia's Women: Accommodation, Resistance, Transformation*, edited by Barbara Evans Clements, Barbara Engel, and Christine Worobec (Berkeley: University of California Press, 1991).

28. Ransel, *Mothers of Misery*, chapter 7.

29. T. Ivanovskaia, "Deti v poslovitsakh i pogovorkakh russkogo naroda," *Vestnik vospitaniia*, 19(1908): 121.

30. A. N. Martynova, "Life of the Pre-Revolutionary Village as Reflected in Popular Lullabies," *The Family in Imperial Russia: New Lines of Historical Research*, edited by David L. Ransel (Urbana: University of Illinois Press, 1978), p. 176.

31. Ibid.

32. For a start, one could look at the article by Stephen P. Dunn, "The Family as Reflected in Russian Folklore," *The Family in Imperial Russia: New Lines of Historical Research*, edited by David L. Ransel (Urbana: University of Illinois Press, 1978), pp. 153–170, and the references cited therein.

33. O. P. Semenova-Tian'-Shanskaia, *Zhizn' "Ivana": Ocherki iz byta krest'ian odnoi iz chernozemnykh gubernii* (Zapiski Imperatorskogo Russkogo Geograficheskogo Obshchestva po otdeleniiu etnografii, vol. 39, St. Petersburg, 1914), especially chapter 4.

34. Ben Eklof, *Russian Peasant Schools: Officialdom, Village Culture, and Popular Pedagogy, 1864–1914*, (Berkeley, 1986).

35. Quoted in James Bowen, *Soviet Education: Anton Makarenko and the Years of Experiment* (Madison, 1965), p. 36.

36. A recent review of these schemes can be found in Wladimir Berelowitch, "Modèles familiaux dans la Russie des années 1920," *L'évolution des modèles familiaux dans les pays de l'est européen et en U.R.S.S.*, edited by Basile Kerblay (Paris, 1988), pp. 25–40.

37. Their story is told in a novel based on close observation of the children, dubbed "the unsupervised" (*besprizornye*), by Vyachelav Shishkov, *Children of the Street*, translated by Thomas P. Whitney (Royal Oak, Mich., 1979). A near-contemporary study was done by Vladimir Zenzinov, *Bezprizornye* (Paris, 1929), which is now available in English as *Deserted: The Story of the Children Abandoned in Soviet Russia*, translated by Agnes Platt (Westport, Conn., 1975).

38. For his history and an extensive bibliography, see Bowen, *Soviet Education*.

39. See the important studies of Soviet attitudes based upon interviews with Soviet citizens who escaped to the West after World War II: H. Kent Geiger, *The Family in Soviet Russia* (Cambridge, Mass., 1968), especially chapters 10 and 11.

REFERENCES

Bowen, James. *Soviet Education: Anton Markarenko and the Years of Experiment*. Madison, 1965.

Brine, Jenny, Maureen Perrie, and Andrew Sutton, eds. *Home, School and Leisure in the Soviet Union*. London, 1980.

Dunn, Patrick. " 'That Enemy Is the Baby': Childhood in Imperial Russia." In *The History of Childhood*, edited by Lloyd deMause. New York, 1974, pp. 383–405.

Eklof, Ben. *Russian Peasant Schools: Officialdom, Village Culture, and Popular Pedagogy 1864–1914*. Berkeley, 1986.

Engel, Barbara Alpern. *Mothers and Daughters: Women of the Intelligentsia in Nineteenth-Century Russia*. Cambridge, 1983.

Froese, Leonhard. *Ideengeschichtliche Triebkräfte der russischen und sovjetischen Pädagogik*. Heidelberg, 1956.

Geiger, H. Kent. *The Family in Soviet Russia*. Cambridge, Mass., 1968.

Gromyko, M. M. *Traditsionnye normy povedeniia i formy obshcheniia russkikh krest'ian XIX v.* Moscow, 1986.

Hellie, Richard. *Slavery in Russia, 1450–1725*. Chicago, 1982.

Kerblay, Basile, ed. *L'évolution des modèles familiaux dans les pays de l'Est européen et en U.R.S.S.* (Cultures & sociétés de l'Est, 9). Paris, 1988.

Kliuchevskii, V. O. "Dva vospitaniia." *Russkaia mysl'* 14:3 (1893):79–99.

Kon, I. S. *Rebenok i obshchestvo (istoriko-etnograficheskaia perspektiva)*. Moscow, 1988.

Makarenko, Anton. *The Road to Life: An Epic of Education*, translated by Ivy and Tatiana Litvinov. 3 vols. Moscow, 1955.

Okenfuss, Max J. *The Discovery of Childhood in Russia: The Evidence of the Slavic Primer*. Newtonville, Mass., 1980.

Raeff, Marc. *Origins of the Russian Intelligentsia: The Eighteenth-Century Nobility*. New York, 1966.

Ransel, David L. *Mothers of Misery: Child Abandonment in Russia*, Princeton, N.J., 1988.

———, ed. *The Family in Imperial Russia: New Lines of Historical Research*. Urbana, 1978.

Semenova, L. N. *Ocherki istorii byta i kul'turnoi zhizni Rossii pervaia polovina XVIII v.*, Leningrad, 1982.

Semenova-Tian'-Shanskaia, O. P. *Zhizn' "Ivana": Ocherki iz byta krest'ian odnoi iz chernozemnykh gubernii* (Zapiski Imperatorskogo Russkogo Geograficheskogo Obshchestva po otdeleniiu etnografii, vol.39). St. Petersburg, 1914.

Shabaeva, M. F. *Ocherki istorii shkol i pedagogicheskoi mysli narodov SSSR XVIII v.— pervaia polovina XIX v.* Moscow, 1973.

Tovrov, Jessica. *The Russian Noble Family: Structure and Change*. New York, 1987.

Szeftel, Marc. "Le statut juridique de l'enfant en Russie avant Pierre le Grand." *Recueils de la société Jean Bodin pour l'histoire comparative des institutions*. Vol. 36. Brussels, 1976, pp. 635–656.

Wachtel, Andrew Baruch. *The Battle for Childhood: Creation of a Russian Myth*. Stanford, 1990.

Zenzinov, Vladimir. *Deserted: The Story of the Children Abandoned in Soviet Russia*, translated by Agnes Platt. Westport, Conn., 1975.

19

THE UNITED STATES

Joseph M. Hawes, Constance B. Schulz,
and N. Ray Hiner

The amount of historical scholarship on children in the United States has increased dramatically since the 1970s. This work covers a wide variety of topics and touches on the American experience from colonial times to the present. In the late 1970s and early 1980s much of the research focused on the colonial period, but recently there has been an outpouring of scholarly publication about children in the progressive era and in the late twentieth century. Some of the themes in the literature on the most recent past include the increasing activity of the federal government in children's lives, the rise of the child-care expert, the increased social importance of the peer group as children spent more and more time with their own age-groups, the transformation of the family as it responded to new economic challenges, and the participation of young children in the market economy as consumers in their own right. One could label the twentieth century the age of the child simply because of the number of programs designed for children and the number of people who make their living doing something with, to, or for children.[1]

Today there are programs for newborns, infants, toddlers, pre-schoolers, afterschool activities, and summer work for adolescents. There are special television series for children of all ages, organizations of all kinds, marketing strategies designed to identify and tap the buying power of specific groups of children and young people. All of this suggests that "childhood" has expanded as a social construct and reflects the radical changes experienced by American society since the seventeenth century. Thus children growing up today face very different and in some ways more complicated conditions, choices, and responses than did children of the colonial era.

The literature on the history of American children that has appeared since the early 1980s has, like childhood itself, become more specialized. No new broad synthesis has appeared; nor is there an interpretation that incorporates this entire literature. Instead, recent scholarship is characterized by study of particular aspects of the lives of children in greater depth.

REFERENCE WORKS

The most comprehensive guide to the literature of the history of children in the United States is *American Childhood: A Research Guide and Historical Handbook* (1985), edited by Joseph M. Hawes and N. Ray Hiner.[2] The purpose of this chapter is to supplement rather than summarize that earlier work. Consequently only a few of the most significant works discussed there are considered here. Although more limited in scope, Bernard Mergen's *Play and Playthings* (1982) also is a valuable reference work.[3] It provides a history of children's play (broadly defined) and a comprehensive guide to the literature on that topic.

The history of childhood is a relatively new field, but the range and depth of recent scholarship have made possible the publication of several collections of documents and scholarly essays.

COLLECTIONS OF PRIMARY MATERIALS

The standard collection of documents concerning the history of American children is the now classic *Children and Youth in America: A Documentary History*, edited by Robert Bremner and others and published in three volumes from 1950 to 1974.[4] This comprehensive collection includes a wide variety of primary sources and provides excellent coverage topically, chronologically, and regionally. It also includes lists of important events in the history of childhood and a large bibliography. A particular strength of this collection is its treatment of legislation pertaining to children.

Less extensive collections of primary sources include Philip Greven's *Child Rearing Concepts 1628–1861: Historical Sources*, a collection of writings about child rearing, and James Axtell's *The Indian Peoples of Eastern America: A Documentary of the Sexes*.[5] The Axtell volume is organized around the life cycle and includes both early and contemporary accounts as well as the editor's discussion of the historical validity of the documents. Axtell's work is vital for an understanding of the history of native American childhood.

Still another collection of basic documents relating to children is *American Families: A Documentary History*, edited by Donald M. Scott and Bernard Wishy.[6] Scott and Wishy embrace no single interpretation of the history of the family, but seek instead to introduce readers to the range and diversity of family history. This collection contains excerpts from classic pieces of child-rearing advice. Taken together, these works provide a set of primary materials that illustrate many of the experiences of children in the United States. The principal strength of these collections is the focus on public matters. Although they contain private documents, most of this material remains unpublished and unexploited.

COLLECTIONS OF SCHOLARLY ARTICLES AND ESSAYS

Anthologies constitute another major component of the literature on the history of American children. Two of the most recent examples of this genre have the same primary title: *Growing Up in America: Children in Historical Perspective* (1985), edited by N. Ray Hiner and Joseph M. Hawes, and *Growing Up in America: Historical Experiences*, edited by Harvey J. Graff and published in 1987.[7]

A somewhat older but valuable work is *Regulated Children/Liberated Children: Education in Psychohistorical Perspective*, edited by Barbara Finkelstein. This volume is made up of original essays and is notable for the range and diversity of methodologies included.[8] *Familes and Children*, the 1985 proceedings of the Dublin Seminar for New England Folklife, is a slightly different sort of anthology. According to the editor, the seminar, which covered topics from the seventeenth to the nineteenth centuries, "examined a broad range of artifactual decorative arts, documentary, archeological, and pictorial evidence in an attempt to identify the uniqueness of New England's demographic history, to explore its child nurturing and tutelage practices, as well as to reconstruct its traditions of courtship and everyday family life."[9] Unfortunately no similar works for other regions of the country currently exist.

Similar to *Families and Children* but broader in scope is *Loving, Parenting, and Dying: The Family Cycle in England and America, Past and Present*, edited by Vivian C. Fox and Martin H. Quitt.[10] The essays in this collection are organized around the family life cycle concept. The introductory chapter of this collection includes extensive references.

CHILDREN DURING THE COLONIAL AND EARLY NATIONAL PERIODS

Historians who have studied children in the seventeenth century have concentrated on the English-speaking peoples in New England and the Chesapeake. With the notable exception of recent work by James Axtell and Margaret Szasz on American Indian children, neither race nor gender considerations have received the attention they deserve.[11] Nor have class differences among seventeenth-century children received adequate attention. For the eighteenth century the coverage of children and childhood by historians has broadened to include children of African slave families, the urban working class, and the families of German immigrants, New York Dutch families, and Pennsylvania Quakers. But the basic focus continues to be on children and families of the predominantly English-speaking elites.

Children in Early American Families

Edmund Sears Morgan's *The Puritan Family* (1944) and his *Virginians at Home* (1952) were among the first works in early American history that included significant discussions of parental attitudes toward their children, the behavior of children within the family, and the interplay between family members of differing generations in an age when nearly half the entire population was composed of children under the age of sixteen. Morgan's analysis replaced the antiquarian, descriptive approach to colonial children and the family that marked early studies. Heavily influenced by his familiarity with the Puritan religious context and based almost exclusively on literary evidence, Morgan's books are gracefully written and still contain useful insights into colonial children and families, but their interpretive framework has been superseded, though not entirely supplanted, by recent studies influenced by the "new social history."[12]

John Demos, in *A Little Commonwealth* (1970), was one of the first of the new social historians to examine the experience of children within seventeenth-century New England families. In this work Demos used quantitative "community reconstitution," psychological theory, and anthropological approaches to the study of material culture in Plymouth Colony. He described a community without clear distinctions between the nature or roles of children and adults, where a shared communal experience was rooted in lack of privacy in the home only partially mitigated for both children and adults by ready access to an extensive outdoor environment. For Demos the modern perception of adolescence as stressful breaking away from childhood dependence into adult responsibility had little meaning in such a setting.[13] The analysis of demographic and genealogical data on which Demos built his description of Plymouth contributed during the 1970s and 1980s to a burgeoning cottage industry of family and community history studies, but none looked as closely as did Demos at the role of children within the family in New England. Because their focus is on the institution of the family within the locus of particular communities, no clear synthesis concerning children emerged from these studies. They do agree, however, that the demographic profile in New England was one of large families, with relatively low parental death rates (especially in the seventeenth century), and increasing intergenerational tensions as available land for division among adult sons declined in the eighteenth century. These factors led to changing patterns of courtship, premarital pregnancy, adolescent struggles for independence, and inheritance. But while acknowledging change over time, these studies disagree "about the nature and duration of childhood, the quality of childhood experiences, and the influence of parental attitudes and practices on children" during the seventeenth century.[14]

More recent work on colonial families has focused more directly on children and on areas other than New England. Darrett and Anita Rutman have observed that because of relatively low mortality rates in New England and the tragically high death rates in the Chesapeake, especially in the seventeenth century, children in New England lived in a parental situation, whereas Chesapeake children lived in a kinship situation.[15] Important essays by Lorena Walsh, Lois Green Carr, Allan Kulikoff, and the Rutmans describing the experience of children in Chesapeake society appeared in two anthologies growing out of conferences held in 1974 on seventeenth-century Maryland and the Chesapeake.[16]

Daniel Blake Smith (*Inside the Great House*) and Darrett and Anita Rutman (*A Place in Time*) have examined family life and the changing role of children within it for different groups in Chesapeake society. Smith describes an elite planter class in which eighteenth-century children received autonomy and affection. The Rutmans describe an economically stratified Middlesex County, Virginia, society within which high mortality rates and an agricultural economy created complex family structures. Many of these families included sibling and half sibling offspring of several adults, with extended kin networks having responsibility for protecting the people and the inheritances of children among the subsistence and middling planters as well as the elite. In his *Tobacco and Slaves* Allan Kulikoff treats black and white children in Prince George's County, Maryland, more briefly in his examination of family inheritance and work patterns.[17]

For the early nineteenth century the historical focus has continued to move southward. Jan Lewis, in *The Pursuit of Happiness*, described the middle-class parental expectations of a declining elite in postrevolutionary Virginia, noting that the children in these increasingly child-oriented families were protected and loved, but failed to develop the independence and imaginative skills characteristic of their revolutionary forefathers. Jane Turner Censer, analyzing *North Carolina Planters and Their Children*, also finds strong emotional bonds between parents and among parents and children, much like the companionate marriage and the child-oriented values expected with a modern family.[18]

Early American Attitudes Toward Children and Child Rearing

The study of family history has become a forum for discussion of changing attitudes toward children. An important recent development in women's history, the discussion of childbearing and childbirth, offers similar insight into the attitudes of parents toward infancy and children. Where family studies portray a growing parental affection for their children, studies of childbirth and the childbearing experience reveal a tension between parental affection and love of infants, and fear caused by high death rates among both mothers and infants. Recent scholarship, however, suggests that earlier studies that concluded that parents were indifferent to very young children because of the threat of infant mortality were mistaken; parents did love and mourn for the infants they bore and far too often lost. But at the same time, the attitudes of mothers who feared death in childbirth led to a dramatic change, beginning early in the nineteenth century. These mothers sought to make childbirth safer by calling on the assistance of male physicians to lessen the danger to themselves and their newborn infants. Catherine M. Scholten explores this issue in her ground-breaking study *Childbearing in American Society, 1650–1850*. In a broad interpretive work, *Brought to Bed: Childbearing in American Society, 1750–1950*, Judith Walzer Leavitt examines changes in the childbirth experience from the late colonial period to the mid-twentieth century.[19]

Many family history studies include extended discussions of the child-rearing strategies that families of a particular region, time period, or language and cultural group chose to follow. For the colonial and early national periods one significant study addresses child rearing directly. Philip Greven's *The Protestant Temperament* has been criticized for ignoring the impact of change over time and differences of wealth or status when assigning permanent value to the three child-rearing strategies that he labeled "evangelical," "moderate," and "genteel." Nevertheless, his detailed descriptions of these strategies, and the impact each had on the lives of children, proved to be the starting point for much of the recent discussion of child-rearing practices.[20]

Demographic Realities for Early American Children

Although much of the work cited above under the category "Family Studies" relied in part on the use of demographic data for its interpretations, Robert V. Wells made the demographic analysis of family patterns in all the colonies the explicit basis for his study of *Revolutions in Americans' Lives*. Wells' most important contribution is his argument for the existence of a revolutionary demographic transition of declining fertility that led to smaller families, and more concentration of parental attention and expectations on their fewer children. This transition is integral to an understanding of the attitudes of adults toward children, and the ways in which children and childhood affected adults. When exactly did this transition occur and why? Did a change in parental attitudes toward children lead to more effective use of existing birth control methods, or did improved ability to limit childbirth result in a change in family size and then to changed parental attitudes? Were women, men, or both the decision-makers in successful family limitation, and how important were fears of the dangers of childbirth in influencing such decisions?

The work of Wells and other historical demographers is central to historians' understanding of the conditions that shaped the development of children and the societal perceptions of childhood. Children in colonial and early national society lived different lives from modern children in part because there were more of them in proportion to adults; even with high infant death rates few children grew to adulthood as only children, and thus the existence of other children within the household and the community was an important condition of childhood before 1800. The circumstances that shaped these demographic patterns—birth rates, infant mortality, the dangers of childbirth and other causes of parental death, the factors that affected child health—are thus closely associated with the larger patterns of demographic change in studies of the conditions affecting children.[21]

Infant and child mortality was an important factor shaping the conditions of childhood until well into the nineteenth century. Infants who survived childbirth were nursed, usually by their mothers, although among the wealthier families they might have been suckled by a wet nurse. Some wealthy Southern families, like those of Eliza Lucas Pinckney, used slave mothers as wet nurses for their own offspring. The immunity thus gained did not prevent a seventeenth-century mortality rate for infants under one year that reached as high as 30 percent in New England; the death rate for children in the seventeenth century was consistently higher in the Chesapeake than in New England. Infant mortality rates in rural areas and the South did not decline significantly before the American Revolution; moreover, periodic epidemics (such as those in 1702, 1721, 1730, and 1752) swept away young children, who were particularly susceptible to smallpox, yellow fever, intestinal disease, influenza, and the peculiarly child-fatal diseases of scarlet fever and diphtheria. The latter was so virulent in the mid-eighteenth century that at least one New England community was reported to have lost all its children under the age of fifteen. To these dangers were added still others for slave children. According to Kenneth Kiple and Virginia King, deficiencies in the slave diet created a mortality rate for slave children double that of their white counterparts.[22]

It was this high probability of death for children that created for many New England children and their parents the particular theological problems that Peter G. Slater described in his *Children in the New England Mind in Death and Life*. For New England children the actuality of frequent childhood deaths meant both an immediacy to the preaching of Calvinist clergy (whether ''Old Light'' or ''New Light'') about hell and damnation, and a more practical result of reducing somewhat the size of large families. Ray Hiner demonstrated the practical impact of high infant and child mortality on the conditions in which children live by a chart illustrating the family of Cotton Mather in the seventeenth century: although two of his three wives bore him sixteen children in twenty-six years, only twice did the household contain more than two children under the age of five.[23]

The Education of Early American Children

The first two volumes of Lawrence Cremin's monumental study, *American Education*, provide the most comprehensive treatment of the education of Euro-American children. Cremin says that there was limited development of formal educational institutions in the seventeenth century, primarily in New England, that served traditional community needs for literate lay people and an educated clergy. In the eighteenth century three distinctive forms of educational institution emerged below the collegiate level: the ''English'' or common grammar school, with its emphasis on practical subjects; the ''Latin School,'' which focused on classical languages, preparing young men for college; and the ''academy,'' which added classical and occasionally collegiate subjects to basic reading and ciphering. Wealthier families, particularly in the South, where a lower density of population made it difficult to establish formal schools, hired tutors for their children. Although educational levels for children were lower in the South, even on the South Carolina frontier, dissenter and Anglican clergy sometimes provided a rudimentary common school education.[24]

James Axtell, in *The School Upon a Hill*, argued that by the end of the eighteenth century, most New England grammar schools used less physically punitive and rigid discipline than they had earlier: some schools included a few young girls among their students. The groundwork was thus laid for a dramatic transformation in the form and function of the institutions that delivered education beginning in the early nineteenth century: education increasingly became an essential component of preparing young Americans for republican citizenship, capable not simply of inculcating knowledge, but of transforming the child.[25]

Another significant book on colonial education is Margaret Szasz's recent study of *Indian Education in the American Colonies*. Her work is an important contribution not only to the history of education, but also to the history of Indian-White relations in the United States. In addition to a discussion of the various European attempts to educate native Americans during the colonial period, Szasz provides an overview of native American educational practices, including a succinct description of child-rearing practices. She notes that two factors played a major role in Indian-white relations in the colonial period: the degree to which European-style education influenced Indian youth and the development of cultural brokers, usually native Americans who understood both cultures.[26]

CHILDREN IN NINETEENTH- AND TWENTIETH-CENTURY AMERICA

A number of changes marked the transition from colonial, preindustrial, early America to modern, urban, industrializing America, and many of these changes involved children. Chief among them were the demographic transitions—the emergence of the urban middle-class family and the beginnings of the decline in the birthrate, which has continued (with one notable exception) to the present. The birth of a new nation, the dawn of a new century, and the appearance of a new system of gender relations all combined to influence the growth and development of children. Some authorities even argue that the modern American concept of childhood was created in this period.

Child-Rearing Advice and Practice

The problem of relating child-rearing advice to the actual practice of child rearing remains a difficult one for historians. Although advice literature does not necessarily reflect the behavior of people, it certainly retains considerable historical significance. First, scholars need to know what advice was available, and second, changing advice is important in its own right. Typically, historians interested in child-rearing advice are interested in other questions besides what kind of care children received.

An early and effective study of advice literature was Anne L. Kuhn's *The Mother's Role in Childhood Education*, published in 1947. Kuhn analyzed the advice given to young mothers in the middle of the nineteenth century and saw in this literature a foreshadowing of "modern parent education."[27]

Child-rearing advice became a fertile ground for historians after the appearance of Bernard Wishy's pathbreaking *The Child and the Republic* in 1968. Since 1985, however, historians have not been as active in this area of investigation. Wishy's work also included considerable discussion of children's literature because of his interest in "religious ideals and moral indoctrination." Wishy saw his work as a contribution to the history of ideas and to "the study of the iconography of the American child, at home, in school, and at prayer, in a period which we have too long mistakenly assumed to have been relatively barren or hopelessly antediluvian in the attention it gave to child care."[28]

Following in Wishy's footsteps, at least with respect to using children's literature to study the transmission of ideas, is Gail Murray's article "Rational Thought and Republican Virtues: Children's Literature, 1789–1820," which appeared in the *Journal of the Early Republic* in 1988. According to Murray, "books written for the instruction and entertainment of children do provide penetrating glimpses into those values a culture holds particularly essential, and thus children become the natural recipients of conscious and unconscious cultural motifs." Murray found that the literature reflected "a society much concerned about its future health and stability." This concern led to "an emphasis on character-building above all other objectives in its instructions to the next generation."[29]

Another classic that stands with Wishy is Charles Strickland's analysis of the child-rearing practices of Bronson Alcott. Alcott observed his children closely, and romantic that he was, he learned a great deal from them. Strickland argues that Alcott's observations mark the beginning of modern child psychology.[30]

Nancy Cott's "Notes Toward an Interpretation of Antebellum Childrearing" (1978) also provides important insight into nineteenth-century advice literature. Cott states that the authors of advice literature "took as their first premise the definitive importance of the events and habits of childhood, especially early childhood." She also found a new concern with the physical health of children, and, following Kuhn, an "affirmation of the mother's predominance." The reasons for this, she argues, is that "the mother's role in child care, like other work roles became more discrete and specialized in the urban/commercial milieu that spawned the childrearing literature." She also says that it is important that family government became the means to produce self-mastery in children rather than an end in itself, and that "parents were encouraged to use invisible restraints or psychological coercions in order to make the child's conscience the real determinant of behavior." Parents were supposed to "convince rather than coerce."[31]

By the twentieth century the government itself was in the business of giving child-rearing advice. Molly Ladd-Taylor provides a study of part of that advice in a look at mothers' letters to the Federal Children's Bureau. Ladd-Taylor's *Raising a Baby the Government Way* includes a sketch of the early history of the Children's Bureau and a discussion of the Bureau's two advice pamphlets, *Prenatal Care* and *Infant Care*. The bulk of Ladd-Taylor's work is taken up with letters that mothers wrote to the Children's Bureau. These letters in turn provide insight into the daily lives of poor women in the early twentieth century.[32]

Particularly useful for the historian is a broad overview of child-rearing advice in the twentieth century, "Do Young Children Need Intellectual Stimulation? Experts' Advice to Parents, 1900–1985," by Julia Wrigley, which appeared in the *History of Education Quarterly* in 1989. Wrigley did a content analysis of 1,017 articles on advice to parents and found a broad set of patterns. Early in the century the authors of advice articles were concerned about the survival of babies and routines for baby management. By the 1930s an emphasis on the emotional development of children had appeared. This in turn paved the way for a focus on the intellectual development of children that began in the 1960s. A common theme for all periods in the twentieth century was that experts warned parents against trying to manage their tasks alone.[33]

Child-Naming Practices

Historians seeking to understand the changing attitudes of parents toward their children have begun to analyze child-naming practices, which permits the historian to study the families of poor children as well as those of the middle and upper classes. Naming patterns can be extracted from genealogical source materials, and linked together for large numbers of illiterate and otherwise historically inarticulate groups as well as for the elite. Such studies also allow historians to compare naming practices among regions, classes, and cultures over time. Name choices not only reflect parents' attitudes toward their children, but also give insight into the embeddedness of a generation within a matrix of larger familial and community values. This is among the newest of the historical work directly relating to children and childhood; it is not yet available in monograph form, but is represented in the journal literature in important studies by Daniel Scott Smith, Cheryl Ann Cody, and others.

Smith pioneered this form of historical inquiry in an article first published in 1977 based on a study of the names of 7,500 children of Hingham, Massachusetts, between 1641 and 1880. He concluded that changes in the pool of common names and the declining practice of assigning names of deceased children to later-born siblings reflected a loss of traditional Puritan parental and community control to more individualistic, secular Yankee forces. Borrowing Smith's methodology, and applying it to a comparative study of African-American slave families and the families of plantation owners in South Carolina, Cody concluded that both the names themselves and the naming patterns—use of birth-day and extended maternal or paternal kin names—were distinctive for each group, with the names of the slave children retaining evidence of strong cultural links to African naming patterns.[34]

Children and Families

Probably no area of social history has spawned more new recent work than family history, a relatively new field and, like the history of children, soon to have a guide to the literature, *American Families, a Research Handbook and Reference Guide*.[35] Although family history is a separate field of study, much of the recent scholarship is of obvious interest to the historian of children. Children spend a great deal of time in families (although some social critics would argue that the amount of time children spend with family members has been declining steadily since the colonial period); thus the study of this institution necessarily involves the study of children. Family historians cannot function effectively without knowledge of the history of children and vice versa.

The best overview of the history of the American family is *Domestic Revolutions*, by Mintz and Kellogg, which was published in 1988.[36] John Demos has recently collected a series of significant essays concerning the history of the family in *Past, Present, and Personal*.[37] In addition to these general works, several important but highly specialized works are now available. Michael Grossberg's *Governing the Hearth: Law and Family in Nineteenth Century America* defies easy classification, but is essential for an understanding of the changing legal status of children and of legal processes that affect children, such as adoption, apprenticeships, and guardianship.[38] Another important legal study is "We, the Family: Constitutional Rights and American Families," by Martha Minow, which appeared in the *Journal of American History* in December of 1987.[39]

The study of ethnic families has been enhanced by Richard Griswold de Castillo's *La Familia*, which is the major source of information available concerning Hispanic children in the United States.[40] A useful collection of scholarly essays is *Ethnic Families in America*.[41] The classic treatment of black families in the United States is Herbert Gutman's *The Black Family in Slavery and Freedom*.[42]

One way to study families (and, by extension, children) who leave no manuscript records is indirectly through the use of statistics. The demographic approach to the study of the history of the family has produced a wealth of scholarly work. For the nonspecialist the best general introduction to the demographic approach is the previously cited work by Robert Wells, *Revolutions in American's Lives* (1982).[43] An important, although speculative, recent work is *Society and Family Strategy*, by Mark Stern.[44]

It is not possible in the space allotted to this chapter to discuss a large number of the recent works on the history of the family in the United States, but certain works stand out because of their bearing on the history of children. Notable among these studies is Glen Elder's significant *Children of the Great Depression*, a classic cohort study in the field of family history. Elder sought to trace the impact of the Great Depression on both individuals and family life in general. Elder followed his conclusion that the Great Depression was a positive influence on children's lives with the observation that "from the perspective of children and their productive potential, our urbanized, affluent society represents an over-manned environment: the young members of a surplus category which is mainly restricted to vicarious contact with the occupation routines of life."[45] Although Elder's work stands alone because of the breadth and depth of the research methodology, Elaine Tyler May's *Homeward Bound: American Families in the Cold War* is similar because of the data base she used. Her study focuses on a later period, and argues that there was a conceptual link between the foreign policy of containment and efforts to contain sexuality in the family.[46]

Other important work on the idea of the family and on family violence has added to our knowledge of changes inside the family and between the family and society as a whole. Charles Strickland has added immensely to our knowledge of the family by looking at one particular family and the idea of family in an important body of literature in *Victorian Domesticity*.[47] Elizabeth Pleck's *Domestic Tyranny* is an excellent example of thoughtful and creative historical scholarship. Pleck's work documents the changing social climate for the regulation and punishment of domestic violence and in the process provides a history of child abuse as well. She also provides an excellent guide to American social policy regarding families. In conclusion she observes that

from the vantage point of more than three hundred years of American history, the family has become a less hierarchical institution. It is no longer viewed as a little kingdom but as an intimate grouping of individuals bound by affection and companionship. Children are seen as having rights to minimum standards of care and to physical and emotional safety. They are no longer expected to submit to parental commands with unquestioned obedience. . . . These changes, however, have not reduced family violence.

An equally significant treatment of the history of family violence is Linda Gordon's *Heroes of Their Own Lives* (1988), which focuses primarily on Boston. Gordon sees a strong relation between child welfare reforms and gains for women in the period before 1920. She also believes that the entire question of child welfare can benefit from a feminist analysis. In the process of studying such topics as child protection, child abuse and neglect, incest, and wife-beating, Gordon provides new insight into the difficulties of a "social control" interpretation of welfare efforts, arguing that the meaning of welfare is far more complex and fluid.[48]

Education

The history of education and the history of children are closely related, if not inseparable, fields, and scholars in one field frequently find their work cited in the other. If education is the process by which a society recreates itself across generations, then children are both the objects and the vehicles for that recreation. From the point of view of the historian of education the history of children is the study of one side of the teaching-learning equation; for the historian of childhood the study of the history of education is the study of the people, institutions, and processes that occupy a major (and increasing) portion of children's lives.

A number of important studies in the history of education in the United States have recently appeared, including the concluding volume of Lawrence Cremin's broad multivolume work, which must surely be judged the most comprehensive history of American education.[49] These recent works deepen our understanding of the relation between educational institutions and the larger society, and they take us inside particular institutions so that we can appreciate the processes of change within schools and their impact on children.

Cremin's trilogy is especially significant because of the broad scope of each volume and the fact that he takes a comprehensive, national view of the history of American education. Cremin is able to achieve this breadth in part because of the definition of education he uses, "the deliberate, systematic, and sustained effort to transmit or evoke knowledge, attitudes, values, skills, and sensibilities, a process that is more limited than what the anthropologist would term enculturation or the sociologist socialization."[50] Cremin's work may be read as a kind of cultural history of colonial America; he begins in 1607 and carries volume one down to the end of the American Revolution. Cremin's second volume continues the story from the end of the Revolution to the centennial year; the third volume, published in 1988, brings the story to 1980. According to Cremin, his second volume sought to depict the development of "an authentic American vernacular in education," which in turn "proffered a popular *paideia* compounded of evangelical pieties, democratic hopes, and utilitarian striving."[51] The third volume emphasizes "the transformation and proliferation of educative institutions as the United States became a metropolitan society." In addition, Cremin touches on a broad range of other topics: the export of American culture and civilization to other parts of the world, and the role of "progressive reformism" in schools and colleges and "in the establishment of a host of educationally oriented social service agencies." He also analyzes the role of the media, the transformation of institutions like libraries into educational agencies, and the function of education in a host of other agencies such as the military. Cremin concludes that "by advancing liberty and choice, American schools and colleges also tried to advance equality of economic opportunity," and notes that family background still had an enormous influence on the successes of young people in American society. Still, he contends that schools "were able to advance opportunity in significant ways for a significant proportion of the population." He also argues that "an increasing standardized, indeed metropolitanized, schooling provided one important foundation of common language, common knowledge, and common values throughout the society."[52]

At the level of more particular or monographic scholarship recent work on the history of the high school is especially significant. These works include Reed Ueda's, *Avenues to Adulthood*, which focuses on the history of the high school in Sommerville, Massachusetts, from the middle of the nineteenth century to the present. Ueda's purpose was to determine the extent to which the high school aided upward social mobility. Instead of assisting members of the working classes in their efforts to improve their status, Ueda found that "the principal beneficiaries of a high school education and the mobility it enhanced were the children of Yankee white collar and skilled employees who comprised the majority of secondary students."[53] Ueda also studied the rise of a peer culture in the high school, the creation of a junior high school, and the way the school changed when it became a mass institution.

Another important recent study of a high school is David Labaree's *The Making of an American High School*. In his study Labaree finds that "the high school was founded to produce citizens for the new republic but quickly became a vehicle for individual status attainment," a view that is not necessarily in conflict with Ueda's work.[54] Both Ueda and Labaree agree that high school attendance conferred status on the students who were able to attend. Both also would agree that attendance did not lead to new status, but confirmed the existing status of those who attended. Labaree believes that Central High School of Philadelphia was an unusual institution in two respects. Until recently it was an all-male school, and it was an elite high school throughout most of its history. Central High School (and most American high schools, Labaree would argue) was able to maintain its exclusiveness by making use of a tracking system, reserving the most demanding classes for the ablest student, while providing vocational or practical classes for the weaker students.

Tracking has become a feature of American high schools, but there has been little analysis of its historical development. To remedy that defect Joel Perlman studied the public high schools of Providence, Rhode Island, during the period from 1880 to 1930. Perlman found that "tracking had always existed in the public high school system. However, in the nineteenth century it did not sharply distinguish working class children from others in quite the way it did later." Providence began with a single high school with three separate departments: classical, English, and girls. The city added a technical high school and moved the English and classical departments into separate buildings. When the requirements for admission to Brown were modified the classic high school added science and math to their curriculum, and in the meantime it had become co-educational. The English high school then concentrated on a commercial or business course, and the technical high school emphasized manual training. As a result of all these changes the "tracks" correlated with the class level of the students. Upper- and middle-class boys and girls attended the classic high school; lower-class girls went to the English school; and lower-class boys went to the technical high school.[55]

Most of the change that has taken place in the curriculum, structure, and governance, as well as the role and mission of high schools, has occurred since 1940, according to Robert Hampel in *The Last Little Citadel*. Further, Hampel argues that the most sweeping changes occurred from the mid-1970s to the early 1980s. The high schools of the postwar years were still authoritarian, rigid institutions. Recently, however, there has been what he describes as a "necessary liberalization"; "student rights, teacher unions, a comprehensive curriculum, compensatory and remedial programs, and other initiatives empowered different groups unaccustomed to full participation in the schools."[56] In the same period he argues that academic achievements have declined because of easy-going teaching methods. Thus he gives high schools high marks for their commitment to equality but faults them for declining standards.

In an important article in the *Journal of American History*, "Outlawing Teenage Populism: The Campaign Against Secret Societies in the American High School, 1900–1960," William Graebner details the history of secret societies in Buffalo, New York, in the first half of the twentieth century. He notes that school authorities sought to stamp out these youth groups in the name of "a vision of a classless, egalitarian, conflict-free, meritocratic homogeneous society." Graebner defends the secret societies and sees the efforts to eliminate them as part of the desire of high school administrators to promote conformity. He concludes that "what the dominant culture described as insufficient loyalty was, in fact, a deeply felt loyalty to the ethnic groups, religious feelings, social classes, and peer group friendships."[57]

Three new works in the history of education take up topics not often discussed: Wayne Fuller's *The Old Country School*, Lloyd P. Jorgenson's *The State and the Non-Public School, 1825–1925*, and Larry Cuban's *How Teachers Taught*.[58] Fuller sees his work as a "social history of the midwest," an effort to show "how people felt about democracy and education and why they felt as they did, and above all to capture something of their spirit and values, and the hopes and dreams they had for their children."[59] Basically a history of one-room schoolhouses in the nation's midsection, it traces school consolidation, particularly after World War II.

Jorgenson describes his book as "a history of the bifurcation of education into public and non-public sectors, and of the ensuing struggles between the proponents of the two sectors."[60] In the nineteenth century the struggles were known collectively as "the school question." Jorgenson is sharply critical of nineteenth-century Protestant zealots he says controlled the public schools, and notes that even contemporary state education officials still know little about nonpublic schools. He also observes that "historically, the state's interest in requiring universal education has been based on the collective welfare of the state rather than on the individual interests or needs of the child."[61]

Cuban focuses on the behavior of teachers in classrooms and in particular asks whether teaching activity was more teacher-centered or student-centered. He sees a trend in the twentieth century toward more student-centered teaching and pays particular attention to the spread of the ideas of John Dewey. In his analysis he examines five possible explanations for the shift or resistance to it: (1) the schools mirrored larger society; (2) the architecture of building and structure of the administrative system determined how teachers performed; (3) the culture of teaching has resisted change; (4) the ideas teachers have about children's needs have shaped their behavior; and (5) the extent to which reforms were made effective in classrooms. In assessing these explanations Cuban looks at both urban and rural schools and finds considerable variance among them.[62]

Thomas Webber considers the process of education within slavery. *Deep Like the Rivers* is organized around three questions: "First, what was it that whites wanted their slaves to learn and what teaching methods did they employ? Second, what did slaves actually learn? Third, where and from whom did slaves learn what they learned?" The concluding chapter compares a slave plantation with an Indian reservation. By using the methodology of anthropology Webber goes beyond the question of what efforts were made to shape slave values and looks at "the success of slaves in actively creating, controlling, and perpetuating their own education."[63] Webber concludes that some of the white teaching was successful, particularly in the area of job and work skills. At the same time, however, the slaves rejected the efforts of whites to instill values and attitudes because they had created their own culture. Slaves effectively passed this culture on between generations through the community of the slave quarter. "By the time plantation authorities began their attempts to influence the beliefs and values of their slaves," Webber writes, "most slave children had already internalized the themes and behavioral modes of the quarter community. They had learned the language, sung the songs, eaten the food, attended the secret ceremonies, and stored away in their unconscious the imagery, the hopes and fears of their people."[64]

Welfare and Correctional Institutions for Children

Good institutional history also can be good social history, and the history of institutions for children is no exception. Our understanding of social institutions has become more sophisticated, and recent studies of such institutions has yielded a great deal of new information. We understand how institutions reflected both the values of the larger society and the efforts of the people who staffed them. We can no longer maintain a simplistic theory of "social control" as a way of explaining the development of institutions for children; child advocates had a variety of motives, including both a desire to control children and a wish to improve their lives.

Like the study of child-rearing advice, the study of institutions for children has been a rich field that produced many works cited in *American Childhood*. Recently, however, the number of new works in institutional history has been fairly small. Perhaps typical of older institutional studies is Joseph M. Hawes' *Children in Urban Society*, which appeared in 1971. The basic purpose of that work was to trace the evolution of institutions for juvenile delinquents from the creation of the New York House of Refuge in 1825 to the creation of the Juvenile Court in 1899.[65]

Two similar studies, *Love and the American Delinquent*, by Steven Schlossman, and *Stubborn Children*, by John R. Sutton, have recently appeared. Schlossman's purpose was "to trace the origins and nature of publicly sponsored 'progressive' correctional programs." Schlossman found that the progressive system depended heavily on personal relations, which presupposed that the people who staffed the courts would be of a certain cast of mind. "Ideally," he says, "the court was a missionary agent for the educational and moral uplift of the poor. In practice it functioned more often than not as a source of arbitrary punitive authority, and an arena for the evocation of hostile emotions on all sides."[66] Sutton was interested in the origins of the therapeutic approach to child control and that interest led him to undertake a study of the history of the American juvenile justice system. He looked specifically at the timing of major reforms, the content of reforms, and the process by which local innovations became national patterns. Sutton challenges the view of Michel Foucault and others that therapeutic control is primarily an aspect of the modern European state. He believes that the origins of therapeutic control can be found much earlier in the United States and that it reflects "the weakness and ambivalence of official authority."[67]

The classic work on the origins and early workings of the juvenile court is *The Best Laid Plans*, by Ellen Ryerson, which was published in 1978. According to Ryerson, "the creation of the court marked the height of confidence in the possibility of reclaiming delinquents for an orderly and productive social life. Most of the ideas which made this confidence plausible have lost their force in the last three quarters of a century, and the consensus about the child and the state which produced the juvenile court movement has disintegrated." In effect, Ryerson argues that the juvenile court was the epitome of progressivism, while also contending that the failure of the court to retain public confidence reflected the decline in confidence in progressive ideas.[68]

The juvenile court was one of the last institutions to be created in establishing the American juvenile justice system. One important innovation in the middle of the nineteenth century was the creation of a separate, state-funded institution for girls. The creation of the first reform school for girls is ably documented in Barbara Brenzel's *Daughters of the State*, published in 1983. Brenzel describes her work as a "social portrait" of the institution. The original idea for the institution was for it to provide family training for delinquent girls, but over the course of the nineteenth century the institution shifted to a mode of custodial care and harsh discipline.[69]

A recent study of delinquency, James Gilbert's *A Cycle of Outrage*, detailed a national concern with what many believed to be an epidemic of juvenile crime. Self-appointed authorities blamed mass culture for the undermining of American values and the "seduction" of young people into acts of crime and delinquency. Gilbert sees much of the concern about mass culture as coming from a fear of change in American society, including the rise of a defiant (but not necessarily delinquent) youth culture.[70]

Although most of the recent work on institutions for children has dealt with delinquent children, two other studies look at the practice of apprenticeship and the historical development and decline of institutions for dependent children.

According to William J. Rorabaugh, in *The Craft Apprentice*, apprenticeship was

a system of education and job training by which important practical information was passed from one generation to the next; it was a mechanism by which youths could model themselves on socially approved adults; it was an institution devised to insure proper moral development through the master's fatherly responsibility for the behavior of his apprentice; and it was a means of social control imposed upon potentially disruptive male adults.[71]

Rorabaugh focuses on the practice of apprenticeship—what it was like to be an apprentice in the United States from the middle of the eighteenth century through the end of the Civil War.

Saving the Waifs, by LeRoy Ashby, appeared in 1984. Ashby's purpose was to delineate the definition of dependent children used by social workers in the progressive era and to look at some less well known institutions for dependent children. Ashby argues that most child-care workers genuinely cared about their young charges and believed that they were creating a new moral order that would be accomplished through faith in "the rejuvenating power of a cooperative, untied, educated people."[72]

Child Health

The question of children's well-being has always been a central one for parents, but social concern for child health has changed quite dramatically over time. For example, a number of scholars have been sharply critical of the federal government and the medical profession over the discontinuation of the program to reduce infant mortality under the Sheppard Towner Act. Today, compared with Western Europe, the United States has a very high infant mortality rate in part because of the lack of medical care for its poorest citizens. At the same time, the history of efforts to improve child health in the United States includes a number of significant improvements.

Concern for the physical and emotional well-being of children became a public issue in the nineteenth century. One example of that concern was the campaign to eliminate corporal punishment from the schools, as detailed in Myra Glenn's *Campaigns Against Corporal Punishment*, published in 1984.[73]

The focus on child health by parents and physicians began in the nineteenth century with attention directed to childbirth and early nurturing of the infant.

Several recent works have focused on the relation between childbearing and child health while also addressing the issues that this event in the life course represented for mothers. Works by Scholten, Leavitt, and Hofferth have deepened our understanding of the changes in childbirth that took place in nineteenth-century America.

Catherine M. Scholten's *Childbearing in American Society: 1650–1850* was published in 1985, and stressed the improvements in women's legal status in the nineteenth century. Scholten also noted that these developments and a focus on children had the effect of confining women to their homes. At the same time, "bearing and rearing children ceased to be inevitable and natural and became events to be planned, studied, and controlled. Motherhood was no longer simply a woman's private concern but was a matter of public discussion and management."[74]

Sylvia Hoffert also looks at the degree to which birth became a private matter in the nineteenth century. In the preindustrial world childbirth had been a public event, attended by relatives, neighbors, and the midwife. By the nineteenth century, however, among middle-class urban families, birth became increasingly private as male obstetricians replaced the female midwives as the primary birth attendants. Hoffert devotes a chapter to issues of infant nurture, touching on such issues as breast-feeding (which physicians and child-care experts urged), weaning, and infant care and feeding.[75]

In *Brought to Bed* (1986) Judith Walzer Leavitt focuses primarily on the time of the transition from home to hospital birth. She sees birth as "a cultural event as much as a biological one." She also argues that "problems emerged during the middle of the twentieth century because the hospital acted to homogenize the birth experience and make it similar for all women."[76]

Whereas these works touch on the rise of the specialty of obstetrics, Sydney Halpern documents the appearance of pediatrics as a medical specialty in his *American Pediatrics*, published in 1988. Halpern contends that pediatrics is different from other medical specialties because it grew out of a concern for the health of poor children rather than from new scientific discoveries or from a focus on a particular part of the body. Halpern sees a certain irony in pediatrics in the twentieth century because "by 1940, its principal consumers were middle class women, not the working class mothers for whom it was originally designed. The net result was less social control for the poor than professional validation for the affluent."[77] Other factors that partially explain the improvement in child health include changes in infant feeding patterns. Rima Apple's *Mothers and Medicine* documents the changing practices of infant feeding and the rise of "scientific" experts on infant feeding.[78]

An unusual new work in the field of child health, in that it looks at the social reactions to a particular disease over time, is Joan Jacobs Brumberg's *Fasting Girls*. Brumberg's work is in effect a history of anorexia nervosa, an eating disorder that primarily affects young women.[79]

Material Culture and the Study of Children

Thomas Schlereth, one of the most prolific and astute students of the use by historians of material culture as evidence, argues that among the best sources for describing the subjective experience of childhood are objects used and worn by children.[80] Museum curators have been quicker than more traditional historians to make use of articles in their collections to interpret the experience and meaning of childhood in past time. A permanent exhibit at the Smithsonian Museum of American History on "Everyday Life in the Eighteenth Century" includes a well-informed selection of artifacts on child life. For historians and others who cannot visit these museums, the exhibits and the research that helped in their creation are made more accessible by published catalogues, a source that also preserves more ephemeral temporary exhibits, such as that created in 1979 by the Museum of American Folk Art, "Small Folk: A Celebration of Childhood in America." A similar catalogue is Bernard Barenholtz' *American Antique Toys*, which describes the author's personal collection and provides a history of nineteenth-century children's toys.[81]

American portraiture also offers opportunities for deciphering the physical dimension of children's experiences. Karen Lee Calvert has analyzed several hundred portraits to describe an increasingly complex age differentiation among children from the seventeenth into the early nineteenth centuries whose outward manifestation was the clothing they wore and the toys and other objects included in their portraiture.[82]

Children in Action and Social Policy Concerning Children

It should be obvious that children have had a significant influence on adults throughout our history, not only because of their presence in large numbers, but also because of their actions. Children have not been simply passive recipients of the wishes and commands of the adults around them. It has been difficult, though, for historians to study children in action in the past because they have left few records themselves. They certainly left traces of their actions, however, and careful historical research has yielded several interesting and informative studies of children in effect making history.

No work better illustrates American historians' growing sensitivity to the influence and perspective of children than Elliott West's *Growing Up with the Country: Childhood on the Far Western Frontier*. In the development of the West, he says, "children and women played an important part in much that is credited to their fathers and husbands." Children worked; they "formed the center of social and political life"; they adapted readily to the new physical environment; and their growing-up experience eventually helped to shape the development and character of the West itself. According to West, "until its children are heard, the frontier's history cannot be truly written."[83]

It may seem strange to discuss children in action together with social policy, but in fact the two intersect in a number of ways. In the twentieth century young people have gained greater control over important aspects of their own lives (such as dating, courtship, and individual life-styles), while at the same time society as a whole has invested greater and greater sums of money in young people in various forms of education and sought in a variety of ways both to control young people and to enhance their lives.

A particularly important work makes the case for the blending of these two categories. David Nasaw's *Children of the City*, which appeared in 1985, is a study of urban children and the world they created. Unlike most other books on children, it takes a child's point of view as its focus. Nasaw's work also makes unusual use of a variety of source materials, including documentary photographs, autobiographies, and the reports of child-saving reformers. The reformers sought to create and enforce public policy concerning children, while Nasaw describes the response of young people to these efforts.[84]

The question of social policy can be complicated because it involves not only the conscious construction of policy, but also the creation of patterns and cultural directions that involve all sorts of factors. An example of this process and an important work in the history of American childhood is Joseph Kett's *Rites of Passage*, which traces the evolution of the cultural construction of "adolescence" or the process whereby young men left home and learned how to become adult members of American society.[85] Kett's work has recently been supplemented by the work of John Modell, who has placed the study of the maturation of youth in a broader "life course" perspective and argued that there have been major changes in the sequence of events in the life course for young people and that young women now have life courses remarkably similar to those of young men. Modell makes effective use of demographic data and popular fiction to illustrate his points, and concludes that in the twentieth century, "young people . . . have increasingly taken control of the construction of the youthful life course: adult-maintained convention has crumbled, and young people have been left the pieces and much of the mortar needed to construct it afresh."[86]

Still other aspects of social policy involve attitudes about children and their value to society. An intriguing study of this process is Vivianna Zelizer's *Pricing the Priceless Child*, which was published in 1985. She describes "the profound transformation in the economic and sentimental value of children—fourteen years of age or younger—between the 1870s and the 1930s," and argues that "the emergence of this economically 'worthless' but emotionally 'priceless' child has created an essential condition of contemporary childhood." She sees this development as having resulted from a process she labels the "sacralization" of the child, and uses this idea to explain such developments as the regulation of child labor.[87]

The classic work on the history of efforts to regulate child labor is Walter Trattner's *Crusade for the Children*, published in 1970. Trattner's work chronicles the efforts to pass legislation making child labor illegal in the United States in the twentieth century and places this effort in the context of the broad child welfare reform movement of the twentieth century.[88]

Two other works on social policy that make significant contributions to the history of American childhood are Urie Bronfenbrenner's *Two Worlds of Childhood* and Robert Coles' *Children of Crisis*. Coles' classic study of the impact of segregation on children is a powerful and empathic work. Bronfenbrenner's study, a comparison of child-rearing and education philosophy and methods in the United States and the Soviet Union, provides in effect a detailed critical essay on American child rearing in the 1960s.[89]

CONCLUSION

The history of American children needs a theoretically grounded synthetic overview. Collections of documents and scholarly articles, important as they are, simply do not meet this need. Such a work should account for the extraordinary social energy and effort expended on children, while maintaining an awareness of real children in real circumstances. This overview should also help future scholars relate their research to larger themes in the field. In the interim those with an interest in this expanding field must provide their own conceptual schemes and arguments for the significance of their work.

The appearance of new, specialized studies in a wide variety of areas is gratifying, but as in any new field, much remains to be done. In particular the vast possibilities for the use of material and popular culture remain to be exploited. It is thus our hope that by calling attention to newer works in the history of American childhood, we can stimulate further scholarly effort, both in synthetic works and in monographic studies.

NOTES

1. See, for example, Christopher Lasch, *The Culture of Narcissism: American Life in an Age of Diminishing Expectations* (New York: W. W. Norton, 1979); and *The Minimal Self: Psychic Survival in Troubled Times* (New York: W. W. Norton, 1984).

2. Joseph M. Hawes and N. Ray Hiner, eds., *American Childhood: A Research Guide and Historical Handbook* (Westport, Conn.: Greenwood Press, 1985).

3. Bernard M. Mergen, *Play and Playthings, a Reference Guide* (Westport, Conn.: Greenwood Press, 1982).

4. Robert H. Bremner et al., eds., *Children and Youth in America: A Documentary History*, 3 vols. (Cambridge, Mass.: Harvard University Press, 1970–1974).

5. James Axtell, ed., *The Indian Peoples of Eastern America: A Documentary History of the Sexes* (New York: Oxford University Press, 1981); Philip Greven, ed., *Child Rearing Concepts: 1620–1861: Historical Sources* (Itasca, Il.: F. E. Peacock, 1973).

6. Donald M. Scott and Bernard Wishy, eds., *American Families: A Documentary History* (New York: Harper & Row, 1982).

7. N. Ray Hiner and Joseph M. Hawes, eds., *Growing Up in America: Children in*

Historical Perspective (Urbana: University of Illinois Press, 1985), and Harvey J. Graff, ed., *Growing Up in America: Historical Experiences* (Detroit: Wayne State University Press, 1987).

8. Barbara Finkelstein, ed., *Regulated Children/Liberated Children: Education in Psychohistorical Perspective* (New York: Psychohistory Press, 1979).

9. Peter Benes, ed., *Families and Children*, vol. 10 (1985) of the *Annual Proceedings of the Dublin Seminar for New England Folklife* (Boston: Boston University Scholarly Publications, 1987), pp. 5–6.

10. Vivian C. Fox and Martin H. Quitt, eds., *Loving, Parenting, and Dying: The Family Cycle in England and America, Past and Present* (New York: Psychohistory Press, 1980).

11. Axtell, ed., *Indian Peoples of Eastern America*; Margaret Szasz, *Indian Education in the American Colonies, 1607–1783* (Albuquerque: University of New Mexico Press, 1989).

12. Edmund Sears Morgan, *The Puritan Family: Essays on Religious and Domestic Relations in Seventeenth Century New England* (Boston: Little, Brown, 1944), and *Virginians At Home: Family Life in the Eighteenth Century* (Charlottesville: Colonial Williamsburg, 1952). An example of earlier studies is Alice Morese Earle, *Child Life in Colonial Days* (New York: Macmillan, 1899).

13. John Demos, *A Little Commonwealth: Family Life in Plymouth Colony* (New York: Oxford University Press, 1970).

14. Ross W. Beales, Jr., "The Child in Seventeenth Century America," in Hawes and Hiner, *American Childhood*, p. 24.

15. Darrett B. Ruman and Anita H. Rutman, "Of Agues and Fevers: Malaria in the Early Chesapeake," *William and Mary Quarterly*, 3rd series, 10 (1976): 31–60.

16. See Aubrey C. Land, Lois Green Carr, and Edward C. Papenfuse, eds., *Law, Society, and Politics in Early Maryland: Proceedings of the First Conference in Maryland History, June 14–15, 1974* (Baltimore: Johns Hopkins University Press, 1977), and Thad W. Tate and David L. Ammerman, eds., *The Chesapeake in the Seventeenth Century: Essays in Anglo-American Society* (Chapel Hill: University of North Carolina Press, 1979).

17. Daniel Blake Smith, *Inside the Great House: Planter Family Life in Eighteenth Century Chesapeake Society* (Ithaca, N.Y.: Cornell University Press, 1980); Darrett Rutman and Anita Rutman, *A Place in Time: Middlesex County, Virginia, 1650–1750* (New York: W. W. Norton, 1985); Allan Kulikoff, *Tobacco and Slaves: The Development of Southern Culture in the Chesapeake 1680–1800* (Chapel Hill: University of North Carolina Press, 1986).

18. Jan Lewis, *The Pursuit of Happiness: Family and Values in Jefferson's Virginia* (New York: Cambridge University Press, 1983); Jane Turner Censer, *North Carolina Planters and Their Children, 1800–1860* (Baton Rouge: Louisiana State University Press, 1984).

19. Catherine Scholten, *Childbearing in American Society, 1650–1850* (New York: New York University Press, 1985); Judith Walzer Leavitt, *Brought to Bed: Childbearing in American Society, 1750–1950* (New York: Oxford University Press, 1986); see also Jan Lewis and Kenneth A. Lockridge, " 'Sally Has Been Sick': Pregnancy and Family Limitation Among Virginia Gentry Women, 1780–1830," *Journal of Social History* 22 (Fall 1988):5–19.

20. Philip Greven, *The Protestant Temperament: Patterns of Child-Rearing, Religious Experience, and the Self in Early America* (New York: Alfred A. Knopf, 1977).

21. Robert V. Wells, *Revolutions in Americans' Lives: A Demographic Perspective on the History of Americans, Their Families, and Their Society* (Westport, Conn.: Greenwood Press, 1982).

22. Kenneth F. Kiple and Virginia Himmelsteib King, *Another Dimension in the Black Diaspora: Diet, Disease, and Racism* (New York: Cambridge University Press, 1981).

23. Peter Gregg Slater, *Children in the New England Mind: In Death and in Life: From the Puritans to Bushnell* (Hamden, Conn.: Archon Books, 1977), particularly Pt. 1, "The Dead Child"; and Nancy Schrom Dye and Daniel Blake Smith, "Mother Love and Infant Death, 1750–1820," *Journal of American History* 73 (1986):329–353; N. Ray Hiner, "Cotton Mather and His Children," in Finkelstein, ed., *Regulated Children*, pp. 24–43.

24. Lawrence Cremin, *American Education: The Colonial Experience, 1607–1783* (New York: Harper & Row, 1970), and *American Education: The National Experience, 1783–1876* (New York: Harper & Row, 1980).

25. James Axtell, *The School Upon a Hill: Education and Society in Colonial New England* (New Haven, Conn.: Yale University Press, 1974).

26. Szasz, *Indian Education in the American Colonies*.

27. Anne L. Kuhn, *The Mother's Role in Childhood Education: New England Concepts, 1830–1860* (New Haven, Conn.: Yale University Press, 1947).

28. Bernard Wishy, *The Child and the Republic: The Dawn of Modern American Child Nurture* (Philadelphia: University of Pennsylvania Press, 1968), pp. x, xi.

29. Gail S. Murray, "Rational Thought and Republican Virtues: Children's Literature, 1789–1820," *Journal of the Early Republic* 8 (Summer 1988):159–177.

30. Charles Strickland, "A Transcendentalist Father: The Child-Rearing Practices of Bronson Alcott," *Perspectives in American History* 3 (1969):5–73.

31. Nancy F. Cott, "Notes Toward an Interpretation of Antebellum Childrearing," *Psychohistory Review* 7 (1977–1978):5, 7, 9. 14, 15.

32. Molly Ladd-Taylor, *Raising a Baby the Government Way: Mother's Letters to the Children's Bureau, 1915–1932* (New Brunswick, N.J.: Rutgers University Press, 1986).

33. Julia Wrigley, "Do Young Children Need Intellectual Stimulation? Experts' Advice to Parents, 1900–1985," *History of Education Quarterly* 29 (Spring 1989):41–75.

34. Daniel Scott Smith, "Child-Naming Patterns and Family Structure Change: Hingham, Massachusetts, 1640–1880," *Journal of Social History* 18 (Summer 1985):541–565; Cheryl Anne Cody, "There Was No 'Absolom' on the Ball Plantations: Slave Naming Practices in the South Carolina Low Country, 1720–1865," *American Historical Review* 92 (June 1987):563–596. See also Edward H. Tebbenhoff, "Tacit Rules and Hidden Structures: Naming Practices and Godparentage in Schenectady, New York, 1680–1800," *Journal of Social History* 18 (1985):567–585, and Larry M. Logue, "Modernization Arrested: Child-Naming and the Family in a Utah Town," *Journal of American History* 74 (1987):131–138.

35. Joseph M. Hawes and Elizabeth Nybakken, ed., *American Families, a Research Handbook and Reference Guide* (Westport, Conn.: Greenwood Press, forthcoming).

36. Steven Mintz and Susan Kellogg, *Domestic Revolutions: A Social History of Family Life* (New York: Free Press, 1988).

37. John Demos, *Past Present, and Personal: The Family and the Life Course in American History* (New York: Oxford University Press, 1986). As noted above, there are some basic documentary collections, notably the work by Scott and Wishy. Other

works previously discussed that also fall into this category include Benes, ed., *Families and Children*, and Fox and Quitt, eds., *Loving, Parenting, and Dying*.

38. Michael Grossberg, *Governing the Hearth: Law and Family in Nineteenth Century America* (Chapel Hill: University of North Carolina Press, 1985).

39. Martha Minow, "We, the Family: Constitutional Rights and American Families," *Journal of American History* 74 (December 1987):959–983.

40. Richard Griswold del Castillo, *La Familia: Chicano Families in the Urban Southwest* (South Bend, Ind.: Notre Dame University Press, 1984).

41. Charles H. Mindel and Robert Habenstin, eds., *Ethnic Families in America: Patterns and Variations* (New York: Elsevier, 1981).

42. Herbert Gutman, *The Black Family in Slavery and Freedom, 1750–1925* (New York: Pantheon Books, 1976).

43. Wells, *Revolutions in Americans' Lives.*

44. Mark Stern, *Society and Family Strategy: Erie County, New York* (Albany: State University of New York Press, 1987).

45. Glen H. Elder, Jr., *Children of the Great Depression* (Chicago: University of Chicago Press, 1974), p. 292.

46. Elaine Tyler May, *Homeward Bound: American Families in the Cold War* (New York: Basic Books, 1989).

47. Charles Strickland, *Victorian Domesticity: Families in the life and Art of Louisa May Alcott* (University: University of Alabama Press, 1985).

48. Elizabeth Pleck, *Domestic Tyranny: The Making of Social Policy Against Family Violence from Colonial Times to the Present* (New York: Oxford University Press, 1987), p. 201; and Linda Gordon, *Heroes of Their Own Lives: The Politics and History of Family Violence, Boston, 1880–1960* (New York: Viking Press, 1988).

49. Lawrence A. Cremin, *American Education: The Metropolitan Experience, 1876–1980* (New York: Harper & Row, 1988). The other two volumes are *American Education: The Colonial Experience, 1607—1783* (New York: Harper & Row, 1970) and *American Education: The National Experience, 1783–1876* (New York: Harper & Row, 1980).

50. Lawrence A. Cremin, *American Education: The Colonial Experience, 1607–1783* (New York: Harper & Row, 1970), p. xiii.

51. Lawrence Cremin, *American Education: The National Experience, 1783–1876* (New York: Harper & Row, 1970); *American Education: The Metropolitan Experience, 1876–1980* (New York: Harper & Row, 1988), p. xi.

52. Cremin, *Metropolitan Experience*, pp. 672–673.

53. Ree Ueda, *Avenues to Adulthood: The Origins of the High School and Social Mobility in an American Suburb* (New York: Cambridge University Press, 1987), p. 185.

54. David F. Labaree, *The Making of an American High School: The Credentials Market and the Central High School of Philadelphia, 1838–1939* (New Haven, Conn.: Yale University Press, 1988), p. 1.

55. Joel Perlman, "Curriculum and Tracking in the Transformation of the American High School: Providence, R.I., 1880–1930," *Journal of Social History* 19 (1985–1986):29–55.

56. Robert L. Hampel, *The Last Little Citadel: American High Schools Since 1940*, Third Report from a Study of High Schools Co-Sponsored by the National Association of Secondary School Principals and the Commission Education Issues of the National Association of Independent Schools (Boston: Houghton Mifflin, 1986), p. 140.

57. William Graebner, "Outlawing Teenage Populism: The Campaign Against Secret

Societies in the American High School, 1900–1960,'' *Journal of American History* 74 (September 1987):412, 435.

58. Wayne E. Fuller, *The Old Country School: The Story of Rural Education in the Middle West* (Chicago: University of Chicago Press (1982); Lloyd P Jorgenson, *The State and the Non-Public School 1825–1925* (Columbia: University of Missouri Press, 1987); Larry Cuban, *How Teachers Taught: Constancy and Change in American Classrooms, 1890–1980* (New York: Longman, 1984).

59. Fuller, *Old Country School*, p. viii.

60. Jorgenson, *State and the Non-Public School*, p. vii.

61. Ibid., pp. 217–218.

62. Cuban, *How Teachers Taught*, pp. 9–10, 43.

63. Thomas S. Webber, *Deep Like the Rivers: Education in the Slave Quarter Community, 1831–1860* (New York: W. W. Norton, 1978), pp. xi, xii.

64. Ibid., p. 261.

65. Joseph M. Hawes, *Children in Urban Society: Juvenile Delinquency in Nineteenth Century America* (New York: Oxford University Press, 1971).

66. Steven Schlossmann, *Love and the American Delinquent: The Theory and Practice of "Progressive" Juvenile Justice, 1825–1920* (Chicago: University of Chicago Press, 1977), pp. 4, 188.

67. John R. Sutton, *Stubborn Children: Controlling Delinquency in the United States, 1640–1981* (Berkeley: University of California Press, 1988), pp. 4, 256.

68. Ellen Ryerson, *The Best-laid Plans: America's Juvenile Court Experiment* (New York: Hill & Wang, 1978), p. 14.

69. Barbara Brenzel, *Daughters of the State: A Social Portrait of the First Reform School for Girls in North America, 1856–1905* (Cambridge, Mass.: MIT Press, 1983).

70. James Gilbert, *A Cycle of Outrage: America's Reaction to the Juvenile Delinquent in the 1950s* (New York: Oxford University Press, 1986).

71. W. J. Rorabaugh, *The Craft Apprentice: From Franklin to the Machine Age in America* (New York: Oxford University Press, 1986).

72. LeRoy Ashby, *Saving the Waifs: Reformers and Dependent Children, 1890–1917* (Philadelphia: Temple University Press, 1984), p. 209.

73. Myra C. Glenn, *Campaigns Against Corporal Punishment: Prisoners, Sailors, Women and Children in Antebellum America* (Albany: State University of New York Press, 1984).

74. Scholten, *Childbearing in American Society*, pp. 98–99.

75. Sylvia D. Hoffert, *Private Matters: American Attitudes Toward Childbearing and Infant Nurture in the Urban North, 1800–1860* (Urbana: University of Illinois Press, 1989).

76. Leavitt, *Brought to Bed*, p. 218.

77. Sydney A. Halpern, *American Pediatrics: The Social Dynamics of Professionalism, 1880–1980* (Berkeley: University of California Press, 1988), p. 153.

78. Rima D. Apple, *Mothers and Medicine: A Social History of Infant Feeding 1890–1950* (Madison: University of Wisconsin Press, 1987).

79. Joan Jacobs Brumberg, *Fasting Girls: The Emergence of Anorexia Nervosa as a Modern Disease* (Cambridge, Mass.: Harvard University Press, 1988).

80. See Thomas Schlereth, ''The Material Culture of Childhood: Problems and Potential in Historical Explanation,'' *Material History Bulletin* 21 (1985):1–14.

81. Barbara Smith, ed., *After the Revolution: The Smithsonian History of Every Day*

Life in the Eighteenth Century (New York: Pantheon, 1985, 1987); Sandra Brant and Elissa Cullman, *Small Folk: A Celebration of Childhood in America* (New York: E. P. Dutton and the Museum of American Folk Art, 1980); Bernard Barenholts, *American Antique Toys: 1830–1900* (New York: Harry N. Adams, 1980).

82. Karen Lee Calvert, "Children in American Family Portraiture, 1670–1810," *William and Mary Quarterly*, 3rd series, 39 (1982):87–113.

83. Elliott West, *Growing Up with the Country: Childhood on the Western Frontier* (Albuquerque: University of New Mexico Press, 1989), pp. 245–247.

84. David Nasaw, *Children of the City, At Work and At Play* (Garden City: Anchor-Doubleday, 1985).

85. Joseph Kett, *Rites of Passage: Adolescence in America, 1790 to the Present* (New York: Basic Books, 1977).

86. John Modell, *Into One's Own: From Youth to Adulthood in the United States, 1920–1975* (Berkeley: University of California Press, 1989), p. 326.

87. Vivianna Zelizer, *Pricing the Priceless Child: The Changing Social Value of Children* (New York: Basic Books, 1985), p. 3.

88. Walter I. Trattner, *Crusade for the Children: A History of the National Child Labor Committee and Child Labor Reform in America* (Chicago: Quadrangle Books, 1970).

89. Urie Bronfenbrenner, *Two Worlds of Childhood: U.S. and U.S.S.R.* (New York: Russell Sage Foundation, 1970); Robert Coles, *Children of Crisis*, vol. 1. *A Study of Courage and Fear* (Boston: Little, Brown, 1964). Also see William M. Tuttle, *Homefront Children: The Second World War in the Lives of an American Generation* (forthcoming).

REFERENCES

Scholarly Collections (Documents and Essays)

Axtell, James, ed. *The Indian Peoples of Eastern America: A Documentary History of the Sexes.* New York: Oxford University Press, 1981.

Benes, Peter, ed. *Families and Children*, vol. 10, 1985, of the *Annual Proceedings of the Dublin Seminar for New England Folklife.* Boston: Boston University Scholarly Publications, 1987.

Bremner, Robert H., et al., eds. *Children and Youth in America: A Documentary History.* 3 vols. Cambridge, Mass.: Harvard University Press, 1970–1974.

Finkelstein, Barbara, ed. *Regulated Children/Liberated Children: Education in Psychohistorical Perspective.* New York: Psychohistory Press, 1979.

Fox, Vivian C., and Martin H. Quitt, eds., *Loving, Parenting, and Dying: The Family Cycle in England and America, Past and Present.* New York: Psychohistory Press, 1980.

Graff, Harvey J. *Growing Up in America: Historical Experiences.* Detroit: Wayne State University Press, 1987.

Greven, Philip, ed., *Child-Rearing Concepts: 1620–1861: Historical Sources.* Itasca, Il.: F. E. Peacock, 1973.

Hiner, N. Ray, and Joseph M. Hawes, eds. *Growing Up in America: Children in Historical Perspective.* Urbana: University of Illinois Press, 1985.

Scott, Donald M. and Bernard Wishy, eds. *American Families: A Documentary History*. New York: Harper & Row, 1982.

Works Discussed

Apple, Rima D. *Mothers and Medicine: A Social History of Infant Feeding 1890–1950*. Madison: University of Wisconsin Press, 1987.

Ashby, LeRoy. *Saving the Waifs: Reformers and Dependent Children, 1890–1917*. Philadelphia: Temple University Press, 1984.

Axtell, James. *The School Upon a Hill: Education and Society in Colonial New England*. New Haven, Conn.: Yale University Press, 1974.

Barenholtz, Bernard. *American Antique Toys: 1830–1900*. New York: Harry N. Adams, 1980.

Brant, Sandra, and Elissa Cullman. *Small Folk: A Celebration of Childhood in America*. New York: E. P. Dutton and the Museum of American Folk Art, 1980.

Brenzel, Barbara. *Daughters of the State: A Social Portrait of the First Reform School for Girls in North America, 1856–1905*. Cambridge, Mass.: MIT Press, 1983.

Bronfenbrenner, Urie. *Two Worlds of Childhood: U.S. and U.S.S.R.* New York: Russell Sage Foundation, 1970.

Brumberg, Joan Jacobs. *Fasting Girls: The Emergence of Anorexia Nervosa as a Modern Disease*. Cambridge, Mass.: Harvard University Press, 1988.

Calvert, Karen Lee. "Children in American Family Portraiture, 1670–1810." *William and Mary Quarterly*, 3rd series, 39 (1982):87–113.

Censer, Jane Turner. *North Carolina Planters and Their Children, 1800–1860*. Baton Rouge: Louisiana State University Press, 1984.

Cody, Cheryll Anne. "There Was No 'Absolom' on the Ball Plantations: Slave Naming Practices in the South Carolina Low Country, 1720–1865." *American Historical Review* 92 (June 1987):563–596.

Coles, Robert. *Children of Crisis*, vol. 1. *A Study of Courage and Fear*. Boston: Little, Brown, 1964.

Cott, Nancy F. "Notes Toward an Interpretation of Antebellum Childrearing." *Psychohistory Review* 7 (1977–1978):4–20.

Cremin, Lawrence A. *American Education: The Colonial Experience, 1607–1783*. New York: Harper & Row, 1970.

———. *American Education: The National Experience, 1783–1876*. New York: Harper & Row, 1980.

———. *American Education: The Metropolitan Experience*, 1876–1980. New York: Harper & Row, 1988.

Cuban, Larry. *How Teachers Taught: Constancy and Change in American Classrooms, 1890–1980*. New York: Longman, 1984.

Demos, John. *A Little Commonwealth: Family Life in Plymouth Colony*. New York: Oxford University Press, 1970.

———. *Past, Present, and Personal: The Family and the Life Course in American History*. New York: Oxford University Press, 1986.

Dumas, David W. "The Naming of Children in New England, 1780–1850," *New England Historical and Genealogical Register*, 132 (1978), 196–210.

Dye, Nancy Schrom, and Daniel Blake Smith. "Mother Love and Infant Death, 1750–1820." *Journal of American History* 73 (September 1986):329–353.

Elder, Glen H., Jr. *Children of the Great Depression*. Chicago: University of Chicago Press, 1974.

Fuller, Wayne E. *The Old Country School: The Story of Rural Education in the Middle West*. Chicago: University of Chicago Press, 1982.

Gilbert, James. *A Cycle of Outrage: America's Reaction to the Juvenile Delinquent in the 1950s*. New York: Oxford University Press, 1986.

Glenn, Myra C. *Campaigns Against Corporal Punishment: Prisoners, Sailors, Women and Children in Antebellum America*. Albany: State University of New York Press, 1984.

Graebner, William. "Outlawing Teenage Populism: The Campaign Against Secret Societies in the American High School, 1900–1960." *Journal of American History* 74 (September 1987):411–437.

Greven, Philip. *The Protestant Temperament: Patterns of Child-Rearing, Religious Experience, and the Self in Early America*. New York: Alfred A. Knopf, 1977.

Griswold del Castillo, Richard. *La Familia: Chicano Families in the Urban Southwest*. South Bend, Ind.: Notre Dame University Press, 1984.

Grossberg, Michael. *Governing the Hearth: Law and Family in Nineteenth Century America*. Chapel Hill: University of North Carolina Press, 1985.

Gutman, Herbert. *The Black Family in Slavery and Freedom, 1750–1925*. New York: Pantheon Books, 1976.

Halpern, Sydney A. *American Pediatrics: The Social Dynamics of Professionalism, 1880–1980*. Berkeley: University of California Press, 1988, p. 153.

Hampel, Robert L. *The Last Little Citadel: American High Schools Since 1940*. Boston: Houghton Mifflin, 1986.

Hawes, Joseph M. *Children in Urban Society: Juvenile Delinquency in Nineteenth Century America*. New York: Oxford University Press, 1971.

Hiner, N. Ray. "Cotton Mather and His Children." In Barbara Finkelstein, ed., *Regulated Children/Liberated Children: Education in Psychohistorical Perspective*. New York: Psychohistory Press, 1979, pp. 24–43.

———. "Cotton Mather and His Female Children: Notes on the Relationship between Private Life and Public Thought." *Journal of Psychohistory* 13 (Summer 1985):33–49.

Hoffert, Sylvia D. *Private Matters: American Attitudes Toward Childbearing and Infant Nurture in the Urban North, 1800–1860*. Urbana: University of Illinois Press, 1989.

Inscoe, John C. "Carolina Slave Names: An Index to Acculturation." *Journal of Southern History* 43 (1983):527–554.

Jones, Landon. *Great Expectations: America and the Baby Boom Generation*. New York: Ballantine Books, 1980.

Kemp, John R., ed. *Lewis Hine: Photographs of Child Labor in the New South*. Jackson: University Press of Mississippi, 1986.

Kett, Joseph. *Rites of Passage: Adolescence in America, 1790 to the Present*. New York: Basic Books, 1977.

Kiefer, Monica. *American Children Through Their Books, 1788–1835*. Philadelphia: University of Pennsylvania Press, 1948.

Kiple, Kenneth F., and Virginia Himmelsteib King. *Another Dimension in the Black Diaspora: Diet, Disease, and Racism*. New York: Cambridge University Press, 1981.

Kuhn, Anne L. *The Mother's Role in Childhood Education: New England Concepts, 1830–1860*. New Haven, Conn.: Yale University Press, 1947.

Kulikoff, Allan. *Tobacco and Slaves: The Development of Southern Culture in the Chesapeake 1680–1800*. Chapel Hill: University of North Carolina Press, 1986.

Labaree, David F. *The Making of an American High School: The Credentials Market and the Central High School of Philadelphia, 1838–1939*. New Haven, Conn.: Yale University Press, 1988.

Ladd-Taylor, Molly. *Raising a Baby the Government Way: Mother's Letters to the Children's Bureau, 1915–1932*. New Brunswick, N.J.: Rutgers University Press, 1986.

Land, Aubrye C., Lois Green Carr, and Edward C. Papenfuse, eds. *Law, Society, and Politics in Early Maryland: Proceedings of the First Conference in Maryland History, June 14–15, 1974*. Baltimore: Johns Hopkins University Press, 1977.

Leavitt, Judith Walzer. *Brought to Bed: Childbearing in American Society, 1750–1950*. New York: Oxford University Press, 1986.

Lewis, Jan. *The Pursuit of Happiness: Family and Values in Jefferson's Virginia*. New York: Cambridge University Press, 1983.

Lewis, Jan, and Kenneth A Lockridge. " 'Sally Has Been Sick': Pregnancy and Family Limitation Among Virginia Gentry Women, 1780–1830.'' *Journal of Social History* 22 (Fall 1988):5–19.

Logue, Larry M. "Modernization Arrested: Child-Naming and the Family in a Utah Town.'' *Journal of American History* 74 (June 1987):131–138.

Manfra, Jo Ann, and Robert R. Dykstra. "Serial Marriage and the Origins of the Black Stepfamily: The Rowanty Evidence.'' *Journal of American History* 72 (June 1985):18–44.

May, Elaine Tyler. *Homeward Bound: American Families in the Cold War*. New York: Basic Books, 1989.

Mergen, Bernard M. *Play and Playthings, A Reference Guide*. Westport, Conn.: Greenwood Press, 1982.

Mindel, Charles H., and Robert Habenstin, eds. *Ethnic Families in America: Patterns and Variations*. New York: Elsevier, 1981.

Minow, Martha. "We, the Family: Constitutional Rights and American Families.'' *Journal of American History* 74 (December 1987):959–983.

Mintz, Steven, and Susan Kellogg. *Domestic Revolutions: A Social History of Family Life*. New York: Free Press, 1988.

Modell, John. *Into One's Own: From Youth to Adulthood in the United States, 1920–1975*. Berkeley: University of California Press, 1989.

Morgan, Edmund Sears. *The Puritan Family: Essays on Religious and Domestic Relations in Seventeenth Century New England*. Boston: Little, Brown, 1944.

———. *Virginians at Home: Family Life in the Eighteenth Century*. Charlottesville: Colonial Williamsburg, 1952.

Murray, Gail S. "Rational Thought and Republican Virtues: Children's Literature, 1789–1820.'' *Journal of the Early Republic* 8 (Summer 1988):159–177.

Nasaw, David. *Children of the City, At Work and At Play*. Garden City: Anchor-Doubleday, 1985.

Perlman, Joel. "Curriculum and Tracking in the Transformation of the American High School: Providence, R.I., 1880–1930.'' *Journal of Social History* 19 (1985–1986):29–55.

Pleck, Elizabeth H. *Domestic Tyranny: The Making of Social Policy Against Family Violence from Colonial Times to the Present*. New York: Oxford University Press, 1987.

Rorabaugh, William J. *The Craft Apprentice: From Franklin to the Machine Age in America*. New York: Oxford University Press, 1986.

Rutman, Darrett, and Anita Rutman. "Of Agues and Fevers: Malaria in the Early Chesapeake." *William and Mary Quarterly*, 3rd series, 10 (1976):31–60.

———.*A Place in Time: Middlesex County, Virginia, 1650–1750*, vol. 2. *Explicatus*. New York: W. W. Norton, 1985.

Ryerson, Ellen. *The Best-laid Plans: America's Juvenile Court Experiment*. New York: Hill & Wang, 1978.

Schlereth, Thomas. "The Material Culture of Childhood: Problems and Potential in Historical Explanation." *Material History Bulletin* 21 (1985):1–14.

Schlossman, Steven. *Love and the American Delinquent: The Theory and Practice of "Progressive" Juvenile Justice, 1825–1920*. Chicago: University of Chicago Press, 1977.

Scholten, Catherine. *Childbearing in American Society, 1650–1850*. New York: New York University Press, 1985.

Slater, Peter Gregg. *Children in the New England Mind: In Death and in Life: From the Puritans to Bushnell*. Hamden, Conn.: Archon Books, 1977.

Smith, Barbara, ed. *After the Revolution: The Smithsonian History of Every Day Life in the Eighteenth Century*. New York: Pantheon, 1985, 1987.

Smith, Daniel Blake. *Inside the Great House: Planter Family Life in Eighteenth Century Chesapeake Society*. Ithaca, N.Y.: Cornell University Press, 1980.

Smith, Daniel Scott. "Child-Naming Practices, Kinship Ties and Change in Family Attitudes in Hingham, Massachusetts, 1641–1680." *Journal of Social History* 18 (Summer 1985):541–565.

Stern, Mark. *Society and Family Strategy: Erie County, New York*. Albany: State University of New York Press, 1987.

Strickland, Charles. "A Transcendentalist Father: The Child-Rearing Practices of Bronson Alcott." *Perspectives in American History* 3 (1969):5–73.

———.*Victorian Domesticity: Families in the Life and Art of Louisa May Alcott*. University: University of Alabama Press, 1985.

Sutton, John R. *Stubborn Children: Controlling Delinquency in the United States, 1640–1981*. Berkeley: University of California Press, 1988.

Szasz, Margaret. *Indian Education in the American Colonies, 1607–1783*. Albuquerque: University of New Mexico Press, 1989.

Tebbenhoff, Edward H. "Tacit Rules and Hidden Structures: Naming Practices and Godparentage in Schenectady, New York, 1680–1800." *Journal of Social History* 18 (Summer 1985):567–585.

Trattner, Walter I. *Crusade for the Children: A History of the National Child Labor Committee and Child Labor Reform in America*. Chicago: Quadrangle Books, 1970.

Ueda, Ree. *Avenues to Adulthood: The Origins of the High School and Social Mobility in an American Suburb*. New York: Cambridge University Press, 1987.

Webber, Thomas S. *Deep Like the Rivers: Education in the Slave Quarter Community, 1831–1865*. New York: W. W. Norton, 1978.

Wells, Robert. *Revolutions in Americans' Lives: A Demographic Perspective on the*

History of Americans, Their Families, and Their Society. Westport, Conn.: Greenwood Press, 1982.

Wishy, Bernard. *The Child and the Republic: The Dawn of Modern American Child Nurture*. Philadelphia: University of Pennsylvania Press, 1968.

Wrigley, Julia. "Do Young Children Need Intellectual Stimulation? Experts' Advice to Parents, 1900–1985." *History of Education Quarterly* 29 (Spring 1989):41–75.

Zelizer, Vivianna. *Pricing the Priceless Child: The Changing Social Value of Children*. New York: Basic Books, 1985.

INDEX

abandonment, 289–291, 425, 482; of children in nineteenth-century France, 289; of infants, 425, 482; of infants in Brazil, 147, 159; of infants in medieval Europe, 38–39; of infants in Russia, 482; reasons for in nineteenth-century France, 290, 291. *See also* infanticide

Abbott, Andrew, 108

Abdine, Dr. Zahira, 462

Abelard, Peter, 33

ability grouping (in schools), 504

Aboriginal children, neglect of in Australian scholarship, 102

abortion, 7, 38, 290, 292, 294, 364, 396, 397, 400; in Brazil, 147; as child abuse in nineteenth-century France, 290; condemnation of by medieval Christian church, 38; end of prohibition of in France, 294; penalties for in France, 292

Abu Seoud, Hind, 459

Academics, 99

academic talent, fostering of in later imperial China, 82

academies, 497

accidental death of children, 56, 67 n.15, 243; in early modern Europe, 56; in medieval England, 243

Acholi people of East Africa, 226

Act of 1601 (English) and apprenticeship, 62

adab (Islamic discipline of children), 451, 454

address: forms of for children in France, 290; forms of in Portugal and Brazil, 153

Adelaide, 104, 109

Adelaide group of Australian historians of education, 111–112

administrators, high school, 505

adolescence, 6, 17, 32–34, 36, 39–40, 42, 44, 55, 64, 69 n.43, 112, 113, 242, 243, 286, 316–319, 350, 453, 464, 491, 494, 504, 511; in antiquity, 17; definition of in medieval Europe, 34; difficulty of defining in early modern Europe, 64; in early modern Europe, 242; and expectations toward in eighteenth-century Europe, 65; female, absence of in antiquity, 17; German, 316–319; of Guibert of Nogent, 34; in households of medieval aristocrats, 39–40; invention of in Australia, 112; in late nineteenth-century France, 292; in medieval Europe, 32; nature of in early modern Europe, 243; nature of in nineteenth- and twentieth-century England, 243; in New France, 188; and peasants in medieval Europe, 44; short duration of in early twentieth-century America, 113. *See also* youth

adolescents, 32, 33, 36, 39–40, 42, 44, 64, 69 n.43, 286, 350, 491; attitudes toward in Middle Ages, 33; female, in upper-class

CONTRIBUTORS

WALTER ACKERMAN is Shane Family Professor of Education at Ben-Gurion University of the Negev, Beer Sheva, Israel. He has served as Chairman of the Department of Education, Dean of the Faculty of Humanities and Social Sciences, and Director of the School of Continuing Education at that institution. His research centers on the history of Jewish education in the United States and he is currently working on the history of the curriculum of Israeli schools. He is one of the editors of *Erziehung* in Israel, a collection of papers dealing with the development of Israel's public school system. Prior to settling in Israel, he was Vice President for Academic Affairs, University of Judaism, Los Angeles, California.

LINDA CLARK teaches modern European, French, and women's history at Millersville University of Pennsylvania. She has published two books, *Social Darwinism in France* (1983) and *Schooling the Daughters of Marianne: Textbooks and the Socialization of Girls in Modern French Primary Schools* (1984), and various articles on the history of social Darwinism, French education, and French women. Her current research focuses on women's careers in the French civil service.

JOHN DARDESS teaches East Asian history at the University of Kansas. Among his publications are *Conquerors and Confucians: Aspects of Political Change in Late Yuan China* (1973), and *Confucianism and Autocracy: Professional Elites in the Founding of the Ming Dynasty* (1983).

NUPUR CHAUDHURI, James C. Carey Associate of History at Kansas State University, has coedited "Western Women and Imperialism," which appeared in *Women's Studies International Forum*. She has coedited a collection of essays, *Sharing the White Man's Burden: Western Women and Imperialism* (1991). She is now working on a book-length monograph on memsahibs (English wives) in nineteenth-century India.

ELIZABETH FERNEA is Professor of English and Middle Eastern Studies at the University of Texas at Austin. With her anthropologist husband Robert Fernea, she has done field research in Iraq, Egypt, and Morocco. Her books include *Guests of the Sheik: Middle Eastern Muslim Women Speak* (with Basima Bezirgan); *Women and the Family in the Middle East: New Voices of Change*; and most recently *The Arab World: Personal Encounters* (with Robert Fernea). She is currently editing a book on children in the Arab world.

VALERIE FRENCH teaches ancient history at The American University in Washington, D.C. She is the coauthor of *Historians and the Living Past* (1978) and has published a number of articles and essays on early childhood and family life in classical antiquity. She is currently completing a book on Roman childhood.

MARY GIBSON is an Associate Professor of History at John Jay College of Criminal Justice and the Graduate School of the City University of New York. She is the author of *Prostitution and the State in Italy, 1860–1915* (1986) and has published widely on the history of women, sexuality, and crime in modern Italy. Currently, she is working on a book on Italian criminology and policing in the early twentieth century, including a chapter on the development of juvenile courts and reformatories.

MARY MCDOUGALL GORDON holds the Patrick Donohoe Chair in History and is Director of the Women's Studies Program at Santa Clara University. Among her publications are *Overland to California with the Pioneer Line* (1983); *Through Indian Country to California* (1988); and articles on education and the West in such journals as *Journal of Social History*, *Pacific Historical Review*, and *Southern California Quarterly*. Currently she is editing an anthology of gold-rush literature and preparing an article on women in plural marriages in nineteenth-century Mormon society.

SARA HARKNESS is Associate Professor of Health Education and Human Development at Pennsylvania State University. She has done research on children and families in Kenya and the United States.

JOSEPH M. HAWES teaches courses on the history of U.S. children and the family at Memphis State University, where he is Professor of History. He is the author of *Children and Urban Society* and the coeditor (with N. Ray Hiner) of *Growing Up in America*, and *American Childhood*. He is also coediting (with Elizabeth Nybakken) *American Families: A Research Guide and Reference Handbook* (forthcoming from Greenwood Press). He is currently at work on a history of the children's rights movement.

N. RAY HINER is Chancellors Club Teaching Professor of History and Education at the University of Kansas. He has published widely on the history of children and education in the United States and is coeditor (with Joseph M. Hawes) of *Growing Up in America* and *American Childhood*. He is currently working on a book-length study of children in the life and thought of Cotton Mather.

ELIZABETH ANNE KUZNESOF is Professor of Latin American and Brazilian history at the University of Kansas. She is author of *Household Economy and Urban Development: Sao Paulo, 1765 to 1836* (1986) as well as numerous articles on Brazilian social history, and on the history of the family and of domestic service in Latin America.

ASUNCIÓN LAVRIN is a Professor of History at Howard University. She has edited and coauthored *Latin American Women: Historical Perspectives* (1978) and *Sexuality and Marriage in Colonial Latin America* (1989), as well as numerous articles on ecclesiastical and women's history in Latin America from the seventeenth through the twentieth centuries.

SHERRIN MARSHALL most recently edited and contributed to *Women in Reformation and Counter-Reformation Europe: Private and Public Worlds*. She is currently a Program Officer at the fund for the Improvement of Postsecondary Education, U.S. Department of Education, and engaged in a book-length study entitled *Protestants, Catholics, and Jews in the Dutch Republic, 1550–1700*.

MARY JO MAYNES, Associate Professor of History at the University of Minnesota, is the author of *Schooling in Western Europe: A Social History* (1985) and a coeditor of *German Women in the Eighteenth and Nineteenth Centuries* (1986) and *Interpreting Women's Lives: Personal Narrative and Feminist Theory* (1989). She is currently working on a book on working-class lifecourse and working-class autobiography in nineteenth-century Europe.

DAVID NICHOLAS is Head of the Department of History and Geography at Clemson University. A specialist in the social and economic history of medieval Flanders, his publications include *The Domestic Life of a Medieval City: Women, Children, and the Family in Fourteenth-Century Ghent* (1985); *The Metamorphosis of a Medieval City: Ghent in the Age of the Arteveldes, 1302–1390* (1987); *The van Arteveldes of Ghent: The Varieties of Vendetta and the Hero in History*

(1988); and articles in several scholarly publications, including the *American Historical Review* and the *Journal of Medieval History*.

DAVID L. RANSEL is Professor of History at Indiana University and editor of the *American Historical Review*. He is author of *The Politics of Catherinian Russia: The Panin Party* (1975) and *Mothers of Misery: Child Abandonment in Russia* (1988). He is editor of and contributor to *The Family in Imperial Russia: New Lines of Historical Research* (1978) and is currently at work on studies of child care cultures among several ethnic groups of the Russian empire and USSR.

PATRICIA T. ROOKE is a Canada/Killam Research Fellow, Department of Educational Foundations, The University of Alberta. She has published articles on the history of childhood and Canadian child welfare history, coedited *Studies in Childhood History: A Canadian Perspective* (1982), and coauthored *Discarding the Asylum: From Child Rescue to the Welfare State in English-Canada, 1880–1950* (1983) and *No Bleeding Heart: Charlotte Whitton, A Feminist on the Right* (1987).

RUDY SCHNELL is a professor in the Department of Educational Policy and Administrative Studies at the University of Calgary. He has published articles on the history of childhood and Canadian child welfare history, coedited *Studies in Childhood History: A Canadian Perspective* (1982) and coauthored *Discarding the Asylum: From Child Rescue to the Welfare State in English-Canada, 1880–1950* (1983), and *No Bleeding Heart: Charlotte Whitton, A Feminist on the Right* (1987), a biography of Canada's leading child welfare advocate during the interwar years.

CONSTANCE B. SCHULZ is Director of the Applied History Program and Associate Professor at the University of South Carolina. She has taught courses in the history of childhood and the American family. A contributor to *American Childhood, A Research Guide* (1985), she is the creator and editor of *The History of Maryland Slide Collection* (1980), *The History of South Carolina Slide Collection* (1988), and is currently editing the second edition of *The American History Slide Collection* (forthcoming).

CHARLES M. SUPER is Head of the Department of Human Development and Family Studies and Professor of Human Development at Pennsylvania State University. He has done research on children and families in Kenya and the United States.

THOMAS TAYLOR is an Assistant Professor of History at Seattle University. He recently completed his dissertation on "The Crisis of Youth in Wilhelmine Germany." He has written several articles, including "The Transition to Adulthood in Comparative Perspective: Professional Males in Germany and the United States at the Turn of the Century,'' which appeared in *Journal of Social History*.

SELWYN TROEN is the Sam and Anna Lopin Professor of Modern History at Ben-Gurion University of the Negev. He is presently on leave as Weidenfeld Fellow and Senior Associate Member at St. Antony's College, Oxford. His work in the history of education includes *The Public and the Schools: Shaping the St. Louis System 1838–1920* (1975). His most recent publications are in Israeli history: *Redeeming the Captives: National Jewish Solidarity in the Modern Period* (coeditor) (1988) and *The Suez-Sinai Crisis 1956: Retrospective and Reappraisal* (coeditor) (1989).

KATHLEEN S. UNO teaches history at Temple University in Philadelphia, Pennsylvania. She most recently contributed to *Recreating Japanese Women* (1991).